ΝΟΜΟΣ ΡΟΔΙΩΝ ΝΑΥΤΙΚΟΣ

THE RHODIAN SEA-LAW

EDITED

FROM THE MANUSCRIPTS

BY

WALTER ASHBURNER

THE LAWBOOK EXCHANGE, LTD.
Clark, New Jersey

ISBN 978-1-58477-173-9

Lawbook Exchange edition 2001, 2015

The quality of this reprint is equivalent to the quality of the original work.

THE LAWBOOK EXCHANGE, LTD.
33 Terminal Avenue
Clark, New Jersey 07066-1321

*Please see our website for a selection of our other publications
and fine facsimile reprints of classic works of legal history:*
www.lawbookexchange.com

Library of Congress Cataloging-in-Publication Data

Rhodian sea-law.
    Nomos Rodion nautikos = The Rhodian sea-law / edited from
the manuscripts by Walter Ashburner.
        p. cm.
    Originally published: Oxford : Clarendon Press, 1909.
    Includes bibliographical references and index.
    ISBN 1-58477-173-9 (cloth : alk. paper)
        1. Maritime law--History--Sources. I. Title: Rhodian sea-law.
    II. Ashburner, Walter, 1864-1936. III Title.

K1163.R45 R49 2001
343.09'6'09--dc21   00-065551

Printed in the United States of America on acid-free paper

ΝΟΜΟΣ ΡΟΔΙΩΝ ΝΑΥΤΙΚΟΣ

THE RHODIAN SEA-LAW

EDITED

FROM THE MANUSCRIPTS

BY

WALTER ASHBURNER

OXFORD

AT THE CLARENDON PRESS

1909

PREFACE

ALTHOUGH the Rhodian Sea-law has been not infrequently edited, the learned continue to call for a new edition. Goldschmidt says of the Sea-law : ' Es bedarf noch gründlicher Untersuchung.' Zachariä von Lingenthal says of it : 'Sowohl Text als lateinische Uebersezung bedürfen noch wieder-holter kritischer Bearbeitung.' It is to meet this demand that the present edition has been under-taken.

The fullness of the critical apparatus may excite surprise. The object of a critical apparatus, as I con-ceive it, is to enable the earnest student to form his own text. It is therefore an editor's duty to give all the material variants of all the independent manuscripts. It is particularly his duty in a case like the present where there are many passages of which he can give no satisfactory explanation.

The Appendices which follow the text contain, partly, matter which, though it is given in manu-scripts as part of the Sea-law, does not, in my opinion, form part of its original composition, and, partly, matter relating substantially to maritime

affairs which, in some manuscripts, either immediately precedes or immediately follows the Sea-law.

The Commentary is confined, for the most part,
to the discussion of various readings and to matters
of grammar, syntax, and the usage of words. The
papyri throw great light upon the vocabulary of the
Sea-law: I hope it will be found that the Sea-law
occasionally throws light upon the papyri.

The substance of the Sea-law, that is to say, the
legal effect of its provisions, and their relation, on
the one hand, to Roman law and, on the other, to
the Mediterranean maritime law of the middle ages,
is dealt with at large in the Introduction. The
reader who wishes to find my opinion as to the
meaning of any chapter will do well to consult the
first Index, where references are given to every
place in the Introduction in which a chapter of the
Sea-law is considered.

Mr. H. J. Roby has answered my questions on
Roman law, and Mr. T. W. Allen my questions on
palaeography. If I had trespassed oftener on their
kindness, my work would have been less imperfect.
The Reverend J. Wood Brown has read over the
proofs of the Introduction. To all three friends are
due my sincere thanks.

My thanks are also due to the heads of various

libraries or manuscript-rooms for their courtesy in facilitating my researches. I am especially indebted to the Prefect of the Vatican Library, the librarian of the venerable monastery of Grotta Ferrata, the authorities of the Vallicelliana, Laurenziana, and Riccardiana, Signore Levi of the Marciana, and M. Omont of the National Library. The heads of the Court Library at Vienna, the University Library at Leipzig, and the University Library at Messina have kindly permitted me to have photographs taken of manuscripts in their respective collections. The time is gone by for thanking the late Prefect of the Ambrosian Library. Let me at least say that I count it among the happiest results for me of these studies to have seen and spoken with Antonio Ceriani.

ADDENDA ET CORRIGENDA

P. cclxxxix. The Lex Romana Curiensis (XXIV, 7) gives a reward
'iuxta legem' to the salvor of goods. It has been suggested that
the 'lex' is our Sea-law, but see Siciliano Villanueva, p. 156.

P. 48, l. 13. For τοῦ χ′ read τοῦ λ′.

TABLE OF CONTENTS

PAGE

LIST OF AUTHORITIES x

INTRODUCTION xiii

Summary of Contents of Sea-law xiii
Plan of the Introduction xvi

PART I

Manuscripts used for this Edition xvi
a. Manuscripts of the Sea-law xvii
b. Manuscripts of the Synopsis Major . . . xxxi
Method of the Critical Apparatus xxxii
Other Manuscripts of the Sea-law xxxiv
Printed Texts of the Sea-law xli
Principles on which the Text is based xlvi

PART II

Origin of the Sea-law lx
Opinions as to its Origin lxi
The Forty-seven Chapters lxiii
The Titles lxvii
Table of Chapters of Part III lxix
The Nineteen Chapters lxx
The Prologue lxxi
Subsidiary Matter lxxv
Sources of the Sea-law lxxv
Comparison of the Sea-law with other Law . . . lxxvii
a. As regards Offences against Property . . . lxxviii
b. As regards Offences against the Person . . lxxxiv
c. As regards the Punishment of Perjury . . . lxxxvi
d. As regards the Law of Deposit . . . lxxxvii
e. As regards Proof lxxxix
f. As regards Contracts in Writing xc
g. As regards the ἀρραβών xcii
Relation of the Sea-law to Basilica, LIII . . . xcviii

vii

CONTENTS

PAGE

Sources of Basilica, LIII :—
    Indexes of the Basilica xcix
    Venturi's Synopsis xcix
    Ambrosian Synopsis ci
    Synopsis Major ciii
    Other Sources of Basilica, LIII civ
Contents of Basilica, LIII civ
Was the Sea-law an original part of Basilica, LIII . cviii
Summing up of Part II cxii

PART III

Authorities used in Part III cxv
City Statutes and Maritime Statutes cxix
Maritime Custom cxxii
Commercial Documents cxxv
Divisions of Subject cxxix
The Parties to the Maritime Adventure . . . cxxx
Dangers and Difficulties of Navigation cxli
    Dangers from Ignorance and Want of Discipline . cxli
    Closing of the Sea in Winter cxlii
    Dangers from Pirates, &c. cxliii
    Danger from Fire cxlix
    Difficulties in reference to Food and Drink . . cl
The Ship clii
    Its Capacity and Valuation clii
    Its Name clv
    Provisions to insure Safety clvi
The Shipowner clix
    Joint Owners of Ship clxiii
The Mariners clxvi
    Their Pay clxvi
    Their Pacotilles clxxiv
    Their Duties clxxvi
Transportation of Goods clxxix
    Condition of Ship and Crew clxxxii
    Receipt and Loading of Cargo clxxxvi
    Payment of Freight clxxxix
    Unloading of Cargo cxcvii
    Duty to restore the Cargo cxcviii
    Breaches of the Contract of Transportation . . cci

CONTENTS

PAGE

Maritime Loans ccix
   In Greece and Rome ccxii
   In the Sea-law ccxxi
   In the Middle Ages ccxxiii
Partnership between Merchants ccxxxiv
   The Commenda ccxxxvii
   The Societas ccxl
Partnership between Ship and Cargo ccxli
   The Column of Amalfi ccxliv
   The Entega of Ragusa ccxlviii
Average, Jettison, Contribution ccli
Collision cclxxxv
Salvage cclxxxviii

SIGLA CODICUM ccxcvi

TEXT AND APPENDICES 1

TRANSLATION AND COMMENTARY 57

INDEXES :
   I. Chapters of the Sea-law referred to in the Intro-
     duction 126
   II. Greek Words and Phrases 127
   III. Words and Phrases in Latin and other Languages 128
   IV. Subject-matter 128

LIST OF AUTHORITIES

[Another list, containing the authorities used for Part III of the Introduction, is given at pp. cxv–cxix.]

1. LEGAL TREATISES AND WRITERS OF LEGAL HISTORY.

I cite the Epitome Seldeniana by the folios of Selden, 10; the Farmer's Law (νόμος γεωργικός) by the chapters of Marcianus gr. 579, so far as that extends on parchment, and thereafter by the chapters of Marcianus gr. 172 ; and the Soldier's Law (περὶ στρα-τιωτικῶν ἐπιτιμίων) by the chapters of Laudianus gr. 39. For other Byzantine law-books I have used the printed texts. A list of these and of histories of Byzantine law is given in Zachariä von Lingenthal (K. E.), Geschichte des Griechisch-römischen Rechts, Berlin, 1892 [which I cite as Zach. Geschichte] at p. 3. I also cite :—

Ferrini (E. C.), Mercati (J). Editionis Basilicorum Heimba-chianae Supplementum alterum. Lipsiae, 1897 [as FM.].

Le Livre du Préfet, publié par Jules Nicole. Genève, 1893.

Prochiron Legum, pubblicato a cura di F. Brandileone e V. Puntoni. Roma, 1895.

Siciliano Villanueva (L.). Diritto Bizantino. Milano, 1906.

Syrisch-römisches Rechtsbuch, herausgegeben von K. G. Bruns und E. Sachau. Leipzig, 1880.

2. COLLECTIONS OF DOCUMENTS.

The collections of papyri are cited by the current abbreviations. Other collections referred to are :—

Acta et Diplomata Graeca medii aevi. Ediderunt F. Miklosich et I. Müller. Vindobonae, 1860–1890. 6 volumes.

Marini (G.). I Papiri Diplomatici. Roma, 1805.

Mas-Latrie (L. M. de). Traités et documents divers concernant les relations des Chrétiens avec les Arabes de l'Afrique Septen-trionale au moyen âge. Paris, 1866–1872.

Müller (G.). Documenti sulle relazioni delle città Toscane coll' Oriente Cristiano e coi Turchi. Firenze, 1879.

Prologo (A. di G.). Le Carte che si conservano nello Archivio del Capitolo Metropolitano della Città di Trani. Barletta, 1877.

LIST OF AUTHORITIES

Spata (G.). Le Pergamene Greche esistenti nel grande Archivio di Palermo. Palermo, 1861.

Tafel (G.) und Thomas (G). Urkunden zur älteren Handels- und Staatsgeschichte der Republik Venedig. Wien, 1856–7. 3 volumes.

Trinchera (F.). Syllabus Graecarum Membranarum. Neapoli, 1865.

3. OTHER WORKS.

Billeter (G.). Geschichte des Zinsfusses bis auf Justinian. Leipzig, 1898.

Böckh (A.). Urkunden über das Seewesen des Attischen Staates. Berlin, 1840.

Brunner (H.). Zur Rechtsgeschichte der Urkunde. Berlin, 1880.

Camera (M.). Memorie di Amalfi. Salerno, 1876–81. 2 vols.

Canale (M. G.). Nuova Istoria di Genova. Firenze, 1858–64. 4 vols.

Dareste (R.) and others. Recueil des Inscriptions Juridiques Grecques. Paris, 1891–1904. 2 vols.

Du Cange (C. du Fresne). Glossarium ad Scriptores Mediae et Infimae Graecitatis. Lugduni, 1688. 2 vols. [The labours of Sophocles, Κουμανούδης, Herwerden, and others have in no way superseded this work, which I cite as Duc.]

Goldschmidt (L.). Universalgeschichte des Handelsrechts. Stuttgart, 1891.

Goldschmidt (L.). Lex Rhodia und Agermanament in Zeitschrift für das gesammte Handelsrecht, XXXV. Stuttgart, 1888.

Guglielmotti (Padre A.). Vocabolario marino e militare. Roma, 1889.

Moryson (Fynes). An Itinerary. London, 1617.

Pardessus (J. M.). Collection de lois maritimes. Paris, 1828–45. 6 vols. [Cited as Pard.]

Pitti (Andrea). Narrazione di tre Viaggi in Egitto. Firenze, 1893.

Schaube (A.). Handelsgeschichte der Romanischen Völker. München, 1906.

Targa (Carlo). Ponderationi sopra la contrattatione maritima. Genova, 1692.

Wheler (G.). A Journey into Greece. London, 1682.

INTRODUCTION

THE RHODIAN SEA-LAW: SUMMARY OF ITS CONTENTS

AMONG the monuments of Byzantine jurisprudence which have survived no one perhaps is found in more manuscripts than the little treatise on maritime law which is here edited. In the manuscripts its title varies; but it is oftenest described as the Rhodian Sea-law (νόμος 'Ροδίων ναυτικός), and I shall hereafter call it the Sea-law. The subject-matter which is contained under this or a similar title varies in different manuscripts. Pardessus, who edited the book in his Collection de Lois Maritimes, divides it (Tome I, p. 208) into three parts; and I follow this division, as it has been generally accepted, although what he calls the first part does not belong to the original work, and in this edition is relegated to an appendix.

Part I is a prologue, which purports to give a sanction to the Sea-law from the declarations of various Roman emperors. It corresponds more or less closely, as Godefroy has pointed out (De Imperio Maris in Opera Iuridica Minora, Lugd. Bat. 1733, col. 88), to what in Roman law is called an auctoritas, i. e. a statement of the imperial constitutions by which validity is given to a body of laws. Part II consists of nineteen chapters, mostly very short. The first seven determine the shares which the members of the ship's company take in the profits of the maritime adventure. Chapters 8 to 13 are regulations of internal police. They determine the space to be allotted to each passenger; limit the number of servants whom a merchant may bring with him; fix the water allowance, and forbid certain dangerous acts. They are regulations of the sort which are often put up on board a ship for the guidance of passengers. Chapters 14 and 15 limit the captain's liability for a passenger's valuables to the case where the passenger has deposited them with him. Chapter 16 provides a method of valuing ship for general average purposes. Chapters 17 to 19 deal with maritime loans and loans in general. In one or two manuscripts a table of contents is prefixed to this part.

Part III contains forty-seven chapters, which are generally much longer than those of Part II. They deal with various topics of maritime law, and chapters on the same subject are as a rule grouped together. The following gives a rough idea of their contents. Chapters 1 to 8 are occupied with questions of police. Chapters 1 and 2 deal with the theft of a ship's anchors or other tackle, and chapter 3 with thefts by a sailor from a merchant or passenger. Chapter 4 fixes the responsibility as between captain and passengers for going to a place where thefts are frequent. Chapters 5 to 7 relate to fights, whether of sailors among themselves or of captains and merchants with sailors, and fix the responsibility for personal injuries. Chapter 8 deals with the case where captain and crew make away with the ship and the money on board. Chapter 9 deals with jettison and its results, and chapter 10 fixes the responsibility for injury to ship or cargo where one of the parties is to blame. Chapter 11 is couched in a hortatory form. It dissuades merchants from loading heavy and valuable cargoes on old bottoms. It does not sound like the statement of a legal rule, but perhaps it may be understood as limiting the conditions under which the owners of freight are entitled to demand contribution. Chapters 12 to 14 deal with deposits, 13 reproducing in slightly different language chapters 14 and 15 of Part II. Chapter 15 relates to cases where the ship is obliged to put off suddenly and leaves passengers behind. There is an incidental reference in it to deposit, and that no doubt is the reason why it is put in this place. Chapters 16, 17, and 18 deal with maritime loans or maritime partnerships. Chapters 19 to 25 (except chapter 21) deal with the hiring of the ship by the merchant. Chapter 21 deals with contribution between two shipowners or two owners of cargo. Apparently it is inserted here because, like chapter 20, it refers to a case where there is no written contract between the parties.

In the chapters which follow it is more difficult to seize the principle of arrangement, especially as the same chapter often deals with more than one subject. Chapters 26 to 44 (with the exception of chapter 42) deal mainly with the question of contribution, i. e. the extent to which, where there is a maritime loss, ship or cargo in so far as saved are to make good ship or cargo in so far as injured or lost. Under chapter 26 sailors or captains who sleep off the ship are responsible for injuries done to ship in their absence. Chapters 27 to 33 fix the merchant's liability to contribute to injuries to ship either while it is being loaded (27–29), while it is on the voyage (30–32), or after it has been unloaded (33). Chapter 34 fixes the liability for injuries to goods of a character particularly subject to be injured by damp. Chapter 35 provides for contribution where the ship's mast is broken or cut away. Chapter 36 deals with collision between two ships. Chapters 37, 40, and 41 fix the proportions in which, where ship is lost, contribution is to be made by gold, silver, and other articles of great value in small compass. These chapters in part repeat matter which has been dealt with in chapters 30 and 31, and ought logically to follow the latter chapter. Chapters 38 and 39 deal with corn ships or ships carrying provisions, and provide for contribution either where the cargo (38) or where the ship (39) is injured. Chapter 42 gives the captain authority to transfer the cargo to another ship if ship springs a leak. Chapters 43 and 44 contain very general provisions as to contribution. Chapters 45 to 47 deal mainly with salvage and the rewards of salvors.

The forty-seven chapters of Part III are in some manuscripts split up into a greater number; but their substance and order remain practically the same in all the uninterpolated manuscripts. In some manuscripts a table of contents is prefixed, which does not always tally with the contents of the chapters as we have them. After the forty-seven chapters the manuscripts contain as a rule various additional matter, the large majority of them giving three chapters, which I publish in Appendix E.

PLAN OF THE INTRODUCTION.

Such is, stated in brief, the substance of the work which I am editing. In this introduction I propose to consider its text, its origin, and its place in the history of maritime law. The introduction therefore falls into three parts. The first enumerates the manuscripts which have been made use of in forming the text and attempts to ascertain their value; it also deals shortly with other manuscripts of the text known to me, and with the principal editions. The second part deals with the origin of the Sea-law, so far as that can be determined either from internal evidence or from a comparison with other remains of Roman or Byzantine jurisprudence. The third part deals with the relation of the Sea-law to the other monuments of maritime jurisprudence which relate to the Mediterranean basin during the middle ages, and gives a sketch, so far as can be gathered from these materials, of that jurisprudence as it existed between the fall of the Roman empire and the commercial renascence of the thirteenth century.

PART I

MANUSCRIPTS USED FOR THIS EDITION

The Sea-law never appears by itself in the manuscripts. It is always found in conjunction with other treatises, whether of civil or ecclesiastical law. In dealing with the manuscripts which contain the Sea-law, it is unnecessary for the purposes of this work to give a full description of their contents. They are only described here so far as they contain the Sea-law, but the reader is referred, where it is possible, to other works where they are more fully described. The manuscripts on which this edition is based fall into two classes: (a) manuscripts which contain the Sea-law either in whole or in part, (b) manuscripts of the so-called Synopsis Major.

a. *Manuscripts of the Sea-law.*

Of manuscripts belonging to the first class, the following have been used:—

A[1] Ambrosianus F 106 sup. is a palimpsest on parchment. It is described by J. Mercati in Rendiconti del R. Istituto Lombardo, 1897, pp. 821 sqq., and by E. C. Ferrini in the Preface to Basilicorum Libri LX, Vol. VII. Editionis Basilicorum Heimbachianae Supplementum alterum ... Ediderunt E. C. Ferrini, J. Mercati. Lipsiae, 1897.[2] The manuscript, which contains the speeches of the Emperor Leo,[3] in a hand of the thirteenth or early fourteenth century, has been made up out of five earlier manuscripts. The most important of these is an abridgement of the Basilica in a hand of the tenth century. This abridgement contains the Sea-law (Part II, Table of Contents of Part III, Part III). The Sea-law is transcribed in FM, pp. 108-20, with a Latin translation. When I saw the manuscript (June, 1906) the under hand was so faint—no doubt in consequence of the chemicals used to bring it out—that it was impossible for me to read more than a word here and there. I have therefore had to rely, not without misgivings, on the published transcript.

---

[1] The letter prefixed to the description of each manuscript is the sign by which it is referred to in the apparatus criticus.

[2] As I have to refer to this work frequently, I shall henceforth describe it as FM.

[3] This part of the manuscript is described by Martini and Bassi (Catalogus Codicum Graecorum Bibliothecae Ambrosianae. Digesserunt Aemilius Martini et Dominicus Bassi. Mediolani, 1906. Vol. I, p. 421).

INTRODUCTION

B   Vaticanus graecus 2075 = Basilianus 114, on parchment, of the early eleventh century, contains 263 numbered leaves, many of them torn. Its contents are described by Heimbach, Basil. VI, p. 174, and by Zach., J. G.-R., Pars II, p. 267. The Sea-law begins (f. 25 v.) with the title in capitals: κεφάλαια τοῦ νόμου τοῦ ῥοδίου. Table of contents of Part II as given in Appendix B. τὰ κεφάλαια. Part II. F. 26 v. κεφάλαια νόμου ῥοδίου κατ᾽ ἐκλογὴν περὶ ναυτικῶν. Table of chapters of Part III. F. 27 v. κεφάλαια ἀρχὴ τοῦ κεφαλαίου. Part III. After Part III it contains the chapters given in Appendix G. The Sea-law ends f. 35 v.

C   Vaticanus graecus 845, on parchment, in double columns, of the twelfth century. It is described in part by F. Brandileone and V. Puntoni in their preface to Prochiron Legum (Fonti per la Storia d'Italia), Roma, 1895. They give two facsimiles. The Sea-law begins on f. 104 v. Title, κεφάλαια τοῦ νόμου ῥοδίου. Part II. From the end of c. ιη′, C goes on directly (f. 105 r.) to c. 1 of Part III. The contents of f. 106 deal with another subject. The Sea-law begins again on f. 107 and ends on f. 113 r.

D   Vaticanus graecus 844, of the fourteenth century, on paper. It contains (f. 1 r.) ἐξήγησις τῶν ἱερῶν καὶ θείων κανόνων. F. 424 v. ἐνταῦθ᾽ ἀπαρχὴ τοῦ νόμου τοῦ προχείρου. F. 455 r. νόμος στρατιωτικός. F. 457 v. νόμος γεωργικός. The Sea-law begins on f. 461 r. νόμος ῥοδίων ναυτικὸς ὃν ἐθέσπισαν οἱ θειότατοι αὐτοκράτορες ἁδριανὸς ἀντωνῖνος τιβέριος λούκιος σεπτίμιος σεβῆρος περτίναξ ἀεισέβαστοι. Prologue. κεφάλαια τοῦ ναυτικοῦ νόμου. Table of chapters of Part II. Part II. κεφάλαια νόμου ῥοδίου κατ᾽ ἐκλογήν. Table of chapters of Part III. F. 462 r. νόμος ῥοδίων ναυτικός. Part III. The three chapters given in Appendix E. It ends f. 465 r.

E   Vaticanus graecus 847, of the fourteenth century, on paper, bound in two volumes. It is partially described by Iosephus Simonius Assemanus (Bibliotheca Iuris Orientalis Canonici et Civilis. Romae, 1762. Liber Secundus, pp. 576–9). The Epanagoge begins on f. 26 r., the last in the list of titles being μα′ περὶ ναυτικῶν. The leaves are numbered by the original scribe and numbered wrongly. He repeated f. 168 and f. 169. Later on he saw his mistake and corrected it by leaving out two numbers ; hence f. 178 comes immediately after f. 175. F. 169 A v. begins τίτλος μα΄ νόμος ῥοδίων ναυτικὸς ὃν ἐθέσπισαν οἱ ἀεισέβαστοι βασιλεῖς ἀντώνιος ἀδριανὸς τιβέριος λούκιος σεπτίμιος σεβῆρος καὶ περτίναξ οἱ αὔγουστοι καὶ αὐτοκράτορες. Prologue. Part II. After Part II the MS. gives (f. 169 B r.) chapters 46 and 47 of Part III. F. 169 B v. ἐκλογὴ ἐκ τῶν διγέστων. Part III omitting chapters 46 and 47. The three chapters given in Appendix E. The Sea-law ends f. 179 v.

F Palatinus graecus 371, of the fourteenth century, on paper, is described by Henricus Stevenson (Codices Manuscripti Palatini Graeci Bibliothecae Vaticanae, Romae, 1885, p. 239). It contains the Ecloga ad Prochiron mutata, and was made use of by Zach. for his edition (J. G.-R,, Pars IV, Lipsiae, 1865, pp. 49–170). The Sea-law begins (f. 188 v.) πρόλογος ῥωδίου νόμου ἐκτιθὲν ὑπὸ τιβερίου βασιλέως. Prologue. νόμος ναυτικὸς ῥοδίωνος, Part II (abridged). ˙ F. 191 v. νόμος ναυτικὸς ῥοδίωνος ὃν ἐθέσπισαν οἱ θειότατοι αὐτοκράτορες ἀδριανὸς ἀντώνιος τιβέριος λούπιος σεπτίμιος σενῆρος οὐεσπασιανὸς τραϊανὸς περτίναξ ἀεισέβαστοί τε καὶ λόγιοι. Part III (including the four chapters which are given in Appendix D). The three chapters which are given in Appendix E.

f Vaticanus graecus 640, of the fourteenth century, on paper, contains the Ecloga ad Prochiron mutata, and was consulted by Zach. for his edition. It is partially described by Iosephus Simonius Assemanus (op. cit., Liber Secundus, pp. 557–61). The Sea-law begins at f. 345 v. νόμος ναυτικὸς ῥοδίωνος. Part II in an abridged form. Title as in F, but omitting τραϊανός. The following chapters of Part III : 1, 2, 3, 5, 7, 6, 11 (much abridged), 19 (abridged), and 50 of Appendix E. It ends at f. 346 v.

G Vallicellianus E 55, of the fourteenth century, on paper, is described by Heimbach (Ἀνέκδοτα, T. I, p. lxvi), and by E. Martini (Catalogo di Manoscritti Greci esistenti nelle Biblioteche Italiane, Volume II, Milano, 1902, pp. 119 sqq.). The Sea-law begins (f. 238 r.) κεφάλαια τοῦ νόμου τοῦ ῥωδίου κατὰ θάλατταν. Part III. After chapter 47 come chapters numbered νβ' to νζ', which are given in Appendix G.

Ħ Cryptensis Zγ III. This manuscript, which is on parchment, is described by Father Antonio Rocchi (Codices Cryptenses ... digesti ... cura et studio D. Antonii Rocchi, Tusculani, 1883, p. 488), who appears to assign it to the seventeenth century (p. 488). This is evidently a printer's error, as on a later page (p. 490) he assigns the body of the manuscript to the end of the thirteenth or beginning of the fourteenth century. The present learned librarian, with whom I respectfully agree, would put the body of the manuscript at the beginning of the thirteenth century. The Sea-law begins (f. 76 r.) κεφάλαια τοῦ νόμου τοῦ ῥοδίονος. Part III, as far as c. 47, διὰ τὸν κίνδυνον τοῦ βυθοῦ. Then come (f. 83 v.) the chapters given in Appendix G. Then (f. 84 r.) the rest of c. 47. Then Part II as far as the words ὅσον δεῖ συμβαλλομένους ναυκληρίαν, which are treated as the end of c. 18. It ends f. 84 v. F. 110, 111 are in a hand which, according to Father Rocchi, is about a century later than the body of the manuscript. Title, οὗτός ἐστιν ὁ πρόλογος τοῦ νόμου ῥωδίονος ἐκτεθὲν ὑπὸ Τιβερίου βασιλέως περὶ τῶν πλοίων καὶ λοιπῶν καράβων καὶ ναυτῶν καὶ σχοινίων καὶ ἀρμένων. Prologue. Title, νόμος ναυτικὸς ῥωδίονος ὃν ἐθέσπισαν οἱ θειότατοι αὐτοκράτορες ἀδριανὸς ἀντωνῖνος τιβέριος λούκιος σεπτίμιος σευῆρος οὐεσπασιανὸς τραϊανὸς περτίναξ ἀεισέβαστοι κατ' ἐκλογήν. This is followed by ἐὰν πλοῖον ὁρμᾷ ἐν λιμένῃ ἢ ἐν ἀκτῇ ζητεῖ καὶ τοῦτο τὸ κεφάλαιον καὶ τὰ ἕτερα λοιπὰ κεφάλαια τὰ περὶ πλοίων καὶ καράβων εἰς τὸν αὐτὸν νόμον τοῦ ῥοδίονος. Then comes c. 46 of Part III beginning ἐάν τις κάραβον ἀποσώσει; then the four chapters given in Appendix D; then the three chapters given in Appendix E; then τέλος τῶν κεφαλαίων ... καραβίων τοῦ νόμου ῥοδίονος καὶ ταῦτα τὰ κεφάλαια ἐκεῖ ζητοῦνται εἰς τὸν τίτλον ἐκεῖνον τοῦ ῥο̅. Here f. 111 ends.

ħ Cryptensis Zγ V, a small manuscript on parchment,

MANUSCRIPTS USED FOR THIS EDITION

is ascribed by Father Rocchi (op. cit., p. 492) to the twelfth century. The Sea-law begins f. 19 r. κεφάλαια τοῦ νόμου τοῦ ῥωδίου. It contains the first 41 chapters of Part III. The Sea-law and the manuscript end f. 24 v.

J Laurentianus plut. IX, cod. 8, is described by Aug. Mar. Bandinius (Catalogus Codicum Manuscriptorum Bibliothecae Mediceae Laurentianae, Florentiae, 1764, cols. 395–403). It is on parchment, of the middle of the eleventh century. F. 349 v. περὶ στρατιωτικῶν καὶ ἐπιτιμίων. This treatise ends on f. 350 v. with chapter ι'. Between f. 350 and f. 351 some leaves have been torn out. The numbering of the leaves—so Prof. Rostagno assures me—is in the hand of the librarian, Francesco Maria Ducci, who died in 1718. (See Cianfogni, P. N., Memorie della Basilica di S. Lorenzo, Firenze, 1804, p. 125). F. 351 r. begins with Part III of the Sea-law, c. 43 ἐρχέσθωσαν. After c. 47 come the three chapters which are given in Appendix E. The Sea-law ends on f. 351 r.

Of the missing leaves, eight are now in the University Library at Leipzig, and form leaves 9–16 of Lipsiensis graecus 46. This manuscript is cited by Zach. as Bienerianus 4. It is described by V. Gardthausen, Katalog der Griechischen Handschriften der Universitäts-Bibliothek zu Leipzig. Leipzig, 1898, p. 65. F. 13 r. begins with Part II, c. ιη'. Title, κεφάλαια νόμου ῥοδίων κατ᾽ ἐκλογήν. Table of chapters of Part III. F. 13 v. Title, Νόμος ῥοδίων ναυτικὸς κατ᾽ ἐκλογὴν ἐκ τοῦ ια' βιβλίου τῶν διγέστων. Part III. F. 16 v. ends with c. 34, l. 4 ὁ ναύκλη. These leaves are numbered in an old hand 5, 6, 7, 8.

K Laurentianus plut. LXXX, cod. 6, is described by Aug. Mar. Bandinius (Catalogus Codicum Graecorum Bibliothecae Laurentianae, T. 3, Florentiae, 1770, columns 178–186). It is of the fifteenth century, on paper. It contains, among other things, the so-called Epitome Laurentiana, as to which see Zach., J. G.-R., Pars II, p. 272. At f. 206 r. comes Τίτλος ν' περὶ ναυκλήρων καὶ πιστικῶν καὶ ναυτῶν καὶ πανδοχέων καὶ τῆς κατ᾽ αὐτῶν καὶ ὑπὲρ αὐτῶν ἀγωγῆς. Zach. is mistaken in saying (Geschichte,

p. 314, n. 1070) that the words Νόμος ῥοδίων ναυτικός form part of the title. Then come chapters described in Appendix H. Then Part III of the Sea-law. Then other chapters described in Appendix H. The title ends on f. 211 r.

L Laudianus graecus 39 (formerly C 73) is on parchment, and belongs to the end of the tenth or beginning of the eleventh century.[1] It is described by H. O. Coxe (Catalogi Codicum Manuscriptorum Bibliothecae Bodleianae pars prima, Oxonii, 1853, col. 519), and by Zach. ('Ο πρόχειρος νόμος, Heidelbergae, 1837, p. 323), who calls it Laudianus 73. F. 331 r. νόμος 'Ρωδίων ναυτικὸς ὃν ἐθέσπισαν οἱ θειότατοι αὐτοκράτορες 'Αδριανὸς 'Αντωνῖνος Τιβέριος Λούκιος Σεπτίμιος Σεύηρος Περτίναξ ῥωμαῖοι ἀεισέβαστοι. Part II. F. 331 v. κεφάλαια νόμου ῥωδὶ κατ' ἐκλογήν. Table of chapters of Part III. F. 332 r. νόμος 'Ροδίων ναυτικός. Part III Chapters of Appendix E. Ends (f. 338 v.) with the words τέλος νόμου 'Ρωδίονος.

M Marcianus graecus (fondo antico) 172 is described by Antonius M. Zanetti (Graeca D. Marci Bibliotheca Codicum Manu Scriptorum Per titulos digesta . . . 1740

---

[1] Coxe puts it 'sec. forsan xi ineuntis.' According to a manuscript catalogue in the Bodleian of the Laudian Greek manuscripts it was probably written in South Italy at the close of the tenth century. Zach. in Wissenschaft und Recht für das Heer (Byz. Zeitschrift, Band III, Leipzig, 1894, pp. 437 sqq.) dates it at A.D. 903. The manuscript contains a list of Patriarchs of Constantinople, which treats Nicolaus (A.D. 896–908) as being still on the throne. It also contains a portion of the χρονογραφικὸν σύντομον of Nicephorus, giving a list of emperors down to the sole reign of Constantinus Porphyrogennetus (A.D. 944–59), but, according to Zach., the names after Leo the Wise (A.D. 886–912) are in a later hand. (See Dr. William Fischer in Byz. Zeitschrift, Band VIII, p. 169.) This is very doubtful. It is true that Nicolaus is the last in the list of patriarchs (f. 9 v.), but so he is in a similar list in cod. 38 quarto of the Bibliotheca Typographei Synodalis at Moscow, and this manuscript is of the eleventh or twelfth century (Chr. Frid. de Matthaei, Accurata Graecorum MSS. Bibliothecarum Mosquensium Notitia, Lipsiae, 1805, p. 319). It is also true that in the list of emperors (f. 13 r.) after λέων ὁ υἱὸς αὐτοῦ ἔτη the colour of the ink changes from brown to black, but this only means, in my opinion, that the original writing had become faint and was traced over at a later time. The handwriting belongs to the end of the tenth century, at earliest, rather than the beginning.

MANUSCRIPTS USED FOR THIS EDITION

fol. I, p. 100), and by Dr. William Fischer in the Byzautinische Zeitschrift,Band VIII, p. 176. It is on parchment, and was written in A.D. 1175 as appears from the subscription, the beginning of which runs as follows (f. 256 v.): ἐτελειώθη τὸ παρὸν νόμιμον βιβλίον μηνὶ ἰουλίω ἰνδίκτου ὀγδόου ἐν ἔτει ϛχπγ΄ διὰ χειρὸς ϊω εὐτελοῦς νοταρίου. (F. 1 r.) νόμος ῥοδίων ναυτικὸς κατ' ἐκλογὴν ἐκ τοῦ δεκάτου τετάρτου βιβλίου τῶν διγέστου πίναξ σὺν θεῶ τοῦδε τοῦ νόμου περὶ πλοίων (in red capitals). Table of contents of Part III, as I give it in Appendix C. At f. 21 r. of the general index of the volume comes the table of contents of Part II, as I give it in Appendix C. (F. 30 v.) Νόμος ῥοδίων ναυτικὸς κατ' ἐκλογὴν ἐκ τοῦ ιδ΄ β̈ τῶν διγέστων (in red capitals). Part III. (F. 36 v.) ἐκ τοῦ β΄ β̈ τίτλ ια΄ τοῦ κώδι. The chapters given in Appendix E. The chapters given in Appendix F. The Sea-law ends at f. 37 v., and the volume goes on κεφάλαια τοῦ γεωργικοῦ νόμου κατ' ἐκλογὴν ἐκ τῶν ἰουστινιανοῦ βιβλίων κεφὰ̈ πε΄. (F. 230 r.) νόμος ῥωδίων ναυτικὸς ὃν ἐθέσπισαν οἱ θειώτατοι αὐτοκράτορες ἀδριανὸς τιβέριος λούκιος σεπτίμιος σεύηρος περτίναξ ἀεισέβαστοι. Prologue. Part II. After c. ιθ΄ of Part II the manuscript goes on ἐὰν δὲ προσχρείαν (Part III, c. 32), and gives the rest of c. 32 and the whole of c. 33. The Sea-law ends on f. 231 r. It appears from this description that Dr. Fischer is in error when he says (Byz. Zeitschrift, VIII, p. 175) 'Beiden Venezianischen Handschriften fehlen die gewohnheitsrechtlichen Normen des cod. Ambros.'

N Marcianus graecus (fondo antico) 579 is described by Zanetti (op. cit., I, p. 305) and by Dr. Fischer (Byz. Zeitschrift, Band VIII, p. 171). It contains (a) 65 numbered leaves of paper, of which 1, 2, and 65 are blank; (b) leaves of parchment numbered 66 to 194; (c) leaves of paper numbered 195-200, of which only f. 195 contains writing. The part on parchment is of the early eleventh century. Two parchment leaves, numbered 82 and 83, contain a fragment of the Sea-law. These leaves are not in their proper place, but come in the middle of τίτλος κε′ περὶ ἀνατροπῆς διαθήκης καὶ περὶ μέμψεως αὐτῆς κεφάλαια μη′, of which c. κβ′ ends at the bottom of f. 81 v., while c. κγ′ begins at the top of f. 84 r. F. 82 r. νόμος ῥοδίων ναυτικὸς κατ᾽ ἐκλογὴν ἐκ τοῦ ιδ′ β̕ τῶν διγέστων κε ξγ′ (all in capitals). Part III. F. 82 v. ends with κατὰ δύο μῆνας· κατά of c. 9. F. 83 r. begins with the words ἀπὸ τῆς ζάλης αὐτομάτως of c. 43, but the upper part of the leaf has been so badly injured by damp that only a word or two is legible. F. 83 r. becomes clear with the words τοῖς αὐτῶν κληρονόμοις of c. 46. After Part III the manuscript gives the three chapters of Appendix E. The page ends with ἐκ τοῦ θ′ τ̕ τοῦ μζ′ βιβ̕ τῶν διγέστων. The upper part of f. 83 v. is also illegible. The page begins to be clear with the words ἀπὸ πελάγου εἰς τὴν γῆν πλοῖον, and ends with the words εἴπωσιν οἱ ναῦται. See Appendix F.[1]

O Marcianus graecus (fondo antico) 181 is described by Zanetti (op. cit., I, p. 104), who omits to notice the subscription. This is at f. 347 r., and fixes the date of the book at A.D. 1441. F. 207 r. κεφάλαια νόμου ῥοδίων κατ᾽ ἐκλογήν. Table of chapters of Part III. F. 210 r. νόμος ῥοδίων κατ᾽ ἐκλογὴν ἐκ τοῦ ιδ′ βιβλίου τῶν διγέστων. Part III. F. 223 r. The three chapters of Appendix E. The Sea-law ends f. 223 v.

P Paris. graecus 1367 is described by Heimb. (Basil. VI, p. 175) Pard. (I, p. 210) and H. Omont (Inventaire Sommaire des Manuscrits Grecs de la Bibliothèque Nationale. Paris, 1886–98, T. 2, p. 26). It is of the twelfth century, on parchment. F. 49 v. περὶ ναυτικῶν κεφάλαια κατ᾽ ἐκλογήν. Part III, chapters 1–7 inclusive; Part II, chapters 14 (which it treats as part of Part III, c. 7)–17 inclusive. Then (f. 50 v.) it breaks off to another subject. At f. 112 r. it begins with the words μετὰ δὲ ὀκτὼ ἔτη of Part II, c. 18, and finishes Part II. κεφάλαια ῥοδίου νόμου. Table of chapters of

---

[1] Dr. William Fischer published in the Byz. Zeitschrift, VIII, p. 171 sqq., collations of M and N. I have gone over both manuscripts twice, and the reader may rest satisfied that, where my collations differ from those published by Dr. Fischer, mine are correct.

MANUSCRIPTS USED FOR THIS EDITION

Part III. F. 113 r. πρόλογος ῥοδίου νόμου ἐκτεθεὶς ὑπὸ τιβερίου βασιλέως. Prologue. F. 113 v. νόμος ʿΡοδίων ναυτικὸς ὃν ἐθέσπισαν οἱ θειότατοι αὐτοκράτορες ʾΑδριανὸς ʾΑντόνιος Τιβέριος Λούκιος Σεπτήμιος Σευῆρος Περιτίναξ ἀεισέβαστοι κατ' ἐκλογὴν ἐκ τοῦ ιδ' βιβλίου τῶν διγέστων. It ends (f. 118 v.) with the word κουφιζέσθωσαν of c. 40. It will be observed that the first seven chapters of Part III occur twice. In the apparatus criticus I denote the first recension (f. 49 v., f. 50 r.) as P¹ and the second (f. 113 v., f. 114 r.) as P².

Q Paris. graecus 1384, of the twelfth century, on parchment. It is described by Heimbach (G.-R. Recht, p. 281) and by H. Omont (op. cit., T. 2, p. 34). F. 119 v. νόμος ʿΡοδίων ναυτικὸς ὃν ἐθέσπισαν οἱ θεότατοι αὐτοκράτορες ʾΑδριανὸς Τιβέριος Λούκιος Σεπτίμιος Σευῆρος Περτίναξ ἀεισέβαστοι. Prologue. F. 120 r. Part II, without a title. F. 120 v. Part III, without title or table of chapters. The three chapters of Appendix E. It ends f. 127 r.

R Roe 18 is described by H. O. Coxe (op. cit., col. 471) and by Zach. (ὁ πρόχειρος νόμος, p. 315). It is on paper, and was written in 1349. At f. 21 v. in the πίναξ comes β' νόμος ναυτικὸς ἤτοι ὁ τῶν ῥοδίων ἐν κεφαλαίοις μα'. F. 86 r. νόμος ναυτικὸς ἤτοι ὁ τῶν ʿΡοδίων. Part III. The three chapters of Appendix E. It ends (f. 90 v.) τέλος τῶν ναυτικῶν κεφαλαίων.

S Ambrosianus Q 25 sup., on 199 leaves of parchment. It is described by Martini and Bassi (Catalogus Codicum Graecorum Bibliothecae Ambrosianae, Vol. II, p. 755), who date it 's. xi. ex.' According to a note on the first leaf it was brought from Calabria in 1607. It begins (f. 1 r.) with c. 18 of Part III. Part III. Paragraphs of Appendix G. The Sea-law ends on f. 5 r.

T Paris. graecus 1383 is described by H. Omont (op. cit., II, p. 33). It is of the twelfth century, on parchment. The Sea-law begins on f. 203 r. There is no title. Part III. F. 210 r. The three chapters of Appendix E. F. 210 v. The matter described in Appendix I. It ends on f. 211 v. with the words τὸν τόπον ἐκεῖνον.

U Ambrosianus M 68 sup. is on 293 leaves of paper.

INTRODUCTION

The book is much worm-eaten ; the last leaf particularly
so. It is described by Martini and Bassi (op. cit., Vol. II,
pp. 634–6). They date it 's. xiii ex.' I should have put it
a hundred years later. A modern note on the fly-leaf
says, 'Canones Conciliorum et Epistolae SS. PP. Canonicae
cum interpretatione Alexii Aristeni. Cfr. Beveregium in
Pandectis Canonum. 145. Leo Imperator.' F. 145 r. λέων
βασιλεύς. ἀπὸ τοῦ α΄ βιβλίου τῶν διγέστων γ΄ τ περὶ νόμου καὶ
δικαιοσύνης. [Epanagoge aucta]. F. 261 r. αἱ ῥοπαί. F. 279 r.
νόμος γεωργικός. F. 288 r. νόμος ῥοδίων κατ' ἐκλογὴν ἐκ τοῦ ιδ΄
βιβλίου τῶν διγέστων. Part III. The last two of the three
chapters given in Appendix E. It ends on f. 293 v.
A collation of this manuscript with Heimbach's text is
given by FM, pp. 169–71. I have revised this collation
throughout. This is doubtless the manuscript which Zach.
alludes to at p. 174 of his edition of the Epanagoge aucta.

V v Paris. graecus 1356 is described by Pard. (I, p. 210)
and by H. Omont (op. cit., II, p. 22). It is on paper. The
body of the manuscript is of the fourteenth century.
F. 319–26 were written, as appears from the subscription,
in A.D. 1478. F. 277 r. νόμος ναυτικὸς ῥοδίωνος. Part II,
chapters α΄ to ιζ΄. F. 277 v. νόμος ναυτικὸς ῥοδίωνος ὃν
ἐθέσπισαν οἱ θειότατοι αὐτοκράτορες ἀδριανὸς ἀντωνῖνος τιβέριος
λούπιος σεπτίμιος σεβῆρος οὐεσπεσιανὸς τραϊανὸς περτίναξ ἀεισέβαστοί τε καὶ λόγιοι. Part III, chapters 1–3, 7, 6, 11 (as far
as εἰς πλοῖον παλαιόν), 19 ; c. 50 (of Appendix E) as far as
παρεχέτωσαι. The Sea-law ends at f. 279 r. [I denote
this part of the manuscript by V.] F. 319 r. κεφάλαια τοῦ
νόμου τοῦ ναυτικοῦ. Table of contents of Part II. νόμος
ναυτικός. Part II. F. 319 v. κεφάλαια νόμου τοῦ ῥοδίου. Table
of contents of Part III. F. 320 r. νόμος ῥοδίων ναυτικὸς κατ'
ἐκλογὴν ἐκ τοῦ ια΄ β τοῦ διγέστου. Part III. It ends f. 325 r.
[I denote this part of the manuscript by v.]

W Vindobonensis iuridicus graecus 2 is described by
Petrus Lambecius (Commentarii de Augustissima Bibliotheca Caesarea Vindobonensi. Editio altera studio et
opera Adami Francesci Kollarii. Liber Sextus. Vindo-

bonae, 1780, coll. 24–31), by Heimbach ('Ανέκδοτα, T. I,
p. lxxvii), and by Zach. (Nachträge und Bemerkungen zu
den Katalogen des Lambecius-Kollar und von Nessel
über die Handschriften des byzantinischen Rechts in der
Wiener Hofbibliothek, in Zeitschrift der Savigny-Stiftung
(Romanistische Abteilung), T. XIX, p. 59). It is on
paper, of the end of the fourteenth century. F. 200 v.
νόμος ῥωδέων ναυτικῶς κατ' ἐκλογὴν ἐκ τοῦ τεσσαρισκαιδεκάτου
βιβλίου τῶν διγέστων. Part III. F. 202 v. The three chapters of Appendix E. The Sea-law ends f. 203 r.

X Vindobonensis iuridicus graecus 7 is described by
Lambecius (op. cit., coll. 69–74), Heimbach (op. cit., T. I,
p. lxxviii), and Zach. (op. cit., p. 63). It is on paper, of
the end of the thirteenth or beginning of the fourteenth
century. F. 42 r. κεφάλαια ῥοδίων κατ' ἐκλογήν. Table of
contents of Part III. F. 43 r. νόμος ῥοδίων ναυτικὸς κατ'
ἐκλογὴν ἐκ τοῦ ιδ' β τῶν διαγέστων. Part III. The three
chapters of Appendix E. The Sea-law ends f. 46 r.

Y Ambrosianus Q 50 sup. is described by Martini and
Bassi (op. cit., vol. II, p. 761), who assign it to the thirteenth century. It is on paper. F. 353 v. περὶ ῥοδίων
ναυτικὸς νόμος κατ' ἐκλογήν. Part III. F. 361 v. The three
chapters of Appendix E. The Sea-law ends f. 362 v.

Z Codex Francisci Venturii. A manuscript in the
Riccardiana (numbered 2118) contains, among many other
things, a translation of part of the Sea-law, in the hand
of Francesco Venturi,[1] accompanied by a letter from him
addressed to an unknown person and dated 'Di Firenze
il dì 18 di Dec⁶ 1604'. Both the letter and the translation (which contains Part II, table of chapters of Part III,

---

[1] Francesco Venturi was born at Florence in 1576. His mother
was niece of Pietro Vettori. He was made Bishop of San Severo in
1625, resigned in 1629, and became Archdeacon of Florence, where he
died in 1641. His life is in Ughelli, Italia Sacra, VIII, col. 363, and
in Ianus Nicius Erythraeus, Pinacotheca Imaginum Illustrium Viro-
rum, Colon., 1645, II, pp. 25-27; and a list of his works in Dom.
Moreni, Bibliografia ... della Toscana, Firenze, 1805, II, p. 440. He
was a protégé of Scipione Cardinal Cobellucci, who is perhaps the
addressee of the letter. The Cardinal was a jurist and scholar. See
his life in Ianus Nicius Erythraeus, supra, I, p. 71, and Alphonsus
Ciaconius, Vitae Pontificum et Cardinalium, Romae, 1677, IV, 446.

and Part III as far as c. 29 inclusive) have been printed
in the Byz. Zeitschrift, VIII, pp. 183-9. The gentleman
who made the copy for Dr. Fischer 'hat an einigen
Stellen den Wortlaut der Vorrede nicht genau entziffern
können.' This is very true. In the first five lines of his
transcription of Venturi's letter there are the following
mistakes. The manuscript reads 'Molto Ill^r s^r mio'
and not 'Illustrissima Vostra Signoria'; it reads 'in tt^o'
(i. e. in tutto) and not 'Inlt'; 'nautiche' and not 'nau-
tile'; 'scusera' and not 'sensera'; 'state' and not
'stata'; 'loro' and not 'coro'; 'Tholosano' and not
'Holosano'. The transcript of the Sea-law is more suc-
cessful, but the following errors deserve mention. Part II.
(9) For 'cubitum' the manuscript gives 'cubitorum'.
(15) For 'atque in contrib.' the manuscript gives 'atque
ita in contrib.' (17) For 'dederit' the manuscript gives
'dederis'. (18) In this chapter Venturi, finding himself
unable no doubt to make any sense, gives the original
Greek. In my apparatus criticus I note the variants.
Table of chapters. (18) For 'peregrin ...' the manuscript
gives 'peregrinante'. (29) For 'abso .. ta' (which
Dr. Fischer wants to fill up as 'absoluta') the manuscript
gives clearly 'absorta'. 'Absorta' (from 'absorbere') is
a good translation of κλασματισθέντος. (37) For 'vel vectorum' the manuscript has 'et vectorum'. (42) For
'perfracta' the manuscript has 'perforata'.

PART III

Readings in Byz. Zeitschrift.	Readings of manuscript.
2 subripiant	surripiant
inquisito	sic, corrected from explorato
puto	puta
canabinarum	cannabinarum
velum	after velum, magnum has been erased
4 infecto	infesto
5 invitus id cecidit	invitus enim id fecit
7 delibitaverit	debilitaverit
medicam et ei	medicamenta et
8 discururrerit	discucurrerit
9 sempulis	scrupulis

MANUSCRIPTS USED FOR THIS EDITION

Readings in Byz. Zeitschrift.	Readings of manuscript.
11 inquirant	perquirant
16 nec . . . ideo	nec n. (i. e. enim) ideo
21 contraxent	contraxerint
27 venient	veniant
societatem	societati
exspectet	sic, corrected from maneat

Harl. Harley 5675, of the sixteenth century, on paper. F. 163 r. κεφάλαια τοῦ νόμου τοῦ ναυτικοῦ. Table of contents of Part II. Part II. F. 166 r. κεφάλαια νόμου τοῦ ῥοδίου. Table of contents of Part III. F. 169 r. νόμος ῥοδίων ναυτικὸς κατ' ἐκλογὴν ἐκ τοῦ ἐνδεκάτου βιβλίου τῶν διγέστων. Part III. F. 179 r. The three chapters of Appendix E. The Sea-law ends on f. 179 v.

Laud. Laudianus graecus 91, of the early sixteenth century, on paper. It is described by H. O. Coxe (op. cit., col. 579) and by Zach. (ὁ πρόχειρος νόμος, p. 323), who refers to it as Laud. 64. F. 217 (or 220) v. νόμος ῥοδίων κατ' ἐκλογὴν ἐκ τοῦ ιδ' βιβλίου τῶν διγέστων. Part III. Chapters 49 and 50 of Appendix E. It then gives the paragraphs ἐκ τῶν περὶ ὕβρεων, which are printed by Zach. in the preface to his edition of the Epanagoge aucta (J. G.-R., IV, p. 178), and ends (f. 221 or 224 v.) with the paragraph περὶ ἀνατροπῆς δωρεῶν.

Mess. Messinensis 114 is described by G. Fraccaroli (Dei Codici Greci del Monastero del SS. Salvatore che si conservano nella Biblioteca Universitaria di Messina, in Studi It. di Filol. Classica, V, p. 487 et p. 491) and by Salvatore Rossi (Catalogo dei Codici Greci del antico Monastero del SS. Salvatore che si conservano nella Biblioteca Universitaria di Messina, in Archivio Storico Messinese, Tomo IV, Messina, 1903, p. 331). It is assigned by Rossi to the twelfth century, but my friend, Mr. T. W. Allen, from a photograph shown him, was inclined to put it late in the eleventh. F. 139 v. κεφάλαια νόμου ῥωδίων κατ' ἐκλογήν. Table of contents of Part III. F. 141 r. νόμος ῥωδίων ναυτικὸς κατ' ἐκλογὴν ἐκ τῶν βιβλίων τῶν διγέστων. Part III. It ends (f. 146 v.) with the words συμβῇ τι τῶν εἰρη. of c. 29. The photographs of this manuscript did not reach me

xxix

until after my text was in print, and I therefore give its
variants here.   The table of chapters seems to have been
erased, and there I am not always sure of the reading.

(F. 139 v.) κεφάλαια νόμου ῥωδίων κατ᾽ ἐκλογήν   Tit. 4 περα-
τόρων (?) (f. 140 r.) Tit. 5   Tit. 7 πήρωσιν . . . ἐργασαμένων]
τύφλωσιν ἐργασαμένων ἢ αἰδοίων (?) κύλλωσιν ποιήσαντος   Tit. 8
ναύτου Tit. 9 ἐπιβατῶν περὶ] ἐπιβάτου καὶ περὶ   Tit. 11 ναυλου-
μένων] ναναναυλουμένων   Tit. 12 ἐν οἴκῳ] οἴκω   Tit. 16 ἐνδανει-
σθέντων   Tit. 17 χρισθέντος   Tit. 20 συμφωνήσαντος ὁρήσαντος
Tit. 21 κοινῶν ἀντιλεγῶντων ἀλλήλος (f. 140 v.) Tit. 22   Tit. 23
καὶ ἐμπ. π. γόμ.] καὶ γόμον   Tit. 24 ἐμπόρων καὶ μετ. γεν.] om.
Tit. 25 τοῦ ἐμπ.   Tit. 27 ἢ κοινωνίας] κοινωνία   Tit. 30 καὶ τοῦ
ἐμπόρου   Tit. 32 ἐκνορίζειν   Tit. 33 om.   Tit. 34 βέστιν ἀντλι-
άσμων (?) φορτίων βλάβης   Tit. 36 ἑτέρου πλοίου καταδιδόντος
(f. 141 r.) (Tit. 37) καὶ ἐπιβάτων σωθέντος   Tit. 38 καὶ ζάλη κατα-
λειφθέντων   Tit. 39 βουλήσαντος   Tit. 41 σωθ. ἢ συναπολ.]
σωθέντων   Tit. 43 ποιήσαντι   Tit. 44 αὐχενίων   Tit. 45 πελάγου
Tit. 47 ἐκ τοῦ βυθοῦ Titulus tertiae partis νόμος Ῥωδίων ναυτικὸς
κατ᾽ ἐκλογὴν ἐκ τῶν βιβλίων τῶν διγέστων   c. 1 1 ὁρμᾷ   2
κατασχεθῆ ὁ κλ. καὶ ὁμ.   4 κατὰ om.   c. 2 2 (f. 141 v.) ὁρμοῦντος
9 σχοίνων   10 ἀρμενίων διλοιπῶν   c. 3 3 τὼ τὰ συλα παθόντι
5 ἐὰν δὲ] ἐὰν   7 μάλιστα σύλα χρυσίων εἰ   c. 4 2 (f. 142 r.) τοῦ
ναυκλήρου   4 ὁ ναυκλ. τοῖς συλ. τὸ ἅπερ ἀπόλεσαν   6 τὴν ζημίαν
οἱ ἐπιβ.   c. 5 3 εἰς κεφ.] τὴν κεφ.   ἢ] ἢ καὶ   6 χρόνου] καιροῦ
καὶ ἐπιμ.] αὐτοῦ   c. 6 4 ἢ om.   c. 7 1 τῶν ναυκλήρων   2
                                                          o o
πυρώσει   4 (f. 142 v.) ὑπὲρ δὲ   5 κοίλης χρυσίνους] ν ν εἰ δὲ
καὶ   6 ἐστιν   7 post τοῦ θανάτου addit ὡς ὕποπτος   c. 8 5
ἡ τούτων ἐκτίμησις ἱκανὸν ποιήσουσι   6 τοῦ χ.] ἐν τῶ χρόνω   7
ναυκλήρω   9 post ποιείτωσαν addit ἀναμφιβόλως   c. 9 5
ἐκτιματούσθωσαν   7 πλείονας   10 (f. 143 r.) ἀγόμενος   12
ἐφάρπαγῆ   14 σὺνψισμὸν συνβαλλέσθωσαν   15 κέρδοκοινωνία
c. 10 6 καὶ τῆ τοῦ   8 τοῦ om.   c. 11 1 ἐκβαλλέτωσαν   2
(f. 143 v.) παλέον εἰ δὲ βάλωσιν   4 τὸ om.   5 οἱ om.   6
αὕτω   8 εἰστὸκεραίαν   9 ἄγκυρά   10 σχοῖνα κανναβικὰ
12 μὴ om.   c. 12 3 παραδιδώτω τὴν παραθήκην   4 φυλάττειν om.
7 κα(f. 144 r.) θὼς   c. 13 3 ἄργυρον   c. 15 5 κελεύσι
ἐξηλίσει   9 τῶν ναυκλήρων   10 (f. 144 v.) ἄκυρα   12 τις om.
13 ἐν om.   c. 16 2 ἐπὶ om.   ἔγγεα   3 σωθέντος δὲ   5 ἐπιβουλῆς ἐγγέων   c. 17 2 ἄργυρον ἐγγράψονται   7 σῶα τὰ ἴδια
ἀπολ.] ἀπολ. αὐτὸ σῶον   9 ἐκ om.   10 καθά(f. 145 r.)περ τὸ
κέρδος   c. 18 4 ἔγγεα   5 ἀποδημεῖ   c. 19 2 μετέπειτα] μετὰ
ἀπόλλει αὐτὸν   c. 20 4 ἐὰν μὲν ὁ ναυλούμενος om.   5 οὕτως
τε   6 ἀποδώτω τὸ ἥμισυ   9 ἡ δὲ πρᾶξις usque ad finem cap.]
om.   (f. 145 v.) c 21 1 ἐγγράφως   2 τὰ om.   3 ἐγγράφως
καὶ om.   6 σαβουλάτορ (?)   8 τῶ λόγω μόνω   10 τὰ σωζόμενα δὲ   c. 22 2 καὶ om.   σχοίνων ὁ ἔμπορος] ἔμπορος   5

MANUSCRIPTS USED FOR THIS EDITION

φέρειν   9 (f. 146 r.) συμβολὴν   c. **23** 2 ἔστωσαν παρέχῃ . . . λοιπαζ.] om.   4 συνεγράψατω   c. **24** 3 τὴν ἐμποδίαν   c. **25** 1 τῶν ἐγγεγραμμένων om.   2 δέκα] ιβ´   3 καὶ ἡ δευτ. προθ.] ἕως καὶ δευτέρας προθεσμίας   4 τὸν ναῦλον πληρώσας   5 προσερχέσθω   6 τὸν ναῦλον πλεέτω   c. **26** 5 ἀζημί(f. 146 v.)ους c. **27** 2 κοινωνία   3 τοῦ om.   4 ἐνόρια   6 ἅμα καὶ φ.] καὶ φ. ἅμα   8 ἐλεγχθεὶς   9 τὴν om.   c. **28** 3 πυρκατάκαιᾶς   4 γενέσθαι] post hoc verbum om. usque ad c. **29** 4 ἐφορᾶν c. **29** 6 εἰρη-] finis paginae et codicis

b. Manuscripts of the Synopsis Major.

The Synopsis Major, a work probably dating from the middle of the tenth century (Zach., Geschichte, p. 26; Siciliano Villanueva, p. 110), contains fourteen chapters of Part III of the Sea-law; namely, 2, 3, 7, 9 (as far as κατὰ τιμὴν ὤν), 10, 13, 28, 31, 34, 35, 37, 41, 44, 47. The Synopsis Major was first published by Ioannes Leunclaius, from a manuscript of Ioannes Sambucus (LX Librorum Βασιλικων . . . Ecloga siue Synopsis, Basil., 1575 fol.). Carolus Labbaeus emended the text from manuscripts at Paris— chiefly Paris. gr. 1351 (Caroli Labbaei Observationes et Emendationes in Synopsim Basilicων. Parisiis, 1607. 12mo). A new edition of the Synopsis Major was published by Zach. (J. G.-R., Pars V, Lipsiae, 1869), but, although he gives a long list of manuscripts in his Prolegomena, his text seems to be based on the published editions, and on a Leipzig manuscript which was written at Venice in A.D. 1541 (Prolegomena, p. xi). I have thought it necessary, therefore, to collate the chapters of the Sea-law which are given by the Synopsis Major in some ancient manuscripts of that work. These are the following:—

a Arundel 516 (in the British Museum), on parchment. The catalogue assigns it to the thirteenth century, but it is perhaps earlier. F. 208 r. ἀρχὴ σὺν θεῷ τοῦ ν´ στοιχείου, περὶ ναυτικῶν ἐνοχῶν καὶ παντοίων ἀγωγῶν τῶν κινουμένων περὶ πλοίου καὶ πάντων τῶν ἐν αὐτῷ ἐμπλεόντων ναυκλήρων πιστικῶν ναυτῶν ἐμπόρων τε καὶ λοιπῶν ἐπιβατῶν καὶ περὶ ναναγίου. F. 210 r. ἐν δὲ τῷ η´ τίτλῳ περιέχεται τὰ κεφάλαια τοῦ ῥοδίου νόμου οὗτινος ἐν τῶ β´ κεφαλαίω φησίν (then follows c. 2 of Part III). The chapters end f. 212 r.

b Barroccianus 173 (in the Bodleian Library), on parchment, ' saec. xii et xiii,' according to H. O. Coxe (op. cit., col. 288). F. σξα´ r. ἀρχὴ σὺν θεῶ κτλ., as above, except that it reads πλοίων and αὐτοῖς. F. σξα´ v. ἐν δὲ τῶ νγ´ (sic) τίτλω περιέχεται τὰ κεφάλαια τοῦ ῥοδίου νόμου οὗτινος ἐν τῶ β´ κεφαλαίω φησίν (then follows c. 2 of Part III). The chapters end f. σξβ´ r.

m Marcianus graecus (fondo antico) 173, on parchment, ' saeculi circiter xii,' according to Zanetti (op. cit., I, p. 100). F. 164 v. ἀρχὴ σὺν θεῶ κτλ., as in *b*. F. 165 v. ἐν δὲ τῶ η´ τίτλω κτλ., as in *a*. The chapters end f. 166 v.

p Paris. graecus 1346, on parchment, of the eleventh century. F. 173 r. ἀρχὴ σὺν θεῶ κτλ., as in *b*. F. 174 r. ἐν δὲ τῶ η´ τίτλω κτλ., as in *a*. The chapters end f. 175 v.

r Palatinus graecus 8, on parchment, of the eleventh century. F. 156 v. ἀρχὴ σὺν θεῶ κτλ., as in *b*. F. 157 v. ἐν δὲ τῶ η´ τίτλω κτλ., as in *a*. The chapters end f. 158 v.

METHOD OF THE CRITICAL APPARATUS.

All the statements in this book with respect to any of the manuscripts described above are based on my own examination of the manuscript in question, subject to the following exceptions. For A, I had to be content with FM's transcript, as the original writing is now almost illegible. For the manuscripts at Leipzig (four leaves of J), Vienna (W and X), and Messina (Mess.), I used photographs ; I also used photographs—made by M. Sauvanaud's clear and economical process—to revise my collations of P, Q, and T.

I give a complete collation of the following manuscripts, so far as they contain the Sea-law : A, B, C, D, E, G, J, K, L, M, N, O, P, Q, R, S, T, U, V, X, Y, Mess., *a, b, m, p, r*.[1]

---

[1] The readings of these MSS. are given in the apparatus criticus, with the exception of T, U, and Mess. The readings of T and U are given in an appendix, because they belong to an interpolated class ; the readings of Mess. have been already given.

Where a, b, m, p, r agree, I denote the agreement by Σ. The reader is entitled to infer, where I do not notice a variant of one of these manuscripts, that the manuscript in question agrees with the printed text. In some cases I have expressly noted that one or more manuscripts agreed with the printed text. This is a work of supererogation, done in some leading passages out of tenderness for the learned reader, in order that he may not have the fatigue of going through a process of reasoning to ascertain, by counting the manuscripts which disagree with the printed text, what manuscripts agree with it.

It remains for me to state how far the implied agreement extends between a manuscript of which variants are not given and the printed text. The manuscripts offer great diversities in spelling, accentuation, and breathing. Varieties of accentuation and breathing I only notice in a few exceptional cases. Varieties of spelling I notice in the case of the older manuscripts; except that I do not notice the omission of iota subscript.

I give the spelling of A, B (as far as c. 15 inclusive of Part III), J, L, M, N, P. Where I do not notice a variant of one of these manuscripts, it may be inferred that its spelling (but in the case of B only as far as c. 15 of Part III) agrees with that of the printed text. In the case of the other manuscripts, that inference may not be drawn; with these, I only notice differences of spelling where they throw light upon the origin of a variant or are interesting for other reasons. I do not, as a rule, notice the ordinary contractions or the use of letters to denote numerals. I have noticed them in the early chapters of Part II, where there is the widest diversity as to the numbers.

As regards the manuscripts of which I do not give full collations, I give a complete collation of F as far as chapter 20 of Part III, and for the chapters given in Appendix D. I give a complete collation of f for Part II only. I collate H for Part II, the first twenty-

one chapters of Part III, and the chapters given in
Appendix D. I collate h for the first twelve chapters
of Part III, and for chapters 20 and 21. I give a complete collation of v for Part II, and chapters 9, 19, and
20 of Part III. I give a complete collation of W for
the first fifteen chapters of Part III. Of *Harl.* I give the
readings for chapters 9 and 20 only. Of *Laud.* I only
give the readings where I am doubtful as to the readings
of U, of which *Laud.* is probably a copy. Of Z (i. e. the
vanished original from which Venturi made his translation) I can only give the readings occasionally, as Venturi's
translation is not close, and his knowledge of Greek imperfect. His most curious blunder is the translation of
τὰ ἡμίναυλα as ' nobis naula ' or ' nostra naula '.

With some of the oldest manuscripts, viz. B, C, J, L, M,
N, P, Q, Mess., I have noted where each page begins. I
have not done so with regard to A because FM do not
give the beginning of each page with sufficient precision.
The following table, which is derived from their statements, is only approximately accurate :—

f. 64 r. begins with		Title of Part II.
64 v.	,,	c. ιθ', 2.
20 r.	,,	Title of c. 27.
20 v.	,,	c. 1, 5.
37 r.	,,	c. 7, 3.
37 v.	,,	c. 11, 6.
50 r.	,,	c. 16, 5.
50 v.	,,	c. 22.
58 r.	,,	c. 28.
58 v.	,,	c. 34, 5.
59 r.	,,	c. 39.
59 v.	,,	c. 44.

OTHER MANUSCRIPTS OF THE SEA-LAW

There are many manuscripts of the Sea-law in existence in addition to those used for this edition. I give
a short list of manuscripts not used by me, derived partly
from my own examination, partly from a list given by
Zach. (Geschichte, p. 314), and partly from notices in

xxxiv

catalogues. The list does not pretend to be exhaustive, but it may be found useful by future editors. The manuscripts are arranged by countries.

ITALY.

There are three manuscripts in the Vatican library which I have not used—Vaticanus graecus 1168, Vaticanus graecus 1185, and Palatinus graecus 55. Vaticanus graecus 1168 is the only one of these which I have seen. It contains (beginning at f. 109 v.) the third part of the Sea-law entituled κεφάλαια τοῦ νόμου τοῦ ῥοδίου. Although it is on parchment, and in a hand which might be of the twelfth century, it gives a poor text, and omits many phrases and chapters, e. g. chapters 10, 16, and 20. The others are both of the sixteenth century; the Palatine manuscript is described by Stevenson (op. cit., p. 28). According to Zach. ('Ανέκδοτα, p. 176, n. 4, Epanagoge, p. 56) it is a copy of Marcianus gr. 181 (my manuscript O).

According to Zach. (Geschichte, p. 314, n. 69) the Sea-law is found in Vallicelli F 47. This is a slip. I have examined the manuscript carefully, and it does not contain the Sea-law or any part of it.

In the monastery of Grotta Ferrata there are three manuscripts which contain the Sea-law. Two of these—H, h—have been already dealt with. The third—Cryptensis Zγ VII—is described by Father Rocchi (op. cit., p. 493), and I have examined it. It is of the fifteenth century, on paper, much worm-eaten. The Sea-law begins (f. 124 v.) κεφάλαια τοῦ νόμου τοῦ . . . δίου τίτλος. Part III. Then come:—

λζ′ ἐὰν διὰ τὸ κουφισθῆναι . . . οὐχ ὁρᾷ τῇ κοντριβουτίονι (= Appendix G (a), (b), (c)).

τοῦ β′ τίτλου του ιβ′ βιβλίου τοῦ κ^ω.

λη′ ὁ ἁρπάζων . . . ἀποδιδότω (= Appendix E, c. 48).

ἐκ τοῦ θ′ τίτλου τοῦ μθ′ βιβλίου τῶν διγέστων.

λθ′ οἱ ἐκ τῆς ἐλεεινοτάτης . . . παρεχέτωσαν (= Appendix E, c. 50).

μ′ ὁ δὲ βαρυτέρα πραῖδα . . . ἐκπέμπονται (= Appendix E, c. 50).

μα′ ἀπολλυμένου τοῦ πλοίου . . . ἀποβληθῶσιν (= Appendix G (ƒ)).

μβ′ τοῦ πλοίου ναυαγήσαντος . . . ὡς μὴ μετακομίσας (= Appendix G (g)).

μγ′ ὁ ναύλαρχος . . . ὠφεληθήσεται (= Appendix G (h)).

This is followed by Part II, the chapters of which are numbered consecutively (μδ′, &c.). The Sea-law ends (f. 131 v.) with the words οὐ δεῖ συμβαλλομένους ναυκληρίαν. So far as I have examined it, its readings agree with H.

Zach., in his list, cites a Neapolitan manuscript by the number 202. This manuscript, as appears from a statement of Zach. elsewhere (Delineatio, p. 40), and from Niccola Alianelli (Delle antiche consuetudini . . . delle Provincie Napolitane, Napoli, 1871, p. xvii. n. (1)), is now numbered II C. 6. It is no doubt identical with the manuscript described under that press-mark by Salvatore Cyrillus (Codices Graeci MSS. Regiae Bibliothecae Borbonicae, Tomus I, Neapoli, 1826, p. 233), who says that it is on paper, in folio, of the end of the fifteenth century, and that it contains ' Epistolas Canonicas et Πρόχειρον manuale legum '.

FRANCE.

Among the Paris manuscripts of the Sea-law I have already dealt with 1356, 1367, 1383, and 1384. But these are not all. Zach. also cites in his list 1368, 1381 A, 1391, and 1720. Of these I have not examined 1368 or 1381 A because, according to M. Omont's Inventaire, neither 1368 (Inventaire, II, p. 26) nor 1381 A (Inventaire, II, p. 32) contains the Sea-law. 1351 A, which is not in Zach.'s list, does contain some rules of maritime law, although not the Sea-law, and perhaps Zach. put 1381 A for 1351 A by a slip of the pen. I have examined 1351 A, 1391, 1720, and suppl. gr. 1236 ; and the following notes, where other sources are not mentioned, are based on my own observations.

Paris. graecus 1351 A, of the fifteenth century, contains (according to the Inventaire, II, p. 21) 'collectanea
iuridica legum rusticarum, navalium, canonum aposto-
lorum et synodorum, &c. (337 v.)'. The only trace of
'leges navales' is at f. 349 v., where there are several passages which have found their way from Book LIII of the
Basilica, e. g. B', ϛ', θ'.

Paris. supplément grec 1236 is assigned by M. Omont
(MSS. du Supplément Grec, p. 64) to the fourteenth to
nineteenth centuries, and is described as being ' copie (en
partie) de Mynas '. The Sea-law, which extends from
f. 152 v. to 156 v., is in a nineteenth century hand.

Paris. graecus 1720, which was copied by Manuel
Dimiri (Inventaire, II, p. 129), forms the basis of Zach.'s
edition of the Ecloga ad Prochiron mutata (J. G.-R.,
Pars IV, pp. 49–170). The Sea-law is given in this work
in an interpolated form, and I prefer to base my text of
that form, so far as I deal with it in my apparatus criticus, or in Appendices A and D, upon earlier and better
manuscripts.

Paris. graecus 1391 deserves more attention. It is
described by Pard. (I, p. 163, n. 2, and more fully VI,
p. 482), and shortly by M. Omont (Inventaire, II, p. 37).
It is of the thirteenth century. The following account
of its contents, so far as they relate to maritime law, supplements, and to some extent corrects, that given by
Pard. at VI, p. 482–3. F. 228 r. νόμος ῥωδίων ναυτικὸς ἐκ
τοῦ βιβλίου τῶν διγέστων (in the margin κϛ') Part III.
' En général,' as Pard. justly says, ' cette copie est fort
incorrecte. Plusieurs chapitres sont mutilés ; quelque-
fois des omissions de mots et même de lignes détruisent
le sens ; les chapitres X, XIII et XXXV n'y sont point
à leur place.' It may be added that c. 9 begins with the
words ἐὰν δέ τις ἐπὶ πράσει ἄγεται, and that c. 31 and c. 34
are also left out. F. 233 v. The three chapters of Appendix
E. Sentences from Theophilus (see Pard.) F. 234 r. Chapters 10, 13, and 35 of Part III. F. 234 v. Paragraphs,
most of which are given by Pard. I, p. 192. (See his

corrections, VI, p. 483.) He does not mention that, after paragraph ϛ′ of his text, there comes a rubric περὶ ναυαγίου καὶ ἀποβολῆς καὶ συνεισφορᾶς (in the margin κζ′). These paragraphs are followed by chapters 7, 9 (as far as κατὰ τιμὴν ὤν), 10, 13, 28, 31, 34, 35, 37, 41, 44, 47 of Part III, i. e. most of the chapters which are given in the Synopsis Major, and these chapters reproduce, although very carelessly, the text which I cite as Σ. The Sea-law ends f. 237 v.

Spain.

Zach. only cites one Spanish manuscript—Scorialens., II, X, 6. E. Miller (Catalogue des Manuscrits Grecs de la Bibliothèque de l'Escurial, Paris, 1848) mentions (p. 35) R, III, 17 'en papier de coton et du XIVᵉ siècle ', as containing the Laws of the Rhodians. Charles Graux and Albert Martin (Notices sommaires des MS. Grecs d'Espagne et de Portugal, Paris, 1892) refer to two—Archivo Histórico Nacional, at Madrid, 163, 3, of the sixteenth century, partly written by Darmarius (p. 22), and Bibl. du Palais at Madrid, F, written in 1562 by Darmarius (p. 69). They compare the former manuscript with Matritensis, 139. Iriarte's Catalogue (Regiae Bibliothecae Matritensis Codices Graeci MSS. Joannes Iriarte . . . excussit. Volumen Prius. Matriti. 1769, fol.) does not go up to this number.

Netherlands.

In the Catalogus librorum . . . Bibliothecae Publicae Universitatis Lugduno-Batavae. Lugd.-Bat, 1716,fol., there is mentioned (p. 392) among the Vossian manuscripts, ' Legis Rhodiae nauticae synopsis ex undecimo libro Digestorum varia scriptura. In Charta 19.' The learned librarian of the University Library at Leiden (S. G. de Vries) was kind enough to inform me that this is the only manuscript of the Sea-law in his library, and that it is of the fifteenth century.

In addition to the leaves once torn from the Laurentian manuscript (my J) there are three manuscripts of the Sea-law at Leipzig. They are all described by V. Gardthausen (Katalog der Griechischen Handschriften der Universitäts-Bibliothek zu Leipzig, 1898). No. 43 is on paper, of the sixteenth century. F. 142 r. νόμος ʿΡοδίων κατ᾽ ἐκλογήν. Part III. Chapters given in Appendix E. It ends f. 147 v. (p. 57). No. 44 is on paper, of the sixteenth century. F. 121 r. (no title). Part III as far as c. 39 τὸν τόπον ἐκεῖνον. It ends f. 126 r. (p. 61). No. 45 is on paper, of the fourteenth century. F. 87 v. νόμος ʿΡοδίων ναυτικός. It apparently contains the table of contents of Part III and Part III (p. 64). These manuscripts, as well as No. 46, which contains the fragment from J, once belonged to Biener, and are often quoted by Zach. under his name.

There are two manuscripts of the Sea-law at Munich, numbered 149 and 303 in Hardt's Catalogue (Catalogus Codicum Manuscriptorum Graecorum Bibliothecae Regiae Bavaricae. Auctore Ignatio Hardt. Monachii, 1806), and there described, the former at Tom. II, p. 160, and the latter at Tom. III, p. 236. Mr. T. W. Allen has been kind enough to examine these manuscripts for me; and the following account, so far as it supplements or corrects the Catalogue, is derived from him. No. 149 is on paper, of the fifteenth century, measuring 295 × 210 mm. F. 148 r. apparently contains the last chapter of Part II. F. 151 r. νόμος ῥοδίων ναυτικὸς κατ᾽ ἐκλογὴν ἐκ τοῦ ἐνδεκάτου βιβλίου τῶν διγέστων. Part III. The chapters of Appendix E. The Sea-law ends f. 164 r. From the readings which Mr. Allen gave the manuscript appears to be worthless. No. 303 is on parchment, and (according to Hardt) of the thirteenth (according to Mr. Allen) of the fourteenth century. It measures 19 × 140 mm. The title of the whole book is νόμος κατ᾽ ἐκλογήν. There is a table of contents at f. 1 v., the last entry in which, unnumbered but = 50, is νόμος ῥωδίων ὁ κατὰ θάλασσαν. F. 181 r. no title, but in a space of one line, m. rec., νόμος ῥωδίων. The chapters are unnumbered, beginning ἐὰν πλοῖον ὁρμᾶ (Part III, c. 1) and ending (f. 188 r.) with a chapter which begins ναυαγήσαντος and ends ἐξεμπτυσμοῦ (=Appendix I (d)). After this comes

ἐκ τοῦ πρώτου τ̇ τοῦ νγ΄ ββ̇^λ τῶν βασι^λ, and then c. 39 of Part III as far as τὸν τόπον ἐκεῖνον. The book ends f. 188 v. From this account, as well as from an examination of select places which Mr. Allen made, it is clear that the manuscript belongs to the class of T, U, and Laud. It may be a copy of T.

There is a fragment of the Sea-law at Vienna, philos. gr. 90, which contains (f. 108 r., 109 r.) Part III, cc. 39–47, and the three chapters of Appendix E. It is described by Lambecius (op. cit., lib. VII, col. 344–62). It is on paper, and, according to Zach. (Nachträge und Bemer-kungen, in Zeitschrift der Savigny-Stiftung, XIX, p. 76), of the fifteenth century. According to Zach., it contains the following note on f. 108 r. in the hand of Sambucus, to whom it once belonged: ' Omnino desunt hic undecim quaterniones, quas Leunclavius accepit et restituet.'

RUSSIA, GREECE, AND THE EAST.

Zach. cites two Moscow manuscripts—Mosquens. 56 and 302. This is not quite correct if we may trust Chr. Frid. de Matthaei, Accurata Graecorum MSS. Bibliothe-carum Mosquensium . . . Notitia, Lipsiae, 1805. Accord-ing to him, in the library of the Holy Synod, codex 301, on paper, of the fifteenth century, contains ' Rhodiorum νόμον ναυτικόν' (p. 194). In the Bibliotheca Typographei Synodalis, codex 38 quarto, on parchment, of the eleventh or twelfth century, contains : f. 215 νόμος ναυτικός· ναυκλήρῳ μισθοῦ μέρη β, f. 216 νόμος ῥοδίων ναυτικὸς κατ' ἐκλογὴν ἐκ τοῦ ἐνδεκάτου βιβλίου τῶν διγέστων· ἐὰν πλοῖον ὁρμᾷ ἐπί. It ends f. 222 (p. 320). Codex 56 quarto is of the fifteenth or sixteenth century and, according to Matthaei, does not contain the Sea-law. Zach. also cites from his own knowledge two manuscripts at Mount Athos—'Ιβήρων 21 and Λαύρας 6. The former is on paper, of the fourteenth century, and appears to contain merely fragments of the Sea-law (Zach. 'Ανέκδοτα, p. xiv). The latter is on parchment, of the twelfth century (Zach. 'Ανέκδοτα, p. xviii). There is another of the eleventh or twelfth century at Mount Sinai (V. Gardthausen, Catalogus Codicum Graecorum Sinaiticorum, Oxford, 1886, p. 228 [1]). There is a sixteenth-century manuscript of the Sea-law at Patmos (Σακκελιων (Ιω) Πατμιακη Βιβλιοθηκη, Athens, αωη', p. 201), and a fifteenth-century manuscript at Athens (Κατάλογος κωδίκων τῆς βιβλιοθήκης τῆς βουλῆς in Νέος Ἑλληνομνήμων, T. I, p. 227).

PRINTED TEXTS OF THE SEA-LAW

The Sea-law was first published by Simon Schard in 1561, together with αἱ ῥοπαί and the Soldier's and Farmer's laws. This is the title of the book : ' De Varia temporum in iure civili observatione, Eustathii . . . Libellus. Item Leges Rhodiorum navales, militares et Georgicae Iustiniani : quarum priores ambae nunc primum, Georgicae autem multo emendatiores & auctiores quam antea, iuxta exemplar D. Antonii Augustini eduntur. Opera & studio Simonis Schardii I. C. Basiliae, per Ioannem Oporinum.' The date, 1561, is at the end of the book, which is a small 8vo. Schard had a proper opinion of the works which he was bringing out for the first time, and went so far as to attribute the distressed state of the world at that epoch to the neglect in which they had fallen. ' Quis etenim non videt,' he says in his dedication (a 5), ' quantis incommodis miseri ex legum Georgicarum neglectione obruantur, quamque commercia legum navalium despicientia concutiantur ? ' His notes, though few, are learned, and he illustrates the Sea-law with success from other maritime codes. His language about the

---

[1] I owe this reference to Dr. William Fischer (Byz. Zeitschrift, Band VIII, p. 167).

manuscripts is vague. In his dedication (a 3) he says, of the leges navales, militares atque georgicae, 'non tantum ad exemplar Augustinianeum ... illas describi curavi, sed & cum aliis exemplaribus quae in Urbe,' i.e. Rome, 'inveniebantur, per ocium ipse studiose contuli.' The Prologue, which he published in the shorter form, was not in all his copies. 'Nam nec in eo quod nobis Florentiae consequi licuit, nec in altero eorum quod Romae in Vaticana invenitur, extabat. Veruntamen cum & in exemplari... D. Antonii Augustini, & in altero Vaticanae Bibliothecae id invenerim, quale id fuit, hisce legibus praemittendum censui' (p. 272). According to Zach. (Geschichte, p. 314, n. 1067) the four manuscripts which Schard made use of were probably Laur. IX, 8 (my J), Vatic. gr. 847 (my E), 1168, and 1185 (formerly No. 170 of A. Augustinus). It is clear that Schard based his text upon the copy of Augustinus. As I have not seen Vatic. gr. 1185, I cannot say whether that is the copy in question. It is probable that his language about a careful collation of other manuscripts is exaggerated, and that he merely looked into them here and there. There is evidence tending to show that he made some use of Vatic. gr. 844 (my D). The next text of the Sea-law is in the Ius Graeco-Romanum of Leunclavius (Iuris Graeco-Romani tam canonici quam civilis Tomi duo. Iohannis Leunclavii Amelburni ... studio ... eruti ... nunc primum editi cura Marquardi Freheri I.C. MDXCVI. Francofurti. fol.). The Sea-law is at Vol. II, pp. 265–77. By the side of the title, in the margin, is printed 'Ex. Franc. Pithœi bibliotheca'. Leunclavius does not simply copy Schard. Schard's readings often go into the margin, and it may be inferred that in such cases the text is based upon the manuscript of François Pithou. Fabrot, in his edition of the Basilica, inserts Part III of the Sea-law—including the table of contents and the chapters which I give in Appendix E—as the eighth title of Book LIII. It extends from p. 651 to p. 671 of Volume VI (Βασιλικων Tomus VI, Carolus Annibal Fabrotus ... Latine vertit & Graece edidit.

Parisiis. 1647. fol.). Fabrot sticks closely to the text of Leunclavius, and gives frequent variants from a ' C. Pet.' If this manuscript belonged to the collection of Paul Petau, it should now be in the Vatican. Petau's library was bought by Isaac Vossius for Queen Christina of Sweden (Sylloge Epistolarum a viris illustribus scriptarum. Leidae, 1727. T. 3, pp. 591, 604), but there is no manuscript of the Sea-law among the Codices Graeci Reginae. Possibly it is the manuscript at Leiden, where other manuscripts of Petau are found.

The next edition of the Sea-law was published by Arnoldus Vinnius in 1647. I only know the second edition of this work, which appeared in 1668 and bears the following title: ' V. Cl. Petri Peckii In Titt. Dig. & Cod. ad Rem Nauticam Pertinentes, Commentarii . . . Quibus nunc accedunt Notae . . . Beneficio Arnoldi Vinnii, I. C. Item Leges Navales et Ius Navale Rhodiorum, Gr. Lat. Quod uberius quam antea . . . edidit Iohannes Laurentius, I. Ctus. Amstelodami, 1668.' Small 8vo. The text is that of Leunclavius. His notes (which chiefly refer to variants) are given in italics. Schard's notes are also given, in Roman type. This edition also contains the variants of a manuscript belonging to Nicolaus Heinsius, D. F. (i. e. Danielis filius). According to Zach. (Geschichte, p. 314, n. 1067) this is the manuscript of Isaac Vossius, which is now at Leiden. But this cannot be; for the manuscript at Leiden is on paper (see *ante*, p. xxxviii), while it is expressly stated that the manuscript of Heinsius is ' scriptus in membrana codex' (p. [10]). The readings of Heinsius' manuscript agree as a rule with those of my J. It is possible that he once owned the eight leaves which are now at Leipzig.

I have not seen any eighteenth-century edition of the Sea-law. According to Pard. (I, p. 229) it is printed at the end of one of the editions of Targa's Ponderazioni, 'avec une quantité de fautes qui la rendent ininintelligible.'

The Sea-law was printed four times in the nineteenth

century. The first time was by Pard., who published in his first volume (I, pp. 209–60) an introduction, text, translation, and commentary. The respect which is due to the memory of this great man must not blind us to the defects of his edition. The text is in substance that of Leunclavius. The critical apparatus gives the readings of Heinsius' manuscript and of four Paris manuscripts— 1356, 1367, 1391, and 1720. The Paris manuscripts were collated for Pard. by two young and incompetent friends (see p. 210, n. (1)). The commentary is confined in the main to two points. First, it indicates the relations between the Sea-law and the law of the Corpus Iuris and the Basilica. Secondly, it points out discrepancies between different parts of the Sea-law. Pard. is always lucid and sensible; but he neglects many of the questions which present themselves at once to a reader of the Sea-law.

Heimbach published Part III of the Sea-law, together with the table of contents and the chapters which I give in Appendix E, in his edition of the Basilica, as title 8 of Book LIII. He merely reprints the text of Pard.

Zach. published the Sea-law as title 40 of the Ecloga ad Prochiron mutata (J. G.-R., Pars IV). Unfortunately in the Ecloga ad Prochiron mutata the text of the Sea-law is largely altered, and Zach. based his text upon a late and bad manuscript (Paris. graecus 1720).

A happier era opened for the Sea-law in 1897, when FM published their second supplement to Heimbach's edition of the Basilica. In this work they rendered an inestimable service to the Sea-law, and also a serious disservice. The service was this. They transcribed and published a text of the Sea-law from a tenth-century palimpsest, Ambrosianus F 106 sup. (my A)—the oldest manuscript, with the possible exception of L, of which we have knowledge, and probably the best. The disservice was this. They gave a collation with Heimbach's text of another manuscript, Ambrosianus M 68 sup. (my U), which they described as giving 'recensionem optimam

additamentis interpolationibusue omnibus liberam' (p.
169). It must be admitted that two entirely different
recensions of the same book cannot both be 'optimae'. If
one represents the genuine text, the other must represent
a depraved text. Now the text of the palimpsest and the
text of Ambrosianus M 68 sup. differ as widely as any
two texts of the same book can differ. Yet Ferrini-Mercati
say of the text of the palimpsest that it 'genuinam indolem
redolet' (p. ix), that it 'linguam stylumque genuinos
refert' (p. 109, n. 5). There is an inconsistency here. If
the text of the palimpsest is genuine, as I believe it to be,
then the text of Ambrosianus M 68 sup. represents
a thoroughgoing *rifacimento*. In Ambrosianus M 68 sup.
many chapters that appear in the palimpsest and in all
other early manuscripts are left out; others are greatly
abridged or altogether rewritten; sometimes two chapters
are melted into one; words and phrases are constantly
altered. I should not dwell upon this point if the language of Ferrini-Mercati had not led astray an eminent
scholar.

M. R. Dareste published a Greek text of the Sea-law,
with introduction, translation, and commentary, in the
Revue de Philologie for January, 1905. He republished
his article, without the Greek text, in the Nouvelle Revue
Historique de Droit Français et Étranger for July–
August of the same year (Vol. XXIX, pp. 429–48). He
republished both text and article in his Nouvelles Études
d'Histoire du Droit, Troisième Série, 1906, pp. 93–132.
In default of a critical text, which it would be difficult to
establish—says M. Dareste—there is only one means of
obtaining a tolerably satisfactory result: 'C'est de
s'attacher au manuscrit qui paraît le plus ancien et le
meilleur. Ce manuscrit a été étrouvé dans la Bibliothèque
de Milan, où il porte le n° 68. Il paraît être du XIe
siècle' (p. 431 in N. R. Hist.; p. 95 in N. Études).

There is no such manuscript in the Ambrosian library as
'le MS. n° 68', but M. Dareste is evidently referring to
Ambrosianus M 68 sup., and he is as evidently confusing it

with the Ambrosian palimpsest. That is, at the latest, of the eleventh century; but Ambrosianus M 68 sup. is, at the earliest, of the end of the thirteenth century. That is the date assigned to it by the learned authors of the recent catalogue (see *ante*, p. xxvi), and Ferrini-Mercati nowhere suggest that it is of the eleventh century. The text which M. Dareste gives is from Ambrosianus M 68 sup., and his translation is made from that. He seems to be unaware that what he calls the codex rescriptus also contains a text of Part III of the Sea-law, though he knows that it contains a text of Part II. Owing to this regrettable error of M. Dareste, his translation and commentary are not as instructive as one would have expected.

PRINCIPLES ON WHICH THE TEXT IS BASED

An ideal critical text would have for its basis collations of all the known manuscripts which present an independent tradition. A former section of this Introduction shows that there are many manuscripts of the Sea-law in existence, of whose contents and value I have no certain knowledge.

But I shall probably have to excuse myself with the learned reader not for what I have failed to give him in the critical apparatus, but for what I have given him. He will be surprised, and perhaps indignant, at finding so elaborate a collection of variants at the foot of a Byzantine treatise on maritime law, where the language, as he thinks, counts for nothing, and the substance for very little. Assuming, however, that the treatise is worth editing at all, this answer may be made to his complaint. A work of the imagination is composed once for all time. An editor, to produce a correct text, has only to ascertain how the work left the author's hands. To a legal treatise, whether it be a code enacted by public authority or the work of a private hand, different considerations apply. A legal treatise is generally based in part on pre-existing

xlvi

material. Even if it is a code or statute, it is seldom altogether new law. It is generally derived in part from previous law or custom, written or unwritten. And if it is a private work, the part of compilation is generally much larger. Moreover, a law-book is a statement of something which in its nature is constantly changing. If it is a code or statute, it is continually being altered by new legislation, and the new legislation finds its place in the copies of it which are thereafter made. If it is a private treatise, it is continually being brought up to date by alterations, insertions, and omissions. Venice in the course of thirty years produced three maritime statutes, the second embodying the first with many alterations and additions, and the third doing the same with the second. The critical apparatus which Bonaini has put under the Constitutum Usus of Pisa illustrates the constant changes which were made in that code.

It follows that when we are settling the text of a legal treatise, we have to consider not one question only—what did the author write—but three questions: (a) what was the text of the materials out of which the treatise was made; (b) what was the text of the treatise as originally compiled; (c) what alterations were made in it in the course of centuries. It is obvious that the first question is one which can hardly be answered from the manuscripts. The manuscripts are all copies of the completed work. Bits of the material out of which it was compiled can only find a place in them by accident. As a rule, material so made use of and superseded soon disappears. There is no further occasion for copying it. We have to rely for the most part in reconstructing the original material upon internal evidence or upon other legal treatises *in pari materia*. By good fortune, however, fragments of the original material may be found at the beginning or end of the new work—inserted by some cautious scribe who was not quite sure whether they were superseded. It is possible that the second form of c. 8, which is given in M and N, belongs to this class.

Moreover, a various reading may exceptionally go back to the original material. I suspect that this has happened in c. 20, 10 (see Commentary). More fruitful as a rule is the comparison of the later manuscripts. The Sea-law exists in a great many manuscripts. It was copied right through the centuries; it was copied in the East and in South Italy. This is in striking contrast to the other mediaeval works of maritime law. The Ordinamenta of Trani exist only in printed texts; the table of Amalfi in one manuscript and a fragment of another; the maritime statutes of Ancona only in three manuscripts; the maritime statutes of Zeno (Venetian) only in three. Prima facie we should be entitled to infer that the Sea-law was in great demand, and that from the tenth to the fifteenth century it represented living law. But there are several circumstances which militate against this view. To state briefly the conclusions which may be drawn from a comparison of the manuscripts, the case stands thus.

The oldest manuscripts of the Sea-law present substantially the same text. Although there are some differences between them which point to the existence of different recensions, the greater part of the variants are such as may reasonably be attributed to pure carelessness. It must be remembered that a law book was never copied with as much care as a classical author. There is no magic in the words. One expression will serve the turn as well as another so long as it conveys the same meaning.

The differences between the later and the earlier manuscripts fall under three heads. (1) The changes due to carelessness have naturally mounted up in the course of centuries, but they have not mounted up to any large extent. Some of the later manuscripts are very carefully written. (2) The number of conscious changes is considerable. Some of these changes are simply due to the desire of making the language clearer. Obsolete words are replaced by modern ones; the grammar is regularized; clumsy phrases are straightened out, obscure ones are made clear. None of these changes affect the substance of the Sea-law. (3) Some of the manuscripts represent what is practically an abridgement. Chapters are left out and others largely cut down. But though the Sea-law dwindles in some of the manuscripts, its substance is never altered, and only in one case enlarged. The four obscure chapters which I give in Appendix D are, so far as I know, the only addition which is found in the manuscripts. The Sea-law, so far as its legal effects were concerned, remained substantially the same from the beginning of its career to the end.

What is the conclusion from all this? If a law-book is copied century after century with no changes or only with changes of form, it shows two things. (1) The law-book is still of practical importance. No doubt with the Sea-law we must not attach too much weight to the re-copyings. As a rule it only occupies a small space in the manuscripts where it is found; and if great part of a manuscript continued of practical importance, as was often the case here, a scribe who was copying it, especially a Byzantine scribe, would naturally go on to copy the whole, without considering too closely whether some pages were obsolete and useless. This remark applies especially to copies made in the monasteries. In the Byzantine empire the spheres of civil and ecclesiastical law were never sharply discriminated. The same manuscript often contained treatises belonging to both jurisdictions. The Sea-law was sometimes no doubt copied merely because it was found attached to a manuscript of the Canons. On the other hand, the Sea-law, as I have said, bears the marks in the later manuscripts of constant and minute revision. Now you may copy something which is useless, but you do not as a rule take the pains to bring it up to date in matters of language and grammar. You do not produce abridgements of what is obsolete. The Sea-law must, even down to the fifteenth century, have represented the maritime law for some parts of the Mediterranean. (2) The second conclusion which we may draw from the unchangeableness of the Sea-law is that the circumstances with which it dealt did not materially change from the time of its original composition until near the time when it ceased to be copied. Our other evidence, such as it is, points in the same direction. There seems to have been very little alteration, except for the worse, in the navigation and commerce of the Mediterranean between the eighth and thirteenth centuries. It is with the thirteenth century that the commercial renascence begins, which made the literary and artistic renascence possible.

For a detailed examination of the manuscripts this is not the place. The Sea-law, as the reader has seen, occupies as a rule a small space in the manuscripts which I have examined, and in order to estimate finally their relations and importance they must be taken as a whole. My only object here is to state shortly the principles which have guided me in framing my text. One thing is clear. It is hopeless on the materials before me—it would probably be equally hopeless if I had collations of the whole of the manuscripts used—to try to arrange them in families. For a reputable family-tree to be constructed, each manuscript can have only one father. The Byzantine law-book is as a rule *vulgo quaesitus*. The copying of legal manuscripts was no doubt a flourishing trade at Constantinople, as it was at Bologna, and they who corresponded to the *stationarii* of the latter town must have always kept a stock of the leading textbooks in hand. If the Sea-law had to be copied the copyist had three or four archetypes to refer to, and could pick and choose his reading from among them. There was another way in which the parentage of a manuscript might be obscured. If a manuscript had to be copied in a hurry, as some of my manuscripts evidently were, it was naturally divided between two or more copyists. A sheet was given to one and a sheet to another, and, as all were copying at the same time, they had to copy from different archetypes. One notices not unfrequently different hands in different

1

sheets. This accounts for the way in which two manuscripts may agree closely during part of a text, and disagree during other part. The system of the *stationarii* was adopted in substance by the monasteries. There were evidently plenty of copies of the Sea-law, as of other Byzantine legal treatises, knocking about in the monasteries of Calabria.

The variants of the manuscripts fall under two heads, (1) those due to carelessness, (2) those made intentionally with a view to improve the grammar or vocabulary or to make the passage clearer. Under the first head come (*a*) the omission or insertion of little words, such as the article, καί, μέν, δέ, ἤ, εἰ, μή; (*b*) confusion between prepositions, &c., whether by themselves or at the beginnings of compound words, e. g. ἐκ, ἐν; ἐν, εἰς; πρό, πρός; παρά, πρό; παρά, περί; ὑπό, ἐπί, ἀπό; καί, κατά; (*c*) substitution of a simple for a compound form, or vice versa, e. g. πλέοντες for ἐμπλέοντες, ψηφισθῆναι for συμψηφισθῆναι; (*d*) transpositions; (*e*) little differences at the end of words, due to the addition or omission of ν or ς, the substitution of α for ω and vice versa; (*f*) use of singular for plural, present for future or aorist, active for middle and vice versa; (*g*) omission of words and phrases, owing in most cases to homoeoteleuton. The many omissions which we find even in the best manuscripts show the haste with which the copying was generally done. Another error, sometimes committed consciously, but more often probably due to carelessness, is the substitution of ναύκληρος for ἔμπορος, and vice versa, which we frequently find in the later manuscripts.

These differences do not help us much in determining the relations between manuscripts. If two manuscripts agree in many cases of this sort, that is some evidence of a relationship, but isolated cases of agreement only show that both scribes were awake or asleep over the same passage. The carelessness in which they unite must be bizarre to justify us in inferring kinship, e. g. as when LDY unite in ἀρμενή(ί)σας for ἀμελήσας, c. 36, 10. Differ-

d 2

li

ences of the other kind are of more weight. It is not impossible that two scribes may once and again light independently upon the same remedy for bad grammar or an obsolete word ; but if two manuscripts go on making the same corrections we are safe in inferring that there is a connexion between them.

Variants of both kinds are very numerous even among the older manuscripts, and there are many cases where it is difficult to say what the true reading was. One case is where words are transposed. What means have we of ascertaining what order of words was acceptable to the Byzantines of the seventh and eighth centuries ? Another case is where sentences are introduced abruptly without καί or δέ. The tradition supports this on some occasions, e. g. c. 9, 9 παῖδες, where many manuscripts read παῖδες δέ; c. 18, 3 ἐὰν μὴ ἔχωσι, where many manuscripts read ἐὰν δὲ μὴ ἔχωσι. In these and similar cases it is really a matter of chance what reading an editor puts in his text and what he relegates to an apparatus criticus ; but his distress at not being able to decide is diminished by the reflexion that it is not of the slightest importance, so far as regards the legal import and significance of the passage, which reading he adopts. There are many obscure places in the Sea-law, but in the great majority of these there is no diversity in the manuscripts, or, where there is diversity, it is due to the conjecture of some late scribe. The worst corruptions of the Sea-law probably arose in its infancy.

I feel less responsibility for the readings which I have put in the text as the learned reader has the opportunity of forming his own. But it will perhaps be of assistance to him in so doing to have some indication of the principles which have guided me in the same task. I have dealt in the Commentary with the most important variants. A few general remarks may be not out of place. Prima facie the oldest manuscripts present the best text. The presumption is weak enough ; but when we find all or most of the oldest manuscripts, though written in different countries and though evidently representing an independent tradition, giving substantially the same text, the presumption is very much strengthened. I should not labour this point were it not that a man of great authority, M. R. Dareste, has chosen to base his text on a manuscript which is not only late in date (end of thirteenth century) but which differs constantly from the consensus of the oldest manuscripts.

The oldest manuscripts unite in certain grammatical peculiarities—irregularities unknown to classical Greek and to Byzantine Greek after the classical revival—and when we find these peculiarities all removed and removed by different expedients in the later manuscripts, we are justified in inferring that these peculiarities belonged to the original text of the Sea-law. If the oldest manuscripts are faithful in preserving these grammatical peculiarities, we are justified in inferring that they will be faithful in greater things ; and I therefore regard a reading which they unite in supporting as being prima facie the better reading. But the oldest manuscripts often differ among themselves. The later manuscripts sometimes give readings which are intrinsically tempting. I confess to a frank eclecticism in the matter. I have followed on the whole the oldest manuscripts, but I have adopted readings from later manuscripts, as I have made conjectures of my own. It remains to say something of the principal manuscripts.

As I say elsewhere (p. cxii) I suspect that there were two editions of the Sea-law, the first and original compilation made by a private hand not later than A. D. 800, and probably a good deal earlier, the second made with a view of fitting the Sea-law for incorporation into the Basilica. I call the second text the vulgate. The vulgate, in my opinion, is the text presented to us by the oldest manuscripts—ABJL—and by the Synopsis Major. The later manuscripts, as a rule, where they differ from the vulgate, differ for the worse. Their differences, as a rule, are due either to carelessness or wilfulness ; and both unfortunate characteristics increase with the centuries. But later as well as earlier manuscripts give us occasionally glimpses of something behind the vulgate. The main question for an editor is the question how often he can get behind it. Very rarely, I fear ; but others may hold a different opinion, and they have most of the material before them.

A, as it is probably the oldest, is also probably the best manuscript of the Sea-law. The following list gives the most important places in which I have not followed its reading [1] :—Part II. c. η΄ ἐν πλοίῳ] ABDZ omit these words. They may be a gloss, as the manuscripts which keep them put them in different places ; c. θ΄ and ιγ΄ πήχεως ἐνός] πήχεως μιᾶς A. The gender of πῆχυς is doubtful. I have followed the preponderance of authority ; c. ια΄ A, with other manuscripts, omits the chapter, evidently owing to the homoeoteleuton ; c. ιδ΄ 3 ἄκυρα εἴτω κτλ.]. Here I have admitted a conjecture ; see app. crit. ; c. ιε΄ 5 καὶ οἱ ναῦται] ABHPZf omit these words. They may be a gloss on ἐμπλέοντες ; c. ιη΄ 6 τελέσῃ] τελευτήσει A ; table, c. 1 κλαπέντων] κλαπεισῶν A. This seems to be a conscious attempt to improve the grammar ; c. 5 κύλλωμα] κήλωμα A ; c. 16 ἐκδανεισθέντων] ἐκδαπανισθέντων A ; c. 20 συμφωνησάντων ... ὁρισάντων] A and most manuscripts give the singular, but the sense requires the plural ; c. 38 σῖτον] σίτου AJ, perhaps another attempt to improve the grammar ; c. 39 βολήσαντος] βολῆς καὶ πόσου A. I cannot explain this. Part III. c. 5, 3 εἰς κεφαλήν] τὴν κεφαλήν A, with most. εἰς κ. seems to me more spirited ; πῶς κυλλώσῃ] προσκυλλώσει A ; c. 8, 1 ἐὰν πλεύσῃ ... καὶ ... ἀποδράσῃ] ἔπλευσεν ... καὶ ... ἀπέδρασεν A, perhaps a conscious alteration intended to make the passage more vivid ; c. 9, 12 στρατεία κοινή] πειρατῶν A. This, if it is the reading of A, looks suspiciously like a gloss. The only other of my manuscripts which has anything like it is R πειρατῶν

---

[1] I differentiate the chapters of Parts II and III by using Greek numerals for the former, Arabic for the latter.

PRINCIPLES ON WHICH THE TEXT IS BASED

κοινή; c. 15, 7 ἕκαστος] ἕκαστος αὐτῶν ABG; c. 17, 11 καὶ
τὰς συνθήκας] κατὰ τὰς συνθήκας AHKZ; c. 20, 7 ἀποδότω]
ἀποδώσει A. The Byzantine fondness for varying the
phrase makes ἀποδότω more probable; c. 25, 5 κατερχέσθω]
κατεχέσθω A (but see app. crit.); c. 26, 4 ἐξωκοιτοῦντας] ἐξω-
κοῦντας A; c. 27, 4 ἐν ὅρια] ἐν ὁρίω ABS, probably a conscious improvement of the grammar; c. 30, 3 ὁ φόρτος]
φορτώσας ACQ; c. 33, 1 ναύκληρος] ἔμπορος A. O gives the
same sense (ναυλούμενος), but the captain must be meant
here; 33, 2 καί τι] ὅ,τι A, clearly made to better the grammar; c. 38, 7 τὰς δὲ ἐξ ἑκατοστάς], see Commentary and app.
crit.; c. 39, 1 ἀρμενίζον] om. A; c. 45, 3 οὗ ἀποσώζει] om.
A with many; c. 46, 6 εὑρίσκει] εὑρήσῃ(ει) ADJ. I omit
here the small points, such as words transposed, article
inserted or omitted, δέ, ἤ, or καί inserted or omitted, instead of προ-... προσ- or vice versa in compound verbs; but
even if these were added the list would not be long; and
in many of these cases, as well as in some of those given
above, it is impossible to say whether A's reading or that
given in the text is the better. Of the late manuscripts
O comes nearest to A. It is on the whole an honestly
written manuscript, and has few interpolations. The
worst perhaps is c. 40, 4 μαργαρίτας] τι τῶν λίθων τῶν πολυτίμων O.

Σ agrees closely with A, but there are more changes
made with a view to improve the grammar or vocabulary; e. g. c. 2, 3 ἀφελόμενοι added; c. 3, 7 ἐὰν καὶ μάλιστα]
καὶ μάλιστα ἐάν Σ; c. 7, 2 κρούσῃ] τρώσῃ Σ, δώσῃ] δῶ Σ;
c. 9, 2 ἐπερωτάτω] ἐρωτάτω ΣΚ, perhaps unintentional;
c. 41, 4 δύο ἢ τρεῖς] om. Σ, probably because it sounds 'unjuristisch'; c. 41, 6 ἅμα τῆς συμβολῆς] ἅμα τῇ συμβολῇ ΣΚ;
c. 47, 3 ἀπὸ δέ] εἰ δὲ ἀπό Σ.

J and L give much the same text as A; indeed J
appears to have the same pagination as A, but they
are both more carelessly written. As regards L,
here are some of its omissions: c. 17, 3 χρεοκοινωνίᾳ]
κοινωνία L; c. 20, 4 ἐὰν μὲν ὁ ναυλούμενος] om. L with
many; c. 20, 7 ἀποδότω] om. DJLvY; c. 30, 2 ἔσται] om.

L ; c. 39, 9 τόπῳ] om. L ; c. 41, 6 πρὸς τὴν ἀπώλειαν ἅμα]
om. DLY. Here are some cases where the scribe misread
words : c. 5, 3 κυλλώσῃ] κολάσει L ; c. 31, 4 βοηθείας] βύθια
DJLY (see app. crit.) ; c. 36, 10 ἀμελήσας] ἀρμενή(ί)σας DLY.
The last instance shows, and many might be added, the
close connexion of D and Y with L, though it is evident
that they are not derived directly from it. L has
omissions (see above) and additions (e. g. c. 11, 10 διαφόρους) which they have not. In J there is also a tendency
to conscious correction, which L is almost entirely free
from : e. g. c. 1, 1 ἐν ἀκτῇ] ἀκτήν J. J has more omissions
than L ; c. 5, 5 τοῦ χρόνου] om. J ; c. 13, 4 ὁ δὲ ναύκληρος
. . . 5 παρεχέτωσαν] om. J. But on the whole J is a better
educated scribe than L, and where he cannot read his
archetype he leaves a gap, which is a sign of candour ;
e. g. c. 9, 8 and c. 20, 2.

B is the head of a family : GHhS. Of S it is probably
parent. After c. 20 K agrees closely with B. B differs
from the other early manuscripts in that it has been carefully gone over and corrected. I cannot always say
whether the corrections are due to the original scribe or
to another; one thing is certain ; that, while some of the
alterations may be corrections of mistakes made in reading the archetype, the majority are derived from an
independent manuscript. GHh sometimes agree with
the unrevised text, sometimes with the revised one ;
S always with the revised one. Here are a few instances :
c. 9, 7 μὴ πλεῖον . . . μιᾶς B1 μὴ πλεῖον καὶ μιᾶς GHh] μὴ
πλεῖον λίτρας μιᾶς B2 ; c. 12, 2 μαρτύρων B1GHh] μαρτύρων
τριῶν B2 ; c. 20, 7 ἀποδότω B1 with most] ἀποδιδότω
B2GKS ; c. 22, 5 χωρῇ τὸ πλοῖον, βαλλέτω· εἰ δὲ μή B2] om.
B1CG (except that CG retain μή) ; c. 27, 3 αὐτῶν B1 and
many] τῶν ναυτῶν B2AGKS ; c. 32, 1 ναυκλήρου B1G] ναύλῳ
B2 ; c. 32, 3 ἔμπορον B1 with most] ναύκληρον B2KS ;
c. 36, 2 ἢ χαλάσαντος om. B1G ; c. 36, 7 ἀμελήσας ποιῆσαι
B1 with others including G] ἀμελήσας τοῦτο οὐ ποιήσῃ B2S.
There are very few omissions in B. The principal are
c. 9, 15 εἰ δὲ σύμφωνον to end ; c. 12, 2 καὶ πιστικῷ ; c. 29, 4

PRINCIPLES ON WHICH THE TEXT IS BASED

τοῦ πλοίου; c. 41, 3 εἰς τὴν ἀπώλειαν; c. 43, 5 φορτίων. Of these the first two are perhaps traces of an earlier recension (see Commentary). In c. 20, 2 B with its family and C adds ποιῶν, evidently to improve the grammar, but it is generally free from corrections of this sort. It gives words or forms of words different from my text in the following places: c. 7, 3 κήλην] κηλήτην BH*h*; c. 21, 6 σαβουράτου] σάβουρον B with many; c. 29, 3 πειρατείας] πειρατίου BS; c. 33, 1 θεὶς] θήσας BGS; c. 36, 7 κραυγάς] κραυάς BS; c. 36, 10 βιγλεοφόρος] βη(ι)γλάτωρ BGS; c. 37, 4 δότωσαν] δοσάτωσαν B with many. Some of these are merely dialectical peculiarities; others perhaps come from an earlier recension.

Among the older manuscripts, P also represents the vulgate, but in a debased form. It might almost, so far as its readings go, be of the fourteenth century. It runs particularly wild in the table of contents. Other instances of carelessness or corruption are: c. 4, 3 συμβῇ συληθῆναι] συμβουληθῆναι; c. 16, 5 ἐγγαίων] γονέων; c. 37, 2 γραμμάτια] ἐξάρτια; c. 38, 8 ἀποβολῆς] ἀπωλείας; c. 39, 7 ἐβούλετο] ἠδύνετο. Fortunately it seems to have left no progeny.

M and N agree very closely together, and E belongs to the same family, but leans rather towards N. R begins to agree with this class after c. 20. There is a wide gap between these manuscripts and the manuscripts with which I have been dealing. A, B, J and L are all comparatively free from conscious corrections. The differences between them, where they are not simply due to mistake, point to the existence of a recension, earlier than the vulgate, of which most traces have perished. In the manuscripts with which I am now dealing the differences due to carelessness are much more numerous, and the differences not due to carelessness appear to me as a rule signs of a conscious effort to improve the vulgate. Of N only a fragment exists. It omits c. 2, 6 καὶ τὰ ἐν τῷ πλοίῳ which M gives. In other respects there is very little difference between them. M omits single words, and it tends to leave out the prepositions at the beginning of compound words, but on the whole it is carefully written. The following readings deserve notice : Part II. c. ε΄ μέρος ἐν ἡμίσυ] μέρος (ἡ) ἥμισυ τέταρτον ὄγδοον (ὄγδ. om. Q) CEMQ. This seems to point to a different recension ; c. η΄ ἐν πλοίῳ (πλοῖον) is added by CEMP. I have put ἐν πλοίῳ into the text, but it may be a gloss ; c. ιγ΄ γυναῖκας . . . λαμβάνειν τόπον] γυνὴ . . . τόπον λαμβανέτω EMQ and nearly CD, an intentional correction of the grammar. Part III. c. 1, 1 ἢ ἐν ἀκτῇ] ἐν ἡμέρα ἢ ἐν ἀκτῆ M. The scribe took ἐν ἀκτῆ for ἐν νυκτί, and then emended ; c. 2, 11 ὁ τὰ σύλα ποιήσας] τοῖς τὰ σύλα (τὴν ζημίαν E) παθοῦσιν EMN ; c. 5, 4 κρούσας] κυλλώσας MN ; c. 7, 3 τὰ ἰατρεῖα] τὰ ἰατρικά EKMN ; c. 10, 10 ἐρχέσθωσαν] ποιείτωσαν M ; c. 11, 12 γοργούς] γρηγορούς M ; c. 12, 4 ὁ δεξάμενος φυλ.] ὁ δεχόμενος ἐν τῷ φυλ. M : c. 15, 5 ἐξειλήσῃ] τὰ ἄρμενα ἐξιλίσῃ M ; c. 19, 2 ἀπόλλειν] ἀπώλλυσιν αὐτόν M ; c. 19, 3 ἄλλην] διάλυσιν M ; c. 27, 8 μαρτύρων τριῶν] τῶν τριῶν μαρτύρων M ; c. 29, 1 ἐν τῷ τόπῳ ὅθεν συγγρ.] ἔνθα γρ. τόπῳ M and nearly R ; c. 38, 2 διφθ.] διφθ. καλάς EMR ; c. 38, 11 διπλᾶ κτλ.] M gives a different phrase, apparently derived from c. 3 ; c. 40, 11 M adds καὶ τὴν ἀποκατάστασιν, ER give nearly the same ; c. 42, 6 διδότω] ὁ ναύκληρος διδότω EMR ; c. 43, 3 M (with which N apparently agrees) inserts a long phrase. E inserts ἔρημον συμβῆ γενέσθαι. These readings look like attempts to fill up a gap. For the most part the readings which are peculiar to M, N and E do not look like relics of a text earlier than the vulgate. After the three chapters of Appendix E, M and N add a series of provisions (Appendix F). Some of these (η΄, θ΄, ι΄) are paraphrases of passages in the Digest ; others (δ΄, ε΄) appear in a fuller form in some late manuscripts (see Appendix D), and evidently were additions to the Sea-law, but not an original part of it ; ς΄ seems an abridgement of c. 46 of the Sea-law, and ζ΄ is another version of c. 8. It is impossible to say whether it is an older form than that of the vulgate. In some cases ER unite as against M, e. g. c. 38, 1 ζάλῃ] χαλάζῃ ER ; c. 40, 10 τελείτωσαν] ποιείτωσαν ER. Possibly they give us N's reading.

CQ agree closely with one another, and they show traces of relationship on the one side to B and on the other to EMN. Of the two Q agrees more closely with M than C does. They are both very carelessly written—constantly omitting words and phrases, and leaving out or adding letters and syllables at the beginning, middle, or end of words with reckless impartiality. The following readings deserve notice: Part III. c. 4, 4 I have added τὰ σύλα on the authority of C; it or something like it is certainly needed; c. 6, 3 καὶ οὐκ ἐνάγεται added by C for clearness' sake; cp. c. 14, 5 where C adds τουτέστι τὴν γλῶτταν τεμνέσθω; c. 12, 3 παραδιδότω] ποιήτω C; c. 13, 2 παρατιθέσθω αὐτό] ἀποδιδότω αὐτῶ εἰς παραθήκην C; c. 13, 5 παρεχέτωσαν] ἐχέτωσαν τῶ συληθέντι C; c. 15, 11 οἱ ναῦται ἔφυγον] οἱ ἐπιβάται τοῦτο ἐποίησαν CQ, cp. the reading of X; c. 21, 7 τέταρτον μέρος] δίμερος C (i. e. δ′ μέρος, cp. c. 45, 3 πέμπτον μέρος, where J reads ἐμέρος); c. 24, 3 ἀπόλλειν] ὑποβάλλει Q; c. 27, 8 ἐλεγχθῇ] δειχθῆ CQ; c. 35, 3 ἔμποροι] προροῖ C, i. e. ἐμ was left out, and then ποροι corrected into the nearest maritime word; c. 37, 2 γραμμάτια] πράγματα CQX; c. 38, 1 καταληφθῇ] καταβληθῆ(εῖ) CQX; c. 38, 8 ἅμα τοῦ πλοίου καὶ τοῖς ναύταις] καὶ οἱ ναῦται ἅμα τοῦ πλοίου CM in order to improve the grammar; Q, though it gives the same reading, leaves in καὶ τοῖς ναύταις; c. 39, 9 χρήζω] θέλω CQ; c. 46, 6 καθὼς ἐν ἀληθείᾳ εὑρίσκει] καθὼς παρέλαβεν ἐν ἀληθεία CEQ. These examples, which might be greatly augmented, are enough to show not only the carelessness of this tradition, but also its readiness to make corrections and add glosses. So far as intentional changes go C is the worse offender; for carelessness both are about on a par.

Mess. contains fewer blunders than C and Q, but in point of intentional corrections it does not leave them behind. The reader who glances over its *varia lectio* as given on p. xxx will see how many alterations and additions there are; I may refer him particularly to c. 4, 4; 5, 6; 7, 7; 8, 9; 16, 3; 17, 7; 25, 3. Most of these are not found elsewhere.

Of the later manuscripts which are not professedly abridgements O is perhaps the best, and D and Y come next. X agrees with P in some curious errors; e. g. c. 34, 5 ἡ ἔκθεσις] μὴ ἔκθεσις PX; c. 36, 7 ἀμελήσας ποιῆσαι] καὶ (om. X) ἀμέλειαν ποιήσας PX; and in others with CQ (see *ante*). K is seriously interpolated. R, on the whole, belongs to the MN type. Of all these manuscripts it may be said that wherever they come across a word which they do not understand they substitute the first word that comes into their head; e. g. c. 15, 5 ἐξειλήσῃ] ἐξελκύσῃ D; εὐλυτώσῃ K; φύγῃ R.

We sink to a yet lower level in T, U, Laud., to which may be added Monac. gr. 303 (see p. xl). I have put their readings together in Appendix I. A rapid glance is enough to show that the vulgate is the basis of the text; and that that has been corrected throughout with a view to conciseness and lucidity. Let M. Dareste, who prints and translates from the text of U, compare chapters 9 and 10 in my text with what U gives, and he will admit at once that U is not merely an abridgement but an unintelligent one.

I ought to have collected the readings of FƒV in an Appendix instead of leaving them in the critical apparatus, as they also represent a revision and abridgement of the Sea-law. The text on which they worked seems to have belonged to the MN class.

PART II

ORIGIN OF THE SEA-LAW

The reader will have observed that in the manuscripts used for this edition there are the greatest diversities both as to the title and as to the contents of the Sea-law. He will have seen, however, that most of these manuscripts contain the forty-seven chapters which in this edition are printed as Part III. In some manuscripts Part III is given in an abridged form, chapters being omitted in whole or in part; in other manuscripts some chapters are split up so that the total number appears larger ; chapters are occasionally transposed ; but on the whole the forty-seven chapters of Part III form the most stable element in the fluctuating tradition.

Some manuscripts prefix a table of chapters to Part III. Some manuscripts contain, generally before Part III or before the table of chapters, a series of nineteen chapters (mostly very short) which in this edition are printed as Part II. In this edition Part II, the table of chapters to Part III, and Part III are treated as standing on the same footing, and as forming one consecutive text. Other matter, which is contained in various manuscripts, either under the same title as the matter given above or under a similar title, is relegated in this edition to various Appendices. There will be found, among other things, (*a*) a Prologue, known to some previous editors as Part I, (*b*) various chapters or groups of chapters which, in different manuscripts, are either added at the end or intercalated among the chapters of Part III.

The first question suggested by this variety in the tradition is, what is the relation of the various parts or fragments one to another. And this question cannot well be separated from another question, namely, what is the date at which, and the circumstances under which, each part or fragment assumed the form in which we now possess it.

OPINIONS AS TO ITS ORIGIN.

Before considering the evidence from which an answer may be obtained, it will be convenient, in order that the reader may see the points to which his attention should be directed, to enumerate the principal answers which have been given in the past. The early views as to the origin of the Sea-law are stated by Pardessus (I, pp. 24–31) with his usual lucidity, and need not be restated here. One observation, however, may be made. Even those who held that the Prologue (or Part I) contained a narrative of historical facts, and that Parts II and III represented the customs of Rhodes as collected under the circumstances narrated in the Prologue—even those who, while throwing the Prologue overboard, maintained that Parts II and III, or at least that Part III justified the title assigned to them in most of the manuscripts—were forced to admit that these documents had suffered a sea-change in the course of centuries, and that, in the form in which we have them, they are a work of the middle ages. A cursory perusal of the Sea-law is sufficient to convince any one of that.

The view of Pardessus is the first that demands attention. He points out at length the absurdities of the Prologue, and ends by declaring it the work of ' un faussaire ignorant ou maladroit' (I, p. 217). This view of the Prologue is accepted on all hands (Zach., Geschichte, p. 318, who dates the Prologue at the time of the Macedonian emperors). Part II, according to Pardessus, is a 'recueil d'usages nautiques, probablement rédigé pour l'utilité des gens de mer' (p. 217). 'Cette série de chapitres, sans appartenir à la législation positive ni en faire partie, s'y rattachoit comme un livre de pratique se rattache à la loi dont il offre les développemens ou le supplément usuel' (p. 218). According to Zach. (Geschichte, p. 318) Part II was put together and attached to the main body of the Sea-law at the same time as the Prologue. As regards Part III, Pard. thinks that it was composed before the Basilica, and that it is probably a private compilation (p. 220). He even suggests a name for the author—Rhodion—as some of the manuscripts call it νόμος 'Ροδίωνος (p. 221). He is clear that it was not an integral part of the Basilica, and that it had no official character (p. 222. See also pp. 165–72).

Zach. has had several views on the subject of the Sea-law. I content myself with his earliest and his latest. His first view was this. Many manuscripts of the Ecloga contain, by way of supplement to the Ecloga, an appendix consisting of various fragments taken from the Digest, the Code, and the Novels, and also the three νόμοι—the Farmer's law, the Soldier's law, and the Sea-law. This supplement was probably compiled in the eighth or ninth century, and the three νόμοι in question are probably the work of the learned person who compiled the supplement (Delineatio, pp. 31, 32; Ἀνέκδοτα, p. 176). Zach.'s last view was this. While he continued to think that the Soldier's law was a private work, he thought that the Farmer's law and the Sea-law—Part III, that is to say, of the Sea-law—were works of public authority, and were probably enacted by one of the Isaurian emperors, Leo or Constantine Copronymus (Geschichte, p. 250 (Farmer's law), p. 316 (Sea-law), Wissenschaft und Recht für das Heer, in Byz. Zeitschrift, III, p. 437 (Soldier's law). Zach. agrees with Pard. in holding that Part III was not an original part of the Basilica, although it found its way into manuscripts of the Basilica at an early time—evidently before the composition of the Synopsis Major—as the eighth title of Book LIII (Geschichte, pp. 318, 319). Other learned persons, who have occupied themselves with this subject, generally accept one of the opinions of Zach. Heimbach (Geschichte, pp. 277, 278, 281) takes Zach.'s earlier view, but differs from him in holding that Part III formed an original part of the Basilica. Vito La Mantia wavers between the two views (Cenni Storici su le Fonti del Diritto Greco-Romano, pp. 13, 14). Siciliano Villanueva refrains from expressing an opinion (Diritto Bizantino, pp. 50–5).

These opinions are stated without the reasoning on which they are based, simply in order that the reader may see around what points the controversy—if it can be called a controversy—centres. I now propose to deal separately with each part or alleged part of the Sea-law.

The Forty-seven Chapters.

I begin with the forty-seven chapters which are printed as Part III. These chapters, whatever their date may be, form an original literary composition. Whatever their sources may be, they have been put into their present form either by one man or by a group of men acting in unison. That is to say, they are not a mere mechanical juxtaposition of enactments, customs, decisions, but the materials of which they are composed have been carefully gone over and worked up with a view of producing a literary unity. This may be proved (a) by their order, (b) by their style.

(a) The chapters are arranged on the whole in a logical order, and chapters relating to the same subject-matter come together. To see this the reader has only to refer to the synopsis which I have already given of their contents (pp. xiv–xv). It is true that violence has been used in some cases to bring a chapter into the place which it occupies; but this, while it may throw some light upon the materials from which Part III is made up, does not in the least militate against the view that it is a literary composition. For instance, chapters 1 to 8 deal with questions of police—thefts, fights, fisticuffs, and murder. C. 4 is out of place here, as it deals with the responsibility of the captain or passengers, as the case may be, for insisting on going to a place where thefts are frequent. It does not deal, like the other chapters, with questions between the criminal and the party aggrieved. Again, chapters 12 to 15 deal with deposits; but chapter 15 looks as if it originally applied to a case, common in all ages, when a merchant or passenger went on shore and was left behind owing to the unexpected departure of the ship. There is a reference in the beginning to slaves whom the captain has taken in deposit, and there is a reference at the end to the case where a merchant or passenger has left behind somebody else's slave whom he has taken in deposit. These incidental and subsidiary observations have been made use of to bring the chapter under the head of deposit. Chapters 16 to 18 deal with loans. Chapters 19 to 25, subject to one exception, deal with the contract of hiring between the captain and the merchant. Here again a chapter has been intercalated. C. 21, which deals with contribution, is put after c. 20, because, like c. 20, it refers to a case where there is no agreement in writing. Chapters 26 to 44 deal in substance with contribution. It is difficult to establish an order within this group, except that cc. 26–33 deal exclusively with injuries to ship. Chapters 45 to 47 deal with salvage. It is obvious that this order (loose as it is) cannot have been the effect of chance. Some one must have been at the pains to arrange the chapters with a certain regard for logical sequence.

(b) The style of the work confirms the impression which is derived from the order of the chapters. A main characteristic of the legal draftsman in the middle ages was his passion for varying the phrase. A modern par-liamentary draftsman uses in a statute the same word to designate the same thing, however often it occurs, because, if he used a different word, the Court would draw the inference that different things were designated. They who had the task of interpreting statutes in the middle ages evidently did not hold this view. Thus, in the mari-time statute of Tiepolo (Stat. maritt. Venez., pp. 52 sqq.), each successive chapter is introduced by a different word of enactment: *statuentes statuimus* (c. 1), *ordinamus* (c. 2), *sancimus* (c. 3), *decernimus* (c. 4), *asserimus* (c. 5), *man-damus* (c. 6), *decernimus* (c. 7), *dicimus* (c. 8), *affirmamus* (c. 9), *mandamus* (c. 10), and so forth. In fact it may be laid down that where a statute does not exhibit this rhetorical form the statute is not a unity; no date can be assigned to it as a whole; it is merely a mechanical agglomeration of provisions of different epochs.

Part III of the Sea-law exhibits the love of variety in a remarkable degree. Where the same thing has to be stated more than once, it is always stated in a different way; either a different word or a different syntactical form is used. In the Commentary attention is called to this point on many occasions. Here it will suffice to point out the various forms which are employed for the words of enactment. (a) The imperative is the commonest form, but (b) sometimes the future is used, e. g. δώσει ὁ κρούσας (c. 7); κατασχεθήσονται (c. 8); ἀποδώσει, and in the same phrase ὑπομενέτω (c. 14) ; ἔσται (c. 18); ἀποδώσει, and in the same phrase ἀποδιδότω and ἀποδότω (c. 20); ἔσται, and in the same phrase ἐρχέσθω (c. 22); ἀποδώσει (c. 46). (c) The infinitive is not infrequent: ἀζήμιον μένειν (c. 17); ἀπόλλειν, and in the same phrase ἀποδιδότω (c. 19 and c. 24); ἐφορᾶν ... ἀζημίους μένειν, προσφέρειν (c. 26) ; ἐφορᾶν, and in the same phrase ἐρχέσθωσαν (c. 29) ; ἀπαιτεῖν, and in the same phrase ἐρχέσθωσαν (c. 32) ; ἀκίνδυνα εἶναι, but in the phrase before it εἰσκομιζέσθω and in the phrase after it ἐρχέσθωσαν (c. 33); ὑπεύθυνον εἶναι, and in the same phrase ἀζήμιοι εἴτωσαν (c. 34); ἐφορᾶν and ἐρχέσθω (c. 36) ; ἀκίνδυνον εἶναι and ἀπολαμβανέτω (c. 39). (d) The aorist is sometimes found; ἑαυτὸν ἀπώλεσεν (c. 11 and c. 36). (e) The legal proposition is. occasionally introduced as if it depended on some other authority; κελεύει ὁ νόμος (c. 1); κομιζέσθωσαν κατὰ τὸν νόμον (c. 18); ἔδοξε, i. e. 'it has been held' (c. 17).

There are several manuscripts of Part III which cannot be later than the end of the tenth or beginning of the eleventh century, and these manuscripts differ so far among themselves as to show that the text must have been in process of transmission for some considerable period. On the authority of the manuscripts alone, we are forced to put the composition of Part III not later than the beginning of the ninth century. It is more difficult to fix the terminus before which it cannot have been composed. So far as the vocabulary and grammar are concerned, it cannot well be earlier than the seventh century. The materials for comparison are wanting here, as it can only be compared with other legislative monuments, and there is a gap in the Novels between a novel of Heraclius (A. D. 620-9) and a novel of Leo and Constantine (A.D. 776-80). It is clearly later than the Novels of Justinian.

Part III is singularly wanting in indications which would enable us to fix a date. There is no reference to

place unless such is to be found in the doubtful word
ἐκπορίζειν (Table, c. 32). There is no reference to judicial
authorities or to judicial process, except in the word ἐκδικεῖν, which is perhaps not the true reading (c. 20). There
is no reference to administration, except in the vague
word τέλος (c. 21). Neither the references to coins nor to
wares are of any avail in fixing a date. We are thrown
back upon a comparison of the legal principles contained
in Part III with those contained in the Pandects and in
the Byzantine textbooks. But before passing to these it
is necessary to deal with an authority which would give a
far higher antiquity not only to Part III but to Part II—
namely, the titles which are contained in the manuscripts.

TITLES OF THE SEA-LAW.

The titles which are given either to the Sea-law as
a whole, or to its different parts, may be classified under
four heads. 1. In some manuscripts it is described as
the law of the Rhodians or the Rhodian law. 2. In
some cases a list of emperors is added who have established (ἐθέσπισαν) it. 3. It is sometimes described as an
excerpt from the Digest; and sometimes the eleventh or
the fourteenth book of the Digest is specified. 4. It is
sometimes described as the law of Rhodion.

The last title occurs as early as L, which adds τέλος νόμου
'Ρωδίονος after the chapters of Appendix E. It is also given
in H before Part III and in some later manuscripts. It is
safe to regard this as a mere graphical error; and we may
dismiss the conjecture of Pard., who wished to add another
name to the shadowy list of Byzantine legal writers.

The first title is the important title. It is found in
the earliest and best manuscripts. Moreover, in two
chapters of Part II (c. ιζ', ιη') there is a reference to the
Rhodian Law as the authority for the legal propositions
therein stated. It is clear that Part III, in the form
in which we possess it, has nothing to do with the Rhodians; and it is not difficult to see the ground on which the
title and the references are based. Dig. XIV, 2, 9 contains

e 2   lxvii

INTRODUCTION

a remark of the emperor Antoninus, ἐγὼ μὲν τοῦ κόσμου κύριος, ὁ δὲ νόμος τῆς θαλάσσης. τῷ νόμῳ τῶν Ῥοδίων κρινέσθω τῷ ναυτικῷ, ἐν οἷς μήτις τῶν ἡμετέρων αὐτῷ νόμος ἐναντιοῦται. It goes on τοῦτο δὲ αὐτὸ καὶ ὁ θειότατος Αὔγουστος ἔκρινεν. (Antoninus, according to Godefroy, is Antoninus Pius, and Augustus is the reigning emperor, i. e. Marcus Aurelius. De imperio maris, col. 82.) This passage forms the first fragment of Book LIII of the Basilica: τὰ ναυτικὰ ἤγουν τὰ κατὰ θάλασσαν τῷ ῥοδίῳ νόμῳ κρίνεται ἐν οἷς αὐτῷ μὴ ἕτερος ἐναντιοῦται νόμος. It is obvious that any learned person who was making a collection of rules of maritime law would be strongly inclined to call his book the Rhodian law, in order to add to its authority.

The existence of this passage also explains why in many manuscripts Part III is described as an excerpt from the fourteenth book of the Digest. (ια′, which some manuscripts give, is evidently a graphical error.) It is true that Part III is not an excerpt, but it will not do to press the language too closely, and the phrase in substance is merely intended to connect Part III with this important passage in the Digest. Moreover, the Farmer's law, which is still less of an excerpt than the Sea-law— which in fact has little or nothing to do with the legislation of Justinian—is described in the oldest manuscripts as κατ᾽ ἐκλογὴν ἐκ τῶν (τοῦ) ἰουστινιανοῦ βιβλίων (βιβλίου).

The list of emperors who have established the Sea-law occurs as early as L, i. e. not later than the end of the tenth century, while there is no trace of the Prologue until the middle of the twelfth. L's list (before Part II) gives Adrianus Antoninus Tiberius Lucius Septimius Severus Pertinax. P (before Part III) gives the same list, but writes Antonius for Antoninus. E (before the Prologue) agrees with P, but puts Antonius before Adrianus. D, M, Q (before the Prologue) agree with L, except that they leave out Antoninus. FʄV (before Part III) add Vespasianus and Trajanus between Septimius Severus and Pertinax. Pard. treats each of these names as referring to a different emperor. It is worth observing that Septimius Severus on inscriptions is normally called Lucius Septimius Severus Pertinax, and that he is normally described as the son of Marcus Antoninus, the grandson of Antoninus Pius, the great-grandson of Hadrianus, and the great-great-grandson of Trajanus. If we assume the author of the title to have got his names from an inscription of Severus, every name would be accounted for but Tiberius, which may be a copyist's error for Trajanus. It is possible—as Dr. Ashby suggests to me—that the author got his names from an imperfect inscription, which he wrongly filled out. Why an inscription of Septimius Severus was made use of it is impossible to say. It is also possible that Antoninus refers to Caracalla, and that the names have been got from some inscription belonging either to Caracalla and his father or to Caracalla alone. It is evident that Caracalla liked to be described as a sea-lord—perhaps because he had once escaped from a shipwreck (Spart. Vit. Caracallae, 5, 8). C. I. G. 3484 τὸν γῆς καὶ θαλάσσης δεσπότην αὐτ. Καίσ. Μ. Αὐρ. Σεουῆρον Ἀντωνεῖνον ; C. I. G. 3485 ; Oppian. Halieut. III, 4, in addressing Caracalla, σοῖς μὲν γὰρ ὑπὸ σκήπτροισι θάλασσα | εἰλεῖται καὶ φῦλα Ποσειδάωνος ἐναύλων. If the author of the Sea-law came across an inscription referring to Caracalla as master of the sea, he would naturally have been tempted to make use of that emperor as an authority for his compilation.

TABLE OF CHAPTERS OF PART III.

There seems no reason for doubting that the table of chapters of Part III was composed at the same time as Part III and formed an integral part of it. It is found in the oldest manuscripts ; its omission by the later ones is merely a mark of neglect. It was a regular custom in Byzantine times (see Commentary) to prefix a πίναξ to law books.

It is true that there are some discrepancies between the table and the text. The title of c. 7 speaks only of ναυτῶν ; the text of ναυκλήρων ἢ ἐμπόρων ἢ ναυτῶν. The title of c. 8 in most MSS. has ναύτου; the text has ναυτῶν. The title of c. 26 speaks of ναυτῶν; the text has ναυτῶν ἢ ναυκλήρων. The title of c. 34 speaks of βέστην; the text has ὀθόνην ἢ βέστην. The omissions in the table may be simply due to a desire to economize space. In two cases the table adds something which is not in the text. The title of c. 21 has ναυκλήρων; in the text there is no statement that the partners are ναύκληροι. The title of c. 32 has ἐν τῷ ἐκπορίζειν; there is nothing of this in the text. But such discrepancies as these, and more serious ones, often occur between a table of chapters and its text. In some cases they may be due to the fact that the compiler of Part III, while modifying the material which he took into his text, preserved unaltered the title which he found in his authority. They are not sufficient to rebut the presumption in favour of a common origin for the table and Part III.

The Nineteen Chapters.

The relation of Part II to Part III is a difficult question. Chapters α' to ζ' deal with the division of the profits arising from the maritime adventure between the persons concerned in the navigation. There is nothing in Part III inconsistent with the existence of such a division. On the contrary, the close relation which is found throughout Part III between captain and mariners presupposes that they all had shares, varying indeed in amount, in the profits arising from the ship. Chapters η' to ιε' contain regulations for the conduct of merchants and passengers on board ship. They are matters of the internal regulation of the ship, and the compiler of the Sea-law may well have thought that, while they were too trivial for insertion in a code, they might be found useful by navigators. Chapters ιδ', ιε' appear in a slightly different form in Part III. Chapter ιϛ' lays down the principles on which ship is to be valued for the purpose of contribution. It may be brought into connexion with c. 9 of Part III, which also determines how certain classes of property are to be valued for the same purpose. Chapters ιζ' to ιθ' deal with loans ; ιη' refers pretty clearly to loans on land.

So far as the tradition is concerned, Part II is as authentic as Part III. There is no ground in the tradition for attributing a later origin to it. It is possible that the compiler of Part III found these chapters in the materials on which he was working, that he considered them in some cases superfluous, and in others insignificant or perhaps of transitory application, and that he therefore discarded them from his finished work, while at the same time retaining them in a subordinate position, as it were, by way of Appendix. It is also possible that they belonged to the original edition of the Sea-law, and that they were cut out at the time of the revised edition or vulgate (see pp. liii, cxiii). Some manuscripts prefix a table of chapters, which I give in Appendix B. Others give titles at the head or side of some of the chapters. Some of these titles, e. g. that of c. ιε' : περὶ ὅρκου ἀπαραιτήτου, are perhaps contemporary with the chapter. Most of them are of no importance, merely reproducing the first two or three words of the chapter.

THE PROLOGUE.

The Prologue, which editors have heretofore placed in the forefront of the Sea-law, is given in the manuscripts in two forms, a shorter and a longer. For the longer as well as for the shorter there is twelfth-century authority. The fact that the Prologue is not found in any of the earliest manuscripts is strong evidence that it is a work of later date than Part III or Part II ; but more important than the question of its date is the question of its veracity.

Godefroy, in a tract De Imperio Maris—I cite it from his Opera Iuridica Minora, Lugd. Bat. 1733—undertakes the defence of the Prologue. He describes it as an eximium fragmentum (col. 88), though he admits that in the form in which we possess it it is merely an abridge-

ment of a lost original, and he suggests that it was put
together by Michael Psellus or some contemporary. The
first remark to make about it is that, whichever we adopt
of the two forms in which it is handed down, it is in
several places unintelligible. It is easy to see this from
the literal translation which I give later. Godefroy's
comments are on a text which is largely conjectural, and
he acknowledges that there are gaps in several places.
To mention a few of the places in which he departs from
the tradition: p. 40, l. 12 he reads ἐνδείξασθαι οὐδέν.
Διήγημα. παραπέμψῃς κτλ.; l. 26 he reads ὑπάτῳ καὶ ὑπατι-
κοῖς τοῦτον προσαγορεύουσιν, and puts a full stop at l. 28
'Ρώμη. (He also [p. 41, l. 30] puts a stop at φαιδροτάτων.)
For καὶ σφραγίσας (l. 32) he reads ὃς καὶ αὐτὸς σφραγίσας, and
puts a full stop at l. 33 συγκλήτου. He inserts a large bit
from Dig. XIV, 2, 9 before l. 36 ὁ δὲ νόμος. We are now
in a position to understand his interpretation. He describes the work as an auctoritas, i. e. a statement of the
imperial constitutions by which validity is given to
a body of laws (col. 88). It begins, he says, with a constitution which Tiberius ' edidisse dicitur post relationem
in senatu vel interlocutionem in consistorio habitam, ex
consilio seu sententia Neronis' (col. 91). Tiberius here is
the emperor Claudius, and Antoninus is the consul of
A.D. 53. For the thirty-second (λβ′) year of tribunician
power Godefroy would read the twelfth or thirteenth
(ιβ′ or ιγ′). In that year the Rhodians recovered their
autonomy at the request of Nero (Tacit. Ann. XII, 58;
Suet. Claud. 25, Nero, 7). Godefroy makes a gap after
l. 8 ἐρχέσθωσαν. 'Hic iam censere iussis senatoribus vel
consistorianis'—there is nothing of this in our text—
'Nero, oratione sumpta, sententiam dixit'. Nero, according to Godefroy, is the future emperor. 'Nihil scilicet
opus esse, ea quae ab imperatore iam antea scilicet con-
stituta fuissent, commendare . . . Mox sententia seu
propositio Neronis sequitur, διήγημα, id est, διήγησις seu
narratio et propositio.' Nero's opinion is, ' mitti videlicet
oportere quosdam Rhodum, investigaturos quidnam in

legibus moribusque Rhodiorum positum esset, quidque ibi observaretur (quod πράξεων appellatione hic designatur) circa navigantes,' &c. We must supply, according to Godefroy, that the plan was approved, the commission sent out, and that it returned with a report in writing. Line 22 ταῦτα πάντα κτλ., he interprets 'Tiberium tandem ea omnia firmasse, firmataque Antonino Consuli tradidisse, ceterisque consulibus qui ad eum salutatum venerant. Et quidem Romae'. Vespasian 'dicitur oblatas sibi a consulibus Leges Rhodias SCto firmasse ... sic enim orationes principum SCtis firmari mos erat'. Vespasian's only known connexion with the Rhodians is that he deprived them of their autonomy (Suet. Vesp. 8), and Godefroy cannot show any relation between the other emperors who are mentioned and the island.

I have stated these views of Godefroy at length out of respect for the man who, as Mommsen has said, has never been excelled in his knowledge of Roman legal antiquities; but on this occasion Godefroy is not convincing. It is impossible to prove that the things cannot have happened which are described in the Prologue; and the complete silence of all our authorities about them—although they are things which would naturally have been mentioned—is not enough of itself to destroy their possibility. But we are at least justified in saying that they are highly improbable. Godefroy begins by an arbitrary change of the text. Prima facie the first emperor meant is Tiberius. The thirty-second year of his tribunician power is A.D. 30–31 (Clinton, Fasti Romani, I, p. 14). Some authors place the Passion in the sixteenth year of Tiberius, which corresponds with the thirty-second year of his tribunician power; and the author of the Prologue, if we assume that he was merely a mystifier, may have been thereby induced to fix upon this date. But if Tiberius is Tiberius, who is Nero? The later recension changes this to Νηρεύς—a sea-god. Of the consuls Laurus (or Claurus or Clarus) and Agrippina there appears to be no trace. The second recension speaks of Clarus and Alexander as consuls in the reign of Hadrian. Some authorities, but, what is curious, only Western ones, insert Clarus and Alexander after Niger and Apronianus, who were consuls in the year in which Trajan died. There is no trace of them in the Constantinople lists (Clinton, Fasti Romani, II, p. 184; Mommsen, Chronica Minora, I, p. 255). It is possible that the Prologue is an exercise composed in the law school which was established at Constantinople in the middle of the eleventh century (Zach., Geschichte, p. 29). The use of ἀπέλυσεν (l. 34), which seems to be used in something like its conveyancing sense (see H. Brunner, Zur Rechtsgeschichte der Urkunde, p. 75), suggests the work of a lawyer. It is easy to imagine a student of the Sea-law embroidering on the title which he found in his manuscript, and which represented the Sea-law as having been sanctioned by a long line of emperors. It is true that there are discrepancies between the Prologue and the titles; but there are striking points of resemblance. If we take the names as they appear in the title of L, Adrianus is in the second recension; Antoninus is a consul (either as Antoninus or Antonius) in both recensions; Tiberius is in both recensions; Λούκιος of L may have been the origin of Οὔλπιος Τραιανός of both recensions. Vespasianus (of both recensions) and Neron (of the 1st) or Nereus (of the 2nd) have no prototypes in L. Vespasianus is found in the title as given in FfV, but as these manuscripts are later than the Prologue they may have borrowed from it.

There is, alas! nothing abnormal in a mendacious prologue being prefixed to a mediaeval maritime code by way of recommendation and advertisement. The Prologue of the Sea-law may be compared with the document which is contained in the manuscripts and early printed texts of the Consulate of the Sea, and which purports to state when its provisions were adopted by various public authorities (see Pard. III, pp. 4 sqq.). It may also be compared with the date, A.D. 1063, which is attached to the title of the Ordinamenta of Trani.

PROLOGUE OF THE SEA-LAW

Subsidiary Matter.

Many manuscripts, including some of the oldest, add three chapters at the end of Part III. These chapters are given in Appendix E. Three manuscripts (D, J, L) give their titles at the end of the table of chapters. These chapters differ, however, from the other chapters of Part III in that they are in substance translations from various passages of the Code and the Digest. Many of the manuscripts which give them state accurately where they come from (see Commentary). These passages may be an integral part of Part III; but they are omitted by some important manuscripts (A, B). The four chapters which are given in Appendix D do not appear in any of the early manuscripts. In the form in which they stand, their tradition does not go behind the thirteenth century; but two of them appear in a more concise form in M and N (see Appendix F), and therefore go back to the end of the eleventh century. They certainly do not belong to Part III in its original form. I have discussed them in the Commentary.

SOURCES OF THE SEA-LAW

We have only got a little way with the Sea-law—and by that term I propose to designate hereafter those chapters which I have printed in the body of my text, namely, Part II, the Table of Chapters of Part III and Part III—when we have ascertained that in its present form it must date from between A.D. 600 and A.D. 800. It is clear at the first reading that it is composed from earlier materials. Whether it is a work of legislative authority or merely a private compilation—a point to which I shall recur hereafter—it is not entirely, perhaps not to any great extent, original. It is possible, without going outside the book itself, to get some idea of the materials of which it is composed. I. We sometimes find, either standing side by side or separated by a short interval, two chapters which deal in substance with the

same subject, although each may contain details peculiar
to itself. It looks as if one of these kindred chapters
belonged to the customs of A and the other to the customs
of B, and as if the compiler of our Sea-law, unwilling to
lose a single point of law, had stuck them both in his
collection. For example, the first part of c. 29 seems to
be a repetition of c. 28. The first part of c. 32 repeats the
passage in c. 27 εἰ δὲ μαρτυρηθῇ κτλ. C. 40 repeats to
a certain extent c. 30 and c. 31. Chapters 41, 43, and 44
are to a great extent mere summings up of what has been
stated before in detail. The same phenomenon is found
in other maritime codes, and is especially noticeable in
the Consulate of the Sea.

II. C. 11 sounds more like a piece of advice to
merchants than a provision in a code. In a later part
of this Introduction I compare it with a chapter in
Pegolotti's Pratica della Mercatura (c. xxx, p. 132), in
which he gives advice to merchants who are intending
to load. So far as any legal rule may be extracted from
c. 11, it is that where a merchant loads on an old ship he
cannot claim contribution if the ship is lost. Again, the
remark in c. 41 ἐὰν δὲ ἐπιβάται κτλ. resembles in its
vagueness a moral precept rather than a rule of law.

III. There are chapters which frankly do not refer to
maritime law at all, and others which evidently did not
originally refer to maritime law, and have only been
compelled to come in by a little gentle violence. C. ιη'
has nothing to do with maritime law; it is rightly
entituled in some of the manuscripts περὶ δανείου ἐν γῇ.
C. 12 professes to refer to deposit ἐν πλοίῳ ἢ ἐν οἴκῳ.
The latter part of the chapter refers exclusively to deposit
on land. It looks as if the chapter originally ran ἐάν τις
παραθῆται, γνωστῷ παρατιθέσθω κτλ. Our author, wishing
to bring it into his compilation, added ἐν πλοίῳ ἢ ἐν οἴκῳ
after παραθῆται and καὶ πιστικῷ—using πιστικός in the sense
of 'captain'—after γνωστῷ. C. 14 again has no special
reference to maritime law.

IV. In two cases there are traces of a double recension.

Chapter 8 is remarkable not only for its obscurity and for the variants of the manuscripts, but also because a different recension exists at the end of M and N (see Appendix F). This recension therefore must date back to the eleventh century. It is there described as being στάσις τοῦ λ΄ διατάγματος, i. e. division (see Duc., col. 1429) of the thirtieth ordinance. We have no other knowledge of the ordinance referred to. The reader has only to compare the two forms to see how important the differences are between them. (They are compared at p. lxxxiii.) It is probable that we are here on the trace of a recension earlier than that of the vulgate ; and this probability is increased by a consideration of the two chapters which precede the second form of c. 8 in M (N is here defective).

The first is cited as στάσις τοῦ ν΄ διατάγματος, and agrees closely with a chapter which is found in one recension of Part III, and which I give in Appendix D as Chapter IV. The next is cited as ἐκ τοῦ μ΄ διατάγματος, and is a shorter form of another chapter which is found in the same recension, and which I give in Appendix D as Chapter III. Our knowledge of Byzantine legislation is unfortunately so imperfect that we cannot say to what date these διατάγματα refer. They must go back to the eleventh century.

There is still another case where we get two forms of a chapter which is found in Part III. C. 13 of Part III corresponds to chapters ιδ΄ and ιε΄ of Part II. There is this curious point about these chapters. The Synopsis Major, as I have said, reproduces fourteen chapters of Part III. In every case but one it gives the same number to these chapters as is given in the best manuscripts of the Sea-law. The exception is c. 13, which it introduces as ἐν τῷ ια΄ κεφαλαίῳ θέμ. ε΄. What this refers to I do not know. (As to θέματα, see Heimb. Basil. VI, p. 118.)

SEA-LAW AS COMPARED WITH OTHER LAW

One resource yet remains for fixing the date and character of the Sea-law and of the elements which compose it—namely, its comparison with other legal monuments.

INTRODUCTION

Zach. finds in the Sea-law points of comparison with the law of the Ecloga. He compares (Geschichte, p. 316, n. 1072) chapters 1–3 with the provisions of the Ecloga with regard to theft, chapters 12–14 with Ecloga, XI, the punishment of perjury in c. 14 with Ecloga, XVII, 2, chapters 12–14, 20 sqq., with the law of the Ecloga in reference to the writing of contracts and the presence of three witnesses, the δάνειον ἐπὶ κοινωνίᾳ of c. 17 with the treatment in the Ecloga (X) of loan and partnership under the same title. 'Unverkennbar,' he says, 'sind die Anklänge an das Recht der Ecloga.' It will be found on examination that the learned man has put his case too strongly.

a. *As regards Offences against Property.*

In the legislation of Justinian the law as to theft was as follows. The owner of a thing stolen had two remedies, the *condictio furtiva* and the *actio furti*, and these remedies were cumulative (Dig. III, 6, 5, 1; XIII, 1, 7, 1; Cod. VI, 2, 12, 1). In the *condictio*, the plaintiff recovered the thing stolen; in the *actio furti*, if the thief was taken red-handed, the plaintiff recovered four times the value of the thing stolen; otherwise he only recovered twice its value (Inst. IV, 1, 5). By the time of Ulpian the actio furti was being superseded by a remedy *extra ordinem*. 'Meminisse oportet (he says) nunc furti plerumque criminaliter agi . . . non ideo tamen minus, si qui uelit, poterit ciuiliter agere' (Dig. XLVII, 2, 93 = Bas. LX, 12, 92; cp. Dig. XLVII, 1, 3 = Bas. LX, 11, 3). The nature of the criminal remedy is indicated by Julian (Dig. XLVII, 2, 57, 1). The thief is brought before the praefectus vigilibus or the praeses. If he is condemned and the stolen property restored, the *quaestio furti* is gone, especially if 'amplius aliquid in eum iudex constituerit'. Light is thrown upon this passage by a scholiast on the corresponding passage of the Basilica (LX, 12, 56). He who hands the thief over to the ἄρχων for punishment, δοκεῖ τὴν τιμωρίαν τοῦ σώματος ἀντὶ τοῦ διπλοῦ ἢ τοῦ τετραπλοῦ αἱρήσασθαι.

But if he only hands him over to be beaten until he confesses, the plaintiff does not thereby relinquish his claim to
double. It appears from this that the two remedies were
mutually exclusive. The person wronged had to choose
between the cash and the lash. The normal punishment
of a thief appears to have been whipping (Dig. XLVIII,
19, 10, 2 = Bas. LX, 51, 10, 2). Aggravated forms of
theft were punished with special severity (saccularii and
derectarii, Dig. XLVII, 11, 7 = Bas. LX, 22, 7 ; nocturni
and balnearii, Dig. XLVII, 17, 1 = Bas. LX, 12, 54). It
is clear that, although a person robbed was not obliged
to take criminal proceedings, he would be strongly
tempted to do so where the thief was not a person of
substance. It is also clear that mariners as a rule were
not treated with much consideration by the law. In
wreck inquiries they and even their captain might be
tortured. Theod. XIII, 9, 2, 3.

The remedy under the lex Aquilia might be pursued
concurrently with the *condictio furtiva* (Dig. XLVII,
1, 2, 3). Under the lex Aquilia the damages were double
if the wrongdoer denied, single if he confessed (Dig. IX, 2,
23, 10). Besides the (*directa*) *actio legis Aquiliae*, there
were analogous actions, *utilis*, and *in factum* (Inst. IV, 3, 16),
and according to Ulpian (Dig. IX, 2, 29, 5) ' si funem quis,
quo religata nauis erat, praeciderit, de naue quae periit, in
factum agendum '. Now where this passage is reproduced
in the Basilica (Synopsis Ambrosiana, LIII, Β', θ', FM,
p. 100) ' in factum agendum ' is rendered by εἰς τὸ διπλοῦν
καταδικάζεται. And this or a similar expression is the normal
translation given by the Basilica for the *actio in factum*
of the lex Aquilia. Dig. IX, 2, 11, 5 'si non tenuit, in
factum agendum ' = Bas. LX, 3, 11 εἰ δὲ μὴ κρατῶν ἠρέθισε, τῇ
ἀγωγῇ τῇ τὸ διπλοῦν ἀπαιτούσῃ ; Dig. IX, 2, 41 pr. ' utilius est
in factum et iniuriarum agi ' = Bas. LX, 3, 41 ἐνάγεται τῇ
ἀγωγῇ τῇ τὸ διπλοῦν ἀπαιτούσῃ καὶ τῇ περὶ ὕβρεως ; Dig. IX, 2,
49 pr. ' in factum actione tenebitur ' = Bas. LX, 3, 49
ὑπόκειται τῇ τὸ διπλοῦν ἀπαιτούσῃ ἀγωγῇ.

The action of theft lies not only against the actual

thief, but against any person by whose *ope consilio* the theft was committed (Inst. IV, 1, 11 ; Dig. XLVII, 2, 50, 3 ; Dig. L, 16, 53, 2). Where *A* commits a theft by the *ope consilio* of *B*, both are liable (Inst. *supra*). But *B*, to make him liable, must have given actual physical assistance to *A*, e. g. held a ladder for *A* to climb up or lent him burglar's tools. *B* is not liable if he merely recommends and encourages *A* to commit the theft (Inst., *supra*. There seems to have been some doubt on this matter. See passages from Dig., *supra*). In the Byzantine law books, *ope consilio* is as a rule expressed by σπουδῇ καὶ συμβουλῇ (Theophilus, IV, 1, 11, ed. Reitz, p. 737 ; Schol. ad Bas. LX, 14, 1), or συμβουλῇ καὶ συνεργείᾳ (Bas. LIII, 1, 31 ; LX, 14, 1).

An action for theft also lay *iure honorario* against the exercitor of a ship for thefts committed by the sailors on board ship. This action was *in duplum* (Dig. XLVII, 5).

Let us now compare the rules laid down in regard to thefts in the first three chapters of Part III with the rules of Roman law. C. 1 lays down that the thief of anchors who is caught and confesses gets a whipping (see Commentary) and makes good the damage twofold. It is fairly clear that his liability is not confined to the value of the anchors, but includes the consequential damage whatever it may be. At first sight this passage is inconsistent with the principles laid down above. (i) Where the wrongdoer suffers in his person, the victim forgoes his right to more than the replacement of the damage done. (ii) Where the wrongdoer confesses his guilt, the right to recover twice the damage disappears. The chapter may be brought into harmony with Roman law as follows. Where it is said that the thief is to make good the damage κατὰ τὸ διπλάσιον, it merely means that he is to make it good by virtue of the actio in factum analogous to the actio legis Aquiliae. As we have seen, this was regularly described by the Byzantines as ἡ τὸ διπλοῦν ἀπαιτοῦσα ἀγωγή. If this is so, the provision of this chapter both accords with Roman law and is precisely analogous to a provision of the Farmer's law, c. 30 : 'he who cuts the bell from a cow or sheep and is recognized as the thief is whipped. If the beast is lost, he must make it good.'

C. 2 deals with two points. The first is this. Sailors steal the anchors of another ship by the will (βουλήσει) of their captain. The ship is thereby lost. The captain who directed the theft to take place (ὁ τὰ σύλα ἐπιτρέψας γενέσθαι) must make the damage good, i. e. replace the ship and its contents. Nothing is said as to the sailors being punished, but this omission is probably due to their being included under c. 1.

It seems that, in Roman law, an *actio in factum* on the analogy of the lex Aquilia would lie against the captain in this case (Dig. IX, 2, 37, 1 ; L, 17, 169). It is not a question of *ope consilio*, which would be expressed otherwise (see *ante*, p. lxxx), but of direct command. C. 2 goes on to say that he who steals part of the ship's tackle must make it good twofold. Here there is no question of corporal punishment, and the thief would therefore be liable *in duplum* in the *actio furti.*

C. 3 again deals with two points. A sailor, by command of the captain, steals from a merchant or passenger. The captain makes good the thing lost twofold, and the sailor receives a hundred blows. Now, if we treat the ναύκληρος here as equivalent to the exercitor of Roman law, the passage would disagree with Roman law in two respects. Under Roman law the exercitor would be liable *in duplum* whether the theft took place by his order or not ; and under Roman law the person robbed could not pursue his remedy concurrently against both the exercitor and the sailor. He would have to elect between the two (Dig. XLVII, 5, 1, 3). On the other hand, if we treat the ναύκληρος as equivalent to the magister, there is nothing in the passage inconsistent with Roman law. The magister is not liable by virtue of his office for thefts committed by sailors ; but he would be liable *in duplum* if the theft took place by his command (see authorities above).

The second point in c. 3 is this. If the sailor commits the theft of his own accord and is caught or convicted by witnesses, he receives a sound whipping and makes good the thing stolen. This, as I have shown, would be the normal result of proceedings taken *extra ordinem* by the person wronged.

It appears therefore that these chapters are not necessarily to be brought down to the period of the Ecloga. It is indeed true that the Ecloga punishes theft with personal chastisement (XVII, 10–17), but so did the legislation of Justinian, as I have shown, and in other respects the provisions of the Sea-law as to theft agree much more closely with Roman law than with the Ecloga. In ordinary cases of theft, according to the Ecloga (XVII, 11), the thief on the first occasion, if he is free and well off, restores the thing stolen and twice its value in addition; the poor thief is beaten and banished. For the second offence the hand is cut off; but whether this applies to the rich as well as to the poor thief is not clear.

In the Farmer's law theft is variously dealt with. The thief of agricultural implements pays so much per diem from the date of the theft (c. 22, 62); the thief of straw makes it good twofold (c. 35). As a rule corporal punishment is inflicted. In ordinary cases this takes the form of a whipping, either with or without a fine (c. 30, 33, 34, 41, 60, 61). Where the offence is repeated or of an aggravated kind, or the offender is a slave, the punishment is more severe, e. g. cutting off the hand (c. 44), blinding (c. 42, c. 63 M), or the gallows (c. 46, 47).

There are two more places in the Sea-law dealing with theft. C. 38 provides that a sailor who robs when jettison is taking place is to lose his profit (i. e. the percentage given him for salvage services) and make good the thing stolen twofold. This is in accordance with the ordinary *actio furti*. Persons who stole on the occasion of a shipwreck were liable to make good the thing stolen fourfold or singlefold, as the case might be, and were also exposed to severe corporal penalties (Dig. XLVII, 9).

C. 8 is difficult, and the existence of another version (see *ante*, p. lxxvii) does not diminish its difficulty. The provisions of the chapter in the ordinary text are shortly as follows. The captain in charge of the ship runs away into another country with money by will of the sailors. Their property is to be seized and sold. If the proceeds of sale do not reach the value of the ship and the profits of the money, the captain and sailors are to be hired out until the balance is made good. The version given in Appendix F differs in the following particulars. (1) The seizure and sale include not merely the property of the fugitive mariners but also their wives and children. (2) If they do not make good the ship and profits of the money (?), the property seized is to be sold, and the captain and sailors to be put to death. (3) If the shipowner forgoes his right to have them put to death, they are reduced into slavery for his benefit. (4) The sailors are expressly made responsible for yielding to the captain.

In the ordinary version the claim against the captain and seamen is treated as an ordinary debt, and the creditor's rights are substantially those which he gets by process of execution in the legislation of Justinian. The only peculiarity is that the services of the debtors are let out for the creditor's benefit, but there is nothing in this inconsistent with the legislation of Justinian, having regard to the low position which mariners then occupied. The language of the other version is very obscure. According to the natural meaning of the words the wives and children of the mariners are to be sold as well as their property ; and if the proceeds of sale do not satisfy the debt, the mariners, unless the shipowner relents, are put to death. This is extraordinary, if we are to treat this as merely process of execution for an ordinary debt. It is clear that creditors sometimes under the terms of the contract of loan took possession of the children of the debtor or other free persons by way of pledge, and obliged them to perform servile offices. By various provisions debtors are forbidden to enter into such a contract or creditors to take advantage of it (Cod. IV, 10, 12 ; 43, 1 ; VIII, 16 (17), 6). Novel CXXXIV, 7, after reciting the existence of a practice in parts of the empire under which creditors took the children of their debtors in pledge and employed them for servile offices or hired them out, prohibits it, under severe penalties both pecuniary and corporal. This provision is reproduced in Basilica, XXIII, 2, 3 ; Ecloga, X, 3 ; Epit. Seldeniana, f. 61 v., 62 r.; Ecloga priv. aucta, XI, 9 ; Ecloga ad Proch. mutata, XII, 3. If creditors could not assert this claim under their contract, it is unlikely that they could assert it when their rights were being enforced by the court. It is evident that in this version of c. 8 the act of the captain and crew is treated as criminal. The Code (XI, 2 (1), 5 (7), repeating Theod. XIII, 5, 33) provides : ' qui fiscales species suscepit deportandas, si recta navigatione contempta litora devia sectatus eas auertendo distraxerit, capitali poena plectetur.' Possibly chapter 8 originally applied to the case contemplated by the Code, and was modified to suit the case of a private owner. If this be so, the original form of the chapter, or at least the earlier form, would be that given in Appendix F, and the ordinary version would be a humanitarian recension.

b. *As regards Offences against the Person.*

Chapters 5 to 7 of the Sea-law deal with offences against the person. They provide as follows. (C. 5) Sailors are fighting. *A* wounds *B*. *A* must pay *B*'s doctor's bills and expenses and his wages for the whole time of his illness and convalescence. (C. 6) Sailors are fighting. *A* strikes *B*. *B* strikes back. Even if *A* dies *B* is not liable. (C. 7) A captain, merchant, or sailor puts out some one's eye or causes a hernia. The offender must pay the doctor's bills and twelve gold pieces for the eye, ten for the hernia.

C. 5, which evidently refers to temporary injuries, is strictly in accordance with the provisions of Roman and Byzantine law. C. 7, which deals with permanent injuries,

is not equally so. Under Roman law the damages to which
a freeman was entitled in respect of an injury included
his doctor's bills, the expenses of his cure, and 'operas
amissas quasque amissurus quis esset inutilis factus—
operas quibus caruit aut cariturus est ob id quod inutilis
factus est' (Dig. IX, 1, 3; 3, 7; cp. Dig. IX, 2, 7 pr.).
This principle is also laid down in the Byzantine authorities : Bas. LX, 2, 3; 4, 7; Proch. XXXVIII, 61;
Epanag. XXXIX, 60; XL, 80; Epit. Seldeniana, f. 175 v.
It follows that, where the injury was transient, the
offender would only have to pay the wages of which the
injured man was actually deprived. C. 5 may be a reminiscence of Exod. XXI, 18, 19. The verses are given
in the Collatio, II, 1, but the author of the Sea-law must
have known them in the original Greek, to which his
language bears some resemblance. Where the injury
was permanent, the amount payable would depend upon
the diminution in the injured man's wage-earning capacity. In c. 7 of the Sea-law it is a definite sum, varying
with the injury. There are provisions of a similar
character in the Ecloga ad Proch. mutata, XVIII, 31-8.
C. 32 runs: ὁ τυφλώσας ὀφθαλμὸν τοῦ πλησίον δώσει αὐτῷ
σίκλους τριάκοντα. 37 ὁ ψωρὸν ποιήσας δωσάτω νομίσματα ιβʹ.
ὡσαύτως καὶ τὰς ἰατρείας καὶ τὰ ἀναλώματα ὅλου τοῦ ἐνιαυτοῦ.
Similar provisions are found in other manuscripts of
Byzantine law (see Zach., Prolegomena ad Proch., p. clii ;
La Mantia, Cenni Storici, p. 93). Such a system is unknown to the legislation of Justinian, and La Mantia
may possibly be right in assigning to it a Lombard origin
(Cenni Storici, *supra*). The Greek translation of the
edict of Rothari, fragments of which were published by
Zach. in 1835, and by Bluhme in M. G. H., Leges, vol. IV,
is probably not earlier than the ninth century, but the
influence of the Lombard law on the Sea-law may go
back before that. The Lombard law, however, attached
more importance to the loss of an eye than the Sea-law
does. The Greek version contains the following passage :
c. 9 ἐάν τις ἑτέρῳ ὀφθαλμὸν ἐκβάλῃ, διὰ τεθνεῶτα ἐκτιμείσθω

INTRODUCTION

κατὰ τὴν ἰσότητα τοῦ προσώπου καὶ ἡμισότης τῆς τιμῆς αὐτοῦ ζημιούσθω ᾧ τοίνυν τὸν ὀφθαλμὸν ἐξέβαλεν (M. G. H., Leges, IV, p. 232). This is c. 48 of the Edict of Rothari. Apparently to put out a man's eye cost half as much as to kill him.

C. 7 goes on to say that if the man who is kicked dies, he who kicked him is liable to be tried for his death. This is not in accordance with Roman law, in which 'uoluntas spectatur, non exitus' (Dig. XLVIII, 8, 14). Where *A* causes *B*'s death by accident, *A* is either not punished at all or, if he has been guilty of carelessness, is subjected to a light punishment (Cod. IX, 16, 1 ; 4 (5) 'Eum, qui adseuerat homicidium se non uoluntate, sed casu fortuito fecisse, cum calcis ictu mortis occasio praebita uideatur, si hoc ita est ... omni metu ... uolumus liberari.' Dig. XLVIII, 8, 1, 3 'leniendam poenam eius, qui in rixa casu magis quam uoluntate homicidium admisit'). Where these provisions are repeated in the Basilica, it is laid down that the killer is to receive moderate chastisement, μετρίως or συμμέτρως σωφρονιζέσθω (Bas. LX, 39, 13 ; 17).

Chapter 6 lays down the principle that he who kills another in self-defence incurs no liability. This is in accordance with Roman law (Dig. XLVIII, 8, 1, 4 ; IX, 2, 4 ; Cod. IX, 16, 2, 3 (4) and with the Byzantine authorities (Proch. XXXIX, 39 ; Epanag. XL, 41 ; Proch. Legum, XXXIV, 37 ; Epit. Seldeniana, f. 173 v.). Whether the facts as stated in the chapter would have brought the case, according to Roman law, within the principle of self-defence, is another matter. In Roman law self-defence is only a justification where the person attacked has no other means of saving himself (Dig. XLVIII, 8, 9).

c. *As regards the Punishment of Perjury.*

In c. 14 a depositary who denies the deposit and is proved to be a liar, not only makes it good twofold—as to which see later—but is punished for perjury. One manuscript (C) adds that the penalty is to have the tongue cut out. In c. 27 a partner who denies the existence of the partnership and is convicted of falsehood by three witnesses, pays the penalty of his denial. It is observable that, apart from C, there is no statement of what the penalty is.

In the Ecloga (XVII, 2) perjury in legal proceedings is punished by cutting out the tongue, and the same law is laid down in other Byzantine textbooks (Proch. XXXIX, 46; Epanag., XL, 70), and in the Farmer's law (c. 28). Zach. (Gesch., p. 335) compares the rule of the Ecloga with the Sea-law, and contrasts it with the jurisprudence of Justinian, which, according to him, is based on the principle that perjury in itself is not a matter for the temporal judge. Zach. here goes too far. It is clear that in later Roman law perjury, whether in civil or in criminal proceedings, and whether by a witness or by a party, was normally visited with corporal punishment (Cod. IV, 20, 13 = Bas. XXI, 1, 37; Dig. XXII, 5, 16 = Bas. XXI, 1, 15; Collatio, VIII). In some cases whipping is specified as the punishment. (Dig. XII, 2, 13, 6 = Bas. XXII, 5, 13; Nov. CXXIII, 20.) The statement in the Code (IV, 1, 2) on which Zach. relies, although it is repeated in some Byzantine textbooks (e. g. Schol. ad Epanag., p. 214), was evidently eaten up by exceptions.

d. *As regards the Law of Deposit.*

C. 12 provides: a man makes a deposit in a ship or in a house. Let him deposit with a person known to him and trustworthy (γνωστῷ καὶ πιστικῷ) before three witnesses. If the thing deposited is valuable, the deposit is to be made in writing. (These points are dealt with later.) The depositary to relieve himself (*a*) must prove that the deposit was stolen, and (*b*) swear that there was no fraud on his part. C. 13 deals with deposits on board ship, and is considered hereafter. C. 14 provides that he who denies a deposit[1] either under oath or in writing must, if the deposit is afterwards found on him, make it good twofold and suffer the penalty of perjury.

There was a difference in Roman law between ordinary deposits and deposits made on board ship. The law as to ordinary deposits was this. The depositary was only liable for *dolus*, unless he received remuneration, in which case he was liable for *culpa*, or unless there was a special contract making him liable for *culpa* and *periculum*. But no contract could relieve him from his liability for *dolus* (Dig. XIII, 6, 5, 2; XVI, 3, 1, 6, 7, 35; XLIV, 7, 1, 5; Inst. III, 14, 3). Where the depositary was not liable except for *dolus*, he was not liable if the deposit was burnt or stolen (Collatio, X, 3, 1; 8, 1). It was a mark of *dolus* if the depositary did not take as much care of the goods deposited as he did of his own (Dig. XVI, 3, 32 'nec enim salua fide minorem is quam suis rebus diligentiam praestabit'). Where the deposit was necessary, i.e. where it was made in an emergency and the depositor had no opportunity of choosing his man, his remedy was *in duplum*—apparently not only where the depositary denied that any deposit had been made but also where, while admitting that it had been made, he refused to return it on demand made at the proper time (Dig. XVI, 3, 1, 1; 3, 18; Collatio, X, 2, 7).

The Roman law as to deposits on board ship was different. That law and its relation to c. 13 of the Sea-law are dealt with hereafter (pp. clix, cc).

Now c. 12 deals professedly with deposit either on land or sea, and if that was its original form it is inconsistent with Roman law. It is probable, however (see *ante*, p. lxxvi), that it originally applied to ordinary cases of deposit, and, if so, it is in principle consistent with Roman law. It also agrees with the provision of the

---

[1] ἀρνήσηται αὐτήν is vague. It probably means 'denies that the deposit was ever made'. It might also mean 'denies his liability', whatever the ground for the denial might be.

DEPOSIT IN THE SEA-LAW

Syro-Roman Law Book, § 127 (see note by Bruns, p. 294), which relieves the depositary if he can prove that the deposit was burnt or stolen. In the Ecloga (Tit. XI) the depositary is relieved if he can prove that the deposit was burnt or stolen together with goods of his own. In Roman law, as stated above, the fact that the depositary's goods were also lost was evidence that there was no *dolus*. It is an easy transition for a rule of evidence to become a principle of law.

C. 14 is not consistent with Roman law. In Roman law the *actio depositi in duplum* only applied to the necessary deposit. In this chapter it apparently applies to every case of deposit in which the depositary denies on oath or in writing (?) that the deposit has been made. C. 14 is in accordance with the Ecloga (Tit. XI), which applies in terms both to the ordinary and to the necessary deposit (δι' οἱανδήποτε πρόφασιν ἢ φόβον), and which imposes a twofold liability upon the depositary who denies the deposit; and a provision to this effect is found in other Byzantine textbooks, e.g. Epit. Seldeniana, f. 82 r.; see also the note in BGH and P. London, II, p. 206 (A. D. 124).

e. *As regards Proof.*

The Sea-law as a rule, where it is referring to proof, for the purpose of fixing either a civil or a criminal liability, refers vaguely to witnesses: c. 2, 4 τούτων οὕτως ἐν ἀκριβείᾳ ἀποδεικνυμένων; 3, 5 κατασχέθη δὲ ἢ καὶ διὰ μαρτύρων ἐλεγχθῇ; 6, 4 μαρτυρηθῇ; 27, 4 μαρτυρηθῇ; 36, 9 εἰ ταῦτα οὕτως μαρτυρηθῶσιν. On one occasion it refers to confession of an accused party; c. 1, 2. On three occasions three witnesses are referred to. In c. 12 a deposit should be made before three witnesses, and, if the thing deposited is valuable, also in writing. If the captain tries to overload the ship, the merchant should protest in the presence of three witnesses (c. 22). A partner who denies the existence of the partnership requires three witnesses to convict him (c. 27).

The passages requiring three witnesses are compared

by Zach. (Gesch., p. 290, n. 958; p. 316, n. 1072) with a provision of the Ecloga (XV, 1) by virtue of which compromises (διαλύσεις) require three witnesses. But Zach. might have compared them with many places of the legislation of Justinian, and even of earlier legislation. Cod. VIII, 17 (18), 11, 1 A creditor who has an idiochiron can only enforce a right of pledge or hypotheca in concurrence with a public instrument if the idiochiron is subscribed by three witnesses (A.D. 472). Cod. IV, 2, 17 = Bas. XXIII, 1, 61 An instrument of loan or a release for an amount over fifty pieces of gold is only valid if subscribed by three witnesses *probatae opinionis* (A.D. 528).[1] Cod. IV, 29, 23, 2 A woman cannot oblige herself on behalf of some one else unless the instrument is public and subscribed by three witnesses (A. D. 530). See also Cod. IV, 20, 15, 6; 21, 20, 1; Nov. CXVII, 2; and especially Nov. LXXIII, 1 = Bas. XXII, 4, 1 (A.D. 538), which provides that a deposit is to be made before three witnesses. It is clear that in the legislation of Justinian most, if not all, private instruments required the subscriptions of three witnesses; and that there was a tendency not to admit proof of solemn acts which might form the foundation of judicial proceedings unless they were proved by three witnesses. The three cases in which the Sea-law requires three witnesses come under one or other of these heads. Where the Farmer's law speaks of witnesses, it prescribes two or three (ἀναμεταξὺ δύο καὶ τριῶν μαρτύρων c. 3; ὑπὸ δύο καὶ τριῶν μαρτύρων c. 28, where, however, some of the best manuscripts leave the phrase out). The Farmer's law agrees in this point with the Syro-Roman Law Book (see Bruns' note at p. 276).

f. *As regards Contracts in Writing.*

C. 12 requires a deposit to be made in writing if the thing deposited is of large amount. There is no pro-

---

[1] Zach. cites (Gesch., p. 398) as if it were new law ('folgende eigenthümliche Stelle') a passage from a manuscript which merely reproduces this rule.

vision to this effect in Roman law, but it is clear that in such cases the depositary generally gave an acknowledgement in writing to the depositor. See Dig. XVI, 3, 24, 26.

C. 17 implies that the contract of partnership therein described is in writing (l. 2 ἐγγράψηται, l. 8 τῶν συνθηκῶν).

C. 21 provides that contracts of partnership between two captains (?) are not valid unless they are in writing and subscribed. A constitution of the emperor Leo A.D. 472 (Cod. VIII, 17 (18), 11) deals among other things with contracts made 'societatis coeundae gratia', and declares them valid (so far as regards personal claims by one party against another) if they have the subscriptions of the parties, whether the body is written by the parties or by a notary or third person, and whether there are witnesses or not.

C. 19 provides: A hires a ship from B and gives an ἀρραβών. If A declines to carry out the contract, he loses the ἀρραβών. If B declines to carry it out, he loses the ἀρραβών and as much again. Nothing is said in this chapter about the contract being in writing. C. 20 provides that a contract for the hire of a ship is not valid unless it is in writing and subscribed by both parties. There are many passages which take it for granted that contracts of charter-party are in writing. C. 22, 3 κατὰ τὰς συνθήκας τῶν ἐγγράφων; c. 23, 1 ἐὰν συγγράψωνται, κύρια ἔστω; c. 25, 1 τῶν ἡμερῶν τῶν ἐγγεγραμμένων; c. 29, 1 ἐν τῷ τόπῳ ὅθεν συγγράψονται; c. 30, 8 τὰ ἡμίναυλα ἀπὸ τῶν ἐγγράφων; c. 32, 6 καθὼς συνεγράψαντο κύρια ἔστω; c. 39, 10 ἐν τοῖς ἐγγράφοις.

In Roman law, contracts of letting and hiring are governed by the same rules as contracts of sale (Inst. III, 24 pr.), and contracts of sale may be valid although not in writing (Inst. III, 23 pr.). But where the parties contemplate the execution of a contract in writing, then the contract is not valid unless certain formalities have been complied with. There are two classes of written contracts, (a) those done by the parties themselves, (b) those done by a tabellio. The second class does not concern us: there is no direct reference to a tabellio in the Sea-law.

According to the Code (IV, 21, 17) instruments of the first class must be 'in mundum recepta subscriptionibusque partium confirmata'. Neither party can make any claim 'vel a scheda conscripta vel ab ipso mundo, quod necdum est impletum et absolutum'. According to the Institutes (III, 23 pr.) instruments of the first class must be 'conscripta vel manu propria contrahentium vel ab alio quidem scripta a contrahente autem subscripta'.

These passages are neither clear nor consistent; but the better opinion appears to be (a) that an instrument to be valid only required the subscription of the party to be charged thereby, (b) that it required his subscription even though the body of it was in his writing. (As to the second point, see *contra* Brunner, Urk., p. 59). As regards the first point, the ordinary charter-party contains a number of terms, some imposing liabilities upon the letter and some imposing liabilities upon the hirer. It therefore must have been executed in duplicate, one copy for the letter and one for the hirer; and either each copy must have been signed by both parties or the letter's copy must have been signed by the hirer and the hirer's by the letter. (See Brunner, p. 60.)

g. *As regards the ἀρραβών.*

As regards the ἀρραβών, c. 19 evidently refers to a complete and enforceable contract. It looks as if the penalties imposed took the place of any other claim under the contract; that is to say, it looks as if the letter could not, if the hirer refused to take the ship, recover any more from him than the ἀρραβών which was already in the letter's hands, and as if the hirer could not, if the letter refused to supply the ship, recover more from him than the ἀρραβών and as much again.[1] The ἀρραβών (Lat. *arra*, *arrha*, sometimes also in the plural) in Greek law served a double purpose. It was used in contracts of purchase

---

[1] Bruns agrees with this view of the passage (Syr.-Röm. Rechtsbuch, p. 220).

or hire or in contracts *ejusdem generis,* e. g. espousals. It was evidence of the completion of the contract; it served to bind the bargain. A contract might be binding although there was no ἀρραβών; probably the fact that an ἀρραβών had been given was conclusive evidence that the contract was complete (Theophrast. apud Stob. Flor. XLIV, 22).

Where the ἀρραβών was merely intended to serve as evidence that the parties had left the stage of negotiation and that the contract was complete, it need not be a thing of any pecuniary value. A ring would do. But the ἀρραβών served another purpose; or, to speak more correctly, there was a second reason for giving something on the completion of a contract; and this was to give the party to whom the thing was given a hold upon the party by whom it was given, so that, if the latter failed to perform his part of the contract, the other party might have something in hand which he could keep in lieu of being put to his action for damages. In this case it was necessary that the thing given should have real pecuniary value. In contracts of purchase or hire, it was normally the purchaser or hirer who gave the ἀρραβών to the vendor or letter. If the purchaser or hirer fulfilled his part of the bargain by paying the price, the ἀρραβών went as part payment; if he did not, it remained in the hands of the vendor or letter (Theophrast. l. c.). If, on the other hand, the vendor refused to perform his part of the contract by handing over the property, it was not equally clear how the purchaser was to be indemnified. According to Theophrastus (l. c.) under Thurian law the vendor had to pay the whole purchase price; in other cases the purchaser had a right of action, presumably for damages.

The same distinction appears in Roman law. There is the arra, which is evidence that the parties have entered into a contract, and which may be, and generally is, an object of small value (Dig. XVIII, 1, 35 pr.; Inst. III, 23 pr.). Where the contract was evidenced by writing, this arra was unnecessary and cannot have been much used. There is the arra which in the case of purchases is paid over by the purchaser to the vendor to secure him against the purchaser's neglect or refusal to carry out the contract. This arra was generally a sum of money bearing a considerable proportion to the whole purchase money payable. If the contract went on, this arra went in part payment. This arra, whether the contract was verbal or in writing, must have been accompanied as a rule by a provision determining what was to be done with it under the various circumstances that might arise.

The common form of provision was no doubt to this effect. If the purchaser failed to perform his part of the contract, the vendor was entitled to retain the arra (Dig. XVIII, 3, 4, 1; 6 pr.; 8; Cod. IV, 54, 1). If the vendor failed to perform his part, he was obliged to return the arra and as much again. The rights of the parties under this provision might be made to supersede their rights under the general law in respect of breaches of contract, or they might be exercisable concurrently therewith. But, where there had been no part performance by the party aggrieved, it is probable that his right, in the one case to retain the arra, in the other to recover it and as much again, superseded his rights under the general law. It is unlikely that the arra was often purely penal; it is unlikely, that is to say, that the vendor, while retaining the arra, or the purchaser, while recovering it and as much again, could recover damages beyond or obtain any other relief.

The ἀρραβών occurs not infrequently in the papyri, and, so far as they go, they support the view taken above. In a contract of service of A.D. 99 (Fayûm Towns and their Papyri, p. 226) a servant receives ἀργυρίου δραχμὰς δέκα ἐξ ἀρραβόνα ἀναπόριφον. If she fails to carry out the contract, she promises to restore to the employer τὸν ἀρραβόνα διπλοῦν. In a contract of service of A.D. 550 (P. Oxyrhynchus, I, p. 225) a servant receives λόγῳ ἀρραβῶνος χρυσοῦ νομίσματα τέσσαρα ἥμισυ. If he breaks the contract, he pays it back and as much again; if he is wrongfully dismissed, he keeps it.

P. Raineri, 19, p. 55, is the claim in a suit brought A.D. 330 by one woman against another for specific performance of a contract for sale of land. The plaintiff agreed to sell land to the defendant—συνεθέμην πρὸς αὐτήν. The defendant παρέσχεν μοι εἰς λόγον ἀρραβῶνος three pieces of gold. If the defendant will not take the land and pay the balance of the purchase money, the plaintiff claims ἀπολέγεσθαι αὐτὴν τοῦ ἀρραβῶνος. Mitteis, who discusses the subject at length (pp. 68 sqq.), thinks that the contract here was verbal.

The passage of the Code referred to before (IV, 21, 17) also deals with arrae. In the beginning it puts contracts relating to the giving of arrae (*dationis arrarum*) on the same footing as contracts of sale. In the end it provides as follows: For the future, if any arrae have been given, on the occasion of making a purchase, whether in writing or without writing, then, although there is no special provision what is to be done with the said arrae if the contract does not proceed, he who promised to sell, if he refuses the sale, must restore them twofold, and he who agreed to buy, if he withdraws from the purchase, loses the arrae given. The language of this provision is not free from doubt. (See Bruns [Syrisch-Römisches Rechtsbuch, p. 220] and Mitteis [*supra*].) But prima facie it refers to cases where the parties contemplate a formal contract in writing, and where arrae have been given on the occasion of the informal arrangements which preceded the execution of the formal contract. Those informal arrangements may or may not be in writing; they must be of such a character that, but for the provision of the Code previously referred to, they would constitute a valid enforceable contract. Having regard to that provision, they do not. But the parties to those arrangements, although having no rights under them if they are not accompanied by arrae, have the rights given by the Code if they are accompanied by arrae.

INTRODUCTION

The corresponding passage in the Institutes, which is also the subject of discussion, seems to me to have the same effect as that of the Code. The Institutes (III, 23 pr.) provide that where a contract in writing is contemplated then, unless the prescribed formalities have been complied with, there is a *locus poenitentiae*, and either party can withdraw from the purchase without penalty. They may, however, only withdraw without penalty, if nothing has been already given by way of arrae ('ita tamen impune recedere eis concedimus nisi iam arrarum nomine aliquid fuerit datum'). If arrae have been given then, whether the sale has been made in writing or not in writing, the purchaser who refuses to fulfil his contract loses what he has given, the vendor restores it and so much again, although there is no express provision about arrae.

It is observable that these provisions only apply where the parties have made no express agreement as to arrae, and they do not negative the right of the parties to make express agreements, whether in accordance with or varying from the rules laid down above. There is nothing in these provisions to prevent the parties to a valid enforceable contract from entering into any agreement they please as to the disposition of the arrae. Subject to this, that where the parties contemplate a contract in writing, the terms which relate to arrae must comply with the formalities prescribed in the passages of the Code and Institutes cited above.

The object of the passage in the Code seems only to have been this. The Code invalidated various forms of contract which had theretofore been perfectly valid. While abolishing as a general rule all right of action under these forms of contract, it left one remedy to the parties, that arising out of the arra. With regard to contracts which remained valid, the Code left the law as it was before.

Where a provision, such as that relating to the arra, becomes of common form in a certain class of contract, it is an easy transition for textbooks and legislators to lay down that it is implied in every contract belonging to that class.

The Syro-Roman Law Book lays down [1] (p. 52 of Translation), 'If a man buys a thing or hires a property and gives as arrha a certain sum of money, neither purchaser nor vendor is allowed to withdraw. If the vendor does withdraw, he gives twice the amount of the arrha which he has received. If the purchaser will not buy, the arrha which was taken from him is not returned to him.'

The Ecloga (IX, 2) lays down the same rule with regard to an ἀρραβών given ἐν οἱῳδήποτε πράγματι ἢ συν‑αλλάγματι. The Prochiros (XIV, 2), Epanagoge (XXIII, 2), and Basilica (XXII, 1, 76), simply reproduce, though not with precision, the passages from the Code or Institutes.

C. 19, therefore, in my opinion, does not contain any new law. If the hirer refuses to take the ship, the letter keeps the ἀρραβών and has no other claim against the hirer. He cannot sue for the balance of the freight. If the letter breaks the contract, the hirer can sue for the return of the ἀρραβών and as much again, but for nothing more. C. 24 differs from c. 19 in that there has been part-performance by the letter. The ship has started. If the merchant wishes to return he loses the ἡμίναυλα. If the captain breaks the contract he restores the ἡμίναυλα and as much again. Notwithstanding this difference, the similarity of the language raises the suspicion that τὰ ἡμίναυλα = ὁ ἀρραβών. In the only classical charter-party which we possess (P. London, III, p. 219; see p. clxxix),

---

[1] This is the form in the Paris MS. The form in the London MS. (p. 17 of Translation) leaves out the passage, 'neither purchaser nor vendor is allowed to withdraw.' Bruns, who regards the Paris form as the original, thinks that under it the party aggrieved has the option 'entweder auf die Erfüllung des Vertrages zu dringen oder aber den Rücktritt zuzulassen und dann die Arrha zu lucriren' (p. 217). I doubt this. I think that the words 'neither purchaser nor vendor is allowed to withdraw', if they are original, must be understood with reference to the sentence immediately following; i.e. neither of them may withdraw except on the terms hereinafter stated.

the total freight is 100 drachmai, and forty are paid on the execution of the contract. The proportion must have constantly varied, and it is possible that τὰ ἡμίναυλα does not necessarily mean one-half of the total freight payable, but simply that proportion, whatever it might be, which was payable by way of ἀρραβών.

RELATION OF SEA-LAW TO BASILICA, LIII

Heretofore I have been comparing the Sea-law with other legal monuments in matters not distinctively of maritime law; I propose now to make the comparison in matters of maritime law. The Sea-law is not the only monument of Byzantine maritime law. We possess, although only in fragments, Book LIII of the Basilica; and this book deals in the main with maritime law— partly with branches of maritime law which are not touched in the Sea-law, and partly with branches which are also treated in the Sea-law. There has been some discussion as to the relation between the Sea-law and Book LIII of the Basilica, and there are in the main two opinions about it. One opinion is that the Sea-law or part of it formed an original and integral part of Book LIII. This opinion was held by Fabrot and the brothers Heimbach. It does not necessarily follow that the Sea-law was originally composed with a view of forming such part. It may have been composed at an earlier date and taken into Book LIII, either as it stood or with modifications. The other opinion is that the Sea-law did not form an original part of the Basilica. According to Zach., the Sea-law was not incorporated into Book LIII of the Basilica by the framers of that work, but was added to some manuscripts of it by copyists at a later date. In order to provide materials for a decision on this question, it is necessary to say something about the external history of Book LIII of the Basilica, and to collect the ancient testimony as to what it contained. It exists, as I have said, only in fragments, and there is no manuscript of it as such.

THE INDEXES OF THE BASILICA.

There are two indexes, one complete and one partial, of the books and titles of the Basilica. The complete index is in Coisl. 151 (fol. 1–18 b).[1] There is an index of the last fifteen books with the heading τοῦ τετάρτου τῶν νόμων τεύχους πίναξ in Paris. gr. 1357, fol. 123 a–128 a (Heimbach, G.-r. Recht., p. 317). In Coisl. 151 the index of Book LIII (I cite it from Pard. I, p. 157) runs as follows:—

Βιβ. νγ´ τῶν Βασιλικῶν· ἔχει τίτ. ζ´.

α´ περὶ ναυκλήρων καὶ πιστικῶν καὶ ναυτῶν καὶ πανδοχέων, καὶ τῆς κατ᾽ αὐτῶν ἢ ὑπὲρ αὐτῶν ἀγωγῆς.

β´ περὶ πλοίου ἐκδικουμένου.

γ´ περὶ ναυαγίου καὶ ἁρπαγῆς καὶ ἀποβολῆς καὶ συνεισφορᾶς.

δ´ περὶ πλοίου ληγατευομένου ἢ ἐν χρήσει διδομένου ἢ ὁμολογουμένου.

ε´ περὶ δανεισμάτων διαποντίων.

ϛ´ περὶ ἁλιέων καὶ ἁλιείας καὶ δικαίου θαλάσσης.

ζ´ περὶ πράσεως καὶ ἀγορασίας οἴνου.

The index of Paris. gr. 1357 agrees substantially with the index given above, except that it adds:—

Τιτλ. η´ τὰ κεφάλαια τοῦ νόμου τῶν ῾Ροδίων· κεφάλαια νόμου ῾Ροδίων κατ᾽ ἐκλογὴν ἢ περὶ ναυτικῶν. (I cite from Pard. I, p. 158. Pard. takes the second η for a numeral.)

Our knowledge of Book LIII, apart from these Indexes, was formerly derived almost exclusively from the paragraphs contained in that title of the Synopsis Major which dealt with nautical matters. It has been materially enlarged by two discoveries made within recent years.

VENTURI'S SYNOPSIS.

Codex Riccardianus 2118[2] is a *zibaldone*, i. e. a collection of fragments of various character bound together. Towards the middle of the volume (which is not paged)

---

[1] A MS., according to M. Omont, of the fourteenth century (Inventaire, T. III, p. 145).

[2] Not 211 as FM constantly describe it. My statements about the MS. are based on my own examination.

there are the following documents. First come eight leaves, of which the first seven contain what is evidently a Latin translation, not indeed of Book LIII of the Basilica, but of an abridgement of that book. These leaves are numbered 1 to 7; the eighth is blank. Then follow six leaves containing a translation of part of the Sea-law by Francesco Venturi. With that I have already dealt (p. xxvii).

The translation of the abridgement of Book LIII is not in Venturi's hand, but it contains corrections in his hand. There are six titles, which appear in the manuscript as follows :—

Liber quartus, tit⁸ pˢ De exercitoribus magistris nautis et cauponibus et actione quae ipsis vel adversum ipsos competit.

Titulus secundus lib. tertii De nave defendenda.

Titulus tertius lib. IIII De naufragio raptu iactu et contributione.

Libri tertii tit. quintus De legato usu et confessione navis.

Lib. 3 tit. 6 De pecunia traiectitia.

Tit⁸ sept⁸ lib. 3 De piscatoribus piscatione et iure maris.

It will be seen that these titles correspond to the first six titles of Book LIII as given by the two manuscripts which preserve an index of the Basilica. Under each title comes a series of paragraphs, which are only numbered in the first two titles.[1] The manuscript was discovered by Zach., and was published by him in the Monatsberichte der Königlich Preussischen Academie der Wissenschaften zu Berlin aus dem Jahre 1881, Berlin 1882, pp. 13–34: Über eine lateinische Übersetzung von Buch 53 der Basiliken. It was published again from a new copy of the manuscript made for FM at pp. 180–5 of their book. It is a surprising coincidence that the

---

[1] The numbering seems to have been done by Venturi himself. The numbering of the MS. differs from the numbering in FM, pp. 180 sqq. Par. 1 in the printed text of Title 1 is not numbered in the MS.; 2 of the printed text is numbered 1 in the MS., and so on ; 26, 27, 28 of the printed text are 25 in the MS., 36 and 37 of the printed text are 33 of the MS. Hence 45, the last paragraph of the printed text, is 41 in the MS. In the second Title, pars. 4 and 5 of the printed text are 4 in the MS.; 8 and 9 are 7. Hence the 13 paragraphs of the printed text are 11 in the MS.

c

learned Italian who transcribed the manuscript for FM should have made in his transcript every error which is found in Zach.'s text; it is not so surprising that he should have added errors of his own. Here are the principal differences between the manuscript and the text given by FM:—

Reading of FM.	Reading of MS.
P. 180, Title I.	
Title adversus	adversum
2 pertinet	pertinent
8 navigiis	aliis navigiis
15 de damno	damno
P. 181.	
20 enim	etenim
22 praescripsit praefinivitque	This was the original reading, corrected by Venturi into praescripta praefinitaque sint
29 illatis	inlatis
39 duobus millibus	duum millibus
P. 182, Title II.	
7 ὁ ἀqήλιος	ὁ ἀζήνιος is the original reading, corrected by Venturi into ὁ ἀζήλιος
10 clavus	clavum
11 et principale esse	esse et principale
13 abene	aberrem (probably)
P. 183, Title III.	
7 alia	alio
10 dominus	dominis
11 servavit	servarit
13 in dolo	de dolo
P. 184.	
28 dimittuntur	dimittantur
ceteris	ceteris delictis
Title V.	
4 ex parte	in una parte (probably)
P. 185, Title VII.	
1 sibi	tibi
7 molem	molum
9 retiaque exsiccare	rectiaque exiccare

AMBROSIAN SYNOPSIS.

Codex Ambrosianus F 106 sup. has been already described (p. xvii). The abridgement of the Basilica, which it contains, fortunately includes part of Book LIII. The abridgement of Book LIII, which is given in FM, pp. 97–107, contains the first two titles complete. The headings of these are as follows:—

BIBΛION NΓ΄, TITΛOC A΄.
περὶ ναυκλήρων καὶ πιστικῶν καὶ ναυτῶν καὶ πανδοχέων καὶ τῆς κατ᾽ αὐτῶν ἢ ὑπὲρ αὐτῶν ἀγωγῆς.
TITΛOC B΄ BIBΛIOY NΓ΄.
περὶ πλοίου διεκδικουμένου.

The third title (the heading of which is περὶ ναυαγίου καὶ ἁρπαγῆς καὶ ἀποβολῆς καὶ συνεισφορᾶς) breaks off in the middle; the fourth is wanting, and only the latter part of the fifth has survived. The sixth and seventh are complete. Their headings are:—

TITΛOC Ϛ΄ BIBΛIOY NΓ΄.
περὶ ἁλιέων καὶ ἁλιείας καὶ δικαίου θαλάσσης.
TITΛOC Z΄ BIBΛIOY NΓ΄.
περὶ πράσεως καὶ ἀγορασ[ίας] οἴνου.

The paragraphs under each title are numbered, but the numbering is not consecutive. Thus in the first title there are forty numbered paragraphs, but the last number is ρε΄. In the second title there are ten numbered paragraphs, and the last is numbered ιγ΄. In the third title, which, as I have said, is imperfect, there are ten numbered paragraphs, the last being numbered ιε΄. In the sixth title there are eight numbered paragraphs, the last being numbered θ΄; and in the seventh sixteen, the last of which is numbered ιθ΄. It is probable that these numbers refer to the original numbering of the paragraphs in the complete text of the Basilica.

The relation between the text of the Ambrosian palimpsest and the text from which Francesco Venturi made his translation is very close. Where a comparison is possible, it may almost be said that the two texts are identical, if we bear in mind that we have to get at Venturi's original through the translation of a man who was not perfectly acquainted with Greek in a copy made by a scribe who could not always read his employer's handwriting.

There is only one paragraph in the Ambrosian palimpsest which is not given by Venturi (Tit. E´, fr. ιε´). There is no paragraph in Venturi which is not given in the palimpsest, so far as the palimpsest exists. In both texts the paragraphs occur in the same order.

SYNOPSIS MAJOR.

Before the discovery of Venturi's translation and of the Ambrosian palimpsest, the principal source for the restoration of Book LIII was the so-called Synopsis Major (see Heimbach, G.-r. Recht, pp. 420-8). In this work, which goes back to about the middle of the tenth century, select paragraphs from the Basilica were arranged in titles due to the compiler of the Synopsis and set in alphabetical order. The only exception to the alphabetical order was the title περὶ τῆς ὀρθοδόξου πίστεως τῶν Χριστιανῶν, which came first. These titles do not necessarily correspond to the titles of the Basilica. In the πίναξ, which in the manuscripts of the Synopsis Major precedes the text, the first title under the letter N runs as follows :—

Περὶ ναυτικῶν ἐνοχῶν καὶ παντοίων ἀγωγῶν κινουμένων περὶ πλοίων τε καὶ πάντων τῶν ἐν αὐτοῖς πλεόντων ναυκλήρων πιστικῶν ναυτῶν ἐμπόρων τε καὶ λοιπῶν .ἐπιβατῶν καὶ περὶ ναυαγίου (e. g. Palat. gr. 8, f. 5 v. ; Marc. gr. 173, f. 14 r.).

This title is repeated with unimportant differences in the body of the work, and most, if not all, manuscripts add : ἀνάγνωθι β νγ´ οὗτινος ἐν τῷ α´ κεφαλαίῳ φησίν. Under this heading come in succession the various titles of Book LIII, and under each title a certain number of paragraphs.

The paragraphs are much fewer than in the Ambrosian Synopsis ; but there are some paragraphs in the Synopsis Major which are not in the Ambrosian Synopsis ; other paragraphs again are given at greater length or in another form. The two Synopses are evidently independent.

The paragraphs in the Synopsis Major are numbered but not consecutively. The numbering agrees on the whole—the exceptions are generally in the first title—with the numbering of the Ambrosian Synopsis, thus strengthening the probability that the numbers of the Ambrosian Synopsis are the original numbers of the Basilica.

OTHER SOURCES OF BOOK LIII.

As I have already pointed out, some manuscripts at the end of the Sea-law add paragraphs on nautical matters which are derived from the Basilica. Most of these paragraphs are to be found either in the Ambrosian Synopsis or in the Synopsis Major. Other Byzantine textbooks add one or two paragraphs, and a few may be gathered from the works of Cujas, who had access to manuscripts of the Basilica more complete than any now existing. (See especially Zach. in Monatsberichte der K. Preuss. Acad. der Wissenschaften zu Berlin aus dem Jahre 1881, p. 14).

CONTENTS OF BOOK LIII.

Book LIII of the Basilica does not contain any new law, if we assume that the Sea-law does not form part of it. It is simply a mechanical *rifacimento* of those passages in the Digest and Code which seemed to its compilers to bear on nautical law. The following summary will show the reader the system on which Book LIII is arranged.

The summary is in tabular form. In the first column come the numbers of the titles and chapters in Venturi's Synopsis[1]; in the second and third the numbers of the corresponding titles and chapters in the Ambrosian Synopsis and in Heimbach's text respectively. In the fourth are cited the passages of the Corpus Juris which the chapters paraphrase.

---

[1] I cite according to the numbering of the MS. which, in the first two titles, does not agree with the numbering in FM (see p. c). In the later titles, the paragraphs are not numbered in the MS., and I adopt FM's numbering.

RELATION OF SEA-LAW TO BASILICA, LIII

Titles and chapters in Venturi's Synopsis.	Titles and chapters in Ambrosian Synopsis.	Titles and chapters in Heimbach's text.	Corresponding places in Corpus Juris.
Tit. I.	Tit I.	Tit. I.	
no number ..	a'	1	D XIV, 2, 9
1	β'	β' (shorter form)	D XIV,1,1,15,16
2	γ'	. .....	D XIV, 1, 1, 5
3	γ'	δ'	D XIV, 1, 1, 1
4	ε'	. .....	D IV, 9, 1, 2
5	ϛ'	ϛ''	D IV, 9, 1, pr. 1
6	ζ'	ζ' (shorter form)	D IV, 9, 1, 3
7	η'		D IV, 9, 1, 4
8	θ'		D IV, 9, 1, 5-7
9	ι'		D IV, 9, 1, 8
10	ια'		D IV, 9, 3, pr.
11	ιζ'		D IV, 9, 3, 5
12	no number ..		D IV, 9, 4, pr.
13	ιη'		D IV, 9, 4, 1, 2, 5, pr.
14	κ'		D IV, 9, 5, 1
15	κϛ''		D IV, 9, 7, pr.
16	κζ'		D IV, 9, 7, pr.
17	κθ'		D IV, 9, 7, 5
18	λ'		D IV, 9, 7, 6
19	no number ..	ιε'	D XIV, 1, 1, 2
20	no number ..	ιϛ''(muchfuller)[2]	D XIV, 1, 1, pr. ; 1, 7; 1, 8-10
21	μ'		D XIV, 1, 1, 12
22	μη'		D XIV, 1, 1, 25
23	νϛ''		D XIV, 1, 5, 2
24	νη'		D XIV, 1, 6, 1
25	νθ'		D XIV, 2, 10, pr.
no number ..	no number ..		D XIX, 2, 15, 6
no number ..	ξ'		D XIX, 2, 19, 7
26	ξβ'		D XIV, 2, 10, 2
27	ξε'		D XIX, 2, 13, 2
28	ξϛ''		D XIX, 2, 31
29	ξθ'		D XXXIX, 4, 11, 2
30	ο'		D XLIV, 7, 5, 6
31	ογ'		D XLVII, 5, 1, 6
	οϛ''		D XLIII, 16, 1, 7
32	οζ'		{ D XLVIII, 6, 3, 6 / D XLVIII, 7, 1, 2

[1] *a'* in Heimbach's text is not a fragment of the Basilica, but simply part of the title in the Synopsis Major.

[2] Heimbach gives after ιϛ'' three chapters, ιζ', κε' μ. γ', and λα', which are not in either Venturi's or the Ambrosian ynopsis. The first and second correspond to D XIV, 1, 1, 3 and ι XVII, 1, 26, 6. The third, which corresponds to D XLVII, 5, 1, 3-6, is also found substantially in Basilica LX, 14, 1, where the scholiast says τὸ παρὸν κεφ. κεῖται ἀπαραλλάκτως βιβ. νγ' τιτ. α'. κεφ. λα' (οα' Fabrot).

Titles and chapters in Venturi's Synopsis.	Titles and chapters in Ambrosian Synopsis.	Titles and chapters in Heimbach's text.	Corresponding places in Corpus Juris.
33	οη'		D XLVIII, 12, 2, 1, 2
34	no number		D XLIX, 14, 46, 2
35	πδ'		C I, 2, 10
36	πε'	λθ'	C IV, 25, 4
37	4'		C XI, 2, 1
38	4α'		C XI, 2, 3
39	4γ'		C XI, 2, 5
40	ρ'		C XI, 8, 9
41	ρε'		C VI, 62, 1
Tit. II.	**Tit. II.**	**Tit. II.**	
1	α'		D VI, 1, 3, 1
2 (?)	δ'	δ'	D VI, 1, 36, 1
3	no number	no number	D IX, 2, 27, 24
4	ϛ'	ε'	D IX, 2, 29, 2
no number	no number	no number	D IX, 2, 29, 3
5	ζ'	no number	D IX, 2, 29, 4
6	η'	no number	D IX, 2, 29, 4
7	θ'	no number	D IX, 2, 29, 5
no number	no number		D XIV, 1, 1, 6
8	ι'		D XXI, 2, 44; L 16, 242
9	ια'	ια'	D XXXIII, 7, 29
10	ιβ'		D XLI, 1, 26, pr.
11	ιγ'		D XIII, 7, 30
Tit. III.	**Tit. III.**	**Tit. III.**	
1	α'	α' (in part)	D XIV, 2, 1; 2, pr. 1
2	no number	no number (in part)	D XIV, 2, 2, 2, 3
3	γ'	γ'	D XIV, 2, 2, 4
4	δ'		D XIV, 2, 2, 5
5	ε'		D XIV, 2, 2, 6
6	η'		D XIV, 2, 2, 8
7	ι'		D XIV, 2, 4, 1
8	ια'		D XIV, 2, 4, 2
9	ιβ'	ιβ' (fuller)	D XIV, 2, 5, pr.
10	ιδ'	no number	D XIV, 2, 6
11	ιε'	ιδ'	D XIV, 2, 7
12	MS. fails till Tit. V.		D XIV, 2, 8
13			D XIX, 5, 14, pr.
14			D XIX, 5, 14, 2
15		ιθ'	D XLI, 1, 9, 8
16			D XLI, 1, 44
17			D XLI, 1, 58
18			D XLI, 7, 7
19		κβ' (in part)	D XLI, 2, 21, 1, 2

Titles and chapters in Venturi's Synopsis.	Titles and chapters in Ambrosian Synopsis.	Titles and chapters in Heimbach's text.[1]	Corresponding places in Corpus Juris.
20	. . . . . .	. . . . . .	D XLVII, 2, 43, 11
21	. . . . .	κε′	D XLVII, 9, pr.; 1, 5 / D XLVII, 9, pr.; 8
22	. . . . .	. . . . .	D IX, 3, 6, 3
23	. . . . .	. . . . .	D XLVII, 9, pr.
24	. . . . .	. . . . .	D XLVII, 9, 3,
25	. . . . .	. . . . .	D XLVII, 9, 3, 8
26	. . . . .	λα′	D XLVII, 9, 3, 8
27	. . . . .	. . . . .	D XLVII, 9, 4, pr.
28	. . . . .	. . . . .	D XLVII, 9, 4, 1
29	. . . . .	. . . . .	D XLVII, 9, 4, 2
30	. . . . .	λθ′ (in part). .	D XLVII, 9, 5
31	. . . . .	. . . . .	D XLVII, 9, 6
32	. . . . .	. . . . .	D XLVII, 9, 7
33	. . . . .	. . : . .	D XLVII, 9, 8
34	. . . . .	. . . . .	D XLVII, 9, 12, pr.
35	. . . . .	. . . . .	D XVI, 3, 1, 1
36	. . . . .	. . . . .	C XI, 2, 3
37	. . . . .	. . . . .	C XI, 6, 1
38	. . . . .	. . . . .	C XI, 6, 2
Tit. V (should be IV).	The MS. fails.	Tit. IV.	
1	. . . . .	. . . . .	D XXI, 2, 36
2	. . . . .	β′	D XXX, 24, 4
3	. . . . .	. . . . .	D XXXII, 88, 1, 2
4	. . . . .	. . . . .	D VII, 4, 10, 7
5	. . . . .	. . . . .	D XLV, 1, 83, 5 / D XLVII, 3, 98, 8
Tit. VI (should be V).	The MS. fails.	Tit. V.	
1	. . . . .	α′	D XXII, 2, 1
2	. . . . .	. . . . .	D XXII, 2, 2
3	. . . . .	. . . . .	D XXII, 2, 3
4	. . . . .	. . . . .	D XXII, 2, 6
5	. . . . .	. . . . .	D XXII, 2, 7
6	. . . . .	. . . . .	D XXII, 2, 8
7	. . . . .	. . . . .	D XIV, 1, 7, pr.
8	. . . . .	. . . . .	D XLII, 5, 24, 1 / D XLII, 5, 26
9	. . . . .	. . . . .	D XLII, 5, 34

[1] Chapters μβ′, μγ′ and μη′ in Heimbach's text do not correspond to anything in Venturi's Synopsis. μβ′ and μγ′ practically repeat κε′ (first part); μη′ comes from D XLVIII, 7, 1, 1, 2.

Titles and chapters in Venturi's Synopsis.	Titles and chapters in Ambrosian Synopsis.	Titles and chapters in Heimbach's text.	Corresponding places in Corpus Juris.
10	number wanting	ιγ′ ιδ′	D XX, 4, 5, & 6
wanting . . .	ιε′	ιε′	C IV, 32, 26, 2
11	ιϛ′	. . . . . .	
12	ιη′	. . . . .	C IV, 33, 2 (1)
13	ιθ′	ιη′	C IV, 33, 3 (2)
14	κ′	. . . . .	C IV, 33, 4 (3)

The sixth and seventh titles of Book LIII do not concern the present subject. The sixth deals with fishers and fishing and private rights in the sea; the seventh with the purchase and sale of wine. Pard. is astonished, not without reason, to find this title in a book which professes to deal exclusively with maritime law. Zach. explains the difficulty as follows (Paralipomena ad Basilica, Lipsiae, 1893, p. 7): 'Nimirum Basilicorum auctores in hos ultimos libros ac titulos congesserunt quaecunque ad ea respicerent quae sub dispositione praefecti urbi essent. Pertinebant eo non solum quae inter magistrum navis, nautas, eos qui merces navigio imponerent vel in eo iter facerent litigiosa fieri solebant, unde παραθαλασσίτης inter officiales praefecti recensetur. Praeterea praefecto cura erat commercii vini, uti e libro Eparchicorum nuper a Nicole Genevi reperto et edito didicimus: cuius rei causa inter officiales ἐπόπτης videtur nominari. Unde iam explicatum est cur hoc loco titulus de vini commercio in Basilicorum libro LIII insertus sit, et simul argumentum peti potest legem Rhodiam primitus a Basilicis alienam fuisse. Nam Basilicorum auctores inepte fecissent si post titulos ius navale illustrantes titulum de emptione venditione vini ab eo argumento alienum posuissent, deinde vero ad rem navalem reversi leges Rhodias collocassent.'

WAS THE SEA-LAW AN ORIGINAL PART OF BOOK LIII?

We are now in a position to discuss the question whether the Sea-law formed an original and integral part of the Basilica. Some of the evidence has already been adverted to. I deal first with the evidence in favour of the view that the Sea-law did so form part. 1. According to the table of contents of the Basilica which is given in Paris gr. 1357, the eighth title of Book LIII was the law of the Rhodians (p. xcix). 2. In both Venturi's Synopsis and the Ambrosian Synopsis, Parts II and III (including the latter's table of contents) are evidently treated as a part of the Basilica. It is true that in neither of these Synopses, as we possess them, is there an express statement to that effect. But in the Ambrosian Synopsis they are in the manuscript which contains the Basilica; and it is highly probable that Venturi's translations of Book LIII and of the Sea-law were made from one and the same manuscript. 3. However this may be, the Synopsis Major treats Part III of the Sea-law as an integral part of Book LIII. The evidence for this has been already stated (p. xxxi). It is true that it only gives fourteen chapters, but it treats those chapters, as we see from the numbers which it prefixes to them, as parts of a larger whole. 4. The scholiasts of the Basilica cite chapters of the Sea-law as from Book LIII. Schol. Bas. XXII, 5, 44 (ed. Heimb. II, p. 565) ζήτει . . . βιβ. νγ´ κεφ. ιγ´ τοῦ νόμου τῶν 'Ροδίων; Schol. Bas. XXIII, 1, 62, n. 8 (ed. Heimb. II, p. 654) ζήτει βιβ. νγ´ κεφ. ιδ´ τοῦ νόμου τῶν 'Ροδίων; Schol. Bas. XXVIII, 2, 1 (ed. Heimb. III, p. 156) τὸ αὐτό φησιν . . . βιβ. νγ´ διγ. ιθ´ τοῦ νόμου τῶν 'Ροδίων. Zach., who cites the two last passages, thinks that they suggest that Book LIII contained the Sea-law and nothing else. What they really suggest, in my opinion, is that the Sea-law, though forming part of Book LIII, was not brought under any τίτλος, but formed, as it were, an Appendix. 5. Paris gr. 1384 and Monac. gr. 303 treat chapter 39 of Part III as coming from Book LIII. (See p. xl and Appendix I.) 6. The author of the Tipucitus apparently treats Parts II and III of the Sea-law as forming the eighth and ninth title respectively of Book LIII (Heimbach's ed. of Basilica, V, p. 119, n.; Pard. I, p. 259). 7. The Synopsis Minor quotes indifferently from Book LIII and from the Sea-law.

Part III, c. 7 = Syn. Minor, N 66; Part III, c. 28 = Syn. Minor, N 67; Part III, c. 47 = Syn. Minor, N 68.

These authorities prove that very soon after the composition of the Basilica, Part III of the Sea-law was found in some manuscripts of it either as the eighth title of Book LIII or at least as part of that Book. They do not prove more than this, but, admitting this, it is difficult to resist the conclusion that Part III of the Sea-law was incorporated in the Basilica from the beginning; and there is some evidence, as we have seen, for holding that Part II and the table of contents of Part III were also so incorporated.

I turn to the evidence which points in the opposite direction. 1. In the table of contents of the Basilica which is given by Coisl. 151, Book LIII has only seven titles (see p. xcix). 2. The forty-eighth title of Michael Attaliates (Leuncl. II, p. 43; Pard. I, p. 194), which is professedly based on Book LIII of the Basilica, contains no quotations from the Sea-law. This title, however, only contains twelve short chapters. 3. It is singular, as Zach. points out (see *ante*, p. cviii), that, if the Sea-law formed an original part of the Basilica, it should have been placed after the title dealing with the sale of wine. 4. The preface of the Basilica only professes in substance to arrange the matter of the Corpus Juris—the Digest, Code, and Novels—in a better order. It does not profess to add new law. And in the books of the Basilica which we possess there are no interpolations on a large scale extraneous to the Corpus Juris. It is true that rules of the Ecloga have found their way into the πρόχειρος νόμος, and from there into the Basilica (Heimbach, Prolegomena Basil., p. 140), but these are merely isolated fragments.

It is apparent that these arguments are mainly arguments from probability, and cannot of themselves outweigh the direct testimonies to the contrary which I have set out. A point of more substance remains.

The law of contribution as laid down in Book LIII of the Basilica, title 3, is in strict accordance with Roman law. In fact that title, so far as it deals with contribution, is merely a paraphrase of Dig. XIV, 2. The Sea-law, while in some chapters it lays down rules not inconsistent with Roman law, has an entirely different doctrine of contribution. I deal with this at length hereafter; it is sufficient now to say that in the Sea-law every maritime disaster for which no one is to blame forms the subject of contribution. Under Roman law the wreck of ship does not entitle the owners to contribution from cargo; under the Sea-law, if the owners are not in default, it does. Under Roman law loss of cargo, except where it is jettisoned to save other cargo and ship, does not entitle its owners to contribution from other cargo and ship. In the Sea-law all losses of cargo not due to the owner's default entitle him to contribution. Pard. finds it impossible to imagine that the compilers of the Basilica should have admitted into their work two doctrines so entirely unlike, and based on inconsistent principles. On this two remarks may be made. (*a*) There are contradictory provisions in parts of the Basilica which are indubitably genuine (see Heimbach, G.-r. Recht, pp. 280, 337 ; Zach., Gesch., p. 341, n. 1186). (*b*) We must distinguish various forms of inconsistency. The Sea-law never refuses to grant contribution where Roman law grants it. Every case of contribution under Roman law is also a case under the extended doctrine of the Sea-law. It is true that there is a difference in the system of valuing goods lost or saved : certain classes of property have a fixed valuation in the Sea-law, but this is a matter of administration and not of principle. The Sea-law simply widens the sphere of contribution. Roman law, followed in the Basilica, admits contribution in cases *a*, *b*, *c*, and therefore by implication rejects it in cases *d, e, f* : the Sea-law admits it in all. Now where one provision merely applies another to cases which the other did not touch, there is nothing unusual in putting the one beside the other in a code or statute. True that the limited provision is in substance superseded, and that, when the compilers of the Basilica admitted the Sea-law into Book LIII, they ought to have struck out many of the provisions of title 3, but lawyers, especially those who are consolidating former legislation, are very loath to hold that an enactment is completely superseded unless it is definitely repealed. The difficulties of Pard. do not seem to me insuperable.

There is another ground for maintaining that the Sea-law in its present form was an original part of the Basilica. The Sea-law fills up gaps in the law of the Basilica. It deals with matters which that law does not deal with at all, or deals with only imperfectly. The Sea-law does not destroy; it fulfils. Without anticipating the sketch of maritime law which occupies the third part of this Introduction, I may say this. The Sea-law deals with maritime offences which are not dealt with in the Basilica. If we reject the three chapters of Appendix E, it does not deal with maritime offences which are dealt with in the Basilica. It deals at length with charter-parties, which are hardly touched upon in the Basilica. It adds important illustrations of the law of collision to those given in the Digest and copied from the Digest into the Basilica. It deals with salvage and the salvor's reward—matters of which there is nothing in the Basilica. On the whole there is very little overlapping as between the Basilica and the Sea-law, and one is tempted to think—merely from a consideration of the two works—that the Sea-law, if it was not composed, was at least adapted to take a place in the Basilica.

SUMMING-UP OF PART II

The evidence brought forward in this and the preceding part has led me to the following conclusions. No one who has read the evidence will fail to perceive how much guesswork there is in them. The Sea-law was probably put together by a private hand between A.D. 600 and A.D. 800. It cannot have been put together much later, because (as I have said) the differences between the earliest manuscripts point to a transmission which has extended over some time. There is no reason for connecting it in any way with the Ecloga. The points of similarity which Zach. discovered disappear on examination.

The Sea-law was put together from material of very different epochs and characters. Some of it was possibly from treatises in the nature of a 'Complete Merchant', guides to a gentleman engaging in business (c. 11). Other parts may come from enactments of Byzantine Caesars; but the mass of it must be derived from local customs. Some provisions which originally had nothing to do with maritime affairs have been doctored in order to bring them within the purview of the Sea-law. There are traces of a South Italian origin for some of the chapters. Part III of the Sea-law, as we have it, was evidently composed to be a part of Book LIII of the Basilica. Part III and Book LIII fit in together and form a complete body of maritime law, while each separately is imperfect. I therefore infer that a second edition of the Sea-law was made either by, or under the direction of, the men who compiled the Basilica. Perhaps at this time Part II was severed from Part III. Our texts represent in substance the second edition—what I call the vulgate—but there are traces of the earlier one or even of the texts out of which the earlier one was composed.

The great difficulty in my hypothesis is this. The Sea-law is found in many manuscripts. It is very often found in conjunction with two other little treatises—the Farmer's law and the Soldier's law—neither of which has any connexion with the Basilica. If the Sea-law existed before the Basilica, as I suggest, and was only taken into it in a modified form, why do we not find the unmodified form in manuscripts of which the tradition appears to be quite independent of the Basilica? An answer perhaps is, that, in the law stationers' shops and the monasteries where the Sea-law was copied, there was generally a pretty complete legal library, and that, when it came to copying a manuscript which gave the unmodified text of the Sea-law, that form was regularly substituted which was not only more compact but which also had received the imperial approbation.

The company in which the Sea-law is often found in the manuscripts—the Farmer's law and the Soldier's law—gives us little or no help in solving the problem of its origin. There is no reason for attributing a common origin to the three books except this juxtaposition in the manuscripts. In character they are entirely distinct. The Soldier's law, or, to give it the title which is commoner in the manuscripts, the law concerning military punishments ($\pi\epsilon\rho\grave{\iota}$ $\sigma\tau\rho\alpha\tau\iota\omega\tau\iota\kappa\hat{\omega}\nu$ $\dot{\epsilon}\pi\iota\tau\iota\mu\acute{\iota}\omega\nu$), is to a great extent a paraphrase of passages in the Digest and the Code. Its other sources are dealt with by Zach. in his essay 'Wissenschaft und Recht für das Heer vom 6. bis zum Anfang des 10. Jahrhunderts' in the Byzantinische Zeitschrift, III, pp. 437 sqq. These sources are clearly indicated by the author of the table of contents which appears in L and in Vall. F 47, and the chapters are distinguished which come from the Digest or the Code and those which come $\dot{\epsilon}\kappa$ $\tau o\hat{v}$ (or $\tau\hat{\omega}\nu$) 'Ρούφου καὶ τῶν τακτικῶν. The Farmer's law has no table of contents in any manuscript which I have seen. Its style is very different from the Sea-law's. The chapters are generally short and pithy; many of them deal with agricultural offences and inflict punishments, pecuniary or corporal or both. It refers to judicial authorities, οἱ ἀκροαταί (c. 7, 37, 62 M), to taxes (ὁ δημόσιος λόγος, c. 18, 19), and to φόλλεις (c. 22, 62), none of which are mentioned in the Sea-law.

PART III

AUTHORITIES USED IN THIS PART

In this, the third Part of my Introduction, I propose
to compare briefly the maritime law of the Byzantine
empire, treating for this purpose the Basilica and the
Sea-law as forming one system, with the maritime law
of the Mediterranean states in the early middle ages, so
far as it can be gathered from those sources which come
nearest in age to the Basilica and the Sea-law. There is
a long interval of time between the Byzantine authorities and the earliest of those sources. No communal
statute goes back in its existing form before the middle
of the twelfth century. There are very few commercial
documents of earlier date. To avoid being charged with
a lack of the historical spirit for attempting to illustrate
a code of law by materials dating the oldest of them
three hundred years after it was compiled, let me say
this. The date at which a statute received its present
shape is not necessarily the date of the law which it
contains; and the form of a commercial document may
easily be centuries older than the document itself. So
long as the conditions which make the law remain unaltered, the law itself remains unaltered. Between the
ninth and the thirteenth centuries there was probably
less change in the conditions of commerce and navigation
than there has been in the last twenty-five years.

Before speaking generally of the materials which exist
for ascertaining the ancient maritime law of the Mediterranean, I give a list of the texts which I have used,
prefixing to each the short title by which I cite it :—

Table of Amalfi, Consuetud. Amalfi. Tavola e Consuetudini di Amalfi were edited by Tommaso Gar from a
Vienna manuscript in Archivio Storico Italiano, prima

serie, Appendice, T. 1, pp. 257-89. The Tavola and c. 14 of the Consuetudini are also given, mainly after Gar, in Alianelli (Niccola), Delle antiche Consuetudini e Leggi marittime delle Provincie Napolitane, Napoli, 1871, pp. 101-36, with a commentary. The Tavola is also published (from Alianelli) in Camera (Matteo), Memorie di Amalfi, Salerno, 1876, T. 1, pp. 210-17. Camera gives variants from another manuscript, T. 1, p. 537 n., and adds some chapters from still another manuscript, T. 1, pp. 535-7. He also gives the Consuetudini from a fourteenth-century manuscript more complete than the Viennese, T. 1, pp. 457-71.

Amalric. Notules commerciales d'Amalric (not Al-maric), in Blancard (Louis), Documents inédits sur le commerce de Marseille au moyen âge, Marseille, 1884-5. 2 vols.

St. Ancon. Statuti Anconitani del mare, del terzenale e della dogana, e patti con diverse nazioni, a cura di C. Ciavarini, Vol. I, Ancona, 1896. Pard., V, pp. 116-98, published ninety-seven chapters of a maritime statute of Ancona, which were copied for him (as he says) from the Portulario of Graziozo Benincosa, a manuscript written in 1457. The subscription of this manuscript states that it was copied from a 'libro del MCCCXCVII' (Pard., V, p. 101). Ciavarini refers to three manuscripts all in the Archivio storico comunale of Ancona. The first contains among other things the Statuti del mare in eighty-eight chapters. It is entituled on the back of the binding in a modern hand 'Statuta MSS. 1397 Mare'; but there does not appear to be anything to identify it with the 'libro del MCCCXCVII'. Ciavarini calls this manu-script C, and apparently—though he never says so—bases his text upon it. He gives the variants of M, a manu-script which contains only thirty-two chapters of the maritime statute, and of B, the manuscript used by Pard. Ciavarini calls it the Portolano of Grazioso Benincasa, and dates it between 1435 and 1445. It will be observed that Ciavarini prints only eighty-eight chapters as against

AUTHORITIES USED IN THIS PART

the ninety-seven of Pard. Pard. does not give Ciavarini's 88 (De aliis statutis . . . cassandis). Chapters 88 to 97 of Pardessus are not in Ciavarini.

Baracchi. Baracchi (Antonio), Le carte del mille e del mille cento che si conservano nel R. Archivio notarile di Venezia, in Archivio Veneto, VI, p. 293; VII, pp. 80, 352; VIII, p. 134; IX, p. 99; X, p. 332; XX, pp. 51, 314.

Barcelona Ordinance. Ordonnance sur la Police de la Navigation de 1258, in Pard., V, pp. 339–46.

Consuetud. Bari. The original edition, from which I cite, is in Commentarii super Consuetudinibus Preclarae Civitatis Bari . . . autore Domino Vincentio Maxilla ab Atella, Patavii, 1550, fol. The chapters which relate to maritime affairs are printed in Pard., VI, 625–6 (from an edition of 1596), and in Alianelli, op. cit., p. 150, from the edition of 1550.

St. Cattaro. The chapters of the Statutes of Cattaro which relate to maritime affairs are printed in Pard., V, pp. 96–8, from the edition of 1616.

Consulate of the Sea. The Consulate of the Sea is published in Catalan with a French translation in Pard., II, pp. 49–368, and with an English translation in the Black Book of the Admiralty, edited by Sir Travers Twiss, Vol. III, London, 1874, pp. 35–657. For the Italian translation I have used the edition published at Venice, 1737, 4to, with the commentary of Giuseppe Maria Casaregi.

St. Curzola. Statuta et Leges Civitatis et Insulae Curzulae (1214–1558), opera Prof. D^ris J. J. Hanel, Zagrabiae, 1877.

Actes génois. Actes génois d'Arménie, published by Desimoni in Archives de l'Orient Latin, Paris, 1881–4, T, 1, pp. 434–534, and Actes génois de Famagouste, published by him in Archives de l'Orient Latin, T. 2 Documents, pp. 3–120. These were continued in the Revue de l'Orient Latin, vols. 1 and 2.

Leges Genuenses. Historiae Patriae Monumenta, Tomus XVIII. Leges Genuenses inchoaverunt Cornelius

INTRODUCTION

Desimoni, Aloisius Thomas Belgrano, explevit et edidit
Victorius Poggi. Turin, 1901, fol.

Off. Gazarie of Genoa. Imposicio Officii Gazarie of
Genoa, published in Monumenta Historiae Patriae,
Leges Municipales. Turin, 1838, cols. 305–430.

St. Lesina or *St. Phara* in Statuta et Leges Civitatis
Buduae, Civitatis Scardonae, et Civitatis et Insulae Le-
sinae, opera Prof. Simeonis Ljubić, Zagrabiae, 1882–3.

Manduel. Les Chartes Commerciales des Manduel, in
Blancard, op. cit., T. 1, pp. 1–258.

St. Massil. Statuta Massilie, in Méry (Louis) et Guindon (F), Histoire ... des Actes ... de la Municipalité de
Marseille, T. 2, Marseille, 1843, p. 81—T. 4, Marseille,
1845, p. 282.

Pegolotti. La Pratica della Mercatura, scritta da
F. B. Pegolotti, in Della Decima e delle altre Gravezze, &c.,
T. 3, Lisbona e Lucca, 1766.

St. Pera. Statuti della colonia Genovese di Pera, in
Miscellanea di Storia Italiana, Torino, 1870, t. XI, pp. 513–
780. The chapters on maritime affairs in Pard., VI,
pp. 587–595, whose text I cite.

*Breve Curiae Maris, Pisa; Breve dell' Ordine del Mare,
Pisa; Const. Usus, Pisa.* The Breve Curiae Maris Pisanae
Civitatis is in Statuti inediti della Città di Pisa ... rac-
colti ... per cura del Prof. Francesco Bonaini, Vol. III,
Firenze, 1857, pp. 345–445. The Breve dell' Ordine del
Mare is in the same volume, pp. 447–643. The Consti-
tutum Usus Pisanae Civitatis is in Vol. II, Firenze,
1870, pp. 811–1026.

Pisano. Il Liber Abbaci di Leonardo Pisano, pubblicato
... da Baldassarre Boncompagni, Roma, 1857.

St. Ragusa. Liber Statutorum Civitatis Ragusii com-
positus anno 1272 ... Nunc primum in lucem protule-
runt V. Bogišić et C. Jireček. Zagrabiae, 1904.

Sacerdoti. Sacerdoti (Adolfo), Le colleganze nella
pratica degli affari e nella legislazione Veneta, in Atti
del R. Istituto Veneto, T. LIX, P. 2, pp. 1–45.

St. Scardona. See St. Lesina, *supra.*

AUTHORITIES USED IN THIS PART

Scriba. Notulario di Gio. Scriba, in Historiae Patriae Monumenta Chartarum Tomus II. Turin, 1853, fol., cols. 285–989.

St. Spalato. Statuta et Leges Civitatis Spalati, opera Prof. D^ris J. J. Hanel, Zagrabiae, 1878.

C. Tortosa. Libre de les Costums de Tortosa. Texto que da á luz D. Bienvenido Oliver. Madrid, 1881.

Ordin. Trani. Ordinamenta . . . maris edita per consules civitatis Trani, in Pard., V, pp. 237–51, and Alianelli, op. cit., pp. 53–64.

Consolat. Trapani. Consolato del Mare e dei Mercanti . . . di Messina e di Trapani, pubblicati p. c. di Vito La Mantia, Palermo, 1897, pp. 3–7.

St. Ziani, St. Tiepolo, St. Zeno. Gli Statuti Marittimi Veneziani fino al 1255. Editi a cura di Ricc. Predelli e Adolfo Sacerdoti. Venezia, 1903.

St. Zara. Book III, c. 40, and Book IV, c. 1–81, in Pard., VI, pp. 605–22.

CITY STATUTES AND MARITIME STATUTES

The dates at which the statutes were reduced to the form in which we possess them is in many cases fixed by statements in the statutes themselves. Here is a list of the principal cases where the date is so determined, and where there is no reason to question its genuineness [1] :—

1156–60 Constitutum Usus (Pisan) ; [2]
1214 Curzola (earliest part) ;
1227 Ziani (Venetian) ;
1229–36 Tiepolo (Venetian) ;
1255 Zeno (Venetian) and Marseille ;
1258 Barcelona ;
1272 Ragusa and Tortosa ;
1298 Breve Curiae Maris (Pisan) ;
1312 Spalato ;

[1] Pard. (VI, 629) gives a chronological list of all the statutes or parts of statutes published by him.
[2] As to the date of this important body of law, see Schaube (Adolf), Zur Entstehungsgeschichte des Pisanischen Constitutum Usus, in Zeitschrift für Handelsrecht, XLVI.

1313–44 Off. Gazarie (Genoa);
1331 Phara (Lesina);
1345 Consolat. Trapani.[1]

In this list I have omitted several documents, the date of which is doubtful. One of these is the Ordinamenta of Trani. This work bears on the face the date of 1063, but this date is abandoned by most scholars.[2] The lost Latin original, from which the existing Italian translation was made, may go back to the beginning of the fourteenth century; it cannot well be earlier. The Table of Amalfi is in two parts, one Latin and one Italian. The Italian chapters are probably not earlier than the middle of the fourteenth century; the Latin may go back to the time when Amalfi was an independent duchy; i. e. before A.D. 1131 (see Alianelli, p. 77; Schupfer, op. cit., p. 435). The statutes of Cattaro (see Pard. V, p. 17), Pera (see Pard. VI, p. 583), and Zara (see Pard. VI, p. 605) belong to the early fourteenth century; Ancona, perhaps, to the middle, and the Consulate of the Sea to the end (see Goldschmidt, p. 208). These dates, I repeat, are the dates at which the statutes assumed their existing form. Many of them (e. g. the Consulate of the Sea) contain large masses of much earlier material.

The Consulate of the Sea, unfortunately, is not in a state now to be of much help in the investigation of mediaeval maritime law. There is a great deal of it: it is very verbose. Every principle is laid down two or three times, always with some difference; and every rule is accompanied by elaborate reasons, mostly futile. It must be admitted that there is an ancient nucleus of custom; but the greater part of the work consists of ingenious suggestions by learned men, which were probably never practised by any mariner or enforced by any court. No maritime code of the middle

---

[1] But see La Mantia, p. ix.
[2] It is supported, however, by Professor Schupfer (Storia del Diritto Italiano, 2nd ed., pp. 424–33) and Professor Ciccaglione (Storia del D. I., vol. II, p. 86).

ages has such an air of unreality about it. Until it has been separated into its constituent parts, it must be used with great caution.

The mediaeval city-statute embraced the whole field of administrative law and a great part of private law. It is, as a rule, in the form in which we possess it, a regular code—that is to say, not a mere succession of enactments arranged chronologically or according to chance, but a system of enactments, arranged logically, in groups and sub-groups, and professing to be the work of one or several revisors. The revisors sometimes give us in the preface to their work an account of the principles upon which they proceeded. It is enough to cite that given by the revisors of the Constitutum Usus, the most undoubtedly ancient and perhaps the most important of all mediaeval statutes.[1]

The city of Pisa, according to the Prologue of the Constitutum Usus, had its unwritten customs by the side of the lex, a mixture of Roman and Lombard law. Previsores were appointed yearly to judge matters of custom. As there was great diversity in these judgments, the Pisans determined to write down their customs. In 1156 they elected for the first time sages, called constitutores,[2] whose duty it was to correct what had to be corrected, to separate matters of custom from matters of law, and to commit the whole to writing. This committee was continued by yearly appointments—no doubt with alterations in the personnel—till the work was finished. They had from time to time published separate provisions made by them; but the Constitutum Usus was not published as a whole till 1160. No other written constitutum de

---

[1] Constitutum Usus (Pisan) Prologus (Bonaini II, p. 813), with the additions made from Vaticanus lat. 6385 in Gaudenzi (Augusto), A proposito di un nuovo manoscritto del Costituto Pisano, in R.C. della R. Accademia dei Lincei, Classe di scienze morali, stor. e filol., serie V, vol. 3, parte 2, Roma, 1894, pp. 692-693. See also the observations of Schaube, op. cit.

[2] 'primi constitutores' must mean (as Gaudenzi thinks) that these were the first to be appointed, and not merely (as Schaube suggests) that they were the first who held office for a year.

usibus was to have any force thereafter except as regards past acts. The Constitutum Usus must have been well arranged at first, but it was frequently revised in the course of the hundred and fifty years which followed its creation, and, as it now stands, it reads like an English textbook which has been through the hands of half a dozen editors.

The enactments which relate to maritime affairs sometimes form a book or part of a book in the general volume of statutes; sometimes they form an independent volume by themselves. The separation of the maritime law into an independent volume was merely a matter of convenience. It is highly convenient to have all the law relating to a particular subject put together in one volume, so that those who are interested in that subject may be able to carry the law about with them. A copy of the maritime law of a state was needed on board the ships of that state; it was also required by the judicial officers of the state abroad, as they had to administer it (Breve Curiae Maris of Pisa, c. 35, 104; St. Ancon., c. 38, 47 end, 84).

In some cases legislation in maritime affairs is confined to administration and police, e. g. the maritime statutes of Venice. In other cases it deals both with matters of administration and with matters of principle. Both in the statutes and in the documents there is constant reference to custom, as determining the practice in the absence of positive law.

MARITIME CUSTOM

The Venetian authorities constantly refer to 'usus' or 'consuetudo'. St. Venet. III, 2, p. 39, ed. 1729, 'De quibus volumus secundum consuetudinem observari antiquam'. St. Tiep. A, 7, Expenses of clearing ships from the harbour of Venice are to be borne 'de communi habere navis et etiam de ipsa nave secundum usum'. St. Tiep. A, 26 = St. Zeno 68, Three-fourths of the freight in a certain case

is to be divided among mariners 'secundum usum'. St.
Tiep. A, 35, Repairs to the tackle of a ship are to be borne
'de communi habere navis et etiam de ipsa nave secundum
usum' (cp. St. Zeno, 76, 77). St. Zara, IV, 75, Injury to
goods where ship springs a leak is to be the subject of
average 'secundum usum et consuetudinem diutius appro-
batam'. The same provision is in St. Spalat. VI, 46,
where the words are 'secundum consuetudinem hactenus
observatam'. Sacerdoti, p. 27, Rate of interest is to be
20 per cent. 'secundum usu patriae nostrae'. (Same phrase
in Baracchi, 8, Arch. Veneto, VII, 84, and Baracchi, 95,
Arch. Veneto, XX, 79.) Sacerdoti, p. 32, Ship is to be
supplied with mariners, &c., 'sicut consuetudo est navium
ire per mare.'

The appeal to custom is not confined to Venice: Table
of Amalfi, c. 23, Gains of the maritime adventure are
divisible in shares 'prout est consuetum'. Leges Genuenses, col. 13, 'Secundum quod usus et consuetudo itineris
exigerit'. Breve Curiae Maris of Pisa, c. 7, The consul of
the sea swears: 'omnes reclamationes . . . per Constitutum usus seu per formam Brevis Potestatis vel mei,
diffiniam ; et [si] inde Constitutum vel forma Brevis non
fuerit, secundum bonûm usum civitatis' (where see
Bonaini's note).

It is true that the custom alleged is the local custom ;
but these authorities, which might be largely added to,
clearly point to the existence, if not of a general sea
custom for the whole Mediterranean, at least of a custom
extending beyond the jurisdiction of the individual state.

The existence of such a sea custom is suggested by two
other circumstances, (1) the constant borrowings by one
statute from another,[1] (2) the absence of enactments providing for conflicts of jurisdiction.

1. Many chapters of the statutes of Zara are taken
bodily from the Venetian statutes of Zeno, the only
difference being one in style. The statute of Zara as

---

[1] On this subject, see Lattes (Alessandro), Studii di diritto statutario,
Milano, 1886, pp. 69-108.

a rule is more diffuse and explanatory, and the long periods of the Venetian statute are cut up into short sentences.[1]

There are close affinities between the statutes of Zara and those of Spalato and of Scardona,[2] and again between the statutes of Ragusa and those of Lesina and of Cattaro.[3]

2. The jurisdiction of a state is only limited by its power of enforcing the decrees of its courts. Now as a rule during the middle ages ships which were built within the territory of a state belonged to citizens of the state, were manned by sailors who were citizens, and loaded by merchants who were also citizens. The state, therefore, was able to ensure that all controversies between builders and owners, owners and mariners, or owners and merchants should be tried before its tribunals and decided in accordance with its law. In order the better so to do, the mediaeval maritime state often appointed judicial officers of its own, generally called consuls, in places where its ships were likely to go. In matters of importance there were appeals from the consuls to the home authorities. A citizen of the state who declined to submit to the jurisdiction of his consul was subjected to heavy penalties, which could always be got out of him when he came home.

But there must have been often cases where a question as to a ship of state A was decided by the tribunal of

---

[1] Cp., for example, St. Zara, IV, 23 with St. Zeno, 53; St. Zara, IV, 38 with St. Zeno, 95.

[2] For instance, St. Spalat. VI, 17, 18, 20 = St. Scardon. 24; St. Spalat. VI, 21 = St. Scardon. 23; St. Spalat. VI, 32 = St. Scardon. 47; St. Spalat. VI, 37 = St. Scardon. 17; St. Spalat. VI, 45 = St. Zara, IV, 74; St. Spalat. VI, 46 = St. Zara, IV, 75; St. Spalat. VI, 60 = St. Zara, IV. 1; St. Spalat. VI, 66 = St. Zara, IV, 37 = St. Zeno, 94; St. Spalat. VI, 67 = St. Zara, IV, 38 = St. Zeno, 95; St. Spalat. VI, 68 = St. Zara, IV, 39 = St. Zeno, 96.

[3] St. Phara, V, 2 = St. Ragus. VII, 7; St. Phara, V, 6 = St. Ragus. VII, 32; St. Phara, V, 8 = St. Ragus. VII, 35; St. Phara, V, 9 = St. Ragus. VII, 54; St. Phara, V, 10 = St. Ragus. VII, 56 = St. Cattaro, 379; St. Phara, V, 11 = St. Ragus. VII, 58; St. Phara, V, 12 = St. Ragus. VII, 60; St. Phara. V, 13 = St. Ragus. VII, 63; St. Ragus. III, 16 = St. Cattaro, 70.

state *B*, e.g. if a citizen of state *B* lent money for repairs of the ship and enforced his claim in the tribunals of his own state. And the curious thing is that the statutes are silent on this point.[1] It may be urged that they could not do anything; but they could at least grant reprisals. A more plausible reason for their silence is that the foreign tribunal in such cases probably decided, as a rule, on the same principles as the home tribunal would have decided; and that therefore, as a rule, there can have been no cause for complaint.

COMMERCIAL DOCUMENTS

The commercial documents fall under two heads, (1) documents which we possess in full, (2) documents which we possess in abstract.[2]

1. Few commercial documents have been preserved in the original. It is easy to see why this should be so. A business man only preserves documents which enable him to enforce or to resist a claim. Most commercial documents have a transitory operation. A charter-party is only of legal importance while the voyage is going on or for a short time after. When the goods have been delivered and the freight paid, then, as a rule, the charter-party may be torn up. Even if there are outstanding questions between the parties, which depend upon the interpretation of the charter-party, they are generally settled in a comparatively short time. If *A* lends money to *B* for a commercial operation, the acknowledgement of indebtedness which *B* gives to *A* is only of value to *A* so

---

[1] To prevent misconception, I may point out that while the statutes sternly forbid suits by their own citizens in foreign courts (e.g. St. Zara, IV, 70; Breve Curiae Maris of Pisa, c. 49; St. Ancon. del Mare, c. 43, 48; St. Spalat. VI, 72), they never declare the nullity of proceedings *in rem* taken by a foreign creditor in a foreign jurisdiction against a native ship.

[2] L. Goldschmidt was the first to make much use of mediaeval commercial documents for the history of maritime law. See his Geschichte, p. 258, n. 84. An account of the chief printed collections of documents is given by Schaube, Handelsgeschichte, pp. 107, 108.

long as the money remains unpaid. When *A* gets his money back, he either destroys *B*'s acknowledgement of indebtedness or hands it over to *B*. *B* would naturally keep it for a time, as he would keep a release given him by *A*, because they would be evidence that he had repaid the loan, but they would not be documents to be treasured up by his descendants like the title-deeds to land. It follows that such commercial documents as we possess have only been preserved by accident—sometimes no doubt for the same reason which makes nervous people keep receipted bills long after the statute of limitations has run.

The most important commercial documents which are in print are the Venetian ones published by Sacerdoti and ranging in date from 1072 to 1210. A few more are published by Baracchi. Some from Amalfi of the twelfth and thirteenth centuries are to be found in Camera; but his transcriptions do not inspire confidence. More important are the Chartes Commerciales des Manduel, 151 documents between 1200 and 1253, which are given by Blancard.

2. Many more commercial documents exist in the form of an abstract, and of these there are several printed collections. These documents have been preserved in the following way.[1] When two or more parties wished to enter into a commercial, or other, contract, they went before a notary, who made a note of the principal provisions which they wished inserted. In this note only special provisions are stated in full: matters of common form are either omitted altogether or indicated by a leading word or two. The notary afterwards, on the basis of the note, drew up the instrument which was to serve as the completed contract, and handed it out to the parties concerned either in duplicate or in as many copies as were necessary (Scriba, 701; Amalric, 777 at end). After the public instrument had been prepared, the note

---

[1] See on this subject Ficker (J.), Beiträge zur Urkundenlehre, Innsbruck, 1877, I, § 184; v. Voltelini (H.), Acta Tirolensia, II, 1, Innsbruck, 1899, p. xxvi.

was cancelled by a line drawn across it, but it was not destroyed; hence, if the public instrument was lost, the notary, under order of the Court, might make a second one from his original note (Amalric, 916). If there was a contest as to the genuineness of the public instrument, its genuineness might be proved by comparison with the original note. If the notary who took the note died before he had drawn up the public instrument, another notary was appointed by the Court to draw it up from the dead man's note (Scriba, 412; Blancard, I, p. 100). These notes were either originally made in regular books, or, if they were originally jotted down on separate slips, the slips were collected together in books; and when a notary died his books were either handed over to the successor in his office or were deposited under statutory authority in a public depository.[1] To this circumstance is due the preservation of so many of these books.

The most complete collection of notarial acts is in the Archivio notarile at Genoa.[2] The earliest volume—the Notulario of Giovanni Scriba—extending from 1155 to 1164, has been published as above mentioned, and contains a great number of commercial documents. From the same Archivio come the acts of wandering notaries in Cyprus and Armenia, which were published by Desimoni. The earlier batch is from 1271 to 1279; the later one begins in 1299. I cite mainly from the earlier one.

The Archives of Marseille supply the Notules d'Amalric, which extend from the end of 1247 over a part of the year 1248, and comprise 1,031 abstracts of commercial documents.[3]

In making use of commercial documents to ascertain

---

[1] As to Italy see Pertile (A.), Storia del D. I., VI, p. 304; Paoli (C.), Programma di Paleografia Latina e di Diplomatica, Firenze, 1898, III, p. 276. As to Marseille, see Blancard, I, p. xliv.

[2] See Lustig (G.), Entwickelungswege und Quellen des Handelsrechts, Stuttgart, 1877, p. 226.

[3] A description of the volume in Blancard, I, p. liv sqq.

the law, two points must be borne in mind. 1. The actual commercial facts do not always correspond exactly to the language of the documents. There are several reasons for this. One is that conveyancers get into the habit of using certain forms. The legal effect of these forms has been precisely fixed by decisions or by usage. The conveyancer does not like to alter his language because he does not know what interpretation may be put upon the phrase as altered, while he is certain of the interpretation which will be put upon the original. Hence, although the commercial facts differ from those which the phrase was originally framed to express, the conveyancer goes on using it. There may be an important change in commercial conditions although there is no change in the language of the documents. Nor is this all. The conveyancer sometimes uses phrases with the distinct object of cloaking the facts. We may put the same thing in another way and say that the same series of facts is often susceptible of two legal interpretations, one under which the parties concerned are exposed to legal or social penalties, the other under which they are not. Naturally the conveyancer adopts the innocent interpretation—'ut res magis valeat quam pereat'. This point may be illustrated by the expedients which were adopted when the Church held that the maritime risk did not justify the taking of interest.

2. A contract often contains a term which merely repeats that which the law lays down and which it would impose upon the parties even though they did not express it. This superfluousness is not necessarily bad conveyancing. It is often useful in drawing up a document to insert terms the validity of which is independent of the contract simply in order that the parties may have before them the whole of the law on the subject of their agreement. I merely refer to this point here to show that it is not safe, because an agreement contains a stipulation, to infer that in the absence of that stipulation the law would be otherwise.

cxxviii

INTRODUCTION

DIVISIONS OF SUBJECT

In comparing the maritime law of the Byzantine empire, which I call for shortness the Byzantine system, with the maritime law of the Mediterranean states during the middle ages, which I call the mediaeval system, I shall begin by dealing in general with the various parties concerned in the maritime adventure, and then with the dangers and difficulties of navigation so far as they are reflected in our authorities. I shall then deal in succession with the various elements of the maritime adventure, the ship and its owners, the ship's company, the transportation of goods across the sea, the outside capitalist and maritime loans. In the Roman empire as in modern times the parties to the maritime adventure are sharply distinguished. The shipowner employs the mariners and lets the ship to the merchant. What makes it so difficult sometimes to understand the mediaeval authorities is that these positions are continually melting into one another. The shipowners are often themselves the mariners, and, while in their capacity of mariners they divide one part of the profits, where that system of payment existed, in their capacity of owners they share the other part. The mariners again may be themselves merchants: they, or some of them, load the ship with their own goods, so that you may have a case where the ship is owned, navigated, and freighted by substantially the same persons. It is necessary, therefore, after dealing with owners, mariners, and merchants as if they were distinct in fact as they are in law, to deal with the results which follow in law from the union of several characters in one person; and from this we are led to consider the various partnerships or quasi-partnerships of the mediaeval system. I conclude by dealing with the legal effect of the principal maritime events, jettison and general average contribution, collision, and salvage.

INTRODUCTION

THE PARTIES TO THE MARITIME ADVENTURE

Nothing brings out more clearly the fundamental differences between the Roman, the Byzantine, and the mediaeval maritime systems than a survey of the various classes who, under each system, took part in the maritime adventure. Roman law distinguishes the dominus nauis, the exercitor, the magister, and the nautae. Ulpian defines the exercitor as 'eum ad quem obuentiones et reditus omnes perueniunt, siue is dominus nauis sit siue a domino nauem per auersionem conduxit uel ad tempus uel in perpetuum' (Dig. XIV, 1, 1, 15). The mark of the exercitor, therefore, is that he receives the profits of the ship for his own benefit. He may be owner: he may also have hired the ship from the owner: the hiring may be for a time; it may be for ever.

He who hires a ship as a whole and thereby becomes exercitor is not to be confounded with a merchant who puts in the whole ship's cargo. The merchant, whether he puts in part of the cargo or all, pays over the freight to another: the exercitor, whether he loads the ship with his own goods or not, retains or receives the freight, as the case may be, for his own benefit; his liability to the owner, when he is not the owner, is not a liability to pay freight, but a liability to pay rent; as against all third persons he is owner.

The exercitor appoints the ship's officers, and among others the magister, who is defined by Ulpian as he 'cui totius nauis cura mandata est' (Dig. XIV, 1, 1, 1). Among his duties are to contract for taking cargo or passengers, to buy tackle for the ship, to buy or sell goods, to incur expenditure for repairs, to hire and pay seamen (Dig. XIV, 1, 1, 3, 7). These duties are all concerned with the financial and administrative side of the maritime adventure. An imperial constitution of A.D. 380, which provides for examining by torture, where there is a wreck, selected members of the crew, suggests that the magistri were also concerned with the navigation (Theod. XIII, 9, 3 pr. = Cod. XI, 6 (5), 3, 1 'circa magistros nauium, quibus est scientia plenior, immoretur'). As a rule, however, the navigation seems to have been in the hands of the gubernator (Dig. IX, 2, 29, 4; XIX, 2, 13, 2).

The exercitor might act as his own magister; he was then said *per se exercere*. There might be several exercitores, i. e. several persons among whom the ship's profits were divisible, and each of them might be his own magister or all might unite in appointing one (Dig. IV, 9, 7, 5; XIV, 1, 4, pr., 1). A ship might have several magistri, each performing all the functions of a magister; or again, the exercitor might provide that no one was to act without the consent of the other or others; or he might divide the duties of the magister among several, appointing, e. g., one to let the ship and another to collect sums due (Dig. XIV, 1, 1, 13, 14). These points are dealt with hereafter in considering the liability of the exercitor on the contracts of the magister; they are only mentioned here to show the variety of systems which prevailed.

The Basilica reproduces in substance the definitions of the Digest. As a rule it translates exercitor by ναύκληρος and magister by πιστικός,[1] but there are exceptions. Ναύκληρος is occasionally used as equivalent to magister (Bas. LIII, Α΄, πε΄ = Cod. IV, 25, 4; Bas. LIII, Γ΄, ε΄ = Dig. XIV, 2, 2, 6). It is also used to translate ratiarius (Bas. LIII, Β΄, ιγ΄ = Dig. XIII, 7, 30) and nauicularius or nauclerus (Bas. LIII, Α΄, ϟ΄ = Cod. XI, 2, 1 and elsewhere). In later Byzantine writings the ναύκληρος is sometimes identified with the κυβερνήτης. Duc. (Appx. 139) quotes a manuscript Schedographia in Agapetum, which says: κυβερνήτης, κυρίως ἐστιν ὁ τὸ πλοῖον διεξάγων πρὸς εὔπλοιαν, ὃν οἱ κοινοὶ ναύκληρον φασίν. In P. Fiorentini, 75, p. 157 (A.D. 380), reference is made to a ναυκληροκυβερνήτης πλοίου ἰδίου.

---

[1] In the earlier jurists the Latin is transliterated. Stephanus has ἐξερκίτωρ (ad Bas. XVIII, 1, 13, ed. Zach. p. 172). Magister is rendered μαγίστωρ by Stephanus (ad Bas. XVIII, 1, 13, ed. Zach. p. 173) and μάγιστρος by Theodorus and Thalelaeus (ad Bas. XVIII, 1, 24, ed. Zach. p. 177).

INTRODUCTION

There are, therefore, four possible meanings of the word
ναύκληρος :

(1) The ναύκληρος might be a member of a corporation
corresponding to the corpus nauiculariorum or naucle-
rorum which is dealt with at length in Theod. XIII, 5-9,
and Cod. XI, 2-6. (As to these, see Daremberg et
Saglio, s.v. nauicularii.) In this sense ναύκληροι are
sometimes alluded to by the Byzantine historians, e. g.
Theophanes, p. 757, Bonn, 487, de Boor. (2) He might be
the exercitor. (3) He might be the magister—agent,
whether on board or in port, of the exercitor, concerned
primarily with the financial management of the ship, and
having authority, under conditions hereafter dealt with,
to bind the exercitor by his contracts. (4) He might
simply have control of the navigation.

In the Sea-law there is no clear reference to the πιστικός.
C. 8 speaks of ὁ ναυκληρὸς πιστευθεὶς τὸ πλοῖον. The same
person is called later, according to the better reading,
προναύκληρος, i. e. representative of the ναύκληρος. This
suggests that he corresponds to the πιστικός of the Basilica,
the magister of the Digest. In c. 12 there is a reference
to deposit with a πιστικός. As the chapter stands, he has
nothing to do with the magister nauis. It is possible,
however, that the text has been altered (see *ante*, p. lxxvi).

There are only two references to the owner. One is in
c. 26. If any of the sailors or ναύκληροι—observe the
plural—sleep off the ship and the ship is lost, they make
good the loss to the δεσπότης τοῦ πλοίου. The ναύκληροι
here are perhaps the petty officers. As we shall see hereafter, in the middle ages a big ship often had many
naucleri on board. The other reference to the owner is
in the version of c. 8, which is given by M and which I
reproduce in Appendix F. This strengthens the view
that the ναύκληρος in this chapter is the magister nauis.

As a rule, however, the Sea-law only knows of the
ναύ ληρος. The ναύκληρος, either by himself or in conjunction with the sailors, stands in opposition to the ἔμπορος
(or ἔμποροι) and the ἐπιβάται.

THE PARTIES TO THE MARITIME ADVENTURE

The chapters may be classified under four heads (a) where the ναύκληρος alone appears, (b) where the ναύκληρος and ναῦται are treated as forming one body, (c) where in the same chapter there is a reference at one point to the ναύκληρος and at another to the ναῦται, (d) where a distinction is drawn between the ναύκληρος and the ναῦται.

(a) In c. 9 one ναύκληρος appears to be in command. If he deliberates concerning jettison, he is to ask the passengers. Goods of great value in small compass are to be deposited with the ναύκληρος (c. ιδ', 13). All questions relating to the hiring of a ship are treated as lying exclusively between the ναύκληρος and the ἔμπορος (c. 19, 20, 23, 24, 33, 44). It is he who, if the ship springs a leak, shifts the goods from one ship to another (c. 42). Where the ship is lost and the cargo saved the merchant and passengers are not to give the ship to the ναύκληρος (c. 37). In these chapters ναύκληρος seems to = exercitor.

(b) In other chapters ὁ ναύκληρος καὶ οἱ ναῦται are spoken of as if they formed one body, subject to the same liabilities and entitled to the same privileges. If the ναύκληρος ἅμα τοῖς ναύταις ἀμελήσῃ and there is a loss, ὁ ναύκληρος καὶ οἱ ναῦται must make it good (c. 10, see also c. 27). In a wreck ὁ ναύκληρος καὶ οἱ ναῦται are directed to help in saving the goods (c. 31). Where goods are injured by bilge, in spite of protests by the passengers, ὁ ναύκληρος is liable ἅμα τοῖς ναύταις (c. 34). In a collision ὁ ναύκληρος and οἱ ἐμπλέοντες —evidently the crew—are liable (c. 36). Compare also c. 8.

(c) In some cases the acts of the ναύκληρος appear to impose a liability upon the ναῦται, or vice versa. In c. 15 the same event is alluded to twice ; first, it is said ἐὰν . . . ὁ ναύκληρος ἐξειλήσῃ ; secondly, ὅτι . . . ὁ ναύκληρος καὶ οἱ ναῦται ἔφυγον. In c. 22 if the ναύκληρος overloads, the merchant is to protest before the ναύκληρος and the ναῦται, and the ναύκληρος will be responsible if there is jettison. In c. 39 a ship goes to a place βουλήσει τοῦ ναυκλήρου καὶ τῶν ναυτῶν against the merchant's wish. In the alternative, if the merchant insists on going to the place and the ship is lost, the ναύκληρος is to receive the ship safe from the merchant. See also c. 27.

(d) Lastly, there are certain cases where the ναύκληρος and ναῦται are contrasted. Sailors steal the anchors of another ship βουλήσει τοῦ ναυκλήρου. The ναύκληρος must make the damage good (c. 2). A sailor steals from a merchant or passenger κελεύσει τοῦ ναυκλήρου. The ναύκληρος must make the loss good twofold (c. 3). The ναύκληρος pays the representatives of sailors who are lost in the long-boat (c. 46). The μισθός of the ναύκληρος is twice the sailor's (c. α′), and if there is jettison, the contribution which the ναύκληρος makes in respect of personal effects has a different limit from the sailor's (c. 9).

In these passages the ναύκληρος is spoken of in the singular. The word occurs in the plural in reference to the power of οἱ ναύκληροι to borrow money (c. ιθ′, 16. Οἱ ναύκληροι ναυκληροῦντες in c. ιθ′ sounds like a translation of ' exercitores per se exercentes'). Chapters 7 and 26 show that a ship might have more than one ναύκληρος on board.

One thing is clear. These passages do not give a consistent view of the position of the ναύκληρος. Of course, we must not press the language of the Sea-law too closely. The examples given under (c) show that ὁ ναύκληρος, by himself, is sometimes equivalent in expression to ὁ ναύκληρος καὶ οἱ ναῦται. The fact that in all the chapters which deal with charter-parties the ναύκληρος is spoken of by himself does not necessarily show that he took the freight for his own exclusive benefit. If we construe these chapters in a sympathetic spirit—by which I mean if we admit that the author of the Sea-law seldom succeeded in expressing his meaning with legal precision—and if we construe them in the light which is thrown upon them by later authorities, we may divide them into the following groups. (a) Some show traces of the Roman system, i. e. that in which the owner of ship employed an agent on board, the magister, and in which neither the agent nor the mariners had any proprietary interest in ship nor any right except, where they were not the owner's slaves, to fixed wages. (b) Other chapters go as far as this, that the ναύκληρος and the ναῦται must have a share in the profits of the adventure. (c) Others again suggest that he and they are owners of ship. We should then have the system which was so common in the middle ages—that in which the owners of the ship, who are numerous, all take part in the maritime adventure, one as captain and the others as mariners. This view is supported by the following chapters.

In c. 10, if a maritime loss occurs through the carelessness of the ναύκληρος and crew, they indemnify the merchant. If it occurs through the carelessness of the merchant, he indemnifies the ship. If no one is to blame, ship and goods contribute. C. 27 points, though less strongly, in the same direction. That is to say, in these chapters the ναύκληρος and crew are identified with ship; they are treated as equivalent to it for legal purposes. In c. 38, if a cargo of corn is injured by a gale, the ναύκληρος and ναῦται are to contribute with the merchant. In c. 35 if a ship loses its mast, sailors, merchants, cargo, and ship are to contribute. These chapters do not mean, in my opinion, that any personal contribution is exacted from either the sailors or the merchants; but merely that, just as the merchants contribute in respect of cargo, so the sailors contribute in respect of ship. It is observable that in chapter 35 there is no reference to the ναύκληρος. He seems to be included among the ναῦται. In c. 36, where there is a collision through the fault of ship A, ὁ ναύκληρος and οἱ ἐμπλέοντες of ship A are responsible, and the cargo also comes into contribution.

The mark of the mediaeval as opposed to the Roman system is its fluidity. No category is clearly defined. Whatever class you belong to, you are constantly found performing the functions of another class. As a rule the ship is divided among a number of owners. They are called in Latin portionarii or socii, in Italian parsenevoli, in the Consulate of the Sea personers. There is as a rule no distinction between the owner or owners of ship and the exercitor. It was evidently not the custom for the owners to let the ship out to some third person to run on his own account. There are one or two instances where a single owner lets the ship to a number of exercitores (Amalric, 106 in Blancard, I, p. 305 ; Amalric, 922 in Blancard, II, p. 255. See Targa, p. 29). But as a rule joint owners undertake themselves the administration and navigation of their ship. By a majority in interest they appoint a manager. He is generally one of themselves, probably as a rule that one who has the largest interest in the concern. He is called patronus (It. padrone). Other joint-owners, probably the majority of them, go as mariners. Where this system prevailed the ship did, as a matter of fact, belong to the captain and crew or the captain and some of the crew. But even where this was the normal system there might be mariners who had no proprietary interest in the ship and merely received a share of profits or a fixed wage.

Where the ship had a single owner he often managed it himself. Where he managed it through an agent, the agent was generally called praepositus (Consuetud. Bari, f. 118 of ed. 1550, p. 152 in Alianelli ; St. Zara, IV, 49, 50, perhaps a reminiscence of Dig. IX, 3, 6, 3 and XIV, 1, 1, 7) or suprapositus or superpositus (St. Zara, IV, 50 = St. Spalat., VI, 53 ; St. Ragus., VII, 14 = St. Phara, V, 4).

Whether the manager of the ship was the agent of many or of one, his powers were in substance those of the Roman magister nauis. He collected the receipts of the ship, paid its outgoings, and handed over the balance to the owner or owners. He had in case of necessity a power of borrowing on the credit of the ship, or even of selling it (Authorities, *supra,* and see p. clxv).

The word nauclerus (also nauclerius and naucherius) is used in the earlier authorities as equivalent to the magister nauis, whether he is himself owner or part owner or merely the owner's nominee (Sacerdoti, p. 40 ; St. Massil., IV, 20 ; Breve Curiae Maris of Pisa, c. 76, ed. Bonaini, III, p. 404 ; Salimbene, f. 315 b, ed. Holder-Egger, p. 252). Capitaneus is sometimes used in this sense (Constitutum Usus of Pisa, c. 49, ed. Bonaini.

II, p. 986). Then nauclerus comes to denote the principal officer in charge of the navigation. Then it is used for the whole mass of officers on board of a big ship or galley (Charter-parties of A. D. 1200 and 1241 in Canale, Istoria di Genova, II, p. 523 ; Mas Latrie, Traités, Documents, p. 122 ; Sanudo, Secreta, apud Bongars, Gesta Dei per Francos, II, p. 75 ; Off. Gazarie of Genoa, coll. 324, 325 ; Georges Yver, Commerce et Marchands dans l'Italie Méridionale, p. 148, n. 1 ; Camillo Minieri Riccio, Notizie storiche tratte da 62 registri Angioini, p. 89).

The Italian and Spanish derivatives of nauclerus follow the same development. Nochiero is sometimes the manager of the ship (St. Ancon., c. 12, 36), but it is generally used in contradistinction to padrone to denote the officer or officers in charge of the navigation (Ordin. Trani, c. 14, 15, 23, Targa, c. XIII, p. 46). Notxer has the same meaning in the Consulate of the Sea (c. 17, 79), nauxer in C. Tortosa (IX, 27, 20), and naucher in the Siete Partidas (Pard., VI, p. 21).

An important character of whom there is no trace before the middle ages, is the scriba scriptor or scribanus.[1] Many statutes prescribe that every ship shall have a scribanus, and ships above a certain size are sometimes required to have two (St. Ragus., VII, 2 ; St. Tiep., A, 17 ; St. Zeno, 41 ; St. Zara, IV, 15, 17, 18 ; Barcelona Ordinance 2 ; C. Tortosa, IX, 27, 8, 19). The scribanus is sworn before the public authority (St. Ragus., VII, 2 ; St. Tiep., C, 4 ; St. Zeno, 41 ; St. Zara, IV, 15, 17 ; Ord. Trani, 16 ; Table of Amalfi, 25 ; Breve Curiae Maris of Pisa, 78). In some cases he is examined by the court as to his qualifications (St. Zeno, 41 ; St. Zara IV, 15, 16). He had a book (quaternus, quaderno) in which he was obliged by law to enter the following, among other, particulars. (1) He kept a list of all the cargo, identifying the goods by their distinctive marks, if any, and he was often obliged to

---

[1] He is to be distinguished from the camerarius (L. Pisano, p. 21 ; St. Pis. III, p. 385 ; It. camerlingho, St. Pis. III, p. 512 ; Mas Latrie, Traités, Documents, p. 41) who at Pisa certainly performed some of the functions of the scriba.

give a receipt on demand to each owner of cargo for the goods which belonged to him (St. Ragus., VII, 2 ; 40 (2) ; 67 ; St. Tiep., A, 17 ; C, 4 ; St. Zeno, 41, 42 ; St. Zara, IV, 15, 19). (2) He kept a list of the mariners, noting the day when their service commenced, and entered all agreements between them and the shipowner (St. Ragus., VII, 2, 67 ; St. Zara, IV, 19, 43 ; Breve Curiae Maris of Pisa, 49). (3) He entered the charter-party and all subsidiary agreements between shipowner and merchants (St. Ragus., VII, 8, 37, 67 ; St. Zara, IV, 19).

In some legislations the scribanus, on returning from a voyage, had to hand over his quaternus to the public authority to keep (St. Tiep., C, 4 ; Breve Curiae Maris of Pisa, 57). Faith is to be given to the quaternus. 'Omnis credentia est scribani,' says the statute of Ragusa (VII, 45). All writings made by the scribanus, whether in his quaternus or on separate slips of paper, had the authority of public instruments (Table of Amalfi, 25 ; Breve Curiae Maris of Pisa, 78 ; C. Tortosa, IX, 27, 16).

Originally, no doubt, the scribanus was merely an accountant who relieved the patronus of the clerkly part of his labours. But the authorities cited above show that he soon assumed an independent position, and that he was intended by the statutes to hold the balance between the shipowner on the one hand and the merchants and mariners on the other. This is clearly stated in the summary of his duties given in the Consulate of the Sea, c. 12–15. At Venice the scribanus was required to report to the public authority if the ship was overloaded (St. Tiep., C, 4 ; St. Zeno, 42).

In the Roman system the mercator and the vector are sharply distinguished. Some vessels are cargo boats (onerariae), others passenger boats ($\epsilon\pi\iota\beta\alpha\tau\eta\gamma o\iota$) (Dig. XIV, 1, 1, 12). The distinction is of fact rather than of law. Prima facie, the merchant is the man who ships cargo on board: he may travel with it himself ; he may send a supercargo. The passenger on the other hand takes only personal goods ; but he may also carry in his chest some few odds and ends for sale—goods of great value in small compass—silks or precious stones. The merchant or passenger sometimes serves as a mariner (Dig. IV, 9, 7, 2).

The Sea-law maintains the distinction between the ἔμπορος and the ἐπιβάτης. To deal first with Part III.

(a) It contemplates in the majority of cases one ἔμπορος, who supplies the whole cargo, which is called indifferently γόμος, φόρτος, φορτία, or ἐνθήκη. (No reference to cargo, c. 24, 25, 28, 31; φορτία in c. 20, 29, 33; φόρτος in c. 30, 38; γόμος in c. 23; γόμος and φορτία in c. 10, 22, 27, 39; γόμος and ἐνθήκη in c. 32.)

Although οἱ ἔμποροι are sometimes referred to in the plural (c. 7, 16, 35, 37), none of these cases necessarily implies the presence of more than one ἔμπορος on board. Indeed, c. 37, which, after speaking of τὰ τῶν ἐμπόρων ἢ ἐπιβατῶν, goes on to speak of ὁ ἔμπορος καὶ οἱ ἐπιβάται, shows that the plural must not be pressed.

In none of the chapters which I have cited in the last two paragraphs, with the exception of c. 37, is there any reference to ἐπιβάται.

(b) The ἐπιβάται are referred to exclusively in five chapters. C. 4, which imposes a liability upon the ἐπιβάται, who insist on going to a dangerous place, may be compared with c. 39, which imposes a similar liability upon the ἔμπορος. C. 9 deals with jettison. There is no reference to a cargo, but merely to the goods of the ἐπιβάται and τὰ διαφέροντα τοῖς ναύταις. C. 13, 40, 41 all deal with ἐπιβάται who have goods of great value in small compass. It is to be observed that c. 40 lays down the same provision with respect to ἐπιβάται who have gold and silver as c. 30 and 31 do with respect to ὁ ἔμπορος. In none of these chapters is there any reference to a cargo or to freight. In c. 34 there is a reference to ἐπιβάται if we read with A οἱ ἐπιβάται instead of οἱ ναῦται of the other manuscripts. In that case, οἱ ἐπιβάται would = οἱ τὰ φορτία ἔχοντες, οἱ ἐμβαλλό-μενοι τὰ φορτία. The goods are linen and silk. Compare this with the reference to the ἐπιβάται in c. 40.

(c) In four chapters both are referred to. C. 3 speaks

of thefts from an ἔμπορος ἢ ἐπιβάτης. In c. 11 οἱ ἔμποροι καὶ οἱ ἐπιβάται are recommended not to put large and valuable cargoes into an old ship. In the rest of the chapter οἱ ἔμποροι alone are referred to. In c. 15 ἐπιβάται ἢ ἔμποροι, οἱ ἐπιβάται καὶ ἔμποροι, ἔμποροι ἢ ἐπιβάται are referred to. In c. 37 we have both referred to in reference to the percentage payable in respect of γραμμάτια.

Part II lays down that the ἔμπορος may take two boys on board but must pay their fare (c. η′). Four chapters contain regulations for the conduct of the ἐπιβάτης on board (c. θ′-ιβ′), and two (c. ιδ′, ιε′) give in a slightly different form c. 13 of Part III.

It is evident that the merchant who went with his goods was entitled from the earliest times to a free allowance for personal luggage (Dig. IV, 9, 4, 2 'etsi earum uectura non debetur'). In the Venetian statutes and the statutes of Zara the merchant may carry free a mattress not over a certain weight (St. Ziani, p. 49; St. Tiep., A, 31; St. Zeno, 56; St. Zara, IV, 26), and one chest (St. Ziani, p. 48; St. Tiep., A, 30; St. Zeno, 55; St. Zara, IV, 25).

The Consulate of the Sea draws the following distinction between the mercader (= ἔμπορος) and the pelegri (= ἐπιβάτης). He who carries less than ten quintals pays freight for his person and personal effects and is a passenger, and the shipowner is not obliged to carry his chest, food, or goods, in the absence of special agreement (c. 68 = c. 111 of Italian tr.; cp. C. Tortosa, IX, 27, 3). On the other hand, he who pays for his goods an amount varying with the length of the voyage is a merchant, and the shipowner must carry his chest, bed, servant, and victuals without extra payment, and give him a place to sleep (c. 32, 33 = c. 75, 76 of Italian tr.; cp. C. Tortosa, IX, 27, 24). The rule in Targa's time was that he who paid for his merchandise three times as much as he would have to pay for his person, paid no passage money, and was entitled to a reasonable quantity of luggage free (p. 355).

INTRODUCTION

DANGERS AND DIFFICULTIES OF NAVIGATION

The dangers and difficulties of navigation, so far as they affected the law laid down in our Sea-law and in other maritime codes, may be classified under four heads, (1) dangers arising from want of knowledge or of discipline on the part of those on board; (2) dangers from pirates, land robbers, and wreckers; (3) dangers from fire; (4) difficulties in reference to the provision and preservation of food and drink.

Dangers from Ignorance and Want of Discipline.

There was very little difference, as regards knowledge of navigation, between the different persons on board ship. Scientific knowledge there was none; and in point of experience every one was on much the same level. It was not merely that there was little difference between officers and crew. The merchants had often made many voyages accompanying their goods, and were as well qualified to give an opinion in matters of wind and weather, of coasts and harbours, of shoals and quicksands, as the oldest mariner on board. The inevitable result was that in times of emergency every one did give an opinion, and that the movements of the ship were decided upon in the last resort by a majority. Some legislations attempt to check, or at least to regulate, this tendency to anarchy by providing a committee of navigation—a sort of representative body. Thus the Venetian statute of Zeno (c. 73) prescribes the appointment of five men—the patronus, the nauclerius, and three merchants chosen by the whole body of merchants on board. This body has entire control of the navigation. The maritime statute of Ancona (c. 32) is substantially to the same effect. [Compare rooles d'Oléron, c. 2 (Pard., I, p. 324) requiring the captain to consult the crew.]

The influence of the merchants and passengers upon the

navigation is illustrated in the Sea-law. Apparently the passengers (c. 4) or the merchants (c. 39) can insist on taking the ship into a place notwithstanding the protests of the ναύκληρος. [Cp. Constitutum Usus of Pisa, c. 28, ed. Bonaini, II, p. 915; Consulate of Sea, c. 56, 64.]

How late this state of things lasted is shown by various passages in the Voyages of Andrea Pitti. On one occasion the commander summons the whole ship's company to give their opinion what the land is which they see ('il padrone di nave, ragunato tutto huomo a consiglio, volse il parere di tutti', p. 16). The identity of education and experience in captain and crew accounts also for the loss of all discipline in time of danger. See the accounts in Andrea Pitti of the mariners' behaviour in a great storm: 'Io vedi alcuni marinari vechi cominciare a piangiere e dare ordine a procacciare barile vote per potere sopra esse salvarsi' (p. 15). 'In ultimo rimedio tutti abandonamo la nave gittati in terra ginocchioni, tutti ad alta voce chiamando Sant' Ermo' (p. 40).

Closing of Sea in Winter.

The mediaeval system inherited from the Roman the custom of lying up during the winter months. In classical times navigation was in principle suspended from some time in November till the beginning of March. Cod. I. 40, 6; Veget. IV, 39; Plin. N. H. II, 47 (122); Godefroy on Cod. Theod. XIII, 9, 3, vol. V, p. 121 of Ritter's ed. G. Libri published (Histoire des Sciences Mathématiques, I) a Latin translation of an Arabic calendar, which dates, according to him (p. 171), from the middle of the thirteenth century. It is based, however, on Roman authorities. According to this, the sea is closed on November 7 (p. 451) and opens on March 7 (p. 412). In emergencies, however, voyages were made in the winter. Suet. Claud. c. 18; Cod. Theod. XIII, 5, 34 with Godefroy's note, vol. V, p. 98 of Ritter's ed.; Plin. N. H. II, 47 (125).

What in Roman times was a rule of prudence became

in the middle ages a rule of law. The Pisan Constitutum
Usus lays down (XXVIII, ed. Bonaini, II, p. 919) that, if
a ship is in harbour after the kalends of November, the
owners are not to leave before the kalends of March, without the consent of the merchants who have goods on board
or of the majority of them. The maritime statute of Ancona (c. 77) fixes dates at which ships returning to Ancona
from abroad are to leave the outport. These dates are
evidently fixed with a view of getting the ship in before
December. Where a ship fails to leave at the prescribed
time, and is compelled to winter on the way, the mariners are entitled to their full pay during the winter.
The Statute of Pera (IV, 15) prohibits navigation in the
Black Sea under heavy penalties from the kalends of
December to the middle of March. There are similar
prohibitions in the northern legislations as late as the
fifteenth century. Recess of Hanseatic League of
A. D. 1417, c. 7, 8 (in Pard. II, p. 465), Hamburg Code of
A. D. 1497, c. 14 (in Pard. III, p. 353). 'Antichamente,'
says Targa (p. 70), 'non si permetteva navigare se non
dal principio d'Aprile, sin ad Ottobre ; se bene hora'
[1692] 'si è raffinato tanto questo studio, che con navi si
naviga d'ogni tempo'.

Dangers from Pirates, &c.

The dangers to navigation which arise from man fall
under three heads. First, there are the pirates who attack
the merchantman in the open sea or lurk for it in harbours. Secondly, there are the land-robbers, who cut a
ship's cables or steal its anchors, or snap up a merchant or
passenger or sailor who happens to go on land. Thirdly,
there are the wreckers, and these not merely plunder
ships which have been driven on shore, but sometimes
lure them to destruction by displaying false lights.

Piracy in the palmy days of the empire had practically
disappeared from the Mediterranean. Strabo, III, 5,
p. 144 ; Epictet. Diss. III, 13, 9 ; Plin. N. H. II, 46 (117).
Of more weight than these bits of rhetoric is the rarity

of allusions to pirates in the Digest. The Digest, on the other hand, deals at great length with wreckers, against whom various emperors were obliged to take strong measures. (See especially Dig. XLVII, 9.)

In the genuine part of the Sea-law there is no reference to wreckers. The reason for the omission is, not that wreckers did not flourish, but that the matter was sufficiently dealt with in the Basilica. On the other hand, sea-robbers and land-robbers receive a great deal of attention. Pirates, fire, and wreck are the three normal maritime dangers. The acts of pirates give rise to general average contribution (c. 9) as they do in the Digest (XIV, 2, 2, 3). Land-robbers are often referred to. (1) The land-robber cuts cables or steals anchors (c. 1, 2). (2) The captain who, in defiance of the passengers, brings the ship into a place which is infested with robbers, must make good to the passengers their losses; and if the passengers bring the ship in contrary to the captain's wish they are responsible (c. 4). (3) If some of the passengers go ashore, and the captain has to put off suddenly for fear of robbers, he incurs no responsibility to those left behind (c. 15).[1]

The dangers mentioned in the Sea-law and the Basilica all reappear in the mediaeval codes, but under the mediaeval system the dangers were intensified in two ways. (1) The maritime states granted licences in time of war to the owners of private ships, authorizing them to attack and seize the ships, goods, and persons of the enemy. This was in substance a legalization of piracy. Father Guglielmotti (Vocabolario marino, s. v. corsaro) is concerned to defend the honour of the Italian seaman by distinguishing the corsair, who only attacked the enemies of his country, from the pirate, who attacked all indiscriminately. Two remarks may be made to this, one of language and the other of substance. In the mediaeval documents the words corsair and pirate are often used indifferently. Several of the examples in Duc., Gloss.

[1] Chapters 4 and 15 may also refer to risks from pirates.

Gr., s. v. κουρσεύειν, and in Duc., Gloss. Lat., s. v. cursarii, refer distinctly to pirates. We may add Boncompagni Boncompagnus in Rockinger, Briefsteller, I, p. 154 'de statuto contra cursales atque pirratas'; St. Cattaro, 400 (in Pard. V, p. 98) 'nullus noster ciuis . . . praesumat ire in cursu aut pirata esse . . . saluo si habuerit licentiam communitatis'; Targa, c. lxi 'de corsaria ouero piratica'. The indiscriminate use of the two words points to a close similarity in the characteristics of the two classes. It is true that in law there was a distinction. True also that the corsair, to adopt Father Guglielmotti's terminology, was an honoured citizen of his own state. He was no doubt often a man of exemplary piety. Roustan Beaumont borrows money to go on a pilgrimage ('pro eundo in viagium beate Marie Magdelene'), and charges the debt on the profits which he hopes to make under Providence ('Domino concedente') from a cursus in which he is taking part (Blancard, II, p. 428). But when he dealt with the world even a corsair had to adopt the world's measure. He stripped the merchants whom he seized 'usque ad camisias' (Tafel und Thomas, III, pp. 221, 222), if he did not do worse. When the Pisans in A. D. 1165 asked Trepedecinus, a distinguished Genoese corsair, where he was going, 'I am going,' was the answer, 'to capture you and your goods and persons and to cut off your noses' (Caffaro, Annales, ed. Belgrano, I, p. 176). It must have been at least as difficult for Pisa or Genoa to keep their corsairs within the bounds of legality as it was for the British Government in the eighteenth century to keep their privateers within the terms of the strict instructions which were given them when war broke out.[1]

(2) The mediaeval system of reprisals added another danger to travelling (see Pertile, Diritto Italiano, I, pp. 289 sqq.). A had a claim against B, the citizen of another state, which he found difficulty in enforcing.

[1] See the excellent observations of Mas Latrie, Traités de Paix, Introduction, pp. 94, 95.

A obtained from the authorities of his own state the right to seize the goods of other citizens of *B*'s state until his claim was satisfied.

Of these various dangers we find the following traces in the mediaeval statutes and documents:—

1. The Sea-law never refers to the necessity of carrying weapons on board. In the mediaeval statutes and documents the matter is dealt with as follows:—

(*a*) Some statutes require the ship to carry weapons, their number and character varying with its capacity (St. Ragus., VIII, 78, 79; St. Zeno, 29, 30 = St. Zara, IV, 7–12; St. Ancon. del Mare, 79; Breve Curiae Maris of Pisa, c. 34, in Bonaini, III, p. 369; Pegolotti, p. 132).

(*b*) Others require the nauclerus and mariners to carry arms—sword, and shield and helmet (St. Ragus., *supra*; St. Spalat., VI, 61; St. Tiep., A, 8; St. Zeno, 27, 28 = St. Zara, IV, 5, 6; St. Ancon., *supra*; St. Massil., IV, 19; Barcelona Ordinance, 7, in Pard., V, p. 342).

(*c*) In some cases the merchant is required to carry arms (St. Ancon., *supra*; Breve Curiae Maris of Pisa, *supra*; St. Massil., *supra*; cf. Amalric, 1021, in Blancard, II, p. 305).

(*d*) No statute, so far as I know, requires the ship to carry men-at-arms, but it was customary to take them. Many merchants, says the Consulate of the Sea (c. 78), would not sail unless they knew that men-at-arms were on board. Hence we get provisions in charter-parties to the following effect: there are to be 25 mariners, of whom 10 are to be in armour, and 6 balestrieri (A.D. 1236, Canale, II, p. 342), 70 mariners, of whom 25 are clad in iron, and 12 balestrieri (A.D. 1241, Canale, II, p. 523), 100 mariners, of whom 20 are clad in iron, 20 with balestre, and the rest with lances (A.D. 1248, Canale, II, p. 524), 100 mariners, including 20 balisterii and 60 mariners 'muniti ad ferrum' (Mas Latrie, Documents, Gê es, IX, p. 122 = Canale, II, p. 580).

2. Many statutes deal with the case of a sailor sent ashore on the service of his ship and robbed or captured.

They provide as a rule that he is to receive his wages while he is in captivity, and that his losses are to be made good or his ransom paid by those for whose benefit he was sent—the communitas navis or the shipowner as the case may be (St. Ragus., VII, 31; St. Ancon., 17; Table of Amalfi, 15; Consulate of Sea, 137; compare Appendix D, II, and my commentary). On the same principle, if a merchant goes on land for the service of his mensa and suffers loss or is captured, the mensa is to make the loss good or pay the ransom (St. Ragus., *supra*). The following provisions refer to reprisals. If a ship goes to a city which has pignora over the men of Ragusa, and a merchant or mariner or person of the ship is captured on account of the pignora and suffers loss, the loss is to be made good by the community of the ship (St. Ragus., VII, 32). If merchants are afraid of being captured (*se pignorari*) in a place, the shipowner is not to go there ('non intret in dicto loco suspecto') without their consent (Barcelona Ordinance, 5, in Pard., V, p. 341). Cf. c. 4 of Sea-law.

3. The provisions which prescribe contribution where ships or merchants are ransomed by pirates or corsairs are dealt with hereafter.

4. Both in the statutes and the documents, charter-parties, contracts of loan, &c., there are many references to the frequent necessity for a sudden alteration of the voyage. (Cf. c. 15 of Sea-law.) Such alterations may have been sometimes necessitated by commercial reasons. But in most cases these changes had to be made, as the Statute of Spalato expresses it (VI, 55), 'propter timorem cursariorum et malorum hominum.' Hence it is constantly provided in statutes and charter-parties that the majority of merchants on board are to have the power of altering the destination of the ship (Constitutum Usus of Pisa, c. 28 in Bonaini, II, p. 921 n.; Scriba, 1296; Sacerdoti, p. 38).

5. Another result of these dangers was that the ships which went from Italian ports on commercial expeditions

went generally in batches. At Venice the agglomeration of ships was called a *mudua*. In the twelfth and
thirteenth centuries there were two *mudue* every year
from Venice to Syria and Egypt. One—'mudua pasche
de resurecione' (Sacerdoti, p. 39)—left in spring and
got back in September; the other—'mudua de mense
Augusti' (St. Tiep., B, 2; St. Zeno, 100; Sacerdoti, p. 35)
—left in August, wintered abroad, and returned in May
of next year (Schaube, Handelsgeschichte, pp. 152-4).
There were three *mudue* every year to Romania. The
first to start left in the spring and got back in September;
the second—'mudua Sancti Petri' (Sacerdoti, p. 35)—
left at the end of June and got back in the late autumn;
the third left in August, wintered abroad, and was back
by Easter (Schaube, op. cit., pp. 244-5). The pilgrim
traffic from Venice also went in *mudue* (Schaube, op. cit.,
p. 197).

From Genoa only one caravan went in each year to
Syria and Egypt. It started in September, wintered
abroad, and got back by St. John's Day (Schaube, op. cit.,
pp. 152-4). In time of war, the public authorities
sometimes forbade the departure of these caravans
(Schaube, *supra*).

6. In addition to the expeditions which regularly
started from the principal Italian seaports, two or more
ships might agree to take a voyage together and afford
each other support. This arrangement was called *conserva*
or *conservagium*—a word which seems to have come into
use not before the thirteenth century.[1] The Statute of
Marseille (IV, 23) distinguishes between a *conservagium*
made by shipowners of their own accord and one made
by command of the public authority.[2] The documents in
Blancard contain several references to *conservagium* or
conserva, e. g. Amalric, 858 (vol. II, p. 226); Pièces Com.,

---

[1] In Italian *conserva* is used in the same sense, Viaggi di Andrea
Pitti, p. 34 ; Targa, c. 48, p. 205. The Catalan equivalent is *conservatge*.
Consulate of Sea, c. 48.
[2] See as to this Leges Genuenses, coll. 752.

110 (vol. II, p. 503), but in these the arrangement appears to have been limited to mutual support.

The arrangement between the ships might extend to more than mere support. It might be in substance a partnership. C. 21 of the Sea-law appears to give the first hint of such a partnership, and there are several examples in the middle ages.

In the Statutes of Ragusa (VIII, 64, A.D. 1311), where ships are put in conserva and under the orders of a capitaneus, then, if any loss happens by corsairs, it is spread equally over all the ships and their cargo. In the Statutes of Scardona (c. 24, p. 126) and the Table of Amalfi (c. 38) conserva is expressly described as equivalent to societas. If one of the ships is wrecked, says the Table, or is captured by pirates, 'tunc, sicut lucrum erat commune, ita esset damnum.' Camera (Memorie, I, p. 543) gives an agreement, made in A.D. 1396, between owners of three ships 'conservam insimul faciendi'. They are to give each other support ('esse debent in una defensione'), and if one of them makes a capture, the booty is to be divided between all ('preda quam fecerint dividi debet inter eos scalinum per scalinum'). The 'Societas Navium Bajonensium', the rules of which are printed by Pard. (IV, pp. 283–9), is a very complete example of such a partnership.

Dangers from Fire.

The danger of fire was always present to the mediaeval navigator. The Sea-law supplies several illustrations. Fire is one of the normal dangers along with wreck and pirates. The passenger is prohibited from frying fish (c. ι') and from cutting wood (c. ια')—doubtless in both cases because of the danger of fire. 'It was in vaine to provide any fresh meates,' says Fynes Moryson of one of his journeys by sea, 'because they' (i. e. the mariners) 'would not suffer a fier to be made in so small a barke, wherewith we might dresse them' (Itinerary, London, 1617, p. 259). 'Sopra tutto deve invigilare al fuoco,' says Targa (p. 47) of the *nochiero*, 'acciò per esso non segua danno.'

Difficulties in reference to Food and Drink.

In the Roman system, the merchant or passenger seems to have supplied himself with food ('penus cotti-dianum,' Dig. IV, 9, 4, 2; cf. IV, 9, 1, 6). If there was a dearth, private supplies went into the common stock (Dig. XIV, 2, 2, 2). Sailors were no doubt fed by the exercitor. Part II of the Sea-law throws some light on the subject. The passages just quoted with reference to the danger from fire (cc. ι', ια') suggest that the passenger supplied himself with food and did his own cooking. On the other hand, the provision that he is to take water by measure suggests that there was a common store of water for all (c. ιβ'). Where the merchant supplies a full cargo, the captain is only to take water, victuals (ἐφόδια), and ropes (c. 22). The victuals are no doubt for himself and the mariners; the water may be for all on board. If the merchant delays in loading after a certain time he provides rations for the crew (c. 25). Apparently apart from this the ship would have to provide them.

The mediaeval system with regard to merchantmen is substantially the same. The merchants and passengers take with them their food, wine, and cooking utensils (Consulate of Sea, cc. 30, 63, 76). In the 'Iudicum Vene-torum in causis piraticis contra Graecos decisiones' there are several cases where travellers are robbed of their *arnesia de coquina* (or *cochina*) [Tafel und Thomas, III, pp. 253, 275], or their *arnesia de tabula* [Tafel und Thomas, III, pp. 248, 275]. Perhaps σκεύη in c. 9 refers to cooking utensils. The amount of food, wine, water, and firewood which travellers might take without paying freight is often restricted. As to food, see St. Zeno, 59; St. Zara, IV, 29; St. Spalat., VI, 50; St. Ancon., 83; as to wine and water, St. Ziani in St. Maritt. Venez., p. 48; St. Tiep., A, 33; St. Zeno, 58; St. Zara, IV, 28; as to firewood, St. Ziani in St. Maritt. Venez., p. 49; St. Tiep., A, 32; St. Zeno, 57;

St. Zara, IV, 27. Matters were complicated partly by restrictions on the exportation of food (Authorities, *supra*), partly by protective provisions. A ship could only bring into Ragusa a very limited quantity of wine per head. The surplus was poured overboard and the owner fined (St. Ragus., II, 18)—a provision which must have made for good fellowship in the last days of a voyage.

As regards the sailors, where they went on shares, the expenses of the food were deducted from the gross profits before division (St. Ragus., VII, 30); where they received fixed wages, they were generally fed by the shipowner (St. Zara, IV, 56, 60; St. Pera, IV, 34; St. Massil., IV, 18; Consulate of Sea, cc. 98–100, which prescribes their dietary; Targa, p. 65). Water for merchants and passengers as well as for crew was supplied by the ship (Consulate of Sea, c. 71).

A new system came in with the growth of the pilgrim traffic. The Marseille system may here be taken as a specimen. The business of transporting the pilgrims was in the hands of cargatores, who may be compared with a tourist-agency. They were bound to supply food for the pilgrims—'victualia bona et incorrupta et sufficiencia'— and not to enter into any partnership with the shipowner in reference to the supply (St. Massil., IV, 27). A contract for the supply of food between a cargator and representatives of pilgrims is in Amalric, 165 in Blanc., I, p. 334. The supply must have been a matter of difficulty, as those who went directly by sea from Venice or Marseille had to take food for fifty days, and on the return journey for a hundred (Ludolphus de Sudheim, de Itinere Terrae Sancte in Archives de l'Orient Latin, II, Documents, p. 330).

With merchantmen the problem so far as regards food was easier. Cargo-ships did not as a rule take long voyages in the open. They hugged the coast and put in from time to time. At these stoppages it was often possible to revictual. The water question was much more serious. (Many authorities are collected in Victor Bérard, Les Phéniciens et l'Odyssée, I, pp. 150-5.) Because even where you could get food you might not find water. It is one of the signs of a good navigating lieutenant (*naucher*), says the wise author of the Siete Partidas, to know where fresh water is to be found [Pard., VI, p. 22].

The same author in dealing with the kinds of food to be taken on board ships of war specifies biscuits, salt meat, vegetables, cheese, garlic, onions, and vinegar (Pard., VI, p. 27). Under the Barcelona Ordinance of A.D. 1258, c. 3, the shipowner is to keep a supply of victuals to last for fifteen days. The supply includes bread, wine, salt meat, vegetables, oil, and water (Pard., V, p. 340). As to the food provided on Venetian galleys, see Sanudo, Secreta, II, pp. 60, 61. The ordinary food of the Greek seaman in the seventeenth century, according to Fynes Moryson (p. 259), was onions, garlic, and dried fish.

THE SHIP

The only word used in the Sea-law to denote the ship is πλοῖον. Πλοῖον corresponds to the Latin *navis*, and it must be remembered that there was a distinction throughout classical times and the middle ages between the round ship, propelled mainly by sails and used exclusively for cargo, and the long ship, propelled mainly by oars, and destined originally for military purposes. The latter is in Latin *galea*, Gk. γαλέα. In the thirteenth century the galley was often adopted on account of its speed for the conveyance of goods and passengers. (See Daremberg et Saglio, s. v. *navis*, t. 4, p. 25, n. 3 ; Guglielmotti, Storia della marina pontificia, I, pp. 180, 343.) The principles which are here laid down apply to the merchantman and not to the warship.[1]

Capacity and Valuation of the Ship.

The Sea-law contains an important passage (c. ιϛ′) as to the valuation of ships. The ship, with all its tackle, is

[1] Both classes of ships are figured in Levi (C. A.), Navi Venete da codici, marmi e dipinti, Venezia, 1892.

to be valued at fifty gold pieces for every thousand modii. An old ship is to be valued at thirty gold pieces. In the valuation a reduction is to be made of a third.[1]

This is obscure, but a comparison of earlier and later authorities throws light upon it. There are found in Roman times several methods of reckoning the capacity of a ship: they are measured sometimes in amphorae, sometimes in modii, sometimes in cupae. (See Godefroy ad Cod. Theod. XIII, 5, 28, ed. Ritter, vol. V, p. 92.) In Byzantine times the reckoning is by μόδιοι (Bas. LIII, A′, πδ′; Acta et Diplomata, VI, p. 51, A.D. 1088).

Now where a ship is said to be of such and such capacity, capacity may mean one of two things. It may mean the capacity of the ship, as measured by its displacement; it may mean its capacity for cargo, having regard to the provision made for cargo in the construction of the ship. The two capacities are widely different, and it is difficult to tell in any given case which is referred to.

Where a ship is described as of so many amphorae, it seems to have meant a ship which could conveniently take on board the number of amphorae mentioned (see Dig. XIV, 2, 10, 2). Where the ship is described as of so many modii, did it mean that the ship could conveniently take on board so many modii of grain or that its total displacement was of so many modii? Ulpian, liber singularis, III, 6, speaks of a ship 'non minorem quam decem milium modiorum'. Scaevola (Dig. L, 5, 3, pr.) speaks of ships 'non minores quinquaginta milium modiorum aut quinque pluresve singulas non minores decem milium modiorum'. (I accept Mommsen's correction.) Novell. Theod., VIII 'nullam nauem ultra duorum milium modiorum capacitatem', repeated in Cod. Iust. I, 2, 10; XI, 4, 2. These authorities are not decisive. In the place in our Sea-law, however, μοδισμός seems to denote the displacement reckoned in modii. It is unlikely that the valuation of the ship should depend upon its capacity for cargo.

The distinction between the two systems of reckoning

[1] As to this reduction, see p. 64.

the capacity of ships is well shown in the maritime
Statutes of Venice. A ship is to be estimated in milliaria.
Its capacity in milliaria is important for many purposes,
e. g. the number of anchors, ropes, masts, and sails which
a ship has to take varies with its milliaria. But because
a ship is of 200 milliaria in this sense it does not follow
that it can take goods to the amount of 200 milliaria.
This is shown by St. Tiep., C, 1 = St. Zeno, c. 102. These
enactments, which apply to a ship loading outside Venice,
fix a varying ratio between its total capacity and the
number of cantaria which it can load. A ship of 1,000
milliaria can take a cargo of 1,050 cantaria ; a ship of
200 milliaria can take a cargo of 110 cantaria. There is
an equivalence for every ten milliaria between these
points.[1]

The total capacity of the ship was no doubt ascertained
by calculations made when it was measured. The measuring took place before the ship left the yard. Various
enactments prescribe maxima and minima of length,
breadth, &c., and it is obvious, even where it is not stated,
that obedience to these provisions could only have been

[1] According to the learned Sacerdoti (Statuti marittimi Veneziani,
p. 18) the migliaio is 'libbre 1,000' and the cantaro is '150 libbre
grosse (kilog. 71,224)'. The cantaro is, he says (p. 205), a Venetian
weight. Hence, he adds, to say that for a ship of 1,000 migliaia the load
is not to exceed 1,050 cantari is to fix a proportion of 1,000,000 : 225,000.
I am not sure of this. The cantaro is not a Venetian weight. I do not
find it among Venetian weights either in Pegolotti (p. 134), or Paxi,
Tariffa de Pexi e Mesure, 1503 (in the beginning), or Luca de Burgo,
Summa (p. AA.iiii). It is an over-sea weight as the statute clearly
indicates. At Venice there is a migliaio grosso = 1,580 libbre sottile,
and a migliaio sottile = 1,000 libbre sottile (Pegolotti, p. 134 ; Paxi,
p. a iii). Luca de Burgo makes the migliaio grosso = 1,500 l. sottile
(p. AA iii). It is probably the migliaio grosso that is meant here, as
this seems to have been the shipping *miliarium* (St. Ragus., VII, 39).
The cantaro varied widely. In Constantinople and Pera they used
the Genoese cantaro of 150 Genoese pounds (Pegolotti, p. 14), which
corresponded apparently to 156 libbre sottile (Pegolotti, p. 33). As
to the Genoese cantaro, see also G. B. Zuchetta, Arimmetica, 1600, f. 55.
In Alexandria there were three kinds of cantaro. The cantaro forfori
equalled 140 libbre sottile ; the cantaro levedi equalled 193, and the
cantaro gervi equalled 300 (Pegolotti, p. 61). Another table of
equivalences, which gives nearly the same results, is in Paxi, p. a v.
No secure results can be obtained in these matters until the subject
of mediaeval weights and measures has been thoroughly dealt with.

insured by an official examination of the ship (St. Ziani, C, p. 51 ; St. Zeno, 101 ; Officium Gazarie, cols. 313, 314). The valuation of the ship in money, according to the Sea-law (c. ις') bore a fixed proportion to its capacity but varied with its age. The Mediterranean codes never refer, so far as I know, to a fixed proportion between the capacity of the ship and its value : they provide, however, for its being valued. The valuation of ship was of most importance for cases of general average contribution, and c. ις' seems to confine its use to that. It was important, however, in other cases. For instance, port dues at Ancona were calculated upon the valuation of the ship, one-third of the valuation, however, being deducted for its corredi (St. Ancon. del terzenale, c. 2, p. 78 ; c. 20, p. 89).

The Ship's Name.

Goldschmidt (Geschichte, p. 338) goes rather too far in treating the fixity of the ship's name as one of the distinctions between the mediaeval law of the Romance countries and Roman law. In the first place, ships in classical times had names (Böckh, Urkunden über das Seewesen, pp. 82 sqq. ; Hermann-Blümner, ed. 1882, p. 489, n. 5 ; P. London, II, p. 99 (A.D. 15) κυβερνήτης σκάφης δημοσίας ἧς παράσημος Ἶβις ; P. Grenfell, I, p. 82 (A.D. 220, 221), ship οὗ παράσημον παντόμορφος). Secondly, the mediaeval ships apparently did not have names till nearly the thirteenth century. As regards Genoa, in the Notulario of Scriba the ship is always described by the name of its nauclerus. Canale alludes to a ship with a name in A.D. 1184 (I, p. 382) and another in A.D. 1200 (II, p. 579). As regards Venice, in Baracchi's documents, the first reference to a name is in A.D. 1189 ('de ipsa naue que vocatur leone ', Baracchi, 86; Archivio Ven. XX, p. 57), and even later ships are referred to by the name of their nauclerus (Baracchi, 90, p. 74, A.D. 1190). In Sacerdoti's documents, a ship first has a name in A.D. 1205 (p. 38 ' cum nave que dicitur spigodaglo '. Cf. p. 39 ' cum nave vocata christiana ', in A.D. 1208, and p. 40 ' cum navi

vocata Urso', in A.D. 1210). At Pisa there is a reference
to the Aquila in A.D. 1197 (Müller, Documenti, p. 73) and
to the Grandeorgolio in A.D. 1199 (Müller, Documenti,
p. 77). In Manduel, the ship has no name in a Messina
document of A.D. 1200 (Blancard, I, p. 4), but it has a
name ('in nave de Oliva') in a Marseille document of
A.D. 1210 (Blancard, I, p. 6). Apparently the ship's name
might be changed at the owner's pleasure (Amalric, 997 in
Blancard, II, p. 292 'in quadam nave que dicitur Sanctus-
Blazius, que olim dicebatur Cidona ').

Provisions to insure Safety.

A characteristic of the Mediterranean legislations, as
Goldschmidt points out (Geschichte, p. 338), is the care
which they take in seeing that the ship is seaworthy, and
in preventing overloading. The provisions which deal
with this subject may be divided into provisions (1) as to
the internal arrangements of ships, (2) as to ballasting,
(3) as to the disposition of the goods on board, (4) as to
the packing of goods in the hold, (5) against overloading.

1. The Venetian statutes contain various provisions
which in substance limit the places where cabins may be
made, prescribe the use to which certain cabins are to be
put, e.g. one for keeping the tackle and another for the
sails, and require spaces to be left free for store-rooms, &c.
(St. Ziani, pp. 47, 49; St. Tiep., A, 5; St. Zeno, 18). The
same statutes distinguish the sleeping-places of merchants
and of sailors (St. Zeno, 26).

2. The ballasting is sometimes done by the navigating
officer, who may be sworn by the merchants to ballast
with a view to the ship's safety (St. Zara, IV, 1; St.
Spalat., VI, 60). At Venice it is done under the direction
of a committee composed of the navigating officer and of
representatives of owners and merchants (St. Ziani, p. 46;
St. Tiep., A, 3; St. Zeno, 3). After the ship is ballasted,
no ballast can be taken out except from necessity in
entering port, or with the consent of the merchants or
the committee (St. Zara, IV, 1; St. Spalat., VI, 60; St.

Zeno, 5). Certain heavy articles, such as lead, may be substituted for ballast, in certain cases by the shipowner alone, in others by him with the consent of the merchants or committee (St. Zara, IV, 2 ; St. Tiep., C, 2 ; St. Zeno, 6, 40, 103, 104).

3. There are many enactments prohibiting heavy goods from being placed in various parts of the ship. These present great variety of detail, and therefore only a general notion can be given of their contents. As a rule, where the ship has more than one deck, then the upper deck, or where the ship has only one deck, then that deck is reserved for extremely light goods, such as wrought silks, or for things that go in chests (St. Ragus., VII, 9 ; St. Ziani, p 47 ; St. Tiep., 19 ; St. Zeno, 48, 88 ; St. Ancon., 45 ; 'subtiles merces in capsia de quibus naulum non datur,' St. Mass., IV, 20 ; Barcelona Ordinance, 12, 13, in Pard., V, p. 343).

At Venice only light goods[1] (St. Ziani, p. 47 ; St. Tiep., 19 ; St. Zeno, 48), and at Pisa one-fourth only of the cargo may be placed between the decks (Const. Usus, c. 28, p. 919).

Exceptions are generally made for the food and drink of those on board, which may be placed in the store-room (St. Zeno, 48 ; St. Ancon., 45), and for the ship's tackle, including the carpenter's tools, armour, &c., which may be placed on the upper deck or elsewhere (St. Ziani, p. 47 ; St. Ancon., 45).

Moreover these rules do not apply in some legislations to ships loaded with provisions (St. Ziani, p. 49 ; St. Tiep., 22 ; St. Zeno, 49 ; St. Mass., IV, 20), ships used exclusively for the pilgrim traffic (St. Tiep., 21), or ships confined to special classes of goods, e. g. wood (St. Ancon., 45), horses (St. Mass., IV, 20). An exception is also some-

---

[1] The technical expression in Venice is *imbolium* (It. *imboio*) as opposed to *caricum* or *mercimonia carici*. The meaning of *imbolium* is a thing which you use as a covering for other things—which you spread over them. The Consulate of the Sea (c. 26) contrasts 'roba de pes' with 'roba de bolum, cosa del ambolum'. First and lowest should be laid 'roba de pes'. The Italian version translates 'roba de bolum, cosa del ambolum' by 'roba di viluppo, cosa del viluppo'.

times made in favour of goods taken from a ship in distress (St. Tiep., 25).

Where these provisions are transgressed by the merchant without the shipowner's knowledge, the shipowner is not liable in case of loss or damage for goods improperly placed (St. Ziani, p. 47; Const. Usus, p. 919), and the merchant has no right to contribution where they are jettisoned (see *post*).

The shipowner who wilfully transgresses these provisions is fined, sometimes twice the freight received for the goods (St. Tiep., 48, 49, 50; St. Zeno, 87, 88, 89).

4. As a rule the packing of the cargo in the hold is left to the discretion of the nauclerus and the stevedores, who are bound to pack (*stivare*) with a view to the safety of the ship (St. Ziani, p. 47; St. Tiep., A, 18; St. Ancon., 4, 46; Consulate of Sea, 25, 26).

5. The provisions against overloading are generally based on this principle. A mark is put on the outside of the ship. Then the ship is officially examined after it has been loaded and before it sets sail (St. Zeno, 44-7, 101). The mark must not lie more than a certain depth below the water-line. The depth at which it is allowed to lie varies with the ship's age. If it lies too deep, goods are taken out until the ship rights itself, and the owner is fined—sometimes twice the freight of the goods loaded in excess (St. Ziani, p. 48; St. Tiep., A, 20; B, 1; St. Zeno, 61; St. Ancon. del terzenale, c. 21, p. 90).

There are strictly limited exceptions, e. g. at Venice, in favour of ships which sail within the gulf or ships carrying victuals (St. Zeno, 64, 65), and in favour of a shipowner who takes goods from a ship in distress (St. Zeno, 67).

Similar provisions, but less detailed, are found in other statutes (St. Spalat., Reform., 84, p. 288; Breve Curiae Maris of Pisa, cc. 73, 77, 93; Off. Gazarie of Genoa, cols. 319, 327).

THE SHIPOWNER

The Digest deals at length with the responsibility of the exercitor (1) for goods and other property of which he has undertaken the safe carriage, (2) for injuries done on board ship by the crew to goods or persons, and (3) on contracts made by the magister. These provisions, which are reproduced in the Basilica, may be summarized as follows:—

I. If *A* gives goods to *B* to be carried on board *B*'s ship, and *B* agrees to carry them safely ('saluum fore recipit'), *B* is bound to deliver them at the journey's end in quantity and quality as they were received (Dig. IV, 9, 1 pr.). If *B* fails to do so, *A* has the following remedies against him. (*a*) If *A* has hired the whole ship, *A* has a civil action against *B* *ex conducto*, (*b*) If *A* has only put on board specific goods, his remedy is *ex locato*, (*c*) If *A* paid no freight, his action is *depositi* (Dig. IV, 9, 3, 1). In actions (*a*) and (*b*), *B* is liable for *culpa* and *dolus*; in (*c*) only for *dolus* (Dig. IV, 9, 3, 1), (*d*) *A* has also a remedy against *B* *iure honorario*, and in this action *B* is liable even if the goods were lost or injured without any fault of his own (Dig. IV, 9, 3, 1). He is responsible for the acts of passengers as well as of sailors (Dig. IV, 9, 1, 8; 3, pr.). He is only relieved if the loss or damage occurred by *damnum fatale*, e. g. shipwreck or pirates (Dig. IV, 9, 3, 1).

What is a 'receptio saluum fore'? The exercitor is liable for his own receipts or for those of the magister nauis (Dig. IV, 9, 1, 2). He is also liable for receipts by an agent to whom he has specially directed delivery to be made (Dig. IV, 9, 1, 2), or by agents who from their position have an implied authority to receive (Dig. IV, 9, 1, 3).

The exercitor is taken to receive by the mere fact of the goods being put on board, and there may be a receipt even before the goods are on board (Dig. IV, 9, 1, 8; 3, pr.).

INTRODUCTION

The rule applies not merely to cargo but to the personal luggage of passengers and provisions taken for the voyage (Dig. IV, 9, 1, 6 ; 4, 2). It applies even though the goods do not belong to the person who put them on board, if he has an interest in their safe arrival, e. g. as pledgee (Dig. IV, 9, 1, 7).

The exercitor is not obliged to take any one on board or his goods (Dig IV, 9, 1, 1), and, even where he does, he may relieve himself from responsibility if he announces that the passengers are to look after their own goods, and the passengers consent (Dig. IV, 9, 7, pr.). This passage appears to apply to the next head, but on principle it must belong here.

II. If a sailor on board ship commits a theft or assault, the person robbed or assaulted has a remedy against the exercitor (Dig. IV, 9, 7, pr. ; XLIV, 7, 5, 6; XLVII, 5, 1, pr.). The extent and limits of the remedy are best shown by contrasting it with the remedy in respect of goods which the exercitor undertook to carry safely.

The remedy is not confined to injuries to goods. It extends to personal injuries (Dig. IX, 3, 7, pr.). It is not confined to merchants or passengers, although in fact it is generally available only by them. It applies in favour of a person on board who has paid no fare (Dig. IV, 9, 6, 1), or of a person upon whom something has been thrown from a ship (Dig. IX, 3, 6, 3). It is confined to cases where there is *culpa* or *dolus* on the sailor's part (Dig. XIV, 1, 1, 2). It is confined to cases where the act is committed on board ship : acts done by a sailor off the ship do not affect the exercitor (Dig. IV, 9,. 7, pr.). The exercitor is not liable for the acts of passengers (Dig. XLVII, 5, 1, 6), nor is he liable for acts done by one sailor to another (Dig. IV, 9, 7, 1), but if a merchant or passenger serves as a mariner, the exercitor is liable to third persons for wrongs done by him *qua* sailor, and liable to him for wrongs done him by another sailor (Dig. IV, 9, 7, 2).

The person robbed or injured has two alternative remedies. He has a remedy *iure civili* against the sailor. He has a remedy *iure honorario* against the exercitor, and this is *in duplum* (Dig. IV, 9, 7, 1; XLVII, 5, 1, 2). But if the sailor who misbehaves is the exercitor's own slave, he can relieve himself from liability by handing him over to the plaintiff (Dig. IV, 9, 7, 4; XLVII, 5, 1, 5). Where damages are recovered against the exercitor, he has his remedy over *ex conducto* against the sailor who committed the wrong (Dig. IV, 9, 6, 4). The person aggrieved has, as I have stated, a direct remedy against the sailor; but, if he sues the exercitor, he must transfer to him his right of action against the sailor (Dig. IV, 9, 6, 4); and, if an action brought whether against the exercitor or against the sailor is dismissed, the dismissal operates as a bar to an action against the other (Dig. IV, 9, 6, 4).

Where a sailor steals goods which the exercitor has undertaken to carry safely, the person robbed is not entitled both to sue the exercitor on his receptio and to sue the sailor for theft. He must elect between his remedies. The exercitor in such a case may, subject to certain exceptions, sue the sailor for theft as he has undertaken the risk (Dig. IV, 9, 3, 5; 4, pr.; XLVII, 5, 1, 4).

III. The exercitor is liable on the contracts of the magister made within the limits of his authority. He is not liable on contracts made by a sailor (Dig. XIV, 1, 1, pr. 2).

The language of the jurists seems not quite consistent as to how far a person dealing with a magister is entitled to rely upon his apparent authority. On principle, a contract made by the magister can only bind the exercitor when its subject-matter is within the sphere of the magister's attributions, or when the exercitor has put forward the magister or allowed him to put himself forward as having those attributions. In this case the exercitor is bound on what in English law is known as the principle of estoppel. Ostensible authority in such a case is the same in favour of innocent and diligent third parties as real authority. The jurists appear to say that the exercitor is liable not only on the contracts of a magister whom he has appointed, but also on the contracts of any one to whom the magister has delegated his authority, and this although the delegation was made contrary to the orders of the exercitor (Dig. XIV, 1, 1, 5). On the other hand, if the exercitor limits the magister's authority, he is not liable on a contract made by him in excess of that limit. E. g. he appoints a magister to collect fares ; he is not liable on a charter-party made by him (Dig. XIV, 1, 1, 12). So, if he appoints several magistri and declares that no one is to act without the consent of the others, a contract made with one alone does not bind the exercitor (Dig. XIV, 1, 1, 14). The explanation of these passages perhaps is that, where there is only one magister on board, any person dealing with him is entitled to assume that he has been properly appointed and possesses the whole authority which a magister usually possesses. On the other hand, where there are several magistri in evidence, any person dealing with one is put upon inquiry as to the extent and limits of his authority, and, where a magister is found doing only one class of work, any person dealing with him is put upon inquiry as to why he is not exercising his other normal functions.

As regards money borrowed by the magister, the law stood thus. He must state that the loan is made for the purposes of the ship, and the lender must have reasonable grounds for believing the truth of the statement. E. g. if the magister borrows professedly for repairs, the lender, in order to sue the exercitor, must know that repairs are needed, and that the amount borrowed is not excessive for the purpose ; but he is not obliged to superintend their execution (Dig. XIV, 1, 1, 9 ; 7, pr.).

The party contracting with the magister may at his option sue the magister or the exercitor (Dig. XIV, 1, 1, 17). But if he has sued one he cannot sue the other, and a payment made by one diminishes *pro tanto* the other's liability (Dig. XIV, 1, 1, 24). Where there are several exercitores, each one may be sued *in solidum*, and if they have appointed one of their number magister, any one of the others may be sued on contracts made with him. But where several are acting as magistri each on his own account, contracts made with one do not bind the others (Dig. XIV, 1, 1, 25 ; 4, pr., 1).

In strict law the exercitor could not sue on contracts made by the magister. His only remedy was in strictness against the magister. However, the 'praefecti propter ministerium annonae' and the governors of provinces gave extraordinary assistance to exercitores on contracts made by their magistri (Dig. XIV, 1, 1, 18).

Joint Owners of Ship.

The Roman jurists recognize the division of a ship among several owners ; but what was probably the exception in the Roman empire became the rule of the middle ages. There are two possible ways in which a ship may be divided among several owners. The ship might be divided by metes and bounds. Each owner might have a measured space in part of the ship. Such a division of the ship can hardly ever have existed, although there are cases where a person owns a certain number of receptacles, e. g. casks, on board, and receives freight for them on his own account (compare Amalric, 493, with Amalric, 604, 737). But the regular system was that the ship was divided into notional parts, and that each of the several owners of ship owned one or more of those parts. You owned a twelfth or eighth or sixth in the entire ship. Such a twelfth, eighth, or sixth was also expressible in terms of tonnage. If you owned a twelfth in a ship of a hundred and twenty *meste*, you owned ten *meste*. Now the owner of such a share might deal with his share independently of his co-owners ; but it is obvious that some agreement had to be come to between the co-owners in order that the ship might sail ; and the mediaeval statutes are filled with provisions for bringing about and

1 2

enforcing this agreement and regulating its terms in order to prevent the oppression of a minority.

In the fifteenth and sixteenth centuries the Mediterranean ship is as a rule divided into twenty-four parts or *carati*, and the shares of the owners are reckoned in *carati* (Targa, p. 26).[1] But in the thirteenth century there seems to have been no fixed principle of division with regard to the ships of any state. The ship was divided merely with a view to the immediate convenience of the owners. A ship which was divided in eighths on one voyage might as the result of a sale be divided into twelfths.[2]

One result of the normal division of the ship into parts was the necessity of providing by law for the cases when there was a difference of opinion among the co-owners. No restrictions seem ever to have been put upon the right of a co-owner to deal with his own share. He might, so it seems, sell or pledge his share without the consent of his co-owners, except in so far as they might have a preferential right of purchase (p. clxvi). But the appointment of a common agent to manage ship, the raising of money on the security of ship, and the letting and sale of ship were the subject of precise legislative provisions. The general principle is that the majority in interest of the owners have full power of dealing with the ship, subject to their acting in good faith (cf. Targa, p. 33 and p. 23). As a rule notice has to be given to all the owners before any important step is taken, and some acts can only be legally effected under the superintendence of the Court

---

[1] This division existed in Genoa in the fourteenth century. Jal, Glossaire nautique, s. v. *carattus*.

[2] In Genoa the ship was divided into loca, generally forty (Canale, II, pp. 579, 582; Amalric, 971), but sometimes more and sometimes less (Canale, *supra*; Amalric, 991, 1006). The word is perhaps derived from the Digest, XIV, 2, 2, pr., but at Genoa it denotes a notional division of the ship, while in the Digest it denotes simply the sleeping-place taken by a passenger. In Marseille the regular division is into setzene (Amalric, 480, 481, 539, 584, 616, 939, 991), but there are references to quarters (Amalric, 665, 831, 875) and to eighths (Amalric, 188, 512, 750, 808, 997). In Amalric, 752, the division of the ship is altered on a purchase.

having jurisdiction. The provisions fall under the following heads: —

1. The majority of the owners appoint the manager (St. Ragus., VII, 18). A co-owner who has sufficient technical knowledge has a preferential claim to be appointed (Targa, p. 42). Hence we find that the nauclerus often owns a share (Sacerdoti, p. 40; Scriba, 645; other authorities below).

In the documents we often find cases where one owner receives the shares of the others *in commenda* (see *post*). No doubt this was found a convenient expedient for giving the managing owner a power of disposition over the shares of the others, and for relieving persons who dealt with him from the necessity of inquiring into the extent of his authority. Sometimes the merchants are given the power of choosing the nauclerus (Mas Latrie, Traités de Paix, Documents, p. 39).

2. The majority of the owners may incur necessary expenditure on the ship, and may for that purpose charge the whole ship, including the shares of dissenting members (St. Ragus., VII, 17; Consuetud. Bari, f. 118 of ed. 1550; p. 152 in Alianelli; St. Ancon., c. 3, c. 40). The obscure c. ιϐ´ of the Sea-law probably refers to a case of this kind, see p. 68. As the majority of the owners may do it, so may their agent, the manager, do it (Authorities, *supra*).

3. The majority of the owners may let the ship (St. Ancon., c. 1; Const. Usus, p. 918).

4. Sometimes any joint-owner, and in any event a majority in interest, can insist on the ship being sold. The sale takes place by public auction, and generally under the direction of the Court. Any joint-owner may bid. Notice of the sale is given, and absent parties are bound. The sale is made subject to any existing charter-party. A sale by the Court sometimes has the effect of extinguishing claims of creditors as against the ship and transferring them to the proceeds of sale (St. Zara, III, 40; IV, 46 = St. Spalat., VI, 52; St. Ancon., 6; Cons. Tra-

pani, 9; Table of Amalfi, 35; Const. Usus of Pisa, pp. 916–17; Breve Curiae Maris, c. 79; St. Pera, IV, 20; see Consulate of Sea, 11). In some cases where one owner wishes to sell his share, his co-owners have a preferential right of purchasing it (Consuetud. Bari, f. 56 r.; 118 v.; Goldschmidt, Geschichte, p. 339 n.).

THE MARINERS

The commercial documents give us no help in determining the mariner's[1] position. His engagement was no doubt in most cases merely verbal. It was binding between him and the shipowner when the two had shaken hands or the mariner had received earnest money ('vel per arras vel per fiduciam,' St. Zara, IV, 65; 'arra overo speranza,' St. Ancon., 10; 'facta aliquali solutione seu mutuo, recepta pecunia seu mutuo,' Table of Amalfi, 1, 2; Consulate of Sea, 111). In most cases the only written evidence of the engagement must have been the entry of the mariner's name with the terms of his hiring in the book kept by the scribanus (St. Ancon., 41; Breve Curiae Maris of Pisa, 49, 76; Breve dell' Ordine del Mare, 49, 68; Consulate of Sea, 111). We have therefore to fall back upon the statutes. The information which they supply may be classified under two heads, (1) provisions as to the payment of the mariner, (2) provisions as to his duties.

The Mariner's Pay.

Different classes of the ship's company are referred to in the Sea-law, c. a'–ζ', c. 9 and c. 36. The meaning of the

---

[1] The mariner must be distinguished from the galiotus. A galiotus is a rower in a galley. He was originally recruited by voluntary enlistment, like the mariner, but he evidently belonged as a rule to a lower social stratum. St. Ragus., II, 31; St. Ancon., 81, 82. Duc. s. v. quotes from a chronicle: 'quia viles erant galioti nulliusque nominis,' their loss was not of much importance.

The mariner must also be distinguished from the famuli or fanti, who acted as servants on board. (See p. clxxxvi.)

various designations is considered in the commentary; in this place I only deal with the light which these and other chapters throw upon the condition of the ship's company as a whole. Chaps. α'-ζ' lay down that the captain's μισθός is two parts, while that of other members of the ship's company ranges from one part and a half to half a part. The sailor's μισθός is one part. There are two other places in which reference is made to the sailor's μισθός. C. 5 lays down that if one sailor injures another, the one who dealt the blow is to pay the other his μισθός for the whole time that he is out of work taking care of himself. C. 46 provides that, if the long-boat breaks off from the ship, and the sailors who are in it are lost, the captain is to pay their representatives their yearly wages up to a complete year. It is clear that c. α'-ζ' refer to mariners who sail *ad partem*, who receive, that is to say, an aliquot part of the profits in lieu of wages. The chapters so understood are perfectly plain. They may be illustrated by a concrete instance. Let us suppose that one-half of the net profits of the ship is divisible among the crew, and that there are on board one officer of each class, twenty ναῦται and four παρασχαρῖται. The captain receives two parts; each of the four officers one part and a half – in all six parts ; each of the ναῦται one part—in all twenty parts ; each παρασχαρίτης one-half part —in all two parts. The total number of parts in this hypothetical case will be thirty. The half of the ship's profits available for distribution will be divided into thirty parts, distributed as above. I should not have laboured this point but for the extraordinary language of the lamented L. Goldschmidt (Lex Rhodia, p. 86) : ' Das wahrscheinlich jüngere zweite Hauptstück der pseudo-rhodischen Sammlung spricht c. 1-7 . . . von dem μισθός des Schiffers und der speziell genannten Schiffsoffiziere, welcher auf 2, resp. 1½, 1 und ½ μέροι (sic) festgesetzt ist, so dass sie zusammen 8½ μέροι (sic) haben—wahrscheinlich von der Fracht oder von dem Reisegewinn; aber von welcher Einheit, erhellt nicht, ebensowenig, ob auch das Schiffsvolk (ναῦται) und die Befrachter und in welchem Masse partizipiren.' C. 46, on the other hand, apparently refers to a fixed wage. It seems to contemplate a hiring by the year—commencing no doubt from the time when the sea was presumed to be open to navigation, and going on till it was closed. If in the course of the year a sailor was killed under the circumstances mentioned in the chapter, his representatives were entitled to the wages remaining due to him till the end of the year. No conclusion can be drawn from c. 5 as to the nature of the hiring, but it also rather suggests a fixed wage.

So far the genuine Sea-law. Some manuscripts add four chapters, which I give in Appendix D. As a whole they cannot be traced back before the fourteenth century, but parts are not later than the twelfth. They are very obscure, but they seem to distinguish between three classes of sailors (1) the μερίτης, who receives a share under the terms of a contract (c. I); (2) a sailor who hires himself out, receiving a fixed wage (c. III); (3) a slave who is let out by his master as a sailor (c. IV). We shall meet persons of the last class in the Statutes of Ragusa.

Two statutes—that of Ragusa and of Zara—go into minute detail as to the various systems under which the mariner may be hired. Their provisions may be taken as specimens.

The Statutes of Ragusa distinguish three classes of persons concerned with the navigation of the ship. The scribanus was bound to write all the mariners (1) *tam euntes ad partem*, (2) *quam ad marinariciam*, and (3) *pueros vel conductos* (VII, 2). Each group requires separate treatment.

(1) The statutes nowhere define the proportions in which the profits of the maritime adventure were divided between ship and crew, but according to Gondola, a sixteenth-century jurist, who says that the system existed in his own day, the mariners took half and the ship-

owner half (Stat. Ragus., p. 420). No one is to have an extra share (*honorificentia*) except the nauclerius, who has two shares (VII, 30), just as in our Sea-law. The nauclerius and crew are described sometimes as the nauclerius with his community, sometimes as the nauclerius with his society. The community of the ship is a larger term, including the owner of ship.

If a mariner falls ill before the ship leaves Ragusa, he is not bound to the ship. If he falls ill outside Ragusa and is put ashore, he is entitled to his share for that voyage, as if he were present, and to his expenses, i. e. an allowance for food (VII, 23). If a mariner dies on the voyage, his representatives are entitled to his share for that voyage (VII, 25). If a slave who went as a mariner fled or was captured, his share continued to make profits for his master until the ship came in, but the master was not entitled to have him redeemed (VII, 19).

Interim divisions on account of profits were sometimes made outside Ragusa, but the profits divided were subject to return to make up for subsequent losses (VII, 28). There was no doubt a final adjustment when the voyage was over.

(2) The normal system at Ragusa was evidently that under which the mariners went *ad partem*. The chapters which relate to mariners *ad marinariciam* give the impression of being later additions. The mariner might be hired for the voyage or for a fixed term. If he was hired for the voyage, he was bound to carry it out, going and returning, loading and unloading. If he left the ship, he was liable to return double his wages received or to be received. If the owner did not pay him at the prescribed time, the owner was liable to pay double (VII, 12 ; St. Lesina, V, 3). Where the mariner was hired for a term, and the term ended in the course of a voyage, the mariner was bound to complete the voyage, on the terms of receiving additional payment calculated on the basis of his previous pay (VII, 22). If the mariner fell ill before the ship started, he was bound to restore all advance

pay. If he fell ill during the voyage and was put ashore, or died, he was only entitled to pay for the period of his actual service (VII, 24, 25 ; St. Lesina, V, 5, p. 212).

(3) Gondola does not understand what a *conductus* is (Stat. Ragus., p. 420). The following explanation is therefore offered with diffidence. A ship always required a certain number of sailors; where it went *ad partes* there might be a difficulty in finding men who were willing to take the risk. The shipowner in such a case was obliged to hire sailors. The hired sailor, as between himself and the shipowner, received a fixed wage ; as between himself and the other sailors, he received a share. The shipowner who put him on board either gained or lost, as the case might be, the difference between the wages paid to the sailor and the share of profits which accrued to him and for which he was accountable to his employer. VII, 21, which deals with the flight of a *conductus*, has evidently been much altered. It begins by saying that, where the *conductus* of a shipowner runs away, his share continues to sail for his employer. This was probably the original form of the chapter. Then, as its injustice was felt, it was emended by the addition that the *nauclerius* was to put a substitute on board, whose wages were payable by the shipowner. A second emendation provided that, where no substitute was found, the share of the *conductus* was divisible among the community of the ship. The shipowner instead of hiring a man might send a slave, whose position, as between himself and the other mariners, was equivalent to that of a *conductus*. If he fled or was lost, his share continued to sail for his master, but the nauclerius and his community were not bound to make the loss good (VII, 20).

The Statutes of Zara, with which the Statutes of Spalato substantially agree, are a contrast to the Statutes of Ragusa. The normal system at Ragusa—the 'usus Ragusii' as it is called on one occasion—was that under which the nauclerius and mariners divided between them a proportion—probably as a rule one-half—of the net profits of the maritime adventure. The normal system at Zara and Spalato is that under which the nauclerius and mariners receive a fixed wage from the shipowner. The system of profit-sharing is recognized in one chapter, which lays down that an agreement between crew and owners for putting the ship *ad partem* is binding if reduced to writing (IV, 71), but as a rule the mariner is hired *ad soldum* or *ad marinariciam*. As a rule the mariner was hired for the whole period during which the sea was open, i. e. from March 1 till November 30 (IV, 43), and his wages were payable in thirds ('per terzariam dividendo'), the first payment being due on March 1, the second on June 1, and the third on September 1 (IV, 44). Where the mariner, whenever hired, was bound to remain until the *mudua* of St. Andrew (November 30), he was said to be hired *ad muduam* (IV, 53). The same hiring is called in other statutes *ad terzaria*, from the payment of the wages in three divisions. The mariner might also be hired *ad mensem*, or *ad certum viagium* (IV, 53).

Where the mariner was hired till November 30 and remained on board later, e. g. if the ship was not in Zara by that date, he was entitled to a proportional increase of wages (IV, 43, 76. Cf. St. Spalat., VI, 70). If the ship was in before the 30th, the mariner was obliged to remain by the ship and assist in dismantling it, &c. (IV, 77). If the mariner died in the first period of three months (*in primo terzerio*), his representatives were entitled to his wages for the whole of that period. If he died thereafter, they were only entitled to his wages apportioned up to the day of his death (IV, 63). To this there was an exception. If the mariner was killed in defending the ship or in the course of his service, his heirs were entitled to his wages for the whole period of nine months (IV, 78. Cf. the Sea-law, c. 46, and the Barcelona Ordinance of A.D. 1258, c. 20, in Pard., V, p. 344). If a mariner *ad certum viagium* died within the gulf in the course of the voyage, his

INTRODUCTION

heirs were entitled to the whole of his wages for the
voyage (IV, 62. St. Spalat., VI, 59, is to the same effect, but
omits the limitation 'within the gulf'. See also IV, 78).

A mariner, however hired, who fell ill during a voyage
and was left behind, was entitled to his wages up to the
time of his leaving the ship, and to a small payment (two
soldi parvorum) per day for a month (IV, 61).

The statutes dealt with illustrate in sufficient detail the
various systems of payment which existed in the middle
ages; it would be useless to go through the laws of the
other maritime states with the same minuteness. It will
be enough merely to enumerate the systems which prevailed elsewhere, and to draw attention to some special
points on which the authorities given above are not
sufficiently explicit.

The maritime Statutes of Venice have no trace of the
profit-sharing system. The mariner seems to have been
generally hired for a *mudua*, and to have received part at
least of his pay in advance (St. Zeno, 21, 99; St. Tiep.,
39 = St. Zeno, 80). An owner who fails to pay a mariner
at the appointed time must pay him double (St. Tiep.,
40 = St. Zeno, 81). The Statutes of Ancona recognize
all three systems, payment by a fixed wage and by time,
probably as a rule for the whole season during which the
sea was open (St. Ancon., 20, 54), payment by a fixed
wage and for the voyage (St. Ancon., 7, 10, 44), and payment *a parte* (St. Ancon., 44, 56). The Ordinamenta of
Trani allude both to the mariner at a fixed wage (Ordin.,
1, 3) and to the mariner *a parte* (Ordin., 10, 12). The
Consulate of Trapani, which was based upon that of
Messina, speaks only of mariners at fixed wages (c. 12).
The original form at Amalfi, as will be shown hereafter,
was a system of partnership between ship, cargo, and
crew. In the fourteenth century the three systems existed
side by side. The Table of Amalfi in its Italian chapters
alludes on several occasions to mariners *a soldo* (c. 41,[1]

[1] The mariner *de sodû* in c. 41 is not, as Alianelli suggests (p. 121), a
mariner who stays on dry land, but a mariner who receives fixed wages.

clxxii

52, 53). The regulations as to galleys, which were published by Camera (I, p. 535), speak of mariners going ' a
parte o vero ad rascione de anno ', and again of mariners
going ' ad terzaria, ad parte, o vero a viaggio '. The
mariner who goes ' ad rascione de anno ', i. e. for the open
season, is evidently the same as the man who goes *ad
terzaria*, i.e. at three months' wages (see *ante*, p. clxxi). At
Pisa there is no trace of the profit-sharing arrangement.
The mariner receives a fixed wage whether he is engaged
ad mare clausum, i. e. for the open season, *ad mensem* or
ad viadium (Breve Curiae Maris, c. 49, ed. Bonaini, III,
p. 388; c. 76, III, p. 404).[1] Under the Constitutum Usus,
the wages are subject to reduction if the shipowner does
not get full freight (c. 28, ed. Bonaini, II, p. 911). At
Genoa again the fixed wage seems to be the rule. The
mariner is hired either *ad certum terminum* or *ad viagium*.
If he dies after the voyage is half over, the whole of his
wages are payable (St. Pera, V, 3 ; VI, 8).

The Consulate of the Sea recognizes hiring by the
voyage (c. 84, 116) or by the month (c. 85) and sailing
upon shares (c. 202, 203). It apparently speaks of a
mariner who is paid by the mile (c. 115), but this is
extremely doubtful, although it is accepted both by
Pardessus and by Twiss. ' Il est difficile de deviner,' says
Pardessus, ' comment on arbitroit les distances parcourues '
(II, p. 143). The Portolani of course give mileages,[2] and
many ships no doubt carried a Portolano, but there must
have been great practical difficulties in the way. Perhaps
it is merely a suggestion of the ingenious author, or
authors, of the Consulate, seldom, if ever, put into execution. Mariners also sailed, according to the Consulate,
on the terms of their wages being fixed at the end of the

---

[1] The Pisan regulations, which go into much detail, are collected by
Adolf Schaube, Consulat des Meeres in Pisa, Leipzig, 1888, pp. 94–6.

[2] See Beazley (C. R.), Dawn of Modern Geography, III, pp. 512, 514.
It is just possible that two chapters in the St. of Zara (IV, 53, 54),
which I explain otherwise (p. clxxv), refer to mileage payments. See
also Const. Usus of Pisa, c. 28 (Bonaini, II, p. 913) ' estimatione facta
per miliaria '.

INTRODUCTION

voyage by certain of the ship's officers (c. 181). ' Ce genre
de location,' says the judicious Pardessus, ' devoit être rare
à cause de l'incertitude qu'il laissoit sur les droits de celui
qui s'étoit loué, et de l'arbitraire dans la fixation des
loyers' (II, p. 205).

According to Targa (c. 85, pp. 356 sqq.) four systems
were in use in his time. (1) The mariner was paid by
the month. This was the regular system with big ships.
Three months' pay was generally kept back till the end
of the voyage. Pay ceased if the navigation was interrupted, the mariner only receiving his food. (2) The
mariner was paid a lump sum for the voyage. He also got
his food. In either of these cases, if the shipowners failed
to recover the freight or part of it, the mariner's pay
abated *pro rata*. (3) The gross profits of the voyage were
divided into three parts. One part went to the ship;
another to the person who undertook to feed the mariners
and provide for the defence of the ship; the third went
to the mariners. (4) The commonest system with small
ships was this. The net profits were divided between
ship and mariners in equal moieties; but the ship's half
gave the captain a part equal to what he got from the
mariners' half, and it gave another part to be divided
among the higher officers.[1] The mariners' food under
this system was payable out of the gross profits before
division.

The Mariner's Pacotille.

There is one other point in connexion with the remuneration of mariners. In certain cases the mariner
was entitled to carry a limited quantity of goods free of
freight. In the Statutes of Ragusa there are obscure
allusions to what is called a paraspodia (VII, 29) or para-
spodium (VII, 53). The word appears under the form

[1] The system of *arruolamento a parte* is gradually disappearing in
Italy. See Inchiesta Parlamentare sulla Marina Mercantile, 1881-2,
vol. VII, p. 217, where its loss is regretted.

THE MARINERS

παρασπόρια in Labbé's Veteres Glossae Verborum Iuris (ed. 1606, p. 57 ; ed. 1682, p. 17), as equivalent to κανστρέσια, ἰδιόκτητα. It denotes perhaps an allowance of space which was given to the mariners *ad partem* as a community and in which they are entitled to carry goods free of freight. It apparently does not refer to an allowance given to the individual mariner.

At Zara, a mariner, however hired, was entitled to carry free a limited quantity of goods. This was called his miliare or caricum. The mariner could not put a man in lieu of goods, nor could he sell his right to put in goods except to the patronus or by his consent. If there was no room on board for the mariner's miliare, he was entitled to the freight receivable in respect of the goods which took its place (IV, 67). The mariner's miliare became in this case a percentage of the freight, and might be increased if the shipowner took additional freight. If the shipowner took goods from a vessel in distress, the mariners *ad certum viagium* were entitled to an extra payment proportioned to their miliaria in respect of the additional goods carried (IV, 53). If the ship-owner hired mariners *ad viagium* to go outside the gulf and then changed his voyage, they were entitled to an extra payment proportioned to their miliaria (IV, 54 ; cf. St. Spalat., VI, 55).[1]

Venetian statutes recognize the existence of cargo belonging to mariners (St. Tiep., A, 17 = St. Zeno, 50). At Ancona, a miglaro or cantaro or more than one might be yielded to a mariner. He might load it himself or yield or let it to another (St. Ancon., 52) Under the Consulate of the Sea, a mariner was entitled to the free carriage of goods to the value of half his wages (cc. 86, 88). He could not let his right to a merchant or other mariner (c. 89). In Targa's time the mariner's free allowance, his portata or canterata, might equal his wages (p. 64). Targa

---

[1] As to the regulations of the northern codes on this point, see a note of Pardessus, I, p. 336, n. 3 and the Articles of Queensborough of A. D. 1375 in Pard., IV, p. 206 sqq.

seems to confine the privilege to a mariner hired by the voyage (p. 356).

The Mariner's Duties.

The enactments which deal with the mariner's duties may be arranged under the following heads:—

1. The mariner's duties are not necessarily confined to the actual voyage. It was convenient for the captain to be sure of his men some time before the voyage began. Hence, from the moment that the engagement was entered into, the mariner had to hold himself in readiness. Some statutes forbid him to leave the city from which the ship is to sail (St. Zara, IV, 66 = St. Spalat., VI, 42; Consulate of Sea, 109). In all cases he is bound to turn up as soon as he is summoned; at Pisa a crier went round town to collect the mariners when a ship was about to start (Table of Amalfi, 1, 2, 50; St. Pera, IV, 34; St. Pisani, III, p. 387, 388, 514).

2. In most ports there was a class of persons whose business it was to load and unload ships (their names in Pegolotti, p. xix; Mas Latrie, Introduction, p. 191), and who no doubt resented, even with knives, any interference with their privileges and profits. It is for this reason that as a rule the loading and unloading of cargo is not among the mariners' duties. (It is in St. Zara, IV, 68, 69; St. Lesina, V, 5; St. Ancon., 9.) According to the Consulate of the Sea, 29, they are only bound to load and unload where there are no porters. But the mariners are bound to ballast the ship, to put in the owner's wood, &c. (Authorities, *supra*; Consulate of Sea, 110, 135, 136).

3. In some statutes the mariner is bound to take an oath on making his engagement (St. Zeno, 39, 40; St. Zara, IV, 14; St. Ancon., 8; Barcelona Ordinance, 11, in Pard., V, 342; Consulate of Sea, 16, 109). At Venice the oath is elaborate. The mariner swears not only to perform his duties on the ship, but also to inform the public authorities in cases of certain infractions of the statutes.

4. The mariner during the voyage must obey the person

clxxvi

in command—patronus or nauclerus as the case may be
(St. Ragus. VII, 34 = St. Pharae, V, 7; Consulate of
Sea, 117).

5. The mariner must not go on shore (St. Ancon. 31;
Consulate of Sea, 121) or sleep on shore (Table of Amalfi,
56; St. Massil. IV, 17; Consulate of Sea, 129) at intermediate stations without the consent of the person in
command, and the person in command can only give
leave to a limited number. A certain proportion of the
ship's company must always remain on board (St. Tiep.
D, p. 75; St. Zeno, 32, 33, 34; St. Massil. IV, 17; Barcelona Ordinance, 3, in Pard. V, p. 340). These provisions
throw light on c. 26 of our Sea-law which deals with
the responsibility of ναύκληροι or ναῦται who sleep off the
ship.

6. The Sea-law lays down (c. 31) that where there is
a shipwreck the captain and the sailors are to help in
salving. This rule is repeated in more precise terms in
many statutes. At Zara and Spalato the mariners must
remain by the ship until it is repaired or brought to its
destined place (St. Zara, IV, 56 = St. Spalat. VI, 56). At
Venice they must remain by the ship for fifteen (St. Zeno,
40, 92), at Trani for eight days (Ordin. Trani, 1). At
Venice they receive three per cent. on what they recover
(St. supra).

7. Several statutes lay down the conditions under which
a mariner may leave after he has engaged himself. At
Trani he may leave, (a) if he is made patrone (b) or
nochiero of another ship, or (c) if in the voyage in
question he makes a vow to go to Saint James or the
Holy Sepulchre or Rome (Ordin. Trani, 11). At Amalfi
he may leave if he has an opportunity of bettering himself by taking a position which he has never held before
(Table of Amalfi, 41). The Consulate of the Sea deals
with the subject twice: c. 110, 111. According to Twiss,
c. 110 refers to leaving the ship in the course of the
voyage, and c. 111 to leaving it before the voyage has
begun. This is not clear. It is more probable that we

have here two recensions, as is so frequently the case in the Consulate. According to c. 111 the mariner may leave to take a wife, fulfil a vow, or get a better position.

8. Several statutes give a list of the offences for which a mariner may be dismissed. The Consulate (c. 80) mentions theft, quarrelling, repeated disobedience, or perjury. The Ordinance of Trani (c. 9) omits disobedience and perjury, and adds blasphemy and debauchery (*luxuria*). At Ancona the mariner may be dismissed if he is a thief, traitor, blasphemer, quarrelsome, fraudulent (the MSS. vary between *baractiero* and *bugiarone*), or disobedient (c. 54).[1] [Cp. Off. Gazarie, 412.]

So much for the mariner's duties: it cannot always have been easy to enforce them. The Sea-law, though it refers more than once to misdeeds by sailors—theft, c. 2, 3, 38; Appendix D, I, III, IV; assaults, c. 5, 6, 7; desertion, Appendix D, I—and imposes punishments— corporal as well as pecuniary—never alludes to the existence of a disciplinary power either in the captain or in any committee of officers. Indeed it contemplates in several cases—see especially c. 8—that the crime is committed by the whole ship's company, captain included. The absence of discipline on board the mediaeval merchantman has already been referred to. The provisions which create a domestic forum for offences committed on board are very few.

At Spalato if a mariner makes a *rixa* or *litigium* without arms and without drawing blood, the patronus or nauclerius may whip him so as they do not use arms or draw blood (VI, 58). At Zara if a mariner makes a *rixa* or *litigium*, the patronus nauchlerii and proderii can punish the quarrellers at their discretion (IV, 58). At Pisa if a mariner makes a disturbance on board, the padrone and other officials can put him in irons, and if he resists they

[1] In Fynes Moryson's journey from Venice to Constantinople, the patron, at the beginning of the voyage, makes a solemn oration to the mariners, admonishing them 'to refraine from swearing, blasphemie, and sodomie, under great penaltie' (Itinerary, I, p. 210).

can strike him with hand or stick, even to drawing blood (Breve dell' Ordine del Mare, c. 49 ; Bonaini, III, p. 513). At Genoa the patronus is to carry him 'ligatum et immuselatum' before the nearest magistrate (Off. Gazarie, 415).

TRANSPORTATION OF GOODS

Of the most important maritime contract, the contract for the transportation of goods, there are fortunately not a few specimens in existence, ranging over a long period of time. An abstract of two will form the best introduction to this subject.

Papyrus 948 of the British Museum (P. London, III, p. 219) is a private charter-party of A.D. 236. 1. X, captain of his own ship of a capacity of 250 ἀρτάβαι, lets it to Y for the voyage therein stated. 2. The load is to fill the whole ship. 3. The freight agreed upon is 100 drachmai of silver. X receives 40 on the spot and is to receive the remaining 60 on delivery of the cargo. 4. X will deliver the goods safe and uninjured by sea peril.[1] 5. X has two days to load the goods. 6. He is to remain four days at the port of discharge. If he is kept longer, he is to receive sixteen drachmai per diem (μεθ᾽ ἃς ἐὰν παρακατασχεθῇ λήμψεται ὁ κυβερνήτης ἡμερησίως δραχμὰς δεκάεξ ἑαυτῷ). 7. He is to provide sufficient sailors and the complete equipment of the ship (τοὺς αὐτάρκεις ναύτας καὶ τὴν τοῦ πλοίου πάσην ἐπιχρείαν[2]). The document is subscribed by X, who acknowledges receipt of the forty drachmai.

The other charter-party is given in Mas Latrie, Traités de Paix et de Commerce, Paris, 1866, at pp. 38 sqq. of the Text. It was made at Pisa on August 10, 1263, between

---

[1] The phrase is σῶα καὶ ἀκακούργητα ἀπὸ ναυτικῆς κακουργίας. Is this guarantee confined to acts of the mariners ? In a papyrus of A.D. 138–161 (P. London, II, p. 256) the phrase is : παραδώσω τὸν γόμον σῶον καὶ ἀκακούργητον τῷ ἐμαυτοῦ κινδύνῳ.

[2] The editors suggest ἐπιχορίαν, i.e. ἐπιχορηγίαν, but see my commentary p. 92.

A, B, and C, shipowners, and D, E, F, G, on behalf of themselves and other merchants. The terms are as follows :—

1. The shipowners will provide the ship in good condition and furnished with the tackle specified in the charter-party, thirty-six skilful mariners properly armed, including the nauclerius and scribanus, and six famuli or fantes.

2. The shipowners will set sail from Porto Pisano within ten days from the date of the contract. Before they set sail, they will receive the cargo from the merchants and will load it on board. They will also provide at their own expense lighters for bringing the cargo from Pisa to the ship.

3. Also, before they set sail, the shipowners will make their partners, the sailors, the stevedore, and the nauclerius take an oath to observe the stipulations of the contract.

4. The shipowners will carry the cargo at the customary freight, and will charge no freight for the merchants and their partners, or for their personal goods.

5. When the ship has reached Bugea, the shipowners will put the cargo on land and hand it over to the merchants ' per apertum scriptum ' as they received it.

6. The shipowners will carry no forbidden goods on board.[1]

7. Within ten days from the time when the ship reaches Bugea, the shipowners will begin to load and will load within a month the cargo received from the merchants to the extent of 2500 cantaria. There follow the names of the merchants with the number of cantaria which each provides.

The third deck and the upper poop are to remain free for the merchants and for their personal goods.

8. A price is fixed for freight *per cantarium*. Certain goods—small in amount—are to be brought back gratis for charitable purposes.

9. The cargo is to be brought to the ship at the expense

---

[1] i. e. no goods exposing the cargo to confiscation.

of the merchants. The shipowners will load and stow it properly.

10. The shipowners will receive the cargo on board 'per apertum scriptum'. A weigher appointed by the parties and paid by ship is to weigh the cargo. The ship's scribanus is to write the weight in the ship's cartularium.

11. The scribanus, nauclerius, and camerarius are to swear upon the evangels to maintain the ship, its tackle, and cargo. If in stowing the cargo, wool or sheepskins are compressed beyond a certain amount, their freight is diminished.

12. As soon as the cargo is loaded, the shipowners will start for Porto Pisano and unload the cargo there at their own expense. The shipowners will not demand average for any part of the ship's tackle either on the voyage out or in.

They will not demand freight except for goods delivered to the merchants at Porto Pisano.

13. If a mariner is missing on the voyage, the shipowners will recover him without average ; and they will do the same if part of the tackle is lost or injured. They will ensure that three-fourths of the mariners and the nauclerius remain by the ship until it is completely unloaded. They will have the goods of the merchants written in the ship's quaternus and will restore them *per scriptum.*

14. The shipowners will make the voyage directly from Porto Pisano to Bugea and back. They will not alter the voyage or make any other voyage or take any cargo (except so far as there is room on board) until the cargo loaded at Bugea has been brought back to Porto Pisano.

15. The shipowners swear to observe these terms, except so far as they are prevented by just impediment of God or tempest or except so far as D, E, F, G excuse them. If they fail, they are liable to a penalty of double and to damages.

16. D, E, F, G, on behalf of themselves and the other

merchants, agree to deliver the cargo within the prescribed time, and to pay the agreed freight to the shipowners or their agents or to one of them or to the camerarius of the ship, payment to one of them or to the camerarius being a discharge. Payment is to be made in currency or gold or silver. It is to be made within eight days from the unloading of the ship in Porto Pisano and the delivery of the cargo to the merchants or their agents. If cargo is delivered before payment of the freight, a *cautio* of a bank or banks is to be given for payment.

17. The merchants will observe these terms subject to just impediment of God or tempest or to a concession made (*parabola*) by the shipowners. In default they are liable to a penalty of double the freight and to damages.[1]

These documents indicate the order for treating the matters contained in this chapter. I shall deal (I) with the shipowner's duties in reference to the condition of the ship and of the ship's company, (II) with the receipt and loading of cargo, (III) with the payment of freight, (IV) with unloading, and (V) the shipowner's duty to restore the cargo as received, (VI) with breaches of the charter-party, whether wilful or non-wilful, and whether by the merchant or by the shipowner.

Condition of Ship and Crew.

I. No passage in the Sea-law deals explicitly with the obligation of the shipowner to provide the ship in good state, with its proper tackle and a sufficient number of skilful mariners. But in c. 11 merchants who wish to load great and valuable cargoes are recommended to make certain inquiries. These inquiries are (*a*) if the ship has all its tackle complete, (*b*) if it has sailors τοὺς ἀρκοῦντας ναυτικοὺς γοργοὺς γρηγοροῦντας, and (*c*) τὰ πλάγια μὴ παραλελυμένα. This chapter should be compared with a chapter in Pegolotti's Pratica della Mercatura (c. XXX, p. 132), in which he gives advice to merchants who are

---

[1] Pard. (VI, p. 36) gives from the Siete Partidas a Spanish form of charter-party of the thirteenth century.

about to load. They are to see that the ship is ' fresco e non vecchio', and that it is 'bene concio' and 'bene stagnato'. They are to see that it is well furnished with *alberi, antenne, sarte, agumine, vele*, and *ancore*. They are to see that there are weapons on board in sufficiency according as the voyage is in time of peace or in time of war. They are to see that the ship has a good and experienced *nocchiere di mare*—good and experienced *piloti*—and good and expert mariners and servitors (*fanti*), sufficient in numbers having regard to the size of the ship. Just as Pegolotti in his directions has in mind the ordinary charter-parties of his time, it may be inferred that the passage in our Sea-law is based on the regular forms of Byzantine charter-parties. A reference to mediaeval charter-parties and statutes will bring out some points of comparison and others of difference between the Byzantine and the mediaeval system. I deal separately (*a*) with the condition of the ship, (*b*) with its tackle and (*c*) with its mariners.

a. The only allusion in c. 11 to the condition of the ship is that the merchants should see that τὰ πλάγια are μὴ παραλελυμένα, i. e. that the ship is watertight. The charter-parties generally contain a provision, that the ship is to be *bene concia, calcata* (Mas Latrie, Traités, Documents, p. 39). The statutes are to the same effect. At Venice the ships are to be ' bene conzatas atque càlcatas de foris ' (St. Tiep. A, 1 ; St. Zeno, 1). At Ragusa they are to be ' bene aptatas et calcatas de foris ' (St. Ragus. VII, 1). At Cattaro they are to be ' bene acceptatas et calcatas a lateribus ' (c. 378, Pard. V, p. 97). At Ancona the *patrone* is to *calcare* and *conciare* the ship under the direction of the *nochiero* (St. Ancon. 4). Now to *calcare* a ship is to fill up with tow (*stoppa*) the fissures or seams in its woodwork (Capitolari delle Arti Veneziane a cura di G. Monticolo, vol. 2, pp. 214, 235 ; Boerio, s. v. *incalcar*). This is no doubt what the Sea-law expects to have done when it says that the sides are not to let in water. It is a common provision that all expenses of tow, pitch, &c.,

must be met by the shipowner (St. Tiep. A, 6 ; St. Zeno, 17 ; St. Zara, IV, 3 ; St. Cattaro, 378; St. Ragus. VII, 1).

b. In c. 11 the only reference to *masts* is in the word ἰστοκεραίαν. The ship should have a strong ἰστοκεραίαν. It seems unlikely that while there is a reference to the sail-yard there should be none to the mast, and the true reading is possibly ἱστὸν καὶ ἱστοκεραίαν. It is true that the word regularly used for mast in the Sea-law is καταρτία or κατάρτιον, but ἱστός is a more general expression.[1] The mediaeval charter-parties regularly provide that the ship shall have a certain number of masts (*arbores, alberi*) and sail-yards (*antennae, antenne*), and in some cases add that the masts shall be provided with various fittings, the exact meaning of which is doubtful (Mas Latrie, Documents, pp. 39, 122 ; Canale, II, pp. 342, 580–1 ; Amalric, 549, in Blancard, II, p. 91). The statutes which lay down rules as to the ship's tackle are to the same effect (St. Zeno, 7).

C. 11 refers to ἄρμενα, which are here evidently used in the sense of sails. The charter-parties provide as follows : 7 vele (Mas Latrie, Documents, p. 39), 3 of cotton and 1 of canvas (Canale, II, p. 342), 6 of cotton and 1 of canvas (Canale, II, p. 580), 6 of cotton (Canale, II, p. 381), 1 new artimonus in addition to 5 vella (Actes génois, II, p. 60), 5 vela of cotton (Amalric, 549, in Blancard, II, p. 91). The statutes of Venice and Ragusa contain minute provisions as to the number of sails which ships of different sizes were to carry and the materials of which they were to be composed (St. Tiep. A, 10; St. Zeno, 10, 11 ; St. Ragus. VII, 3 ; cp. Off. Gazarie, 341).

There is nothing in the mediaeval authorities which corresponds with the obligation on the shipowners to supply διφθέρας (as to which, see Commentary, p. 81).

C. 11 provides that the ship is to have ἀγκύρας τε καὶ σχοινία καννάβινα διάφορα. In c. 2 σχοινία τε καὶ καννάβια are included among the ship's tackle. There is a refer-

---

[1] ἱστός, τὸ μέγιστον ξύλον ἡ κατάρτιος λεγομένη ὑπὸ τῶν ναυτικῶν, Etym. Mag. 478, 23. See examples in Duc. s. v. κατάρτιον.

ence in c. 22 to ropes taken by the captain, and in
c. 46 to the ropes which attach the long-boat to the ship.
The charter-parties regularly provide that a ship shall
have so many anchors and so many anchor-cables (*gomene, agumine*), e. g. 15 anchors and 17 agumine (Mas
Latrie, Documents, p. 39), 20 new agumine in addition
to those wetted and 23 anchors (Mas Latrie, Documents,
p. 122), 4 anchors and 4 gomene (Canale, II, p. 342),
22 anchors in going and 25 in returning and 20 gomene
(Canale, II, p. 580), 8 new agumine in addition to 11
already there (Actes génois, II, p. 60), 16 anchors and
20 new gumene (Amalric, 549, in Blancard, II, p. 91),
22 anchors of iron and 28 gomene (Canale, II, p. 581).
There is sometimes allusion to other cordage (Canale, II,
p. 581 ; Amalric, 549).

The statutes of Venice (Zeno, 8) and of Ragusa (VII, 3)
provide that a ship is to have so many anchors, so many
ropes, so many more new ropes kept coiled in reserve
(*in corcoma* or *in corhinam*, see Pard. V, p. 24 n.), and so
many guiding ropes (*indagarii*). The number of each of
these articles required increases with the size of the
ships. The Venetian statute also regulates (Zeno, 9)
the length and thickness of the hempen ropes which are
kept in coil.

C. 11 contemplates the existence on board of αὐχένες
ἐπιτήδειοι—tillers—and temones, timoni are frequently
referred to in the charter-parties, e. g. 2 temones (Mas
Latrie, Documents, p. 39), 2 timoni (Canale, II, p. 342),
2 timoni of oak (Canale, II, p. 581). Oak seems to have
been the regular material (Amalric, 648, in Blancard, II,
p. 134). C. 11 also refers to κάραβοι—barques (see also
c. 46). The charter-parties refer to one or more barques,
i. e. 1 barcha de parisclalmo, 1 gondula (Mas Latrie,
Documents, p. 39), 1 barca (Canale, II, p. 342), 1 big
barcha with sails and 2 with oars (Canale II, p. 581).
Sometimes a barque was hired to serve two galleys
(Amalric, 382, in Blancard, II, p. 14). The Statutes of
Venice prescribe (Tiepolo, A, 1 ; Zeno, 1) that the owners

INTRODUCTION

of ships must supply them with a barcha and a gondola.
The Statutes of Ragusa (VII, 1) and Cattaro (c. 378) only
prescribe a barcha.

The statutes impose heavy penalties where there is
any defect in the ship's tackle as prescribed (St. Tiep.
A, 46; St. Zeno, 14, 16; St. Ragus. VII, 4). They also
forbid an owner to sell any tackle except to buy better
or except to supply ships in distress, and even then he can
only sell with the consent of a majority of the merchants
and mariners (St. Zeno, 37; St. Zara, IV, 13; St. Spalat.
VI, 62).

c. C. 11 alludes to ναύτας τοὺς ἀρκοῦντας ναυτικοὺς γοργοὺς [1]
γρηγοροῦντας. The charter-parties generally specify that
so many mariners 'boni et sufficientes' are to be on board
(Amalric, 57, in Blancard, I, p. 286; Amalric, 382, in
Blancard, II, p. 14; Amalric, 968, in Blancard, II, p. 278;
Actes génois, II, p. 60; 'in arte maris edocti sufficienter
et convenienter armati,' Mas Latrie, Documents, p. 39).
Sometimes a certain proportion of servitors is provided
for (36 mariners and 6 famuli, Mas Latrie, Documents,
p. 39; 16 mariners and 2 famuli, Actes génois, I, p. 466;
55 mariners and famuli, Actes génois, II, Documents,
p. 42; 40 mariners and 5 famuli, Actes génois, II,
Documents, p. 60).

Under the Venetian statutes of Tiepolo and of Zeno
every ship of 200 milliaria is to have twenty mariners,
not counting soldiers and pilgrims and cooks. One more
mariner is required for every additional ten milliaria
(St. Tiep. A, 8-16; St. Zeno, 20). If a mariner dies or
leaves the ship, the owner must supply his place at the
first port (St. Zeno, 20).

Receipt and Loading of Cargo.

II. The next group of stipulations relates to the recep-
tion and loading of the cargo. The shipowner normally

[1] γοργοί may be compared with *gagliardi*, a Venetian term used
in the sixteenth century for sailors of special agility. Jal, Glossaire
nautique, s. v.

agrees to have his ship at the prescribed place and time
ready to load, to load the goods on board with dispatch,
and to pack them with a view to their safety and the
safety of the ship, not to carry cargo in excess of the
prescribed quantity, and not to carry cargo liable to
confiscation. The merchant normally agrees to supply
the cargo agreed upon and to have it ready for loading
at the prescribed place and time. The Sea-law contains
the following provisions on this subject.

C. 22 deals with the obligations of the ναύκληρος. Where
the merchant puts in the whole cargo in accordance with
the contract, the ναύκληρος is only to carry water, provisions, and ropes. If the ναύκληρος wishes to carry
additional cargo, he may only do so if there is room ; if
there is no room and the merchant protests, the ναύκληρος
is responsible if a case for jettison arises ; if the merchant
does not prevent him there is to be contribution.

Chapters 25, 28, and 29 all deal with delay by the
merchant in loading. C. 25 seems to mean this. A
period is fixed by the contract (ἡ προθεσμία) within which
the merchant is to load. When that period is over, the
merchant is allowed ten days' grace (ἡ δευτέρα προθεσμία)
during which he must feed the sailors. After the ten
days' grace is over, 'above all things let the merchant
make up the full freight and go away.' If the merchant
wishes to add a proportionate amount (ποσότης)—not
necessarily an equal amount—to the freight, let him do
so and sail as he pleases. Under c. 28, where the merchant
hinders the ship in the loading and the days of grace run
by, he is responsible for any injury to the ship. Under
c. 29, if the merchant does not provide the cargo at the
prescribed place and the days of grace run by, he is
responsible for any injury to the ship. If the days of
grace are not over when the injury happens there is to be
contribution.

The charter-parties generally fix a time within which
the loading is to take place—two days (P. London, III,
p. 219 ; see *ante*, p. clxxix), a week (Amalric, 374, in Blan-

card, II, p. 9), fifteen days (Amalric, 167, in Blancard, I, p. 335). In Actes génois (I, p. 451) the merchants agree to pay extra freight (400 instead of 300 bissantii) in case of a breach by them of any of the terms of the contract, including a stipulation to load within a certain time. Under the Ordinamenta of Trani (c. 25), where there is no provision in the contract, the merchant has eight days of good weather to load the ship. After that time the ship is at his risk, and the shipowner is entitled to a salary to be fixed by the local consuls.

The system under which the goods were loaded may be illustrated from the statutes of Venice. The merchant gives notice before bringing his goods alongside ; and the shipowner or his representative is to be there to receive them (St. Tiep. A, 17 ; St. Zeno, 50). The loading takes place at the shipowner's expense (St. Zeno, 50). The ship's scribanus writes down the goods, their number and weight, and any marks which the merchant has put upon them [1] (St. Tiep. A, 17 ; St. Zeno, 42). The scribanus at the merchant's request gives him a copy of what he has written (St. Tiep. A, 17 ; St. Zeno, 42). Where the goods are packed up, the merchant may hand them over as *colli* without showing their contents, and in that case the shipowner is not responsible for any deterioration in quality (St. Tiep. A, 17). If the merchant shows their contents before handing them over, the shipowner must restore them as they were received (St. Tiep. A, 17).

The shipowner must have a weighing machine, and weigh the goods, where it is possible. Where they have not been weighed, the weight is fixed by agreement between shipowner and merchant (St. Tiep. A, 17 : St. Zeno, 31, 43).

The copy from the ship's book which the scribanus gives to the merchant is the *apertum scriptum* of the

---

[1] As to the merchant's marks, see Scriba, 644, col. 514, ' res ansaldini hoc signo sunt insignite Ā. res Wilielmi hoc G. res nostre hoc IK '; Scriba, 1321, col. 889 ; Breve Curiae Maris of Pisa 52, in Bonaini, III, p. 391.

charter-parties (Mas Latrie, Documents, p. 39). To trace the steps by which this document turned into a negotiable instrument is not within the scope of this Introduction (see Goldschmidt, Geschichte, pp. 342, 343).

Payment of Freight.

III. The shipowner stipulates to carry the cargo at the agreed freight, and the merchant to pay it at the time, to the persons and in the currency agreed upon. The Sea-law gives no answer to the question on what principles the freight was determined, but the charter-parties and statutes enable us to illustrate the various systems which prevailed.

1. Where the merchants travelled with the cargo, no charge was made for carrying either them or their personal belongings. This applied not only where the cargo was on board but also where the ship was sent out in ballast to the port of loading (Mas Latrie, Documents, p. 39; Amalric, 167, in Blancard, I, p. 335 ; see also *ante*, p. cxl).

2. The ship might be let as a whole for an aggregate price and either for a voyage or by the month (Pièces Commerc. Div. 74 in Blancard, II, p. 443), or the merchant might arrange with the shipowner to carry certain specified goods at a fixed price (Amalric, 978, in Blancard, II, p. 285).

3. In some cases goods were charged a percentage of their value for freight. This applied chiefly to goods of great value in small compass—silks, goods in chests, silver, &c., or to transport in armed galleys (Pegolotti, pp. 140, 141 ; St. Ancon. 39 = Pegolotti, p. 154).

4. In some cases the payment was made in kind, i. e. so much of the cargo carried (L. Pisano, pp. 186, 276).

5. In most cases a merchant who hired a ship or part of a ship could not tell beforehand what goods he was going to load on board. This was especially the case where the goods were to be loaded abroad. Everything depended on the turn of the market. All the merchant

could do was to take either the whole ship or so much space on board for the carriage of his goods. The capacity of the ship or the space so taken was reckoned in certain ideal measures, and the merchant agreed to pay so much for every unit of the measure in question which he took. In the Sea-law (as in the Roman empire) the measure is a μόδιος (c. ις'); at Venice a milliarium or cantarium; at Ragusa a miliarium or centenarium (St. Ragus. VII, 39–41); at Ancona usually a mesta (St. Ancon. 39), but sometimes a cantaro; at Marseille a quintale (Amalric, 167, in Blancard, I, 335 ; Amalric, 374, in Blancard, II, 9).

Now, where goods are transported by sea, the freight is in substance determined mainly by the space which they take up; their weight is a secondary consideration. One would expect therefore that, where the capacity of a ship for cargo is stated, the capacity should be stated in terms of cubic measurement, and that, where a merchant hires part of a ship, he should be said to hire so many cubic feet or whatever the corresponding cubic measure may be.

But in mediaeval charter-parties and maritime codes this is not the case. In them the capacity of a ship is always stated in the terms of measures which on land are measures of weight; and where a merchant hires part of a ship, he hires so many pounds of weight or whatever the corresponding measure may be.

It is obvious that, where a measure of weight is taken to determine the capacity of a ship and where goods pay freight according to weight, the measure must suffer a sea change in coming on board. A ton of feathers cannot be compressed into the same space as a ton of lead. The difficulty is got over in the statutes by elaborate tables of equivalence ; tables which say, in short, that two pounds or three pounds of one thing shall for the purpose of calculating the freight be deemed equal to one pound of another. These tables require explanation.

The capacity of a ship for cargo was originally determined by the quantity which it would hold of the commodity which formed the staple export from the ship's home port. This point is illustrated by an interesting passage of Leonardo Pisano. He has been describing a method of reducing one weight into another. 'This method,' he says (p. 117), 'is very useful in loading ships, when they are loaded with different commodities. The loading varies with the diversity of their weight' (I read *habet modum* for *habent modum*). 'For example, ships which are loaded in Gerba are loaded by cantaria of skins. Now, since there are loaded' (for *ponderentur* I read *honerentur*) 'in the same ship diverse commodities, some of which are heavier and others lighter than skins, while some take up less and others more room, the following provision was made by the ancients. Of alum, which they load in the bottom of the ship, they put two cantaria for one of skins; of sheep-skins, on the other hand, because they are lighter than skins, they put two cantaria for three of skins; of rabbit-skins or of sugar they put one cantare for two of skins.

'In the same way ships which are loaded in Sicily are loaded according to the weight of a collus; and a collus contains one hundred rotuli. They put three cantaria of copper in a collus; of cotton they put one cantare and one-third. Ships which are loaded at Alexandria are loaded by sportatae of pepper, and the sporta is counted at 100 rotuli. The different kinds of commodities are reduced to this sportata in accordance with certain provisions, which it is not necessary to mention; because any one can ask about it when he finds it necessary.'

This passage explains the enigmatical tables of equivalence which are found in various statutes.[1]

These tables inform the merchant who hires so many

---

[1] For instance, in the Statutes of Ragusa, VII, 38-41; Stat. of Tiepolo, C. 2; Stat. Zeno, 103-10; St. Ancon. del Mare, 39, with which compare Pegolotti, pp. 154, 155. See also as to Alexandria, Pegolotti, p. 58 (with which compare a corrupt passage in the Italian version of the Consulate of the Sea, c. 43), and as to Naples, Pegolotti, p. 189. In Naples the unit is one hundred salme of grano.

sporte or milliaria or cantaria or salme or whatever the weight may be, how much of each class of commodity he is entitled to put in in consequence. They do not override special contracts between the merchant and the shipowner; they only operate in the absence of a special contract.

The principle which I have stated above will be made clearer by an example. Let us take sugar. Pegolotti deals with the packing of sugar in two places (pp. 311–13, 364). There were four ways of packing sugar in the middle ages.

Firstly, loaf sugar might be loaded on board ship *a rinfuso*, without being put in a chest (*cassa*) or a barrel (*botte*). Where the loaf was large, it was put in a palm-leaf hat and covered with a palm-leaf covering, and the two were sewed together. It was wrapped round with canvas on which the merchant put his mark. Where the loaf was small, two had one palm-leaf covering. In such a case, if the freight of the sugar was 40 soldi the cantaro, the freight of the sugar, with its wrappings (*invoglie*), came to 42½ soldi the cantaro.

Secondly, loaf sugar might be packed in barrels. No canvas was used; but dry leaves of sugar cane were put in to preserve the sugar and keep it from shifting. Where the sugar net cost 40 soldi for freight, the tare of the wrappings and of the barrels added 33 to 40 per cent.

Thirdly, where the sugar was in very big loaves, it was generally packed in chests. The chest was wrapped outside with cotton, and corded canvas was put on the outside. The tare in this case came to 26⅔ per cent.

Fourthly, sugar dust was made in loaves, but was less cooked and therefore crumbled. The loaf was cut away until it made a cube, and sixteen cubes were then put into a chest which was covered with canvas and corded with a great rope. The tare here came to 17 per cent.

Compare this with the rules laid down in the maritime codes. Under the Statutes of Tiepolo, sugar in hats without chests (Pegolotti's first system) and sugar dust in sacks (not mentioned in Pegolotti) are counted two cantaria for one of imbolium.[1] On the other hand, sugar in chests is counted as imbolium (St. Tiep. C. 2). That is to say, sugar in chests took up roughly twice as much space in proportion to its weight as sugar in hats. The only difference made in the Statutes of Zeno is that in the case of sugar in chests, three cantaria equal two cantaria of imbolium, i. e. it evidently was found to take up less space than had been thought (St. Zeno, 105, 108).

The rule laid down by the Statutes of Zeno, under which four cantaria of sugar dust in sacks would go for the same freight as three cantaria of sugar in chests, is substantially confirmed by a statement of Pegolotti (p. 140) that sugar dust in chests pays 22 soldi grossi *per migliaio* in an armed galley from Venice to Flanders, while sugar in barrels pays 30 soldi.

The Statutes of Ancona only deal with sugar so far as freighted from Cyprus (c. 39). Their provisions are given both in a passage of Pegolotti (p. 155) and in the editions of the statute. According to these, sugar dust in chests (*casse*) or in barrels (*botte, caratelli*) was freighted at the rate of two cantaria for one cantaro of cotton, which formed the ideal measure. Sugar in loaves, on the other hand, made up without chests or barrels, was freighted *cantaro per cantaro*. This differs from the rule in the Venetian statutes—perhaps because the loaves of sugar from Cyprus were particularly liable to break (Pegolotti, p. 364), and therefore required more room.

It is to be observed that for the purpose of calculating freight the sugar is weighed with its covering, *lordo di tara*.[2] Pegolotti says (p. 313) that the Provenzali in all their contracts contract to pay freight only for the merchandise *netto di tara*, and pay no freight for the wrappings, chests, or barrels in which the merchandise is

---

[1] As to the meaning of *imbolium*, see *ante*, p. clvii.

[2] An equivalent phrase is *incama(e)rata*, Scriba, 1323, col. 890 ; Amalric, 48, in Blancard, I, p. 283 ; Amalric, 528, in Blancard, II, p. 81, and often in the statutes.

contained. Other people, however, he says, pay for the weight of the merchandise with all its *tara*.

6. Where the merchant puts on board more goods than he is entitled to, he must pay for the excess, under some statutes, twice the rate which he pays on the rest of his goods (St. Ragus. VII, 40 ; St. Zara, IV, 30), under others, twice the highest rate which is payable on the ship (St. Zeno, 60).

The Sea-law nowhere lays down explicitly the times at which and proportions in which freight was payable, but it is possible from a consideration of several of its provisions to gather what was the custom on the subject. There are frequent references to τὰ ἡμίναυλα, τὰ ἥμισυ τοῦ ναύλου, τὰ ἥμισυ ναῦλα—all of which phrases seem to have the same meaning. It is possible that they do not denote an exact half of the freight, but merely a variable proportion. C. 20 is reserved for future consideration, as it deals with penalties for breach of contract. From c. 24 it is clear that τὰ ἥμισυ ναῦλα were paid at or before the beginning of the voyage. C. 27 is to the same effect. It refers to a ship which is on its way to be loaded. If it is lost in a storm, the captain is to retain τὰ ἡμίναυλα. Nothing is said as to ἡμίναυλα in the case where the ship is lost through the carelessness of the crew or captain. Possibly the provision as to the ἡμίναυλα applies to both cases. C. 32 appears to be a repetition of c. 27. C. 30 lays down that, where the ship is wrecked with the merchant's goods, he must provide τὰ ἡμίναυλα in accordance with the contract. This phrase probably does not mean that he is bound to pay any freight which he has not paid, but simply that he cannot recover freight already paid. C. 33 seems to mean no more than that, where the merchant has unloaded his goods, the captain is entitled to the whole freight—τὸ ναῦλον εἰς πλῆρες. The merchant is also bound to pay the whole freight where the goods are transferred to another ship (c. 42, but see p. ccviii) or where they are injured by bilge, although in the latter case the captain must make good the injury (c. 44).

The Sea-law refers once to an advance by way of loan of a portion of the freight; with regard to this, the provisions of the contract are to prevail (c. 32).

The charter-parties present wide diversities as to the times at which and proportions in which freight was payable. No doubt the credit and reputation of the hirer accounted in great measure for these diversities. Crusaders seem to have been looked on with suspicion. The cases may be arranged as follows:—

(a) A proportion, not always half, is paid at or before the beginning of the voyage and the remainder at the end. In the charter-party of A.D. 236 the freight is 100 drachmai; 40 is paid on the execution of the contract, the balance on delivery of the goods (P. London, III, p. 219). Freight 150 l.; 100 l. paid before the execution of the contract; the balance at the end of the voyage (Amalric, 106, in Blancard, I, p. 306). Freight 6 l.; 1 l. paid on the execution of the contract, 5 l. at the end of the voyage (Amalric, 922, in Blancard, II, p. 256). Two-thirds on the execution of the contract, the remainder on demand by the shipowner (Actes génois, II, p. 43). Ship sent to be loaded: one-half on the loading and the other half within fifteen days after unloading (Actes génois, II, p. 61).

(b) Sometimes the whole is made payable on the execution of the contract or at least before the departure of the ship (Amalric, 57, in Blancard, I, p. 286; Amalric, 393, in Blancard, II, p. 19; Amalric, 549, in Blancard, II, p. 92; Amalric, 777, in Blancard, II, p. 193; Amalric, 968, in Blancard, II, p. 278; Actes génois, I, p. 466).

(c) The cases are much rarer where nothing is to be paid until the expiration of the voyage (Amalric, 167, in Blancard, I, p. 336; Amalric, 978, in Blancard, II, p. 286).

The statutes naturally do not attempt to lay down any general rules on this matter. Their provisions in respect to payment of freight fall under three heads:—

1. They impose a penalty, e. g. 10 per cent. of the amount due, upon the merchant who does not pay

freight at the times fixed by the contract (St. Zeno, 81, 99).

2. They authorize the shipowner to secure payment of the freight due at the expiration of the voyage either by taking a pledge from the merchant or by retaining goods of his sufficient to cover the amount (St. Spalat. VI, 69; St. Zara, IV, 42 ; St. Ancon. 22).

3. They provide that a claim by the merchant against the shipowner in respect of loss of, or damage to goods, shall not prejudice the shipowner's right to recover the contract freight, on his giving security to the merchant to abide by the determination of the Court on the claim (St. Ancon. 22 ; Breve dell' Ordine del Mare of Pisa, 130 ; Procedure before Consuls of Barcelona, c. 27, in Pard., V, p. 386). This may be compared with c. 44 of the Sea-law.

The shipowner's default in certain cases relieves the merchant from his liability to pay freight.

(*a*) If the shipowner agrees to take goods which he cannot carry, he is bound not only to restore any freight which he has received in respect of them but also to pay the merchant the difference between the freight at which he agreed to carry them and the freight which the merchant has in fact been obliged to pay (St. Ancon. 51).

(*b*) The shipowner's contract to carry the freight is a contract to carry it to the journey's end. If he fails to do that, he is prima facie not entitled to any freight, and, if freight has been paid in advance, the merchant is prima facie entitled to recover it. This principle is laid down in a passage of the Digest (D. XIX, 2, 15, 6), which is repeated in the Basilica (LIII, A', νθ') and in other Byzantine law books. The Sea-law does not adhere to this principle. C. 27 and 32 seem to refer to a case where the ship is on its way to be loaded, and c. 30 refers clearly to a case where the ship has been loaded. In all these cases, if the ship is lost, the captain retains the ἡμίναυλα which have been paid. C. 32 seems to refer distinctly to the passage in the Digest. It says that if an advance has been made the contract of the parties is to prevail.

TRANSPORTATION OF GOODS

There are two ways in which these provisions might be reconciled. (a) It might be said that the passage of the Digest only refers to an advance made in addition to the normal part payment, i. e. if the merchant advances that part of the freight which under the contract is to be paid at the end of the voyage he may recover that, while he cannot recover the half (or whatever it may be) which was paid on the execution of the contract. (b) It might be said that the passage of the Digest refers to a case where the loss of the goods was due to the shipowner's default, while in the Sea-law the shipowner is throughout assumed to be free from responsibility. Neither of these reconciliations is satisfactory. The mediaeval authorities throw little light upon the subject. The Statute of Ancona seems to say (c. 58) that no freight is payable where cargo is lost, although freight already paid cannot be recovered back.[1]

Unloading of Cargo.

IV. The reciprocal obligations of the merchant and shipowner with respect to unloading varied with the provisions of the charter-party, and, in default of such provisions, with the custom of the port. The shipowner is under the obligation of delivering the cargo to the merchant and the merchant of taking delivery; but there was naturally no uniform practice as to where delivery was to be made.

Where the goods were taken off the ship in lighters,[2] as was generally the case, the merchant seems to have been obliged as a rule to provide the lighters, and to bring them to the ship; while the shipowner was under the obligation of bringing the goods up from the hold and loading them on to the lighters (St. Zeno, 50).[3]

---

[1] As to payment of freight in respect of things jettisoned, see hereafter, p. cclxxvi.

[2] The duties of lightermen are laid down minutely in Breve Curiae Maris of Pisa, c. 83.

[3] The Ordinamenta of Trani seem to lay down (c. 17) that where the shipowner has unloaded merchandise into a *barcha* his responsibility for it ceases.

INTRODUCTION

Under the Statutes of Venice, Zara, and Spalato (which may be taken as specimens), when the shipowner had merchandise ready at the ship's porta, he was to give notice to the merchant, and the merchant had to take delivery on that or the following day. He was liable to pay the shipowner a sum either fixed or varying with the quantity of goods for every day's delay, except in case of storm or unless the goods were damaged (St. Zeno, 52; St. Zara, IV, 22; shorter form in St. Spalat. VI, 64). A time was fixed by the public authority within which a ship had to be wholly unloaded, and the shipowner who failed to unload within the time was fined (St. Zeno, 85; St. Zara, IV, 36).

Duty to restore the Cargo.

V. In dealing with the shipowner's obligation to restore the merchants their property at the end of the voyage, it is necessary to distinguish between (a) merchandise and (b) personal effects of merchants, e. g. gold, silver, and precious stones.

(a) The authorities relating to merchandise may be arranged under three heads: (i) the shipowner's liability for cargo which he fails to return, (ii) his liability for injuries done to cargo during the voyage, (iii) his liability for injuries done to cargo in loading or unloading it.

(i) The Sea-law does not deal with the shipowner's liability to restore the cargo. The reason no doubt is because it is dealt with fully in the Basilica, which simply paraphrases the provisions of the Digest set out above (p. clix). In the Pisan charter-party of A.D. 1263 the shipowners promise to restore the merchants their goods *per apertum scriptum* as they have received them (*ante*, p. clxxxi), but the insertion of such an obligation in the charter-party must in most cases have been unnecessary, as it was generally provided for by statute.

Some statutes speak as if the shipowner's obligation was absolute provided that the goods have been written by the scribanus in his quaternus or cartularium (St.

Ragus. VII, 6; St. Phara, V, 1; St. Pera, V, 14; St. Massil. IV, 26, p. 127; C. Tortosa, IX, 27, 9. The Ordin. Trani, 16, speak as if the scrivano was personally liable). In other statutes the shipowner is excused in case of violence, fire, tempest, or jettison (St. Tiep. A, 17; St. Zeno, 51; St. Zara, IV, 21; St. Spalat. VI, 63; C. Tortosa, II, 17, p. 97). According to the Venetian statute of Zeno (c. 48) extending that of Tiepolo (A, 17) the shipowner is not responsible for camlets or silks loaded on the upper deck, if placed there by consent of the merchant.

(ii) The Sea-law speaks on several occasions of ἀντλία and its consequences. C. 34 deals with a ship which carries ὀθόνη or βέστις. If the ship lets in water (ὑπεραντλήσῃ) the captain is to inform the owners of cargo in order that they may bring up their goods. If the passengers give notice to the captain and he fails to take precautions, the captain and crew are liable. On the other hand, if the captain and crew give notice to the cargo owners and they fail to take precautions, the captain and crew are not liable. C. 38 deals with a corn-ship. If there is a gale, the captain is to supply skins and the sailors are to work at the pumps. If they are remiss and the cargo is wetted by the ἀντλία, the sailors are fined. If the cargo is injured by the gale, the loss is borne by the captain and sailors in conjunction with the merchant. C. 44 provides that if the cargo is injured by a storm there is to be contribution. If it is injured by ἀντλία, the captain is to deliver the goods ξηρὰ μέτρῳ καθὼς παρέλαβεν, i. e. he must make up for any deficiency in quality or quantity.

The mediaeval authorities are to the same effect. It has already been stated (p. clxxxiii) that it is the shipowner's duty to see that the ship is well *calcata*. Many statutes lay down that, if any damage arises to cargo through bad *calcatura*, the shipowner is liable unless he can prove that the damage arose through the storm (*per fortunam temporis*) (St. Ragus. VII, 6; St. Tiep. A, 17; St. Phara, V, 1). This strictly speaking is illogical, though the meaning is clear. Others more correctly lay down that, if the cargo is damaged by bad *calcatura*, the shipowner is absolutely liable (St. Spalat. VI, 45 ; St. Zara, IV, 74 ; St. Ancon. 4, beginning). Others again lay down that where cargo is injured by water the shipowner is liable ; but most add that he can relieve himself from liability by proving that it was wetted in putting out a fire or through storm (St. Zeno, 53 ; St. Zara, IV, 23 ; St. Spalat. VI, 65 ; St. Pera ,V, 13 ; C. Tortosa, IX, 27, 20, 21). The Consulate of the Sea indulges as usual in hair-splitting distinctions (cc. 19-21). It also deals with injury to cargo from rats (cc. 22, 23)—a point not alluded to by earlier authorities. Some statutes go into great detail as to the process for estimating damage done to goods (St. Zeno, 53 ; St. Zara, IV, 23 ; Breve Curiae Maris of Pisa, c. 46).

(iii) Some statutes also impose a liability upon the shipowner for injuries done to merchandise in the process of loading and unloading it (St. Zeno, 54 ; St. Zara, IV, 24 ; St. Ancon. 53).[1]

(b) The Sea-law deals with personal effects of passengers both in Part II and Part III. Chapters ιδ' and ιθ' are repeated in almost identical language in chapter 13. Chapters ιδ' and ιε' speak only of gold and silver. Chapter 13 mentions gold, silver, or anything else. The provision would no doubt include pearls or precious stones. The chapters provide that the captain is not responsible for such effects of a passenger unless they have been deposited with him ; but the captain, sailors, and possibly the other passengers are to clear themselves by oath. The doctrine here laid down apparently prevailed

---

[1] I may point out a curious misunderstanding. The words in the Venetian statute are ' de quolibet sacco banbacii ... quod de nave cum discaricabitur extractum fuerit per pilum'. Pard. (V, p. 41, n. 2) presumes ' qu'il s'agit de l'extraction par le moyen de leviers ou autres moteurs'. He takes back this view later (VI, p. 612, n. 1). The learned Sacerdoti, however, in his glossary to St. maritt. Venez. explains *pilum* as ' leva od altro motore'. That the words *extrahi per pilum* mean 'to have its wrappings torn ' is shown both by the language of St. Zara, IV, 24, and by the corresponding provision of St. Ancon. 53.

through the middle ages. In the Assempre of Fra Filippo of Siena (Siena 1864, c. 47, p. 178) there is a story of a wine merchant who adulterated his wine and made large gains thereby. He goes on board ship carrying his property in a sealed bag. The captain tells the passengers as they arrive 'Whoever has money is to commend it to me (*me gli accomandi*) and give it me to keep; otherwise let him keep it at his own risk and fortune'. The wine merchant puts the bag on a bench in front of the captain. It is seized by a monkey, who carries it up to the masthead, opens it, takes out the coins one by one and smells them. After smelling he throws into the sea the coins which represent the dishonest profits, while he lets those fall on the deck which represent the wine merchant's original capital.[1]

Breaches of the Contract.

VI. A contract for the transportation of goods by sea has this peculiarity, that its execution is often interrupted or made impossible by causes quite beyond the control of the parties. Hence the distinction is in this case particularly important between (A) wilful and (B) non-wilful breaches of the contract.

Wilful Breaches of Contract.

A. Various breaches and their consequences have been already considered in dealing with the obligations prescribed by the charter-party. But there are some general considerations, which apply to all breaches of the charter-party, whether by the merchant or by the shipowner, and which are most fitly dealt with together.

The parties to a contract may leave to the general law the determination of what shall happen if a provision of the contract is broken. They may, and generally do,

---

[1] The monkey is an instrument of divine justice in a very similar story in *Le Novelle Antiche*, ed. Biagi, Firenze, 1880, No. 133, p. 129.

prefer to settle the question for themselves, by imposing a penalty upon the transgressing party for the benefit of the other.

Chapter 20 of the Sea-law, after laying down that contracts for the hire of a ship are not valid unless they are in writing and subscribed by the parties, goes on to say that they may add penalties, if they wish (as to the word ἐπιτίμια see the Commentary). It then provides what is to happen if they do not add penalties and if there is a breach of contract by either of them. The text here is corrupt. (1) In a certain event, the hirer is to give the half freight to the captain. (2) If the captain commits a breach of contract (ψεύσηται), he is to give the half freight to the merchant. (3) If the merchant wishes to take out the cargo, he is to give the whole freight to the captain.

There is another possible interpretation of this chapter. It might be said that ἐπιτίμια is used here not in the strict sense of penalties arising on a breach of contract, but in the sense of provisions, whether penal or otherwise, for the payment or repayment of freight due under the contract. In that case the chapter would run: (1) When the hirer provides the cargo, let him pay half the freight. (2) If the captain commits a breach of contract, he is to restore the half freight which he has received. (3) On taking out the cargo at the end of the voyage, the hirer is to pay the full freight.

The mediaeval charter-parties (like other contracts) contain as a rule a general penal clause. In Amalric, 106 (in Blancard, I, p. 307) only the hirers (who also supplied the crew) stipulate a penalty, which is made equal to the whole freight (two-thirds of which had been paid), and the payment of which does not relieve them from their obligations under the contract. In most cases both parties enter into the penal clause, and in addition give a pledge of all their goods present and future (e. g. Actes génois, I, p. 466). In one case the penalty is to be applied for a public purpose (Amalric, 57, in Blancard, I, p. 286).

TRANSPORTATION OF GOODS

In order to understand the equities which a shipowner would have against a merchant who wilfully neglected or refused to carry out his contract in whole or in part, it is necessary to bear in mind the mediaeval conditions of commerce. Where the expedition was a long one, there was generally a short period of time every year within which the voyage had to be undertaken in order that the ship might get home before winter set in. If the ship-owner did not get a cargo within that time, he might easily lose his opportunity for the whole season. A merchant who promised a cargo and delayed delivering it would probably prevent the shipowner from looking elsewhere until it was too late. There is therefore nothing inequitable in requiring a merchant who has been guilty of grave delay to indemnify the shipowner by paying him the whole freight. Even this would not always be a complete indemnity. The freight did not always represent the whole probable profits of the voyage. There would be in addition the profits derived from the traffic in goods belonging to the shipowner or shipowners; and casual profits arising from derelicts. It was therefore just that, if a merchant wished to retain his hold on the ship, he should be required to add a percentage to the agreed freight. Of course the other party to the contract is bound here, as in every case of contract, to use due diligence in minimizing the damages. The shipowner is bound, when he finds that one cargo fails him, to try to secure another; and, if he succeeds, the freight which he receives from that will on equitable principles operate to diminish either *pro tanto* or altogether the liability of the first merchant. The case is altogether different with vessels which go on short coasting voyages. If the merchant takes such a vessel and repudiates the contract before he has put his goods on board, there is no equity in making him pay the whole freight. The shipowner will probably get another fare in a few days' time and will be amply compensated for his enforced idleness by a moderate proportion of the original freight.

INTRODUCTION

Let us consider the regulations of the Sea-law in the light of these observations. Chapter 20 appears to lay down that, if the merchant wishes to take out his cargo, he shall give the whole freight to the captain. The natural meaning of these words is, if he wishes to take out his cargo before the voyage begins. Another interpretation is possible, as I have said (p. ccii), but this one is not only more probable in itself; it is also consistent with other passages. Chapter 25 appears to lay down that, if the merchant is guilty of undue delay in loading, he is liable to pay the whole freight (see p. clxxxvii). Chapter 23 is fortunately clear. Where the merchant agrees to provide a full cargo and does not, he pays freight on the deficiency. This rule accords completely with a passage of the Digest (XIV, 2, 10, 2) which is reproduced in the Basilica, LIII, A', ξβ'.

Chapter 24, on the other hand, contains a different rule. If the captain, after receiving the half freight, has set sail and the merchant wishes to return (ὑποστρέψαι), the merchant loses the half freight. On the other hand, if the captain commits a breach of contract, he is to restore the half freight and so much again.

It is perhaps not fanciful to hold that, while chapters 20, 23, and 25 refer to a case where the shipowner runs the risk of losing his whole voyage through the merchant's misconduct, chapter 24 refers to a case where the shipowner is fully indemnified if he is paid for the time when his ship is occupied.

The Ordinamenta of Trani contain provisions resembling those of c. 24. If the merchant refuses to give the cargo at all, he pays one-fourth of the freight (c. 7). If he insists on having his cargo back before the ship leaves harbour, he pays one-half of the freight (c. 6). If the ship starts and then returns, and the merchant takes out his cargo, he must pay the whole freight (c. 5). If a ship lets in water in course of loading, the merchants are not bound to go on loading (c. 29). If a ship is loaded, or in course of loading, and it is found out that there is a corsair about, the merchants are not entitled to have their goods back except on the terms of guaranteeing the ship's ransom (c. 32. This is very obscure).

Under the statute of Pera (VI, 7) a merchant must pay the whole freight if he wishes to unload the cargo after it has been loaded.

These provisions lay down a rule of thumb justice, which is only tolerable in small transactions, where an arbitrary assessment of damages saves the parties the trouble and expense of having them ascertained by the Court. In other statutes the matter is determined on strict principles of equity. At Ancona, if the merchant fails in whole or in part to load the cargo which he promised to load, he is bound to pay the whole freight, provided the shipowner leaves an empty space on board sufficient to hold the cargo in question (c. 51; see also c. 28). In the Constitutum Usus of Pisa, which is followed in the statute of Marseille, the true principles are stated in detail.

The shipowner has the ship ready at the appointed place and time. The merchant, without reasonable excuse, fails to load it. He is liable to pay the whole freight; but if the shipowner succeeds in letting the ship, the merchant is only liable to pay the difference, if any, between the freight which he agreed to pay and that which the shipowner actually got (Const. Usus, c. 28, in Bonaini, II, p. 913; St. Massil. IV, 8).

If the contract provides a penalty, the merchant must pay that so as it does not exceed twice the agreed freight (Const. Usus, *supra*).

The merchant is also liable for failure to load if the shipowner, although he is not at the appointed place at the appointed time, is there at a reasonable time thereafter. By reasonable time is meant such a time as will enable the merchant to bring back his cargo before the ensuing winter (Const. Usus, *supra*; St. Massil. IV, 8).

The Consulate of the Sea, as is its usual custom, deals with the matter in several groups of chapters which are inconsistent one with the other.[1] According to c. 38 where the merchant abandons the voyage before putting anything on board he must pay the shipowner's expenses in connexion with the voyage. If he abandons the voyage after having begun to load he pays half the freight. According to c. 39, where the merchant abandons the voyage before bringing his goods to the port of embarkation, he only pays the shipowner's expenses ; if he has brought his goods to the port of embarkation before he abandons the voyage, he pays one-third of the freight. If he abandons the voyage after having begun to load or after having loaded in full, but before the ship sets sail, he pays half the freight. If he abandons the voyage after the ship has set sail he pays the whole freight. C. 39 looks like a revised edition of c. 38, and both may be compared with C. Tortosa, IX, 27, 25, 26. According to c. 57 a merchant who puts on board less than he has agreed pays freight for the deficiency (cp. C. Tortosa, IX, 27, 37, p. 464).

So far I have spoken of breaches of contract by the merchant : it remains to speak of the shipowner's. Most of these have been already dealt with : there only remains his failure to provide ship or to provide space for the cargo. The Sea-law uses vague language in speaking of breaches of contract by the ναύκληρος. If he plays false (ψεύσηται) let him give the half freight to the merchant (c. 20). This can hardly mean that he is merely to give back the half freight which he has received. C. 24 is clearer. If there is a contract in writing and the ναύκληρος does not conform to it (ἄλλην ποιήσῃ) let him give back the half freight and as much again.

The legislations of Pisa and Marseille deal with the matter as follows. A shipowner who agrees to have a ship at a certain place by a certain time fails, through

---

[1] Until these groups have been separated, it is hopeless to make much use of the document for historical purposes. In the chapters dealing with freight, for instance, it is clear that c. 35 is continued by c. 60, and c. 36 by c. 59, and that cc. 35, 60 belong to a different group of customs from cc. 36, 59. See the observations of Pardessus, II, p. 83, n. 4.

wilful default, to reach the place at the time. If the contract contains a penalty, the shipowner must pay it up to the amount allowed by law. If there is no penalty, he is liable in damages to the merchant (Const. Usus, c. 28, in Bonaini, II, p. 914; St. Massil. IV, 8).

One point remains as to breaches of contract. It has already been said (p. xcvii) that the Sea-law follows Roman law in its doctrine of the arra. If a contract is accompanied by an arra, the party who has given the arra can escape all liability under it by abandoning the arra; the party who has received it can escape all liability by returning it with so much again. This rule must have some limit, but where it is to be put is not quite clear. Can the shipowner relieve himself in this easy way after the merchant has loaded his goods? Can the merchant relieve himself after the shipowner has prepared his ship to receive them? The rule would be highly inequitable unless it was confined to cases where nothing substantially has been done by the other party in execution of the contract.

The Statutes of Ragusa, which are followed by the Statutes of Curzola, discriminate between the function of the arra as binding the contract and its function as affording a method of relief from the contract. If the arra is a nominal sum, one folarus, the contract is binding and the merchant who abandons the ship except in case of death must pay the whole freight to the shipowner. If, on the other hand, the merchant gives more than one folarus by way of arra, the shipowner must content himself with the arra (St. Ragus. VII, 37; see also VIII, 17; St. Curzulae, I, c. 35, p. 15; II, c. 38, p. 36. The folarus, Gk. φόλλις, was a small copper coin. See Index, St. Ragus., p. 435).

The Constitutum Usus of Pisa, which is followed in substance by the Statute of Marseille, places the doctrine on a reasonable basis. Where an arra has been given, then, if the shipowner wilfully fails to supply the ship, the merchant may at his choice recover either the arra

INTRODUCTION

and so much again or the actual damages suffered. If
the merchant wilfully fails to take the ship, he is liable
for the actual damages suffered, up to the amount of the
whole freight, credit being given him for the arra which
he has paid (Const. Usus, c. 28, in Bonaini, II, p. 914 ; St.
Massil. IV, 9 ; see also A nalric, 968, in Blancard, II,
pp. 278, 279).

Non-wilful Breaches of Contract.

B. The Sea-law nowhere deals explicitly with the question what relieves a party to the contract from liability
for failure to carry out its terms—in other words, what
constitutes a *iustum impedimentum*. One chapter, however (c. 42), bears upon the subject. A ship springs a
leak, and the goods are taken out. The captain has two
alternatives. He can have his ship repaired and carry
the goods in it to the prescribed market, or he can
tranship the goods. There is a doubt as to the subject
of the last sentence in the chapter. Does it say that the
merchant is to pay the full freight, or that the captain is
to pay it ? If we insert ὁ ἔμπορος, which might easily fall
out after ἐμπόριον, it simply means that the merchant
is not relieved from his obligation to pay the freight by
the change of boats. If we supply ὁ ναύκληρος from the
conditional sentence or add it with some MSS., it must
mean that the captain is to pay the freight of the
substituted boat. In this case he might be mulcted in
the excess, if any, of what he pays over what he receives
(see a note of Pardessus, I, p. 326, n. 1). The Digest deals
in two places with the consequences of transhipping
goods, but only as regards the liability of the original
shipowner where the second ship is lost with the goods
(Dig. XIV, 2, 10, 1 ; XIX, 2, 13, 1). The original shipowner is justified in transhipping, according to Paulus,
'si nauis eius uitium fecerit sine dolo malo et culpa eius'
(Dig. XIV, 2, 10, 1).

What constitutes a *iustum impedimentum* must depend

on the circumstances, and the definitions which are sometimes given in the statutes (e. g. Const. Usus of Pisa, 28, in Bonaini, II, p. 914; St. Massil. IV, 9) cannot be extended beyond the particular case to which they are applied.

MARITIME LOANS

The six chapters in the Sea-law which deal with loans (cc. ιζ'–ιθ' of Part II, cc. 16–18 of Part III) are, perhaps, the most obscure among their obscure compeers. To deal with them at all we must understand the leading rules of classical law with regard to maritime loans. Questions relating to maritime loans fall under two heads : I, questions as between lender and borrower; II, questions as between different classes of lenders. Both these heads are dealt with in Roman law and in the Basilica; the Sea-law deals only with the first. I therefore confine myself to that.[1]

A maritime loan—as it existed during the period dealt with here—had some peculiarities which distinguished it from an ordinary loan. In an ordinary loan, if made for a legal purpose, the borrower is unconditionally bound to restore the amount lent, with or without interest, as the case may be. The destination of the money lent is immaterial to the lender. If the borrower builds a house with it and the house is burnt down, or buys slaves and the slaves run away, the lender's absolute right to repayment is in no wise affected. In a maritime loan the destination of the loan conditioned the right of the lender to be repaid. A maritime loan—in the jurisprudence of Greece, Rome, and the middle ages—was a loan made to a shipowner, or a merchant trading at

---

[1] The chief passages in Roman and Byzantine law dealing with priorities as against ship or cargo are : Dig. XX, 4, 5 pr.; 6, pr., 1; reproduced in Syn. Ambr. LIII, E', 10; Syn. Vent. LIII, V, 10; Syn. Major, LIII, V, ιγ', ιδ'. Priorities as regards distribution of assets are considered in Dig. XLII, 5, 26 reproduced in Epit. XVII, 13; Dig. XLII, 5, 34 referred to by Schol. ad Bas. XXIII, 1, 25.

sea, and made for the purpose of the maritime adventure. It was made, e. g., to build or buy or repair a ship, or pay seamen's wages, or buy a cargo to be put on board ship, or meet expenses connected with the cargo. Now the material on which the loan was expended, the ship or the cargo, was necessarily subject to maritime risk, and, as a rule, the borrower was not in a condition to repay the loan until the maritime risk had been run, and the ship or cargo or that into which the cargo had been converted was safe at home. If a man borrowed money to build, buy, or repair a ship, he could not, as a rule, repay the loan until the ship had earned freight. If he borrowed money to purchase cargo, he could not, as a rule, repay the loan until he had sold the cargo. Whether from kindness to the borrower or from some other reason, it was settled that in a contract of maritime loan the lender took the maritime risk; and this is the leading distinction between a maritime loan and other loans.

Although the terms in which the loan was expressed remained substantially the same from the age of Demosthenes till the thirteenth century, there are differences in the wording of the documents, which do not necessarily imply corresponding differences in the legal effect of the transaction. The application of the money lent is seldom referred to in the documents. In the Greek documents there is a hypothecation of ship or cargo, as the case may be, and the loan is made repayable upon the safe arrival of the subject hypothecated. Hence the loss or destruction of that, as it destroys the obligation, takes away any claim against the borrower personally or against his other property. In the mediaeval documents the loan is generally expressed to be repayable if the ship, or if the ship or the greater part of its cargo, arrives safe. There is sometimes, but not normally, a specific hypothecation.

In the documents, therefore, the loan often resembles an ordinary loan upon a contingency, and there is evidence that both in antiquity and the middle ages the forms of a maritime loan were made use of for contracts which were purely aleatory. There is nothing illegal prima facie in a purely aleatory contract of loan. There is nothing illegal in A lending money to B upon the terms of being repaid only on the happening of an event in which neither A nor B has any interest, pecuniary or moral. But such a contract must be clearly distinguished from contracts upon a contingency where the contingency is connected with the parties, e. g. a loan to be repaid only if the borrower receives a legacy, and still more must it be distinguished from contracts upon a contingency where the contingency is directly connected with the loan, as in the true maritime loan. With the maritime loan, repayment is contingent not merely upon the happening of an event which necessarily puts the borrower in funds to repay, but definitely upon the safety of that into which the money lent has been converted, the ship which it has repaired, the cargo which it has purchased.

Another distinction between the maritime loan and the ordinary loan has been already adverted to.

A loan may be accompanied by a pledge of property belonging, or to belong to, the borrower. Such a pledge does not prima facie affect the rights of the parties to the contract; it only affects the remedies of the lender. It is an additional security. If the personal remedy against the debtor proves fruitless, the creditor may (in some cases) retain the pledge in satisfaction of the debt, (in other cases) sell the pledge and pay himself out of the proceeds of sale. The right of resorting to the pledge belongs to the pledgee in preference to other creditors. The loss or destruction of the pledge does not prima facie diminish the creditor's rights; it only narrows the sphere of his remedies, and his personal right against the debtor remains as before.

But in a maritime loan, the existence of the obligation depends upon the continued existence of the property pledged or hypothecated till the expiration of the period during which the maritime risk is running. If ship or cargo, as the case might be, perished during the voyage, the lender not only lost his right to recover the amount secured out of ship or cargo ; he also lost all other rights against the borrower in respect of the loan. The loan was wholly extinguished.

Maritime Loans in Greece and Rome.

As regards classical Greece, two speeches of Demosthenes (Adv. Phormionem, Adv. Lacritum), and one attributed to him (In Dionysodorum), deal exclusively with this subject. In Adv. Lacritum a form of maritime loan is given. It is doubtful whether this is the actual document to which the speech refers.[1] It looks as if the writer had a model before his eyes, which he adapted to suit the circumstances of the speech. However, the model was evidently a good one, and may be taken to represent the law not later than the third century B.C.

A maritime loan was a loan upon security, and the security, τὸ ἐνέχυρον or τὸ ὑποκείμενον, might be a ship, or its freight, or a cargo (ship in Adv. Zenoth., p. 886 ; In Dionysod., passim ; freight in Adv. Lacrit., p. 933 ; cargo in Adv. Phorm. and Adv. Lacrit., passim, see esp. pp. 914, 930). The loan was made either for a double voyage, which, where an Athenian was the lender, must have been from Athens to a foreign port and back to Athens, or it was made for a single voyage, whether outward or inward. The loan for the voyage out and back was called δάνειον or ἀργύριον ἀμφοτερόπλουν (pp. 914, 6 ; 1284, 20) or τὰ ἀμφοτερόπλοα (p. 915, 10, where however S and other manuscripts have ἑτερόπλοα). The loan for one voyage only was called ἀργύριον ἑτερόπλουν (p. 1291, 25) or τὰ ἑτερόπλοα (pp. 909, 25 ; 914, 3, 27). Where the loan was to be paid in an out-port, it was customary for the lender to sail in the same ship as the borrower (pp. 909, 24 ; 914, 28 ; 942, 4).

[1] See Dareste, Inscriptions, I, p. 297 ; Billeter (G.), Gesch. des Zinsfusses, p. 32 n. ; E. Drerup in Jahrbücher für Class. Phil. 1898, p. 320.

MARITIME LOANS

There was a regular form for contracts of maritime loan. They were made κατὰ τοὺς ἐμπορικοὺς νόμους (p. 924, 10). The principal provisions were as follows.

1. The journey to be taken is laid down and a power is given to the borrower, under circumstances, of varying it (pp. 926, 1; 1284, 12).

2. The rate of interest is specified and it is made to vary with the journey actually taken (pp. 926, 4; 1284, 14; 1286, 25; see Böckh, Staatshaushaltung, I², p. 151 (193)).

3. The subject of the security is identified, e. g. three thousand jars of wine, to sail from Mende or Scione in the twenty-oared ship, Hyblesius master (pp. 926, 6; 928, 24).

It seems to have been the rule that the property hypothecated should be of the value of twice the loan—at least in cases where the loan was for both the outward and inward voyage (pp. 908, 24; 928, 26). Apparently lenders for one voyage only did not require so large a margin (p. 909, 1).[1]

4. The borrowers declare that they owe no money to any one on the security of the property hypothecated, and that they will not borrow anything more upon it (pp. 926, 9; 930, 4).

In ordinary cases it is immaterial to a lender whether other people lend upon property already hypothecated to him, as securities rank in ordinary cases in the order in time of their creation. A different rule prevails in maritime law. A loan there is generally made for salvage purposes, and a lender who comes last in time, as his

---

[1] A peculiar use of the word ὑποθήκη has occasioned some difficulties. It means not only the aggregate property subject to the security, but also the difference between the value of that and the amount of the loan, the margin in fact. If A lends 20 minas on property worth 30, there is a ὑποθήκη of 10 minas. Examples of this use are ἐπὶ ἑτέρᾳ ὑποθήκῃ (p. 908, 21), 'on a margin of as much again'; οὐ γὰρ τὴν ὑποθήκην παρέσχετο (p. 909, 6), 'he did not provide a margin'; ὑποθήκην οὐκ ἔχων (p. 914, 1), 'having no margin'; οὐ παρασχόντα τὰς ὑποθήκας (p. 922, 5), 'not leaving any margins'; ὡς ὑπαρχούσης αὐτοῖς ὑποθήκης ἑτέρων τριάκοντα μνῶν (p. 928, 26), 'as if they had a margin of other thirty minas.'

money is deemed to have saved the property for the benefit of all parties, including prior lenders, is given priority over them as against the security.

5. Where the voyage was both outward and inward, and the subject of the security was a cargo, the borrowers bound themselves to sell it at the out-port, to buy other goods with the proceeds of sale, to load the goods bought on board ship—generally the ship which had been used on the out voyage—and bring them back to the home port (pp. 909, 26; 926, 10; 931, 13; 933, 16; 935, 19). The goods so bought were hypothecated to the same extent as the goods taken out.

The contract of Adv. Phormionem appears to have given the borrower a right to relieve himself of liability by paying the loan with interest to the captain in the out-port; but it is impossible to say what the precise terms were (pp. 908, 15; 914, 7, 26; 916, 17, 25; 917, 14).

6. Where the subject of the security is a ship, the repayment of the loan is made contingent upon the ship coming safe to port (pp. 883, 17; 1212, 4; 1283, 19; 1292, 15). When it is cargo, the repayment is made contingent upon the safety of the cargo (p. 926, 12).

7. Payment is to be made within twenty days after the ship comes in (pp. 926, 15; 931, 3). According to the contract inserted in Adv. Lacritum, the borrowers were entitled to make a deduction from the amount payable in respect of (a) jettison made by those on board by common vote; (b) payments made to enemies (p. 926, 16). There is no reference to this provision in the speech itself; but that does not militate against its genuineness.

8. The lenders are to have control of the property hypothecated in its integrity until actual payment (pp. 926, 20; 931, 4; 1294, 8, 20, 28).

9. If the borrower fails to pay within the twenty days, the lenders may raise the debt by hypothecation or sale at market price of the property subject to the security (p. 926, 21).

In Adv. Apaturium, Demosthenes describes the various

steps which were taken by the lenders on a ship to realize their security. The lenders, who had lent 40 minas, were taking possession (ἐνεβάτευον εἰς τὴν ναῦν, p. 894, 8). They are paid off by a third party, who apparently makes a purchase of the ship until the loan is paid (p. 894, 27). He sets guards over the ship (p. 895, 17) which is eventually sold for 40 minas (p. 896, 5).

10. There was also a personal remedy against the borrower (pp. 885, 20; 1293, 16; 1296, 20). The contract inserted in Adv. Lacritum provides that, if the property subject to the security fails to meet the debt, the lenders may exact the balance from the borrowers and from all their property, on land and on sea, as if judgment had been given against them and they were not in time.[1] Each borrower may be sued separately (p. 926, 25).

11. Although the contract inserted in Adv. Lacritum does not contain a penal clause, such a clause must have been usual. It evidently provided that, if the borrower failed to perform any of the stipulations of the contract, he became liable to pay a sum equal to twice the amount lent with interest (pp. 915, 1; 916, 26; 1286, 3; 1289, 8; 1291, 6; 1294, 7; 1296, 4, 18).

12. The contract inserted in Adv. Lacritum[2] contains a provision not elsewhere referred to. If the ship carrying the goods is wrecked and hypothecated goods are saved, let what survives be common to the lenders (p. 927, 8).[3] The provision seems hardly applicable to this contract. It seems to apply to the case of a number of independent lenders, each lending upon a separate item of cargo. If part of the cargo is lost, what is saved is divisible among the lenders *pro rata*. This looks suspiciously like the doctrine under which every loss was turned into a general average loss. (See p. cclix.)

---

[1] A similar phrase in Inscriptions Juridiques Grecques, p. 318, lines 31 and 40; p. 324, line 3.

[2] The special provision beginning with the words ἐὰν δὲ μὴ εἰσβάλωσι (p. 927, 3) is discussed by Böckh, Staatshaushaltung, I², p. 152 (194). As it refers to a special voyage, it need not be discussed here.

[3] I adopt A's reading.

13. The contract finally provides that its terms are to govern the matter (pp. 927, 10; 937, 15).[1]

When the loan was paid off, the documents which evidenced it were destroyed (τὰς συγγραφὰς ἀνειλόμεθα, pp. 896, 10; 916, 10. Cf. Inscriptions Juridiques Grecques, Index, s. v. ἀνελέσθαι).

There is no complete Roman specimen of a contract of maritime loan, although Scaevola (Dig. XLV, 1, 122, 1) gives an abstract of one. On the other hand, the law of the subject is laid down with some fullness.

Maritime loans are dealt with in a title of the Digest (XXII, 2 'de nautico faenore') and another of the Code (IV, 33 'de nautico fenore'). To understand the object of the provisions which these titles contain, it is necessary to know two rules which in Roman law related to loans in general.

1. Before Justinian the rate of interest in ordinary cases was limited to 12 per cent.; but in a maritime loan there was no limit to the rate which the lender could exact while the maritime risk continued (Paul. Sent. II, 14, 3).

Justinian in A.D. 528 lowered the rate of interest in ordinary cases, making it vary with the character and quality of the lender, and he also fixed a maximum of 12 per cent. for maritime loans (Cod. IV, 32, 26, 2).

2. It was the law, both before and after Justinian, that as a rule interest could not be enforced on a loan of money unless there was a distinct stipulatio to that effect (Dig. XII, 1, 11, 1; XIX, 5, 24; Cod. IV, 32, 3). One exception

---

[1] These passages supply some evidence against the authenticity of the contract which is inserted at p. 925, 27. The contract says merely: κυριώτερον δὲ περὶ τούτων ἄλλο μηδὲν εἶναι τῆς συγγραφῆς. In the text (p. 937, 15) we have ἡ μὲν γὰρ συγγραφὴ οὐδὲν κυριώτερον ἐᾷ εἶναι τῶν ἐγγεγραμμένων, οὐδὲ προσφέρειν οὔτε νόμον οὔτε ψήφισμα οὔτ' ἄλλ' οὐδ' ὁτιοῦν πρὸς τὴν συγγραφήν. Now these latter words were a regular form in acknowledgements of debt, and no doubt occurred in the real συγγραφή. Inscriptions Juridiques Grecques, p. 316, line 41; p. 320, line 45; p. 324, line 27. It looks as if the composer of the contract had taken the latter words in the text as mere verbiage, and had therefore omitted them.

to this rule was interest on a maritime loan during the continuance of the maritime risk (Dig. XXII, 2, 7).

We may now proceed to the Roman law of maritime loans.

1. A contract of maritime loan in Rome as in Greece is not a gambling contract. It is a contract upon a contingency, but the contingency is one in which the parties have a pecuniary interest. *Traiecticia pecunia* is defined by Modestinus (Dig. XXII, 2, 1) as money which is carried over sea, or goods bought with the money and carried over sea. Money which is spent in the place where it is lent is not *traiecticia*. The destination of the money determines the character of the contract. It follows from this definition that, if A lends money to B to be employed in building a house, and B agrees to repay the money with interest if C's ship comes in, this is not a maritime loan, although the repayment depends upon a maritime event. It is no more a maritime loan than if the repayment were made to depend on C becoming consul. There is nothing illegal in a contract of the latter class, but it is doubtful whether in such a contract the lender would be entitled (before Justinian) to unlimited interest, and (after Justinian) to interest at 12 per cent., or whether interest could be claimed without a stipulation.

2. Maritime interest can only be contracted for during the continuance of the maritime risk. The risk begins, as a rule, at the day fixed by the contract for the departure of the ship; it ends, as a rule, when the ship comes in (C. IV, 33, 2 (1); 5 (4)). The former of these events within certain limits is within the power of the parties: the latter not. The risk, therefore, though it may be made to begin on a prescribed day, can only be made to determine on an uncertain day, i. e. whenever the ship comes in (Dig. XXII, 2, 3, 4, 6).

There is nothing illegal in a contract for the loan of money to be carried over sea, the borrower as in other contracts taking the risk. Only in this case the lender is not entitled to maritime interest (C. IV, 33, 3 (2) ; 5 (4)), and, if interest is claimed, it can only be claimed in virtue of a stipulation. Moreover, on a maritime loan, after the determination of the risk, interest can only be claimed at the ordinary rate and in virtue of a stipulation.

3. A maritime loan generally contained a pledge or hypothecation. The pledge or hypothecation might be (a) of the goods purchased with the money lent or to be purchased with the proceeds of sale of these goods, or (b) of other goods belonging to the borrower sailing on other ships (Dig. XXII, 2, 4), or (c) of the borrower's land.

The existence of such a pledge or hypothecation did not enlarge the lender's rights. (a) He could not retain the property pledged or hypothecated as a security for interest beyond what he would otherwise be entitled to (Dig. XXII, 2, 4 pr.). (b) If a maritime loss occurred, the lender had no rights against property pledged or hypothecated (Dig. XXII, 2, 6).[1] The advantage to the lender of a pledge or hypothecation was this. If the obligation of the borrower became absolute, the lender might enforce it more readily against property pledged or hypothecated, e.g. if the property primarily pledged was lost or if its proceeds of sale did not satisfy the amount due (Dig. XXII, 2, 6).

4. No doubt Roman like Greek documents of loan provided for a penalty if the loan with interest was not punctually paid. There are several passages in these two titles referring to a penalty, but none which states of what the penalty consisted. It is clear that, so far as it became due upon non-payment of the loan and interest, it cannot have been fully enforceable. The loan and interest only became payable if the maritime risk was over. After default in payment, interest might continue to run by virtue of a penal condition, but nothing more could be enforced by virtue of such a condition than

[1] The first part of the passage which is given in Synopsis Ambr. LIII, E', ιϛ', and in Synopsis Vent. LIII, VI, 11, and which comes from the Code, is to the same effect.

ordinary interest, i.e. before Justinian at the rate of 12 per cent. (Theod. II, 33, 1), and under his legislation at a rate varying from 4 to 8 per cent. (Dig. XXII, 1, 9 pr.; 1, 44; Cod. IV, 32, 15 and 16).

5. The contract often provided for the presence on board of a slave or servant of the lender, in Greek the κερμακόλουθος (see Cujacius, Obs. et Emend. V, 38). The passages which refer to him are obscure.

It is obvious that a provision throwing the expenses of his salary or his keep upon the borrower might have been used to defeat the restrictions upon the rate of interest. It is probable that a passage which is found in Synopsis Ambr. LIII, E′, ις′ and in Synopsis Vent. LIII, VI, 11, and which comes from the Code deals with this point. As it stands it is illogical; if we fill it up as Paul Krüger proposes (Zu den Basiliken, in Zeitschrift der Savigny-Stiftung, XIX, 192, at p. 197), it lays down that, where creditors do not run the maritime risk, they are not entitled to more than the ordinary interest, and it makes no difference whether they sail themselves or have the so-called κερμακόλουθος on board. Two other passages which deal with him (Dig. XXII, 2, 4, 1; XLIV, 7, 23) are evidently interpolated. It is clear that he had no implied authority by virtue of his position to alter the terms of the contract of loan (Dig. XLV, 1, 122, 1).

A Novel (106) of A.D. 540 throws light upon the variety of systems which prevailed. It is to this effect. Certain lenders on maritime loan had petitioned to have the custom of maritime loans settled by public authority. The Eastern prefect by the emperor's order convoked the captains who were concerned in maritime loans to ascertain the ancient custom. They reported that there were several systems. One was this. For every νόμισμα which the lender gave, he put on board one μόδιος of corn or barley. He paid no duty on this to the officers of customs. In addition he received one gold coin by way of interest for every ten lent. He ran the maritime risk. Another system was this. The lender took one-eighth of each νόμισμα by way of interest.[1] The loan was made until the ship came back safe, and the amount receivable by way of interest was the same whatever might be the duration of the voyage. The ship might be away for a year or more: it might be back within a month. In either case the lender got his 12½ per cent. If a ship returned in time, a lender might obtain 12½ per cent. upon his capital more than once in a single season, as the loan was made not for a fixed period, but for each maritime adventure (καθ' ἕκαστον φόρτον). After the ship came back, the borrower had twenty days' grace before any demand was made for capital or interest, i. e. until he had time to sell his cargo. In default of payment, the lender was entitled to interest at 8 per cent. (τὸν ἐκ διμοίρου τῆς ἑκατοστῆς τόκον), i. e. the interest which Justinian allowed men in business to receive. The loan became a land loan, the lender being no longer exposed to maritime risks.

The emperor sanctions contracts made in these forms and declares that they are to prevail in mercantile suits. He repealed these provisions however the year after (Novel 110).

The Byzantine authorities present, as usual, an ungodly jumble. The Ecloga appears to place all loans on the same footing. It provides thus. A makes a loan to B on land or on sea. A is to receive back his loan at the time fixed by the agreement, and B cannot set up a hostile invasion or shipwreck or any other cause as against A's claim (X, 1). Zach. is right in saying (Gesch., pp. 301, 312) that the Ecloga never alludes to interest on money. On the other hand it is nowhere distinctly forbidden. The other Byzantine law-books give an uncertain sound (Zach., Gesch., pp. 312, 313). The emperor Nicephorus I appears to have lent money at a high rate—over 16 per cent.—to the ναύκληροι of Constantinople (Theoph.,

---

[1] This is equivalent to τὰ τρία κεράτια mentioned later, the νόμισμα being divided into twenty-four κεράτια. Zach., Geschichte, p. 310.

MARITIME LOANS

p. 487, De Boor).[1] The Basilica restored the legislation
of Justinian (Zach., Gesch., p. 312).

Maritime Loans in the Sea-law.

I turn to the Sea-law. C. ιζ´ is a direction not to write
down 'loans which are made on property at sea where
the loan is unconditionally repayable out of property
on land'. Ἔγγαια καὶ ἀκίνδυνα, as I point out in the Commentary (p. 67), is equivalent to Latin phrases like 'sal-
vos in terra sine omni periculo' (Baracchi, 46, in Archivio
Veneto, VIII, p. 150, A.D. 1168). Now this, if we do not
press the language too closely, is strictly in accordance
with Roman law. It is true that money might be lent
at sea on the footing of the borrower taking the maritime
risk; only the lender in such a case was not entitled to
maritime interest. This chapter evidently contemplates
the normal case, that in which the lender takes maritime
interest, and in this sense it is true that he must take the
maritime risk. This chapter was probably removed from
Part III of the Sea-law as being superfluous.

C. ιη´ has nothing to do with maritime law. Indeed,
it is described in some MSS. as 'concerning a loan on
land'. It seems to mean this. A lender pays interest
regularly for eight years. After that he has a misfortune.
He is no longer liable to pay interest. A conjecture may
be hazarded as to the term of eight years. It was laid
down by Justinian that on a loan to a husbandman of
grain, &c., he paid by way of yearly interest one-eighth of
the produce lent (Cod. IV, 32, 26, 2; Nov. Just. 32).
This rule is reproduced in the Byzantine law-books (Bas.
XXIII, 3, 76; Ecloga P. A. XI, 13; Epanag. A. XXII,

---

[1] The passage is explained by Gfrörer, A. F., Byzantinische Ge-
schichten, II, p. 407. I agree with his explanation except as follows:
ἀνὰ χρυσίου λιτρῶν δώδεκα does not mean that he lent each of them
twelve pounds of gold. The amount lent probably varied with the
individual. The words are an explanation of ἐπὶ τόκῳ τετρακεράτῳ.
He lent at 16⅔ per cent. interest, i. e. twelve νομίσματα for every λίτρα
of gold. The λίτρα was divided into 72 νομίσματα. For λιτρῶν probably read λίτρας.

13). It follows that, if the borrower paid regularly, the lender at the end of eight years would have received his capital back; and Justinian also lays down that, where interest has been paid equal to the original debt, interest ceases to run (Nov. 121, c. 2; 138). C. ιη′ is not so favourable to the borrower as this, as it only relieves him from further payments of interest where his property has been destroyed.

C. ιθ′ is again very doubtful. οἱ ναύκληρου ναυκληροῦντες are probably the joint owners who are in actual command —who *per se exercent*, as the Digest says—as opposed to those who either stay at home or go as common seamen. The chapter seems to give them a power of borrowing money on the security of the ship if they own three-fourths in value of it (see Commentary). This rule is in substantial agreement with the provisions of other maritime codes (St. Ragus. VII, 17; Consuetud. Bari, f. 118, ed. 1550; p. 152, ed. Alianelli). The last part of the chapter evidently refers to the κερμακόλουθος of Roman law, but it is not clear what he is to do.

C. 16 of Part III is the worst chapter of all. Zach. thinks it is an interpolation (Gesch., p. 314). Would that it were so, but it is given in all the oldest MSS. Pard. says: 'le sens de cette décision est plus facile à saisir qu'une traduction littérale à faire' (p. 247). He takes the sense to be this. Captains and merchants who borrow money on a voyage are not to be bound except on the terms that freight and goods, ship and money come safe, and unless the money runs a risk from sea dangers and from pirates. Money borrowed on this condition is to pay nautical interest. Pard.'s translation does not agree with his Greek text nor his Greek text with the manuscript tradition. But every allowance must be made for editors of this chapter. What makes it so baffling is the apparent want of connexion between its clauses. The title is: 'concerning money which is lent to be carried over sea.' The text falls into four groups. (1) The first goes down to φορτίοις. I should put the words ἔγγαια μὴ χρηέσθωσαν after φορτίοις and translate as follows: 'captains and merchants and whosoever borrow money on the security of ship and freight and cargo are not to borrow it as if it was a land loan,' i. e. are not to borrow it on the terms of its being unconditionally repayable. (2) The second fragment goes from σωθέντος to χρημάτων, 'if ship and money are saved.' (3) The third goes from μή to ἐπιβουλή, 'lest a plot be laid against the money from the dangers of the sea or from pirates.' ἐπιβουλή is very curious. If we read ἐπιβουλῆς, which has some MS. authority, there is no subject to ἐγγένηται. (4) 'Let them pay back the loan from the property on land with maritime interest.' We should expect τὴν χρῆσιν. It is obvious that the chapter is corrupt and that the corruption is deep-seated.

I pass over cc. 17 and 18 for the present, as they contain the first traces of an institution which afterwards rose to great importance as the commenda and which is dealt with hereafter. (See p. ccxxxv.)

It is singular that all the chapters in the Sea-law which relate to loans, whether they are in Part II or in Part III, should be so difficult of interpretation. The explanation may be this. The Basilica contains an elaborate and consistent doctrine of maritime loan. When the Sea-law was edited with a view to its incorporation in the Basilica, its rules regarding maritime loans, which no doubt represented local customs, had to be brought into harmony with the strait Roman doctrine. Hence these chapters have been particularly tampered with.

Maritime Loans in the Middle Ages.

The mediaeval doctrine of maritime loans is complicated by the ecclesiastical prohibitions against taking interest. These prohibitions about the year 1230 were extended to the case where the lender took the maritime risk (see Goldschmidt, Geschichte, p. 346, n. 52). The thunders of the church did not affect the actual course of commerce.

INTRODUCTION

In the commercial cities of Italy and Southern France, interest was regularly taken on loans, even though the loan was unconditionally repayable, and the rate was as a rule much higher than in classical times. The only effect of the ecclesiastical prohibitions was the adoption of various conveyancing devices which cloaked the real nature of the transactions involved. (See the observations of Schaube, Handelsgeschichte, p. 121). It is convenient on this occasion to keep separate the evidence of the documents from the evidence of the statutes.

The documents distinguish on their face the *mutuum*, the *permutatio* or *cambium*, the *emptio*, the *commenda*—called in Venice *collegantia*—and the *societas*. These various classes of contract have many characteristics in common; they are probably all derived, either in whole or in part, from the ancient maritime loan; the great difference is that while in the first three the person who has the management and control of the fund pays for its use a sum fixed at the execution of the contract, in the last two he pays a proportion of the profit which he makes out of it. The main authority for the *mutuum* is the Notulario of Giovanni Scriba.

I. The amount of the loan is sometimes stated in money, sometimes it is left vague, e.g. 'tot' or 'tantum de rebus tuis', or 'de bonis tuis' (Scriba, 365, 550, 877, 920, 1200; Sacerdoti, p. 32). In a Genoese case it is pepper (Scriba, 680) which seems to have formed an alternative currency in that city.

The borrower sometimes promises to repay a fixed sum (Sacerdoti, p. 24 'inter caput et prodem'; p. 30; Baracchi, 29, in Arch. Veneto, VII, p. 366), sometimes to repay the amount lent with interest, 'de tribus quattuor,' 'de quattuor quinque,' or as the case may be. There is sometimes a provision raising the rate of interest if payment is delayed (Scriba, 621). In one Genoese case the debtor repays 'in pipere et brazili' (Scriba, 339), in another he has the option of repaying either in cash or pepper (Scriba, 880), and in another he repays either in cash or in goods to be approved by the creditor (Scriba, 1087).

There are sometimes provisions for repayment of the loan if the borrower or his ship does not start before a certain date (Scriba, 828, 880, 884, 885, 1485).

The forms of the *emptio* or the *permutatio* were sometimes adopted to cloak a transaction of loan and evade the canon law. In an ordinary maritime loan the money lent was as a rule applied by the borrower in the purchase of goods, and the repayment of the lender depended upon the safe arrival of those goods or the goods into which they had been converted. This transaction may be put in another way. Instead of B buying goods with money lent by A, A buys the goods himself and sells them to B, and the price which B agrees to pay will be (*a*) payable at a future date; (*b*) contingent upon the safe arrival at the place of payment, either of the original goods or the goods into which they have been converted; and (*c*) sufficient to meet the sum paid by A with maritime interest. Thus business goes on as usual and there is no undue strain upon the conscience. Examples of *emptio* are Scriba, 1064; Manduel, 14, 15; Amalric, 68, 973; Actes génois, I, p. 501.

Permutatio or *cambium* is this. If B receives coins from A on the terms of paying coins of a different character at a later date this is merely exchange, like the exchange of wheat for mutton, and there is no taint of usury in it, although the coins returned may be of much greater value than the coins received. *Permutatio* or *cambium* might be made use of not merely where the loan was made repayable in a foreign port and where it would naturally be repayable in the currency of that port, but also where the loan was repayable in the home port. The variety of currencies which circulated in every trading centre made this easy.

II. In all cases of loan there is generally a short interval between the cesser of the maritime risk and the day fixed for payment; e.g. 15 days after the ship comes in (Scriba,

INTRODUCTION

613 ; Manduel, 15 ; Amalric, 109, 522, 973) ; 20 days (Manduel, 14, 72) ; 30 days or one month (Scriba, 332, 333, 452 ; Baracchi, 29; Sacerdoti, p. 24; Manduel, 1; Amalric, 68); two months (Sacerdoti, p. 32). Sometimes payment is to be made 30 days after the ship is unloaded (Scriba, 265).

The borrower sometimes has the option of anticipating payment under discount (Scriba, 759, 805). Where the loan is for the double voyage, the borrower is sometimes given the power, if he alters his voyage, of sending back to the lender the amount due and relieving himself from liability (Scriba, 265, 333; Manduel, 15).

Where the loan is to be paid in an out-port, it is sometimes made payable to the lender or a third specified person (Amalric, 644), sometimes to the lender or his nominee (Scriba, 440, 884; Amalric, 435, 917), sometimes to the lender's agent ('nepoti tuo pro te recipienti' Amalric, 111). Where there is no one at the out-port who can give a discharge, the borrower promises to invest the money due in specified goods (Scriba, 459, 464, 877). In some cases the borrower has the option of deferring payment till the return home (Scriba, 339, 419, 440, 885).

III. In the Genoese documents there is, with one or two exceptions, no special pledge of the goods purchased with the money lent, and no provision that these are to go at the lender's risk, but the loan is made repayable only upon the happening of an uncertain event. If we confine ourselves to the form of the documents, the event may be one in which the borrower has no interest, and no doubt the form of a maritime loan was sometimes made use of for purely aleatory transactions; but in the vast majority of instances the event was evidently one in which the borrower had a direct pecuniary interest. Omitting certain very special cases, the contingencies, where the loan is made for a voyage out and in, may be grouped as follows :—

The loan is made repayable (*a*) if the ship in which the borrower sails goes safe to the foreign port (generally, in the Genoese documents, Alexandria) and returns safe back (Scriba, 332, 445, 452, 550, 591); (b) if A's ship goes safe to the foreign port and returns safe back (Scriba, 460, 661; (c) if the ship in which some third person sails goes safe to the foreign port and returns safe back (Scriba, 632, 708); (d) if A's ship goes safe, and the ship in which the borrower returns comes back safe (Scriba, 613).

In a case coming under (a) it is provided that, if the borrower does not go, then the loan is repayable if A's ship goes safe and the biggest ship which sails from the foreign port to Genoa the next summer returns safe (Scriba, 452).

In a case coming under (b) it is provided that, if A's ship does not go, then the loan is repayable if the ship in which the borrower sails goes and returns safe (Scriba, 661).

All these contingencies evidently refer to the same event, the safety of the money lent or the goods which were purchased with it. It is clear that, where a particular ship is prescribed, it is the ship in which the borrower sailed; and, where the ship in which a third party sails is prescribed, that third party is the partner or servant of the borrower.

In most of the documents the contingency is much more elaborate than those given above. The contracts look forward to payment in the following summer. In Genoa the regular ship caravan to Alexandria generally went out in September, and the merchants who took part in it returned in the following year, arriving at Genoa by St. John's Day (Schaube, Geschichte, pp. 153, 154). It might often happen that in the year following the loan, the event on which repayment depended had become impossible. For example, where the ship prescribed for the return journey is the same as that prescribed for the out journey, that ship might be sold or might alter its route; and in that case it became necessary to specify another ship upon the safe arrival of which the loan should be repayable. Or again, where the prescribed ship is the ship, whichever it may be, in

which the borrower returns, the borrower might not
return; and here again it was necessary to specify some
other ship.

Hence we get a series of alternative contingencies. If
the ship originally prescribed is sold or changes route,
then the loan is repayable (a) if that ship comes back
safe (whichever it may be) in which the borrower or the
greater part of his goods returns (Scriba, 332, 445, 1132);
(b) if that ship comes back safe in which A returns or
loads the greater part of his goods (Scriba, 461, 516, 917,
942); (c) if that ship comes back safe in which the
majority of the merchants or goods return who or which
were in the former ship (Scriba, 460); (d) if that ship
comes back safe in which the majority of the Genoese
merchants or the major part of their goods return
(Scriba, 661, 828); (e) if that ship comes back safe which
in that summer first starts from the foreign port for
Genoa (Scriba, 519, 550, 591, 621, 1200; cp. Sacerdoti,
p. 24).

Again, if the borrower does not return or if A does
not return, we get a further alternative series of contingencies. The loan is repayable (a) if the principal
ship comes safe which starts in that year from the foreign
port (Scriba, 332); (b) if that ship comes back safe which
first starts, as in (e) above (Scriba, 632, 708); (c) if that
ship comes back safe in which the majority return, as in
(c) above (Scriba, 613).

In most cases the contingency is put frankly as a contingency, *salva eunte et redeunte*. In one case payment
is to be made within twelve days after the safe return
of the galley of the commune (Scriba, 912). Perhaps it
was thought unpatriotic to treat the return of the galley
of the commune as an uncertain event.

Where the loan is for an out voyage only the contingency is the safe arrival of (a) the borrower's ship (Scriba,
459, 884, 1124; cp. Sacerdoti, p. 32); (b) the ship of a third
person (Scriba, 670); (c) the ship in which the borrower or
his agent (*nuncius meus*) goes (Scriba, 365, 833, 859, 877);

(d) a ship to be chosen by the parties to the contract (Scriba, 440, 670, 833); (e) the galley of a third person or the majority of the galleys which go to the foreign port (Scriba, 1393); (f) the greater part of the borrower's goods or the goods on board ship (Scriba, 440, 859, 877, 884).

In one case it is provided that, if anything should happen to any of the ships upon whose safe arrival repayment depended, the borrower shall repay in proportion to the amount saved ('pro ea parte quam evadet tibi inde per racionem solvam', Scriba, 828).

In one case on a loan for an out voyage there is an immediate pledge of specified goods then in the lender's possession which the borrowers agree to carry in the lender's name. There is also in default of payment a general pledge of these and the other goods of the borrowers (Scriba, 859). In another case there is an immediate pledge of specified goods. The lender will put them *in commendacionem* of X or Y, and the pledge is to be carried at the risk and fortune of the lender. When they have arrived at the foreign port, the borrower may change the pledge for another of greater value. If the borrower does not change or redeem the pledge, the lender may sell it, pay himself out of the proceeds, and restore the balance to the borrower (Scriba, 1124).

In a contract of loan made at Messina in A.D. 1200 (described as *mutuum*), the loan, which is repayable at Marseille, is received *in fortuna Dei et maris.* There is a pledge of specific goods on board: 'quod magis valent ista pignora quam debitum vestrum est erit ad resegum nostrum; reliquum ad resegum vestrum.' At the end is the clause: 'salva existente nave vel maiore parte rerum navis' (Manduel, 1). In a contract of A.D. 1236 there is the clause 'sana eunte dicta nave vel maiori parte rerum', and also a pledge of specified goods on board, but it is not stated that they go at the lender's risk (Manduel, 72).

In the Marseille documents the loan often assumes the form of an *emptio.* Where a loan was for the double voyage, it was made repayable 'if the said ship goes there in safety or the greater part of the goods, or if the said ship returns in safety or any other in which I come back from the said voyage or the greater part of the goods' (Manduel, 15). As a rule the documents refer to a single voyage. In one case the purchaser pledges the goods bought, 'over which the purchase price ought to go and stand at the vendor's risk and their excess value at the purchaser's' (Manduel, 14). No contingency is expressed. In two cases the contingency is: 'if the goods bought go safe which ought to go in the said ship at your [the vendor's] risk and fortune up to the quantity of the purchase price' (Amalric, 68, 973). In one of these cases the goods are pledged (Amalric, 68).

Where the contract is a *permutacio* or *cambium*, the contingency is sometimes the safe arrival of goods which are on board the ship upon whose arrival the loan is made payable. The phrase is: 'if the goods go safe which ought to sail in the said ship at your risk up to the amount of the sum repayable.' The goods are sometimes merely referred to as 'my goods' (Amalric, 109, 111). Sometimes they are specifically described (Amalric, 145, 435, 522, 644, 657, 917). The contingency clause is always followed by a pledge of the goods in question to secure the loan. Once the goods are declared to be held for the lender on board (Amalric, 644). Once the borrower agrees to pay their freight (Amalric, 917).

The contingency is sometimes the safe arrival of a ship. This is generally put: 'if the ship goes safe, which ought to be at your risk up to the amount of the sum repayable' (Amalric, 416, 939, 977). Another form is: 'if the ship goes safe or the greater part of the goods on the said voyage' (Amalric, 193, 484, 1013). Once the two forms are combined: 'if the ship goes safe or the greater part of the goods, which ship and barrels ought to go at your risk up to the amount of the sum repayable' (Amalric, 1019). The ship or part of it always belongs to the borrower, and in two cases it is expressed that

part of the property subject to the risk had been purchased with the loan (Amalric, 939, 1019).

In these cases there is generally a special pledge of the
ship and of all the borrower's goods present and to come
(e. g. Amalric, 193, 416).   Sometimes the freight is also
pledged (Amalric, 193).   Sometimes only part of the ship
is pledged (Amalric, 977, 1013, 1019).

In one case, although the contingency is expressed to
be the safe arrival of ship, it is really the goods that are
in question; ' salvo tamen eunte dicto bucio vel maiori
parte rerum, in quo bucio implicita mea debent vehi ad
tuum resegum et fortunam usque ad quantitatem ' of the
sum repayable (Amalric, 418.   Here the ship did not
belong to the borrower).

IV. If the borrower makes default in payment, he
becomes liable to a penalty of twice the amount due,
capital and interest (Scriba, 332, 452 ; Sacerdoti, p. 24
' omnia in duplo, caput et prode '). There is often a
general pledge of all the borrower's goods both present
and future to secure the loan and the penalty (Scriba,
332, 452 ; Sacerdoti, pp. 24, 32). The lender is entitled to
enter on the property pledged without judicial process
and to take it at a valuation or to sell it (Scriba,
265, 332, 333, 440, 519; Sacerdoti, p. 32).   There is
sometimes a special pledge, e. g. one-fourth of a ship
(Scriba, 365), the borrower's lands, and then his other
goods (Scriba, 438, 629). The borrower often takes an
oath to pay the loan and interest (Scriba, 440, 445, 452) ;
sometimes there are sureties (Scriba, 685, 833, 895).

In the Venetian documents, after default in payment,
the capital and twice the interest is to bear interest at
20 per cent. (Sacerdoti, pp. 24, 32).

The study of the documents raises some questions.   It
is evident that the mediaeval contract of maritime loan
was identical in its main features with the classical contract.   To take the simplest form, the loan is applied by
the borrower in buying goods.   If they, or other goods
into which they have been converted, survive the mari-

time risk, the lender recovers his loan with interest; if they do not, he loses his money. But the documents do not always, or indeed often, present the transaction in this form.

In the first place, where a loan applied in the purchase of cargo is made repayable if ship or the greater part of its cargo arrives safe, there is a discrepancy between the contingency expressed and the destination of the loan. They do not fit. One would expect a loan applied in the purchase of cargo to be made repayable upon the safe arrival of the cargo purchased or of the cargo into which that has been converted. In such a case, is the loan repayable if the cargo actually purchased is lost, while the ship or the greater part of its cargo arrives safe?

Secondly, there is sometimes an inconsistency on the document itself between the pledge-clause and the contingency-clause. Which is to prevail? These questions were evidently raised in the middle ages, and the statutes throw some light upon the answers to be given.

The Constitutum Usus provides as follows (c. 24, p. 903). B receives a loan from A at the risk (*ad fortunam*) of a ship in which B proposes to go or to put his goods. B does not go or put his goods in the ship and the ship is lost. In this case, B is liable to restore the capital of the loan, unless it was within the knowledge of both parties that B was not to go or put his goods in the ship in question; i. e. if both parties knew that the contract was aleatory, its terms are to be observed (see also c. 27, p. 910). Note that in this case the provisions of the statute override the terms of the contract. Under the terms of the contract, B is not liable if the ship is lost.

A passage in the Customs of Bari (f. 118, ed. 1550, p. 153, ed. Alianelli) appears to be to the same effect. It runs: 'si tamen cum navi pecuniam credidi navigandum & debitor se alio navigio destinavit, creditarum pecuniarum eventus & periculum describitur debitori, nisi aliud inter contrahentes convenisse claruerit.'

There is one case in the Notulario of Scriba where the contract appears to be aleatory. The canons of S. Lorenzo borrow money to buy vestments, and the loan is made repayable 'sano eunte Sardiniam galeotto Puelle et sano redeunte inde' (Scriba, 735). It is possible that the contingency was inserted *per incuriam*—possible also that the men of God who borrowed did not like to oblige themselves to pay interest unless a contingency was expressed.

It is improbable that originally the difference in phraseology between the pledge-clause and the contingency-clause was intended to carry with it any difference in legal effect. It was merely a question of the conveyancer's convenience. Where the out-voyage alone has to be considered, it is easy enough to provide that the actual goods bought are pledged to the lender and sail at his risk. It is not so easy to frame the clause where you have to refer not merely to goods originally bought but to the goods which are to be bought with the proceeds of their sale. Be this as it may, the interpretation of these clauses evidently gave rise to doubts.

The Statute of Marseille (III, 5, ed. Méry et Guindon, IV, p. 32; ed. Pard. IV, p. 265) provides as follows :—

1. There is a special pledge, which is expressed to be at the lender's risk. There is also a provision that the loan is repayable if the ship goes safe or the greater part of the goods loaded on board. If the ship goes safe, the borrower is bound although the special pledge is lost. 2. If there is a special pledge but no provision 'if the ship goes safe, &c.', then the borrower is not bound if the special pledge is lost. 3. If there is no special pledge or only a general pledge of all the borrower's goods, and the provision 'if the ship goes safe', then the borrower is bound if the ship or the greater part of the goods goes safe ; he is not bound if they do not, except to the extent to which he has saved goods of his own on board. 4. If there

is a special pledge and the pledge is saved, then, even
if there is no provision 'if the ship goes safe,' the borrower is bound, but only to the extent of the pledge.

The provisions of the Constitutum Usus with reference
to maritime loans require special mention. The Constitutum Usus fixes the limit of interest in ordinary cases
at 10 per cent. (c. 11, p. 854; c. 49, p. 987). There is
an exception in favour of loans which are made *ad pro-
ficuum maris*. These are dealt with in a special chapter
(c. 24, p. 900). The parties may fix the rate of interest.
Where they do not fix it, the Constitutum lays down
rates which vary with the voyage (c. 25, p. 905). The
peculiarity of the Constitutum is that the rate of interest,
whether fixed by the contract or by statute, is subject
to decrease if the borrower's profits do not reach it. The
borrower is accountable not only for profits which he
has made but for those which, but for his wilful default,
he would have made. The rule applies even though
there is an agreement under penalty to pay interest
although no profits are made, or although the benefit
of the statute is renounced. The rule must have been
hard to work. There is nothing in the chapter or elsewhere to justify Goldschmidt's statement (Gesch., p. 351)
that the Constitutum Usus also knew of maritime loans
at a fixed and invariable rate of interest.

PARTNERSHIP BETWEEN MERCHANTS

The word κοινωνία occurs not infrequently in the Sea-
law, but the context does not as a rule carry us far in
ascertaining its meaning. If by κοινωνία is meant a community of profits and losses in some fund, goods, or
undertaking, two questions present themselves: 1. Who
are the κοινωνοί? 2. What is the subject-matter of the
κοινωνία? The partnership may be a partnership as
between merchants, and the partnership property may
consist in various items of cargo. A partnership exists
of necessity between the joint-owners of ship, and there

may be minor partnerships between two or more of such joint-owners. The owners of several ships may also form a partnership. On the other hand the partnership may be more extended. Where the mariners receive a share in the profits of a ship, there is a partnership between them and the owners of ship. There may also be a partnership between owners of ship, mariners, and owners of cargo. This is not to be confounded with a case where the profits of ship and cargo go in fact to the same persons. The owners of ship may, and often did, load the ship on their own account, and they may, and often did, contribute their personal services in navigating the ship. Whether in such cases accounts were kept in which the ship was credited with freight and the ship's company with wages, is immaterial. A joint-owner who served as a seaman and who had a part in the cargo may not have been concerned to apportion his share of the profits between freight, wages, and earnings of cargo ; but in law his share of the profits was received by him in three distinct capacities.

One chapter in the Sea-law deals distinctly with partnership as between merchants. This is c. 17. Its provisions are these. A gives to B ἐπὶ χρείᾳ κοινωνίας gold or silver. The κοινωνία is for a voyage. A writes down how long the χρεοκοινωνία is to last. B does not return the gold or silver to A within the time fixed ; and it is lost from fire or robbers or shipwreck. A is entitled to recover his property. If within the time fixed there is a destruction from the dangers of the sea, A and B are to bear the loss as they would have shared in the profit according to their parts and according to the contract.[1]

C. 18 refers in terms to a loan (χρησάμενος, τόκοι), but its position after c. 17 looks as if it really dealt with the same class of contract. 'A man borrows money and goes abroad.' This may refer to the man who receives money

---

[1] The Syro-Roman Lawbook (Paris MS., 82) refers to the case where A gives money to B for a business on the terms of equal division of profits. See Mitteis in Abhandl. der K. P. Acad. 1905, p. 40.

ἐπὶ χρείᾳ κοινωνίας. 'When the time agreed upon has expired, let them (the lenders) recover from his property on land according to law. If they cannot recover, the capital of their loan shall be unconditionally repayable, but the interest shall be maritime interest for so long as he is abroad.' This translation is rather forced. I treat ἔγγαια in the second place where it occurs as practically equivalent to ἀκίνδυνα. The arrangement of the chapter is not quite logical. If we treat the words from κομιζέσθωσαν to κομίσωνται as a parenthesis it becomes clearer. If the man who borrows the money does not return it at the appointed time, the money ceases to be liable to maritime risk, just as in c. 17, but maritime interest continues to be payable. The clause beginning with κομιζέσθωσαν would be better at the end. The lender in such a case, i. e. on the money becoming unconditionally repayable, may recover from the man's property on land. I do not think that ἐὰν μὴ ἔχωσι πῶς κομίσωνται in any way limits the generality of ἔσται αὐτοῖς κτλ. That is a statement of principle, equally true whether the lenders succeed in recovering their debt in full or not. The passage may be compared with various provisions both in statutes and documents, relating some to maritime loans and some to maritime partnerships, which unite in saying that, where the borrower or travelling partner does not fulfil the terms of his contract, the advance or share of the other partner, as the case may be, becomes immediately and absolutely repayable with heavy interest, and that the amount with interest may be raised out of all the defaulter's property (Camera, I, p. 433; II, p. xli; Consuetud. Bari, f. 118, ed. 1550, p. 153, ed. Alianelli; especially St. Pera, IV, 4).

C. 21 of the Sea-law appears to refer to a partnership between the owners of two ships. If this is so, it may be compared with the mediaeval *conserva*, which has been already dealt with (p. cxlviii).

The arrangements by virtue of which, during the middle ages, one man managed another's property on the maritime adventure fall under two main heads. 1. The man who goes abroad with the property and deals with it —I call him B—puts nothing himself into the common stock. The whole of that comes from the man who stays at home, and whom I call A. 2. The common stock is supplied by A and B jointly, A generally contributing twice as much as B. This system perhaps had a different origin from the last (see Goldschmidt, Geschichte, p. 272), but in many of its details it closely resembled it. Each form of contract deserves a short description.

The Mediaeval Commenda.

The first form of contract bears many names.

In the Venetian documents and statutes and in the statutes of Ragusa and Spalato it is described as *collegantia* (St. Venet. III, 1, 2, 3; Venetian laws in Sacerdoti, pp. 41 sqq.; St. Ragus. VII, 50; St. Spalat. III, 73). In the Genoese documents it is described generally as *com-(mm)endacio*, sometimes as *accomendacio* (Scriba, 945, 958), sometimes as *societas ad quartam proficui* (Scriba, 243, 340, 426). In Actes génois, I, p. 443, it is described as *accomendacio siue societas*. In the statutes of Ancona it is *recomandigio* (c. 50). It is sometimes spoken of as equivalent to *societas* (Consuetud. Amalfi, c. 14; St. Spalat. III, 73). For convenience' sake I call it *commenda*, which is the usual form, subject to varieties of spelling, at Pisa and Marseille.

The terms of the contract, as gathered from documents and statutes, are in substance the following:—

1. The advance may be, and generally is, in cash, but it may also consist of goods estimated in cash (e. g. Amalric, 479, in Blancard, II, p. 57). It is often described as so many 'librae implicatae in comunibus implicitis meis', i.e. B took various sums from various people and invested them all in goods which formed one common stock. It may also consist of a ship or part of a ship (Scriba, 508; Manduel, 11, in Blancard, I, p. 14; 'medietatem nauis

cum caricho salis et cum compaigna et cum adobo esti-
matam cxxx l.,' Manduel, 62, in Blancard, I, p. 91;
Manduel, 107, in Blancard, I, p. 172; Manduel, 135, in
Blancard, I, p. 218; Amalric, 219, in Blancard, I, p. 356;
Amalric, 233, in Blancard, I, p. 362; Amalric, 358,
in Blancard, I, p. 410; Amalric, 663, in Blancard, II,
p. 139). The contract in these cases was sometimes
a means, as has been already pointed out (p. clxv) of
investing the captain of the ship, generally one of several
joint-owners, with full authority over the shares belonging
to the other owners.

2. The terms on which the advance is to be used are
defined. In some cases B has the widest latitude of
dealing with the property (e.g. Sacerdoti, p. 27); in
others he is closely restricted.

3. When the expedition is over B submits his account
to A within a reasonable time. He is required to swear
to it on A's demand (Sacerdoti, p. 35; St. Venet. III, 1,
2; Établissemens de Montpellier, in Pardessus, IV, p. 255).

4. B is entitled to an allowance for victuals and other
necessary expenditure (Sacerdoti, p. 22). Where B has
received advances from several, his necessary expenditure
is taken out of the advances in proportion to their
amounts (St. Zeno, 112, 113; Venetian enactment of A.D.
1275 in Sacerdoti, p. 43). This is what is meant by the
phrase 'expensas debeo facere per libram' (Scriba, 301,
305).

5. The advance is made at A's risk; that is to say,
where it or part of it is lost without B's default, i. e. by
fire, shipwreck, or pirates, B is not liable to replace what
is lost (St. Ragus. VII, 50; St. Spalat. III, 73; Consuetud.
Amalfi, c. 14; St. Ancon. 88, ed. Pard.; St. Massil. III,
24). Various phrases are used in the documents to express the risk (see Scriba, 508; Sacerdoti, pp. 27, 36,
39; Baracchi, 90; Manduel, 3, in Blancard, I, p. 6.;
Manduel, 5, in Blancard, I, p. 8; Manduel, 40, in Blancard,
I, p. 54).

If the advance or part of it is lost by B's wilful default,

B is personally liable to make the loss good, e. g. if he takes an advance on the footing of trafficking within the Adriatic and goes outside (St. Ragus. VII, 50, cp. Assises de Jérusalem, 41 = ’Ασίζαι τῆς Κύπρου, μβ′; Assises de Jérusalem, 45 = ’Ασίζαι τῆς Κύπρου, μϛ′; St. Massil. III, 19, 20).

6. All gains made by B by virtue of the advance are brought into account (Sacerdoti, pp. 27, 35).

7. Where there has been no loss, the division is as follows. First, the whole of A's advance is replaced. Then the profits are divided in varying proportions, but the normal system is that A takes three-fourths and B one-fourth. B is often said to take the advance 'ad quartam partem lucri' or 'ad quartum denarium de omni lucro' (Baracchi, 90; St. Venet. III, 3; Venetian enactment of A. D. 1276 in Sacerdoti, p. 43; St. Ancon. 21; Consuetud. Amalfi, 14; Camera, I, p. 433; II, p. xli; L. Pisano, p. 114). Other divisions are these: (a) Where B is a relative of A he sometimes gets half the profits (Sacerdoti, p. 27). (b) Not unfrequently in the earlier documents he gets one-third of the profits (Sacerdoti, pp. 12 n. 4, 22, 35). At Ragusa one-third was regarded as B's normal share (St. Ragus. VII, 50). (c) Sometimes B gets one-fourth profits only on part of the sum (Amalric, 29, in Blancard, I, p. 274), and sometimes B's one-fourth is estimated at a fixed sum (Amalric, 444, in Blancard, II, p. 41). (d) In the Genoese documents B often gets simply his wages (conductus), the amount of which is generally specified (Scriba, 261, 302, 1464, 1503). (e) In one case the advance is taken 'absque quarto denario de lucro' (Amalric, 599, in Blancard, II, p. 115). Both parties are Jews. The transaction needs explanation.

8. Where B fails to perform his part of the contract, the documents often contain a penal clause (Sacerdoti, pp. 27, 36, 38; Camera, I, p. 433; II, p. xli), and, (9), the penal sum bears interest at 20 per cent. (Authorities, *supra*).

This contract has a by-form sometimes known as

rogadia or *rogancia*. In a Venetian document of A. D. 976 there is a release, 'de omni collegantia, rogadia, commendatione, prestito atque negociis' (Ficker, J., Forschungen, IV, p. 40), and practically the same phrase in another of A.D. 1038 (Baracchi, 1, in Arch. Veneto, V, p. 315). The *rogadia* is distinguished from the *collegantia* in St. Venet. III, 3, and in enactments in Sacerdoti, p. 43. Under the statutes of Ragusa and of Spalato, a man is not liable for losing a thing given him in *rogantia* if he loses it together with his own goods (St. Ragus. VII, 55; see definition by Gondola at p. 420; St. Spalat. VI, 37). This suggests that the *rogantia* had its origin in the deposit (see *ante*, p. lxxxix). If its distinguishing mark was that the man who took it got nothing for his trouble, it is not surprising that we hear so little about it.

The Mediaeval Societas.

The second form of contract, that in which A contributes twice as much as B, is included in the Venetian documents under the title of *collegantia*. It is more generally known as *societas* (Genoa) or *companhia* (Marseille). Its provisions correspond closely with those of the first form of contract. The following points deserve notice.

1. The partnership property may consist of cash, goods, or shares of a ship. Thus there are partnerships between the owners of two-thirds of a ship and the owners of one-third (Scriba, 328; Sacerdoti, p. 40). Shares in a ship form part of the partnership property in Sacerdoti, pp. 21, 29.

2. B as a rule has a wider discretion than in contracts of the first class. The duration of the partnership is generally fixed, but sometimes it lasts during the pleasure of the parties (Sacerdoti, p. 21).

3. If there is a complete loss not due to default, neither party has any claim against the other. If there is only a partial loss, what remains is divisible in the propor-

tions in which the capital was advanced (Sacerdoti, pp. 21, 30; Baracchi, 25, in Arch. Veneto, VII, p. 363; Amalric, 112, in Blancard, I, p. 311; 236, in Blancard, I, p. 364; 486, in Blancard, II, p. 62).

4. All gains made by B by virtue of the partnership property are brought into account (Sacerdoti, pp. 21, 30). Sometimes B took with him several *commende*, and it is then provided that his share of the profits of these *commende* is to be brought into the partnership account (Scriba, 329, 462, 1046, 1104; Amalric, 112, in Blancard, I, p. 311). His expenses in such cases are spread rateably over the amounts which he has in *commenda* and the partnership property (Scriba, 329, 346, 354).

5. Where there have been no losses, then, after the capital of the parties has been replaced, the profits are divided in equal shares (Scriba, 267, 329; Baracchi, 25, 93; Camera, I, p. 434; II, p. xl).[1]

PARTNERSHIP BETWEEN SHIP AND CARGO

As we have seen, our Sea-law assumes in most of its provisions that the merchant pays freight to the ship-owner, and that there is no direct relation between the merchant and the crew. The crew are paid by the ship-owner; they receive from him either a share in the profits of the voyage or a fixed wage. But, although this is evidently the normal system, there are some traces of another. The word κοινωνία occurs several times in connexions which suggest the existence of a

---

[1] Schaube (Gesch., p. 111, n. 3) corrects *perfectam medietatem* of Sacerdoti's document (p. 21) into *per fictam medietatem* 'mit Bezug darauf, dass es sich um zwei Schiffsantheile handelt, im Gegensatz zu dem sonst gebrauchten *per veram medietatem*.' I see no reason why the profits derived from shares in a ship are not susceptible of actual division as much as any other profits. In Sacerdoti, p. 30, although the partnership property consists of shares in a ship, the division is *per veram medietatem*. I agree with Schaube's correction, but explain it thus. The division in Sacerdoti, p. 21, takes place on the return from a taxegium, although the partnership does not then determine. It is therefore merely a hypothetical division.

partnership between shipowner and merchant, or between shipowner, merchant, and crew. Chapters 17 and 21, in which the word occurs, have already been dealt with (p. ccxxxv). There remain chapters 9, 27, 28, and 32.

C. 27 deals with a ship which is on its way to be loaded by a merchant or κοινωνία. In the table of chapters the word is either κοινωνία or κοινωνός. If the ship is wrecked in a gale, there is contribution between ship and the cargo to be loaded on board; but the captain keeps the half-freight. If a man falsely denies the existence of the κοινωνία, τὴν κοινωνίαν ἀποδιδότω. C. 32 may be another version of c. 27. According to the title, it deals with a ship which is hired or which sails in partnership (κοινωνίᾳ πλέοντος; the text is doubtful). The chapter speaks of a ship on its way to be loaded ἐμπόρου ναύλῳ ἢ κοινωνίᾳ (here again the text is doubtful). If an accident happens, the merchant is not to ask back his half-freight, but the ship and cargo (ἐνθήκη) are to go to contribution. The chapter also alludes to an advance made by the merchant or partner (ὁ τὴν κοινωνίαν). C. 28 deals with an injury to the ship where the loading has been delayed by the merchant or partner (κοινωνός). It would be possible to take κοινωνός, κοινωνία in these chapters as referring to a partnership between the merchants who load; but the more obvious interpretation is that they refer to a partnership between shipowner and owners of cargo. But they do not help us to ascertain the terms of the partnership; and they certainly do not show, as Zach. alleges (Geschichte, p. 317), that partnership between freighter and skipper was the customary form. The normal system in the Sea-law, if we may judge from the care with which it is regulated, is that in which the merchant hires the ship.

Evidence in favour of the view that a partnership often existed between the parties concerned in the maritime adventure is to be found not so much in the passages which refer expressly to partnership as in the elaborate provisions for contribution, which are at variance with the Roman law, and which would be easily explicable on the partnership hypothesis. Some support is given to this hypothesis by a passage which is found in most manuscripts at the end of c. 9. That chapter, as I point out hereafter (p. cclviii), presents the Roman doctrine of contribution with slight modifications. The passage at the end says that, if there is an agreement for sharing in gain, then, after everything on board and the ship have been brought into the valuation, each man is to contribute to the loss according to his share in the gain. It is arguable that this passage was introduced into the Sea-law when the Sea-law was edited with a view to its incorporation in the Basilica, and that it was introduced in order to bridge over the gulf which separated the Roman law doctrine of contribution, as laid down in the Basilica and the rest of c. 9, from the wider doctrine which is found in many chapters of the Sea-law. If there was a partnership between ship and cargo, then there would be nothing inconsistent with Roman law in the extended doctrine of contribution. But even if this passage was so introduced, that does not prove that partnership between ship and cargo lay at the root of the extended doctrine of contribution. The editors of the Sea-law may have brought in the conception of partnership, not because a partnership really existed in most cases, but because that conception would supply a logical justification for rules which would otherwise be inconsistent with fundamental principles of Roman law.

Κοινωνία is represented in mediaeval Latin by *comune, comunitas*. We get these words constantly in the maritime statutes; there was no lack of commonalties in the middle ages at sea as well as on shore. To take Ragusa alone, there is the *comunitas nauis* (St. Ragus. I, 17; II, 18; VII, 21, 31), the whole body of persons who share in the profits of ship,[1] and the *comune marinariorum* (St. Ragus. VII, 1, 20), sometimes also described

[1] In St. Ancon. 66, the 'comunità de la nave' is defined as 'lo navilio con la mercantia'. But in St. Ancon. 17 its meaning is more restricted.

as the *nauclerius cum societate sua* (St. Ragus. VII, 2, 52), the whole body of mariners. I have already dealt with the relations between the joint-owners of ship (p. clxiii) and between the captain and crew (p. clxviii). It remains to deal with the cases where there is a community between ship, crew, and merchants. Details of two systems have been preserved—that described in the Table of Amalfi and the system of the *entega* at Ragusa.

The System of the Colonna.

The Table of Amalfi[1] is in the main a code for ships which go 'ad usum de Rivera' (c. 1); perhaps in its original form it referred exclusively to them.

The custom of the coast was this. The owners of ship, the merchants and the mariners formed a partnership for the conduct of the maritime adventure, the owners giving the ship, the merchants the cargo, and the mariners their services. The whole body of persons interested formed the *societas* or *comunitas*. These words are used interchangeably, and the word *columna* (see later) has often the same meaning. The word *socii* (It. *compagni*) seems to be treated as equivalent to *nautae*. Doubtless any of the shipowners who sailed, with the exception of the managing owner, went as mariners; and so did any merchants who accompanied their goods. The management of the adventure was in the hands of a *patronus*, who was appointed by the shipowners ('patroni de caratis de navigio', c. 7; also called *parsonarii*, c. 9; in Italian, *porzonari*, c. 35).

For the purpose of distributing the gains of the adventure, the following arrangement was made. Each mariner had one share. The *patronus* could not give an

---

[1] Some chapters of the Consulate of Trapani agree closely with chapters in the Table. Table, c. 3 = Consulate, c. 8; Table, c. 10 = Consulate, c. 10 (latter part); Table, cc. 26, 27 = Consulate, cc. 6, 7. But in c. 12 of the Consulate the mariners receive monthly wages.

additional share ('partem de avantagio') to any mariner except the captain (*nauclerius*) and scribe; and then only with the consent of his co-owners (c. 9). The mariner on entering the service generally received an advance on account of his share (c. 1). The advance, as between himself and the other mariners, was made at the risk of the *patronus* (c. 17; cp. Codice Corallino, VI, 14). It was not subject to maritime risk (c. 43). If the sailor ran away he lost his share (c. 16).

The owners of ship had a number of shares varying with the value of their ship. According to a Latin chapter, the ship had a share for every ten salmae of capacity [1] (c. 5). According to an Italian chapter, it had a share for every six and a half ounces of value (c. 36. The amount may be different as the MS. is corrupt). If the ship was in want of repair when it started, its owners had to bear the expenses of putting it in repair (c. 20).

The *patronus* was entitled to take *ad accomandum* from any person and to oblige the ship to any person according to the custom of the coast (c. 7); and the *accomandum* and the ship formed one mass and one body (c. 6). The *accomandum* consisted either of money or of merchandise estimated in money. In some cases the form was gone through of a sale by the merchant to the *patronus* (c. 31). The merchant apparently had a share for every five ounces in value of the *accomandum* (c. 24).

A list was made in which were entered the ship with the number of shares which it carried, the goods of each merchant with their respective values, and the names of the mariners. This list was called the *columna* (It. *colonna*), and the *patronus* was obliged to show it to the mariners and partners when the voyage began and to state at the same time where they were going (cc. 4, 10, 66).

---

[1] The capacity of the ship was determined in measures of corn (Camera, I, p. 535). The salma of corn was about 160 liters (G. Yver, Le Commerce et les Marchands dans l'Italie Méridionale, Paris, 1903, p. 402).

The *patronus* was not entitled to insert in the *colonna* merchandise which had not been valued. Where he carried merchandise which had not been valued, it paid freight as in ordinary cases; if it was sold in the outport, the net proceeds of sale might be inserted in the *colonna* (c. 11, an obscure chapter). The *patronus* could not insert merchandise or men in the *colonna* nor remove them from it without the consent of a majority of the mariners or partners (c. 18, also obscure).

The word *colonna*, which strictly means a column in a page, containing a row of figures,[1] is used in the Table as equivalent to the partnership which is described there (see cc. 19 and 21), and later writers use *contratto di colonna* to denote a contract of partnership, either identical with or resembling the contract of partnership according to the custom of the shore (Targa, c. 36, p. 159; Alianelli, p. 93).

In ordinary cases the profits of the partnership were derived from the gains made by trafficking with the cargo taken in *accomandum*. All gains made during the partnership—'unumquodque lucrum vel invenctum vel ex exercitio quaesitum'—by the *patronus* or any of the mariners or partners also went to swell the *colonna*, subject to a reward, at the discretion of the Court, to the person to whom the gain was due (c. 12). Penalties imposed upon the mariners went into the *colonna* (c. 1).

---

[1] As Alianelli does not understand the meaning of *colonna* (pp. 93, 94), some references may be useful. 'Colonna è ciascuna filza di figure, che stieno una all' altra sopraposte dall' alto al basso' (G. B. Zucchetta, Arimmetica, Brescia, 1600, p. 3); 'Moltiplicare a colonna overo per tavoletta' (Lucas de Burgo, Summa Arithmetice, 1495, fol. 27 v.); 'moltiplicar per cholona' (Piero Borgi, Opera de Arithmeticha, 1517, p. 9 v.); 'partir per cholona' (Piero Borgi, op. cit., p. 16 r.); 'multiplicare per colona' (Tartaglia, Trattato di Numeri, 1556, I, p. 21 r.); 'partire per colona' (Tartaglia, op. cit., p. 29 r). Observe that Lucas de Burgo treats *colonna* as equivalent to *tavoletta*; and compare a passage in the Liber Abbaci di Leonardo Pisano, Roma, 1857, p. 21 'cum autem . . . quis . . . uoluerit colligere summas expensarum navium . . . describat in tabula linealiter pretium unius cuiusque rei.' These passages suggest that Tabula, in the title of the Amalfi document, has nothing to do with the tables of the law or the Twelve Tables, but is simply equivalent to *columna*.

No *patronus* or partner was entitled to take on his own account goods above the value of one ounce. If he did the profits went into the *colonna* (c. 29).

The profits of the *colonna* might also be augmented by the freight of merchandise carried on the ordinary terms (see c. 11), and by the fares paid by passengers. The *viciati* of c. 47 are probably *viaggianti*.

After the voyage (i. e. the voyage out and back) was over, the *patronus* gave his account in Court in the presence of the mariners or partners, and the net profits were divided according to the shares (c. 23). The decision of the consuls was final (c. 39). A consul could increase the share of a person who performed special services to the partnership (c. 12) or the allowance of a mariner or partner who was sent on shore (c. 13). The *colonna* was written in the acts of the Court (c. 30). If goods which had been given in *accomando* proved unsaleable, they might be returned in specie to the *accomandatario* (c. 31).

The Table deals specifically with various expenses which the *colonna* was liable to meet. Such are the allowance given to a mariner or partner sent on shore (c. 14); the doctor's bills of one who fell ill or was wounded (c. 14); the ransom of one who was captured (c. 15); the indemnity of one who was robbed (cc. 15, 45); the expenses of repairing the ship or of replacing tackle (cc. 19, 21, 37).

Wreck is dealt with in several places. Two Italian chapters (cc. 8, 33) provide for the case where the ship is wrecked and can be sold. The proceeds of sale are divided *pro rata* with the rest of the *colonna*. The ship is taken for the purpose of receiving contribution as of its value at the commencement of the partnership. It is not clear from these chapters whether the mariners receive a share of the divisible fund. Three other Italian chapters (cc. 26–28) deal with wreck or capture. If the ship is wrecked or captured, the cargo saved is divided *pro rata*. The mariners are not bound to contribute, but must restore any advance made them (c. 26). If ship is wrecked and can be repaired, the expenses of repairing it are to be borne by the partnership, including therein the mariners' share of profits (c. 27). If the ship is taken and can be ransomed, the ransom is to be borne by the partnership, but the mariners are not bound to contribute (c. 28). The last phrase probably means no more than that they are not bound to contribute personally; the partnership property would naturally include the amount of profits coming to them. C. 47 deals with jettison. The loss is to be made good from profits. So far as the profits are insufficient, or if there are no profits, the loss is to be distributed between the *colonna* and the ship according to their respective shares in profits. (*Colonna* is used here in the restricted sense of cargo.) The mariners are not bound to contribute, but they must restore the expenses of their food and any advance made them. Passengers (*viciati?*) must also contribute in respect of goods or money which they carry. The *patrone* must make good every loss, whether of capital belonging to the *colonna* or of tackle, which arises by his own neglect (c. 44).

The System of the Entega.

In the Table of Amalfi the ruling system is the system described above. In the Statutes of Ragusa, partnership between ship, goods, and mariners is only one of several systems, and is only expressly dealt with in a few chapters.

Franciscus de Gondola, a Ragusan lawyer of the sixteenth century, describes the system as follows (Stat. Ragus., p. 420):—' The *entigum* is the name of a partnership between the merchant and the shipowner. An agreed sum of money was laid down for purchasing goods and loading them on the ship. They were carried abroad and sold and the profits divided in three parts. One part went to the owner of the money, one part to the shipowner, and one part to the crew, or otherwise, as the parties agreed. Losses were distributed in the same proportion. The system and the name is still preserved in maritime Apulia and the neighbourhood.' He says elsewhere (p. 377) that the system was obsolete in his time at Ragusa.

The word *entigum* is not used in the Statutes. The Statutes speak of *entega* (*enticha*), and denote by it the contribution which is made by each merchant to the partnership in question.

The provisions of the Statutes which deal with the subject do not present a consistent whole. It is probable (as is so often the case) that additions have been made from time to time to an original and consistent body of law, and that no attempt has been made to bring the original into harmony with the additions.

The *entega* (ἐνθήκη) is either cash or goods valued in cash (VII, 49), which their owner has entrusted to the captain and crew for them to traffic with on a foreign voyage. Several *entege* belonging to different owners might be, and generally were, entrusted to the same captain and crew. A shipowner or a mariner might have an *entega* on board. Money received for necessary expenses of the ship might be received as an *entega* (VII, 17).

We must distinguish between the capital of an *entega* and the profits arising from it. As between the several owners of *entege*, they formed a common fund; whether they were in the shape of cash or of goods reckoned as cash, they had a common fortune, and any maritime loss was borne by the owners *pari passu* (VII, 44).

As between the owners of *entege* on the one hand and the shipowners and captain and crew on the other, the *entege* went at the owners' risk (VII, 42, 43). To this there was an exception. If a captain and crew received *entege* for a voyage within the gulf, and went outside it without the consent of a majority of owners of *entege*, and a loss occurred, it had to be made good by the captain and crew (VII, 48). And, just as ship and mariners did not contribute to a loss of *entege*, so, if the ship was wrecked, it was to be made good from its own profits and from the profits of the *entege*, but not from their capital (VII, 47). Another chapter provides that, if there is a loss of *entege*, the ship and the mariners are to share in the loss as they would in the gain (VII, 49). This probably merely means that they are to share in the loss to the extent of the profits which they would derive from the maritime adventure, and not that the ship is liable to be sold for the purpose of contributing to the *entege*, or that the mariners incur any personal liability.

Capital losses therefore, as between ship and *entege*, lay where they fell. As regards profits, the law stood thus. The profits arising from the *entege*, and from the freight of the voyage out and back, and the casual profits of the ship, were divisible in certain proportions between owners of *entege*, owners of ship, and mariners. If the voyage was within the gulf, the ship and mariners took two-thirds and the *entege* took one-third (VII, 42). If the voyage was outside the gulf, the *entege* took half and the ship and mariners half (VII, 43). Observe, it is not merely the profits of the *entege* which are thus divided. The profits of the *entege* are thrown into a common fund with the profits of the ship; and the aggregate mass is divided in fixed proportions. The proportions do not vary (as they do in the Table of Amalfi) with the shares held by ship, cargo, and mariners respectively. We must assume, if VII, 42 bears the meaning I have given it, that the *entege* bore a fixed proportion to ship. A ship which carried *entege* might also carry merchandise, which went at the owners' risk, paid freight, and of which the proceeds of sale might be put with the *entege* (VII, 44; cp. Table of Amalfi, c. 11).

The system contemplated by all these provisions is a system under which the management of the maritime adventure is in the hands of the captain and crew—'nauclerius cum suis marinariis.' They are not merely concerned with the navigation; they have control of the cargo, which may be supplied by the shipowner or by third persons. There is some analogy between their position and that of the travelling merchant who takes sums from a number of other merchants and invests them in one indiscriminate mass of goods (see *ante*, p. ccxxxvii). It is their duty to the owners of cargo to make the best of the cargo; and several provisions in the Statutes of Ragusa, like corresponding provisions in the Table of Amalfi with regard to the managing-owner, are concerned with preventing them from acquiring an interest which might conflict with that duty.

AVERAGE. JETTISON. CONTRIBUTION

An *avaria* in mediaeval Latin (see Duc. s. v.) is an expense or loss, and the word was applied specially to losses occurring in the course, or in respect, of navigation. The English word average has the same sense, but like many terms of commercial law it is used in a variety of other significations (see Park on Marine Insurance, 8th ed., I, p. 216). For the present purpose, it is sufficient to say that prima facie all losses occurring in the course, or in respect, of navigation lie where they originally fell (Consulate of Sea, cc. 152, 187; Targa, p. 322). Such a loss in English law is called a particular average. To this rule there are certain exceptions.

1. In the course of the voyage certain extraordinary expenses might fall on ship, and the shipowner might be entitled to charge a proportion of them against cargo. For instance, the Statutes of Ragusa, Phara, and Cattaro lay down that if, in a ship containing merchants, any sum is given by way of benevolence (*strina, strenna*) or for dues (*pedocia, pedochya*) or for any other purpose connected with the ship's safety by the will of the majority of those on board, that sum is to be the subject of average (St. Ragus. VII, 56; St. Lesin. V, 10; St. Cattaro, 379; and cp. Ordin. Trani, 8).

It is not uncommon in commercial documents to find

a provision throwing all *avarie* upon one of the parties. In cases of *commenda* the man who receives the property agrees to return it free from all *avarie* (Manduel, 12, in Blancard, I, p. 16 'mundos ab omnibus dacitis et avariis et de duana'; Manduel, 13, in Blancard, I, p. 17; Manduel, 69, in Blancard, I, p. 104; Manduel, 80, in Blancard, I, p. 121 'mundis de cathena et dacita et omnibus avariis'; Amalric, 88, in Blancard, I, p. 297 'computato ibi naulo et omnibus avariis conductis in nave'). So in cases of 'permutatio sive cambium' (Amalric, 145, in Blancard, I, p. 324; Amalric, 238, in Blancard, I, p. 365; Amalric, 977, in Blancard, II, p. 284). These phrases probably refer only to *avarie* of this class, which are called in English law general average losses.

2. But the word general average loss is used more frequently in a slightly different sense. The averages mentioned above are averages which the shipowner is entitled to throw to a certain extent upon the owners of cargo. The averages with which I am now dealing are losses which may fall on ship or on its tackle or on cargo, and which, wherever they originally fall, form the subject of contribution as between the different parties interested in the maritime adventure. The commonest source of the right to contribution is jettison.

In Roman law the doctrine of jettison is dealt with mainly in the Digest, XIV, 2 'de lege Rodia de iactu', and the rule is laid down clearly by the Roman jurists. 'The Rhodian law provides,' says Paulus (Dig. XIV, 2, 1 pr.), 'that, if goods are thrown overboard in order to lighten the ship, what is sacrificed for the common benefit should be made good by a common contribution.' 'It is settled,' says Hermogenianus (Dig. XIV, 2, 5 pr.), 'that an equity of contribution only exists when there is a common danger, and by the help of jettison the interests of others are protected and the ship is saved.' In the light of these statements of the principle, we may inquire, first, in respect of what property and under what conditions must the loss be incurred in order to be a general average loss; secondly, from what property may contribution be claimed; thirdly, how is property valued for purposes of contribution; and fourthly, what is the machinery for enforcing it.

I. The ordinary case of a common sacrifice is where goods are thrown overboard in a storm to lighten the ship (Dig. XIV 2, 1 pr.). The same principle applies where goods are transhipped into a lighter to lighten the ship, and the lighter sinks (Dig. XIV, 2, 4 pr.; Paul. Sent. II, 7, 4). Where goods are thrown overboard which covered other goods, and the goods exposed get wet, they are entitled to contribution to the extent to which they were deteriorated by the wetting (Dig. XIV, 2, 4, 2).

But the sacrifice must have the effect of ensuring the common safety. That is, in Roman law, the essential condition. Thus, where the ship is wrecked, and goods are brought up by divers for a reward, their owners cannot claim contribution in respect of the reward paid (Dig. XIV, 2, 4, 1). There is no contribution where slaves are lost at sea or die on board or throw themselves overboard (Dig. XIV, 2, 2, 5). But contribution takes place if the common safety is ensured at the moment, though the ship is wrecked later on. Goods brought up from the wreck contribute to goods which were thrown overboard at an earlier date (Dig. XIV, 2, 4, 1; Paul. Sent. II, 7, 3 (2)).

The Roman jurists evidently hesitated at first to grant contribution in respect of injuries to ship. Paulus did not admit it where an injury was done to the ship or tackle unless it was done 'voluntate vectorum vel propter aliquem metum'[1] (Dig. XIV, 2, 2, 1). On the other hand

---

[1] Mommsen is inclined to omit *vel*. The corresponding phrase in Paulus (Sent. II, 7, 2 (3) is 'ipsis (sc. *vectoribus*) arborem salutis causa eruentibus.' If it is kept, he interprets it of the passengers compelling the captain by threats to cut the mast. *Vel* is supported by the Synopsis Ambrosiana (LIII, 3, *a'*, p. 101). May it not have been inserted in the text of Paulus to bring it into harmony with the statements of the other jurists? In that case 'propter aliquem metum' would = 'removendi communis periculi causa.'

INTRODUCTION

Papinian and Hermogenian admit the right to contribution where the mast is cut down or other tackle destroyed to save ship and goods (Dig. XIV, 2, 3 pr.; 5, 1). Here again the condition is the attainment of the common safety. There is no contribution where the ship is obliged by storm to put in at an intermediate port and execute repairs (Dig. XIV, 2, 6 pr.), nor where the ship is wrecked and some of the goods are saved (Dig. XIV, 2, 5 pr.; 7 pr.).

As regards pirates, Paulus lays down (Dig. XIV, 2, 2, 3): ' si nauis a piratis redempta sit, Servius Ofilius Labeo omnes debere aiunt: quod uero praedones abstulerint, eum perdere cuius fuerint, nec conferendum ei, qui suas merces redemerit '. There are here two distinctions: (a) a distinction between the case where the ship is redeemed and the case where a man redeems his own goods; (b) a distinction between *piratae* and *praedones*. The latter distinction, which however the Synopsis Ambrosiana does not notice (LIII, Γ', β', FM., p. 102), is probably between sea robbers and land robbers; and this distinction throws light upon the other one. If a merchant goes ashore and has to pay ransom, he has no case for contribution. If pirates board a ship and let it go on receiving the passengers' cash and jewels, there is a case for contribution.

II. Everything is liable to contribute which has received a benefit from the sacrifice. Goods are liable to contribute even though they did not load the ship (e. g. gems, pearls) and therefore would not in any circumstances have been thrown overboard. Articles of domestic apparel or ornament are liable to contribute, but not consumable stores. The ship is liable to contribute. But free men are not liable to contribute merely because their lives have been saved, because free bodies cannot be valued (Dig. XIV, 2, 2, 2). It is nowhere stated that freight is liable to contribute.

III. For the purpose of ascertaining what each contributor has to pay, a valuation is made both of the things sacrificed and of the things saved. The things sacrificed are to be valued as of their value at the time of the loss, without taking into account the profit which, in the case of merchandise, might have been obtained by their sale. The things saved are to be valued at the price which they would fetch on sale (Dig. XIV, 2, 2, 4). Where goods get wetted on the occasion of a common sacrifice, the extent of their liability depends on the way in which they get wetted. If they get wetted simply because they are lying in a corner and the water comes in, they are to contribute according to their value as diminished by the wetting, i. e. their selling price. If, on the other hand, they get wetted because the removal of the goods which are sacrificed exposes them to the water, they are entitled to contribution in respect of the diminution in value as much as if they had been thrown overboard: while they are only bound to contribute in respect of their value as diminished (Dig. XIV, 2, 4, 2).

IV. The persons who ought to make contribution are under no direct liability to the persons entitled to enforce it. The only remedy of the latter is against the captain; it is for him to sue the owners of goods saved. The captain may also, if sued by the owners of goods lost, retain the goods saved until they contribute their share. But he is not obliged to do so (Dig. XIV, 2, 2 pr.). His liability is limited by what he can get from the passengers. He incurs no liability by letting a passenger go who afterwards turns out insolvent (Dig. XIV, 2, 2, 6). If contribution has been made, and goods which were thrown overboard are afterwards recovered by their original owners, those who have contributed may sue the captain to compel him to recover from those to whom payment has been made (Dig. XIV, 2, 2, 7).

So far as we can see from the scanty remains of Book LIII, title 3, of the Basilica, the Basilica adopts without alteration the principles of contribution laid down in the Digest. Our Sea-law, however, deals with contribution from an entirely different point of view.

This difference has formed with some scholars the principal ground for denying that the Sea-law could have been an original and integral part of the Basilica. It is therefore necessary to examine closely wherein the difference consists.

What is the *aequitas* on which the Roman lawyers base the claim to contribution? The following conditions, it would seem, must concur in order to raise it. 1. There must be a loss of, or damage to property— whether ship, tackle, or cargo. 2. The loss or damage must have been incurred intentionally, with a conscious view of saving other property. If the mast is cut down, the equity may arise; if the mast is blown down, it cannot. 3. The loss or damage must have produced the intended effect; the sacrifice must have brought about the common safety.

One point here requires to be dwelt on, in order to avoid a misunderstanding. Where it is said that the loss or damage must have been incurred intentionally, it is not necessarily implied that the owner of the property lost or damaged should have any intention in the matter. The intention is that of the person or persons in control of the ship. They have the power, and they make the sacrifice in the way most convenient to themselves. Where it is a case of jettison, they throw over the heaviest goods or those nearest at hand. It is immaterial whether the owner of the goods consents. He may see the danger as well as the others and see that it is most expedient to throw his goods over, and in that case he may make the sacrifice willingly. But his equity does not depend upon his eagerness. It really depends upon the inevitableness of the sacrifice.

If A voluntarily makes a sacrifice for the benefit of B, e. g. if he pays the premiums on B's life policy in order to prevent its forfeiture, he has no equity to be reimbursed by B. Unless he can make out a claim against B under contract, he must be content with the cold satisfaction of his own benevolence. Jettison of goods in a common peril stands on a different footing. Something must be sacrificed, or the whole will go to the bottom. It is the compulsion exerted upon the owner of the goods sacrificed in the first instance by nature, and in the second instance by his fellow travellers, which gives him his claim to contribution. The Roman jurists, who never dwelt upon circumstances which were legally immaterial, never deal with the actual facts of the jettison. They recognize that the act might be done by some other than the owner (Dig. XIX, 5, 14), but, whether it was done by the owner or by some one else against the owner's will, the legal result was the same, so long as it was done intentionally, and so long as it produced the desired effect.

The chapters in the Sea-law which deal with contribution—setting aside those in which there is distinct reference to a partnership (κοινωνία) and which have been already considered (pp. ccxxxv, ccxxxvi, ccxlii)—may be classified under three heads. 1. Some chapters deal with jettison proper, and in these, although there are subordinate provisions which modify or add to the rules of Roman law, there is nothing at variance with the general principle of sacrifice for the common safety on which the Roman law is based. 2. Intermingled with these chapters are others which lay down an entirely different rule. Many accidents may happen to a ship or its cargo, whether on the sea or in harbour. The ship may be wrecked, run into, burnt, or attacked by pirates. The cargo may be lost, wetted, or plundered. Now the Sea-law lays down in many places that, where there is a loss of this nature for which no one is to blame, ship and cargo, so far as saved, are to contribute to ship and cargo, so far as lost. There is no question here of a sacrifice for the common safety. It is only necessary that a loss shall occur in the course of the maritime adventure for which neither the owner of the property lost nor any other partaker in the maritime adventure can be held responsible. The result of the principle is

INTRODUCTION

that, by entering into the maritime adventure, you insure
to a certain extent the ship on which you sail and the
goods of your co-adventurers, while on the other hand
you are insured to the same extent by the owners of
ship and the other goods on board. 3. There is still
a third group of chapters in the Sea-law which are
generally treated as introducing a new rule of contribution, but which, in my opinion, have nothing to do
with contribution. Where shipwreck took place, there
was always a danger that the captain and crew might
avail themselves of the opportunity to plunder the merchants and passengers—especially passengers who carried
with them goods of great value in small compass. To
obviate this danger the rule was adopted that, where
there was a shipwreck and such goods were saved, their
owner should pay a proportion of their value to the captain and crew. The proportion varied with the character
of the goods. The payment was not in any sense a contribution to the shipowner. It was, on the contrary,
a bribe to the captain and crew not to plunder the goods,
an incentive to them to protect them. I pass to a detailed examination of the chapters in the Sea-law which
fall under these three heads.

I. Of the chapters which speak of jettison (ἐκβολή or
ἀποβολή) two (cc. 9, 38) clearly refer to jettison in the
strict sense in which *iactus* is used in the Digest.

Chapter 9 deals distinctly with Roman jettison and
introduces the following modifications of Roman law.
(a) The captain before jettison is to ask the passengers
who have goods on board, and they are to vote what
is to be done. (b) The personal luggage contributes as
it does in Roman law, but a pecuniary limit is placed
upon the valuation according as the luggage belongs to
the captain or a passenger, to a ship's officer or to a
common sailor. (c) Slaves contribute as they do in
Roman law, but they are to be valued at a fixed amount,
three minas for a passenger's body-slave, two minas for
a slave who is merely merchandise. (The text here is

doubtful.) Chapter 38 introduces another modification of the Roman law. (*d*) When there is jettison the merchant is to throw first and then the sailors are to take a hand. As regards these provisions (*a*) and (*d*) will be dealt with hereafter; (*b*) and (*c*) are simple rules of convenience. It is obvious that an arbitrary valuation made by statute or an arbitrary limit imposed by statute upon a valuation saves trouble and expense and removes opportunities for dispute, and that such a valuation is therefore to be recommended when it works no substantial injustice.

Chapter 22 may refer to a case of jettison in the strict sense. It provides that, if the captain overloads the ship in spite of the merchant's protests and there is jettison, the captain is responsible. If the merchant has not protested contribution takes place.

Chapters 35, 43, and 44, although they speak of jettison, probably come under the next head.

II. In contrast with the chapters dealt with above, and which, as I have shown, are not inconsistent with the principles of the Roman law, stands a group of chapters which lay down a different and inconsistent principle. The loss of the ship or its tackle, according to the Roman law, gave no right to contribution. According to these chapters the loss of the ship or its tackle gives a right to contribution from cargo unless the loss has arisen from the default of the captain or the captain and crew. The loss of the cargo, according to Roman law, did not give any right to contribution. According to these chapters the loss of cargo gives a right to contribution from ship and from other cargo unless the loss has arisen from the default of the owner of cargo. The rule applies as between the ship on the one hand and the cargo on the other, and as between different parts of the cargo *inter se*. The rule is nowhere laid down as applying to the personal luggage of passengers which, as will be shown hereafter, is governed by different considerations. The phrases used for the subject-matter of contribution are:

τὰ σωζόμενα μέρη τοῦ πλοίου καὶ τῶν φορτίων (c. 10); τὰ σωζόμενα τοῦ πλοίου ἅμα καὶ φορτίοις (c. 27); τὰ ἐκ τοῦ πλοίου
σωζόμενα καὶ τοῦ φόρτου (c. 30); τὰ σωζόμενα πάντα (c. 31);
τὰ τοῦ πλοίου καὶ τῆς ἐνθήκης (c. 32); τὰ εὑρισκόμενα ἐν τῷ
πλοίῳ ἅμα τοῦ πλοίου (c. 33); πάντα (c. 39). These phrases
all come to the same thing. In some cases the Sea-law,
instead of speaking of the objects for which or from
which contribution is claimed, speaks of the persons for
whom or from whom it is claimed: πάντες οἱ ναῦται καὶ οἱ
ἔμποροι καὶ τὰ φορτία καὶ τὸ πλοῖον σωθέντα εἰς συμβολὴν
ἐρχέσθωσαν (c. 35); ἐπιγινωσκέτωσαν τὴν ζημίαν ὅ τε ναύκληρος
καὶ οἱ ναῦται ἅμα τῷ ἐμπόρῳ (of an injury to cargo) (c. 38).
These phrases do not refer to any personal liability of
captain or crew or merchant: they are merely picturesque
ways of putting what is put impersonally in other places.

Contribution in these chapters arises where there is
any injury to, or loss of ship, tackle, or cargo which is not
imputable to any of the parties to the maritime adventure. Where the injury or loss is imputable to the owner
of the property injured or lost, he has no claim to contribution. Where it is imputable to some one else, the
claim of the owner of the property injured or lost is not
contribution but indemnity. The cause of the injury or
loss is sometimes described generally as a sea danger
or sea event: τι τῶν κατὰ θάλασσαν κινδύνων (c. 30); τῶν
κατὰ θάλασσαν (c. 32). Sometimes it is particularized as
a storm: ζάλη (cc. 27, 38), or as piracy, fire, or wreck
πειρατεία ἢ πυρκαϊὰ ἢ ναυάγιον: (cc. 28, 29).

The rule apparently comes into operation as soon as
the ship starts from its home port, although it has not
yet picked up the cargo; and it continues to operate until
the cargo is unloaded at its place of destination. Chapter
27 refers to a case where the ship is on its way to be
loaded and provides as follows. (a) If the ship is wrecked
through carelessness of the sailors or captain, cargo lying
in warehouses is not liable to contribute. (b) If the ship
is wrecked in a gale, what is saved from the ship together
with cargo is to come into contribution. This must mean

that the cargo waiting to be loaded is liable to make contribution. Chapter 32 is obscure, but is probably to the same effect. Chapter 29 applies to the case where the ship is in harbour waiting to be loaded. If anything happens and the merchant is not in default there is to be contribution. The language is vague. It is not stated whether goods not yet loaded on board are liable to contribute. Chapter 33, on the other hand, applies to the case where the merchant has unloaded his goods in the place fixed by the contract, and provides that, if anything happens to the ship thereafter, the goods which have been unloaded are not liable to contribute either to the rest of the cargo or to the ship. Contribution can only be claimed as between ship and goods which are still on board.

There is nothing in Part III of the Sea-law dealing with valuation apart from c. 9. In Part II, c. ىٯ' deals with the valuation of ship. That chapter has been already considered (p. cliii). The Sea-law never deals with procedure in this connexion.

III. Chapters 30, 31, 37, 40, and 41 deal in the main with a subject which is not to be confused with contribution. Under Roman law the personal effects of travellers by sea, including articles of great value in small compass, which they may carry on their persons or as part of their personal luggage, are entitled to receive and bound to make contribution on the same footing as any part of the cargo. In c. 9 of the Sea-law this provision is repeated with respect to the clothing, bedding, &c., of passengers, except that a limit is fixed to the valuation. It is generally, but wrongly, supposed that chapters 30, 31, 37, 40, and 41 carry out the rule of the Digest except that they fix a limit to the amount to be exacted from such articles respectively.

Their provisions are shortly as follows : c. 30 provides that the merchant in case of shipwreck is to pay one-tenth of his gold if he is saved without clinging to any of the ship's spars. If he has to cling to a spar to be saved he pays one-fifth. C. 31 provides that the merchant in case of shipwreck is to pay one-fifth of his silver. C. 37 applies both to merchants and passengers, and provides that instruments of indebtedness are to pay one-fifteenth. C. 40 applies exclusively to passengers, and fixes the proportions which they are to pay: one-tenth of gold, one-fifth of silver, and one-tenth of whole silks or pearls. C. 41 appears to sum up in a general way the contents of cc. 37 and 40. 'If there are passengers on board and the ship is lost, but the passengers' goods are saved, let the passengers make a payment (ἐπιφερέτωσαν) towards the loss of the ship.' It also prescribes in a very vague way payment by passengers who have not lost to those who have. Now, if these are cases of contribution, there is this initial difficulty. If gold is to pay 10 per cent. of its value, silver 20 per cent., &c., whatever be the contribution required, it is obvious that these articles may contribute a much larger amount than, on any equitable consideration, could be required from them.

In my opinion the percentage payable in respect of gold, silver, &c., by the owner has nothing to do with contribution. It is a reward payable to the captain and sailors, partly for their exertions in assisting to save the articles in question, partly for their self-restraint in not knocking the merchant or passenger on the head and possessing themselves of his belongings. It must be remembered that there was no hard and fast line between the mariner and the pirate. In the Mediterranean, piracy, until a much later period than the date of the Sea-law, was the resource of the young, active, and resolute among the sea-faring population. The merchant service was manned to a great extent by pirates who were getting too old for that honourable calling. There must always have been some danger that the temptation of a large booty would revive the habits of youth; it was the object of these provisions to offer a counterpoise to such temptation.

This view is fortified by a careful consideration of

their language. Chapters 30 and 31 deal with the case where the merchant has loaded the whole ship. They draw a contrast between the contribution which takes place between ship and cargo and the payment to be made in respect of gold or silver: τὰ ἐκ τοῦ πλοίου σωζό-μενα καὶ τοῦ φόρτου εἰς συμβολὴν ἐρχέσθωσαν, τὸ δὲ χρυσίον κτλ. (c. 30); τὰ σωζόμενα πάντα εἰς συμβολὴν ἐρχέσθωσαν ἑκάτερα, τὸ δὲ ἀργύριον κτλ. (c. 31). In c. 30 the proportion which the merchant has to pay depends on whether he was saved by clinging to a spar or not. The natural tendency of the predatory mariner would be to thrust the merchant off while retaining his pocket-book; the merchant who is allowed to get to shore on a spar pays just twice the proportion of the merchant who reaches the shore unaided. In c. 31 the captain and crew are directed to assist in the salvage. This is not a mere exhortation. Probably remissness on the part of a captain or sailor would disentitle him to his percentage. C. 37 applies not merely to a merchant but to merchants or passengers. It is distinctly said that they are not to give the ship to the captain, which is probably a loose way of saying that they are not to contribute in the strict sense.

The words used with regard to the payment to be made are vague: δεκάτας ἀποδιδότω, πέμπτας ἐπιφερέτω (c. 30); πέμπτας ἐπιδιδότω (c. 31); πεντεκαιδεκάτας παρε-χέτωσαν (c. 37); δεκάτας παρεχέτω, πέμπτας ἐπιφερέτω, δεκάτας ἐπιφερέτωσαν (c. 40). It is true that in c. 40 there are phrases which suggest that this is a case of συμβολή. τὰ δὲ ὁλοσηρικὰ . . . εἰς συμβολὴν ἐρχέσθωσαν . . . οἱ δὲ μαργαρῖται . . . τελείτωσαν τὴν ἀπώλειαν (c. 40). These phrases show nothing more than that a certain confusion existed in the minds of the compilers of the Sea-law.

Two other passages may be brought into connexion with the view expressed above. C. 38 is obscure, but it seems to mean this. Where the cargo is injured by tempest, the captain and crew are to contribute to the loss; but the captain, together with the ship and crew, are to receive a certain proportion—probably 6 per cent.—of what is saved. This suggests that the proportion, whatever it may be, is a direct payment to the captain and crew. The same chapter provides that a sailor who commits theft is to lose all his gain, which must mean his share in the proportion aforesaid. C. 45 provides that where a ship is lost, he who saves anything and brings it to land is to receive one-fifth.

These chapters, therefore (cc. 30, 31, 37, 40, 41), may be definitely removed from the law of general average contribution to the law of salvage, under which head some parallels will be adduced from other mediaeval codes.

Natural equity does not satisfy Goldschmidt (Lex Rhodia) as a foundation for the doctrine of contribution. 'Ganz und gar auf jede dogmatische Konstruktion ist endlich verzichtet, wenn die Kontributionspflicht direct auf "aequitas"—natürliche Billigkeit—zurückgeführt wird' (p. 56). If by a 'dogmatische Konstruktion' he means a reasoned and reasonable body of rules, the answer is that the Roman lawyers, who based their doctrine of contribution on natural equity, had no difficulty in forming one. But whether natural equity is or is not a sufficient logical foundation for the doctrine, it is not necessarily the historical one, and Goldschmidt prefers to find this not in equity but in contract. According to him contribution had its origin in an agreement to which the shipowner and the owners of cargo were parties, and which had for its effect to unite in one aggregate mass, for the purpose of supporting the risks of the maritime adventure, the ship and the various articles which made up the cargo.

The authorities often speak of consultations or parleyings between captain, crew, and freighters or between some of these as a usual, or necessary, prelude to jettison. The Sea-law itself does in c. 9. Such a consultation may, as Goldschmidt admits (pp. 328–31), be looked at from any one of three points of view. 1. It may be a necessary condition of the existence of contribution: 'ein formeller Vertragsakt.' That is to say, unless there is a consultation, and unless that is followed by an agreement between the parties concerned, one party can have no right, in case of jettison, to claim contribution from another. 2. It may be evidence—perhaps the only admissible evidence—that the circumstances have concurred which alone justify jettison : ' ein formeller Beweisakt.' That is to say, unless there is consultation, or consultation followed by agreement, the Courts will assume, in case of dispute, that the peril had not arisen which made jettison necessary. 3. It may be a mere measure of prudence : ' eine blosse Zweckmässigkeitsmassregel.' That is to say, the captain, before making jettison, consults the crew or the passengers or both, not because their consent is legally necessary but because they are likely to know quite as much about the matter as he does—because there are men among them whose nautical experience and knowledge of winds and weathers is probably as great as his own, and also because, whatever their knowledge or experience may be, they will probably insist on having their opinion asked and their decision followed, whether the captain wish it or no. Now, as Goldschmidt says (p. 331), it requires a close analysis of each body of law to ascertain which of these points of view the law in question takes when it prescribes consultation or consent before jettison. Although in itself— I still quote Goldschmidt—the first view appears to be the earlier, because it lies at the root of the law of contribution, whose existence is presupposed by the other views—nevertheless the first view is only carried out completely and unambiguously in the Consulate of the Sea and the cognate Customs of Tortosa—i. e. in Catalan Law.

In the Consulate of the Sea, according to Goldschmidt, the partnership in the risk which leads to contribution, whether it is a partnership between ship and cargo or between cargo belonging to different freighters, is always founded on agreement or the fiction of agreement. The agreement is made, according to the circumstances of each case, between the captain and the freighters. In cases of danger the consent of a majority of the freighters is sufficient. If there is no call upon the ship for contribution, the agreement is made between the freighters exclusively. If there are no freighters or representatives of the freighters on board, the captain by a legal fiction assumes the position of sole freighter or owner of the whole cargo. In this case he has to summon the ship's officers and crew, but they act not as mere advisers. As the captain is supposed to act on this occasion on behalf of the freighters or owners of cargo, so the ship's officers and crew are supposed to represent the shipowners, and thereby a contract becomes possible. The contract is described as *ceremonia*, and it consists in the declaration that the one object (ship, cargo) shall stand in with the other, shall join in making good any injury to it. This agreement is called agermanament: the act is 'agermanar la nau ab l'aver' and vice versa, or 'agermanar una roba ab altra'. Agermanament is an act of fraternization, but it is not persons who are made brethren but things. It is the same legal conception which called forth the fraternization of Germanic antiquity with its reciprocal obligation of help—it is the same in which lies the germ of the Scandinavian, and probably also of the West Germanic Schutzgild, and further of the Kaufgild or Hanse (p. 344). This act of fraternization, whether it took place at the time of loading or, as was much more usual, in the presence of the common danger— whether it was carried out by a real contract or by the captain alone—was the legal act which in the eye of the law produced the partnership in the risk (p. 351). Agermanament must not be confused with the later germinamento. Agermanament is a genuine, though very peculiar, partnership for the exclusive object of bearing the danger in common. Germinamento, on the other hand, is a jettison which takes place with the consent of the freighter or the crew or both together, and it is based exclusively on a statutory power given to the majority of those interested for a common purpose.

AVERAGE. JETTISON. CONTRIBUTION

So far Goldschmidt, with whom I respectfully disagree. The Consulate of the Sea, or other Catalan legislation, is not a sufficiently firm basis to build such a theory on. The doctrine of agermanament, as it appears there, may be the relic of a remote past; it may equally well be a product of the misplaced ingenuity of some one among the compilers of the Consulate. In dealing with that work we must not forget the part of mere invention, and, because a theory which appears there is unreasonable or fantastic, it is not safe to assume that it is a relic of German legal antiquity. In order to ascertain the real meaning and legal effect of the consultations between captain, crew, and passengers which are sometimes required by the mediaeval statutes, it is necessary to pass in review their provisions on this subject[1]; and we shall in so doing come across several passages which throw light on the Sea-law. Before, however, turning to the statutes, one passage should be mentioned of an earlier date, which may refer to general average contribution.

A cook in Diphilus (apud Athen. 291 f, Kock II, p. 554) is giving a list of the kinds of employer to seek or to avoid :—

> ναύκληρος ἀποθύει τις εὐχήν, ἀποβαλὼν
> τὸν ἱστὸν ἢ πηδάλια συντρίψας νεώς,
> ἢ φορτί' ἐξέρριψ' ὑπέραντλος γενόμενος·
> ἀφῆκα τὸν τοιοῦτον· οὐδὲν ἡδέως
> ποιεῖ γὰρ οὗτος, ἀλλ' ὅσον νόμου χάριν·
> ὁμοῦ δὲ ταῖς σπονδαῖσι διαλογίζεται
> τοῖς συμπλέουσιν ὁπόσον ἐπιβάλλει μέρος
> τιθείς, τά θ' αὑτοῦ σπλάγχν' ἕκαστος ἐσθίει.

What is meant by the share which falls upon his fellow-travellers? One explanation is this. Where a vow is made on board ship for the benefit of the whole ship's company, the expenses of carrying it out are

---

[1] On this occasion I also refer to some northern statutes.

apportioned rateably among those for whose benefit it was
made (cp. Statutes of Riga, XI, 5, in Pard. III, p. 509).
This may be all that is meant. It is, however, singular
that the cook should mention the cutting down of the
mast and the jettison of cargo—both cases for general
average contribution. On the other hand, the shattering
of the rudder sounds more like an accident.

The statutes fall into two groups. 1. Some of them,
e. g. the maritime statutes of Ancona, the Constitutum
Usus of Pisa, present a complete theory of the law of
general average contribution. 2. Others again, e. g.
Ragusa, Venice, Zara, Spalato, only deal with isolated
points in the law. They presuppose a custom—*consuetudo* or *usus* (St. Zara, IV, 75 ; St. Spalat. VI, 46 ;
St. Tiep. A 35)—by which the cases are governed, and
the statutes merely intervene where there is a dispute as
to the terms of the custom—'ut omne prorsus litigium
tollatur', St. Zara, IV, 55—or where it is found necessary
to modify it.

In classifying the testimony of the statutes, I follow
the division which I adopted in dealing with Digest
XIV, 2. After arranging the statutory material under
the first three of the four heads given in p. cclii, I shall
deal with those statutes which in their theory of contribution differ widely from the common type.

I. We have seen that, according to the Sea-law (c. 9),
with which the Συγγραφή in Adv. Lacritum (p. 926, 16)
closely agrees, the captain before making jettison is to
take a vote of the passengers who have goods on board.
We have also seen that, according to c. 38, when there
is jettison the merchant is to throw first, and then the
sailors are to take a hand. The statute of Ragusa (VII,
58) speaks as if jettison was not valid unless made with
the consent of the captain and of a majority of those on
board. C. 87 of the maritime statutes of Ancona admits
contribution in two cases. (1) The ship in a storm
throws goods overboard after deliberation by the owner,
captain, and merchants on board or the majority of

them. (2) A loss is incurred in order to ransom the ship or cargo after a similar deliberation.

According to the Ordinamenta of Trani, if there is a storm and there are no merchants on board, the shipowner is entitled to throw cargo overboard with his own hand. He cannot be questioned because he does it to save the persons on board and the rest of the cargo (c. 26). If a ship is attacked by corsairs and there are no merchants on board, the shipowner may make a compact with the corsairs, giving them gold, silver, or part of the cargo to save the ship and the rest of the cargo (c. 27, cp. c. 31).

The Table of Amalfi deals first with a ship which sails under the system of the *colonna*. If after consultation jettison is found necessary, the owner is to throw first and then give permission to the comrades to throw (c. 47). The Table deals secondly with a ship which has been hired by merchants. If jettison becomes necessary, the owner is to take counsel with the merchants or, if the merchants are absent, with their agents, and explain to them the necessity of jettison. The merchant, is to throw first. If neither the merchant nor any representative is present, the owner may throw after consultation with the captain and majority of the comrades (c. 48). If the merchant from avarice refuses to make jettison, the owner after taking counsel with the captain and other good men of the ship may do it himself (c. 49).

The Constitutum Usus of Pisa (c. 29) distinguishes between 'iactus cum concordia' and 'iactus sine concordia'. (1) There is a storm. A majority in number of the owners of cargo (*henticales*) or, if there are none on board, a majority of the mariners agree to make jettison. He who throws overboard without agreement is liable for the goods thrown. If an owner of goods thrown makes a claim against the mariners who were not owners of cargo for improper jettison, they can only protect themselves by swearing that they threw 'sine fraude et pro timore iudicii'. (2) Jettison made 'sine

INTRODUCTION

concordia' is valid if made 'propter inminens et repentinum periculum', e. g. if the ship is going on the rocks.

The statutes of Genoa require, as a condition for contribution in case of jettison, the consent of a majority of the merchants or owners of cargo (St. Pera, V, 25 ; Officium Gazariae, A. D. 1441, c. 98 in Pard. IV, p. 521 ; Leges Genuenses, 739, 793). The statute of Marseille (IV, 30) simply reproduces in abstract the Constitutum Usus of Pisa. According to the customs of Valencia (IX, 17, 7 ; Pard. V, p. 336) and Tortosa (IX, 27, 30) there must be an agreement of the crew and merchants or a majority of them, and one of the merchants must begin. The Barcelona Ordinance c. 27 (Pard. V, p. 362) requires the consent of a majority of the merchants. If there are no merchants or representatives of merchants on board, a majority of the crew must consent.

According to the Rooles d'Oléron, the captain, before he throws goods overboard, must ask the consent of their owners. But he may throw without their consent if he and three of the crew on reaching the port of discharge take an oath 'qu'il nel faisoit de nul malice mès pur saufver leurs corps, la neef et les darrées et les vyns' (Rooles d'Oléron, 8 in Pard. I, p. 328; Jugemens de Damme, 8 in Pard. I, p. 375). This provision looks as if it were borrowed from the Constitutum Usus of Pisa. Where the shipowner cuts the mast or cables, he must call the merchants and show them that the measure is necessary to save ship and cargo (Rooles d'Oléron, 9 ; Jugemens de Damme, 9).

According to other Northern statutes, there is no right to contribution where the masts or the cables are cut unless there has been a previous agreement (Law of Hamburg of A. D. 1270, c. 22 in Pard. III, p. 346 ; Law of Lubeck of A. D. 1299, c. 24 in Pard. III, p. 410 ; Law of Riga of A. D. 1270, c. 162 in Pard. III, pp. 506, 509). This is evidently taken straight from the Digest : 'nisi voluntate vectorum.' (See p. ccliii.)

cclxx

None of the provisions which I have hitherto cited
supports the contention of Goldschmidt. According to
him, they are relics of an earlier stage, in which the
right to contribution in case of jettison depended not on
equity but on contract. There is no trace of that in
these cases. It cannot, so far as they go, be put any
higher than this, namely, that the consent or acquiescence
of the majority on board is necessary to show that a case
for jettison has arisen. If a merchant alleges that his
goods have been thrown without necessity and that
therefore he is entitled to be indemnified by the shipowner, you answer him by proving consent. If a merchant alleges that another man's goods were thrown
without necessity and that therefore he is not bound
to make contribution, again you answer him by proving
consent. The Roman lawyers lay down the principle.
The jettison must be 'removendi communis periculi
causa'. The mediaeval codes answer the question; what
is to prove that there was a *commune periculum* and that
the act was done *removendi causa*? On this view, the
necessity for consent is a development, and not a sur-
vival.

The Digest lays down (XIX, 5, 14, pr.) that he who
throws another man's goods into the sea to save his own
is not liable to an action; if he did it without cause,
he may be sued *in factum*; if he did it from malice, he
may be sued *de dolo*. This passage applies only to an
owner of cargo; various statutes extend its provisions
to a mariner, or lay the law down in general terms. He
who throws goods overboard without the consent of the
nauclerius and a majority of those on board must indemnify their owners (St. Ragus. VII, 58; St. Phara, V,
11). If a mariner or *viciato* throws without licence of
the owner or merchant, he must make good the damage
himself (Table of Amalfi, 48).

The statutes in determining when contribution may
be claimed follow as a rule the strict doctrine of Roman
law. It is universally admitted that if cargo is thrown

overboard to lighten the ship, the cargo thrown is entitled to contribution from ship and the rest of cargo.

The rule of Roman law imposing contribution if the ship is ransomed by pirates is generally followed (St. Ragus. VII, 7 'si adveniret quod navis ... dampnum aliquod haberet per cursarios'; St. Phara, V, 2 'si aliquod navilium ... per piratas vel per cursarum esset acceptum'; Ordin. Trani, 3 'se la mercatantia dela nave fusse robata da corsari'; see also 27; Consuetud. Bari, f. 118, ed. 1550; p. 153, ed. Alianelli, where read 'emptica tamen empticae conferet (text, *conferret*) spoliatae etsi expressim (text, *expressum*) pirata (text, *pro rata*) dixerit se illius empticam ablaturum'; Consolato of Trapani, c. 6).

The statute of Ancona (c. 87) makes a distinction. There is contribution if the ship or goods are ransomed. There is no contribution if corsairs take goods or merchandize from a ship. This distinction is evidently based on the Digest (XIV, 2, 2, 3). According to the statute of Lubeck, there is no contribution where the goods of some merchants are taken by pirates (Pard. III, p. 415).

Where a ship makes jettison or cuts the mast or runs ashore in order to escape pirates or corsairs, contribution might be claimed on the principles of Roman law, although these cases are not expressly mentioned in the Digest.

The statutes contain various provisions which, though not found in the Roman authorities, are not inconsistent with them. Goods ought to be, but are not, written down in the manifest (*quaternus*). They are taken by pirates or thrown into the sea. Their owners cannot claim contribution (St. civil. Venet. VI, 68; C. Tortosa, IX, 27, 39). Where the owner of gold, silver, pearls, or other articles of great value in small compass does not assign them to the shipowner, captain, or *scrivano*, and a case for contribution arises either by reason of corsairs or storm, these goods cannot claim it (Ordin. Trani, c. 23). Where goods improperly carried on deck are jettisoned, their owner under the statute of Marseille (IV, 20) cannot claim contribution if they were so carried with his consent. Under the Genoese law, where they are jettisoned, the damage is to be made good by the shipowners notwithstanding any agreement between them and the merchants (St. Pera, V, 10; Off. Gazariae, c. 8 in Pard. IV, p. 464; Leges Genuenses, 737, 792; accord probably St. Ancon. 45, 86). Some statutes provide that goods on deck are to be thrown first (Breve dell' Ordine di Mare of Pisa, c. 81; Off. Gazariae, *supra*; Law of Berghen of A.D. 1274 in Pard. III, p. 32; Icelandic Law in Pard. III, p. 74).

The Sea-law lays down (c. 22) that, where the ναύκληρος overloads in spite of the merchant's protest, and there is jettison, the ναύκληρος is responsible. There are passages to the same effect in other statutes. The statute of Spalato (VI, 73, p. 231), after stating the law as above, adds that, if the merchant is responsible for overloading, he must make good any damage. The Table of Amalfi (c. 49) agrees with the Sea-law.

The following provisions are inconsistent with Roman law, but in agreement with the extended doctrine of the Sea-law. If cargo is damaged by water without any default of the shipowner, the damage is to be the subject of average (St. Spalat. VI, 46; St. Zara, IV, 75, where a passage has dropped out in Pard.'s text).

In the statutes of Ragusa, Phara, Spalato, and Venice, any loss of, or injury to tackle is the subject of contribution (St. Ragus. VII, 7; St. Phara, V, 2; St. Spalat. VI, 51; St. Tiep. A, 35). In the statutes of Venice, with which those of Zara partly agree, the regulations are complicated. The law originally stood thus. Where a ship was hired to merchants, injury to, or loss of tackle was the subject of contribution as between cargo and ship; where it was hired to pilgrims, the injury or loss was borne exclusively by the ship. Distinctions were afterwards introduced based on (*a*) the cause of the injury or loss, (*b*) the character of the tackle (St. Tiep. A, 36, 37 = St. Zara, IV, 31; St. Zeno, 74-79).

In other statutes loss of, or injury to tackle is either

expressly excluded from contribution (St. Ancon. c. 46) or only gives a right to contribution when the tackle is destroyed or injured to save persons, goods, and ship (Ordin. Trani, cc. 2, 22).

In the Pisan charter-party of A.D. 1263 the shipowners agree not to demand contribution in respect of tackle (Mas Latrie, Documents, p. 41).

According to the customs of Bari, a pilgrim ship is not subject to the law of contribution (f. 118, ed. 1550; p. 152, ed. Alianelli).

II. The next question is, from what may contribution be claimed. The general principle is that whatever remains of the maritime adventure after the loss, whether ship, cargo, or personal luggage, must contribute to the loss. This is put sometimes by saying that the loss is to go *per varea* or *ad varea* (St. Spalat. VI, 46; St. Zara, IV, 75; Ordin. Trani, 2, 3, 26). In other cases *varea* is defined. It is said that the loss is to be made good out of the cargo on board and the ship. Sometimes a deduction of one-third is made from the valuation of the ship.

Under the statutes of Ragusa, a loss from jettison or corsairs is to be made good 'per varea de habere invento in ipsa nave et eciam de ipsa nave, appreciando eam tercius minus'. A loss to tackle is to be made good 'de comuni habere navis et eciam de ipsa nave, appreciando dictam navim . . . et prohiciendo ipsam tercium minus' (St. Ragus. VII, 7). Under the statute of Tiepolo, a loss to tackle is to be made good 'de communi habere navis et etiam de ipsa nave secundum usum ' (St. Tiep. A, 35).

Under the statutes of Phara, a loss to tackle is to be made good 'de communi sive de mercatione et navilio sive ligno, secundum erit aestimatum '. A loss from jettison or corsairs ' similiter vadat per avariam ' (St. Phara, V, 2). Under the statutes of Spalato, where there is a loss to tackle, ' fiat contributio inter patronum et mercatores pro rata parte ' (St. Spalat. VI, 51). Under the statutes of Tiepolo, the expenses of getting the ship out of the harbour of Venice are to be borne ' de communi habere navis et etiam de ipsa nave secundum usum' (St. Tiep. A, 7).

In the Ancona statute the phrase is that the loss must 'gire a varea soldo per livera per lo valore de tucte le mercantie del navilio cum lo valore de la nave sbactendo el valore del terzo de la nave per lo corredo' (St. Ancon. 87).

These phrases are clear enough; but in some cases we get merely a reference to the *commune habere navis*, and the question arises whether this is meant to include the ship as well as the goods on board.

Under the statutes of Spalato, Zara, and Venice, the expenses of lightening a ship to enable it to get into harbour and any damage done to goods taken out are to be borne by the *commune habere navis*, subject to any special contract made between merchants and shipowners (St. Spalat. VI, 67; St. Zara, IV, 38; St. Zeno, 95. The statutes vary in details). The same statutes provide that if a ship is robbed, the loss falls on the *commune habere navis*. If the loss is afterwards recovered, the *commune habere* gets the benefit (St. Spalat. VI, 68; St. Zara, IV, 39; St. Zeno, 96; cp. Ordin. Trani, 3). In these cases it is probable that contribution is to be made exclusively from cargo (see St. Tiep. A, 46, and St. Ancon. 17).

I return to the cases where contribution is complete, i. e. where ship contributes as well as cargo. The following points require notice.

1. Under the Sea-law (c. 9), where contribution is claimed in respect of personal luggage, a limit is put upon the valuation; and there is probably also a limit in the case of slaves. There is no trace of a limit in other maritime codes.

2. Although goods which ought to be, but are not written in the ship's *quaternus* cannot claim contribution, yet it may be claimed against them (St. civil. Venez. VI, 68; cp. Ordin. Trani, 23).

The same rule prevails with regard to goods improperly loaded on the upper deck (St. Ancon. 86).

3. It has been seen that in many legislations a deduction of one-third is made from the valuation of the ship, and this deduction is sometimes expressed to be in respect of the tackle, which is not liable to make contribution (St. Ragus. VII, 7; St. Ancon. 86, 87; Ordin. Trani, 22). We have seen that in our Sea-law (c. ιϛ') a deduction of one-third is made from the value of the ship when it comes into contribution. Under the custom of Valencia of A. D. 1250 the ship contributes for one-half its value (IX, 17, 7, in Pard. V, p. 336). This is followed in the Barcelona Ordinance of A. D. 1340 (c. 29 in Pard. V, p. 363).

4. The Mediterranean customs have little to say about freight. C. 25 of the maritime statutes of Ancona, which seems to apply to a case of jettison proper, provides that no freight is to be paid of things lost, and that the freight of things saved is not liable to make contribution. Under the Constitutum Usus of Pisa (c. 29) freight unpaid is liable to make contribution. Under the Barcelona Ordinance of A. D. 1340, the shipowner is entitled to receive freight of things jettisoned, and is liable to contribute in respect of freight, less the expenses required for gaining it, e.g. seamen's wages (c. 30 in Pard. V, p. 363). Under the Rooles d'Oléron, the ship or the freight contributes at the shipowner's choice (cc. 8, 31; Jugemens de Damme, 8), and freight is payable of goods lost as well as of goods saved (Rooles d'Oléron, 31). In one of the versions of the Rooles d'Oléron, the decision whether ship or freight contributes is made by the merchants (Customs of Amsterdam, 2, in Pard. I, p. 406). In all these cases, except the Barcelona Ordinance, the freight appears to be gross freight.

5. There is some difficulty in the authorities with regard to the liability of mariners, because it is not always clear whether, when they are made liable, it is intended to impose a personal liability or merely a liability in respect of their pacotilles; moreover, does the personal liability merely extend to wages unpaid, or may wages already paid be recalled?

According to Pard. (I, p. 243, n. 3) the Sea-law imposes a personal liability upon the mariners. I have already explained (p. cclx) why I do not agree with this view. By the law of Spalato (VI, 51) mariners who have no merchandise on board are not liable to contribute to a loss of tackle. Mariners' wages are not liable to contribute where merchandise is taken by corsairs (Ordin. Trani, 3). At Amalfi, whether the ship sails under the system of the *colonna* or is let to merchants, mariners are not liable to contribute (cc. 47, 48). On the other hand, under the statutes of Zara (IV, 55) mariners contribute if the loss is above ten librae; and by an amendment made in A. D. 1281 to the Pisan Constitutum Usus (c. 29; cp. Breve Curiae Maris, 115) mariners' wages contribute. Under the Rooles d'Oléron the mariner's free allowance of goods is not subject to contribution up to one ton, if he works with zeal to save the ship (c. 8; Jugemens de Damme, c. 8). Under some northern laws his free allowance is not subject to contribution if the jettison does not exceed half a last (Law of Hamburg of A. D. 1270, c. 27 in Pard. III, p. 347; Law of Lubeck of A. D. 1299, c. 29 in Pard. III, p. 411, see p. 415; Law of Riga of A. D. 1270, c. 167 in Pard. III, p. 507, see p. 510).

6. In the customs of Bari (f. 118, ed. 1550; p. 152, ed. Alianelli) a distinction is made between the *parabulusum*, possibly the mariner's venture, and the cargo. If the *parabulusum* was put in by the master's consent, and an agreement is made with pirates, everything on board is bound *pro rata*. If the *parabulusum* was on board without the master's consent, it neither makes contribution to, nor receives it from the cargo.

7. Under the Table of Amalfi, *viciati* on board with merchandise, money, or other goods are liable to contribute (cc. 47, 48). Various explanations have been proposed of *viciati*: it may simply = *viaggianti*.

III. It will be remembered that under Roman law goods lost and goods saved were valued on different principles. In the middle ages two systems prevailed.

(*a*) Both classes of goods were valued at their cost price (Assizes of Jerusalem, c. 42; Ἀσίζαι τῆς Κύπρου, ed. Sathas, c. μγ´, p. 47; St. Ancon. 86).

(*b*) Both classes of goods were valued at their sale price, i.e. what they actually fetched or would have fetched at the port of discharge (Const. Usus of Pisa, c. 29; Breve Curiae Maris of Pisa, c. 115; Breve dell' Ordine del Mare of Pisa, c. 81; Barcelona Ordinance, cc. 28, 29 in Pard. V, p. 363; Rooles d'Oléron, 8; Law of Berghen of A. D. 1274, c. 8 in Pard. III, p. 33; Code of Lubeck of A. D. 1240, c. 88 in Pard. III, p. 401).

There is the same variety as regards the valuation of the ship. At Amalfi it was to be valued as of its value when it left port (Table, c. 54); at Pisa and Barcelona as of its value at the port of discharge (Authorities above).

In order to get a complete view of the doctrine of contribution in the middle ages, it is necessary to refer shortly to some legislations which deal with the subject systematically.

The maritime statute of Ancona contains two important chapters dealing with average. C. 87 agrees in substance with the Digest. On the other hand, c. 86 lays down rules for contribution which do not appear to be found in any other body of maritime law. It applies wherever a ship is wrecked or injured at sea and there is cargo on board. There are in this case two kinds of contribution, (1) as between ship and merchandise, (2) as between different kinds of merchandise *inter se*. (1) The ship is valued, and one-third is taken off the valuation for the tackle, which is not liable to contribute. The merchandise is valued according to its cost at the port of loading. Ship is then to contribute to merchandise and merchandise to ship 'soldo per livera'. (2) On the other hand, merchandise does not contribute to merchandise unless it is of the same character or falls within the same category. Thus soap saved contributes to soap lost, and oil saved to oil lost; but not soap saved to oil lost. Goods which are under the 'coverta viva' do not contribute to goods which are above the 'coverta viva', but may claim contribution from them. But goods in chests ('avere de cassecta'), e.g. gold, silver, pearls, precious stones, wearing apparel, which are above the 'coverta viva', neither make nor claim contribution.

The Ordinamenta of Trani contain several provisions with regard to contribution besides those already mentioned. They are very obscure. The work is translated from the Latin; and the translator did not always understand his original, nor his printers their copy.

C. 1 appears to say that if a ship, big or little, goes ashore and the poop is separated from the prow, the merchandise on board is not bound to make the ship good ('emendare la nave'). If the ship is not cut in two from poop to prow, the merchandise on board is bound to make the ship good. If the original really meant this, we have a new principle, namely, that where there is a total wreck and part of the cargo is saved, there is no contribution; but that there is contribution in case of a partial wreck. It is possible, however, that the original meant something else. If there is jettison and the ship is wrecked, there is no contribution: if the ship is saved, there is contribution. The chapter (whatever it means) is to be brought into comparison with c. 4. If an undecked barque goes ashore and breaks up, the cargo is not bound to make the barque good. If it is in the open sea and in a storm, and the mariners throw cargo overboard to escape, the cargo thrown may claim contribution. This rule is only laid down with regard to an undecked barque: it must apply *a fortiori* to a ship.

The Consulate of the Sea treats of contribution in several places with its accustomed verbosity. Some chapters merely reproduce, with modifications, the Roman law, and with these I deal first.

I. Where goods are thrown overboard in a storm or to escape from armed ships, the goods saved and the ship contribute (c. 51). The goods both saved and lost are valued as follows. If the jettison took place during the

first half of the voyage, they are valued at their cost price.
If it took place during the second half, they are valued at
their value in the port of arrival (c. 52). Freight does not
contribute unless the shipowner demands freight of goods
jettisoned (c. 53). The shipowner is not to make jettison
until the merchant has thrown something. An agreement
written by the ship's scribe on this occasion is as valid as
if made on land (c. 50). C. 54 contains another but not
inconsistent version of the Roman doctrine. Where
jettison is required, the shipowner is to address the merchants in the presence of the mate (*notxer*) and crew, and
explain the necessity of jettison. If the merchants or
a majority agree, jettison takes place. The provisions of
c. 50 are then repeated as to one of the merchants throwing first, and as to the validity of agreements made
between shipowner and merchants, and written by the
ship's scribe or witnessed by the mariners. If there are
no merchants on board, the shipowner can make a valid
jettison with the advice of the mate, other joint owners
(*personers*) and crew. In this case he is said to be a merchant. The chapter professes to have been made to
provide for the emergency of no merchant being on board.
It does not provide for the emergency of the merchants
or a majority refusing to agree to jettison. C. 66 in the
first part repeats in substance the provisions of c. 54 as to
the right of the shipowner to jettison where no merchants
are on board. He is to act with the advice and consent
of all the crew. C. 66 in the second part provides that if
the ship has to be run ashore for fear of armed vessels or
by reason of tempest, agreements made are to have the
same validity as if made in time of jettison.

C. 64 provides shortly that, if the shipowner leaves
behind an anchor or part of the ship's tackle to escape an
armed ship, goods and ship contribute. C. 185 deals with
the case where the shipowner has to ransom a vessel. There
must be an agreement with the merchants. If there is
no merchant on board, the shipowner is to take counsel
with the steward (*panesos*). Then there is contribution.

The same principle applies if the shipowner has to give a forced contribution (*strena*). If there is no agreement, the shipowner pays it out of his own pocket. C. 186 seems another form, but with additions, of c. 185.

In all these cases ship contributes on the basis of half its value.

The mariner's free allowance contributes where he bought it with his own moneys; but it only contributes for half its cost, to the extent to which it was bought out of wages advanced (c. 87). Goods which are worth more than their declared value can only claim contribution at their declared value, but are liable to contribute at their real value (c. 212). In none of these chapters is there any reference to agermanament.

II. Another group of chapters are 150, 151, 152, to which may be added 187.

These chapters are based on a different principle. The Consulate lays down more than once that where there is a loss, whether of ship or cargo, prima facie the loss lies where it falls. ['Si empressio ne convinences no y haura alguna, qui perdut haura per perdut se haura anar' (c. 152). 'Si entre ells agermanament fet no sera, ... qui struch sera, struch se romandra' (c. 187).] To this principle there are three exceptions: (*a*) where the loss is incurred for the common safety and has the effect of insuring it; (*b*) where the loss is occasioned by the act or default of some person other than the owner of the property lost; (*c*) where there is an agreement between those who share in the maritime adventure that ship and cargo, or cargo *inter se*, shall form a common mass for the purpose of bearing losses, or that cargo shall bear the losses of ship, without the obligation being reciprocal. It is with the last class of exceptions that these chapters of the Consulate deal.

C. 150 [cp. C. Tortosa, IX, 27, c. 32] is the most important. A ship has to run aground.

(*a*) The owner in command must propose to the merchants, in the hearing of the scribe, mate, and mariners, 'that the ship go over the cargo, and the cargo over the ship.' The merchants or a majority assent. Then, if the ship breaks up, the cargo saved is to give to the shipowner—*donar* is the word used—the whole valuation of the ship as agreed between him and the merchants or settled in default of agreement by experts. From the valuation is to be deducted the tackle (*exarcia*), and whatever is saved from the ship. If the ship does not break up, but is damaged, then the expenses of repairing the damage are to be met by contribution from the ship, valued as above, and the cargo saved.

(β) Instead of proposing that the ship go over the cargo and the cargo over the ship, the shipowner may simply propose that the ship go over the cargo saved, and the merchants may assent. Then if the ship is damaged, the damage is to be made good by the cargo saved: *a fortiori*, if the ship breaks up, its value is to be made good by the cargo saved.

(γ) The merchants may announce to the shipowner 'that cargo lost is to make with cargo saved', and the shipowner and the merchants or a majority of them assent. In this case there is contribution between goods saved, goods lost, and the price which the shipowner has received as an indemnity for his ship.

C. 151 deals mainly with the question of freight, where the ship goes ashore. If no cargo is saved, no freight is payable. If some of the cargo is saved, then (a) if the shipowner demands freight of goods lost as well as of goods saved, he is entitled to it, but he must contribute in respect of it to goods lost; (β) if he only demands freight of the goods saved, he is not bound to contribute. This agrees substantially with c. 53.

If there is no agreement between shipowner and merchants in anticipation of the ship going ashore, the merchants are not bound to contribute to ship if lost or damaged. If there is an agreement, the merchants are bound, and the shipowner can retain cargo to satisfy their obligation. There is no reference in this chapter to agermanament: the words used are 'convinenca o empressio'.

C. 152 deals first with the case where part of the cargo is unloaded and the rest either costs more to unload or is lost. There is no contribution between the different items of cargo unless the merchants had previously agreed ' that each item should help the other '.

C. 152 further provides that if the ship is lost or injured, and the shipowner and the merchants united the goods with the ship and the ship with the goods ('agermanaran l'aver ab la nau . . . e la nau . . . ab l'aver'), then goods saved must assist to compensate the ship.

C. 187 deals with the case where the ship meets enemies' vessels who carry off part of the cargo. Prima facie, the shipowner is not entitled to retain cargo saved in respect of freight of cargo lost. On the other hand, if the owners of cargo united (agermanaran) the cargo, so that one part should answer for the other ('que la una roba fes a l'altra'), either when they loaded or in anticipation of being robbed, then goods saved are reckoned with goods lost, i. e. contribute to the loss. If the shipowner and merchants are at war with the country of the vessels which carried off the cargo, then the body of the ship is to be reckoned with goods saved and goods lost; and the shipowner is to have his proportion of the freight. Observe the way in which in c. 187 various principles are laid down incidentally. The main object of the chapter is to determine the shipowner's right to freight; but it also lays down rules as to contribution between goods. It is perhaps part of a judgement.

It is provided in several places that, where there are no merchants on board, the owner in command may act as a merchant if he acts in consultation with the mate, the scribe, and the mariners (c. 150), or, as it is put elsewhere, with the advice of all the ship's company or the majority of them.

III. There are some chapters dealing with this subject which probably are later than the rest of the Consulate. C. 239 deals at large with jettison. It distinguishes two kinds of jettison, jettison akin to shipwreck and ordinary jettison. In jettison akin to shipwreck, the danger is so imminent that the goods have to be thrown over without previous consultation. The ship in this case contributes for two-thirds its value. If on the same occasion the ship loses its anchors, cables, or boats, it is entitled to contribution, although in case of ordinary jettison it would not be entitled.

In a case of ordinary jettison, i. e. where there is time for consultation, if the merchant throws overboard without consultation, he is not entitled to contribution. If the shipowner throws overboard without consultation, he is bound to indemnify the merchants.

After a case of extraordinary jettison, where tackle is left behind with the consent of the merchants, or has to be repaired, the shipowner is entitled to contribution from the cargo, and the body of the ship contributes for one-half its value.

C. 251 deals at length with the contribution of freight in cases of jettison.

The last stronghold of the doctrine of consultation is Targa. He (c.58, p.249 sqq.) divides jettison into two kinds: (1) jettison which takes place after previous deliberation between the captain and merchants or other persons on board; and (2) that which takes place where there is no time for deliberation, and where everybody throws overboard what comes into his hands. He illustrates the first case by an imaginary scene in which the captain calls together on the poop the officers, merchants, and passengers, and sets forth the imminent danger, which can only be avoided by lightening the ship. ' On hearing which, they cried with one voice " Yes, and let what is saved make good what is lost " '. There was in Targa's time no difference in point of legal effect between the two cases. The ship in both cases contributed for one-half of its value, although, in strictness of law, it ought to contribute for two-thirds where the jettison was made without consultation (p. 252). The consultation before jettison was in Targa's time very rare. In an experience of sixty years he had only known four or five cases, and in every one of these there were suspicions of fraud (p. 253 'in ognun di questi vi è stato da critticare per esser parsi troppo premeditati'. Cp. Park on Marine Insurances, 8th ed., p. 279 : 'Too close a compliance with forms at a period of supposed danger has very justly excited a suspicion of fraud.')

COLLISION

The Digest puts some cases of collision in the title (IX, 2) · ad legem Aquiliam', and these cases are reproduced in a generalized form in the Basilica (Synopsis Ambrosiana, LIII, B', δ'-θ', and Synopsis Venturiana, LIII, 2, 3-7). There was no special Roman law of collision. It was governed by the ordinary rules. If A's ship ran into B's and sank or injured it, or if A's ship stood in B's way and B's ship ran against it and was sunk or injured, the only question was, was there *culpa* or *dolus* on the part of those who were navigating A's ship. If *culpa* or *dolus* could be imputed to them, they were liable to an action, either *legis Aquiliae* or *in factum.* Their exercitor might be liable on the grounds stated in p. clx ; but not otherwise. If A's ship ran into B's, and it was an inevitable accident, B had no remedy (Cases in Dig. IX, 2, 29, 2-5).

The Sea-law deals with collision in only one chapter (c. 36). It takes the case where one ship [A] is in full sail, while the other [B] is at anchor or has slackened sail. It states three possibilities : (1) A knocks against B in the daytime. All the damage regards the captain of A and those on board. The cargo of A also contributes, how is not clear. (2) A knocks against B at night. Unless B gives notice of his presence,[1] A incurs

---

[1] Under the mediaeval statutes of Riga (Pard. III, p. 508) where ships A and B collide at night, and A has its lantern lighted but B not, B must pay all the damage caused to A.

no liability. (3) It is not so clear what the third possibility is. Probably it is a development of the second. Even though B gives no notice of his presence, yet if A is negligent in his sailing, or does not keep a proper look out, A must save B harmless.

This chapter in one respect merely illustrates, in another it modifies the doctrines of Roman law. It illustrates them by giving additional instances of *culpa*, which take their place by the side of those given in the Digest and repeated in the Basilica. It modifies them by altering the nature of the liability. Its language unfortunately is not free from doubt. Where it says that the damage regards the ναύκληρος and the ἐμπλέοντες, it might be maintained that this merely repeats the provisions of the Digest, viz., that the gubernator or ducator and sailors are liable under the lex Aquilia. But it is more probable, having regard to the juxtaposition of the cargo, that the ναύκληρος and the ἐμπλέοντες represent the ship. It is not clear whether cargo is only liable in default of ship, or whether ship and cargo contribute *pari passu*. The phrase εἰς συμβολὴν ἐρχέσθω supports the latter view.

There is little about collision in the Mediterranean codes. The maritime statutes of Ancona deal with the subject on two occasions (c. 19, 59). Where a ship is properly anchored, good watch kept, and the captain (*patrone*) and navigating officer (*nochiero*) perform their duties properly, it incurs no liability if it damages another ship. Where it does incur liability, the liability falls on the owners, but the navigating officer has to pay ten per cent. of the damage. His total liability, however, is not to exceed one hundred livere.

The Constitutum Usus of Pisa has a chapter (c. 31) 'de dampno navis dato ab altera navi'. The chapter gives a number of concrete cases of collision—some based upon examples in the Digest, but mainly referring to collisions in harbour. It does not add anything to Roman law. The chapter excludes all liability in cases of inevitable accident; and it is careful to add, in cases where one ship is to blame, that, while the ship which is to blame must make good the damage to the ship injured, it is not itself entitled to anything if it gets injured at the same time. It is not clear how the liability is borne.

All these provisions imply that it is easy to determine where the blame lies, and they generally also imply that the whole blame lies on one side. The Rooles d'Oléron appear to be the first body of legislation which lays down special rules for a collision where it is impossible to fix the liability. Ship B, which is at rest, is struck by ship A, and some casks of wine on B are staved in. The captain and crew of A swear that they are not in fault. The damage done to B is divided between the ships, and the damage done to the wine is divided between the cargoes (c. 15). This article is repeated in the Jugemens de Damme, c. 15, and the laws of Wisby, cc. 29–31. It is not clear from these places whether the two ships form one mass for the division of the damage while the two cargoes form another, or whether ships and cargoes are aggregated together. The provision is equally applicable where both ships and both cargoes are damaged by the collision.

A somewhat similar rule prevailed at Hamburg (Pard. III, p. 332 ; Statute of 1270, c. 21, in Pard. III, p. 345), Lubeck (c. 131, Pard. III, p. 402), and Riga (Pard. III, p. 508) in the thirteenth century. The rule was that, where one ship struck another, and the captain and crew of the striking ship swore that they were not to blame, the striking ship only bore half the damage. This doctrine is modified in the Hamburg statute of A. D. 1306 (Pard. III, pp. 348, 349). (*a*) It applies not merely where the one vessel is sunk or damaged, but also where it is struck, and has to make jettison to avoid sinking. (*b*) The cargo on board the ship which did the damage is not liable, and the owner's liability in respect of his moiety does not exceed the value of the ship and tackle.

The Consulate of the Sea deals with the matter with its usual diffuseness (cc. 155–158). It gives a number of cases, some evidently borrowed from the Constitutum Usus of Pisa. It also provides for the division of damages between the two ships in cases of inevitable accident (c. 155), or where both are to blame (c. 157). The damages in these cases are apportioned by experts.

SALVAGE

In Roman law, where goods were thrown overboard in a storm to lighten the ship, the better opinion was that they continued to belong to their original owners. The point was, were they thrown over ' derelinquentis animo ', and Paul (Dig. XIV, 2, 2, 8), Julian (Dig. XIV, 2, 8 pr. ; XLI, 7, 7), Gaius (Dig. XLI, 1, 9, 8), and Javolenus (Dig. XLI, 2, 21, 2) answer in the negative. Ulpian thought that as a rule he who jettisoned his goods did it ' derelinquentis animo ' (Dig. XLVII, 2, 43, 11), but the view of the majority is adopted in the Institutes (II, 1, 48), Theophilus (II, 1, 48 (85)), and the Basilica. It follows from this that he who takes things jettisoned *lucrandi animo* is a thief (Dig. XLI, 1, 9, 8 ; XLVII, 2, 43, 11).

It is even clearer that, if a ship is wrecked, goods cast ashore cannot be considered as derelict (Dig. XLI, 1, 58 ; 2, 21, 1), and that he who takes such goods is a thief (Dig. XLVII, 9, 3 pr.). Moreover, he who stole on the occasion of a shipwreck was liable to restore the goods stolen fourfold, if sued within a year (Dig. XLI, 1, 44 ; XLVII, 9, 1 pr.), and was also liable in some cases to criminal proceedings (Dig. XLVII, 9, 4, 1). A ship wrecked, or things cast ashore from a wreck, were not claimed by the fiscus, but were restored to their owners (Cod. XI, 6, 1).

These rules are reproduced in the Basilica, but one important matter is not touched upon, namely, the right of the salvor or finder of goods to receive a reward for his exertions in salving or recovering them. The Sea-law deals with this matter in several chapters. First, it provides, in c. 38, if my conjecture is right, that where a corn ship is caught in a gale and the captain and crew have to exert themselves to save the cargo, the captain with the ship and the sailors receives 6 per cent. of whatever is saved. Secondly, it provides, in several chapters, that where a merchant or passenger has goods of great value in small compass and there is a wreck, he has to pay a percentage of the goods saved to the captain and crew, such percentage varying with the character of the goods. This matter has been already dealt with (p. cclxii). Thirdly, the Sea-law deals explicitly in its last three chapters with the salvor or finder and his reward.

(C. 45). If a ship is destroyed on the high sea, he who brings anything safe to land receives one-fifth (c. 46). He who saves the ship's boat receives one-fifth (c. 47). If gold or silver or anything else is raised from a depth of eight fathoms the salvor receives one-third; if from a depth of fifteen he receives one-half. Where things are thrown from the sea on the land or found within one cubit of the land the finder receives one-tenth.

In illustrating these chapters from the mediaeval authorities, the cases may be grouped under four heads. I. Claims of the crew or others in cases of wreck. II. Claims for bringing in derelicts. III. Claims in respect of goods found. IV. Apportionment of property found among several.

I. Several statutes give rewards to mariners who display zeal in saving goods on the occasion of a wreck. At Venice they get 3 per cent. in value of the goods salved (St. Zeno, 40 end, 92), at Pisa 5 per cent. (Constitutum Usus, c. 30 in Bonaini, II, p. 924). According to the Rooles d'Oléron, no agreement made between merchants and mariners at the time of a wreck is valid, but the mariners are entitled to a percentage fixed by the Court (Art. 4, a later addition, see Pard. I, p. 326, n. 2).

INTRODUCTION

A letter from the consuls of Hamburg of about A.D. 1261 (cited in Pard. III, p. 332) lays down the law as follows. If there is a wreck and the sailors at the request of the merchants assist in saving the cargo, they are entitled to a percentage of its value varying, according to the danger incurred, from one-thirtieth to one-tenth.

C. 45 of the Sea-law is vague, but appears to apply in favour of any person who brings goods safe to land from a ship which is lost at sea. In the Byzantine Empire, when a ship was wrecked on the coast, the inhabitants were apparently entitled to a percentage varying with the locality for bringing goods safe to land. [Καὶ ἃ δὲ ἐκβάλλουσιν οἱ Ῥωμαῖοι βοηθήσαντες ἵνα ἔχητε κἀκεῖνα παρασχόντες κατὰ τὸν τύπον τοῦ τόπου πρὸς αὐτοὺς τὸν μισθόν. Treaty of A.D. 1192 between Isaac Angelus and Pisa in Müller, Documenti, p. 44 ; Latin in Dal Borgo, Diplomi Pisani, p. 153.] The men of Curzola are entitled to one-fourth of what they save from a wreck (St. Curzulae, I, c. 10, p. 9).

II. With regard to bringing in boats, there is little in the authorities. If a boat is found waterlogged (*turgida*), the crew having been drowned or having abandoned it, he who brings it into harbour or other place of safety is entitled to a reward fixed by the court (St. Zara, IV, 45 ; St. Spalat. VI, 21). Under the statutes of Wisby (in Pard. III, p. 120) he who brings a derelict to land is entitled to one-half the proceeds of sale of ship and cargo.

III. Claims in regard to goods found, whether at the bottom of the sea or floating on the water or on the beach, are dealt with at length by the authorities.

The Statutes of Zara provide as follows (IV, 45) :—If a thing is lost or thrown from a ship, and is found at the bottom ('subter fundum aquae'), one-half goes to the finder, the other half to the shipowner (?). If it is found floating on the surface ('natans super aquam'), the finder gets one-third ; the rest goes to the shipowner (?). The things found are to be brought into the harbour of Zara. Agreements between shipowner and finder are binding.

The Ordinamenta of Trani run as follows:—He who finds goods floating on the sea ('roba in mare che andasse torgida') must assign them to the court with a written inventory within three days of finding them. If the owner appears, the finder has half. If the owner or his representative does not appear within thirty days, the finder has the whole (c. 19). Goods found under water go, as to two-thirds to the finder, and as to one-third to the owner (c. 20. The words 'de robe che habia signale' at the end of this chapter are really the title of the next.) Where goods are found which have a mark, no one is to touch them, under penalty of paying three times their value or more, at the discretion of the court (c. 21).

The Statute of Ancona (c. 60) is corrupt. It reads thus:—'Et qualunqua trovasse et condurà nel porto d'Ancona alcuno avere notando in mare la mità sia de collui che lo trovasse in fondo de mare et l'altra parte sia de collui che la trova, et li doi parti sia del singnore de la cosa.' It is clear that the statute means to make the usual distinction between things found on the surface of the water and things sunk to the bottom. We should probably read something like this:—'Et qualunqua trovasse et condurà nel porto d'Ancona alcuno avere notando in mare, la mità sia de collui che lo trovasse e l'altra parte [sia del singnore de la cosa. Et qualunqua trovasse] in fondo de mare [alcuna cosa e la condurà nel porto d'Ancona, la terza parte] sia de collui che la trova, et li doi parti sia del singnore de la cosa.' The statute goes on to say that, where the thing found has a mark, the finder has no claim to a reward, but it is suggested that the owner should give him something. There are special provisions for the case where the object is found within a certain distance of the harbour of Ancona. He who finds it within these limits receives, if he finds it floating, 'tre soldi per livera' (16⅔ per cent.), and if he finds it at the bottom, 'doi soldi per livera' (10 per cent.). If the owner does not claim the goods within six months, the balance is applied to the harbour of Ancona.

t 2

INTRODUCTION

The Constitutum Usus of Pisa (c. 30) makes a distinction between (*a*) things found floating on the sea ('ita quod ducat illud havere mare'); (*b*) things found at the bottom; (*c*) things found on the beach. (*a*) Of things found floating on the sea, the finder retains one-fourth. Of gold, gems, pearls, &c., he may only retain one-eighth, and of silver one-sixth. (*b*) Of things found at the bottom, the general rule is that the finder retains one-eighth; but of iron and lead he may retain one-fourth, of brass, tin, and steel one-sixth, of silver one-twentieth, of gold, gems, and pearls one-thirtieth. (*c*) Of things found on the beach, the finder may retain one-twelfth; but of gold, gems, and pearls he may retain only one-fortieth, and of silver one-thirtieth. This provision confirms my view that the percentages which the Sea-law makes payable in respect of gold, silver, pearls, silks, &c., are payable not by way of contribution but in respect of salvage services.

The Consulate of the Sea treats the matter in an exceptionally long and confused chapter (c. 207). It deals successively with the following cases:—(1) goods found on the beach or in harbour, either (*a*) floating in the water, or (*b*) cast up on land; (2) goods found in a gulf or on the open sea; (3) goods found at the bottom. 1. (*a*) The finder of these goods produces them before the public authority, which retains them for a year and a day. At the end of that time, if the true owner does not appear, one-half goes to the finder, one-quarter to the public authority, and one-quarter is to be applied for the benefit of the owner's soul. (*b*) In this case the finder's reward is determined by the good men of the place where the goods have been found. 2. With regard to these reference is made to a former chapter, which apparently does not exist. 3. Goods found at the bottom of the sea are not to be sold or alienated, because as goods lying at the bottom they always await their owner ('perco com roba que iaura a fons, totavia espera son senyor'). The finder's reward is determined by the public authority and by two good men of the sea. Where goods are found which have been lost for a year and a day, they belong to the finder. The confused language of the Consulate leaves it doubtful whether the true owner, if he prove his ownership after that time, can insist on having the goods handed over to him.

The bizarre remark that goods at the bottom of the sea are waiting for their owner is also found in the Assizes of Jerusalem, c. 46 ('pour ce que l'avoir qui est au fons atent son seignour'), and of Cyprus ('Ασίζαι τῆς Κύπρου, ed. Sathas, c. μζ', p. 50; c. μη', p. 299).

The Swedish statutes of Wisby (in Pard. III, p. 120) provide as follows :— (*a*) He who finds goods floating on the sea, out of sight of land, receives one-half; in sight of land, one-third. (*b*) He who finds goods at the bottom receives one-third. (*c*) He who finds goods at sea which he can reach by wading, or who finds them on the beach, receives one-eighth. Pard. cites (III, p. 120, n. 4) a passage from the code of the isle of Gothland (see Pard. III, p. 91) which is much to the same effect. The provisions of the Statutes of Hamburg (c. 20, Pard. III, p. 345), Lubeck (c. 14, Pard. III, p. 408), and Riga (c. 160, Pard. III, p. 506 ; see also p. 512) merely offer differences of detail.

IV. Some statutes provide for the apportionment of property found where the find has been made by the whole body of those on board. At Ragusa and Phara, one-fourth goes to ship, one-fourth to cargo, and one-half is divisible among the mariners and merchants, apparently *per capita* (St. Ragus. VII, 35 ; St. Lesina, V, 8, p. 212). At Zara one-half goes to the shipowner, one-half is divided among those on board equally (St. Zara, IV, 72). At Spalato the proportions are one-third to the shipowner and two-thirds among those on board (St. Spalat. VI, 44).

ΝΟΜΟΣ ΡΟΔΙΩΝ ΝΑΥΤΙΚΟΣ

SIGLA

I. *Codices* τοῦ νόμου

A = Ambrosianus F, 106, sup.
B = Vaticanus graecus 2075 = Basilianus, 114
C = Vaticanus graecus 845
D = Vaticanus graecus 844
E = Vaticanus graecus 847
F = Palatinus graecus 371
f = Vaticanus graecus 640
G = Vallicellianus E, 55
H = Cryptensis Z γ III
h = Cryptensis Z γ V
J = { Laurentianus plut. IX, cod. 8
{ Lipsiensis (bibl. univ.) graecus 46
K = Laurentianus plut. LXXX, cod. 6
L = Laudianus graecus 39 (olim C 73)
M = Marcianus graecus 172
N = Marcianus graecus 579
O = Marcianus graecus 181
P = Paris. graecus 1367
Q = Paris. graecus 1384
R = Roe 18
S = Ambrosianus Q, 25, sup.
T = Paris. graecus 1383
U = Ambrosianus M, 68, sup.
V = Paris. graecus 1356 f. 277 r.–f. 279 r.
v = idem codex f. 319 r.–f. 325 r.
W = Vindobonensis iuridicus graecus 2
X = Vindobonensis iuridicus graecus 7
Y = Ambrosianus Q, 50, sup.
Z = Codex quo usus est Franciscus Venturius
Harl. = Harleianus 5675
Laud. = Laudianus graecus 91

II. *Codices Synopsis Maioris*

a = Arundelianus (Mus. Brit.) 516
b = Baroccianus (Bibl. Bodl.) 173
m = Marcianus graecus 173
p = Paris. graecus 1346
r = Palatinus graecus 8
Σ = lectura codicum *a, b, m, p, r*, praeter eos de quibus aliud
traditur

Methodus qua usus sum in exornando apparatu critico e praefatione mea satis patet.

ccxcvi

PARS SECUNDA

ΤΑ ΚΕΦΑΛΑΙΑ ΤΟΥ ΝΟΜΟΥ ΤΟΥ ΡΟΔΙΟΥ

α΄ ναυκλήρου μισθὸς μέρη δύο.

β΄ κυβερνήτου μισθὸς μέρος ἓν ἥμισυ.

γ΄ πρωρέως μισθὸς μέρος ἓν ἥμισυ.

δ΄ ναυπηγοῦ μισθὸς μέρος ἓν ἥμισυ.

ε΄ καραβίτου μισθὸς μέρος ἓν ἥμισυ.   5

ϛ΄ ναύτου μισθὸς μέρος ἕν.

ζ΄ παρασχαρίτου μισθὸς μέρος ἥμισυ.

Titulus De titulo secundae partis maxima codicum varietas. Titulum quem posui dat B, qui post indicem addit: τὰ κεφάλαια. In aliis codicibus ita est : τὰ κεφάλαια τοῦ νόμου τῶ νόμου τῶν ῥοδίων A : κεφάλαια τοῦ νόμου ῥοδίου C : κεφάλαια τοῦ ναυτικοῦ νόμου D : νόμος Ῥωδίων ναυτικὸς ὃν ἐθέσπισαν οἱ θειότατοι αὐτοκράτορες Ἀδριανὸς Ἀντωνῖνος Τιβέριος Λούκιος Σεπτίμιος Σεύηρος Περτίναξ ῥωμαῖοι ἀεισέβαστοι L : νόμος ναυτικὸς ῥοδίωνος VFf : κεφάλαια τοῦ νόμου τοῦ ναυτικοῦ et (post indicem) νόμος ναυτικός v

Apud EMQ nullus titulus cum pars secunda prologum sine intervallo subsequatur; Z habet 'Capita legis Rhodiensium'.

1-7 Ordo capitulorum α΄-ζ΄ apud codices turbatus. Sicut in textu praebent ABCvZ ; D ita : α΄β΄γ΄δ΄ϛ΄ζ΄ε΄ ; E ita : α΄β΄δ΄ϛ΄γ΄ε΄ζ΄ ; LF ita : α΄β΄γ΄δ΄ϛ΄ε΄ζ΄ ; M ita : α΄δ΄β΄γ΄ϛ΄ε΄ζ΄ ; Q ita : α΄β΄γ΄δ΄(quod ut partem capituli γ΄ tractat) ϛ΄ε΄ζ΄. Non numerantur capitula huius partis in BCL

1 α΄. F praeponit περὶ ναυκλήρου μισθοῦ   ναυκλήρω BELM : ναυκλήρο CQ   μισθῶς B : μισθῶ LQ   μέρει β΄ BL : μέρη β΄ CQ : μέρη ... Z 2 κυβερνίτου B : κυβερνίτη E : κηβερνίτη Q   μισθῶς B : μισθῶ L : om. Vf μέρος αϛ΄ B : μέρει αϛ΄ Lv : μέρη ἕνα ἥμισυ MQ : μέρη β΄ C : μέρος α΄ H : μέρος ἓν VFf   3 προρέως ABv : (f. 231 v.) προρέος M : προραίω L : πρωραίου V : προρέου F : πρωρέου f   μισθῶ L   μέρος αϛ΄ B : μέρος αυ΄ C : μέρος ἓν υ΄ D : μέρει αϛ΄ Lv : μέρη ἕνα ἥμισυ MQ : μέρος α΄ in textu, addito in margine ἥμ̅ H : μέρος ἓν VFf   4 ναυπηγῶ B : καὶ ναυπηγοῦ Q   μισθῶ L : om. Vf   μέρος αϛ΄ B : μέρος αυ΄ CD : μέρει αϛ΄ L : μέρη ἕνα ἥμισυ MQ : μέρος, omisso numero, H : μέρος ἓν VFf 5 Capitula ε΄ϛ΄ζ΄ in textu omittit, addit in margine inferiore, capitulum ε΄ capitulo ϛ΄ postponens H   καραβήτου BCMQ : καράβου HVFf : post καραβίτου E addit τυχὸν   μισθῶ L   μέρος ... B : μέρος ἓν DZ : μέρει ... L : μέρη ἥμισυ τέταρτον Q : μέρος ἥμισυ τέταρτον ὄγδοον CE :

μέρη ἥμισυ τέταρτον ὄγδοον M : μέρη β΄ η̅ H : μέρη δύο Vf : μέρει δύο F 6 Cap. ϛ΄ addit in margine B : omittunt Vf   ναύτη AB   μισθῶ L μέρει α΄ L : μέρη ἓν Q : μέρη αϛ΄ v   7 Cap. ζ΄ addit in margine B παρασχαρίτου CEFHLQv] παρασχαρήτου M : παρασκαρίτου Vf : παρα-

η΄ ἐμπόρῳ ἔχειν ἐξὸν ἐν πλοίῳ παῖδας δύο· τὸ δὲ ναῦλον διδότω.

θ΄ ἐπιβάτου τόπος μῆκος πήχεων τριῶν, πλάτος πήχεως ἑνός.

5 ι΄ ἐπιβάτης ἐν πλοίῳ ἰχθὺν μὴ τηγανιζέτω· ὁ ναύκληρος αὐτῷ μὴ συγχωρείτω.

ια΄ ἐπιβάτης ἐν πλοίῳ ξύλα μὴ σχιζέτω· ὁ ναύκληρος αὐτῷ μὴ συγχωρείτω.

ιβ΄ ἐπιβάτης ἐν πλοίῳ ὕδωρ μέτρῳ λαμβανέτω.

10 ιγ΄ γυναῖκας ἐν πλοίῳ λαμβάνειν τόπον πήχεως ἑνός· τὸ δὲ παιδίον τὸ τέλειον πήχεως τὸ ἥμισυ.

σχαρίτη AB   μισθῶ L : om. V ƒ   μέρους ἥμισυ B : μερίδος τὸ ἥμησυ C : μέρει ϛ΄ L : μέρη ἥμισυ MQ : μέρη 5 v : μέρος ϛ΄ Fƒ : μέρους 5 V 1 Cap. η΄ omittit L : in Q habet numerum ζ΄ et sequentia capitula semper uno numero inferiora sunt   εἰ ἐμπόρω D   ἐξὼν BHM   ἐν πλοίῳ omittunt ABDZ : ἐν πλείω ἐξεῖν C : ἐν πλοῖον ἐξὼν Q   Pro ἐμπόρῳ . . . πλοίῳ F legit ἔμπορος ἔχει εἰς πλοῖον : Vƒ legunt ἔμπορος εἰς πλοῖον ἔχει   παῖδας] πόδας DZVƒ   τὸ δὲ ναῦλον] τὸν δὲ ναῦλον CQF : εἰς δὲ τὸ πλέον τὸ ναῦλον Vƒ   2 ἀποδιδότω FƒV. Post διδότω C addit ὁ ἔμπορος   3 θ΄ In H ordo capitulorum est : θ΄, ιβ΄, ιγ΄, ι΄, ιδ΄. In FV ordo est : θ΄, ιγ΄, ι΄, ια΄, ιβ΄, ιδ΄ : in ƒ ordo est : θ΄, ιγ΄, ιβ΄, ιδ΄   μῆκος omittunt BCHQ : ἐν πλοίῳ μῆκος F : μῆκος ἐν πλοίῳ Vƒ   4 πήχεων γ΄ CHLM : πίχεως γ΄ B   πήχεως ἑνός] πήχεως ἑνός M : πηχέου ἑνός Q : πήχεως μιᾶς AD : πίχυν α΄ B : πηχ α΄ L : πυχήν μίαν C : α΄ H, i. e. omittit πήχεως   5 In B cap. ι΄ post ιγ΄, in C post ια΄ ponitur ; omittit ƒ   ὁ ἐπιβάτης D   ἰχθὺν post τηγανιζέτω ponunt FV   τιγανιζέτω BL : τυγανιζέτω DEMF   ὁ ναύκληρος . . . συγχωρείτω] τοῦ ναυκλήρου αὐτοῦ μὴ συγχωροῦντος BC : omittit V   7 Cap. ια΄ omittunt AHLZƒ   ὁ ἐπιβάτης D   ξύλον Dv   μὴ σχιζέτω] μὴ σχηζέτω CQ : μὴ σχύζεται F : οὐ σχίζει V   καὶ ὁ ναύκληρος D   ὁ ναύκληρος . . . συγχωρείτω] ὁ ναύκληρος αὐτοῦ μὴ συγχωρῶν B : τοῦ ναυκλήρου αὐτῶ μὴ συγχωροῦντος C : τοῦ ναυκλήρου αὐτοῦ συγχωροῦντος H : omittunt FV   8 συγχωρήτω M.   9 Cap. ιβ΄ omittit C : bis dat Q primum in textu deinde in margine : ante cap. ι΄ ponit F   ἐπιβάτης ἐν πλοίῳ omittit E   ὁ ἐπιβάτης D   ἐν πλοίον Q   μέτρον ELvVƒ
Post μέτρῳ habuit H : λαμβανέτω ὀγκι δύο quae postea erasa sunt λαμβανέτω] Q in marg. addit ὀγκίας δύο, F idem addit sed in textu : Vƒ addunt οὐγγίας δύο   10 Cap. ιγ΄ in L ut pars cap. ιβ΄ tractatur, in V ante cap. ια΄, ιβ΄ ponitur   γυναῖκας . . . τόπον] γυνὴ ὁμοίως ἀλλὰ καὶ τό πον L   γυναικὸς A : γυναῖκα BH : γυνὴ CEMQ : ἡ γυνὴ D   λαμβανέτω τόπον CD : τόπον λαμβανέτω EMQ   πήχεως ἑνός] πήχεος ἑνός B : πήχεως μιᾶς ADH : πῆχυν ἕνα E : πῆχ α΄ L : πήχυν μίαν MQ : πήχυν αϛ΄ C   11 τὸ τέλεον L : τὸ τελίω H : τέλειον CM : τέλιον Q : τὸ μὴ τέλειον (nondum adultus) Z. Verba τὸ τέλειον omittit E   πῆχυ τὸ ἥμισυ L : πήχεως ὕ E   Capitulum totum ita praebet v :—γυνὴ ἐν πλοίῳ ὕδωρ μέτρον λαμβανέτω καὶ τόπον πῆχυν ἕνα,

2

ιδ΄ ἐὰν εἰσέλθῃ ἐπιβάτης ἐν πλοίῳ καὶ ἔχῃ χρυσίον,
παρατιθέσθω αὐτὸ τῷ ναυκλήρῳ· εἰ δὲ μὴ παραθέμενος
εἴπῃ, ὅτι χρυσίον ἀπώλεσα ἢ ἀργύριον, ἄκυρα εἴτω τὰ
λεγόμενα ἐπεὶ τῷ ναυκλήρῳ οὐ παρέθετο.

ιε΄ ὁ ναύκληρος καὶ οἱ ἐπιβάται καὶ οἱ ναῦται ὁμοῦ 5
ἐμπλέοντες ὅρκον εὐαγγελίων παρεχέτωσαν.

ις΄ εἶναι τὴν χιλιάδα τοῦ μοδισμοῦ χρυσίνων
πεντήκοντα μετὰ πάσης τῆς ἐξαρτίας αὐτοῦ καὶ εἰς
συμβολὴν ἐρχέσθω, τοῦ δὲ πλοίου τοῦ παλαιοῦ χρυσίνων τριάκοντα. καὶ ἐν τῇ τιμήσει τὸ τρίτον μέρος κουφι- 10
ζέσθω, καὶ οὕτως εἰς· συμβολὴν ἐρχέσθω.

ιζ΄ ὁ νόμος κελεύει· τὰ ἐν τῇ θαλάσσῃ δεδανεισμένα

τὸ δὲ τέλειον παιδίον πήχεως ἥμισυ: ita praebent VFƒ:—γυναικὸς τόπος ἐν
πλοίῳ πῆχυς (πήχει F) μία, τοῦ δὲ πτιδὸς τοῦ τελείου τὸ ἥμισυ (πήχεις
ἥμισυ F) 1 M titulum (numero α΄ insignitum) περὶ ἐπιβάτου ἐν
πλοίῳ: v περὶ ἐπιβάτων ἐν πλοίῳ: Q περὶ ἐπιβάτων habent. P (f. 49 v.) ad
hoc capitulum (cui nullum numerum dat) ab capitulo septimo partis
tertiae nullo intervallo transit εἰσέθη A: εἰσέλθοι CE: εἰσέλθης M
εἰς πλοῖον D ἔχει BCLM 2 πα(f. 26 r.)ρατιθέσθω B
παραθέσθω VFƒ αὐτῷ BCMQv: αὐτὰ L (f. 105 r.) ὁ δὲ μὴ C εἰ
erasum in H 3 εἶπε A: εἴπι F: εἴποι CEHVƒ ἀπόλεσα BM
ἄργυρον B ἄκυρα] ἄκηρα M: ἢ ἄγκυραν Vƒ ἤτω LMFƒ: ἴτω
V: εἰ B: εἶναι H: εἴη Q: εἰσι E τὰ λεγόμενα ἐπεὶ τῷ ναυκλήρῳ] πάντως
τὰ τοῦ ζητοῦντος E τὰ λεγόμενα soli servant BH 4 ἐπεὶ] omittunt
BHv: ἐπὶ ceteri τὸ ναυκλήρῳ B: τῶν ναυκλήρων A: ναυκλήρῳ v Ante
οὐ inserunt ἀ D: ὁ ceteri 5 M titulum (numero β΄ insignitum)
περὶ ὅρκου καὶ ἀπαραιτήτων: Lv περὶ ὅρκου ἀπαραιτήτου: Q περὶ ὅρκου παρα-
τίτου: E περὶ τιμῆς πλοίου, habent. In PVFƒ hoc cap. ut pars ultimi
tractatur ὁ δὲ ναύκληρος VFƒ καὶ οἱ ναῦται post ἐπιβάται ponunt
CEMQ, post ναύκληρος DLvVF: omittunt ABHPZƒ ὁμοῦ οἱ H
6 εὐαγγελίων B: εὐαγγελικὸν C: εὐαγγελίον LMQv: ἐν εὐαγγελίῳ E:
εὐαγγελίου VFƒ ἐχέτωσαν CMQ VFƒ addunt αἰτῷ 7 M
titulum (numero γ΄ insignitum) περὶ τιμῆς πλοίου ῥωδίου: DQv eundem,
sed sine numero: L περὶ τιμῆς πλοίου habent: cap. omittunt Vƒ δεῖ
εἶναι D χηλιάδαν L μωδισμοῦ L χρυσίον BDHPvVF: χρυσίον
MQ: χρυσίου C 8 ἐξαρτήσεως A αὐτῶν F καὶ om. L
9 συμβουλὴν MF: βολὴν v ἔρχεσθαι L τοῦ δὲ πλοίου . . .
11 ἐρχέσθω] om. F τοῦ δὲ παλαιοῦ πλοίου E πλοῖον C χρυσίων DLv: χρυσίον CMQ: χρύσου BH 10 Supra τριάκοντα scriptum
est in Q ἐνενίκοντα τιμήσι B: τημίση C: τιμίσει L: διατιμήσει αὐτοῦ E
τοῦ γ΄ μέρους H τρί(f. 120 v.)τον Q 11 (f. 50 r.) εἰς συμβολὴν F
συμβουλὴν v: συμπλοκὴν MQ 12 M titulum (numero δ΄ insignitum)
περὶ δανείων θαλάσσης: LQv περὶ δανείου θαλάσσης: C περὶ δανίου ἐν
θαλάσσῃ: E περὶ δανείων habent τὰ ἐν τῇ θαλάσσῃ] ἐν τῇ (τί B)
θαλάσσῃ τὰ BH δεδανισμένα L: δανεισμένα BHMQ: δανειζόμενα VFƒ

B 2 3

ΝΟΜΟΣ ΡΟΔΙΩΝ ΝΑΥΤΙΚΟΣ

ἔγγαια καὶ ἀκίνδυνα μὴ γραφέτωσαν, εἰ δὲ καὶ ἐπιγράφουσιν, ἄκυρα εἴτω ἐπὶ τὸν ῥόδιον νόμον· τὰ δὲ ἐν
ἀγροῖς ἢ ἐν ὄρεσι δανειζόμενα ἔγγαια καὶ ἀκίνδυνα
ἐπιγραφέτωσαν κατὰ τὸν ῥόδιον νόμον.

5 ιη΄ ἐὰν δανείσηταί τις ἐν τόκοις καὶ εἰ ἔτη ὀκτὼ
τελέσῃ τοὺς ἐννόμους τόκους, μετὰ δὲ ὀκτὼ ἔτη συμβῇ
ἀπώλειαν γενέσθαι ἢ πυρκαϊὰν ἢ διαρπαγὴν βαρβάρων,
τῶν τόκων διάλυσις γινέσθω κατὰ τὸν ῥόδιον νόμον· εἰ
δὲ μὴ τελέσῃ τοὺς τόκους ἐκ τῶν νομίμων, τὰ ἔγγραφα
10 κύριά ἐστι κατὰ τὰς προτέρας συνθήκας, καθὼς τὸ
ἔγγραφον προφέρει.

ιθ΄ οἱ ναύκληροι ναυκληροῦντες, συμβαλλομένου

1 ἔγγαια BCHLP*v*] ἔγγυα EMQ : ἔγγεα AD : ἔγκεα F : ἄγγεα V*f*   ἀκήνδυνα
B   γραφέτωσαν] γραφέσθωσαν CDE : γράφεσθαι V*f*   Post hoc verbum
V*Ef* addunt κατὰ τὸν ῥόδιον νόμον et sic parti secundae finem faciunt
ἐπιγράφουσιν] ἐπιγραφῶσιν P : ἐπιγραφέτωσαν BH   2 ἄκυρα . . .
νόμον] κατὰ ῥόδιον νόμον ἄκυρα εἰ B : κατὰ ῥόδιον νόμον ἄκυρα εἶναι H   ᾖτο
L   τὸν ῥώδιον M : τῶν ῥοδίων APZ   νόμων PZ   ἐν τοῖς ἀγροῖς P
3 ἢ ἐν ὄρεσι omittit Z   ἢ ἐν] ἢ C : καὶ ἐν *v*   ὄρεσιν BL   ἔγγαια
BCLMP*v*] ἔγγυα EQ : ἔγγεα AD : in textu omittit, addit in margine
ἔγγαια H   καὶ om. *v*   ἀκήνδυνα B : κίνδυνα *v*   4 ἐπιγραφέσθωσαν
E   κατὰ τ. ῥ. ν. omittit D   τὸν omittit P 1 (f. 50 v.)   τὸν ῥώδιον L : τῶν
ῥοδίων AP   νόμων AP   hic finit P 1 (f. 50 v.)   5 Cum hoc
capitulo incipit J (f. 13 r.) numero ϛ΄ in margine addito : titulum LQ*v*
περὶ δανείου ἐν γῇ : C περὶ δανίου ἐν γῇ καὶ περὶ τοκετῶν habent. In M
cap. ut pars praecedentis tractatur quamquam prima littera vocis ἐὰν
rubro colore depingitur.   ἐὰν δὲ E   Post ἐὰν addit τις C   δανείσηταί
τις ex coni. scripsi] δανείσῃ ABDHQ : δανήσει CJ : δανίσει L : δανείσει M :
δανείσοι E   εἰ om. CD   ἔτη τελέσῃ] ἐπιτελέσῃ H et fortasse Z   ἔτει
A : ἔτι BCEM*v* : τι Q : om. DJ   ὀκτὼ ex coni. addidi   6 τελέσῃ
L] τελέσει BJM : τελέσοι E : τελευτήσει A : τελευτήσῃ *v*   τοὺς ἐνόμους
τόκους M : τοὺς ἐννόμω τόκους J : τοῖς ἐννόμοις (f. 331 v.) τόκους L : τοὺς
τόκους τοὺς ἐννόμους B : τοὺς ὄρκους (sic) τοὺς ἐννόμους H   Post τόκους
D addit τὰ ἔτη   μετὰ] Hic incipit P 2 (f. 112 r.)   ὀκτὼ ἔτη] εἰ ἔτι H
συμβεῖ BC : om. A   7 ἀπόλειαν BM   ἁρπαγὴ M : ἀρπαγὴ Q   8 τὸν
τόκον M   ἢ διάλυσις EMQ : ἢ διαλύσης C : διαλύσει H   γενέσθω JLM
τῶν ῥοδίων AZ   9 τελέσῃ AJ] τελέσει BLMP : τελέσοι E : τελευτήσει *v*   ἐκ om. P   10 ἐστιν BLM : ἔστω (sunto) Z   προτέρους
H : πρώτερον C : πρότερον MQ   προφέρει τὸ ἔγγραφον E   11 προσ-
φέρει BCHMQ   post προφέρει C nullo intervallo relicto ad cap. 1
partis tertiae vadit   ABH addunt ὅσον (οὐ A) δεῖ συμβαλλομένους
ναυκληρεῖν (ναυκληρίαν H) ut partem praecedentis capituli; idem
repperit in Z   Venturius cum scribat 'quantum oporteat hos qui con-
trahunt exercere'.   DJ addunt ὅσον δεῖ συμβάλλεσθαι   Hic finit H
12 Capitulum Graece dat Z   Titulum L ὅσον δὴ συμβαλλομένους

4

PARS SECUNDA

τοῦ πλοίου μὴ ἔλαττον τοῦ τριμερίτου, ὅπου ἐὰν ἀπο-
στέλλωνται, καθὸ δεῖ χρήματα χρηννύειν καὶ ἀποστέλλειν
ἐπὶ πλοίου κατὰ θερείαν καὶ κατὰ πλοῦν, καθὼς ἂν
συνεγράψαντο κύρια ἔστω· ὁ δὲ χρήσας τὰ χρήματα
ἐπιπεμπέτω ἄνθρωπον ὃς ἂν ἐπιχρήννυται.

INDEX CAPITULORUM PARTIS TERTIAE

ΚΕΦΑΛΑΙΑ ΝΟΜΟΥ ΡΟΔΙΟΥ ΚΑΤ' ΕΚΛΟΓΗΝ
ΠΕΡΙ ΝΑΥΤΙΚΩΝ

α΄ περὶ ἀγκυρῶν πλοίου κλαπέντων.

β΄ περὶ ἀγκυρῶν καὶ λοιπῶν ἐξαρτίων κλαπέντων.

γ΄ περὶ ναύτου κλοπὴν ἐργασαμένου.

δ΄ περὶ πλοίου ἀπὸ κλεπτῶν ἢ πειρατῶν σύλα
ὑπομείναντος.   5

ε΄ περὶ ναυτῶν ἐν μάχῃ κύλλωμα ἐργασαμένων.

ϛ΄ περὶ ναυτῶν ἐν μάχῃ φόνον ἐργασαμένων.

ναυκληρεῖν : P ὅσον δεῖ συμβάλλειν τὸν ναύκληρον : EMQυ περὶ ναυκλήρων
(ναυκλήρου υ) καὶ ναυτῶν habent   ναυκληροῦντος υ   συμβαλλομένου]
τὰ συμβαλλόμενα υ   1 μὴ ἔλασσον JLM : μὴ ἐλάσσων P   τοῦ
τριμερήτου L   ἀποστέλλονται BJLMZ : στέλλωνται D   2 καθὸ δεῖ]
καθὼ δεῖ B : καθὸ δὴ DLMQZ : ὁδοχῇ P   δεῖ om. υ   χρεινννοὴν B :
χρωννύειν E : χρινννύειν JL : χρεῖν νύειν P : χρονννύειν Q : χρῆν νάειν Z
3 ἐπὶ πλοίου] ἐπὶ πλοίων P : om. L   κατὰ θ.] καὶ θ.MQ   θερείαν
scripsi] θερίων ABCDJLMQυ: θερίων E : θηρίων P : θήριον Z   καὶ om.
Q   καθὼς] καὶ καθὼς D : καθόσον P   ἂν] οὖν Z   4 συνεγράψαντο L (f. 231 r.) ὁ δὲ χρήσας M   ὁ δὲ] εἰ δὲ L   5 ἐπιπεμπέτω]
ἐπιβλεπέτω P   ὡς ἂν ELPZ   ἐπιχρίνυται B : ἐπιχρώννυται E :
ἐπιχρίννυται JLMZ : ἐπιχρεινννύτο P : ἐπιχρείννυται Q
Titulus] Titulum exhibui qualis in B reperitur, cum quo congruit
(ut videtur) Z   (f. 26 v.) κεφάλαια B   νόμου om. X   ῥοδίων AJOX :
ῥωδι L   περὶ ναυτικῶν om. DJLOX   P habet solum κεφάλαια ῥοδίου
νόμου
1 Titulis nulli numeri in D; in B cum numero θ΄ incipiunt
ἀγκυρῶν] ἀγκύρων codices mei antiquiores ut semper   πλοίου
post κλαπ. ponit D   κλαπεισῶν A   2 ἀγκυρῶν καὶ λοιπῶν om.
P   λυπῶν B   4 Post κλεπτῶν addit in margine ἢ λιστῶν
B   πηρατῶν L   σύλα] ita semper codices mei antiquiores
5 ὑπομεινάντων L   6 X numero ε΄ titulum dat qui ad numerum
ϛ΄ pertinet, numero ϛ΄ qui ad η΄   ἐν μάχῃ om. P   κύλλωμα BJL]
κύλωμα P : κύκλωμα DO : κήλωμα A   ἐργασαμένου D   7 ἐν μάχῃ om. D

ΝΟΜΟΣ ΡΟΔΙΩΝ ΝΑΥΤΙΚΟΣ

ζ΄ περὶ ναυτῶν ἐν μάχῃ πήρωσιν ὀφθαλμοῦ ἢ αἰδοίων κήλωσιν ἐργασαμένων.

η΄ περὶ ναυκλήρου καὶ ναυτῶν ἀλλοτρίαν λαβόντων ἐνθήκην καὶ σὺν τοῦ πλοίου ἀποδρασάντων.

5 θ΄ περὶ ναυκλήρου καὶ ἐπιβατῶν περὶ ἀποβολῆς βουλευομένων.

ι΄ περὶ πλοίου ζημίαν ἢ ναυάγιον ὑπομείναντος.

ια΄ περὶ ἐμπόρων πλοῖα ναυλουμένων.

ιβ΄ περὶ πάσης παραθήκης διδομένης ἐν πλοίῳ ἢ ἐν 10 οἴκῳ.

ιγ΄ περὶ παραθήκης χρυσίου ἀντιλεγομένης.

ιδ΄ περὶ παραθηκαρίου τὴν παραθήκην ἀρνησαμένου.

ιε΄ περὶ ἐμπόρου ἢ ἐπιβάτου ἢ δούλου παρατιθέν-
15 τος καὶ ἐν ἀκτῇ ἀπομείναντος, τοῦ πλοίου ἀποφυγόντος δι᾽ ἐπήρειαν ἢ καταδρομὴν λῃστῶν.

ις΄ περὶ χρημάτων ἐπιποντίων ἐκδανεισθέντων.

ιζ΄ περὶ χρυσίου καὶ ἀργυρίου ἐπὶ κερδοκοινωνίᾳ χρησθέντων.

20 ιη΄ περὶ τοῦ χρήματα ἐκδανεισαμένου ἐπὶ προθεσμίᾳ καὶ ἀποδημήσαντος.

1 ναύτου P   ὀφθαλμῶν D   2 αἰδοίων] ἐδοίων B : οἱανδήποτε P   κύλωσιν BJL : κύλωσιν P : κοίλωσιν D : κύκλωσιν O   ἐργασαμένου P   3 ναυτῶν P] ναύτου ceteri   λαβόντος JL   4 ἀποδράσαντος JL   5 ναυκλήρων JX   ἐπιβάτου BZ   καὶ ante περὶ addunt BL   περὶ ἀποβ. βουλ.] καὶ ἀποβολῆς σκυλευομένων DJ : καὶ ἐπιβολῆς P   6 βυλευομένων L : βουλευομένου B   X verba περὶ ἀποβ. βουλ. ut titulum novi cap. (η΄) tractat. Deinde numero θ΄ titulum dat qui ad ι΄ pertinet et sic deinceps   7 ἢ ναυάγιον] ἢ ναυαγίου X : ναυαγίου D   8 πλοῖον Z et ex πλοῖα correctum B : πλοίῳ J : πλοίων O : πλοίου P   ναυλούμενον P   9 ἐν πλοίου P   ἢ ἐν οἴκῳ om. P   12 (f. 112 v.) ιδ΄ P   παραθηκαρίου τὴν om. X   παραθήκης X   14 ἢ ἐπιβάτου] ἢ supra lineam inserit B   παρατεθέντος LP   15 ἀκτὶ BJ : ἀντι L   ἀποφυγόντος] ἀποδράσαντος P   16 ἐπίρειαν B : ἐπήριαν J   ἐπήρειαν ἢ om. PZ   καταδρ. λῃστῶν] ἐπιδρομὴν λῃστῶν P : λῃστῶν καταδρομὴν J : λῃστῶν ἐπιδρομὴν D   Post λῃστῶν O addit ἐνεχθέντων   17 (f. 332 r.) ις΄ L   ἐπιποντίου X   ἐκδανισθέντων L : ἐκδαπανισθέντων A   18 κερδωνκοινωνία L : κερδεικοινωνίας B : κερδουκοινωρίας J : κερδουκοινωνίας P : κέρδοσκοινωνοίας X   19 χρισθέντων JL : χρησθέντος BPX   20 τοῦ addidit recentior manus in B   χρήματα correctum ex χρημάτ . . . apud B : χρῆμα P : χρήματος X   ἐκδανησαμένου L   21 καὶ ἀποδημήσαντος

6

INDEX CAPITULORUM PARTIS TERTIAE

ιθ´ περὶ τοῦ ναυλωσαμένου πλοῖον καὶ ἀρραβῶνα δεδωκότος.

κ´ περὶ τοῦ ναυλωσαμένου πλοῖον καὶ ἐγγράφως συμφωνησάντων ἢ καὶ ἀγράφως ὁρισάντων.

κα´ περὶ δύο κοινωνῶν ναυκλήρων ἀλλήλοις ἀντι- 5 λεγόντων.

κβ´ περὶ ἐμπόρου τὸν γόμον ὅλον τοῦ πλοίου ναυλωσαμένου.

κγ´ περὶ ναυκλήρου καὶ ἐμπόρου περὶ γόμου συγγραψαμένων. 10

κδ´ περὶ ναυκλήρου καὶ ἐμπόρου συγγραψαμένων καὶ τὰ ἡμίναυλα δοθέντα καὶ μεταμέλους γινομένους.

κε´ περὶ ἐμπόρου πρὸς τὰ ἔγγραφα ὑπερπροθεσμήσαντος.

κϛ´ περὶ πλοίου κλασματισθέντος τῶν ναυτῶν 15 ἐκκοιτούντων.

om. P   1 P coniungit in unum ιθ´ et κ´ ita: ιθ´ περὶ τοῦ ναυλωσα-
    ϋ
μένου πλοῖον καὶ ἐγγράφως συμφωνησάντων ἢ ἀγράφως γνωρησάντων: κ´.
περὶ deinde spatium vacuum   τοῦ om. B   ἀραβῶνα J: ἀραβῶνος X
2 δεδοκότος J: ἐκδεδωκότος O: διδόντος L   3 τοῦ ναυλωσαμένου πλοίον]
ναυλοῖον quod in ναυλωσαμένου πλοῖον correxit B: ναυλωσαμένου πλοῖον
L: τῶν ναυλωσαμένων πλοῖον D: τοῦ ναυλουμένου πλοῖον X   4 συμφωνησάντων DJL] συμφωνήσαντος ceteri   ἢ καὶ ἀγράφως ὁρισάντων D]
ἢ ἀγράφως ὠρισάντων J: ἢ ἀγράφως ὁρησάντων L: ἢ καὶ ἀγράφως ὁρίσαντος
A: ἢ καὶ ἀγράφως ῥίσαντος X: omittunt O et prima manus B, ubi
recentior manus addidit ἢ ἀγράφος ὁρίσαντος. De Z non liquet
5 δύο κοινονῶν L: κοινῶν δύο X   7 γόμον] νώμον X   τοῦ πλοίου
om. P   9 καὶ om. A   καὶ ἐμπόρου om. J   περὶ] καὶ περὶ L:
om. D   γόμου] γόμους B: τοῦ γόμου PX: τοῦ γόμους L: τὸν γόμον D:
τοὺς γόμους J   συγγραψαμένου J   11 X qui hucusque (ut iam
dictum est) semper uno numero retardat, numero κδ´ eum titulum dat
qui in textu numero κε´ assignatur. Tituli subsequentes hunc in X
locum habent: κϛ´ omittitur: κζ´ = κϛ´ X: κη´ = κε´ X: κθ´ = κζ´
X: λ´ = κη´ X: λα´ omittitur: λβ´ = κθ´ X: λγ´ = λ´ X: λδ´ = λα´
X: λε´ = λβ´ X: λϛ´ = λη´ X: λζ´ = λγ´ X: λη´ et λθ´ = λδ´ X:
μ´ = λε´ X: μα´ = λϛ´ X: μβ´ = λζ´ X: μγ´ = λθ´ X et sic deinceps
συγγραψαμένων καὶ] συγγραψαμένου BL: om. P   12 τὰ ἡμίναυλα
δοθέντα L: τὰ ἐν ἡμηνναύλα δοθέντα A: τῶν ἡμιναύλων δοθέντων J
(f. 27 r.) δωθέντα B   καὶ μεταμέλους γινομένους] καὶ μεταμέλους
γινομένων AX: μετάμελος γηνόμενος B: μεταμέλου γενομένου DJL et
fortasse Z: μεταμελῶν γινομένων O: om. P   13 πρὸς] εἰς D
ὑπερπροθεσμίσαντος J: ὑπερποθεσμήσαντος D   15 O dat: κϛ´ περὶ

7

ΝΟΜΟΣ ΡΟΔΙΩΝ ΝΑΥΤΙΚΟΣ

κζ΄ περὶ πλοίου κλασματισθέντος εἰς γόμον ἀπερχομένου ἐμπόρου ἢ κοινωνίας.

κη΄ περὶ πλοίου κλασματισθέντος ἐξ αἰτίας ἐμπόρου ἢ κοινωνοῦ.

5 κθ΄ περὶ πλοίου κλασματισθέντος πρὸ τῆς προθεσμίας τῶν ἐγγράφων ἢ μετὰ τὴν προθεσμίαν.

λ΄ περὶ πλοίου πεφορτωμένου διαλυθέντος, τοῦ ἐμπόρου σωθέντος χρυσίον ἐπιφερομένου.

λα΄ περὶ πλοίου παθόντος καὶ μέρος τοῦ φόρτου 10 σωθέντος.

λβ΄ περὶ πλοίου ναυλωθέντος ἢ κοινωνίᾳ πλέοντος καὶ ἐν τῷ ἐκπορίζειν κλασματισθέντος.

λγ΄ περὶ πλοίου μετὰ τὴν ἐκβολὴν κλασματισθέντος.

λδ΄ περὶ πλοίου βέστην κομίζοντος καὶ ἀπὸ ζάλης 15 ἢ ἀντλίας βλάβης τῶν φορτίων γινομένης.

λε΄ περὶ πλοίου ἀποβολὴν τῆς καταρτίας ὑπομείναντος.

λϛ΄ περὶ πλοίου ἐν τῷ ἀρμενίζειν ἕτερον καταδιδόντος πλοῖον.

ναυτῶν ἢ ναυκλήρων ἐκκοιτούντων ἐκ τοῦ πλοίου καὶ ἀπολείας γενομένης. Tituli subsequentes hunc in O locum habent : κϛ΄ = κζ΄ O : κζ΄ = κη΄ O : κη΄ = κθ΄ O : κθ΄ = λ΄ O : λ΄ = λα΄ O : λα΄ = λβ΄ O : λβ΄ = λγ΄ O : λγ΄ = λδ΄ O et sic deinceps   B titulos numerorum κϛ΄ et κζ΄ transponit   In L vacuum spatium inter κλασματισθέντος et τῶν ναυτῶν relinquitur   16 ἐγκοτούντων D : om. L   1 (f. 13 v.) κζ΄ J D titulos numerorum κζ΄ et κη΄ transponit   κλασθέντος O   ἀπερχόμενον BP   2 ἐμπόρου om. J   κοινωνοῦ BPZ   3 κη΄ om. B   4 κοινῶν L : κοινωνίας DX   5 πρὸ τῆς προθ. usque ad finem tituli] om. P   7 πεφορτομένου BJL : φορτωμένου P 8 χρυσίον ἐπιφ.] om. X   ἐπιφέροντος P   9 παθώντος L   μέρους O   τοῦ om. J   φορτίον A   11 λβ΄ in margine additum apud B et lectu difficillimum   ναυλοθέντος B   ἢ κοινωνίᾳ πλέοντος] om. P   κοινωνίαν JL : κοινωνῶν O : κοινωνίας X   πλεόντων JLOX   12 ἐν τῷ] om. L   ἐκπορίζειν JL] ἐκπλωρίζειν P : ἐκπρορίζειν X : εἰσπορίζειν D : ἐμπορίζειν AOZ   13 P numero λγ΄ eum titulum dat qui revera ad numerum λδ΄ pertinet.   Deinceps uno numero retardat usque ad numerum μ΄ cui eum titulum dat qui revera ad numerum λγ΄ pertinet 15 ἢ ἀντλίας ... usque ad finem tituli] βλαβέντος P   ἀντλίας] ἀνταίας D   φόρτων X   γενομένης J   16 ὑπομήναντος L   18 ἕτερον πλοῖον καταδιδόντος AO : ἑτέρω πλοίω (correctum ex ἕτερον πλοῖον) καταδιδόντος B : ἑτέρου καταδιδόντος (καδίδοντος J) πλοίου DJL : ἑτέρου καταδιδόντος P,

8

INDEX CAPITULORUM PARTIS TERTIAE

λζ΄ περὶ πλοίου κλασματισθέντος, τὰ δὲ τῶν ἐμπόρων καὶ ἐπιβατῶν σωθέντα.

λη΄ περὶ πλοίου σῖτον πεφορτωμένου ἐν ζάλῃ καταληφθέντος.

λθ΄ περὶ πλοίου πεφορτωμένου βολήσαντος τῆς 5 ἐνθήκης σωθείσης.

μ΄ περὶ πλοίου ναυαγήσαντος καὶ μέρος τι τοῦ πλοίου καὶ τῆς ἐνθήκης σωθέντων.

μα΄ περὶ πλοίου διαφθαρέντος, τὰ δὲ τῶν ἐπιβατῶν σωθέντα ἢ συναπολεσθέντα. 10

μβ΄ περὶ πλοίου τρυπήσαντος φορτία κομίζοντος.

μγ΄ περὶ πλοίου ἐκβολὴν ποιήσαντος τοῦ γόμου καὶ τῶν ἐξαρτίων.

μδ΄ περὶ πλοίου ἐκβολὴν τῆς καταρτίας ἢ τῶν αὐχένων ἐν ζάλῃ ὑπομείναντος. 15

με΄ περὶ τοῦ ἀποσώζοντος ἐκ τοῦ πελάγους εἰς γῆν τι ἐκ πλοίου ναυαγήσαντος.

μϛ΄ περὶ τοῦ ἀποσώζοντος κάραβον ἐκ πλοίου ἀπορρήξαντος.

μζ΄ περὶ τοῦ ἀποσώζοντός τι ἐκ βυθοῦ ἐκ πλοίου 20 ναυαγήσαντος.

qui πλοῖον omittit   1 τὰ δὲ τῶν] τῶν δὲ X   ἐμπόρων καὶ] om. P
2 σωθέντων BX   3 X λη΄ et λθ΄ in unum coniungit cum numeri
λη΄ verba tria postrema (ἐν ζάλῃ καταλ.) numeri λθ΄ prima tria (περὶ πλ.
πεφ.) omittat   σῖτου πεφορτωμένου DLO : σῖτον πεφορτώ(ο B)-
μενον BP : σῖτου πεφορτω(ο J)μένου AJ   ἐν ζάλῃ BDJP : καὶ
ἐν ζάλῃ ALOZ   καταλειφθέντος AJP   5 (f. 332 v.) λθ΄
L   πεφορτομένου BJL   βολήσαντος] βουλήσαντος DX : βολῆς καὶ
πόσου A   7 τι om. J   8 σωθέντος X : σωθείσης DP. De J dubito
9 (f. 113 r.) μ΄ P (Vide quae adnotavi ad lineam 13 praecedentis
paginae) φθαρέντος P   Post ἐπιβατῶν DJ addunt καὶ τῆς ἐνθήκης   10
σωθέντων L   ἢ συναπολεσθέντα] ἢ συναποπλεύσαντα J : om. X   11 περὶ
τοῦ πλοίου D   τριπήσαντος X : τριπηθέντος P   κομίζοντα J   12 καὶ
τῶν ἐξαρτίων om. P   14 Post ἐκβολὴν B ποιήσαντος addit   τῆς om.
P   ἢ τῶν αὐχένων ἐν ζάλῃ om. P   15 αὐχενίων D   ἐν ζάλῃ om. Z
                                                                    εἰ
ὑπομηναντος J : ὑπομήναντος L : ὑπομένοντος ADO : om. B   16 ἀποσώζοντός τι P   ἐκ πελάγου X   εἰς γῆν τι] om. P   17 ἐκ τοῦ πλοίου DX
18 (f. 27 v.) μϛ΄ B   τοῦ om. B   Post ἀποσώζοντος addunt τι DJ et
κάραβον (D) sive τὸν κάραβον (J) post ἀπορρήξαντος ponunt   ἐκ τοῦ
πλοίου X   19 ἀπορρίξαντος J : ἀπορήξαντος B : ἀπορίξαντος L   20 τοῦ

ΝΟΜΟΣ ΡΟΔΙΩΝ ΝΑΥΤΙΚΟΣ

PARS TERTIA

ΑΡΧΗ ΤΟΥ ΝΟΜΟΥ

α´ ἐὰν πλοῖον ὁρμῇ ἐπὶ λιμένα ἢ ἐν ἀκτῇ καὶ σύλα
πάθῃ τῶν ἀγκυρῶν καὶ κατασχεθεὶς ὁ κλέπτης ὁμολο-

ἀποσ.] ἀποσ. P βυθοῦ] τοῦ βυθοῦ ΑΟΧ ἀπὸ πλοίου J DJL addunt:—
μη´ περὶ τοῦ ἁρπάζοντός τι ἀπὸ ναυαγίου (ἐκ ναυαγίου D). μθ´ περὶ τοῦ
ἀναγκάζοντος τὸν ναύκληρον πλεῦσαι. ν´ περὶ τῶν πραίδας (πραίδαν D) ποιούν-
των ἀπὸ ναυαγίου (εἰς τὰ ναυάγια L)

Titulus. Titulum dedi qualem exhibet A cum quo congruit ut videtur Z ('Principium legis' Vent.) alii aliter:—κεφάλαια ἀρχὴ τ κεφαλαίου B :
νόμος ῥοδίων ναυτικός DL: ἐκλογὴ ἐκ τῶν διγέστων E : νόμος ναυτικὸς
ῥοδίωνος ὃν ἐθέσπισαν οἱ θειότατοι αὐτοκράτορες ἀδριανὸς ἀντώνιος (ἀντωνῖνος V) τιβέριος λούπιος σεπτίμιος σευῆρος οὐεσπασιανὸς τραϊανὸς (τραϊανὸς
om. *f*) περτίναξ ἀεισέβαστοί τε καὶ λόγιοι F*f*V : κεφάλαια τοῦ νόμου τοῦ
ῥωδίου (ῥοδίονος H) κατὰ θάλατταν (κατὰ θ. om. H*h*) GH*h* : νόμος ῥοδίων
(ῥωδέων W) ναυτικὸς (ναυτικῶς W : ναυτικὸς om. O) κατ᾽ ἐκλογὴν ἐκ τοῦ ιδ´ (ια´
J*v*: τεσσαρισκαιδεκατου W: ἐνδεκάτου Harl.) βιβλίου τῶν διγέστων (διαγέστων X: διγέστων *v*) JMN (qui κεφάλαια ξγ´ addit) OWX*v* Harl.: περὶ ναυτικῶν κεφάλαια κατ᾽ ἐκλογήν P (f. 49 v.) : νόμος ῥοδίων ναυτικὸς ὃν ἐθέσπισαν οἱ
θειότατοι αὐτοκράτορες, ἀδριανὸς ἀντόνιος τιβέριος λούκιος σεπτήμιος σευῆρος
περιτίναξ ἀεισέβαστοι, κατ᾽ ἐκλογὴν ἐκ τοῦ ιδ´ βιβλίου τῶν διγέστων P (f.
113 v.) : νόμος ναυτικὸς ἤτοι ὁ τῶν ῥοδίων R : περὶ ῥοδίων ναυτικὸς νόμος
κατ᾽ ἐκλογήν Y Nullus titulus apud CQ: titulum codicum TU
vide in appendice I

Numeratio capitulorum. Eam capitulorum distributionem quam
in textu adhibui praebent, paucis mutatis de quibus suo loco
dicam, ABJLOPSWXZΣ. In CEFK capitula non numerantur. In
D c. 12 recepit per errorem numerum ιγ´ : sequentia capitula
semper uno numero praeeunt usque ad c. 36, quod numero
caret. Cum verbis ἐὰν ἄβροχα capituli 40 D novum cap. incipit
(μα´); sequitur ut c. 47 numerum μη´ habeat. G verbis ἐὰν δέ τις
κλέψει capituli 2 capitulum γ´ ; verbis ἐὰν δὲ ναύτης capituli 3 capitulum ε´ ; verbis ἐὰν δὲ τοῦ ναυκλήρου capituli 4 capitulum ζ´ ; verbis τῶν
δὲ ἐκριπτομένων capituli 47 capitulum να´ incipit. Capitula quae post
c. 47 in G sequuntur et de quibus in Appendice G egi numeros in
G habent νβ´ usque ad νζ´. Apud M nova distributio. Verbis ἐὰν δέ
τις κλέψει capituli 2 c. γ´ ; verbis ἐὰν δὲ ναύτης capituli 3 c. ε´ ; verbis
ἐὰν δὲ τοῦ ναυκλήρου capituli 4 c. ζ´ ; verbis ἐὰν ἔχει capituli 11 c. ιε´ ;
verbis ἐὰν δὲ τοῦ χρόνου capituli 17 c. κβ´ ; verbis ἐὰν τὸ ἓν πλοῖον capituli 21 c. κζ´ ; verbis ἐὰν δὲ καὶ παρέλθῃ capituli 25 c. λβ´ incipit.
Capitulis 44 et 45 eundem numerum (να´) per incuriam dat. Itaque
numerus νγ´ capitulo 47 adhibetur, cui in tabula quam in Appendice
C dedi rectius numerus νδ´ datur. In hac tabula sicut in textu
decem capitula quae sequuntur novam numerationem habent (α´
usque ad ι´) Apud N c. 47 numerum νε´ habet, et in capitulis
quae sequuntur eadem numeratio continuatur ita ut quod in M α´
est in N numerum νϛ´, quod in M β´ in N numerum νζ´
habeat. In Q verbis ἐὰν δὲ ναύτης capituli 3 c. δ´; ἐὰν τὸ ἓν πλοῖον
capituli 21 c. κγ´ ; ἐὰν δὲ παρέλθῃ capituli 25 c. κη´ incipit. Itaque c.

γήσῃ, τοῦτον κελεύει ὁ νόμος βασανίζεσθαι καὶ τὴν
προσγενομένην ζημίαν ἀπολογεῖσθαι κατὰ τὸ διπλάσιον. 5

β′ ἐὰν βουλήσει τοῦ ναυκλήρου οἱ ναῦται σύλα
ποιήσωσιν ἀγκύρας πλοίου ἑτέρου ὁρμοῦντος ἐν λιμένι
ἢ ἐν ἀκτῇ καὶ συμβῇ ἐντεῦθεν ἀπώλειαν γενέσθαι τοῦ
πλοίου τοῦ τὰς ἀγκύρας συληθέντος, καὶ τούτων οὕτως
ἐν ἀκριβείᾳ ἀποδεικνυμένων, πᾶσαν τὴν προσγενο- 5
μένην ζημίαν ἔν τε τῷ πλοίῳ καὶ τὰ ἐν τῷ πλοίῳ σῶα
ἀποδιδότω ὁ ναύκληρος ὁ τὰ σύλα ἐπιτρέψας γενέσθαι.
ἐὰν δέ τις κλέψῃ σκεύη πλοίου ἤ τι τῶν ἐν τῷ πλοίῳ

47 numerum να′ habet. In R verbis ἐὰν δέ τις κλέψει capituli 2 c. γ′;
ἐὰν δὲ ναύτης capituli 3 c. ε′; ἐὰν ὁ λαμβάνων capituli 17 c. κ′ incipit.
Itaque c. 18 numerum κα′ et c. 19 numerum κβ′ habent; sed per errorem capitula 20 et 21 eosdem numeros habent. Verbis ἐὰν δὲ μὴ capituli 30 c. λβ′ incipit; omittitur c. 35; verbis εἰ δὲ ἁρμενίζοντος capituli
39 c. μβ′ incipit. Capitulo 47 numerum ν′ dat. In Y verbis ἐὰν ἔχῃ
capituli 11 novum capitulum incipit (ιβ′). Capitula sequentia semper
uno numero praeeunt usque ad cap. 30, quod per errorem numerum
κβ′ habet.

α′ 1 ὁρμῇ MN] ὁρμᾷ ABJLP: ὁρμήσῃ K: post ἀκτῇ ponit D λιμένα ἢ]
λιμένη C: λιμένα ἐν ἡμέρα ἢ M ἐν ἀκτῇ] ἐν ἀκτὶ LQ: ἀκτὴν J 2 πάθοι
E κατασχεθείς] κατασχεθῇ EKMNP²WFV ὁμολογήσῃ]
ὁμολογήσει BJLP¹: καὶ ὁμολογήσῃ KFV: καὶ ὁμολογήσει MNP²W: ἢ ὁμολογήσῃ E 3 τοῦτο MN post quod ponunt interpunctionem 4 προσγινομένην BJLMNP¹ ἀπολογεῖσθαι] ἀπολογίσεται C: ἀπαιτεῖσθαι G
κατὰ] εἰς C διπλοῦν K β′ Capitulum in Σ sic introducitur: ἐν δὲ
τῷ η′ τίτλῳ περιέχεται τὰ κεφάλαια τοῦ ῥοδίου νόμου οὗτινος ἐν τῷ β′ κεφαλαίῳ
φησιν 1 βουλήσει] εἰδήσει V σύλα ποιήσωσιν] σύλα ποιήσωσιν L:
συμποιήσωσι J ἀγκύρας ex ἀγκύρα manu recentiore corr. P¹:
ἀγκύρα C: ἀγκύρων ORF: εἰς ἄγκυραν V ἑτέρου om. X ὁρμῶντος
ALMNP¹P²: ὁρμόντος BJ ἐν λιμένη BJQ: ἐν λίμνη Hh: εἰς λιμαῖνα M
3 ἀκτῇ] ἀκτὶ JLQ Addunt ἀφελόμενοι Σ συμβεῖ BP²: συμβαίη E συμ-
(f. 105 v.)βῇ C ἀπωλίαν L: ἀπώλεια XYFV γινέσθαι B τοῦ
πλοίου τοῦ] ὁ X 4 τοῦ τὰς] καὶ τούτων in M rasura trium litterarum συλληθέντος J καὶ τούτων... ναύκληρος] καὶ τούτων τὴν ζημίαν
σῶαν ἐπιδώσει ὁ ναύκληρος V ἀκριβία B: ἀκρυβεία J 5 (f. 114 r.)
ἀποδεικνυμένων P² ἄπασαν Q προσγινομένην JLMNP²: προσ-
γεναμένην X 6 ἐν τῷ πλοίῳ AEHJKNORFY: ἐντός τε τοῦ πλοίου K
καὶ τὰ... 8 πλοίῳ] om. X καὶ τὰ ἐν τῷ πλοίῳ] καὶ τὼ ἐν τῷ πλοίῳ C:
καὶ τοῖς ἐν τῷ πλοίῳ DK: om. EHhNOP²RF σῶαν EORF:
ἅ σῶα W: om. K 7 ἀποδιδώτω M: ἀποδιδότο P¹: ἀποδιδίτω C
(f. 121 r.) ὁ τὰ σύλα Q ἐπιτρέψας γενέσθαι] ἐπιτρεψάμενος C
8 (f. 14 r.) ἐὰν δέ τις J Cum verbo ἐὰν novum capitulum (γ′) incipiunt
GhMNR δέ om. FV κλέψει A: κλέψοι E: κλύσει W: post
σκεύη ponit K σκεύη πλοίου] πλοῖον V ἤ τι τῶν] ἤ τι τῶ C:

11

χρηματιζόντων, τουτέστι σχοινίων τε καὶ κανναβίων
10 ἢ ἁρμένων ἢ διφθερῶν καὶ καράβων καὶ λοιπῶν, διπλᾶ
ἀποδιδότω ὁ τὰ σῦλα ποιήσας.

γ´ ἐὰν ναύτης κελεύσει τοῦ ναυκλήρου κλοπὴν
ποιήσῃ ἐμπόρου ἢ ἐπιβάτου καὶ καταληφθεὶς κατασχεθῇ, ὁ ναύκληρος διπλᾶ ἀποδιδότω τοῖς τὰ σῦλα
παθοῦσιν, ὁ δὲ ναύτης λαμβανέτω ξυλαγώγια ἑκατόν.
5 ἐὰν δὲ ναύτης αὐτοβούλως συλήσῃ μὲν κατασχεθῇ
δὲ ἢ καὶ διὰ μαρτύρων ἐλεγχθῇ, σφοδρῶς βασανιζέσθω,
ἐὰν καὶ μάλιστα τὰ σῦλα χρυσίον ᾖ, καὶ τὴν ἀποκατάστασιν τῷ συληθέντι ποιείτω.

εἴ τοι τῶν M   ἐν] om. DY   9 τουτέστι ... usque ad finem
capituli] σχοινίον τυχὸν ἢ ἄρμενον διπλᾶ ἀποδώσει αὐτά V   τουτέστιν
BLN: (f. 31 r.) τουτέστιν M   σχοινίων ... λοιπῶν] σχοινίον ἢ
ἄρμενον ἢ διφθέρων καὶ πλοίων καὶ καράβων F   σχοινίων ... ἁρ-
μένων] σχοινίων καὶ ἁρμενίων καὶ κανναβίων O   σχοινίων EJNP²h]
σχοινίον HM: σχυνίων C: σχοίνων sive σχοινῶν ceteri   τε καὶ] ται
καὶ B: καὶ R: om. J   καναβίων RΥΣ: κανναβίνων E: καναβίνων WX
10 (f. 333 r.) ἢ ἁρμένων L   διφθέρων codd. plerique: διαφθέρων X   ἢ
καράβων K   καὶ λοιπῶν] καὶ τῶν λοιπῶν MNΥ: καὶ λειπῶν X: λοιπῶν C:
καὶ λοιπὰ Hh: om. W   11 ἀποδιδότω B   ὁ τὰ σῦλα ποιήσας] τοῖς τὰ
σῦλα παθοῖσιν MN: τοῖς τὴν ζημίαν παθοῦσιν E   γ´ Titulus huius cap.
in Σ ἐν δὲ τῷ γ´ κεφαλαίω   1 ναύτης] τις EN: ναῦτις mr   κελεύσῃ
L: κλέψῃ (sic) W   2 ποιήσει JLM: ποιήσοι E: ἐμποιήσῃ V   ἐμπόρων H   ἢ ἐπιβάτου] om. FV   καταληφθεὶς] καταλειφθεὶς Jp:
καταλυφθεὶς M: ληφθεὶς R (quod post κατασχέθη ponit): om. V   3
ἀποδιδότω ... παθοῦσιν] ἀποδώσει αὐτά V   ἀποδιδότω B   τὰ
σῦλα] τὰ, quod in αὐτὰ correxit recentior manus X   4 πεπονθῶσι Y
οἱ δὲ ναῦτε (ναῦται Υ) λαμβανέτωσαν JΥ   ναύτης] addit ὁ τὴν κλοπὴν
ἐργασάμενος et omittit λαμβανέτω D   ξυλαγωγίας H, qui in margine
habet ἐν α ξυλαγωγῶν   ξυλαγώγα X   5 ἐὰν δὲ] ἐὰν EKMNP²WΥb
Principium novi capituli in GMNR (ε´) et Q (δ´)   ἐὰν δὲ ... μαρ-
τύρων] εἰ δὲ αὐτοβουλήτως τοῦτο ποιήσει καὶ κατασχέθη ἢ (καὶ V) ὑπὸ
μαρτύρων FV   ὁ ναύτης OR   αὐτέβουλος M   αὐτοβούλως
post συλήσει ponit Υ   συλήσῃ μὲν] συλίσει μὲν M: συλήσοι μὲν
E: συλήσῃ DJ: συλήσει LQΥ: συλήσας Σ   κατασχεθῇ] συληφθῇ
W   6 δὲ om. Σ   (f. 50 r.) ἢ καὶ διὰ P   ἢ διὰ MN: ἢ μὲν
διὰ X   ἐλεγχθεί L: ἐλεγχθείη E   βασανίζεται Q: βασανίζεσθαι
W   7 ἐὰν καὶ μάλιστα ... usque ad finem cap.] om. R   ἐὰν καὶ
μάλιστα ... ῇ] om. FV   ἐὰν καὶ μάλιστα] καὶ μάλιστα ἐὰν Σ: ἐὰν δὲ
καὶ μάλιστα K: ἐὰν καὶ κάλλιστα X   τὰ σῦλα] σῦλα CEGHMNP²W:
In B τὰ addit recentior manus: τὰ συληθέντα D: συλλάβῃ K: om. h
χρυσίου CEGHMNh: χρυσίω P¹: χρυσίων P²: χρυσίως X   ᾖ] ἦν B
(sed ex ἢ correctum) JΣ: εἶ h: ἢ Υ: om. KX   καὶ τὴν] ἢ τὴν X
8 τῷ συλ.] τῶν συληθέντων MP²   ποιήτω BJ: ποιήσει FV: ποιήσει

12

PARS TERTIA

δ´ ἐὰν ἐν τόπῳ συλωμένῳ ἢ ληστευομένῳ κατάξῃ
πλοῖον, μαρτυρουμένων τῶν ἐπιβατῶν τῷ ναυκλήρῳ
τὴν τοῦ τόπου αἰτίαν καὶ συμβῇ συληθῆναι, ἀποδιδότω
ὁ ναύκληρος τὰ σῦλα τοῖς συληθεῖσιν. ἐὰν δὲ τοῦ
ναυκλήρου ἀπομαρτυρουμένου καταγάγωσιν οἱ ἐπιβάται 5
τὸ πλοῖον καὶ συμβῇ τι, ὑποκείσθωσαν οἱ ἐπιβάται τὴν
ζημίαν.

ε´ ἐὰν ναῦται μαχὴν ποιήσωσι, λόγοις ποιείτωσαν
καὶ μηδεὶς κρουέτω τὸν ἕτερον. ἐὰν δὲ καί τις κρούσῃ
εἰς κεφαλὴν καὶ ἀνοίξῃ ἢ ἑτέρως πῶς κυλλώσῃ, παρεχέτω ὁ κρούσας τοὺς μισθοὺς τοῖς ἰατροῖς καὶ τὰ
ἀναλώματα τῷ ἀδικηθέντι καὶ τὸν μισθὸν ὅλου τοῦ 5
χρόνου τῆς ἀργίας καὶ ἐπιμελείας.

supra quod ποιείτω atramento rubro scriptum est K   δ´ 1 ἐν τόπῳ]
ἐ τόπω ἐν D : τόπω X   συλουμένω LP¹P²RX : συλημένω MN : συλου-
μένων J : σύλου F   λιστευομένω M : λη”τευομένω F : ληστευομένων
JQ   κατάξει LM : κατάρξοι E : κατάρξει Y   2 μαρτυρουμένω P¹ :
διαμαρτυρουμένων D   (f. 28 r.) τῶ ναυκλήρω B   τῶ ναυκλήρω post
αἰτίαν ponit Y   3 τοῦ τόπου] τούτου X : τόπου W   καὶ] addit
recentior manus in Q : ἐκεῖνος δὲ ἀμελήσας K   συμβῇ συλ.] συμβουληθῆναι P² : συμβῇ σῦλα γενέσθαι D : συμβῇ συληθῆναι O   ἀποδότω
EKN : ἐπιδιδότω F   4 τὰ σῦλα solus servavit C : omittunt ceteri
συληθῆσιν M : συλληθεῖσιν P¹   ἐὰν] GMN novum cap. (ζ´) incipiunt   εἰ F   5 μαρτυρουμένου C : ἐπιμαρτυρουμένου F : προ-
γα
μαρτυρουμένου τὴν τοῦ τόπου αἰτίαν D   καταγωσιν J : κατάγωσιν R
6 τὸ πλοῖον . . . οἱ ἐπιβάται] om. Y   τοῦ πλοίου M   καὶ] καὶ
εἰ D   ὑποκείσθωσαν] E addit καὶ ἀποδιδώτωσαν   οἱ ἐπιβάται
τὴν ζημίαν BDJL] τὴν ζημίαν (ζυμίαν F) οἱ ἐπιβάται AEFOP¹P²WX : οἱ
ἐπιβάται τῇ ζημία Q : τῇ ζημία (ζυμία C) οἱ ἐπιβάται CGHhMNR : τῇ
τοιαύτη ζημία οἱ ἐπιβάται K   ε´ In Z cap. ϛ´ venit ante cap. ε´   1
μαχὴν ναῦται Y   ποιήσωσι μαχὴν K   ποιήσωσιν BLMP¹   ποιήτωσαν BJL   2 μηδεὶς . . . ἕτερον] μὴ θάτερος κρουέτω θάτερον K
κρουέτω] κρούση MN   ἐὰν δὲ καί τις κρούση] om. Ch   ἐὰν δέ τις
GHOP¹P²RX : εἰ δέ τις KFV   κρούση (κρούσει J) εἰς κεφαλὴν
DJLY] εἰς κεφαλὴν κρούσει Q : κρούση (κρούσει AKX) τὴν κεφαλὴν
ABKMNOP¹RX : κρούσοι τὴν κεφαλὴν E : κρούση τῆς κεφαλῆς P²W :
κρούσει κατὰ κεφαλῆς FV : τῇ κεφαλῇ G : κρουτήσει τὸν
ἕτερον τὴν κεφαλὴν H   3 εἰς κεφαλὴν καὶ] καὶ τὴν κεφαλὴν C : τὴν κεφαλὴν καὶ h   καὶ πλεῖν (sc. πληγὴν) ἀνοίξει D   ἀνοίξει AJL : ἀνύξη BP² :
ἀνύξει P¹ : πλήξη K   ἕτερος B : ἑτέρω P²   πῶς κυλλώση EGH]
πῶς κυλλώσει BChJQX : πῶς κυλώση OP² : πῶς κοιλώση DR : πῶς κωλύσει
P¹ : πῶς κολάσει L : πῶς κοιλλώσει F : πῶς κοιλώσει K : πῶς κυκλώσει W :
πῶς κακώσει V : προσκυλλώσει A : κυλώση M : κυλλώσει N   (f. 82 v.)
παρεχέτω N : παρασχέτω Q   4 κρούσας] κυλλώσας MN : πλήξας K
τὸν μισθὸν XFV   τοῦ ἰατροῦ X   τὰ om. MN   5 ἀναδόματα P²

13

ϛ´ ἐὰν ναῦται μαχὴν ποιήσωσι καί τις κρούσῃ
λίθῳ ἢ ξύλῳ πάλιν δὲ ὁ κρουσθεὶς πατάξῃ τὸν πρῶτον
κρούσαντα, ὡς βιασθεὶς ἐποίησεν. εἰ δὲ καὶ θάνῃ
ὁ κρουσθεὶς καὶ μαρτυρηθῇ ὅτι πρῶτος ἔκρουσεν ἢ
5 λίθῳ ἢ ξύλῳ ἢ σιδήρῳ, ὁ πατάξας αὐτὸν καὶ
θανατώσας ἀκίνδυνος ἔστω· ὃ γὰρ ἠθέλησε ποιῆσαι
ἔπαθεν.

ζ´ ἐάν τις τῶν ναυκλήρων ἢ ἐμπόρων ἢ ναυτῶν
κρούσῃ τινὰ γρόνθον καὶ πηρώσῃ ἢ λὰξ δώσῃ καὶ
συμβῇ κήλην ποιῆσαι, δώσει ὁ κρούσας τὰ ἰατρεῖα
καὶ ὑπὲρ μὲν τοῦ ὀφθαλμοῦ χρυσίνους δώδεκα ὑπὲρ

ἀδικιθέντι L   τοὺς μισθοὺς Q   ὅλον DHJP²R   τοῦ χρόνου] om. J
χρόνου καὶ τῆς P¹   ἀργείας MN: ἀναργυρίας X   καὶ ἐπιμελείας] καὶ om.
Q: αὐτοῦ V   ϛ´ (f. 107 r.) ϛ´ C   In FV cap. ζ´ ante cap. ϛ´ ponitur
1 ποιήσωσιν BLMNP¹P²   τις κρούσει AL: τῆς κρούσῃ B: τις κρούσοι
E: τις ἐξ αὐτῶν κρούσει K: κρούσῃ τις FV   2 λίθω ξύλω A: λίθου ἢ
ξύλου P²W: λίθον ἢ ξύλω X: ξύλω ἢ λίθω ZY: ξύλου ἢ λίθου F: ξύλω ἢ
πλίνθω V: ἢ ξύλῳ om. E   πάλιν δὲ] καὶ πάλιν MN   κροσθεὶς M
πατάξει AL: πατάξοι E: κρούσει W   τὸν πρῶτον] τὸν τὸ πρῶτον A:
τὸν πρώτως DJKORY: πρῶτον in textu omittit H et in margine ita
addit τὸν πρῶτον   (f. 114 v.) πρῶτον κρ. P²   πρῶτον κρ.] προ-
κρούσαντα E   3 ὡς om. E   ὡς βιασθεὶς ... ὁ κρουσθεὶς] ὁ βιασθεὶς καὶ ἀποθάνη ὁ κρουσθεὶς K: ὡς βιασθεὶς καὶ ἀποθάνη F: καὶ θανατώσας
αὐτὸν V   ἐποίησεν] πεποίηκεν MN   καὶ οὐκ ἐνάγεται addit C
θάνει L: θάνοι E: ἀποθάνη CJ: ἀποθάνει BGHhQY   4 ὁ κρουσθεὶς] ὁ
πρῶτος κρούσας Y   μαρτυριθεῖ L: μαρτυριθῇ P¹   μαρ(f. 121 v.)-
τυριθεῖ Q   πρῶτον EKMNOP²WF: πρώτως DRY: ἐκεῖνος πρῶτον
V   ἔκρουσε J   ἢ λίθω ... θανατώσας] om. FV   ἢ λίθου
ἢ ξύλου ἢ σιδήρου P²W: ἢ ξύλω ἢ λίθω ἢ σιδήρω Z   5 ἢ ξύλῳ] om. Q
πατάξας] κρούσας K   6 ἀκίνδυνος B   ἔστω] ἔσται N   Addit V
ὁ θανιτώσας: F ὁ θανατώσας αὐτόν   ὃ γὰρ ... ἔπαθεν] om. E
ἠθέλησεν BLMNP¹P²: θέλησε D: ἤθελε FV   ποιῆσαι] om. MN, sed in
M verba ὃ γὰρ ἠθέλησεν ἔπαθεν scripsit recentior manus supra litteras
quae evanuerant   7 καὶ ἔπαθεν K   ζ´ Titulus cap. in Σ: ἐν δὲ τῷ
ζ´ κεφαλαίω   1 τῷ ναυκλήρω ἢ ἐμπόρω AJL: κρούσοι
E: κρούσας V: τρώσῃ Σ, praeter b qui στρώσει habet   γρόθον WY:
γρόνθω BCEGHhJKRΣ (praeter b): γρόνθου P²   καὶ] om. V   πη-
ρώσει AJ: πληρώσῃ E: πληγώσει Q   δώσῃ ... ποιῆσαι] κρούσας
κελητώσει V: δώσας κελητόσει F   δώσει AJLP²: δώη H: δῶ Σ: om.
Y   καὶ συμβεῖ M: ἢ συμβεῖ C: συμβαίη E   3 κήλην EP¹P²Oς]
κίλην ADLNR: κοίλην CJKWY: κύλην MQR: κύλιν X: κύλλην G:
κηλήτην B: κηλίτην H: κοιλίτην h   ποιήσε M: ποιήσει X   δώσει]
δώσῃ P¹P²: δόσῃ N: διδότω D: δώτω E: ἀποδώσει V   τὰ ἰτρεῖα A:
τὰς ἰατρείας BCGHhWFV: τὰς ἰατρείας ex τὰ ἰατρεία correctum Q: τὰ
ἰατρικὰ EKMN: τὴν ἰατρείαν X   4 μὲν om. GX   ὀφθαλ-
μοῦ] ὀφθαλμοῦ δώσει FV   (f. 333 v.) χρυσίνους L: χρυσίους M
χρυσίνους ex χρυσίους correctum mr   ὑπὲρ ... δέκα] om. Y

δὲ τῆς κήλης χρυσίνους δέκα. εἰ δὲ ὁ τὸ λὰξ κρου- 5
σθεὶς ἀποθάνῃ, ἔνοχος ἔσται ὁ κρούσας τῆς δίκης τοῦ
θανάτου.

η΄ ἐὰν πλεύσῃ ὁ ναύκληρος πιστευθεὶς τὸ πλοῖον
καὶ εἰς ἄλλην χώραν ἀποδράσῃ μετὰ χρυσίου βουλήσει
τῶν ναυτῶν, τὰ μὲν οἰκεῖα αὐτῶν ἅπαντα, κινητὰ ἀκίνητα καὶ αὐτοκίνητα, ὅσα ὑπάρχει αὐτοῖς, κατασχεθήσονται. καὶ ἐὰν μὴ αἱ τούτων ἐκτιμήσεις τὸ ἱκανὸν 5
ποιήσωσι τοῦ πλοίου καὶ τῆς ἐργασίας τοῦ χρόνου ἐν
τῷ πιπράσκεσθαι αὐτά, οἱ ναῦται ἅμα τῷ προναυκλήρῳ
μισθούσθωσαν καὶ τὴν ἀποπλήρωσιν τῆς ζημίας
ποιείτωσαν.

5 τῆς] om. MNP²W. In mr τῆς additur supra lineam manu recentiore κήλης ADEOP¹P²R] κίλης BLN : κοίλης ChJKW : κύλης MQXF :
κύλλης G χρυσίους M : om. FV δέκα] ' sex decim ' Venturius εἰ
δὲ ... usque ad finem cap.] om. V 6 ὁ τὸ λὰξ] ὁ τῷ λὰξ P¹P² :
ὁ τῇ λὰξ Ε : ὁ λὰξ AKMNQRΣ : τῷ λὰξ C τὸ λὰξ om. J κρουσθεὶς]
λαβὼν Υ 6 ἀποθάνει BLMN : om. F ἔνοχος post ὁ κρούσας ponit
R ἐστιν P² Post ἔσται F addit θανάτου ὁ κρούσας ...
δίκης] τῇ κρίσει καὶ τῇ δίκῃ ὁ κρούσας K τῆς δίκεις B : τῇ δικῇ p
In margine huius cap. habet Σ ὅτι ὑπὲρ τοῦ ὀφθαλμοῦ δώδεκα νομίσματα, ὑπὲρ κήλης δὲ [ὑπὲρ δὲ κήλης] νομίσματα δέκα παρέχεται ποινή
Post hoc cap. P¹ vadit ad c. ιδ΄ Partis secundae η΄ 1 ἐὰν πλεύσῃ ...
πιστευθεὶς] ἐὰν ὁ ναύκληρος πιστευθῇ F ἐὰν πλεύσῃ] ἔπλευσεν Α : ἐὰν
πλεύσει LMQ πλεύσῃ ὁ] om. Χ τοῦ πλοίου K : τὰ πλοῖον B
2 καὶ] om. EPW εἰς ἄλλην χώραν] om. EKPWF ἀποδράσει
BLMNQ : ἀπέδρασεν Α : ἀποδράσοι E βουλήσει τῶν ν. μ. χ. AD
χρυσίων F βουλήσῃ JP 3 καὶ τὰ μὲν οἰκεῖα Q οἰκία L
πάντα L κιν. ἀκιν. καὶ αὐτοκίν.] om. Ηh κύνητα Q ἀκί-
νητα] ἀκύνητα Q : ἢ ἀκίνητα BCW : καὶ ἀκίνητα EMNF : om. J 4 καὶ
αὐτοκίν.] addit in margine N, post ὅσα ὑπάρχει αὐτοῖς ponit F : om. W
αὐτωκύνητα Q καὶ ὅσα R 5 (f. 28 v.) καὶ ἐὰν μὴ B καὶ ἐὰν
μὴ] ἐὰν δὲ μὴ L : καὶ εἰ μὴ ἦν L μὴ om. Υ αἱ τούτων ἐκτιμήσεις
DJY] εἰ τούτων ἐκτιμήσης B : ἐκ τούτων ἐκτίμησις X : ἡ τούτων ἐκποίησις
E : ἡ (sive ἢ HP : sive εἰ W) τούτων ἐκτίμησις ceteri, quorum nonnulli
(sicut P) post ἐκτίμησις comma ponunt τὸ ἱκανὸν ποιήσωσι
JLQ] τὸ ἱκανὸν ποιήσουσι DX : τὸ ἱκανὸν ποιήσοιτο O : τὸ ἱκανὸν οὐ ποιήσωσι
Υ : τὸ ἱκανὸν ποιήσῃ R : ἱκανὸν ποιήσουσιν MN : ἱκανὸν ποιήσωσι PW :
ὁ
ἱκανὸν ποιήσῃ AGHh : ἱκανων ποιήσει B : ἱκανὸν ποιήσει C : ἱκανὸν ποιήσοι
E : ἱκανοποιήσει F : ἱκανὴ διὰ K 6 τὸ πλοῖον καὶ τὴν ἐργασίαν F
καὶ τοῦ χρόνου A ἐν τῷ] ἐν τὸ L : ἐντὸς Q 7 (f. 14 v.) οἱ ναῦται
J προναυκλήρῳ ADEJKLPYZ] πρωτωναυκλήρῳ Q : πρωτοναυ-
κλήρω W : πωναυκλήρω F : ναυκλήρω BCGHhMNOR : ναυναυκλήρω X
8 ἀναπλήρωσιν X ζυμίας Q ut semper 9 ποιήτωσαν BJL Extat
apud M altera recensio huius cap., quam in Appendice F dedi

15

ΝΟΜΟΣ ΡΟΔΙΩΝ ΝΑΥΤΙΚΟΣ

θ΄ ἐὰν περὶ ἐκβολῆς βουλεύσηται ὁ ναύκληρος,
ἐπερωτάτω τοὺς ἐπιβάτας οἷς χρήματά ἐστιν ἐν τῷ
πλοίῳ. ὅ,τι δὲ ἐὰν γένηται, τοῦτο ψῆφον ποιείτωσαν.
συμβαλλέσθωσαν δὲ εἰς συμβολὴν καὶ τὰ χρήματα·
5 στρώματα δὲ καὶ ἱμάτια καὶ σκεύη πάντα ἐκτιμάσθω,
καὶ ἐὰν γένηται ἐκβολή, τῷ ναυκλήρῳ καὶ τοῖς ἐπιβάταις μὴ πλείονος λίτρας μιᾶς, κυβερνήτῃ δὲ καὶ
πρωρεῖ μὴ πλείονος ἡμιλίτρου, ναύτῃ γράμματα τρία.
παῖδες καὶ εἴ τις ἄλλος συμπλέει μὴ ἐπὶ πράσει
10 ἀγόμενος †κατὰ τιμὴν ὤν· ἐὰν δέ τις ἐπὶ πράσει ἄγηται
†κατὰ δύο μῆνας. κατὰ τοῦτο δὲ καὶ ἐὰν χρήματα

θ΄ Titulus capituli in Σ : ἐν δὲ τῷ θ΄ κεφαλαίῳ   1 περὶ ἐκβολῆς] ἐκ περι-
βολῆς EN   βουλεύσειται B : βουλεύεται C : δουλεύσεται F   2
ἐπερῶτα CEHhMN : ἐρωτάτω ΚΣ (sed in m recentior manus ἐρ. in ἐπερωτάτω correxit) : om. Q   τοὺς ἐπιβάτας om. Q : τοῖς ἐπιβάταις bX
τὰ χρήματα PF : σχήματα X   εἰσιν BEGHhY   3 ὅτι δὲ ἂν BG
γένοιτο hX : γίνεται F   τούτῳ LMQ : τοῦτο καὶ R : τόσῳ A
ποιήτωσαν BJLMPQ   4 συμβαλέσθωσαν Ab : συμβουλεύσθωσαν NX :
συμβαλέτωσαν W   εἰσυμβολὴν Q   συμβουλὴν ChPWX   χρή-
ματα] χρήματα δὲ L   5 στρώματα ... ἱμάτια] om. X   στρόματα
BCL   καὶ ἱμάτια] καὶ ἡμάτια B : ἱμάτια O   σκεύει BL   ἐκτιμάσθωσαν CGK : ἐκτετιμείσθωσαν Y   6 ἐκβολὴν X   τῶν ναυκλήρων CJLY Harl. : τοῖς ναυκλήροις Kv   τῶν ἐπιβατῶν F : τοῖς ναύταις K   7 (f. 107 v.) μὴ πλέον C   πλείονος AEKNOPR] πλείωνος M :
πλεῖον post quod rasura unius litterae B : πλεῖον GHhJLQv Harl. :
πλέον CDYΣ   λίτρας μιᾶς] B in textu habet /Ἰμιᾶς et in margine
/Ἰλίτρας μιᾶς : λήτρας μιᾶς LM : λιτρὸς μιᾶς CQXY : μιᾶς λίτρας F :
καὶ μιᾶς GHh   κυβερνίτῃ δὲ B : κυβερνήτι δὲ M : κυβερνίτῃ δὲ N :
καὶ κυβερνήτῃ δὲ CJQv Harl. : καὶ κυβερνίτῃ δὲ LY   8 προρῇ
BCG : προρὶ J : προρεῖ LMNY : πρωροῖ X : πλωρεῖ R   μὴ πλείονος
ἡμιλ ... συμπλέει] om. W Harl.   μὴ πλείονος ἡμιλίτρου] om. GHh
πλείωνος C : πλείωνος MQ : πλεῖον AR : πλέον BΣ   ἡμηλήτρου L :
εἱμιλίτρου MO   ναύται EKNP   γράμματα τρία παῖδες] om. J,
spatio vacuo relicto   γράμματα] γρύμματα (quod per compendium
scribitur) νομίσματα v   9 παῖδες CKLOPQRvF] παῖδας EMN : παῖδες
δὲ ABDGHhΣ   συμπλέη JL : συμπλεύσει Q   μὴ om. Z (?)
πράσῃ B : πρώσει X : πρᾶσιν EMN   10 ἀγόμενος ... πράσει] om.
HhP   κατὰ τιμὴν ὤν] κατὰ τὴν τιμὴν ὄν C : κατὰ τιμὴ ὤν X : κατὰ
τρίμηνον OR : ἕκαστος κατὰ τρίμηνον K. Cum his verbis finit cap. Σ
Post haec verba in M spatium vacuum c. 2 cent   ἐὰν δέ τις] Principium novi cap. (ιγ΄) apud N   τις] om. CQ   πράσῃ BJ :
πρᾶσιν EMN   ἄγηται] ἄγεται JLMNOPQRvWYF : ἄγειτε B : ἄγετε C :
ἄγειτα Hh   11 καὶ κατὰ F   μῆνας (ACELQY) sive μῆνας (JNPRF)
codices plerique : alii (BHv) verbum per compendium (μμ΄) scribunt :
μηνῶν h : μέρη G   κατὰ τοῦτο ... usque ad finem cap.] om. Z   κατὰ
τοῦτο] τοῦτο R Cum voce κατὰ finem habet f. 82 v. apud N   καὶ om. F   ἐὰν]

16

ἀφαρπαγῇ ὑπὸ πολεμίων ἢ λῃστῶν ἢ †στρατεία κοινὴ
σὺν τῶν διαφερόντων τοῖς ναύταις, καὶ ταῦτα εἰς τὸν
συμψηφισμὸν εἰσερχέσθωσαν καὶ κατὰ τὸ αὐτὸ συμ-
βαλλέσθω. εἰ δὲ σύμφωνον κερδοκοινωνίας ἐστί, μετὰ 15
τὸ ἄπαντα συμψηφισθῆναι τὰ ἐν τῷ πλοίῳ καὶ τὸ
πλοῖον, κατὰ τὸ κέρδος ἕκαστος ἐπιγινωσκέτω καὶ τὴν
προσγενομένην ζημίαν.

ιʹ ἐὰν ναύκληρος ἅμα τοῖς ναύταις ἀμελήσῃ καὶ
συμβῇ ζημίαν ἢ ναυάγιον, ὁ ναύκληρος καὶ οἱ ναῦται
ὑποκείσθωσαν τῷ ἐμπόρῳ εἰς τὴν ἀπόδοσιν τῆς ζημίας.
εἰ δὲ ἀπὸ ἀμελείας τοῦ ἐμπόρου συμβῇ ἀπώλειαν τοῦ
πλοίου καὶ τοῦ γόμου γενέσθαι, ὑποκείσθω ὁ ἔμπορος 5
ἐν τῇ ζημίᾳ τοῦ ναυαγίου καὶ τοῦ πλοίου, εἰ δὲ τοῦ
ναυκλήρου μὴ ἐμποδίσαντος μηδὲ τῶν ναυτῶν μηδὲ

εἰ K   χρημάτων ΕΗhΚΜ   12 ἐφαρπαγῇ CQ : ὑφαρπαγεῖ Μ : ὑφαρπαγῇ Χ : ὑφαρπάσῃ J : ὑφαρπαγῇ ἢ Ε : ἁρπαγὴ Κ   (f. 115 r.) ὑπὸ
πολεμίων Ρ : ὑπὸ πολε(f. 122 r.)μίων Q   ἢ λῃστῶν] ἢ λισῶν ΒΜΧ :
λῃστῶν F   στρατεία κοινὴ ΒΗJΚLPQ] στρατία κοινὴ CΕGhMνΧ Harl. :
στρατείας κοινῆ D : πειρατῶν Α : πειρατῶν κοινῆ R : κοινῇ O   13 σὺν τοῖς
διαφέρουσι DK   τὸν om. JLY   14 συνψιφισμὸν Β : συμψηφισμῶν
L : ψιφησμὸν C : ψηφισμὸν hK : ψισφισμὸν Q   ἐρχέσθωσαν
CJMOQRY   καὶ κατὰ τὸ αὐτὸ συμβαλλέσθω] om. ΕΚΜΡWF   καὶ
om. J   καὶ κατὰ] καὶ τὰ Χ   τῷ αὐτῶ Β   συμβάλλεσθαι J :
συμβουλέσθω L : συμβαλέσθωσαν ΒGY : συμβαλλέσθωσαν CHhQΧ : συνερχέσθωσαν καὶ συμβαλλέσθωσαν ν Harl.   15 εἰ δὲ σύμφωνον . . . usque ad
finem cap.] om. ΒGHh   συμφωνία Χ   κέρδηκοινωνίας CLY :
κέρδεικοινωνίας Jν Harl. : κέρδοικοινωνίας Q : κέρδωκοινωνίας F   ἐστιν
LMP   16 τὸ ἄπαντας Ε : ἅπαν FΧ   ψηφισθῆναι DJLνY Harl. :
ψιφησθῆναι Q : ψηφισθῆναι C : συμψήφισμα Χ   τὰ] τοὺς Ε   τῶν Χ
supra lineam addit Q, om. DY   καὶ τὸ πλοῖον] om. ΕΜΡWF   17
τὸ κέρδος] τὸ κέρδους C : τοῦ κέρδους Q : κέρδος ν Harl.   ἑκάστου DJY :
ἕκαστον ΟF : καὶ ἕκαστος R   καὶ] om. LM   18 προσγινομένην JP
ιʹ Titulus cap. in Σ :--ἐν δὲ τῷ ιʹ (ζʹ mr) κεφαλαίῳ   1 ἅμα] σὺν Κ
ναύταις] συναύταις Μ : συνναύταις Ε   συ(f. 32 r.)ναύταις Μ   ἀμελήσῃ . . . ναυάγιον] om. W   ἀμελήσει LΜ : ἀμελήσοι Ε   2 συμβεῖ
                                                                    a
Β : συ Χ   ζημίαν] καὶ ζημίαν Β : ζημί DR : ζημία JΟmp : ζημεία
G   3 (f. 334 r.) τῷ ἐμπόρῳ L : τὸ ἐμπόρω Β   εἰς om. ΕΚΜ
τῆς ζημίας τὴν ἀπόδοσιν Κ   ἀπόδωσιν ΒJLMP   4 ἀπὸ ἀμελείας]
ὑπὸ ἀμελείας CQYαpr (ubi ύ in ras.) : ὑπὸ ἀμελίας ΒL   τῷ ἐμπορῷ
                                                                    λ
Μ   συμβεῖ Β   ἀπόλεια MQ : ἀπώλεια hK : ἀπωλίαν L : ἀπω´ W : loco
huius vocis inserit Χ :--ζημίαν ἢ ναυάγιον τὰ σωζόμενα μέροι   5 καὶ τοῦ
γόμου] om. ΚΡ   γενέσθαι] om. Κ   6 ἐν] om. JK   τι
ζημία Β   καὶ τοῦ] καὶ τῇ τοῦ ΑΒDGLYΣ   εἰ δὲ . . . 9 πλοίου]
om. Χ   εἰ δὲ καὶ CQ   τὸν ναύκληρον PW   7 μὴ] μὶ Β

ΑΘΗΒ.   C   17

τοῦ ἐμπόρου συμβῇ ζημίαν ἢ ναυάγιον, τὰ σωζόμενα
μέρη τοῦ πλοίου καὶ τῶν φορτίων εἰς συμβολὴν
10 ἐρχέσθωσαν.

ια΄ φορτία μεγάλα καὶ πολύτιμα μὴ ἐμβαλλέτωσαν
οἱ ἔμποροι καὶ οἱ ἐπιβάται εἰς πλοῖον παλαιόν. εἰ δὲ
ἐμβάλωσιν, ἐὰν τοῦ πλοίου ἀρμενίζοντος πάθῃ ἢ διαφθαρῇ, ὁ φορτώσας τὸ παλαιὸν πλοῖον ἑαυτὸν ἀπὸ γῆς
5 ἀπώλεσεν. ὅταν δὲ οἱ ἔμποροι ναυλῶνται, ἐπερωτάτωσαν
ἀκριβῶς παρὰ τῶν ἄλλων ἐμπόρων τῶν πρὸ αὐτῶν ἐπι-
πλεόντων καὶ οὕτως ἐπιβαλλέτωσαν τὰς ἐνθήκας, ἐὰν
ἔχῃ τὸ πλοῖον πᾶσαν τὴν ἐπιχειρίαν τελείως, ἱστοκεραίαν ἰσχυρὰν ἄρμενά τε καὶ διφθέρας ἀγκύρας τε

ἐμποδήσαντος LMP   μηδὲ] καὶ K   ναυτῶν] om. h   μηδὲ
τοῦ ἐμπόρου . . . ναυάγιον] om. Q   8 τῶν ἐμπόρων OR   συμβῇ]

συμβεῖ B : γένηται K   ζημίαν] ζημία KPRmpr : ζημι DJbF : ζημεία
G   σωζόμενα M   μέρει M : μέρει ἢ L   9 καὶ τῶν φορτίων om. H
τῶν φορτίων] φορτίων MPFW : τοῦ φόρτου J : τῶν ναυτῶν K   Post
φορτίων rasura duarum litterarum in M   εἰσυμβολὴν Q   συμβουλὴν hX   10 ἐρχέσθωσαν] ἐρχέσθω F : ποιείτωσαν M   ια΄ (f. 29 r.)
ια΄ B   1 πολίτημα D : πολυτίμητα h   ἐμβαλέτωσαν A : ἐπιβαλλέτωσαν CHOR : ἐπιβαλλέσθωσαν QFV : βαλέτωσαν K   2 καὶ οἱ] καὶ
EH   ἐπιβάται] hanc vocem in M recentior manus cancellavit et
ἐπίβαι suprascripsit   Cum verbo παλαιόν cap. finit V   εἰ
δὲ ἐμβάλωσιν] εἰ δὲ ἐμβάλλουσι K : εἰ δὲ ἐὰν βάλλωσιν PF : εἰ δὲ ἐὰν βάλ-
λοντες W : εἰς δὲ βάλωσιν sed litterae εἰς δὲ β supra rasuram sunt M :
εἰ δὲ βάλωσιν BEGHhLOQRX : εἰ δὲ βάλλουσιν CY : ἐὰν (quod post
cancellatur) εἰ δὲ βάλωσιν J : εἰ οι εἰ δὲ βάλωσιν D   3 ἐὰν] om.
EMPFW : καὶ K   πάθῃ ἢ] om. ORY   πάθει M : πάθη τι K : πάθοι EF
διαφθαρεῖ LM   4 φορτώσας B   τὸ πλοῖον τὸ παλαιὸν CJQX
παλαιὸν] om. DY   πλοῖον] om. OR   ἀπὸ γῆς ἑαυτὸν R
ἑαυτὸν] om. J   ἀπὸ γῆς] ἀπὸ τῆς γῆς ACGHhF : om. D   5 ἀπώλεσεν
B   ὅταν] ὅτε K   ναυλοῦνται BEGHLMP : αὐλοῦνται C
ἐπερωτήτωσαν MP : ἐρωτάτωσαν F   6 παρὰ] περὶ K   παρὰ τῶν
ἄλλων ἐμπόρων] ἑτέρους ἐμπόρους Y   τῶν πρὸ αὐτῶν] πρὸ αὐτῶν A :
τῶν παρ' αὐτῶν L : καὶ τῶν πρὸ αὐτὰς ἢ C   αὐ(f. 108 r.)τὰς ἢ C
πλεόντων D : ἀποπλευσάντων F   7 ἐπιβαλέτωσαν AJ : ἐπιβαλλέσθωσαν
Q : ἀποβαλλέτωσαν F   τὰς] om. CEKMPQWF   θήκας quod
supra lineam in ἐνθήκας correxit Y   ἐνθήκας] E addit ἢ ἐρώτησις
αὕτη   ἐὰν ἔχει CJLMQ : ἐὰν ἔχοι E : ἐὰν δὲ ἔχῃ AGHKF : ἐὰν δὲ
ἔχει B   Principium novi capituli in M (ιε΄) et in Y (ιβ΄)   8 πλεῖον
Y   τὴν om. F   ἱστοκεραίαν] ἱστοκερέαν J : ἱστῶ κεραίαν
X : εἰστοκερέαν CLF : εἰστοκεραιὰν Q : ἱστὸν κεραίαν DWY : ἱστὸν
καὶ κεραίαν BH : ἱστὸν καὶ κερέαν Gh : ἱστίον κεραίαν OR : ἰσοκεραίαν
K : κεραίαν M : εἰστὸκαιρέαν τελείαν P   9 ἄρμενά τε] ἐν ἀρμάταις

18

καὶ σχοινία καννάβινα διάφορα καὶ καράβους ἐξηρτισ- 10
μένους αὐχένας ἐπιτηδείους καὶ ναύτας τοὺς ἀρκοῦντας
ναυτικοὺς γοργοὺς γρηγοροῦντας τὰ πλάγια μὴ παραλελυμένα. καὶ ἁπλῶς οἱ ἔμποροι τὰ πάντα ἐπιζητείτω-
σαν καὶ οὕτως ἐπιβαλλέτωσαν.

ιβʹ ἐάν τις παραθῆται ἐν πλοίῳ ἢ ἐν οἴκῳ, γνωστῷ
καὶ πιστικῷ παρατιθέσθω ἐπὶ μαρτύρων τριῶν. ἐὰν δὲ
ᾖ τὸ θέμα βαρύ, ἐγγράφως τὴν παραθήκην παραδιδότω.
ἐὰν δὲ εἴπῃ ὁ δεξάμενος φυλάττειν αὐτὴν ὅτι ἀπώλετο,
δεῖ δειχθῆναι τὴν διωρυγὴν ἢ τὰ σῦλα πόθεν ὑπέστη 5
καὶ ὀμνύειν ὅτι αὐτὸς οὐκ ἐδολιεύσατο. ἐὰν δὲ μὴ δείξῃ,
καθὼς παρέλαβεν ἀποδιδότω σῶα.

ιγʹ ἐὰν εἰσέλθῃ ἐπιβάτης εἰς πλοῖον καὶ ἔχῃ χρυσίον
ἢ ἕτερόν τι, παρατιθέσθω αὐτὸ τῷ ναυκλήρῳ. εἰ δὲ μὴ

X   10 καὶ (bis)] om. X   σχονία C : σχοίνας HhPW : σχοῖνα
ABGX   καννάβηνα L : κανάβηνά ται B : καννάβια MPR : καννάβιά
τε GHh : καναβικὰ F   καὶ καράβους] καράβους K   καράβους διαφόρους
L   ἐξηρτησμένους CO : ἐξιρτισμένους L : ἐξηρτημένους ADEKQR :
ἐξηρτιμένους X   11 αὐχένας] καὶ αὐχένας D : αὐχένας τε F : αὐχενία R   ἐπι-
τιδίους BLM : ἐπιτήδεια R   τοὺς ἀρκοῦντας] ἀρκοῦντας Q : κάλους καὶ
ἀρκοῦντας C   12 ναυτικοὺς] εἰς ναυτικὸν K : om. F   γοργοὺς] γρηγορούς
M   (f. 15 r.) γρηγοροῦντας J   τὰ πλάγια μὴ παραλελυμένα] om. CJORY
μὴ τὰ πλάγια E   μὴ παραλελυμένα] om. M   μή] om. BDGHhLQW
13 τὰ om. CQ   ἐπιζητήτωσαν AJ : ἐπιζητήσωσαν P : ἐκζητείτωσαν O
ἐπιζητεί(f. 122 v.)τωσαν Q   14 ἐπιβαλέτωσαν A : ἐπιβαλλέσθωσαν M :
ἐμβαλέτωσαν KF : ἐπιβαλλέστωσαν h   ιβʹ 1 εἴ τις CDJLQY   παραθῆ
BF   In B ται additur supra lineam manu recentiore   γνωστίκω
E   2 καὶ πιστικᾷ] καὶ πιστῶ PR : καὶ πιστικῶ πιστικῶς C : τῶ πιστικῶ Y :
om. BGHh   παραθέσθω EKMPF : παραδιδότω Y   τριῶν addit recentior
manus in B : om. GHh   ἐὰν δὲ ᾖ] καὶ εἰ μὲν εἴ Y   3 ᾖ τὸ θέμα] εἰς τὸ
θέαμα C : ᾖ τὸ θέαμα F : εἴη τὸ θέμα X   διδότω KR : ποιήτω C : διαδότω X
4 ἐὰν δὲ εἴποι EF : εἰ δὲ εἴποι K (f. 115 v.) εἴπη P ὁ δεξάμενος φυλάττειν] ὁ
φυλάσσων F : δεξάμενος] δεχόμενος EKPW : δεχόμενος ἐν τῶ M : παραδεχόμενος
Q   φυλάττην B : φυλάσσειν JLMP : φυλάττων X   αὐτὴν] ταύτην EKMPWF
αὐτὰ D   ὅτι ἀπώλετο] ἀπώλετο δὲ R : om. O   ἀπώλωντο D : ἀπολέσθη X
5 δεῖ] om. X   διορυγὴν BJLMP : διοριγὴν X : ὀρυγὴν QY   ᾖ] καὶ B
supra rasuram Y : εἰς PFW   ὁπόθεν GHh : τὸ πόθεν MPWF : πώθεν, ante
quod rasura unius litterae B   ὑπέστη] ὕπεστιν A   6 ὀμνύει X   ὅτι
αὐτὸς] ὅτι ὡς M : αὐτοὺς P   ἐδολιεύσατω M : ἐδολεύσατο LX : ἐδουλεύσατο
CO   εἰ K   δείξει JL : δίξει C   7 παρέλαβεν αὐτὰ Q   ἀποδιδότω
σῶα] ἀποδιδότω σῶαν R : ἀποδῶτω σῶα Q : σῶα ἀποδιδότω ABGH : ἀποδότω
σῶα JF   ιγʹ Cap. in Σ sic introducitur ἐν δὲ τῶ ιαʹ κεφαλαίω θέματος εʹ F
cap. omittit   1 ἐὰν δὲ EJLMP   εἰσέλθω L : εἰσέλθοι CE   ὁ ἐπιβάτης mpr:
ἐπιβάτοις Q   ἐμπλοΐω CQ   ἔχει AJ : ἔχοι E   χρυσὸν K : τὸ χρυσίον r

c 2   19

παραθέμενος εἴπῃ ὅτι χρυσίον ἀπώλεσα ἢ ἀργύριον,
ἄκυρα ἔστω τὰ παρ᾽ αὐτοῦ λεγόμενα. ὁ δὲ ναύκληρος
5 καὶ οἱ ναῦται ὁμοῦ οἱ ἐμπλέοντες ὅρκον παρεχέτωσαν.

ιδ΄ ἐάν τις δεξάμενος παραθήκην ἀρνήσηται αὐτὴν
καὶ μαρτυρηθῇ ἐν αὐτῷ καὶ ἐὰν ἐν καιρῷ εὑρεθῇ ἐν αὐτῷ
τῷ ὀμόσαντι ἢ ἐγγράφως ἀποταξαμένῳ, διπλῆν ταύτην
ἀποδώσει, τῆς δὲ ἐπιορκίας τὴν τιμωρίαν ὑπομενέτω.

ιε΄ ἐὰν πλοῖον φέρῃ ἐπιβάτας ἢ ἐμπόρους ἢ δούλους
παραθήκην λαβὼν ὁ ναύκληρος ἐλθὼν ἐν πόλει τινὶ ἢ
ἐν λιμένι ἢ ἐν ἀκτῇ, ἐὰν ἐξελθόντων τινῶν ἐκ τοῦ πλοίου
συμβῇ διωγμὸν λῃστῶν ἢ πειρατῶν ἐπιδρομὴν γενέσθαι
5 καὶ κελεύσας ὁ ναύκληρος ἐξειλήσῃ, σωθῇ δὲ τὸ πλοῖον

2 παρατιθέσθω αὐτὸ] ἀποδιδότω αὐτὸ εἰς παραθήκην C   αὐτῷ AJPYab: αὐτὰ
L: om. K   3 παραθέμενον p: παρατιθέμενος BH   εἴποι CDEHK
χρυσὸν K: τὸ χρυσίον P   χρυσί(f. 32 r.)ον M   ἀπώλησα A:
ἀπόλεσα M   ἢ] καὶ Y   ἄργυρον BGHK: τὸ ἀργύριον E   4 ἔστωσαν
BHKY: ἔστι C   λεγώμενα B: λεχθέντα K   ὁ δὲ ναύκληρος ...
παρεχέτωσαν] om. J   (f. 29 v.) ὁ δὲ ναύκληρος B: ὁ ναύκληρος H   5 οἱ
ναῦται] οἱ ἐπιβάται in textu, in margine ÷ οἱ ναῦται habet H   ὁμοῦ] om.
O   ὁμοῦ καὶ CMY   οἱ ἐμπλέοντες] ἐμπλέοντες LQ: εἰσπλέοντες K: om. OR
ὅρκῳ Q   παρεχέτωσαν] ἐχέτωσαν τῷ συληθέντι C: διδότωσαν K   ιδ΄
(f. 334 v.) ιδ΄ L   Cap. omittit K   1 ἐὰν δέ τις D: ἐὰν δὲ ὁ F   τις] της B
παρακαταθήκην H: τὴν παραθήκην F   ἀρνεῖται MPW: ἀρνῆται EF: καὶ ἀρνήσηται R   ταύτην F   2 καὶ μαρτ. ... ἀποδώσει] ἐγγράφως ἢ μεθ᾽ ὅρκου καὶ
μετὰ ταῦτα μαρτυριθῇ ἐν αὐτῷ, τὴν μὲν παρακαταθήκην διπλῆν ἀποδώσει Y
μαρτυρηθῇ ... καὶ ἐὰν] om. F   μαρτυριθῇ BLP: μαρτυριθεῖ M: μαρτυρισθῇ C
καὶ ἐὰν ... αὐτῷ] om. C   καὶ ἐὰν ἐν κ. εὐ.] ἐὰν ἐν κ. εὐ. J: καὶ ἐν κ. εὐ. X:
καὶ ἐάν ποτε κ. εὐ. D: καὶ εὑρεθῇ ἐν καιρῷ GH   εὑρεθεῖ L: εὑρεῖν τῷ]
ἐν αὐτῷ LOR: ἐν αὐτῷ καὶ τὸ Q: ἐν αὐτῷ τε τῶ E   3 ὀμώσαντι BQ: ὠμόσαντι
P: ὠμώσαντι L   ἢ ἐγγραφος B: ἢ ἔγγραφον Q: ἐγγράφως ἢ L   ἀποταξάμενος EMPW   διπλοῦν E   4 ἀποδώσει] ἀποδώσῃ M: ἀποδιδώτω
X: ἐπιτελέσει F   ἐπιορκίαν W   τὴν om. W   τιμωρείαν M   ὑπομετ-
νέτω G   Post hanc vocem BGH addunt πᾶσα (πᾶσα γὰρ G) παρακαταθήκη
                                                                         ο
ἐξ ἀρνήσεως διπλασιάζεται.   B habet in margine σχ i.e. σχόλιον   C addit
τουτέστι τὴν γλῶτταν τεμνέσθω   ιε΄ 1 φέρει JLM: φέροι E: ἐπιφέρει Q:
ἐπιφέρῃ Y   ἢ δούλους ἢ ἐμπόρους E   δοῦλος Q   2 παραθήκη X   λαβὼν ὁ ναύκληρος] λαβὼν ὁλοκλήρως E   ναυκληριακὸς Q
ἐπὶ πόλει τινὶ X   πόλι L   3 καὶ ἐν λιμένι W   λιμένη B   (f. 108 v.)
ἢ ἐν ἀκτῇ] ἀκτὶ JL: ἀκτω M   ἐὰν] ἐξ αὐτῶν DY   τοῦ] om.
E   4 συμβεῖ B: καὶ συμβῇ MF   διογμὸν B: διογμῶν L: διωγμῶν M
                                                                πειρατῶν
λιστῶν B   ἢ] καὶ K   πηρατῶν AL: πηρετῶν Q: παραιτῶν G:
παραυτῶν H   ἐπιδρομῇ PY: ἐπιδρομὴ ex ἐπιδρομὴν corr. C   γενέσθαι
om. K   5 καὶ κελεύσας] κεκελεύσας C   ἐξειλήσῃ] ἐξηλήση J: ἐξη-
λήσει ALQY: ἐξειλίσει P: ἐξειλήσοι E: τὰ ἄρμενα ἐξιλίση M: ἐξελκύση D:

20

PARS TERTIA

καὶ τὰ τῶν ἐπιβατῶν καὶ ἐμπόρων κομιζόμενα, ἀπολαμβανέτω ἕκαστος τὰ ἴδια αὐτοῦ καὶ τὰ τῶν ἐξελθόντων εἴδη καὶ σκεύη ἀπολαμβανέτωσαν. εἰ δὲ θελήσῃ τις τῷ ναυκλήρῳ ἀμφισβητῆσαι ὅτι ἐν ἀκτῇ ἔασεν αὐτὸν ἐν τόπῳ ληστρικῷ, ἄκυρα ἔστω τὰ παρ᾽ αὐτοῦ λεγόμενα, 10 ὅτι διωκόμενος ὁ ναύκληρος καὶ οἱ ναῦται ἔφυγον. εἰ δὲ ἐμπόρων ἢ ἐπιβατῶν τις δοῦλον ἐν παραθήκῃ ὄντα ἀλλότριον ἔασεν ἐν οἱῳδήποτε τόπῳ, τὴν ἀποκατάστασιν τῷ κυρίῳ αὐτοῦ ποιείτω.

ιϛ´ οἱ ναύκληροι καὶ οἱ ἔμποροι ὅσοι δ᾽ ἂν χρήσωνται χρήματα ἐπὶ πλοίου ἔγγαια μὴ χρηέσθωσαν καὶ ναύλῳ καὶ τοῖς φορτίοις, σωθέντος τοῦ πλοίου καὶ τῶν χρημάτων, μὴ ἐγγένηται τοῖς χρήμασιν ἐκ τῶν θαλασσίων κινδύνων ἢ πειρατῶν ἐπιβουλή. ἐκ τῶν ἐγγαίων ἀποδι- 5 δότωσαν χρημάτων χρῆσιν ναυτικοῖς.

εὐλυτώσῃ K : φύγῃ R   σωθῇ] σωθεί M : σῶα J   6 και τὰ τῶν] και τῶν EPW : τὰ τῶν GM   καὶ τῶν ἐμπόρων G   κομιζόμενος X : τὰ κομιζόμενα E   7 ἕκαστως B   Post ἕκαστος addunt αὐτῶν ABG τὰ ἴδια αὐτοῦ καὶ] om. CQ   καὶ τὰ] κατὰ E   τὰ τῶν ἐξελθόντων . . . σκεύη] οἱ ἐξελθόντες F   τὰ τῶν ἐξελθόντων] τούτων ἐξελθώτων M : τὰ τῶν ἐξελθον (sic) H   8 εἴδη καὶ] ἤδη καὶ LM : ἤδει καὶ QX : εἴδη ἢ H : ἢ καὶ O : om. R   σκέβει X   εἰ θελήσει δέ τις E   θελήσει τις AJP : θέλει τις Q : θέλῃ τι C   9 τῷ ναυκλήρῳ] τῶν ναυκλήρων ALXYZF : τῶῦ ναυκλήρωῦ J, duobus punctis supra ultimam litteram harum vocum positis, scilicet expungendi causa : τῶν αὐκλήρων Q   καὶ ἀμφισβητῆσαι F   ἀμφισακτίσαι L : ἀφισβητήσαι X   ὅτι] ὁ W   ἐν ἀκτὶ JL : ἐν νυκτὶ GH   εἴασεν DEHKMR : ἔσασεν A : ἐάσας F   αὐτοὺς BGHK : αὐτὸ PY : αὐτὰ R : με F : om. M   10 ἐν τῷ τό(f. 123 r.)πω Q   λιστρικῷ B   ἄκυρα . . . λεγόμενα] καὶ ἄκυρα τὰ τούτου λεχθέντα K   ἔστωσαν BGHY   παρ᾽ αὐτῶν H   11 διοκόμενος B : διωκώμενος M   οἱ ναῦται ἔφυγον] οἱ ἐπιβάται τοῦτο ἐποίησαν CQ : οἱ ναῦται τοῦτο ἐποίησαν X   12 εἰ δὲ ἐμπόρων ἢ ἐπιβατῶν] ἐὰν ἔμποροι ἢ ἐπιβάται F   ἢ] καὶ MR : μὴ Q   τις cum edd. addidi δούλων EKMOPRWX   ἐν] om. E   14 παραθήκει B   ὄντων ἀλλοτρίων EKMOPRW   13 εἴασεν DEKL : ἴασαν J : οἴασεν Y : ἔσασεν A : ἐάσονται F   ἐν] om. HF   οἱοδήποτε B : οἱωδήποτε L   τρόπω CEMQWF   14 τῷ ἰδίω κυρίω R   αὐτοῦ] αὐτῶν KP : τούτου F   ποιήτω J : ποιείτωσαν KF   ιϛ´ (f. 116 r.) ιϛ´ P   cap. omittit F   1 καὶ ἔμποροι P   ὅσοι ἂν DX   χρήσονται JLMP   2 χρήματα om. E   ἔγγεα AD : ἔγγυα ELP : ἐγγέου H   χριέσθωσαν CLMOQ : χρήσθωσαν EK : χράσθωσαν R : χρησάσθωσαν DXY   ναῦλα sive ναῦλά EGMP : ναυ J   3 ἀλλὰ σωθέντος R   4 μὴ ἐγγένηται] εἰ δὲ ἐγγένηται R   5 ἢ] καὶ M   πηρατῶν BL : τῶν πειρατῶν K   ἐπιβουλὴν CDLQY : ἐπιβουλῆς P : ἐπιβου J : ἐπιβολὴ KM   ἐγγέων

21

ΝΟΜΟΣ ΡΟΔΙΩΝ ΝΑΥΤΙΚΟΣ

ιζ′ ἐάν τις δώσῃ ἐπὶ χρείᾳ κοινωνίας χρυσίον ἢ
ἀργύριον καὶ ταύτην κατὰ πλοῦν καὶ ἐγγράψηται καθὼς
ἀρέσει ἕως πόσου χρόνου τῇ χρεοκοινωνίᾳ, ἐὰν ὁ λαμβάνων τὸ χρυσίον ἢ τὸ ἀργύριον πληρωθέντος τοῦ
5 χρόνου μὴ ἀποστρέψῃ αὐτὸ τῷ κυρίῳ αὐτοῦ καὶ συμβῇ
ἀπὸ πυρὸς ἢ λῃστῶν ἢ ναυαγίου περιπεσεῖν, ἀζήμιον
μένειν τὸν κύριον τοῦ χρυσίου καὶ σῶα τὰ ἴδια ἀπολαμ-
βάνειν. ἐὰν δέ, τοῦ χρόνου τῶν συνθηκῶν μὴ πληρωθέντος, συμβῇ ἐκ τῶν κατὰ θάλασσαν κινδύνων ἀπώ-
10 λειαν γενέσθαι, καθάπερ τοῦ κέρδους ἔδοξε καὶ τὰς
ζημίας πρὸς τὰ μέρη καὶ τὰς συνθήκας ἀναδέχεσθαι.

ιη′ ἐάν τις χρήματα χρησάμενος ἀποδημήσῃ, ἐξελθόντος τοῦ χρόνου οὗ ἐὰν συνθῶνται, κομιζέσθωσαν
ἐκ τῶν ἐγγαίων κατὰ τὸν νόμον. ἐὰν μὴ ἔχωσι πῶς

ADH : ἐγγύων E : γονέων P   ἀποδιδώτωσαν A : ἐπιδιδότωσαν
DY   6 χρημάτων] χρήματα τῶν C : χρήματα BEGM   χρυσὸν
Q : χάριν D   ναυτικῶς CQX : ναυτικήν J   ιζ′ Cap. omittit K
1 ἐὰν δέ τις M   δώσει AJ   δώσῃ ἐπὶ] ἐπιδώσει Q   χρείᾳ
κοινωνίας] χρειακυνωνίας B : χρέοι κοινωνίας M : χροίακοινωνίας Q   2
(f. 30 r.) καὶ τοῦτο B : τοῦτο BGH : ταυ X   In D carta ita abrasa est ut
vox legi nequeat   (f. 15 v.) κατὰ πλοῦν J : κατὰ ἀπλοῦν EPF
ἐγγράψεται BG : ἐγγράφεται DJY : ἐγγράφετε L : ἐγγράψονται MPQ :
ἐγγράψωνται EORF   3 ἀρέσῃ P : ἀρέσοι E : εὑρέσῃ M   ἕως]
καὶ ὡς DY   χρόνου] χρόνον οὗ C : χρό J in fine lineae : om. QF   τῇ]
om. Q   χρεωκοινωνία JPF : χρ . . κυνωνι . . B priore rasura postea
cum litteris ια impleta : χρεῶκοινωνίας G : χρέους κοινωνία Q : τοῦ χρέους
κοινωνία EM : χρεῶσκοινωνίας C : κοινωνία L   ἐὰν] καὶ ἐὰν E   R
incipit novum cap. (κ′)   ὁ λαμβάνων] λαμβάνων C : ἐλάμβάνον (?) L :
ὁ λαβὼν D   4 (f. 33 r.) πληρωθέντος M   5 ἀποστρέψει LM : ἀπο-
στρέψοι E   αὐτῶ BGL : om. Q   τοῦ κυρίου ΗΜ   6 ἀπὸ] ἀπὸ
B : αὐτῶ G : αὐτὸ Η   πυρὸν C   ἢ λιστῶν M : καὶ ληστῶν E
ναυαγίω QR   παραπεσεῖν DEJLY   ἀζύμιον M   7 μένειν] μένει
Q : μὲν εἶναι E : εἶναι PF   τῶ κυρίω Q   (f. 335 r.) τοῦ χρυσίου L
τὰ ἴδια σῶα D   ἴδια] ὕδια C   8 ἐὰν δὲ... usque ad finem capituli]
om. C   ἐὰν δὲ] ἐὰν J : εἰ δὲ F   Principium novi cap. (κβ′) apud M
τὸν χρόνον Q   πληρωθέντων BLX   9 συμβῇ τι DJY : τοῦ συμβῇ O
Post συμβῇ addidi ex coni. ἐκ   τῶν] τὸν ABCHLQX : τοῦ P : τὸ F :
om. EM   κινδύνων] κίνδυνον ABCEHLX : κινδύνου PF   ἀπώλιαν
L : καὶ ἀπώλειαν E : ἀπώλεια MY : om. Q   10 τὸ κέρδος DJMY
ἔδοξεν LM   καὶ] οὕτως καὶ Q   11 μέρει M   καὶ] κατὰ AHKZ
ἐνέχεσθαι OR   ιη′ Cum hoc cap. incipit S : capitulum om. K   1
ἀποδημήσῃ AJ : ἀποδημήσοι E   ἐξελθόντος L : καὶ ἐξελθόντος EM
2 τοῦ χρόνου] χρόνου EP : om. M   οὗ ἐὰν] ἐὰν CQR   (f. 109 r.)
ἐὰν συνθῶνται C   3 ἐγγέων ADHKP : ἐγγυῶν ER : ἀγγείων F

PARS TERTIA

κομίσωνται, ἔσται αὐτοῖς τὰ μὲν χρήματα ἔγγαια, οἱ
δὲ τόκοι ναυτικοὶ παντὸς τοῦ χρόνου ὅσον ἀποδη- 5
μήσει.

ιθ′ ἐὰν πλοῖον ναυλώσηταί τις δώσῃ δὲ ἀρραβῶνα
καὶ μετέπειτα εἴπῃ· χρείαν οὐκ ἔχω, ἀπόλλειν τὸν
ἀρραβῶνα. ἐὰν δὲ ὁ ναύκληρος ἄλλην ποιήσῃ, ἀποδιδότω τῷ ἐμπόρῳ διπλοῦν τὸν ἀρραβῶνα.

κ′ ὃς ἂν πλοῖον ναυλώσηται, ἔγγραφα συνεσφραγισμένα κύρια εἴτω· εἰ δὲ μή, ἄκυρα· γραφέτωσαν δὲ καὶ
ἐπιτίμια, ἐὰν θέλωσιν. ἐὰν δὲ μὴ συγγράψωνται καὶ
ψεύσηται ὁ ναύκληρος ἢ ὁ ναυλούμενος—ἐὰν μὲν ὁ ναυλούμενος παρέχῃ τὰ χρήματα † οὕτω τε τοῦ ἐπιφόρτου, 5

(f. 123 v.) ἐγγαίων Q   ἢ κατὰ C   τὸν νόμον] τῶν νόμων A : νόμον X
ἐὰν δὲ DGHJLRYF   ἔχωσιν LP : ἔχονται M   τὸ πῶς S   4 κο-
μίσονται JLMP : κομίσαι Y   ἔστω EGH : ἔστωσαν F   τὰ μὲν ...
χρόνου] om. H   ἔγγεα ABDHKPX : ἔγγυνα ER : ἄγγεα F   5 ναυτικοὶ τόκοι D   ναυτικοὶ] om. Q   τοῦ] om. M   ἀποδημεῖ
EMOPQRXF   ιθ′ 1 πλοίω X   ναυλώσῃ τις KV   δώσῃ
δὲ] δώσει δὲ AJLP : καὶ δώσει V : δώσῃ F   ἀραβῶνα J : ἀρράβωναν
S   2 καὶ μετέπειτα ... ἀρραβῶνα] om. HFV   μετέπειτα] μετὰ
ταῦτα EGMOPQRX   εἴπει BCS : εἶποι ALQv   ἀπόλλειν DLOS]
ἀπώλειν X : ἀπόλλει ABKQ : ἀπώλλει P : ἀπώλει G : ἀπόλλησι C : ἀπώλειν
αὐτὸν J : ἀπόλλειν αὐτὸν E : ἀπώλλειν αὐτὸ Y : ἀπόλειν αὐτὸν v : ἀπόλλυσιν
αὐτὸν M : ἀπολύειν αὐτὸν R   3 ἀραβῶνα J : ἀρράβονα S   ἐὰν δὲ] δὲ
addit supra lineam B : om. H   ἐὰν δὲ ... ποιήσῃ] εἰ δὲ ὁ ναύκληρος
ἄλλως ποιήσῃ F : ὁ δὲ ναύκληρος ἄλλω ναυλώση V   ἄλλην ποιήσῃ]
ἀνατροποίσει X (?)   ἄλλην] ἄλλη L : ἀλλαχοῦ R : ἀλλαχόθεν v : διάλυσιν
M : πάλιν τοῦτο K   ποιήσει JLM   4 τῷ ἐμπόρῳ] post ἀρραβῶνα ponit
v : omittunt FV   ἀραβόνα B : ἀραβῶνα J : ἀρραβόναν S   κ′ 1 ὃς
ἂν πλοῖον (πλοιω X) ναυλώσηται codd. plerique] ὃς ἂν ναυλώ(ή M)σηται
πλοῖον MR : ἐὰν πλοῖον ναυλώσηται P : ἐὰν πλοῖον αὐλώσηται C : ἐὰν
ναυλώσηταί τις πλοῖον Y : ἐὰν ναυλώσῃ τις πλοῖον E : ἐάν τις ἐγγράφως
ναυλώσηται πλοῖον F : ἐγγρ. συνεσφρ.] μετ' ἐγγράφων συνεσφραγισμένων
Y   ἔγγραφα] ἐγγράφως MP post quod comma ponunt : ἔγγραφος X :
ἄνευ ἔγγραφα J : εἰ ἔγγραφα E : om. F   ἐσφραγισμένα GM   Post
συνεσφραγ. addunt ποιῶν BCGHhKS   2 κύρια ... ἄκυρα] ἄκυρα ἤτω,
quod sequitur spatium vacuum J   καὶ κύρια M   εἴτω] ἤτω GKF :
εἰ O : ἔστω EMR   εἰ δὲ μή] εἰ μὴ P : ἐὰν δὲ μὴ L   ἄκυρα G   γραφή-
τωσαν P : ἐγραφέτωσαν S   3 θέλωσι J : ἐθέλωσιν E : θελήσουσιν X   ἐὰν
δὲ μὴ] Principium novi capituli in O, quod usque ad finem c. κα′ venit
μή] om. PF   συγγράψονται JLMP : συνγράψωται S : γράψωνται K :
γράφονται D   4 ψεύσωνται KF   (f. 116 v.) ψεύσηται P   ὁ ναυκληρος ἢ ὁ
ναυλούμενος] om. F   ἢ ὁ ναυλούμενος] om. Q   ὁ ναυλούμενος] ὁ ναυλόμενος
J : ναυλώμενος Hh : ὁ ναυλωσάμενος G   ἐὰν μὲν ὁ ναυλούμενος] om.
EGHhLPQX   ἐὰν μὲν] ἐὰν μὲν οὖν O : ἐὰν μὲν v : εἰ μὲν KF   5 παρέχῃ
BHhJKLMQSvX : ψεύσηται παρέχει F : παρέχοι E : παρεῖχε G : παρέσχῃ

23

ἀποδιδότω τὰ ἥμισυ τοῦ ναύλου τῷ ναυκλήρῳ. ἐὰν δὲ
ὁ ναύκληρος ψεύσηται, ἀποδότω τὸ ἥμισυ ναῦλον τῷ
ἐμπόρῳ· ἐὰν δὲ θελήσῃ ὁ ἔμπορος τὰ φορτία ἐξελέσθαι,
ἀποδώσει τὸ πᾶν ναῦλον τῷ ναυκλήρῳ. ἡ δὲ πρᾶξις
10 ἔσται τούτων τῶν ἐπιτιμίων καθάπερ εἰ ἐκδικήσει τίς
τινα.

κα´ ἐὰν κοινωνίαν ποιήσωσιν ἀγράφως δύο καὶ
ἀμφότερα τὰ μέρη καθομολογήσωσιν ὅτι κοινωνίαν καὶ
ἄλλου καιροῦ ἐποιήσαμεν ἀγράφως καὶ πίστιν ἑαυτοῖς
ἐφυλάξαμεν καὶ τὸ τέλος πάντοτε περὶ μιᾶς ἐνθήκης
5 ἐτελέσαμεν—ἐὰν τὸ ἓν πλοῖον συμβῇ τινα παθεῖν ἢ
σαβουράτον ἢ πεφορτωμένον, τὰ σωθέντα τῷ παθόντι
τέταρτον μέρος ἐπιφερέτω, ἐπειδὴ ἔγγραφα οὐ προ-

A: ἔχει C: μὴ παρέχῃ R   χρείματα P   οὕτω τε] ita EJMQRXY:
οὐ τότε OPF: οὕτως τε D: τοῦτό τε BCGSv: τοῦ τότε K: τοῦτο δὲ L:
τότε AHh   τοῦ ἐπιφόρτου] τῶ ἐπιφόρτω X: τοῦ φόρτου D: ἐπὶ φόρτου
C   6 ἀποδιδότω] ἀποδότω BhKOPSF: ἀποδώτω CHQX   τὰ ἥμισυ
CGHhKLOPvXF] τὰ ἥμησυ BS: τὰ εἴμισυν M: τὰ ἡμίσειω Y: τὰ ἡμίση
ER: τὰ ἥμισι D: τὸ ἥμισυ AJQ   ναύλου] ναύτου EQ (in Q supra
ras.)   τῶναυκλήρων Q: τωνκλήρω S: τοῦ ναυκλήρου F   εἰ δὲ F   7
ψεύσεται J   ἀποδότω HhMOPRXF] ἀποδώτω CEQ: αποδότω B: ἀποδιδότω GKS: ἀποδώσει A: om. DJLvY   τὸ ἡμισόναυλον C: τὸ ἥμησι-
ναύλον X: τὸ ἥμισυ ναύλω Q: τὸν ἡμισυναῦλον Y: τὸ ἥμισυ τοῦ ναύλου K:
τὸ εἱμίσυνον τοῦ ναύλου M   8 ἐμπόρῳ] ναυκλήρῳ K: γαύχληρῳ ἐμπόρω P
ἐὰν δὲ] ἐὰν KS   (f. 30 v.) ἐὰν δὲ B   θελήσει JLM: θέλησι ex θέλη
correxit P: θελήσοι E   ἔμπορος ex ναύκληρος correxit G   τὰ om. ES
ἐξελέσθαι τὰ φορτία F   9 ἀποδιδότω G   τὸν πᾶν ναῦλον CY: τὸ
πᾶν ναύλω Q: τὸ ναῦλον πᾶν Hh: τὸ ναῦλον P   ἡ δὲ πρᾶξις . . . τινα]
om. EMOPQRX   εἰ δὲ πρᾶξις J: εἰ δὲ πράξεις D   10 ἔσται] ἔστω
A   τῶν ἐπιτιμίων] ἐπιτιμίον S   εἰ . . . τινα] ἐκδικησάτω F   εἰ]
καὶ BCGHhKS: om. DJLvY   ἐκδικήσοι DJLvY   τίς] om. DJvY
κα´ 1 ἀγράφως DGLMOY] ἀγράφως ex ἐγγράφως corr. J: ἀγγράφως, cuius
tres primae litterae in rasura sunt E: ἐγγράφως ABCHhPQRSXZ
δύο] Q addit in margine ναύκληροι   καὶ] ἢ καὶ X   2 τὰ om. X
μέρει M   καθομολογήσουσιν J   3 ἄλου J   ἀγράφως ADLP] ἐγράφως
J: ἐγγράφως BCEGHhMOQRSXY   ἑαυτοῖς] ἐν αὐτοῖς C: εἰς ἑαυτοὺς
O: αὐτοῖς J: αὐτοῦ K (?)   4 καὶ τὸ τέλος . . . ἐτελέσαμεν] om. O
πάντωστὲ Y   5 (f. 33 v.) ἐὰν M   ἐὰν] Principium novi cap. apud
M (κζ´) et apud Q (κγ´)   συμβαίη E   τινα] τινά τι GHh: τι DEMORY:
om. K   ἢ σαβουράτον] ὦσαβουρον M   6 σαβουράτον] σαβου-
ράτων Q: σαυράτον E: σάβουρον BCGHhJOS: σαβουρέον P: σαβηναρατον X   Post σαβηναρατον repetit συμβεῖ τινα παθεῖν X   πεφορτομένον
J: περιφορτωμένον K   τὸ σωθὲν O: τῷ σωθέντι J   τῷ παθόντι]

φέρουσιν ἀλλὰ λόγῳ μόνῳ κοινωνίαν συνετάξαντο. τὰ
δὲ ἔγγραφα σφραγιζόμενα βέβαια καὶ ἰσχυρὰ ἔστωσαν
καὶ τὰ σωζόμενα τοῖς ἀπολλυμένοις συνερχέσθωσαν. 10

κβ΄ ὁ ναύκληρος μὴ ἀγέτω πλὴν ὕδατος καὶ ἐφοδίων
καὶ ἀφ᾽ ὧν χρῶνται σχοινίων τὰ πλοῖα, ἐὰν ὁ ἔμπορος
ἐμβάληται τὸν γόμον ὅλον κατὰ τὰς συνθήκας τῶν
ἐγγράφων. καὶ ἐὰν θελήσῃ ὁ ναύκληρος φορτία ἄλλα
ἐπιφέρειν μετὰ ταῦτα, ἐὰν μὲν χωρῇ τὸ πλοῖον, βαλλέτω· 5
εἰ δὲ μὴ χωρεῖ, ὁ ἔμπορος ἐπὶ μαρτύρων τριῶν ἀντι-
τασσέτω τῷ ναυκλήρῳ καὶ τοῖς ναύταις καί, ἐὰν ἐκβολὴ
γένηται, τῷ ναυκλήρῳ ἔσται· ἐὰν δὲ μὴ κωλύσῃ ὁ
ἔμπορος, εἰς συμβολὴν ἐρχέσθω.

κγ΄ ἐὰν συγγράψωνται ὁ ναύκληρος καὶ ὁ ἔμπορος,
κύρια ἔστω· ἐὰν δὲ ὁ ἔμπορος μὴ παρέχῃ τὸν γόμον
πλῆρες, τῶν λοιπαζομένων παρεχέτω τὰ ναῦλα, καθὼς
συνεγράψαντο.

om. X   7 τέταρτον ... προφέρουσιν] τέταρτον φέρουσιν Q. In margine additum μέρος ἐπι   τέταρτον μέρος] δίμερος C   ἐπιφέρεται
C: ἐπιφερέσθω X: ἐπιφερέτωσαν Υ   ἔγγραφον X   προσφέρουσιν
LPX: φέρουσιν BCGHhS: δεικνύουσιν K   8 λόγῳ μόνῳ] λόγῳ μόνον
BLO: λόγου μόνον P: λόγων μόνων S: τῶ λόγῳ μόνῳ R   καὶ κοινωνία QX
9 ἔγγραφα] (f. 109 v.) ἄγραφα C: ἐγγράφως EG   (f. 335 v.) σφραγιζόμενα L   βέβαια ... σωζόμενα] om. Qh   10 καὶ GLMOR] εἰ A:
om. BCHKPSXZ   καὶ τὰ σωζόμενα] καὶ τὰ σωζόμενα M: τὰ δὲ σωζόμενα
EJ: τὰ σωζόμενα δὲ DY   ἀπωλυμένοις G   συνεχέσθωσαν Q: συνεισ-
ερχέσθωσαν EMPR   κβ΄ (f. 16 r.) J   1 μὴ ἀγέτω] post τὰ πλοῖα ponit
G: μὴ ἀγαγέτω AMP   2 καὶ ἀφ᾽ ὧν DY soli: ἐφ᾽ ὧν EM: ἀφ᾽ ὧν ceteri
σχοινίων] post τὰ πλοῖα ponit M: σχοινῶν Q: σχοίνων sive σχοινῶν
BCEGLORSY   ἐὰν δὲ JR   ὁ ἔμπορος] ἔμπορος MO: ἔμπροσθεν R: ὁ
ἔκπορος Q: ὁ ναύκληρος E   3 ἐμβάλει(f. 124 r.)ται Q: ἐμβάλλεται G:
ἐκβάληται X: ἐμβάλλη P   γῶμον M   ὅλον] om. J   κατὰ] καὶ CM
4 γραφῶν P   καὶ ἐὰν] καὶ εἰ K: ἐὰν DEQY   θελήσει JLM   5 ἐὰν
μὲν] εἰ μὲν K: ἐὰν C   χωρῇ ... εἰ δὲ μὴ] Addit in margine B ita χωρὶ
τῶ πλοίων βαλλέτω ἢ δὲ μὴ: omittunt CG praeter μὴ quod servant ambo
χωρῇ] χωρεῖ JM: χορῇ L: χωροῖ E: ἐγχωρῇ R   βαλέτω A: ἐμβαλέτω O
6 εἰ δὲ μὴ χωρεῖ]ἐὰν δὲ μὴ χωρεῖ Q: εἰ δ᾽ οὖν K (?) Post χωρεῖ addit τὸ πλοῖον
P   ὁ ἔμπορος] om. Q   ἐπὶ τριῶν μαρτύρων Q   ἐπιτασσέτω Q: ἀντιτασσέσθω ERX   7 τῷ] τῶν S   καὶ τοῖς ναύταις ... ναυκλήρῳ] om. S
συνναύταις P   8 ἔστω M: ἔσται ex ἔστω correctum J   κωλύσει JL:
κωλύσοι E: κολήσει X   9 ἔμπορος ex ναυκλήρος corr. G   εἰς συμβ. ἐρχ.]
συμβολὴ γενέσθω E   εἰς om. Y   συμβουλὴν X   ἔρχεσθαι D: ἐρχέσθωσαν
KX   κγ΄ 1 συγγράψονται JLMP: συγγράφωνται ER   οἱ ναύκληροι C
καὶ οἱ ἔμποροι M   2 ἔστωσαν Υ   ἐὰν δὲ] ἐὰν Q   παρέχει LM:

κδ´ ἐὰν ὁ ναύκληρος λαβὼν τὰ ἥμισυ ναῦλα πλεύσῃ
καὶ βουληθῇ ὁ ἔμπορος ὑποστρέψαι ἔγγραφα δὲ συνε-
σφράγισαν, διὰ δὲ τὴν ἐμπόδιον ἀπόλλειν τὸν ἔμπορον
τὰ ἡμίναυλα. ἐὰν δὲ ὁ ναύκληρος τῶν ἐγγράφων γενο-
5 μένων ἄλλην ποιήσῃ, διπλᾶ ἀποδιδότω τὰ ἡμίναυλα.

κε´ ἐὰν ἡ προθεσμία τῶν ἡμερῶν τῶν ἐγγεγραμμένων παρέλθῃ, ἕως ἡμερῶν δέκα παρεχέτω ὁ ἔμπορος
τὰς σιταρχίας τῶν ναυτῶν. ἐὰν δὲ παρέλθῃ καὶ ἡ
δευτέρα προθεσμία, πρὸ πάντων πληρώσας τὸ ναῦλον
5 ὁ ἔμπορος κατερχέσθω. εἰ δὲ θελήσει ὁ ἔμπορος προσθεῖναι ποσότητα τῷ ναύλῳ, διδότω καὶ ἐμπλεέτω καθὼς
ἐὰν δόξῃ.

κϛ´ ἐάν τινος τῶν ναυτῶν ἢ ναυκλήρων ἐκκοιτοῦντος

παρεχέτω G   3 πλῆρες BMQS] πλῆρες K: πλήρης GLP: πλῆρις C:
πλῆρεις J: πλήρη ADEOR   τῶν λειπαζομένων BES: τῶν λιπαζομένων
GQY: τὸν λοιπαζόμενον L   τὰ ἔναυλα J: τὸ ναυλῶ Q: τὸν γόμεν
τ ναυ X   καθὰ P   4 συνεγράψαντο CDEJPQR] συνεγράψαντω L:
συνεγράψατο ABGKMOSXY   κδ´ (f. 117 r.) κδ´ P   1 λαβὼν] om. E
τὰ ἥμισυ ναῦλα ABC] τὰ εἱμισύναυλα M: τὰ ἡμίση (ex ἥμισυ corr.) ναῦλα
E: τὰ ἡμησιναυλα X: τὰ ἡμίση ναῦλα DKR: τὸ ἥμισυ ναῦλον G: τὰ ἡμίναυλα Q
πλεύσει JLM   2 βουληθεῖ L   συνεσφράγησαν LMP: συνεσφραγίσαντο
DO: συνεσφραγίσθησαν J   3 διὰ δὲ] διὰ K   τὴν ἐμποδίαν QX: τὸ ἐμπόδιον
KMR: τι ἐμπόδιον D   ἀπώλλειν D   ἀπόλλειν J: ἀπόλλειν G: ὑποβάλλει Q
(f. 32 r.) ἔμπορον B   τῶν ἐμπόρων S: τὸν ναύκληρον E   4 τὰ ἡμῖν ναῦλα
A sicut alibi: τὰ ἡμηναῦλα L: τὰ εἱμίναυλα M: τὰ ἥμισυ ναῦλα CG: τὰ ἡμίση
ναῦλα EK   ἐὰν δὲ] Principium novi cap. (κε´) apud BS. Vadit usque ad
finem cap. κε´   ναύκληρος] ἔμπορος X   τῶν ἐγγρ. γεν.] om. G   γινομένων JMP   5 ἄλλως D: ἀλλαχοῦ R   ἄλλην post ποιήσῃ ponit C   ποιήσει
JLM   διδότω διπλᾶ D   ἀποδότω X   τὰ ἡμίν ναῦλα Q: τὰ ἡμηναῦλα
L: τὰ εἱμίναυλα M: τὰ ἥμισυ ναῦλα C: τὰ ἡμίση ναῦλα K   κε´ 1 ἡ om. G
τῶν] om. Q   γεγραμμένων BCKOQSX   2 παρέλθει L: παρέλθοι EGY
ὡς CP   παρεχέτο M   ὁ addit supra lineam B   3 σηταρχίας BSX: σι-
ταρκίας EK: σιταρχίας γασ. (?) Q   ἐὰν δὲ] Principium novi cap. apud M
(λβ´) et apud Q (κη´)   ἐὰν δὲ] ἐὰν P   παρέλθει L: παρέλθοι GY:
καὶ παρέλθη M   καὶ] om. G   ἡ] om. CEMOQRX   4 πρὸ πάτων Q:
om. X   τὸν ναῦλον CMOY: τὰ ναῦλα BGKS   5 ὁ ἔμπορον (sic) J
τερχέσθω X: κατεχέσθω A solus, quod vereor ne sit error typothetae,
cum in versione scribatur ' exeat '   εἰ δὲ] ἢ Q   θελήσῃ P:
θέλει CQ   ὁ ἔμπορος θελήσει E   προσθῆναι AJP: θῆναι C
6 ποσότητα] om. S   τῷ ναύλῳ DJLPQX] τὸ ναῦλον ABERSZ:
τὸν ναῦλον CGK: τῶν ναύλων M: καὶ τὸν ναῦλον O   διδότω καὶ]
om. DJLPY: ἐπιδιδάτω καὶ Q   πλεέτω K   καθὼς ἂν QX   κϛ´
Post κϛ´ ponunt BGKS   Numerum capituli omittit J   (f. 110 r.)
κϛ´ C   1 τῶν ναυκλήρων ἢ τῶν ναυτῶν G   τῶν ante ναυκλ. addit Y

26

PARS TERTIA

ἐκ τοῦ πλοίου συμβῇ ἀπώλειαν γενέσθαι τοῦ πλοίου
νυκτὸς ἢ ἡμέρας, πᾶσαν τὴν ζημίαν ἐφορᾶν τοὺς
ἐξωκοιτοῦντας ναύτας ἢ ναυκλήρους· τοὺς δὲ εἰς τὸ
πλοῖον μείναντας ἀζημίους μένειν· τοὺς δὲ ἀμελήσαντας 5
προσφέρειν τῷ δεσπότῃ τοῦ πλοίου τὴν διὰ τῆς αὐτῶν
ἀμελείας προσγενομένην ζημίαν.

κζ´ ἐὰν πλοῖον ἀπέρχηται εἰς γόμον ἐμπόρου ἢ
κοινωνίας, συμβῇ δὲ τὸ πλοῖον παθεῖν ἢ διαφθαρῆναι
κατὰ ἀμέλειαν ναυτῶν ἢ τοῦ ναυκλήρου, ἀκίνδυνα εἴτω
τὰ φορτία τὰ ἐν ὅρια κείμενα. εἰ δὲ μαρτυρηθῇ ὅτι
ζάλης γενομένης ἀπώλετο, εἰς συμβολὴν ἐρχέσθωσαν 5
τὰ σωζόμενα τοῦ πλοίου ἅμα καὶ φορτίοις, τὰ δὲ
ἡμίναυλα κατεχέτω ὁ ναύκληρος. ἐὰν δέ τις ἀρνήσηται
τὴν κοινωνίαν καὶ ἐλεγχθῇ ὑπὸ μαρτύρων τριῶν, τὴν
μὲν κοινωνίαν ἀποδιδότω, τῆς δὲ ἀρνήσεως τὴν τιμωρίαν
ὑπομενέτω.   10

ναυκλήρω C: ναυκλήρου J   ἐκκιτοῦντος Q: ἐξωκοιτοῦντος P   2 ἐκ]
om. CDMQY   συμβεῖ M   ἀπώλεια M: ἀπώλεια Q   τοῦ
πλοίου] om. CEMQR   3 ἢ καὶ ἡμέρας G   (f. 34 r.) τὴν ζημίαν M
ἐφορᾶν τούσκ.]   ἔξω κ. ἐφορᾶν K   ἐμφορᾶν S   4 ἐξωκοιτοῦντας
BDGPS] ἐξοκοιτοῦντας CJLQ: ἐξοικοιτοῦντας M: ἐξωκιτοῦντας O: ἐξοι-
κοιτόταςX: ἐκκοιτοῦντας R: ἐξωκατοικοῦντας E: ἔξωκοῦντας A   ναύτας]
om. P   ἢ τοὺς ναυκλήρους O: σὺν ναυκλήροις X   τοὺς δὲ εἰς
... μένειν post 7 ζημίαν ponit Q   εἰς τὸ πλοῖον] ἐν τῷ πλοίῳ EMR :
om. C   5 μήναντας L   ἀζημίους ... ἀμελήσαντας] om. G   μέ-
νειν] εἶναι E   οἱ δὲ ἀμελήσαντες Y   6 προσφέρειν ... τὴν διὰ]
om. S   προφέρειν K   Post προσφέρειν addit ταῦτα C   τὴν
ex τῆς corr. J   διὰ τῆς] δι᾽ αὐτῆς M   7 ἀμελείας αὐτῶν D   προσγινομένην JL: προσγινομένειν M   Post ζημίαν addit ἀπαιτηθήσονται
Y   κζ´ (f. 124 v.) λ´ ἐὰν πλοῖον Q   1 ἀπέρχεται P   2 κοινωνίαν
EP: κοινωνία O   συμβεῖ L   παθεῖν ἢ] om. Y   3 παθεῖν τι DJK
(f. 336 r.) ἢ διαφθαρῆναι L   διαφθαρεῖναι A   3 ναυτῶν EMOQR]
αὐτῶν CDJLPY: ἢ αὐτῶν X: τῶν ναυτῶν AB (sed ex αὐτῶν sec. manu
correctum) GKS   τοῦ] om. E   εἴτω] ἤτω GKX: ἔστω O : ἢ
JLP: εἰ DY: εἶναι MR   4 τὰ ἐν ὅρια κείμενα] τὰ ἐνόρια κείμενα
EGJKLOXY: τὰ ἐνόρεα κείμενα MP: τὰ ἐνορικήμενα Q: τὰ ἐνορκίμενα C:
τὰ ἐν ὁρίῳ κείμενα ABS: τὰ ἐν ὡρείῳ κείμενα D: τὰ ἐν ὡραίοις κείμενα R
μαρτυριθεῖ L: μαρτυριθῇ MP   5 γινομένης LMP   ἀπολετο
M   εἰς συμβ.] ἢ συμβολὴν X   6 σωζώμενα M   τῷ πλοίῳ R.
καὶ om. E   τοῦ φορτίου K   7 εἰμίναυλα M : ἡμιναυλία O : ἡμισί-
ναυλα C   κατὰ δεχέτω CQ   ἀρνήσεται L   8 καὶ ἐλεγχθῇ
... κοινωνίαν] om. RX   καὶ ἐλεγχθῇ] καὶ ἐλεγχθεῖ L: καὶ ἐλλεγχθῇ
M: ἐλεγχθῇ δὲ K: καὶ δειχθῇ CQ   τῶν τριῶν μαρτύρων M   9

27

κη΄ ἐὰν πλοῖον ἐν τῇ ἐμβολῇ ἐμποδισθῇ ὑπὸ τοῦ
ἐμπόρου ἢ κοινωνοῦ πληρωθείσης τῆς προθεσμίας, καὶ
συμβῇ ἀπὸ πειρατείας ἢ πυρκαϊᾶς ἢ ναυαγίου ἀπώλειαν
γενέσθαι τοῦ πλοίου, ὁ τὴν ἐμπόδιον ποιήσας ἐμφερέτω
5 τὰς ζημίας.

κθ΄ ἐὰν ὁ ἔμπορος ἐν τῷ τόπῳ ὅθεν συγγράψονται
μὴ παράσχῃ τὰ φορτία πληρωθείσης τῆς προθεσμίας,
καὶ συμβῇ ἀπὸ πειρατείας ἢ πυρκαϊᾶς ἢ ναυαγίου
ἀπώλειαν γενέσθαι, ἐφορᾶν πᾶσαν τὴν ζημίαν τοῦ
5 πλοίου τὸν ἔμπορον. ἐὰν δὲ μὴ πληρωθέντων τῶν
ἡμερῶν τῆς προθεσμίας συμβῇ τι τῶν εἰρημένων, εἰς
συμβολὴν ἐρχέσθωσαν.

λ΄ ἐὰν ὁ ἔμπορος φορτώσας τὸ πλοῖον, χρυσίον δὲ
ἔσται μετ᾽ αὐτοῦ, καί τι τῶν κατὰ θάλασσαν κινδύνων
συμβῇ παθεῖν τὸ πλοῖον καὶ ὁ φόρτος ἀπόληται καὶ

ἀποδώτω E   τιμωρείαν M   **κη΄** (f. 16 v.) κη΄ J   1 ἐν τῇ] om.
S   ἐμπολῇ BGS: ἐκβολῇ MQ: συμβολῇ X: πόλει K   ἐμποδισθῇ]
συμποδισθῇ D: ἀποδείχθη P: post κοινωνοῦ ponit J   ὑπὸ τοῦ] ὑπὸ K:
ἀπὸ τοῦ G: om. O   2 κοινωνικοῦ D   πληρωθήσις M   καὶ]
om. J   (f. 32 v.) καὶ συμβῇ B   3 πηρατείας A: πυρατί.. as Q:
πειρατηρίας E: πειρατηρίου K: πηρατῶν B (sed ὦν supra rasuram) S
ἢ ἀπὸ πυρκαϊᾶς C   ναγίου O   4 γενέσθαι] Post hoc verbum Q et
E omittunt usque ad c. 29, 4 γενέσθαι. Sed Q post c. 30 dat c. 29
(quod numero κγ΄ notat) usque ad l. 5 ἔμπορον. Sequitur in Q tantum
modo omitti c. 28, 4 τοῦ πλοίου usque ad finem capituli, repeti autem
c. 29, 4 ἐφορᾶν ... 5 τὸν ἔμπορον   τὸ ἐμπόδιον DKMR: τὴν ἐμπόδον
X   ἐμφερέτω] εἰσφερέτω A: προσφερέτω KX: ἀφαιρέτω b   5 τῆς
ζημίας J: τὴν ζημίαν C   **κθ΄** (f. 117 v.) κθ΄ P: (f. 125 r.) idem cap.
sed numero λγ΄ Q   1 ὁ om. Q   ἐν τῷ τόπῳ ὅθεν συγγράψονται] ἔνθα
γράψονται τόπω M: ἔνθα συγγράψωνται τόπω R   ὅθεν] ὅνθεν S:
ὅθε O: ἔνθα Y   συγγράψωνται A: ἐγγράφεται Q   2 παράσχει M:
παρέχει M: ἔχει Q   πληρωθήσης M: πληρωθὴς Q   προθεσμίας...
πειρατείας ἢ] om. K   3 ἀπὸ] ἀπόλει S   (f. 110 v.) ἀπὸ πειρατείας
C   πηρατείας A: πηρατίας LQ: πειρατίου BS: πειρασιου X: πειρατηρίου G   4 ἀπόλεια Q   γενέσθαι] R addit τοῦ πλοίου   τὴν
ζημίαν] om. M   τοῦ πλοίου] om. BGS   5 ἐὰν] εἰ DJKLY   μὴ]
om. CEMRS   πληρωθεισῶν OR   6 καὶ συμβῇ Q   7 ἐμβολὴν
O   ἐρχέσθω JPR   **λ΄** 1 χρυσίον ... αὐτοῦ] χρυσίον ἔχει μετ᾽ αὐτοῦ
J: ἔχει δὲ χρυσίον μετ᾽ αὐτοῦ D: χρυσίον ἔχῃ μεθ᾽ ἑαυτοῦ R: ἔχων δὲ
χρυσίον μετ᾽ αὐτοῦ Y   χρυσίον M   2 ἔσται] ἐστιν GP: om. L
τῶν] τὸν B   κατὰ supra lin. add. P   κατὰ τὴν θάλασσαν G
κινδύνων] om. EMR: κίνδυνον B   3 παθεῖν] om. M   τοῦ πλοίου
M   ὁ φόρτος BGJKORS] ὁ φορτώσας DELMPXY: φορτώσας ACQ
ἀπόληται] ἀπώληται J: ἀπώλειται GMY: ἀπωλείτε L: ἀπόλειται DO:
28

τὸ πλοῖον διαλυθῇ, τὰ ἐκ τοῦ πλοίου σωζόμενα καὶ τοῦ
φόρτου εἰς συμβολὴν ἐρχέσθωσαν, τὸ δὲ χρυσίον τοῦ 5
ἐμπόρου ἐκκομιζέτω μεθ᾽ ἑαυτοῦ, δεκάτας δὲ ἀποδιδότω.
ἐὰν δὲ μή τι τῶν σκευῶν τοῦ πλοίου κατασχὼν ἐσώθη,
τὰ ἡμίναυλα ἀπὸ τῶν ἐγγράφων παρεχέτω· εἰ δέ τι
τῶν σκευῶν τοῦ πλοίου κατασχὼν ἐσώθη, πέμπτας
ἐπιφερέτω. 10

λα΄ ἐὰν ὁ ἔμπορος φορτώσῃ τὸ πλοῖον καί τι συμβῇ
τῷ πλοίῳ, τὰ σωζόμενα πάντα εἰς συμβολὴν ἐρχέσθωσαν
ἑκάτερα· τὸ δὲ ἀργύριον ἐὰν σώζηται, πέμπτας ἐπι-
διδότω· ὁ δὲ ναύκληρος καὶ οἱ ναῦται βοηθείας
παρεχέτωσαν εἰς τὸ σῶσαι. 5

λβ΄ ἐὰν πλοῖον ἐπὶ γόμον ὑπάγῃ ἐμπόρου ναύλῳ
ἢ κοινωνίᾳ καὶ τῶν κατὰ θάλασσαν συμβῇ, τὰ μὲν
ἡμίναυλα μὴ ἀπαιτεῖν τὸν ἔμπορον, τὰ δὲ τοῦ πλοίου

ἀπόλλεται Q: ἀπόλυται C: ἀπόλλυται K: ἀπώλλυται P   4 διαλυθεῖ LM
τὰ ἐκ τοῦ] τὰ δὲ τοῦ CQ   καὶ τοῦ] καὶ ἐκ τοῦ M   5 φορτίου Q
συμβουλὴν C   6 ἐκκομιζέτω DJOPX] ἐγκομιζέτω A: ἐκκομιζέσθω
ELR: ἐγκομιζέσθω M: ἐγκομίζειν CQ: εἰ ἐκομίσατο BKS: εἰ ἐκομήσατο G
μεθ᾽ ἑαυτοῦ] μετ᾽ αὐτοῦ G   αὐτὸ G   δεκάτας δὲ] δεκάτας BGS: δεκα
—τίας supra ras. K   ἀποδότω G   7 (f. 34 v.) ἐὰν δὲ μὴ M   ἐὰν δὲ
μή] Principium novi cap. apud O (λα΄) et apud R (λβ΄)   ἐὰν] εἰ K
δὲ] om. P   καὶ κατασχὼν S: μετασχὼν P   8 τὰ ἡμίναυλα...
ἐσώθη] om. EMY   ἡμήναυλα L   ἐχέτω J: παρεχέτωσαν X
εἰ δέ τι... ἐπιφερέτω] om. CQX   τι] τις S   9 πέμπτα
M   λα΄ Titulus in Σ: ἐν δὲ τῷ λα΄ κεφαλαίῳ   λα΄ et λβ΄ unum cap.
faciunt in O numeratum λβ΄   1 φορτώσει JLM: φορτώσοι E: φορτώσας CQ   τὸ om. M   συμβεῖ τι B: συμβῇ τι GJKS: συμβαίη
τι E   2 τοῦ πλοίου BGS: τὸ πλοῖον QXY   σωζώμενα M   ἅπαντα
CQ: ἅπαντες X (?)   εἰσυμβολὴν J   3 ἐὰν] ἑαυτῷ E   σώ-
ζεται P   πέμπτοις P: πέπτας Q   ἐπιδότω M: ἀποδιδότο C:
ἀποδιδότω O   4 ὁ δὲ] ὁ μὲν ab   βύθια JLY: βυθὶ D: βυθίας MO:
βυσθίας Q: βοήθειαν K   5 παρεχέτω S: περεχέτωσαν M   εἰς τὸ
σώζεσθαι M   λβ΄ (f. 336 v.) λβ΄ L   1 ὑπάγοι ἐπὶ γόμον E: ὑπάγει ἐπὶ
γόμον X   ὑπάγῃ] ὑπάγει J: ὁρμᾷ K   ἐμπόρου ναύλῳ ἢ] om. P
ἐμπούρου S   ναύλῳ] Ita B sed in rasura, ubi stabat (si non erro)
ναυκλήρου: ναύλου ELM: ναύλα QX: ναυ J: ναυκλήρου G   2 κοινωνία
Q: κοινωνίαν PX   καί τι τῶν COQXY: καί τη τῶν BS: sed in B τη
supra lineam additum   τὴν θάλασσαν O   συμβῇ τι DEMR
3 ἡμήναυλα L: εἱμίναυλα M   μὴ] om. CDQY   ἀπετεῖ Q: ἀπετεῖν
L   τὸν ἔμπορον] In B stetit τὸν ἔμπορον, quo postea eraso, τὸν ναύκληρον scriptum est: τοναύκληρον S: τὸν ναύκληρον K   τοῦ om. X

καὶ τῆς ἐνθήκης εἰς συμβολὴν ἐρχέσθωσαν. ἐὰν δὲ
5 καὶ προχρείαν δώσῃ ὁ ἔμπορος ἢ ὁ τὴν κοινωνίαν,
καθὼς συνεγράψαντο κύρια ἔστω.

λγ΄ ἐὰν ὁ ναύκληρος θεὶς τὰ φορτία ἐπὶ τῷ τόπῳ
τῶν συνθηκῶν καί τι πάθῃ τὸ πλοῖον, τὸ μὲν ναῦλον
εἰς πλῆρες εἰσκομιζέσθω ὁ ναύκληρος ὑπὸ τοῦ
ἐμπόρου, τὰ δὲ ἐν ὅρια ἐκβεβλημένα ἀκίνδυνα εἶναι
5 ὑπὸ τῶν συμπλεόντων τοῦ πλοίου μετὰ τοῦ πλοίου,
τὰ δὲ εὑρισκόμενα ἐν τῷ πλοίῳ ἅμα τοῦ πλοίου εἰς
συμβολὴν ἐρχέσθωσαν.

λδ΄ ἐὰν πλοῖον ὀθόνην ἢ βέστην κομίζῃ, ὁ ναύκληρος
διφθέρας καλὰς παρεχέτω, ἵνα μὴ ὑπὸ χειμῶνος τῇ
ἐπικλύσει τῶν κυμάτων τὰ φορτία ἀδικηθῇ. ἐὰν δὲ τὸ
πλοῖον ὑπεραντλήσῃ, ὁ ναύκληρος εὐθὺς λεγέτω τοῖς
5 τὰ φορτία ἔχουσιν ἐν τῷ πλοίῳ, ἵνα ἡ ἔκθεσις γένηται
τῶν φορτίων. ἐὰν δὲ οἱ ἐπιβάται φανερὸν ποιήσωσι

4 τῆς supra lineam in Y   συμβουλὴν C   (f. 33 r.) ἐὰν δὲ καὶ
B   ἐὰν δὲ] εἰ δὲ JK : in Q principium novi cap. λϛ΄ : incipit M²
(fol. 231 r)   5 καὶ] om. CDM²Q   προχρείαν ADJOPX] προχρίαν
L : πρόχρειαν Ε : πρόχρεαν Ε : προχειρίαν M : προσχρείαν BCGKM²QRS
δώσει JLM² : δόσει Μ : δώῃ R   ἢ] τι ἢ R   τὴν κοινωνίαν] κοινωνος
J   6 συνεγράψαντο] συνεγράψαντω L : συνεγράψατο ADMQ : συνετάξαντο G   ἔστωσαν Y   λγ΄ 1 ἐὰν δὲ ὁ C   ναύκληρος]
ναυλούμενος O : ἔμπορος A   θεὶς] θῆς C : θήσας BGS : θῇ D : θήσῃ Κ :
θείη R : εἰς Y   (f. 111 r.) τὰ φορτία C   ἐπὶ τόπω O : ἐπὶ τὸν τόπον
BGKS   2 καί τι] ὅ,τι A   πάθει LM : πάθοι E   τὸ μὲν ναῦλον
CKMQRY : τὸν μεναῦλον AS : τῶν μὲν ναύλων P   3 εἰς om. BDGKS
πλήρης AL : πλήρις CMQM²S : πλήρεις JP : πλήρυς (?) B : πλήρη Κ
κομιζέσθω EM   4 ἐν ὅρια] ἐνόρια codd. plerique : ἐνόρεια P : ἐν ὠρία
G : ἐν ὁρίω BS : ἐν ὠρείω R : ἐμπόρια D   ἐκβαλλόμενα J   (f. 118 r.)
εἶναι P   5 συνπλεόντων L : πλεόντων JX   τὸ πλοίω M : τῶ
πλοίω CD   μετὰ τὸ πλοῖον O : om. CJM²QX   6 ἅμα τῶ πλοίω
DJLMO : ἅμα τὸ πλοῖον Y : om. CM²QX   7 ἐρχέσθωσαν] K rursus
addit ἅμα τοῦ πλοίου   Hic finit M²   λδ΄ Titulus in Σ : ἐν δὲ τῷ
λδ΄ κεφαλαίω   1 ἐὰν τὸ πλοῖον BGKS : ἐὰν δὲ πλοῖον CQ   ὀθώνην
ALMP : ὀθόνιν Q : ἠθόνην D   βέστιν AB   κομίζει JLMP   2
ἐπὶ χειμῶνος AJPb : ἀπὸ χειμῶνος Y   3 ἐπικλύσει AKOΣ (sed in
mpr ex ἐπικλάσει correctum)] ἐπικλάσει BDGJMPRXY : ἐπικλάσι S :
ἐπικλήσει CELQ   κοιμάτων MPQ   ἀδικιθῇ L : ἀδικηθεῖ M   ἐὰν δὲ
τὸ] ἐὰν δὲ M : ἐὰν τὸ b   4 ὑπεραντλήσει JLM : ὑπεραντλήσοι Ε   ὁ
ναύκλη (Finis f. 16 v.) J   εὐθέως EMR   5 τὰ om. Rb   ἡ
ἔκθεσις] ἔκθεσις ELMR : ἐκθέσεις DY : μὴ ἔκθεσις PX   γένωνται D :
γίνονται Y   6 ἐπιβάται A solus servavit : ναῦται ceteri   (f. 125 v.)

τῷ ναυκλήρῳ καὶ εἶθ᾽ οὕτω βλάβῃ τὰ φορτία, ὑπεύθυνον εἶναι τὸν ναύκληρον ἅμα τοῖς ναύταις· εἰ δὲ
προδιαμαρτύρηται ὁ ναύκληρος ἅμα τοῖς ναύταις ὅτι
τὸ πλοῖον ὑπερήντλησε καὶ ἐκθέσθαι, οἱ δὲ ἐμβαλ- 10
λόμενοι τὰ φορτία ἀμελήσωσι τοῦ ἐκθέσθαι, ἀζήμιοι
εἴτωσαν ὅ τε ναύκληρος καὶ οἱ ναῦται.

λε´ ἐὰν πλοῖον ἐκβολὴν ποιήσηται τῆς καταρτίας
αὐτομάτως ἀποβαλλομένης ἢ κοπτομένης, πάντες οἱ
ναῦται καὶ οἱ ἔμποροι καὶ τὰ φορτία καὶ τὸ πλοῖον
σωθέντα εἰς συμβολὴν ἐρχέσθωσαν.

λϛ´ ἐὰν πλοῖον ἀρμενίζον ἔλθῃ ἐπάνω πλοίου ἑτέρου
ὁρμοῦντος ἢ χαλάσαντος τὰ ἄρμενα ἡμέρας οὔσης,
πᾶσαν τὴν συντριβὴν καὶ τὴν ἀπώλειαν ἐφορᾶν τόν τε
ναύκληρον καὶ τοὺς ἐμπλέοντας. λοιπὸν δὲ καὶ τὸ
φορτίον εἰς συμβολὴν ἐρχέσθω. εἰ δὲ ταῦτα νυκτὸς 5
οὔσης συμβῇ, ὁ τὰ ἄρμενα χαλάσας πῦρ ἁπτέτω.
εἰ δὲ καὶ πῦρ οὐκ ἔχει, κραυγὰς παρεχέτω. εἰ δὲ ἀμε-

φανερὰν Q φανερὰν CQ φανεροποιήσωσιν P ποιήσωσιν LM 7 καὶ]
om. K οὕτως βλαβῇ PΣ : οὕτως βλαβεῖ LM : οὕτως λάβει Q : οὕτως
λάβοι C ὑπεύθυνοι X 8 τὸν ναύκληρον ... ὁ ναύκληρος] om.
CQX εἰ δὲ προδιαμ. ... ναύταις] om. Pb 9 προδιαμαρτύρειται
L ἅμα] ἅμα ἅμα D ὅτι] ὁ Q 10 τὸ] om. G ὑπερήν-
τλησεν LMP ἐκθέσθε GRΣ οἱ δὲ ἐμβ. ... ἐκθέσθαι] om.
GPS οἱ δὲ] εἰ δὲ οἱ b ἐμβαλόμενοι B : βαλλόμενοι M : ἐκβαλλό-
μενοι DQY 11 φορτεία corr. ex χαρτεία C ἀμελήσωσιν L : ἀμελήσουσι Σ praeter b ἀζύμιοι MO : ἀζήμιον C 12 εἴτωσαν]
KLXa : ἔστωσαν CEGMORYp λε´ Titulus in Σ : ἐν δὲ τῷ λε´ κεφαλαίῳ
Cap. in R post λη´ ponitur et λθ´ numerum accipit 1 πλοῖον] om.
C ποιήσει(f. 35 r.)ται M ποιήσειται LM : ποιήσιτε C : ποιήσοιτο EQ
2 ἐπιβαλλομένης G : ἐπιαποβαλλομένης D 3 ἔμποροι] προροί C 4
ἐρχέσθω M λϛ´ 1 ἀρμενίζων L ἔλθει M : ἔλθοι BEKPQY ἐπάνου
M ἑτέρου] om. EY ὁρμῶντος ALM 2 ἢ χαλάσαντος] addit
in margine B, omittit G 3 ἀπώλιαν L (f. 337 r.) τόν τε
ναύκληρον L 4 τοὺς] αὐτοὺς τοὺς O συμπλέοντας EM : πλέοντας
KLO 5 (f. 33 v.) συμβολὴν B. In B margo interior folii 33 ita
abscissa est ut ab linea quinta capituli 36 εἰ δὲ ταῦτα νυκτὸς οὔσης
σ ... βεῖ usque ad lineam secundam capituli 38 διφθέρας παρεχέτω
καὶ ... ναῦται duo sive tres litterae cuiusque lineae deperditae sint
6 ἄρμετνα G 7 εἰ δὲ πῦρ MP κραυὰς BS κραυ(f. 111 v.)γὰς
C εἰ δὲ] ἐὰν δὲ O ἀμελήσας ποιῆσαι ACL] Ita prima manus
B, quod secunda in ἀμελήσας τοῦτο οὐ ποιήσῃ correxit. G cum priore
lectione B congruit, cum posteriore S : ἀμελήσας ποιῆσε Q : ἀμελήσας

λήσας ποιῆσαι καὶ συμβῇ ἀπώλειαν, ἑαυτὸν ἀπώλεσεν,
εἰ ταῦτα οὕτως μαρτυρηθῶσιν. εἰ δὲ καὶ ὁ ἀρμενιστὴς
10 ἀμελήσας καὶ ὁ βιγλεοφόρος ἀποκοιμηθῇ, ὡς εἰς
βράχη ἀπώλετο ὁ ἀρμενίζων καὶ ὃν κρούσει ἀζήμιον
φυλαττέτω.

λζ′ ἐάν τι πάθῃ τὸ πλοῖον καὶ σωθῇ τὰ τῶν ἐμπόρων
ἢ ἐπιβατῶν τὸ δὲ πλοῖον ἀπώληται, τὰ μὲν γραμμάτια
σωζόμενα πεντεκαιδεκάτας παρεχέτωσαν, ὁ δὲ ἔμπορος
καὶ οἱ ἐπιβάται μὴ δότωσαν τῷ ναυκλήρῳ τὸ πλοῖον.

λη′ ἐὰν πλοῖον πεφορτωμένον σῖτον ἐν ζάλῃ καταληφθῇ, ὁ ναύκληρος διφθέρας παρεχέτω καὶ οἱ ναῦται
ἀντλείτωσαν. εἰ δὲ ἀμελήσωσι καὶ βραχῇ ὁ φόρτος

οὐ ποιήσει EMR: ἀμελήσας ταῦτα ποιῆσαι D: ἀμελήσει ταῦτα ποιῆσαι Υ:
ἀμελήσει τοῦτο ποιῆσαι Κ: ἀμελήσῃ Ο: καὶ ἀμέλειαν ποιήσας P: ἀμέλειαν
ποιήσας Χ   8 καὶ συμβῇ ἀπώλειαν] om. EMR   καὶ συμβῇ] συμβῇ
DP   ἀπώλεια OP   ἀπώλειαν γενέσθαι DY   ὤλεσεν CEMOPR
9 οὕτως] om. Ο   μαρτυριθῶσιν LP: μαρτυρηθῇ D   εἰ δὲ καὶ] εἰ δὲ
CQY: ἢ καὶ E   10 ἀμελήσας] ἀμελήσει R: ἀρμενήσας L: ἀρμενίσας DY
βιγλεοφόρος AX] βιγλιοφόρος LY: βιγλαιοφόρος Ο: βιχλεοφόρος M:
βιγλυοφόρος Q: βιγλοφόρος EKR: βιγληφόρος D: αἰγλιοφόρος C: ἐκλεω-
φόρος P: βηγλάτωρ BS: βιγλάτωρ G   ἀποκοιμηθῇ L: ἀποκυμηθῇ B:
ἀποκυμιθῇ C: ὑπνώσας Κ: ἀποκοιμηθεὶς Υ   ὡς] ὁ EM: om. Κ   11
βράχη] βράχει CLP: βράχρη BS: βράχυ Q: βράχος EMR   ἀπώλεσεν Κ
ὁ ἀρμενήζων L: ἀρμενίζων AM: ἀρμενίζον E   ὃν κρούσει] ὃν κρούσῃ M: οὐ
κρούσει C (?): ὁ κρούσει E   ἀζήμιος BDKRS: ἀζύμιος C   Post ἀζήμιον
addit ἑαυτὸν Υ   12 φυλαττέσθω DK   λζ′ Titulus in Σ: ἐν δὲ τῷ λζ′
κεφαλαίω   1 τι] om. M   πάθοι M: πάθοι E   σωθεῖ LM   2 καὶ
ἐπιβατῶν CQ: ἢ τῶν ἐπιβατῶν Ο   τὸ μὲν πλοῖον L: καὶ τὸ μὲν πλοῖον DY
ἀπώληται] ἀπωλείται LM: ἀπολείται Q: ἀπόλληται Κ: ἀπόλλυται DP:
ἀπόλετο C: ἀπολέτω Χ: ἀπόλει A   τὰ μὲν] τὰ δὲ BDGS: καὶ τὰ
Κ   γραμμάτια KL] γραμματεῖα ADEORΣ (praeter b ubi scribitur
γράμμ   ᾳᾳ) γ . . . μάτια B, quod probabiliter γραμμάτια fuit, cum GS id
habeant: γράμματι M: πράγματα CQX: ἐξάρτια P   Ego γραμμάτια potius
quam γραμματεῖα scripsi cum in codd. antiquioribus illa orthographia
praevaleat. In Seld. 10 semper scribitur γραμμάτιον, γραμμάτια, e.g.
fol. 61 r., 62 r., 67 r., 77 r.   γράμματα et πράγματα saepenumero confusa
esse docet clarissimus Bastius ad Greg. Cor. p. 185 n. * * * et p. 803.
3 σωζώμενα M   πεντεδεκάτας M   οἱ δὲ ἔμποροι καὶ ἐπιβάται D
(f. 118 v.) ἔμπορος P   4 δότωσαν ADEORX] δώτωσαν M: δο . . τωσαν
B: δοσάτωσαν KL: δωσάτωσαν CGPQS   τῷ] om. Q   τὸ πλοίω C

λη′ 1 τὸ πλοῖον EQ   πεφορτόμενον L: πεφορτισμένον ER: τὸ πεφορτωμένον Q   σίτου C   ζάλῃ] χαλάζῃ ER   καταληφθῇ] καταληφθεῖ
BL: καταλειφθῇ A: καταβληθῇ C: καταβληθεῖ QX   δὲ διφθέρας S:
διφθέρας καλὰς EMR   3 ἀντλήτωσαν ALMP   ἐὰν δὲ LX   ἀμελήσωσιν LMP: ἀμελήσουσι A: ἀπελήτωσαν C   βραχεῖ AM: βραχὺ

32

ἐκ τῆς ἀντλίας, οἱ ναῦται ζημιούσθωσαν. εἰ δὲ ἀπὸ
τῆς ζάλης ὁ φόρτος ἀδικηθῇ, ἐπιγινωσκέτωσαν τὴν 5
ζημίαν ὅ τε ναύκληρος καὶ οἱ ναῦται ἅμα τῷ ἐμπόρῳ, τὰς δὲ ἐξ ἑκατοστὰς τῶν σωζομένων κομιζέσθω ὁ
ναύκληρος ἅμα τοῦ πλοίου καὶ τοῖς ναύταις. ἀποβολῆς
δὲ εἰς θάλασσαν γενομένης, ὁ ἔμπορος πρῶτος ῥιπτέτω
καὶ οὕτως οἱ ναῦται ἐπιχειρείτωσαν. μετὰ δὲ τοῦτο 10
μηδεὶς τῶν ναυτῶν σύλα ποιήσῃ. εἰ δὲ ποιήσῃ, διπλᾶ
ἀποδιδότω ὁ ἐπιβαλλόμενος καὶ τοῦ κέρδους παντὸς
ἐκπιπτέτω.

λθ´ ἐὰν πλοῖον μεστὸν σίτου ἢ οἴνου ἢ ἐλαίου ἁρμε-
νίζον βουλήσει τοῦ ναυκλήρου καὶ τῶν ναυτῶν χαλα-
σάντων τὰ ἄρμενα καὶ εἰσέλθῃ τὸ πλοῖον εἰς τόπον
ἢ ἐν ἀκτῇ μὴ βουλομένου τοῦ ἐμπόρου καὶ συμβῇ
ἀπώλειαν γενέσθαι τοῦ πλοίου, τὸν δὲ γόμον ἢ τὰ 5
φορτία σωθῆναι, ἀκίνδυνον εἶναι τὸν ἔμπορον ἐκ τῆς

GQXY   4 ἀντλήσεως P   ἀπὸ τῆς ζάλης] ὑπὸ τῆς ζάλης G : ἀπὸ τῆς
βλάβης K   5 ὁ φόρτος] om. EM   ἀδικιθῇ L   6 (f. 126 r.) ὅ τε
ναύκληρος Q   7 τὰς δὲ ἐξ ἑκατοστὰς τῶν scripsi] τὰς δὲ δεκάτας ἢ ἔντας
ἑκάστων A : τὰς δεκάτας τῶν BS : τὰς δεκάτας δὲ τῶν P : τὰς δὲ δεκάτας τῶν
G : τὰς δὲ δεκαδίας τῶν K : τὰς δὲ ἑκατοστὰς τῶν DLMOX : τὰς δὲ ἑκαστω E :
τὰς δὲ ἑκτὰς τῶν Q : τὰς δὲ ἑκτὰς τῶν ER : τὰς δὲ ἑκτῶν C   σωζομένω E
κομιζέσθωσαν EMY : κομίζεσθαι P   8 ἅμα τοῦ πλοίου καὶ τοῖς ναύταις
ABELOPSX] ἅμα τῶ πλοίω καὶ τοῖς ναύταις DR : ἅμα τοῖς ναύταις G : καὶ
οἱ ναῦται ἅμα τοῦ πλοίου CM : καὶ οἱ ναῦται ἅμα τοῦ πλοίου καὶ τοῖς ναύταις
Q : καὶ οἱ ναῦται ἅμα τῶ ἐμπόρω καὶ τῶ πλοίω Y : καὶ οἱ ναῦται K   ἀποβολὴ
Q : ἀπωλείας P   9 γενομένης εἰς θάλασσαν AMX   γινομένης LP
πρῶτον ELMY : πρότον BS : τὸ πρῶτον G : πρότερον K   10 οὕτως] τότε
Y   ἐπιχειρήτωσαν AL : ἐπιχειρίτωσαν MP   μετὰ δὲ τούτων C :
μετὰ δὲ τούτω L   11 τῶν ναυτῶν μηδεὶς EM   σύλα ποιήσῃ] σύλα
ποιήσει L : σύλα ποιεῖτο M : σύλα ποιείτω DER   εἰ δὲ ποιήσῃ] om. QS
Omittit etiam K, sed spatio vacuo relicto   εἰ δὲ καὶ DY   ποιήσει
AP : ποιείσῃ M   διπλᾶ ... ἐκπιπτέτω] λαμβάνειν αὐτὸν ξυλαγώγια
ἑκατὸν καὶ διπλᾶ ἀποδιδώτωσαν οἱ ἐπιβαλλόμενοι καὶ προρίπτοντες τοῦ γόμου
καὶ τοῦ κέρδους παντὸς ἐκπιπτέτωσαν M   12 ὁ ἐπιβ.] ἐπιβ. P   ἐπι(f. 35 v.)-
βαλλόμενοι M   κέρδος L : κέρδου S   παντὸς] αὐτὸς G   λθ´ 1 ἐὰν
δὲ Y   μεστὸν] μετὰ X   σίτον PY   ἁρμενίζων L : ἁρμενίσει P : om. A
2 βολήσει EL : βολήσῃ O : κωλύσῃ Y   3 τὰ] om. Q   καὶ] om. KQ
εἰσέλθοι CEMQY : εἰσελθὼν P   τὸ πλοῖον] om. K : post τόπον ponit R
τόπον τινα K   4 (f. 34 r.) ἢ ἐν ἀκτῇ B   ἀνακτῇ X : εἰσ ἀκτὴν Y
5 ἀπόλειαν M sed l. 11 ἀπώλειαν   6 σωθέντα S   (f. 112 r.) εἶναι
τὸν ἔμπορον C   εἶναι ... πλοίου] ἐστι τὸν ἔμπορον ἐκ τοῦ πλοίου τῆς

ζημίας τοῦ πλοίου, ἐπειδὴ οὐκ ἐβούλετο εἰσελθεῖν εἰς
τὸν τόπον ἐκεῖνον. εἰ δὲ ἀρμενίζοντος τοῦ πλοίου εἴπῃ
ὁ ἔμπορος τῷ ναυκλήρῳ· ἐν τῷ τόπῳ τούτῳ χρῄζω
10 εἰσελθεῖν, τοῦ τόπου μὴ ἐγκειμένου ἐν τοῖς ἐγγράφοις,
καὶ συμβῇ ἀπώλειαν γενέσθαι τοῦ πλοίου τὰ δὲ φορτία
σωθῆναι, ἀπολαμβανέτω ὁ ναύκληρος τὸ πλοῖον σῶον
ἀπὸ τοῦ ἐμπόρου. εἰ δὲ βουλήσει τῶν ἀμφοτέρων
ἀποβάλληται τὸ πλοῖον, πάντα εἰς συμβολὴν ἐρχέ-
15 σθωσαν.

μ´ ἐὰν πλοῖον συμβῇ ναυάγιον παθεῖν καὶ σωθῇ
μέρος τοῦ γόμου καὶ τοῦ πλοίου, ἐὰν οἱ ἐπιβάται
βαστάζωσι μεθ᾽ ἑαυτῶν χρυσίον ἢ ἀργύριον ἢ ὁλοσηρικὰ ἢ μαργαρίτας, τὸ μὲν χρυσίον τὸ σωζόμενον
5 δεκάτας παρεχέτω, τὸ δὲ ἀργύριον πέμπτας ἐπιφερέτω·
τὰ δὲ ὁλοσηρικά, ἐὰν ἄβροχα σωθῶσι, δεκάτας ἐπιφερέτωσαν, ὡς ὅμοια ὄντα τοῦ χρυσίου· εἰ δὲ βραχῶσι,
κουφιζέσθωσαν τὴν ὑποτριβὴν καὶ τὴν ἀποβροχὴν καὶ

ζυμίας X   ἐκ τῆς ζημίας] τῆς ζυμίας Q   7 (f. 337 v.) ἐπειδὴ L
ἠβούλετο K : ἠδύνετο P   εἰς] om. P   8 ἐκεῖνον] om. CQ   εἰ
δὲ ἀρμενίζοντος] Principium novi cap. (μβ´) in R   εἴπῃ . . . πλοίου]
om. P   εἴπει A : εἴποι CKY : εἴπεν EM   9 τόπῳ] om. L
χρίζω LM : θέλω CQ   10 ἐλθεῖν O   τοῦ δὲ τόπου S   μὴ] om. D
ἐγγυμμένου X : ἐγγιμένου Y   11 ἀπόλεια Q   τοῦ πλοίου om. X
τὰ δὲ] τὰ P   12 σωθῇ CEOPQR : σωθέντα G   σῶον] om. C
13 ἀπὸ] ἅμα M   τῶν] om. DKLY   ἀμφοτέρω S   Post ἀμφοτέρων addit
μερῶν O   14 ἀποβάλληται] ἀποβάλλεται AM : ἀπόλληται D : ἀπολεῖται L :
ἀπόληται O : ἀπόληται P : ἀπώλειται Y   τὸ πλοῖον πάντα] om. P   πάντες R
ἐρχέσθω M   μ´ 1 ναυάγειον M : ἐκ ναυαγίου Y   Post παθεῖν addit τι Y
σωθεῖ M   3 βαστάζωσιν L : βαστάζουσιν M   μεθ᾽ ἑαυτῶν] om. P : post
χρυσίον ponunt EKMR   χρυσὸν ἢ ἄργυρον K   ὁλοσηρικὰ]
ὁλωσίρικα L : ὁλοσειρικᾶ OP : ὁλοσίρικα QX : ὁλοσυρικὰ MY : ὁλοσήρηκα
G : σηρικὰ K   4 μαργαρίτας] τι τῶν λίθων τῶν πολυτίμων O   τὸ
σωζόμενον] τὸ σοζόμενον L : τὸ σωζόμενον M : om. O   5 δεκάτας]
addit supra lineam recentior manus in B   παρεχέτωσαν CQ : om. O
πέπτας Q   ἐπιφερέτο M : ἐπιφερέτωσ . . . Q   6 ὁλοσηρικὰ]
ὁλωσίρικα L : ὁλοσειρικᾶ OP : ὁλοσίρικα X : ὁλοσίρυκα Q : ὁλοσυρικὰ M :
ὁλοσίρηκα G : σηρικὰ K   ἐὰν ἄβροχα σωθῶσι] ἄβροχα ὦσιν X
ἀβρόχως L   σωθῶσιν LMP : διασωθῶσιν K   ἐπιφερέτωσαν δεκάτας
K   7 ὡς ὅμοια ὄντα] ὡς ὅμοια τὰ BS : ὡς ὅμοια X : ὡς ὅμοζα ὄντως X :
ὁμοίως τοῖς K   τοῦ χρυσίου] τῷ χρυσίῳ D : ante ὄντα ponunt EMR   εἰ
δὲ καὶ G   βραχῶσιν LM : βροχασθῶσιν X   8 κουφιζέσθωσαν]
Cum hoc verbo finit P   κουφιζέτωσαν X   ὑποτριβὴν] ἀποτριβὴν

οὕτως εἰς συμβολὴν ἐρχέσθωσαν. οἱ δὲ μαργαρῖται,
καθὼς ἐκτιμηθῶσι, χρυσίου φόρτον τελείτωσαν τὴν 10
ἀπώλειαν.

μα΄ ἐὰν πλέωσιν ἐν πλοίῳ ἐπιβάται καὶ ἢ διαφθαρῇ
ἢ ἀπόληται τὸ πλοῖον, τὰ δὲ τῶν ἐπιβατῶν σωθῇ,
ἐπιφερέτωσαν οἱ ἐπιβάται εἰς τὴν ἀπώλειαν τοῦ πλοίου.
ἐὰν δὲ ἐπιβάται δύο ἢ τρεῖς ἀπολέσωσι τὸ χρυσίον
αὐτῶν ἢ τὰ εἴδη, ἀπὸ πάντων λαμβανέτωσαν κατὰ 5
τὴν δύναμιν πρὸς τὴν ἀπώλειαν ἅμα τῆς συμβολῆς τοῦ
πλοίου.

μβ΄ ἐὰν πλοῖον τρυπήσῃ φορτία κομίζον, τὰ δὲ
φορτία ἐξαιρεθῇ, ἐπὶ τῷ ναυκλήρῳ ἔστω, ἐὰν δὲ θελήσῃ
ἐν τῷ πλοίῳ κομίζειν ἐν τῷ συγκειμένῳ ἐμπορίῳ, ἐὰν
τὸ πλοῖον ἐξηρτισμένον ᾖ. εἰ δὲ μὴ ἐξηρτισμένον, ἄλλο

CMQS: ὑποβροχὴν Ε : ἀποβροχὴν Κ   τὴν ἀποβροχὴν] τὴν ἀποτριβὴν Ε :
ἀποτριβὴν Κ   9 συμβουλὴν Χ   ἐρχέσθωσαν] Post hoc verbum
in R vacat mediae lineae spatium, in quo scribitur λήθη   οἱ δὲ
μαργαρῖται . . . ἀπώλειαν] om. G   οἱ δὲ μαργαρῖται] om. CQ   10 ἐκ-
τιμηθῶσιν Μ : ἐκτιμιθῶσιν L   χρυσίον CDQ   τελείτωσαν] ποιείτωσαν ER   11 ἀπώλειαν] Addunt post hoc verbum καὶ ἀποκατάστασιν
Ε : καὶ τὴν ἀποκατάστασιν Μ : εἰς ἀποκατάστασιν R   μα΄ Titulus in
Σ : ἐν δὲ τῶ μα΄ κεφαλαίω (f. 126 v.) μέ΄ Q   1 πλέουσι πλοίω C   καὶ
ἢ] καὶ ADQ   διαφθαρεῖ BCS   2 ἢ ἀπόληται om. Y   ἀπωλεῖται
GLM : ἀπόλυται C : ἀπόλλυται Κ   σωθείη C   ἐπιβαλέτωσαν R
εἰς τὴν ἀπώλειαν] om. BGKS   ἀπώλιαν L   4 ἐὰν δὲ] ἐὰν BS : καὶ
ἐὰν Κ   ἢ δύο Υ   δύο ἢ τρεῖς] δύο ἢ καὶ τρεῖς Ο : om. Σ praeter m, ubi
in margine addidit manus recentior   ἀπολέσωσιν L   τῶν χρυσίων S   5 αὐτῶν] om. G   ἢ] om. DY   εἴδη] ἴδια DEKLMY
ἀπὸ πάντων] om. Κ   (f. 36 r.) κατὰ τὴν δ. Μ   6 τὴν δύναμιν] δύναμιν DLXY   πρὸς] om. CDLY   τὴν ἀπώλειαν ἅμα] om. DLY
τῆ συμβολῆ ΚΣ : τῆς συμβουλῆς ΟΧ : τῆς βολῆς R   μβ΄ 1 ἐὰν δὲ τὸ
πλοῖον S   τρυπήσει LM : τρυπήσοι Ε : τριπήση S   κομίζων LM   2
ἐξαιρεθεῖ L : ἐξερευθῇ Υ   (f. 34 v.) ἐξερεθεῖ Β   (f. 112 v.) τῶ ναυκλήρω C   ἔσται ΕΜ   ἐὰν δὲ θελήσῃ Α] ἐὰν δὲ θελήσει Q : ἐὰν
θελήσει ΟΧ : ἐὰν δὲ θέλη BGKS : ἐὰν δὲ θέλει Ο : ἐὰν θέλη DRY : ἐὰν
θέλει LM : ἐὰν θέλοιεν Ε   3 ἐν τῷ πλοίῳ] ἐπὶ τῶ πλοιῶ Β : ἐπὶ τῶ
πλοιον S : ἐπὶ τὸ πλοῖον Κ : τὸ πλοῖον Ε : πλοῖον C : πλοῖω Q   ἐν τῷ]
ἦν ἐν τῶ S: ἢ ἐν τῶ ceteri. ἢ (sive ἦν) meo Marte omisi   συγγιμένω Υ
ἐμπορω L : ἐμπορείω Β : ἐμπόρω CEMQRX   4 τῶ πλοίω Β   ἐξηρτι-
μένον C : ἐξηρτημένον DEMY : ἐξηρτημένων Q   ᾖ] εἰ CDGLY : ἦν ΑΟ
εἰ δὲ μὴ ἐξηρτισμένον] om. CQ   Post μὴ addunt ἢ GR, post ἐξηρτ. D (ubi
scribitur εἰ) Ο et iterum G   Post ἐξηρτ. addit ἦν Υ   ἐξειρτισμένον

NOMOΣ POΔIΩN NATTIKOΣ

5 δὲ πλοῖον ἐὰν φέρῃ ὁ ναύκληρος εἰς τὸ συγκείμενον
ἐμπόριον, διδότω τὸ πᾶν ναῦλον.

μγ´ ἐὰν πλοῖον ἐπὶ χειμῶνι καταληφθῇ καὶ ἐκβολὴν
ποιήσῃ τοῦ γόμου καὶ κεράτων κλάσιν καὶ καταρτίου
καὶ αὐχένων καὶ ἀγκυρῶν καὶ ἐφολκίων, ταῦτα πάντα
εἰς συμβολὴν ἐρχέσθωσαν ἅμα τῆς τιμῆς τοῦ πλοίου
5 καὶ τῶν σωζομένων φορτίων.

μδ´ ἐὰν πλοῖον ἔχῃ γόμον καὶ ἐν ζάλῃ ἐκβολὴ τῆς
καταρτίας γένηται ἢ τῶν αὐχένων κλάσις ἢ ἀπώλειά
τινος τῶν ἐφολκίων, ἐὰν μὲν ἐκ τῆς ζάλης συμβῇ τὸν
γόμον βραχῆναι, ἀνάγκη πᾶσα εἰς συμβολὴν ταῦτα
5 ἔρχεσθαι. εἰ δὲ ὁ γόμος ἐκ τῆς ἀντλίας πλείω βλαβῇ
καὶ οὐχὶ ἐκ τῆς ζάλης, τὰ ναῦλα λαμβανέτω ὁ ναύκληρος

L: ἐξηρτημένον DY   ἄλλον C: ἄλλω M   5 πλοίω Q   ἐὰν
φέρῃ] ἂν φέρει L: ἐὰν φέρει M: ἐὰν φέροι E: ἐὰν ἐπιφέρει Q: ἐπιφέρει
CD: φέρει Y   ἐν τῶ συγκειμένω ἐμπορίω L   συγγίμενον Y   6
ἐμπορεῖον AB: ἐμπορίω X   διδότω] διδό(ώ Q)τωσαν CQ: ὁ ναύκληρος
διδότω EMR   τὸ πᾶν ναῦλον] τὸ ναῦλον DL: τὸν ναῦλον MY: πᾶν
ναῦλον CQ   μγ´ 1 ἐν χειμῶνι BGK: ἐν χειμόνι S: ἐπὶ χειμωνος (?)
X   καταλειφθῇ EKM: καταληφθεῖ L   καὶ] om. Q   2 ποιήσει LM:
ποιήσοι E: ποιήσετω X   κέρατον CE: κέρατα Q: τῶν κεράτων K
κλάσει CQX: κλάσοι E: κλάσει κλάσει O   καταρτίου] τοῦ καταρτίου K:
καταρτία A: καταρτίων M   3 ἐφαλκίων L, sed in c. 44, 3 ἐφολκίων:
φολκίων X   Post ἐφολκίων inserit E ἔρημον συμβῇ γενέσθαι: inserit
M τὰ μὲν ἀπὸ τῆς ζάλης αὐτόματος ἐκβλησκόμενα, τὰ δὲ αὐτομάτως θραυόμενα
In N incipit f. 83 r. cum verbis ἀπὸ τῆς ζάλης αὐτομάτως sed pars
superior paginae admodum difficile est lectu; cum verbis c. 46, 5
τοῖς αὐτῶν κληρονόμοις omnia clara fiunt.   4 ἐν συμβολὴν X   ἐρ-
χέσθωσαν] ἔρχεται M   (f. 351 r.) ἐρχέσθωσαν J   τῇ τιμῇ M
(f. 338 r.) πλοίου καὶ L   5 σωζωμένων L   φορτίων] om. BGKS
μδ´ Titulus in Σ: ἐν δὲ τῶ μδ´ (μα´ m: μδ´ ex μα´ corr. r) κεφαλαίω
Hoc capitulum bis dat D, sed primum, post (l. 3) ἐφολκίων, scriba
repetit ultimam partem (l. 3 ταῦτα ... l. 5 φορτίων) praecedentis
capituli. Tum errore comperto, rursus dat c. 44   1 ἐὰν ...
γόμον] ἐὰν εἰς πλοῖον ἐν χειμῶνι K   ἔχει LM: ἔχοι E   καὶ] om.
CQX   ἐκβολή] εἰ καὶ ἐκβολή Q: ἐκβολὴν XY   τῆς καταρτίας
Σ praeter m, ubi manus recentior τῆς καταρτίας in τῶν καταρτίων mutavit,
et b, ubi scribitur καταρ articulo omisso: τῶν καταρτίων J   2 ἢ τῶν]
ἢ καὶ τῶν C   ἢ ἀπώλια L: ἢ ἀπόλειαν C: καὶ ἀπόλεια Q   3 τινος]
om. O   ἐὰν μὲν] ἐὰν BGKS   4 βραχύναι E   πᾶσα] πάσει Q:
ταῦτα DEJLMORY   ταῦτα ἔρχεσθαι A] ἔρχεσθαι CDEJMORY: ἐρχέσθω BGKSX: ἐρχέσθωσαν LQ   5 εἰ δὲ] δὲ S   ἐκ] ἐν J   πλείω]
πλίω M: πλεῖον BLSXΣ: πλέον KQR: πλοίω C: πλοῖον O: πλοίονα G:
βραχῆ καὶ Y: om. DJ   βλαβῇ] βραχῆ G: βλαβεῖ L   6 οὐκ CQX
36

καὶ τὰ εἴδη παραδιδότω ξηρὰ μέτρῳ καθὼς παρέλαβεν.

μέ ἐὰν ἐν πελάγει πλοῖον στραφῇ ἢ διαφθαρῇ, ὁ ἀποσῴζων τι ἐξ αὐτοῦ ἐπὶ τὴν γῆν λαμβανέτω ἀντὶ μισθοῦ οὗ ἀποσῴζει τὸ πέμπτον μέρος.

μϛ´ ἐὰν κάραβος ἀπὸ ἰδίου πλοίου τὰ σχοινία διαρρήξας ἀπόληται ἅμα καὶ τοῖς ἐμπλέουσιν ἐν αὐτῷ, ἐὰν οἱ πλέοντες ἀπόλωνται ἢ ἀποθάνωσι, τὸν μισθὸν τὸν ἐνιαυσιαῖον ἀποδιδότω ὁ ναύκληρος εἰς πλῆρες τοῦ ἐνιαυτοῦ τοῖς τούτων κληρονόμοις. ὁ δὲ τὸν κάραβον 5 ἀποσῴζων σὺν τῶν ἐφολκίων, καθὼς ἐν ἀληθείᾳ εὑρίσκει, πάντα ἀποδώσει, λαμβάνων οὗ ἀποσῴζει τὸ πέμπτον μέρος.

μζ´ ἐὰν χρυσίον ἢ ἀργύριον ἢ ἕτερόν τι ἐκ βυθοῦ ἐπαρθῇ ἀπὸ ὀργυιῶν ὀκτώ, λαμβανέτω ὁ ἀποσῴζων τὸ

ἐκ τῆς ζάλης] τῆς ζάλης EM   τω ναυλω L : τοῦ ναύλου X   ναύλαμβανέτω Cp   παραλαμβανέτω Q   7 καὶ τὰ] τὰ δὲ EMR   εἴδη] ἴδη L   παραδιδότω] παραδιδῶτω M : παραδιδότω ὁ ναύκληρος G   μέτρω ξηρὰ J   μετρῶν b : μέτρον M : μέτρα D : om. Q   καθὼς καὶ ELO   μέ 1   ἐν] ἐν τῶ E : om. J   πελάγη JLM   συστραφῇ E   διαφθαρῇ]   διαφθαρεῖ LM : διαστραφῇ C   καὶ ὁ ἀποσῴζων M   2 ἐξ αὐτῶν   BGS   ἐπὶ τὴν γῆν ἐξ αὐτοῦ Q   ἐπὶ τὴν γῆν] ἀπὸ τὴν γῆν M : om.   X   λαμβανέτω post μισθοῦ ponit G   3 οὗ ἀποσῴζει soli servant   DJ] ὁ ἀποσῴζων CELM : ὁ ἀποσῷζον Q : om. ABGKORSX   τὸ πέμπτον   μέρος] τὸ ἔμερος J, id est, τὸ ε´ μέρος   μϛ´ 1 σχοινία] σχοῖνα seu σχοῖνα   ABDGKLSY   2 διαρήξας B   (f. 127 r.) ἀπολεῖται Q   ἀπόλληται   D : ἀπωλεῖται seu ἀπώλειται GJLY : ἀπολεῖται M   ἅμα καὶ] ἅμα D   συμπλέουσιν EJM : πλέουσιν R   3 ἐμπλέοντες M   ἀπόλωνται ἢ]   om. Y   ἀπώλοντο JLX : ἀπόλοντο M : ἀπόλλωνται D : ἀπωλοῦνται   G : ἀπώλοντο R   ἢ ἀποθάνωσι] ἢ ἀποθάνωσιν L : ἢ ἀποθάνουσιν M : ἢ   ἀπέθανον R : om. CE   4 τὸν ἐνιαυσαῖον L : τῶν ἐνιαυσιαίων S   ἀποδιδότω] παρεχέτω R   πλῆρες] πλήρης A : πλήρεις JL : πλῆρις   CMQX : πλήρη D   5 τούτων] τούτου M : αὐτῶν NR   6 ἀποσῷζον   L   σὺν] μετὰ K : om. CDEOQ   ἐφελκαίων S : ὀφολκίων X   καθὼν BGS : καθ᾽ ὧν K   Post καθὼς addunt παρέλαβεν CEQ   εὑρίσκει]   εὑρήσῃ AD : εὑρήσει J : εὗροι Y : om. CEQ   7 ἀποδώσει] ἀποσώζει   MN : ἀποδιδότω G   λαμβάνων] λαμβανέτω MNQ   οὗ ἀποσῴζει   scripsi] ὁ ἀποσῴσας ABGJKLOQRSXY : ὁ ἀποσῴζων DMN : ὁ ἀποδώσας   C : ὁ ἀποδοὺς E   τὸ πέμπτον μέρος] ε´ μέρος J   μζ´ Titulus in Σ : ἐν   δὲ τῶ μζ´ κεφαλαίω   1 χρυσὸν ἢ ἄργυρον K   ἢ ἕτερόν τι] om. R.   Post haec verba rursus dat C ἀργύριον   ἐκ βυθοῦ] post ἐπαρθῇ ponunt   MN : ἐκ τοῦ βυθοῦ D : om. E   2 ἐπαρθῇ ... βυθοῦ] ἐπαρθῇ ἀπὸ   ὀργίων ιε´ λαμβανέτω ὁ ἀποσῴζων τὸ ἥμισυ διὰ τὸν κίνδυνον τοῦ βυθοῦ ἢ   δὲ ἀπὸ ὀργίων η´ λαμβανέτω τὸ τρίτον μέρος C   ὀρ(f. 113 r.)γίων C

37

τρίτον μέρος. ἀπὸ δὲ ὀργυιῶν δεκάπεντε, λαμβανέτω
ὁ ἀποσώζων τὸ ἥμισυ διὰ τὸν κίνδυνον τοῦ βυθοῦ.
5 τῶν δὲ ἐκριπτομένων ἀπὸ θαλάσσης εἰς γῆν καὶ εὑρισκομένων ἢ ἐπιφερομένων ἐπὶ πῆχυν ἕνα, λαμβανέτω
ὁ ἀποσώζων δέκατον μέρος τῶν ἀποσωζομένων.

ὀργυιῶν ΑΣ] ὀργύων BLNS : ὀργιῶν GJQY : οὐργυιῶν Κ : ὠργύων Μ : οὐρ-
γιῶν Χ   ὀκτὼ . . . ὀργυιῶν] om. Χ   (f. 36 v.) ὁ ἀποσώζων Μ
τὸ τρίτον . . . ἀποσώζων] om. ENOQR   3 ἀπὸ δὲ] εἰ δὲ ἀπὸ Σ,
praeter a, ubi legitur ἐὰν δὲ ἀπὸ   ὀργυιῶν ΑΣ (praeter p)] ὀργύων
BLS : ὀργιῶν GJΥp : ὠργυιῶν Μ : οὐργυιῶν Κ   4 (f. 35 r.) τὸ ἥμισυ
Β : εἵμισυ Μ : ἥμισυ μέρος Ο   τῶν] τῶ Q   τῶν δὲ] Principium
novi cap. (να') in G et (μη') in ϛ   5 ἐκριπτουμένων Q : ἐκκρυπτομένων
C : ἐγκρυπτομένων Μ   Post ἐκριπτομένων addit ἐκ τοῦ βυθοῦ Χ   ἀπὸ
θαλάσσης . . . ἐπιφερομένων] om. ΜΝ   καὶ εὑρισκ.] ἢ εὑρισκ. R
6 ἢ ἐπιφερομένων] om. DJLY   ἐπὶ πῆχυν ἕνα] ἐπὶ πύχειν ἕνα Q : ἐπὶ
μίαν πῆχυν Κ : ἐπὶ πήχεως ἕνα Χ   7 τὸ δέκατον b   δέκατον μέρος] ι'
μέρη C : δεκάτου μέρους Χ   σωζομένων JMN : σοζωμένων Q

38

APPENDIX A

PRAEFATIO SIVE PARS PRIMA

Praefatio illa cui v. cl. Pardessus secutus partis primae nomen indidi exstat in duobus recensionibus, una breviore et me iudice antiquiore, altera pleniore. Ambas typis exprimendas curavi : codicum varietatem subieci : addidi insuper editionis quam in Iuris Graeco-Romani parte quarta [p. 162] codice Paris. gr. 1720 potissimum fretus dedit v. cl. Zach. von Lingenthal [Z].

Recensio I

Νόμος 'Ροδίων ναυτικὸς ὃν ἐθέσπισαν οἱ θειότατοι αὐτοκράτορες 'Αδριανὸς Τιβέριος Λούκιος Σεπτίμιος Σεύηρος Περτίναξ ἀεισέβαστοι. 5

Τιβέριος καῖσαρ σεβαστὸς ἀρχιερεὺς μέγιστος δημαρχικῆς ἐξουσίας τῷ τριακοστῷ δευτέρῳ λέγει. ἐντυχόντων μοι τῶν ναυτῶν ναυκλήρων καὶ τῶν ἐμπόρων ἵνα τὰ ἐν θαλάσσῃ καὶ

Recensio II

Πρόλογος 'Ροδίου νόμου ἐκτεθεὶς ὑπὸ Τιβερίου βασιλέως.

Τιβέριος καῖσαρ σεβαστὸς ἀρχιερεὺς μέγιστος δημαρχικῆς ἐξουσίας τοῦ τριακοστοῦ δευτέρου λόγου. ἐντυγχανόντων μοι τῶν ναυκλήρων ἵνα τὰ ἐν θαλάσσῃ ζάλης συμβαίνοντα εἰς

Recensionem breviorem dant D, E, M, Q. *Titulus.* 2 θειώτατοι M : θεότατοι Q   3 Σεβῆρος D E, qui τὸν νόμον ut partem τῆς ἐπαναγωγῆς tractat, titulum sequentem habet :—Τίτλος μα´ νόμος 'Ροδίων ναυτικὸς ὃν ἐθέσπισαν οἱ ἀεισέβαστοι βασιλεῖς 'Αντώνιος 'Αδριανὸς Τιβέριος Λούκιος Σεπτίμιος Σεβῆρος καὶ Περτίναξ οἱ αὔγουστοι καὶ αὐτοκράτορες. Πρόλογος. *Textus.* 2 ἀρχιερεὺς] ἀρχηγὸς E   4 λέγειν Q   τῶναυτῶν Q   τῶν ναυκλήρων D   5 τε καὶ ἐμπόρων E   6 ἐν om. E

Recensionem pleniorem dant F, H, P, Z. *Titulus.* 2 ἐκτιθὲν F : ἐκτεθέντος Z   In H titulus est: οὗτος ἐστιν ὁ πρόλογος τοῦ νόμου ῥωδίονος ἐκτεθὲν ὑπὸ Τιβερίου βασιλέως περὶ τῶν πλοίων καὶ λοιπῶν καράβων καὶ ναυτῶν καὶ σχοινίων καὶ ἁρμένων. *Textus.* 1 Τιβέριος . . . λόγου] In P haec verba litteris uncialibus scripta sunt   3 τοῦ τριακοστοῦ δευτέρου λόγου] om. H   4 Post λόγου F addit ἀποκριθεὶς ὁ νέρων εἶπεν   5 τῇ θαλάσσῃ F H Z   6 ζάλῃ P   7 συμβου-

39

ζάλῃ συμβαίνοντα εἰς συμβολὴν
ἐρχέσθωσαν, ἀποκριθεὶς ὁ Νέρων εἶπεν. μέγιστε σοφώτατε
καὶ ἑδραιώτατε καῖσαρ, τὰ ὑπὸ 10
τοῦ σοῦ μεγέθους καθιστάμενα
ἀναγκαῖον ἡγοῦμαι ἐνδείξασθαι,
οὐδὲν διήγημα παραπέμψας,
ἀκριβῶς ἐν Ῥόδῳ ἐπιζητήσας
καὶ ἀναθέμενος τὰς πράξεις τῶν 15
ἐμπλεόντων ναυκλήρων καὶ ἐμπόρων καὶ ἐπιβατῶν, καὶ ἐνθηκῶν καὶ κοινωνιακῶν καὶ πλοίων
ἀγοράσεων καὶ πράσεων, καὶ
ναυπηγικῶν ἐργασίας, παρα- 20
θηκῶν τε χρυσίων καὶ ἀργυρίων
καὶ εἰδῶν διαφόρων. ταῦτα
πάντα ψήφῳ θεματίσας Τιβέριος καῖσαρ σφραγίσας παρέδωκεν Ἀντωνίνῳ φαιδροτάτῳ 25
ὑπάτῳ. ὑπάτοις τοῦτον προφέ-
ρουσιν ἐν τῇ πανευδαίμονι καὶ
κορυφῇ τῶν πόλεων Ῥώμῃ ἐπὶ
ὑπάτων Λαύρου καὶ Ἀγριππίνου

συμβολὴν ἔρχεσθαι, ἀποκριθεὶς
Νηρεὺς εἶπεν. μέγιστε σοφῶν
καὶ ἑδραιώτατε Τιβέριε καῖσαρ,
τὰ ὑπὸ τοῦ σοῦ μεγέθους καθιστάμενα ἀναγκαῖον ἡγοῦμαι ἐνδείξασθαι, οὐδὲν δὲ διήγημα τῶν
ἐμπλεόντων ἐν Ῥόδῳ παρε-
πέμψατο, ἀλλ᾽ ἀκριβῶς ἐπιζητήσας καὶ ἀναθέμενος τὰς
πράξεις τῶν ἐμπλεόντων ναυκλήρων τε καὶ ἐμπόρων καὶ
ἐπιβατῶν, ἐνθηκῶν τε καὶ κοι-
νωνιῶν καὶ πλοίων πράσεων καὶ
ἀγοράσεων καὶ ναυπηγίας καὶ
ναυτῶν ἐργασίας, παραθηκῶν τε
χρυσίου καὶ ἀργυρίου καὶ εἰδῶν
διαφόρων. ταῦτα πάντα τῇ
ψήφῳ θεματίσας Τιβέριος καῖσαρ
σφραγίσας παρέδωκεν Ἀντωνίῳ
φαιδροτάτῳ ὑπάτῳ. ὑπάτοις
τοῦτο προσφέρουσιν ἐν τῇ πανευδαίμονι καὶ κορυφῇ τῶν πόλεων
Ῥώμῃ ἐπὶ ὑπάτων Κλάρου καὶ

καὶ ζάλῃ om. DE   9 σοφόταται Q
10 ἑδραιότατε Q   καῖσαρ] Τιβέριε
ante καῖσαρ inserunt DE   12
ἀναγκαίων Μ   13 διηγήματα DMQ
παραπέμψεις D   14 ῥώδῃ Μ:
ῥόδῃ Q   16 καὶ ἐμπόρων om.
Ε   17 ἐνθηκῶν] ἐθιακῶν D   ἐνθηκῶν
τε καὶ, sed τε supra lineam Q   18
κοινωνικῶν Ε   19 ἀγωράσεων Q   20
ναυ . . . τῶν Q   Post ἐργασίας MQ
addunt τὸ   παραθίκων Μ   21 χρυσίον Μ: χρυσίου Q   ἀργυρίον Μ:
ἀργυρίου Q   23 ψήφω θεματήσας Μ:
ψηφοθεματήσας D   24 σφραγίσας]
σφραγίσας τε Ε: om. Μ   παρέδωκεν
ante Τιβέριος ponit Μ   25 Ἀν-
τωνίω Ε   φεδρωτάτω Μ   26
προσφέρουσιν Q   29 ὑπάτω λαύρου

λὴν F   ἀποκριθεὶς . . . εἶπεν] om.
FH   8 Νηρεὺς] ὁ Νέρων Ζ   Post
εἶπεν in P reperitur signum ⟋, et
in margine ὁ νέρων   9 ἑδραιότατε
P: ἀνδρειότατε FZ   10 καθιστάμενα
. . . ἐμπλεόντων] addit in margine
F   12 οὐδὲν δὲ] οὐδένα δὲ P:
οὐδὲ FHZ   διηγημάτων ἐνπλεόν-
των HP   17 ἐμπόρων] εὐπόρων P
18 ἐνθηκῶν] ἐθνικῶν F: ἐθνηκῶν Η
19 πλοίων τε καὶ πράσεων P
πράσεων τε καὶ ἀγ. FHZ   20
καὶ ναυπηγίας] ναυπηγίας FHZ   ναυπηγίας τε καὶ Η   23 ταῦτα]
αὐτὰ Z   25 Ἀντωνίῳ] ἀντωνίνω
FH: ἀνθρωπίνω Ζ   26 φαιδρο-
τάτω om. Η   Punctum post
ὑπάτοις ponit Η   27 ἐν om. P

φαιδροτάτων. οὗτοι προσή- ³⁰ Ἀγριππίνου φαιδροτάτων. οὗτοι
νεγκαν μεγίστῳ καὶ αὐτοκράτορι προσήνεγκαν τῷ μεγίστῳ καὶ
Οὐεσπασιανῷ, καὶ σφραγίσας αὐτοκράτορι Οὐεσπασιανῷ τῷ
ἐπὶ τῆς λαμπρᾶς συγκλήτου βασιλεῖ, καὶ σφραγίσας ἐπὶ
Οὔλπιος Τραϊανὸς ἀπέλυσεν τῆς λαμπροτάτης συγκλήτου
εἶναι τὸν νόμον τὸν Ῥόδιον ἅμα 35 ἀπέλυσεν. Οὔλπιος Τραϊανὸς
καὶ φαιδροτάτης συγκλήτου. ὁ ὁ βασιλεὺς ἅμα καὶ τῇ φαιδρο-
δὲ νόμος τῆς θαλάσσης τῷ νόμῳ τάτῃ συγκλήτῳ σφραγίσαντες
κρινέσθω τῷ ναυτικῷ, τὸ δ' αὐτὸ ἀπέλυσαν. Νηρεὺς ὁ βασιλεὺς
καὶ ὁ θεῖος Αὔγουστος ἔκρινεν. σφραγίσας ἀπέλυσεν. αὐτο-
40 κράτωρ Ἀδριανὸς ἐπὶ ὑπάτων
Κλάρου καὶ Ἀλεξάνδρου σφραγίσας ἀπέλυσεν, εἶναι τὸν Ῥόδιον νόμον δίκαιον καὶ ἐπίκρισιν
ἔχοντα. Τιβέριος καῖσαρ εἶπεν,
45 οὐδένα μείζονα κίνδυνον εἶναι
λέγω, τῆς καταρτίου αὐτομάτως
ἐκβεβλημένης, εἰς συμβολὴν
ἔρχεσθαι. ἐὰν δὲ καὶ ἀνάγκη,
ὁ πρωρεὺς καὶ ὁ ναυπηγὸς τὰ
50 σίδηρα προσφερέτωσαν, καὶ
κοπτέτωσαν τὴν κατάρτιον ἵνα
τὸ πλοῖον μὴ καταποντισθῇ, καὶ
ταῦτα εἰς συμβολὴν ἐρχέσθω.

Q 30 φαιδρωτάτων M 32
Οὐεσπασιανοῦ DM Post Οὐεσπ. Q
addit supra lineam τῷ βασιλεῖ
34 Τραινὸς M 35 ῥώδιον M
ἅμα καὶ φαιδρ. συγκ.] ἅμα καὶ φαιδρο-
τάτου συγκλήτῳ M: ἅμα καὶ φεδρο-
τάτης συγκλήτῳ Q: ἅμα τῇ φαιδρο-
τάτῃ συγκλήτῳ D 38 κρινέτω
E τὸ αὐτὸ δὲ E 39 In Q post
ἔκρινεν addidit recentior manus
Π(?)ιρεῦς ὁ βασιλεὺς σφραγίσας ἀπέλυσεν. αὐτοκράτωρ Ἀδριανὸς ἐπὶ
ὑπάτων Κλαύρου καὶ Ἀλεξάνδρου
σφραγίσας ἀπέλυσεν εἶναι τὸν Ῥώδιον
νόμον δίκαιον καὶ ἐπίκρισιν ἔχοντα.

29 Κλαύρου FHZ 31 προσήγα-
γον FHZ 32 οὐασπασιανῶ P
(f. 113 v.) τῷ βασιλεῖ P τῷ om.
Z 33 σφραγήσας P 36 σφρ.
ἀπ. ἅ. κ. τ. φαιδ. συγκ. P 38
νιρεὺς FHZ 39 καὶ αὐτὸς σφραγίσας H 40 Ἀδριανὸς] Τραϊανὸς
P 41 κλαύρου FHZ 44 εἶπεν
om. FHZ 47 ἐκβεβλημένοις P
βολὴν P 49 ὁ ναυπηγὸς FHZ]
ναυπηγὸς P 51 τὸν κατάρτιον FZ :
τὴν κατάρτησιν H 52 μὴ τὸ πλοῖον
FZ 53 ἔρχεσθαι P : ἐρχέσθωσαν
FHZ

41

ΝΟΜΟΣ ΡΟΔΙΩΝ ΝΑΥΤΙΚΟΣ

APPENDIX B

INDEX PARTIS SECUNDAE

In quattuor codicibus (B, D, v, Harl.) indicem partis secundae repperi, quem ex codice B edo, addita varietate codicis D :—

περὶ ναυκλήρου μισθοῦ. περὶ κυβέρνου μισθοῦ.
περὶ προρέως μισθοῦ. περὶ ναυπηγοῦ μισθοῦ.
περὶ καραβίτου μισθοῦ. περὶ ναυτῶν μισθῶν.
περὶ παρασχαρίτου μισθοῦ. περὶ ἐμπόρου μισθοῦ.
περὶ ἐπιβατῶν. περὶ ἐπιβάτου ἰχθὺν μὴ τιγανίζειν.   5
περὶ ἐπιβάτου ξύλον ἐπὶ πλοίου μὴ σκιζέτω.
περὶ ἐπιβάτου μέτρον ἐν πλοίῳ λαμβανέτω.
περὶ γυναικὸς ἐν πλοίῳ. περὶ ἐπιβάτου παραθήκης.
περὶ ὅρκου ἀπαραιτήτου. περὶ τιμῆς πλοίῳ ῥοδίου.
περὶ δανίου ἐπὶ γῆς. περὶ ἐπιβατῶν καὶ ἐμπόρων.   10
περὶ ναυκλήρων καὶ ναυτῶν.

Varia lectio codicis D.   1 κυβερνήτου   3 περὶ ναυτῶν μισθῶν
om.   4 περὶ παρασχαρίτου μισθοῦ om.   5 ἰχθὺν om.   Post
τιγανίζειν addit ἐν πλοίῳ   6 ξύλον ... σκιζέτω] μὴ σχίζειν ἐν πλοίῳ
ξύλον   7 μέτρον ... λαμβανέτω] ἐν πλοίῳ μέτρον λαμβάνειν   8
παρακαταθήκης   10 καὶ om.

APPENDIX C

INDICES PARTIUM III ET II SECUNDUM M

Codex M (f. 1 r.) dat sequentem indicem partis tertiae :—

Κεφάλαια

α′ περὶ τοῦ ἐὰν πλοῖον ὁρμῇ ἐπὶ λημένα ἐν ἡμέρᾳ ἢ ἐν νυκτῇ.
β′ „ „ ἐὰν βουλήσει τοῦ ναυκλήρου οἱ ναῦται.
γ′ „ „ ἐὰν ναύτης κελεύσει τοῦ ναυκλήρου.
δ′ „ „ ἐὰν δέ τις κλέψει σκεύη πλοίου.
έ „ „ ἐὰν ναύτης αὐτοβούλως συλήσει.
ϛ′ „ „ ἐὰν ἐν τόπῳ συλημένῳ ἢ λιστευομένῳ.
ζ′ „ „ ἐὰν τοῦ ναυκλήρου ἀπομαρτυρομένου.

42

η′ περὶ τοῦ ἐὰν ναῦται μάχην ποιήσωσιν.
θ′ „ „ ἐὰν ναῦται μάχην ποιήσωσιν.
ι′ „ „ ἐάν τις τῶν ναυκλήρων ἢ ἐμπόρων.
ια′ „ „ ἐὰν πλεύσει ὁ ναύκληρος πιστευθείς.
ιβ′ „ „ ἐὰν περὶ ἐκβολῆς βουλεύσηται.
ιγ′ „ „ ἐὰν ναύκληρος ἅμα τοῖς συνναύταις.
ιδ′ „ „ ἐὰν φορτία μεγάλα καὶ πολύτιμα.
ιε′ „ „ ἐὰν ἔχει τὸ πλοῖον πᾶσαν τὴν ἐπιχειρίαν.
ιϛ′ „ „ ἐάν τις παραθεῖται ἐν πλοίῳ.
ιζ′ „ „ ἐὰν δὲ εἰσέλθει ἐπιβάτης ἐν πλοίῳ.
ιη′ „ „ ἐάν τις δεξάμενος παραθήκην.
ιθ′ „ „ ἐὰν πλοῖον φέρει ἐπιβάτας.
κ′ „ „ οἱ ναύκληροι καὶ οἱ ἔμποροι ὅσοι.
κα′ „ „ ἐὰν δέ τις δόσει ἐπὶ χρέει κοινωνίας.
κβ′ „ „ ἐὰν δὲ τοῦ χρόνου τῶν συνθηκῶν.
κγ′ „ „ ἐάν τις χρήματα χρησάμενος.
κδ′ „ „ ἐὰν πλοῖον ναυλώσεταί τις.
κε′ „ „ ὃς ἂν ναυλήσεται πλοῖον ἐγγράφως.
κϛ′ „ „ ἐὰν κοινωνίαν ποιήσωσιν ἐγγράφως.
κζ′ „ „ ἐὰν τὸ ἓν πλοῖον συμβῇ τι παθεῖν.
κη′ „ „ ὁ ναύκληρος μὴ ἀγαγέτω πλεῖν ὕδατος.
κθ′ „ „ ἐὰν συγγράψονται ὁ ναύκληρος καὶ οἱ.
λ′ „ „ ἐὰν ὁ ναύκληρος λαβὼν τὰ εἴμισυ ναῦλα.
λα′ „ „ ἐὰν ἡ προθεσμία τῶν ἡμερῶν.
λβ „ „ ἐὰν δὲ παρέλθη καὶ δευτέρα προθεσμία.
λγ′ „ „ ἐάν τινος τῶν ναυτῶν ἢ ναυκλήρων.
λδ′ „ „ ἐὰν πλοῖον ἀπέρχηται εἰς γόμων.
λε′ „ „ ἐὰν πλοῖον ἐν τῇ ἐκβολῇ ἐμποδισθῇ.
λϛ′ „ „ ἐὰν ὁ ἔμπορος ἔνθα συγγράψωνται.
λζ′ „ „ ἐὰν ὁ ἔμπορος φορτώσας τὸ πλοῖον.
λη′ „ „ ἐὰν ὁ ἔμπορος φορτώσει πλοῖον.
λθ′ „ „ ἐὰν πλοῖον ἐπὶ γόμων ὑπάγη.
μ′ „ „ ἐὰν ὁ ναύκληρος θεὶς τὰ φορτία.
μα′ „ „ ἐὰν πλοῖον ὀθώνην ἢ βέστην κομίζει.
μβ′ „ „ ἐὰν πλοῖον ἐκβολὴν ποιήσηται.
μγ′ „ „ ἐὰν πλοῖον ἀρμενίζον ἔλθη ἐπάνω.
μδ′ „ „ ἐάν τι πάθει τὸ πλοῖον καὶ σωθῇ.

43

ΝΟΜΟΣ ΡΟΔΙΩΝ ΝΑΥΤΙΚΟΣ

με΄ περὶ τοῦ ἐὰν πλοῖον πεφορτομένον σίτου.

μϛ΄ ,, ,, ἐὰν πλοῖον μεστὸν σίτου ἢ οἴνου.

μζ΄ ,, ,, ἐὰν πλοῖον συμβῇ ναυάγιον παθεῖν.

μη΄ ,, ,, ἐὰν πλέωσιν ἐν πλοίῳ ἐπιβάται.

μθ΄ ,, ,, ἐὰν πλοῖον τρυπήσει φορτία.

ν΄ ,, ,, ἐὰν πλοῖον ἐπὶ χειμόνι κατά.

να΄ ,, ,, ἐὰν πλοῖον ἔχει γόμων.

νβ΄ ,, ,, ἐὰν ἐν πελάγη πλοῖον στραφῇ.

νγ΄ ,, ,, ἐὰν κάραβος ἀπὸ ἰδίου πλοίου.

νδ΄ ,, ,, ἐὰν χρυσίον ἢ ἀργύριον.

(f. 1 v.) ἐκ τοῦ β΄ βιβλίου τιτλ‧ ια΄ τοῦ κώδικος.

α΄ περὶ τοῦ ὁ ἁρπάζων τι ἀπὸ ναυκλήρου.

β΄ περὶ τοῦ ὁ ἰδικὸν φορτίον ἐπιθεὶς τῶ.

ἐκ τοῦ θ΄ τ τ μζ΄ β τῶν διγέστων.

γ΄ περὶ τοῦ ἐκ τῆς σεληνώτητος τῶν ναυαγ.
στάσις τοῦ ν΄ διατάγματος περὶ δούλου μισθίου.

δ΄ περὶ τοῦ ἐὰν δοῦλος ὑπὸ τοῦ ἰδίου δεσπότου.
ἐκ τοῦ μ΄ διατάγματος ἐλευθέρου μισθουμένου ἑαυτόν.

ε΄ περὶ τοῦ ἐάν τις ἐλεύθερος ἑαυτόν.
περὶ πλοίου διαστραφέντος ἢ φθαρέντος.

ϛ΄ περὶ ἀποσώζοντος ἀπὸ πελάγους.
στάσις τοῦ χ΄ διατάγματος.
περὶ πλοῖον δωθέντος εἰς ναύκληρον ἐκπλεῦσαι.

ζ΄ περὶ τοῦ ἐὰν ὁ ναύκληρος πιστευθείς.

η΄ περὶ τοῦ ἐὰν ναύκληρος μὴ δυνάμενος.

θ΄ περὶ τοῦ ἐὰν πλοῖον ναυαγήσει.

ι΄ περὶ τοῦ πλοίου ναυαγήσαντος.

Index partis secundae reperitur f. 21 r. : -

μβ΄ περὶ νόμων ῥοδίων ναυτικῶν ὃν ἐθέσπισαν οἱ θειώτατοι αὐτοκράτορες ἀδριανὸς τιβέριος λούκιος σεπτίμιος σεύηρος πέρτιναξ ἀεισέβαστοι.

α΄ περὶ τιβέριος κέσαρ σέβαστος.
περὶ ἐπιβατῶν ἐν πλοίῳ.

α΄ περὶ ἐὰν ἔλθη ἐπιβάτης ἐν πλοίῳ.
περὶ ὅρκου καὶ ἀπαραιτήτου.

APPENDIX C

β′ περὶ ὁ ναύκληρος καὶ οἱ ἐπιβάται καὶ οἱ ναῦται.

  περὶ τιμῆς πλοίου ῥωδίου.

γ′ περὶ εἶναι τὴν χιλιάδα τοῦ μοδισμοῦ.

  περὶ δανείων θαλασσίων.

δ′ περὶ ὁ νόμος κελεύει τὰ ἐν τῇ θαλάσσῃ.

ε′ περὶ ἐὰν δανήσει ἐν τόκοις.

  περὶ ναυκλήρων καὶ ναυτῶν.

α′ περὶ οἱ ναύκληροι ναυκληροῦντες.

β′ περὶ ἐὰν δὲ πρόσχρειαν δόσει.

APPENDIX D

QUATTUOR CAPITULA CODICUM FH

Quattuor capitula quae hic edo primus publicavit Pardessus (t. 1, p. 258) codice Paris. gr. 1720 usus, ubi locum habent post partem tertiam τοῦ νόμου et ante tria capitula quae in Appendice E dedi ; mox ex eodem codice publicavit Zachariae in parte quarta Iuris Graeco-Romani, p. 169. Cum ea capitula in F (f. 205 v.–206 v.) et in H (f. 111) invenissem, hos codices quasi fundamenta mei textus posui ; eorum et textus Zachariani (Z) varietatem addidi.

I. ἐὰν ναύτης ἀποτακτάρις ᾖ μερίτης, δεξάμενος μετὰ συνθηκῶν μέρος, πᾶσαν ἐπιταγὴν τοῦ πλοίου ποιεῖν καὶ τοῦ καιροῦ πληρουμένου ἐξὸν κατέρχεσθαι. ἐὰν δὲ θελήσῃ τοῦ καιροῦ μὴ πληρωθέντος ἐξελθεῖν, λαμβανέτω ξυλαγώγια ο′ καὶ οὕτως αὐτὸν πλέειν· εἰ δὲ εὑρεθῇ κλέπτων, λαμβάνειν αὐτὸν ξυλαγώγια ρ′ καὶ τὸ μέρος 5 ἀπολλέτω.

II. ἐὰν ναύτης πεμφθεὶς παρὰ τοῦ ναυκλήρου ἐπὶ ξύλα ἢ ἀλλαχοῦ ὅπου ἂν συνέλθῃ καὶ παραλειφθῇ, ὁ ναύκληρος διαλυέσθω. ἐὰν μὴ συνέρχηται, ἐὰν νεώτερον γένηται κατὰ τοῦ πεμφθέντος, ὁ ναύκληρος διαλυέσθω.

I. 1 ναύτις F   ᾖ scripsi] ἢ FHZ   2 ποιεῖν FH] ποιεῖ Z
πληρωμένου H   3 ἐξὸν F   ἐὰν δὲ] ἐὰν H   θελήσῃ post πληρωθέντος
ponit H   5 λαμβάνειν αὐτὸν] λαμβανέτω H   μέρος] μέρος αὐτοῦ
H   6 ἀπολλέτω H] ἀπολείτω Z : ἀποβαλλέτω F   II. 1 πεμφθεὶς FH]
πεμφθῇ Z   2 ἂν] ἐὰν F   συνέλθῃ H] συνερχέσθω FZ   παραλειφθῇ

ΝΟΜΟΣ ΡΟΔΙΩΝ ΝΑΥΤΙΚΟΣ

III. ἐὰν ναύτης ἑαυτομίσθωτος γενόμενος γινωσκέτω ἑαυτὸν
δοῦλον εἶναι καὶ ἑαυτὸν πεπρακέναι, πᾶσαν δὲ ἐπιταγὴν αὐτὸν
ποιεῖν. καὶ πιστῶς ἐκπεμπόμενος ἐκτελείτω ἀκλόπως ἀκακουρ-
γήτως καὶ σπουδῇ πάσῃ εὐνοῶν ἀξίως, εἰς πλῆρες τὰς ἐπιμισθίας
5 κομιζόμενος. ἐὰν δὲ σύλα ποιήσῃ χρυσίου ἢ ἀργυρίου, ἀπολέσας
τὴν ἐλευθερίαν καὶ μίσθωσιν δοῦλος γενέσθω ἑαυτὸν παραδόσας
εἰς τιμωρίαν.

IV. ἐὰν δοῦλος ὑπὸ τοῦ ἰδίου δεσπότου μισθωθῇ εἰς ἐργαστήριον ἢ εἰς ἐργασίαν, λεγέτω ὁ κύριος αὐτοῦ τὰ τῆς πίστεως αὐτοῦ·
ἐὰν δὲ μὴ εἴπῃ καὶ ὁ δοῦλος σύλα ποιήσῃ καὶ ἀποδράσῃ, τῷ ἰδίῳ
δεσπότῃ καὶ αὐτὰ τὰ σύλα καὶ ἡ φυγὴ καὶ ὁ θάνατος διὰ τοῦ
5 μισθοῦ αὐτοῦ ἐκδιδόσθω.

Η] παρελείφθη F: παρελήφθη Z   διαλυέσθω] διαλασσέσθω F   Post διαλυέσθω punctum ponit Z   συνέρχηται] συνέρχεται FHZ   Post συνέρχεται punctum ponunt FH   3 νεώτερον scripsi] νεώτερος FHZ   4 Post
διαλυέσθω addit H : ἐὰν δέ τις τῶν πεμφθέντων ἀποθάνει, ὁ ναύκληρος θαπτέτω
αὐτὸν τελέσμασι τοῖς αὐτοῦ   III. Hoc capitulum in M forma breviore
repertum dedi in Appendice F   1 γενόμενος] γένηται H   γινωσκέτω H] γινωσκέτο F : γινώσκη τὸ Z   3 ἐκτελείστο F   ἀκακοργήτως
F   4 πάσῃ σπουδῇ Z   5 καὶ αὐτὸς κομιζόμενος H   χρυσίου ἢ ἀργυρίου,
ἀπολέσας τὴν ἐλευθερίαν καὶ μίσθωσιν] χρυσίον ἢ ἀργύριον ἀπολέσας ἃ
ἣν ἐλευθερίαν μάθωσιν F : ἢ χρυσίον ἢ ἀργύριον ἐλευθερίαν μίσθωσιν H :
χρυσίον ἢ ἀργύριον ἀπολέσας, ἀντὶ τὴν ἐλευθερίαν μίσθωσιν Z   Vide
textum codicis M   6 ὡς ἑαυτὸν H   IV. Etiam hoc cap. in
M repertum in Appendice F dedi   1 μιστοθῇ F   2 ἢ εἰς ἐργασίαν H]
om. FZ   3 εἴπῃ καὶ H] εἴποι F: εἴπερ Z   4 καὶ αὐτὰ τὰ σύλα FZ] om.
Η   5 μισθοῦ αὐτοῦ FH] μισθώσαντος αὐτὸν Z

APPENDIX E

TRIA CAPITULA

Post partem tertiam multi codices haec capitula ex-
hibent:—

48. ὁ ἁρπάζων τι ἐκ τῶν ναυκλήρων τὸ τετραπλάσιον ἀποδιδότω.

49. ὁ ἰδιωτικὸν φορτίον ἐπιτιθεὶς τῷ δημοσίῳ καὶ ἀναγκάζων

Addo variam lectionem codicum CDEJLMNOQRTXY. Continent
tria capitula etiam H, Par. gr. 1391, Harl. Capitula 48 et 50 praebet
F, 49 et 50 V et Laud., 50 tantum f.   48. Titulum praebent τοῦ β′
τίτλου ια′ βιβλίου τοῦ κώδικος JR : τοῦ β′ τ τοῦ ια′ βιβλίου τοῦ κώδικος X :

46

ἐπὶ τοῦτο τὸν ναύκληρον μὴ μόνον ζημιούσθω καὶ ἐπὶ τῷ ναυαγίῳ κινδυνευέτω ἀλλὰ καὶ αὐστηρῶς τιμωρείσθω.

50. οἱ ἐκ τῆς ἐλεεινοτάτης τῶν ναυαγησάντων ὑποστάσεως ἁρπάζοντες τὸ εἰτιοῦν ἢ κερδαίνοντες κατὰ δόλον πονηρὸν τὸ τετραπλοῦν τοῖς ἀδικηθεῖσι παρεχέτωσαν· ὁ δὲ βαρυτέρα πρέδᾳ καὶ βίᾳ ἀφέλομενος πράγματα ἀπὸ ναυαγίου μετὰ τὴν τούτων ἀποκατάστασιν, εἰ μὲν ἐλεύθερός ἐστιν, ἐξορίζεται ἐπὶ τριετῆ χρόνον, εἰ 5 δὲ ῥυπαροί τινές εἰσιν, εἰς ἔργον δημόσιον ἐμβάλλονται τὴν αὐτὴν ἐγχρονίαν, εἰ δὲ δοῦλοί εἰσιν, εἰς βαρύτερον ἔργον τοῦ φίσκου ὁμοίως ἐκπέμπονται.

τοῦ β′ τίτλου βιβλίου ια′ τοῦ κώδικος Ο : ἐκ τοῦ β′ βιβλίου τίτλου ια′ τοῦ κώδικος ΜΝ   Capitulum omittunt ΡΤ   1 ἐκ τῶν] ἀπὸ ΜΝ   τὸ om. CX   49. Titulum praebent τοῦ ε′ τίτλου τοῦ κώδικος J : τοῦ ε′ τίτλου τοῦ αὐτοῦ Ν : ἐκ τοῦ ε′ τίτλου τοῦ αὐτοῦ Ο   1 ἰδικὸν ΜΝQ   φόρτον R ἐπιθεὶς DJMNY : θεὶς Ε   καὶ] om. Μ   συναναγκάζων Ε   2 τούτου Ν καὶ ἐπὶ . . . κινδυνευέτω] κἂν ὑπὸ τοῦ ναυαγίου κινδυνευόμενον Υ : om. Q τὸ ναυάγιον ΜΝΟΡΤ : τῶν ναυαγίων C   3 αὐστηρῶς] αὐτὸς στερρῶς CQ : αὐτὸς μᾶλλον στερρῶς Ε   τιμωρείτω C   50. Titulum praebent τοῦ θ′ τίτλου μζ′ βιβλίου τῶν διγέστων J : ἐκ τοῦ θ′ τίτλου τοῦ μζ′ βιβλίου τῶν διγέστων ΝΟ : ἐκ τοῦ θ′ τ τῶν μβ′ β τ ῶν διγέστων Χ : ἐκ τοῦ ἐνάτου βιβλίου μζ′ βιβλίου τῶν διγέστων R   Hoc cap. in Ν legi non potest   1 οἱ] εἰ C ἐλεινότητος CE : σεληνότητος Μ   ὑποστάσεων C : ὑπόστασιν ΕΜQΧ   2 τὸ εἰτιοῦν] εἴτιουν Τ : τὸ οἱονουν R : τὴν οἱανουν Ε   ἢ κερδαίνοντες . . . πονηρὸν] om. Μ   ἢ κερδ.] οἱ κερδ. Χ   τὸ τετραπλοῦν] τὸ τετραπλάσιον Υ : τετραπλάσιον D   3 παρέχουσιν Ε   ὁ δὲ] εἰ δὲ Μ : ὁ CQX   Cum ὁ βαρ. πρ. incipit novum cap. (να′) Χ   πραιδαν Τ   4 βίαν CT ἀφελόμενος . . . ναυαγίου] ἐργασάμενος καί τι ἀπὸ ναυαγίου λαμβάνων Τ ναβαγίου Q : τοῦ ναυαγίου Χ   5 ἐλεύθεροι QΥ   εἰσινΥ   ἐξωρίζονται Υ   τριετεῖ χρόνω Τ   εἰ δὲ ῥυπαροί . . . ἐγχρονίαν] om. O   εἰ δὲ] οἱ δὲ JMX   6 δημοσίου ΕΜ   ἐμβάλλονται . . . ἐγχρονίαν] ἐκβάλλονται ἐπὶ ἐνιαυτω Τ   7 ἔγχρονοι Μ   εἰ δὲ] οἱ δὲ JXY   δοῦλός ἐστιν Ο   εἰς βαρύτερον . . . ἐκπέμπονται] τῷ φίσκω ἐκπέμπονται Τ εἰς] om. J   βαρύτεροι Q   φίσκου] δημοσίου DY   8 ὁμοίως] om. OX ἐκπέμπεται Ο   L addit τέλος νόμου Ῥοδίωνος

APPENDIX F

CAPITULA IN Μ ΕΤ Ν PARTI TERTIAE ADDITA

Post tria capitula quae in Appendice E dedi, Μ ita subsequitur (fol. 36 v.) :—

Στάσις τοῦ ν′ διατάγματος περὶ δούλου μισθίου.

δ′ ἐὰν δοῦλος ὑπὸ τοῦ ἰδίου δεσπότου μισθωθῇ εἰς ἐργαστήριον

47

ΝΟΜΟΣ ΡΟΔΙΩΝ ΝΑΥΤΙΚΟΣ

ἢ εἰς ἐργασίαν, λεγέτω ὁ κύριος αὐτοῦ τὰ τῆς πίστεως αὐτοῦ. ἐὰν δὲ μὴ εἴπῃ καὶ ὁ δοῦλος σύλα ποιήσῃ καὶ ἀποδράσῃ, τῷ ἰδίῳ δεσπότῃ αὐτὰ τὰ σύλα καὶ ἡ φυγὴ καὶ ὁ θάνατος διὰ τοῦ μισθοῦ αὐτοῦ ἐκδιδόσθαι.

Ἐκ τοῦ μ΄ διατάγματος ἐλευθέρου μισθουμένου ἑαυτοῦ.

ε΄ ἐάν τις ἐλεύθερος ἑαυτὸν μισθώσῃ, πιστὰ τηρείτω γνοὺς ἑαυτὸν εἰς δοῦλον παραδόντα. ἐὰν δὲ σύλα ποιήσει χρυσίου ἢ ἀργυρίου, ἀπολέσας τὴν ἐλευθερίαν καὶ μίσθωσιν δοῦλος γενέσθω ἑαυτὸν παραδόσας εἰς τιμωρίαν.

Περὶ πλοίου διαφθαρέντος (f. 37 r.) ἢ στραφέντος.

ϛ΄ τοῦ ἀποσώζοντος ἀπὸ πελάγου εἰς γῆν πλοῖον καὶ τῶν εὑρισκομένων ἐν τῷ πλοίῳ λαμβανέτω πέμπτα.

Στάσις τοῦ χ΄ διατάγματος περὶ πλοίου δωθέντος πρὸς ναύκληρον ἐμπλεῦσαι.

ζ΄ ἐὰν ὁ ναύκληρος πιστευθεὶς πλοῖον εἰς ἄλλην χώραν ἀποδράσῃ μετὰ χρυσίου βουλήσει τῶν ναυτῶν, τὰς μὲν οἰκίας αὐτῶν ἅμα γυναιξὶ καὶ τέκνοις, κινητοῖς τε καὶ ἀκινήτοις, πάντα ὅσα ὑπάρχει αὐτοῖς κατασχεθήσονται. καὶ ἐὰν μὴ τὸ εἰκανὸν ποιήσωσιν τοῦ πλοίου καὶ τῆς ἐργασίας τοῦ χρόνου, τὰ κατεχόμενα ἐν πράσῃ διατιμείσθωσαν, οἱ δὲ ναῦται ἅμα τῷ προναυκλήρῳ τιμωρείᾳ ὑποκείσθωσαν θανάτου. εἰ δὲ βουληθῇ ὁ κύριος τοῦ πλοίου παρακληθεὶς τὴν τιμωρείαν συγχωρῆσαι, δούλους ἰδίους ἀργυρονήτους ἐπιγραφέτωσαν. ἐὰν δὲ εἴπωσιν οἱ ναῦται, οὐ βουλήσει ἡμετέρᾳ ἀπεδράσαμεν, διὰ τὸ συγχωρῆσαι τῷ ναυκλήρῳ, ὑπεύθυνοί εἰσι τῷ δικαστηρίῳ.

η΄ ἐὰν ὁ ναύκληρος μὴ δυνάμενος εἰσελθεῖν ἐν τῷ λιμένι μεταγάγει τὰ φορτία εἰς πλοῖόν σου καὶ ναυαγήσει τὸ σόν, ἐνέχεται ὁ πρῶτος ναύκληρος ἐὰν παρὰ γνώμην τῶν δεσποτῶν τὰ φορτία μετήγαγεν ἢ παρὰ καίρων ἢ εἰς ἀνεπιτίδιον πλοῖον. ἡ δὲ μὴ ἐποίησε ῥαθυμίᾳ, οὐκ ἐνέχεται.

θ΄ ἐὰν πλοῖον ναυαγήσῃ διὰ τὸ μὴ ἔχειν κυβερνήτην, ἐνέχεται τοῖς ἐπιβάταις ὁ ναύκληρος.

ι΄ τοῦ πλοίου ναυαγήσαντος ὁ ναύκληρος ἀποδίδοσι τὰ ναῦλα ἅπερ ἔλαβεν ἐν προχρείᾳ ὡς μὴ μετακομήσας.

N sicut iam dixi tria capitula continet quae in Appendice E dedi, quorum ultimum f. 83 r. terminat. Pars superior f. 83 v. legi nequit. Legibilis fit pagina inde a verbis ἀπὸ

48

APPENDIX F

πελάγου capituli eius cui in M numerus ϛ΄ adicitur. Sequitur capitulum cui in M numerus ζ΄ adicitur. Cum verbis eius capituli ἐὰν δὲ εἴπωσιν οἱ ναῦται pagina finem habet. Perpaucis locis discrepat N a textu quem dat M. In ϛ΄ N legit εἰς τὴν γῆν et πέμπτας. In titulo capituli ζ΄ N legit προναυκλήρω pro πρὸς ναύκληρον et in textu eiusdem capituli τὸν ἱκανὸν pro τὸ εἰκανὸν; πράσει pro πράση; τιμωρία et τιμωρίαν pro τιμωρεία et τιμωρείαν.

APPENDIX G

CAPITULA QUAE IN B ET EIUS SEQUELA INVENIUNTUR

Post capitulum 47 partis tertiae B capitula sequentia exhibet quae cum ad legem Rhodiam nullo modo pertineant et ex aliis fontibus iamdudum nota sint, ego verba prima et ultima solummodo indico. Addo insuper locos apud Synopsim Ambrosianam (= FM), Synopsim Francisci Venturii (= Vent.) et Synopsim maiorem in editione Pardessiana (= Pard.), ubi eadem capitula inveniuntur.

(a) ἐὰν διὰ τὸ κουφισθῆναι . . . ἀποθεραπεύεται τὸ ῥιφθέν (Bas. LIII, Γ, α΄ apud FM p. 101; Vent. p. 182; Pard. p. 187).

(b) κοινοποιεῖται γὰρ ἡ ζημία . . . ὁ μισθωσάμενος αὐτὸ (αὐτῶν B) ζημιοῦται (idem cap. apud FM p. 101; Vent. p. 182).

(c) ση. τὸ αὐτὸ καὶ ὅτε ἀναρυσθῇ παρὰ τῶν πηρατῶν . . . οὐ χώρα τῇ κοντριβυτίονῃ (Bas. LIII, Γ, β΄ apud FM p. 102; Vent. p. 182).

(d) ἐν τῇ κοντριβυτίονῃ τὰ μὲν ἀποβληθέντα . . . ἀποτίμονται (Bas. LIII, Γ, γ΄, apud FM p. 102; Vent. p. 183; Pard. p. 187).

(e) ἐὰν τὰ σωθέντα φορτία . . . τὴν ἁρμόζουσαν κοντριβουτίονα (Bas. LIII, Γ, ια΄, apud FM p. 102, ubi adicitur πλεονάζοντα τὴν ζημίαν, Vent. p. 183).

ΝΟΜΟΣ ΡΟΔΙΩΝ ΝΑΥΤΙΚΟΣ

(*f*) ἀπολλομένου τοῦ πλοίου . . . ἀποβληθῶσιν (Bas. LIII,
Γ, ιβ′ apud FM p. 102; Vent. p. 183; Pard. p. 187, ubi
quaedam adduntur).

(*g*) (f. 35 v.) τοῦ πλοίου ναυαγήσαντος . . . ὡς μὴ μετακόμισας
(Bas. LIII, Α, νθ′ apud FM p. 98; Vent. p. 181; Epanagoge
ΚΔ, θ′; Epit. Seldeniana, f. 78 v.).

(*h*) ὁ ναύλαρχος ἐντὸς ἐνιαυτοῦ μὴ ἀποδείξας τὸ συμβὰν αὐτὸ
(legendum αὐτῷ) ναυάγιον οὐδὲν ἐκ τῶν μετὰ ταῦτα προσενε-
χθεισῶν βασιλεῖ δεήσεων ὀφελεθήσεται (Bas. LIII, Δ, 38 apud
Vent. p. 184 forma tamen expeditiore. Confer etiam Ῥοπαὶ
24, 37).

Eadem capitula apud G et H inveniuntur, paucis admodum mutatis. In G numeris νβ′–νζ′ distinguuntur, cum
ea capitula quae ego (*a*) (*b*) (*c*) numeravi in G uno eo-
demque numero (νβ′) insigniantur. Inveniuntur etiam apud
K cum multis aliis de quibus videas Appendicem H.

APPENDIX H

CAPITULA QUAE IN K INVENIUNTUR

In codice K τὸν νόμον praecedunt et sequuntur multa
capitula quae ex libro LIII Basilicorum hausta sunt.
Titulus hic est (f. 206 r.):—

Τίτλος ν′ περὶ ναυκλήρων καὶ πιστικῶν καὶ ναυτῶν καὶ πανδοχέων καὶ τῆς κατ᾽ αὐτῶν καὶ ὑπὲρ αὐτῶν ἀγωγῆς (= Bas. LIII,
Α, titulus, FM p. 96; Vent. p. 180; Pard. p. 183).

Sequuntur capitula:—

(*a*) τὰ ναυτικὰ . . . ἐναντιοῦται νόμος (Bas. LIII, Α, α′ FM
p. 96; Vent. p. 180).

(*b*) ἐὰν πλοῖον ναυαγήσῃ . . . ναύκληρος (Bas. LIII, Α,
ξε′ FM p. 98; Vent. p. 181; Epanagoge ΚΔ, η′, p. 150;
Epitome Seldeniana, f. 78 v.).

(*c*) ἀκόνα σιδήρου καὶ σίδηρον καὶ ἅλας καὶ σῖτον ἄνευ κεφαλι-
κοῦ κινδύνου τοῖς βαρβάροις πωλεῖν οὐκ ἔξεστιν (Bas. LVI, Α, ι′,
Heimb. V, p. 151; Attal. XXXII sive XLVIII, 4 apud
Leunclavium, II, p. 43; Pard. p. 194).

50

(d) ἐὰν πλοῖόν σου . . . δεσπότης (Bas. LIII, B, ϛ´ apud FM p. 100; Vent. p. 182).

(e) ἐὰν ναῦν βυθίσῃ . . . ἀνέμου (Bas. LIII, B, ζ´ apud FM p. 100; Vent. p. 182; Pard. p. 186).

(f) ἐὰν τὸ σχοινίον . . . καταδικάζεται (Bas. LIII, B, θ´ apud FM p. 100; Vent. p. 182; Pard. p. 186).

(g) πλοῖόν ἐστι . . . καὶ ἡ σχεδία (Bas. LIII, B, θ´ apud FM p. 101; Vent. p. 182).

(h) ἐὰν διὰ τὸ κουφισθῆναι . . . τὸ ῥιφθὲν (= Appendix G (a)).

(i) τὸ ῥιπτόμενον οὐ γίνεται ἀδέσποτον ἀλλὰ τοῦ δεσπότου μένει ἐὰν ἐκβιασθῇ παρὰ τῆς θαλάσσης (Bas. LIII, Γ, η´ apud FM p. 102; Vent. p. 183, sed omissis verbis quinque ultimis. Capitulum plenum exstat apud Attal, XXXII sive XLVIII, 10, apud Leunclavium, II, p. 43; Pard. p. 195).

(j) ἐὰν διὰ τὴν κοινὴν σωτηρίαν ἀποβληθῇ ὁ ἱστὸς ἢ ἄλλο ἐξάρτιον τοῦ πλοίου χώρα τῇ συνεισφορᾷ (Bas. LIII, Γ, ιβ´ apud Pard. p. 187 sed aliis verbis; Attal. XXXII sive XLVIII, 11, apud Leuncl. II, p. 44; Pard. p. 195).

(k) ὁ ἁρπάζων ἀπὸ ναυαγίου ἢ συμπτώσεως ἢ ἐμπρησμοῦ εἴσω μὲν ἐνιαυτοῦ εἰς τὸ τετραπλοῦν, μετὰ δὲ ἐνιαυτὸν εἰς τὸ ἁπλοῦν ἐνέχεται (Bas. LIII, Γ, κε´ apud Vent. p. 183; Pard. p. 188 (κε´), p. 189 (μγ´); cf. etiam Bas. LX, ϛ, λε´ apud Pard. p. 191, Heimb. V, p. 400; Attal. XXXII sive XLVIII, 12, apud Leuncl. II, p. 44; Pard. p. 195).

Hactenus capitula quae partem tertiam τοῦ νόμου praecedunt; sequuntur primo ea capitula quae in Appendice G sub litteris (a) usque ad (h) notavi. Deinde veniunt capitula sex :—

(l) οἱ ἐκ τῆς ἐλεεινοτάτης τῶν ναυαγησάντων ἀποφάσεως ἁρπάζοντες τὸ ὁτιοῦν ἢ κερδαίνοντες κατὰ δόλον πονηρὸν τὸ τετραπλοῦν τοῖς ἀδικηθεῖσι παρεχέτωσαν. ἁρμόζει δὲ ἡ ἀγωγὴ καὶ κατὰ δόλον φαμιλίας· ἁρμόζει δὲ καὶ ἐγκληματικὴ ὑπεξελεύσει (sic). ὁ δὲ τὰ ναυαγήσαντα καὶ ἐκριφθέντα εἰς τὸν αἰγιαλὸν λαμβάνων οὐχ ὑπόκειται τῷ παρόντι ἐδίκτῳ ἀλλ᾽ ἢ φούρτῃ τουτέστιν ἡ κλοπή (extant priora forma diversa apud Venturium, LIII, 3, 21, p. 183; Bas. LX, Κ, α´, Heimb., V, p. 610; Synopsim maiorem, LIII, Γ, κε´, p. 188, ed. Pard.; videas etiam c. 50 quod

ΝΟΜΟΣ ΡΟΔΙΩΝ ΝΑΥΤΙΚΟΣ

dedi in Appendice E. Posteriora (ὁ δὲ τὰ ναυαγήσαντα κ.τ.λ.)
apud Schol. Bas. LX, K, β΄, Heimb. V, p. 611 inveniuntur
et cum Synopsi maiore, LIII, Γ, λθ΄, p. 188, ed. Pard., quo-
dammodo congruunt).

(*m*) ὁ τοὺς οἴακας ἢ ἐν ἐξ αὐτῶν ἀφελόμενος ἐπὶ πᾶσι τοῖς
πράγμασιν ἐνέχεται (apud Venturium exstat LIII, 3, 24, p. 183).

(*n*) ὁ ἁρπάζων κατὰ δόλον καὶ κερδαίνων ἐκ ναυαγίου εἰς ὅσον
ὑπόκειται τῷ ζημιωθέντι τοσοῦτον καὶ τῷ φίσκῳ δίδωσιν (Bas.
LIII, Γ, λα΄ ed. Heimb. V p. 116 ; apud Venturium exstat
LIII, 3, 26, p. 184).

(*o*) ἐπὶ τῶν ναυαγίων ἐὰν βαρυτέρᾳ πραίδᾳ ληφθῶσιν, οἱ μὲν
ἐλεύθεροι ῥοπάλοις τυπτόμενοι ἐπὶ τριετίαν ἐξορίζονται·· οἱ δὲ
δοῦλοι φραγγελούμενοι εἰς μέταλλον πέμπονται· εἰ δὲ μή εἰσι
πολλῆς ποσότητος τὰ ἁμαρτήματα ἢ οὐ τὰ ἁρπαγέντα, καὶ οἱ ἐλεύθεροι καὶ οἱ δοῦλοι ὡς εἴρηται τυπτόμενοι ἀπολύονται. αὗται αἱ
ἀγωγαὶ κληρονόμοις δίδονται, κατὰ δὲ κληρονόμων εἰς τὸ περι-
ελθόν (exstat apud Venturium forma ampliore, LIII, 3, 28,
29, p. 184. Cf. Eustath. XXVI, 8, ed. Zach. p. 201 Videas
etiam c. 50 quod dedi in Appendice E).

(*p*) τὸ σωθὲν ἀπὸ ναυαγίου καὶ ἐμπρησμοῦ καὶ καταπτώσεως
καὶ τεθὲν ἐν ἄλλῳ τόπῳ ὁ κλέψας ἢ ἁρπάσας κλέπτης καὶ ἅρπαξ
ἐστίν (Locus Digestorum est XLVII, 9, 5, pr.).

(*q*) τὴν ἐνεχθεῖσαν εἰς τὸν ἀγρόν μου σχεδίαν βίᾳ τῶν κυμάτων
οὐ δύναται λαβεῖν ὁ δεσπότης αὐτῆς εἰ μὴ περὶ τὴν συμβᾶσαν
ζημίαν ἀσφαλίσηταί μοι (apud Venturium exstat LIII, 3, 33,
p. 184).

APPENDIX I

VARIETAS CODICUM T, U, LAUD.

Cum codices TU recensionem adeo omnibus modis inqui-
natam praebeant ut eorum varietas in apparatum criticum
sine gravi lectorum incommodo admitti non queat, ego in
hunc appendicem reieci. Concordantiam codicum signo
φ notavi. Varietatem codicis Laud., qui de U exscriptus
esse videtur, eis tantum locis admisi ubi de lectione codicis

APPENDIX I

U dubitavi. Codicem Monac. gr. 303 eandem recensionem praebere e relatione Allenii mei compertum habeo.

Titulus. νόμος ῥοδίων κατ᾽ ἐκλογὴν ἐκ τοῦ ιδ΄ βιβλίου τῶν διγέστων U ; vacat apud T.

1 4 ἀπολογεῖσθαι κατὰ τὸ διπλάσιον] διπλασίως διδόσθω φ   2 2 ἀγκύρων φ   4 συλληθέντας T   τούτων . . . ἀποδεικνυμένων] ἀληθῶς δεικνυμένου φ   5 προσγενομένην] γεναμένην φ   6 τὰ ἐν τῷ πλοίῳ] τὰ ἐν αὐτῷ T : τῶν ἐν αὐτῷ U   8 ἐὰν δέ τις] ἐάν τις φ   τῶν ἐν τῷ πλοίῳ] τῶν ἐν αὐτῷ φ   9 τουτέστι . . . λοιπῶν] om. φ   11 ἀπο-διδότω] ἀποδότω U (f. 288 r.). Sed cum membrum sententiae ἄν τις κλέψῃ . . . ποιήσας in principio novae paginae (f. 288 v.) rursus scribat, dat U ἀποδιδότω   3 2 καταληφθείς] om. φ   κατασχεθῇ . . . συλήσῃ] om. U   3 ὁ ναύκληρος . . . παθοῦσιν] διπλᾶ ἀποδιδότω ταῦτα ὁ ναύκληρος T   4 ξυλαγώγια] ξύλα T   5 ἐὰν δέ] ἐὰν T   συλήσῃ] συλλήσας T   κατασχέθη δὲ ἢ καὶ διὰ] κατασχεθῆ ἢ διὰ φ   7 ἐὰν καὶ . . . χρυσίον ᾖ] εἰ μάλιστα χρυσίον εἰ φ   4 1 ἐν τόπῳ] τόπῳ U ἢ ληστευομένῳ] om. T   2 τῷ ναυκλήρῳ] om. φ   4 τὰ σῦλα τοῖς συληθεῖσιν] τὰ συληθέντα φ   εἰ δὲ φ   5 ἀπομαρτ. . . . πλοῖον] μὴ θέλοντος ἐν τῷ τόπῳ εἰσελθεῖν· οἱ ἔμποροι τοῦτο ἀγάγωσι φ   6 τὴν ζημίαν οἱ ἐπιβάται T : τῇ ζημία οἱ ἐπιβάται U   5 1 λόγους U   2 ἐὰν δὲ . . . ἐπιμελείας] εἰ δέ τις κρούσας τὴν κεφαλὴν ἀνοίξει ἢ κυλώσει, δότω τῷ παθόντι τὰς ἰατρείας καὶ τοὺς μισθοὺς τῆς ἀργείας φ   6 2 πατάξῃ] τάξει U   3 κρούσαντα] om. φ   ἢ λίθῳ . . . ἔστω] ἀνεύ-θυνος ὁ δοὺς ἔστω φ   6 ἤθελεν T   7 2 τινὶ φ   δώσει λὰξ φ   3 κύλην T   δώσει] δότω φ   ὁ κρούσας] om. φ   τὰς ἰατρείας φ   4 χρυσίνους] om. φ   5 κύλης T   ὁ λὰξ U   6 ἔνοχος . . . θανάτου] ἔνοχος θανάτου ἔστω ὁ τοῦτο ποιήσας   8 2 ἀποδράσῃ] ἀπέλθῃ φ   βουλήσει τῶν ναυτῶν ante μετὰ ponit φ   μετὰ καὶ χρυσίου U : μετὰ καὶ χρυσίον T   3 τὰ μὲν οἰκεία . . . μισθούσθωσαν] εἰ μὲν ἡ ἅπασα (πᾶσα U) αὐτῶν περιουσία ἐξικανεῖ τῇ τοῦ πλοίου τιμῇ καὶ τῶν ἐν αὐτῷ, ἔστω· εἰ δὲ μήγε, μισθούσθωσαν φ   8 τῆς ζημίας] om. φ   9 et 10 in unum capitulum apud φ conglutinantur, quod sic audit:
ἐὰν περὶ ἐκβολῆς βουλεύσηται ὁ ναύκληρος μετὰ τοῦ ἐμπόρου, καὶ οὐ θελήσει ὁ ἔμπορος, καὶ πάθῃ τὸ πλοῖον, τὴν ζημίαν αὐτὸς ἀποδώσει· αὐτοῦ δὲ μὴ ἐμποδίσαντος μήτε τοῦ ναυκλήρου καὶ τῶν ναυτῶν, συμβῇ δὲ ζημίαν γενέσθαι ἢ ναυάγιον, τὰ σωζόμενα μέρη τοῦ πλοίου καὶ τῶν φορτίων εἰς συμβολὴν ἐρχέσθωσαν.   11 2 ἢ οἱ ἐπιβάται U : ἢ ἐπιβάται T   3 ἐμβάλωσιν] βάλλωσιν T : βάλλουσιν U   ἐὰν] εἰ U   4 φορτίσας U   ἀπὸ γῆς ἑαυτὸν φ   6 ἀκριβῶς . . . ἐπιβαλλέτωσαν] ἀκριβῶς τοῖς πρὸ αὐτῶν πλευσάσασι (πλεύσασι T) περὶ τοῦ πλοίου καὶ οὕτως τὰς ἐνθήκας βαλλέτωσαν (βαλέτωσαν U), εἴπερ ἔχει τελείως καὶ καλῶς πᾶσαν τὴν ἐξόπλισιν αὐτοῦ, καὶ ναύτας τοὺς ἀρκοῦντας αὐτῷ ἐπιτηδείους καὶ ταῦτα τελεία ἔχων καλῶς, βαλλέτωσαν (βαλέτωσαν U) ὡς εἴρηται τὰς ἐνθήκας αὐτῶν. φ   12 1 παραθῆταί τι φ   ἐν πλοίῳ] πλοίω T   ἢ ἐν οἴκω] om. φ   γνωστῷ . . . τριῶν] ἐπὶ πιστῶ καὶ γνωστῶ (καὶ γν. om. U) τιθέσθω πιστικῶ μετὰ ῥ̅ (μάρτυρας U) γ΄ φ   3 ᾖ τὸ θέμα βαρὺ] μέγα ἐστὶν τὸ παρατιθέμενον φ   ἐγγράφως] καὶ γεγ-γράφως U   τὴν παρακαταθήκην διδότω. εἰ δὲ εἴπῃ ὁ ταῦτα δεξάμενος φυλάσσειν ὅτι φ   5 ἢ τὰ σῦλα πόθεν ὑπέστη] καὶ πόθεν τοῦτο ὑπέστη U : om. T   6 εἰ δὲ φ   7 ἀποδιδότω σῶα] δότω φ   13 1 ἐπι-βάτης εἰσέλθῃ φ   3 ἀπώλεσα χρυσίον φ   4 παρ᾽ αὐτοῦ] om. T   5 ὁμοῦ οἱ ἐμπλ.] καὶ οἱ ἐπιβάται καὶ οἱ σὺν αὐτοῖς πλέοντες φ   14 1 Inter παραθήκην et ἀρνήσηται inserunt εἴτε ναύκληρος εἴτε πιστικὸς καὶ φ   αὐτὴν . . . ὑπομενέτω] καὶ διὰ μαρτύρων ἐλεγχθῇ, διπλὴν ἀποδότω τὴν

ΝΟΜΟΣ ΡΟΔΙΩΝ ΝΑΥΤΙΚΟΣ

παραθήκην. εἰ δὲ καὶ (καὶ om. T) ὁμόσει, τὴν τῆς ἐπιορκίας ποινὴν (ποινήν
om. U) πανθανέτω φ   15 1 ἢ ἐμπόρους] ἐμπόρους U : om. T   ἢ δού-
λους] ἢ τυχὸν δούλους φ   2 εἰς παραθήκην φ   καὶ ἐλθὼν φ   ἢ λιμένι φ   3 ἐὰν] καὶ φ   ἀπὸ τοῦ πλοίου φ   5 ἐξυλήσει T : ἐξιλήσει
U   σωθῇ δὲ] καὶ σωθῇ φ   6 τὰ] om. T   κομιζόμενα . . . ἀπο-
λαμβανέτωσαν] φορτία λαμβανέτω ἕκαστος τὰ ἴδια καὶ τὰ τῶν ἐξελθόντων
ἕκαστος λαμβανέτω U : φορτία λαμβανέτω nec plura T   9 ἀμφισβητῆσαι τῷ ναυκλήρῳ φ   αὐτὸν] αὐτοὺς U   10 παρ' αὐτοῦ] om. φ   11
διότι φ   καὶ οἱ ν. ἐφ.] σὺν τοῖς ναύταις ἐξέφυγον φ   12 εἰ δὲ . . .
ἔασεν] εἰ δὲ δοῦλόν τινος ἐν παραθήκῃ λαβὼν ἔασεν φ   14 τῷ
κυρίῳ αὐτοῦ] τῷ τούτου δεσπότῃ φ   16 2 πλοίῳ U   χρησέσθωσαν]
γραφέτω T : γραφέτωσαν U   Cum hoc verbo finis cap. in φ   17 2
καὶ ταύτην] om. φ   ἐγγράψονται T : ἐγγράψωνται U   3 τῇ χρεο-
κοινωνίᾳ] om. φ   λαβὼν φ   4 πληρουμένου φ   5 ἀποστρέψῃ]
ἀποδώσει φ   αὐτὸ τῷ κυρίῳ αὐτοῦ] om. φ   6 ἀπὸ] ἢ ἀπὸ φ   παραπεσεῖν φ   8 ἐὰν δὲ] Principium apud U novi cap. (ιη')   9
ἐκ om. φ   τὸν . . . κίνδυνον T   10 καὶ τὰς ζημίας . . . ἀναδέχεσθαι]
δεχέσθω καὶ τὰς ζημίας φ   18 2 τοῦ χρόνου . . . συνθῶνται] τοῦ συμ-
φωνηθέντος χρόνου φ   3 ἐγγαίων T   κατὰ τὸν νόμον] om. φ   ἐὰν
δὲ μὴ φ   4 κομίσασθαι φ   ἔστω T   ἔγγαια T   5 παντός . . .
ἀποδημήσει] ὅσον χρόνον ἀποδημεῖ φ   19 2 καὶ μετέπειτα . . . ἀρρα-
βῶνα] om. φ   μετὰ ταῦτα T   ἀπώλειν U   ἐὰν δὲ . . . ἀρραβῶνα]
εἰ δὲ ὁ ναύκληρος, διπλασιαζέτω φ   20 omittit φ   21 1 ἐγγράφως
ποιήσωσιν δύο πλοῖα φ   2 καθομολογήσωσιν] καθο T   Tum in T
post vacuum spatium unius lineae subsequitur c. 26.   3 ἐγγράφως φ   4 τὸ περὶ U   7 ἐπεὶ ἐπειδὴ U   8 τὰ δὲ
ἔγγραφα . . . συνερχέσθωσαν] εἰ δὲ ἔγγραφα ἐγένοντο, τὰ σῳζόμενα πάντα
τοῖς ἀπολλυμένοις εἰσερχέσθωσαν U   22 2 καὶ ἀφ' ὧν . . . πλοῖα] καὶ
σχοῖνα καὶ λοιπὰ τὰ τῷ πλοίῳ ἀνήκοντα U   ἐὰν δὲ U   3 ἐμβάλῃ U
τῶν ἐγγράφων] om. U   4 καὶ ἐὰν] καὶ U   5 ἐὰν μὲν] ἐὰν U   6
ἀντιτασσέσθω U   7 καὶ ἐὰν . . . ἔαται] om. U   9 ἔρχέσθωσαν U
23 1 συγγράφωνται U   καὶ ὁ ἔμπορος] om. U   3 τῶν λοιπαζομένων]
om. U   24 1 ἡμίση ναῦλα U   2 ὑποστρέψαι ὁ ἔμπορος βουληθῇ
U   3 ἔμπορον] ναύκληρον U   4 ἐὰν δὲ] εἰ δὲ U   25 3 σιταρ-
κείας U   παρέλθῃ post προθεσμία ponit U   καὶ ἢ] καὶ U   6 τὸ
ναῦλον U   7 ἐὰν δόξῃ] ἔδοξεν U   26 1 ναυκλήρου φ   2 τοῦ
πλοίου] om. φ   3 ἐφορᾶν] ἀφορᾶν T : ἀφορᾶν εἰς U   4 ναύτας ἢ]
ναύτας τε καὶ φ   ἐν τῷ πλοίῳ μένοντας φ   5 τοὺς δὲ ἀμελ. . . . ζημίαν]
om. φ   27 2 κοινωνίᾳ φ   3 ἀμέλειαν τοῦ ναυκλήρου ἢ τῶν ναυτῶν φ
εἴτω] εἶναι φ   4 τὰ ἐνόρια κείμενα U : τὰ ἐνόρια T   6 φορτίοις] τοῖς
φορτίοις U : τῶν φορτίοις T   7 ἐὰν δέ τις] Principium novi cap. apud
φ   τὴν κοινωνίαν] κοινωνίαν φ   9 τῆς δὲ ἀρνήσεως] om. φ   τὴν]
τὴν δὲ φ   28 2 καὶ τῆς προθεσμίας φ   3 ναβαγίου U   4 τὴν
ἔμποδον T   ἐμφερέτω] διδότω φ   29 1 ἐν τ. τ. ὅ. σ.] ἔνθα συγγράψονται τόπῳ φ   2 μὴ π.τ.φ. πληρωθείσης] om. T   3 ἀπὸ π. ἢ
π. ἢ ναυαγίου] om. T   4 ἐμφορᾶν T : ἀφορᾶν U   τοῦ πλοίου] om. T
5 εἰς τὸν ἔμπορον U   μὴ πληρωθέντων] πληρωθέντων T : πληρωθεισῶν U
30 1 ὁ ἔμπορος . . . αὐτοῦ] ἐὰν ὁ φορτώσας τὸ πλοῖον ἔμπορος ἔχῃ μετ'
αὐτοῦ χρυσίον φ   2 κινδύνων] om. φ   3 ἀπολεῖται T : ἀπόλυται
U   6 ἐκκομιζέτω] αὐτὸς ἐκκομιζέσθω φ   7 ἐὰν δὲ μή] Principium
novi cap. in U   8 τὰ ἡμίναυλα . . . ἐπιφερέτω] τὰ ἡμίναυλα ἀπαιτῶν
ἐγγράφων προελθόντων πέμπτας (πέμψας U) ἐπιφερέτω φ   31 2 τῷ
πλοίῳ] ἐν αὐτῷ φ   4 βοηθείας] βυθίας φ   32 omittit φ   33 1
ἐπὶ τὸν τόπον φ   2 τὸν μὲν ναῦλον T   3 εἰς πλῆρες] om. φ
4 ἐνορεία T   5 ὑπὸ . . . πλοίου] om. φ   34 1 ὠθόνην ἢ βέστιν

APPENDIX I

T 2 ὑπὸ χ. . . . ἀδικηθῇ] ὑπὸ χειμῶνος ὑποκλυσθῇ (ὑποκλεισθῇ T) τι
ὑπὸ τῶν ὑδάτων καὶ ἀδικηθῇ (ἀδικηθῆναι T) τι τῶν φορτίων φ   4 εὐθέως
φ   5 ἐν τῷ πλοίῳ] om. U   ἤ] om. φ   6 ἐὰν δὲ . . . φορτία] εἰ
δὲ μηδὲν εἴπη φ   8 ἅμα τοῖς ναύταις] om. φ   9 προμαρτύρηται φ
ἅμα τοῖς ναύταις] τοῖς ἐμπόροις φ   10 ἔκθεσθε U   οἱ δὲ ἐμβ. . . .
ἐκθέσθαι] αὐτοὶ δὲ ἀμελήσω(ου U)σιν φ   12 ἔστωσαν φ   35 3 τὸ
πλοῖον σωθέντα] τὸ σωθὲν πλοῖον φ   36 1 ἀρμενίζοντος T   2 ἄρμενα]
ἄρματα T   4 ἐμπλέοντας] πλέοντας φ   λοιπὸν δὲ] ἀλλὰ φ   6 ἁπτέσθω
φ   7 καὶ πῦρ οὐκ ἔχει] οὐκ ἔχει πῦρ φ   παρεχέτω] ποιείτω φ   8 ποιῆ-
σαι] οὐ ποιήσει φ   καὶ συμβῇ ἀπ.] om. φ   ὤλεσεν φ   10 ἀμελήσει U
καὶ ὁ βιγλ. ἀποκ.] ἀποκοιμηθῆ δὲ (δὲ καὶ U) ὁ βιγλοφόρος φ   ὡς εἰς βράχη] ὡς
(ὡς om. U) εἰς βράχος κρούσας φ   37 omittit U   2 καὶ ἐπιβατῶν
T   ἀπωλεῖται T   γραμματεία T   38 1 ζάλη] γάζη U   καταλειφθῇ φ   2 διφθέρας καλὰς U   6 οἱ om. U (?)   ἅμα τῷ
ἐμπόρῳ] καὶ ὁ ἔμπορος φ   τὰς δὲ δεκάτας ἢ ἔκτας ἑκάστων] τὰς δὲ ἔκτας
τῶν T: τὰς ἐ[κατ]ὰς τῶν U secundum FM: ego solummodo legere
possum τὰς . . . ας τῶν: τὰς ἔκτας τῶν Laud.   8 ἅμα τοῦ πλ. καὶ τοῖς ν.]
ἅμα τοῖς ναύταις καὶ τῷ πλοίῳ φ   10 ἐπιχειρείωσαν] om. φ   11
σύλα . . . κέρδους] σύλα ποιείτω. εἰ δὲ φανεῖ, διπλᾶ ἀποδιδότω (διδότω U)
καὶ τοῦ ἴσως κέρδους φ   39 Priorem partem (usque ad 8 τὸν τόπον
ἐκεῖνον) huius capituli bis dat T.   Secundam recensionem notavi signo
T²   3 καὶ εἰσέλθη] Ita T²: εἰσέλθη φ   τὸ πλοῖον εἰς τόπον ἢ]
Ita T²: om. φ   4 καὶ συμβῇ] om. T²   8 εἰ δὲ] εἰ γὰρ T   9 ἐν]
ὅτι ἐν φ   10 ἐγγράφοις] συμφώνοις φ   11 τοῦ πλοίου T Laud.]
τοῦ μὲν πλοίου U secundum FM: ego invenio τοῦ . . . πλοίου   12
σωθῇ φ   τὸ πλοῖον] om. φ   14 ἀποβάλληται τὸ πλοῖον] τοῦτο
γένηται φ   40 3 μεθ' ἑαυτῶν . . . τὸ μὲν] om. T   χρυσίον μεθ'
ἑαυτῶν U   ὁλοσίρικα U   5 τὸ ἀργύριον T   Cum voce ἀργυ-
ρι‖ον incipit ultimum folium (293) codicis U, quod ita lacerum est ut
multae voces perierint   6 ὁλοσύρικα T   7 ὄντα τοῦ χρυσίου] τοῦ
χρυσίου ὄντα T   τῷ χρυσίῳ ὄντα U   8 τὴν ὑποτριβὴν καὶ τὴν ἀποβροχὴν]
τὴν ἀποτριβὴν φ   9 οἱ δὲ μαργαρῖται . . . ἀπώλειαν] om. φ   41
1 ἢ] om. U   2 ἀπωλεῖται T: ἀπόλυται U   τὰ δὲ τῶν ἐπιβ. σωθῇ]
σωθῆναι δὲ τὰ τῶν ἐπιβ. T: σωθῆ δὲ τῶν ἐπιβ. U   3 ἐπιφερέτωσαν]
συγγινωσκέτωσαν φ   6 πρὸς] καὶ φ   τῇ συμβολῇ U   42 2 ἐπὶ
τῷ ναυκλ. . . . ναῦλον] καὶ μετακομίσει αὐτὰ ὁ ναύκληρος εἰς ἕτερον πλοῖον
αὐτὸς διδότω τὸ (τὸν T) ναῦλον, οἱ δὲ τῶν φορτίων δεσπόται πρὸς αὐτὸν φ
πρὸς αὐτὸν secundum FM omittit U: habet Laud.   De U non potest
iudicium fieri, cum pars paginae hic abscissa sit   43 1 καταλειφθῇ T   2 καταρτίων T: καταρτίου U   4 τῇ τιμῇ U secundum
FM: ego dubito   5 τοῖς σωζομένοις φορτίοις U   44 1 ἐκβολὴ
. . . κλάσις] τῆς καταρτίας (ἀταρτίας U) ἢ τῶν κεράτων γένηται κλάσις
ἢ τῶν αὐχένων φ   2 ἀπώλειαν T   3 μὲν φ   4 ἀνάγκη . . .
ἔρχεσθαι] ἀνάγκη πάντα εἰς συμβολὴν ἔρχεσθαι φ   5 πλέον U (?)
λάβη φ   6 οὐχ T: οὐκ U   7 καὶ τὰ εἴδη] τὰ δὲ εἴδη φ   45
Hic incipit f. 293 v. codicis U, in quo pauca admodum nunc legi
possunt. Ego eam collationem quam fecerunt FM fideliter secutus
tamen, ne lector in errorem inducatur, in his tribus capitulis le-
ctiones Laud. addidi   1 τῷ πελάγει U, si fides FM.   Laud. articulum
omittit   2 ἐπὶ τὴν γῆν] om. φ Laud.   3 οὗ ἀποσώζει] om. φ Laud.
46 1 σχοινία U Laud.] σχοῖνα T   2 ἀπωλεῖται T   ἅμα καὶ τοῖς ἐμπλ. ἐν
αὐτῷ] ἅμα τοῖς πλέουσι T Laud.   3 πλέοντες T Laud.] ἐμπλέοντες U
ἀπώλοντο ἢ ἀπέθανον T Laud.   4 ἀποδιδότω] παρεχέτω φ Laud.   εἰς
τὸ πλήρης T Laud.   5 τούτων] αὐτῶν φ Laud.   6 τῶν ἐφολκίων]

55

ΝΟΜΟΣ ΡΟΔΙΩΝ ΝΑΥΤΙΚΟΣ

τοῖς ἐφολκίοις U Laud.   7 οὗ ἀποσώζει] ὁ ἀποσώσας φ Laud.   τὸ
πέμπτον T Laud.] om. U   47 1 ἢ ἔτερόν τι] om. φ Laud.   2 ἀπὸ
μὲν T Laud.   οὐργυιῶν φ Laud. (bis)   3 λαμβανέτω ὁ ἀποσώζων]
om. φ Laud.   5 ἐκρυπτομένων T   ἀπὸ θαλάσσης . . . ἐπιφερομένων]
om. U Laud.   ἢ εὑρισκομένων T   6 ἐπὶ πύχην μίαν T   7
ὁ ταῦτα ἀποσώζων φ Laud.   τῶν ἀποσωζομένων] om. φ Laud.

Addunt φ Laud. cap. 49, 50, sicut in Appendice E dantur.
Post c. 50 T capitula quaedam praebet quae cum a Zach.
publici iuris facta sint (Ius Graeco-Romanum, Pars IV,
p. 178 Ἐκ τῶν περὶ ὕβρεων . . . p. 179 μίαν ποινήν) et cum
iure maritimo nihil commune habeant, ego omitto. Deinde subsequitur in T :—

(a) Ἐὰν τοῦ πλοίου μὴ δυναμένου μετὰ τοῦ γόμου εἰσελθεῖν
ἐν τῷ ποταμῷ ἢ ἐν τῷ λιμένι μετενεχθῶσιν ἐν τῷ φορτίῳ (sic) εἰς
τὴν σκάφην διὰ τὸ μὴ κινδυνεῦσαι τὸ πλοῖον καὶ ἀπώλειται ἡ
σκάφη, συνεισάγουσιν τοῖς δεσπόταις τῶν ἀποβαλλομένων ὡς
ἀποβολῆς γενομένης οἱ δεσπόται τῶν ἐν τῷ πλοίῳ. εἰ δὲ τὸ
πλοῖον ἀπώλειται, οὐ συνεισάγουσιν οἱ ἐν τῇ σκάφῃ, τοῦ γὰρ
πλοίου σωζομένου ἡ συνεισφορὰ τῆς ἀποβολῆς ἁρμόζει. (Locus
Digestorum est, XIV, 2, 4, pr.)

(b) ἐὰν τὰ σωθέντα φορτία . . . πλεονάζων ἑνὸς τὴν ζημίαν
(Bas. LIII, Γ, ια΄ apud FM p. 102 ; Vent. p. 183 = Appen-
dicis G cap. (e)).

(c) ἀπολυμένου τοῦ πλοίου . . . ἀποβληθῶσιν (Bas. LIII, Γ,
ιβ΄ apud FM p. 102 ; Vent. p. 183 ; Pard. p. 187 = App. G.
cap. (f)).

(d) ναυαγήσαντος τοῦ πλοίου . . . ἑαυτῷ ἔχει ὡς ἂν ἐξ ἐμπτυ-
σμοῦ (sic) (Bas. LIII, Γ, ιε΄ apud FM p. 102 ; Vent. p. 183 ;
Pard. p. 188).

(e) Ἐκ (quaedam quae legi non possunt) ου νγ΄ β $\overset{\lambda'}{}$ τῶν
βασι Ἐὰν πλοῖον μεστὸν σίτου . . . τὸν τόπον ἐκεῖνον (huius
capituli varietatem supra dedi).

56

TRANSLATION AND COMMENTARY

PART II

THE CHAPTERS OF THE RHODIAN LAW

As to the titles which the MSS. give to different parts of the
Sea-law see Introduction, p. lxvii.

κεφάλαια] Both Part II and Part III of the Sea-law are divided
into κεφάλαια. The same holds of the Farmer's and the Soldier's
law. As a rule the smaller textbooks, e. g. the Ecloga, are divided
into τίτλοι, and the τίτλοι into κεφάλαια. The subject-matter of the
Sea-law is so varied that it would have been difficult to arrange
it under τίτλοι. There would be another reason for the absence
of τίτλοι if the text as we have it was arranged in order to come
under a τίτλος of Book LIII of the Basilica.

CHAPTERS 1–7. A master's pay two shares; a steersman's one share and a half; a master's mate's one
share and a half; a carpenter's one share and a half;
a boatswain's one share and a half; a sailor's one share;
a cook's (?) half a share.

The first seven chapters regulate the shares which the various
classes of mariners take in the profits of the maritime adventure.
The word μισθός is used here, not of a fixed wage, but of a divi-
dend arising from profits; it may or may not have the same
meaning in the other cases in the Sea-law where it is used of
sailors (c. 5, 46). On the whole subject of the payment of
mariners see Introduction, p. clxvii.

There are wide differences in the MSS. both as to the order in
which the names come and as to the amount of the respective
shares (see App. Crit.). The most important difference in the
latter case is as to the share of the καραβίτης. This, according
to Av, whose reading I adopt, is $1\frac{1}{2}$; according to CEM, is
$\frac{1}{2}+\frac{1}{4}+\frac{1}{8}=\frac{7}{8}$ (see Bast, Comment. Palaeograph., p. 854); according to Q, $\frac{1}{2}+\frac{1}{4}=\frac{3}{4}$; the later MSS. make it either one or two;
and the amount is left blank in B and L. It looks as if the share
of the καραβίτης was a number which puzzled scribes. If his
share was less than one, we should expect him to come after the

57

ναύτης, who represents unity ; and he is in fact placed after him by several MSS. (DEFLMQ). In the uncertainty as to the meaning of καραβίτης, I have not ventured to change the accepted order.

α′ ναυκλήρου] As to the meaning of the word ναύκληρος and the relation of the ναύκληρος to the ναῦται see Introd., p. cxxxii. The first three names (ναύκληρος, κυβερνήτης, πρωρεύς—an order in which most MSS. are agreed) are arranged in the order of their respective importance. Aristoph. Equites, 542–4 ; Athenaeus, 209 A ; Artemid. Oneirocrit. I, 35 ; Dig. XXXIX, 4, 11, 2. We may assume, therefore, that the other names are arranged on the same principle.

β′ μέρος ἐν ἥμισυ] Some of the best MSS. read μέρη here and throughout. Μέρη is possible. In rows of figures, where the same substantive, e. g. μναῖ, δραχμαί, is repeated before each in the plural, it does not necessarily change to the singular because it precedes unity ; e. g. you may find δραχμαί· ἕξ ; δραχμαί· πέντε ; and so on to δραχμαί· μία. But the more usual course is to alter the substantive ; e. g. Dittenberger, Orientis Gr. Inscr. 674, vol. 2, p. 417 πιττακίου καμήλων ὀβολὸν ἕνα· σφραγισμοῦ πιττακίου ὀβολοὺς δύο, and other cases.

γ′ πρωρέως. Most of my MSS. indicate πρωρεύς as the nom. This and πρωράτης are the classical forms. L and late MSS. indicate πρώραιος or πρώρεος, for which there does not appear to be any other authority.

δ′ ναυπηγοῦ] ναυπηγός is the ship's carpenter. Inscription of A. D. 90, in Dittenberger, Orientis Gr. Inscr. 674, vol. 2, p. 416 ; Edictum Diocletiani de pretiis rerum venalium, 7, 13 (see Blumner's note, p. 108). Every δρόμων is to have on board ναυπηγὸν μετὰ πάντων τῶν ἐργαλείων αὐτοῦ (Leonis Imp. Tactica, c. XIX, § 5). The regular Byzantine word is καλαφάτης (hence It. calafato).

ε′. καραβίτου] καραβίτης apparently is not found elsewhere. Duc. cites καραβιάς, καραβοκύρης, and πρωτοκάραβος. The last of these is an officer of the Byzantine navy.

ζ′. παρασχαρίτου] παρασχαρίτης is the spelling of all my MSS. The word is the same as παρεσχαρίτης. For the change of ε into α, cf. παιδαράστης (De Boor, Index Graecitatis Theoph., p. 764). Duc. explains παρεσχ. as ' cui in navi foci cura incumbit ', citing Eustath. ad Od. ζ (p. 1564, 27) περὶ δὲ ἐσχάρας ἤ παρώνυμος ὁ κοινῶς παρεσχαρίτης λέγεται, δηλοῦται μὲν καὶ ἐν ἄλλοις, ἐνταῦθα δὲ μνηστέον τοῦ εἰπόντος ὅτι βωμὸς μὲν ὁ προσβάσεις ἔχων, ἐσχάρα δέ, ἡ πρὸς βιωτικὴν γινομένη χρῆσιν ἐπὶ γῆς. This passage, however, does not prove his definition.

The identification of the παρασχ(or παρεσχ-)αρίτης with the ship's cook is not free from difficulties. (1) If he was so important a personage as a cook, why should he only get half the wages of an ordinary seaman ? (2) The word ἐσχάρα is never found for the caboose. In Callixenus apud Athenaeum, 204 C, ἐσχάριον is

58

a cradle for launching ships. Eustathius (p. 1575, 42), citing the passage of Athenaeus, says Ἀθηναῖος δὲ καὶ ἐσχάριον παραγώγως οἶδε δι᾽ οὗ καθέλκονται νῆες εἰς θάλασσαν· ὅθεν ἡ ἀπερίεργος γλῶσσα παραφθείρουσα τὸ καινὸν πλοῖον ἀπὸ σκαριόν εἶναί φησι, βουλομένη πάντως ἀπ᾽ ἐσχαρίου εἰπεῖν· ἐσχάριον is therefore the Italian *scaro*, Venetian *squero*. But ἐσχάρα and ἐσχάριον are also used for a platform resting on boats (Athenaeus π. μηχανημάτων in Wescher, Poliorcétique des Grecs, pp. 32, 34).

If παρασχαρίτης is the man concerned with the deck, he would probably correspond to the *famuli* or *fanti* of the mediaeval Italian documents, and to what Charles Molloy (De Iure Maritimo et Navali, 3rd ed., London, 1682) calls (p. 218) ' the *tarpollians*, or those youths or boys that are apprentices obliged to the most servile duties in the ship', and it would be reasonable that he should only receive one-half the sailor's share. Ps.–Chrys. X, p. 760 Montf., p. 906 Gaume, suggests that the παρεσχαρῖται formed a numerous class; now there was only one *coquinator* even on a large galley. Sanudo, Secreta, II, pp. 63, 75.

The ἐσχαρεύς (according to LS) is 'a ship's cook', but the passages which they cite do not prove this. Indeed, the passage from Themistius (195 B), which couples the ἐσχαρεύς with the θαλαμίας, suggests the contrary.

8. A merchant may have on board two boys; but he must pay their fare.

The distinction between the ἔμπορος and the ἐπιβάτης is dealt with in the Introduction, p. cxxxix.

παῖδες here are not necessarily slaves, although in c. 9 they appear to be. There is an interesting contract of service in Amalric, 357 (Blancard, I, p. 409), by which *A* agrees to serve *B* during a voyage in return for food, drink, passage-money, a white tunic, and an outer tunic of fustian.

9. A passenger's allowance of space is three cubits in length and one in breadth.

As to the πῆχυς, Hero's table of lengths appears to have been adopted in Byzantine times. It is given at large in the Geneva MS. of the Livre du Préfet (ed. Nicole, Genève, 1893, p. 69), and in an abridged form by Harmenopulus (II, iv, 12). According to Hero there are two πήχεις: ὁ πῆχυς ἔχει πόδας ⟨δύο⟩ ἤγουν σπιθαμὰς β΄ δίμοιρον [= 2⅔] ἢ παλαιστὰς η΄ ἢ δακτύλους λβ΄ . . . ὁ πῆχυς ὁ λιθικὸς ἔχει σπιθαμὰς β΄ ἢ πόδα ἕνα πρὸς τῷ ἡμίσει ἢ παλαιστὰς ϛ΄ ἢ δακτύλους κδ΄. ὡσαύτως καὶ τοῦ πριστικοῦ ξύλου (Livre du Préfet, p. 70). In the abridged form given by Harmenopulus, and in an Egyptian list of weights and measures of the third or early fourth century, the shorter πῆχυς is alone referred to: ἔχει ὁ πῆχις παλησσὰς ϛ΄, ὁ δὲ παλησστὴς ἔχει δακτύλους δ΄, ὥστε εἶναι τὼν

TRANSLATION AND COMMENTARY

πηχῶν δακτύλων κδ′ (P. Oxyrhynchus, I, p. 77). In another Egyptian list of the same date four πήχεις are mentioned, that of 5 παλεσταί, described as λινουφικός; that of 6, described as δημόσιος καὶ τεκτονικός; that of 7, described as νιλομετρικός; and that of 8, the name of which is wanting (P. Oxyrhynchus, IV, 669, p. 118). Let us hope that the passenger of the Sea-law slept under the longest πῆχυς.

There are differences in the MSS. both as to the spelling and gender of the word. As to spelling: πυχή, which is given in c. θ′ by C. and in c. 47 by Q, may be a South-Italian variant; πυχαις is found in Trinchera, p. 224. As to gender: LS only acknowledge the masculine, but many MSS. (here ACD; in c. ιγ′ ADHMQ; in c. 47 only K) make it feminine.

As to the substance of the chapter: it must be remembered that the τόπος or platea in which the passenger was packed did not correspond to the modern cabin. It was merely a sleeping place. The Statute of Marseille provides (IV, 25) that each pilgrim is to have a place ' duorum palmorum et dimidii canne in latitudine et in longitudine septem palmorum vel sex et dimidii ad minus '. An exception is made for *correterii* (=courtiers maritimes, see Ducange, Gloss. Lat. s. v.), but whether in their favour or not does not appear. This would give the pilgrim about the same space as the Sea-law gives him. The statute, however, goes on to say that two pilgrims are to be put into each place, ' sicut consuetum est eos collocari in nauibus, scilicet uno tenente pedes uersus caput alterius.'

The passenger seems as a rule to have brought with him his own bed and bed-coverings; cp. c. 9 στρώματα. Venetian merchants in 1278 are robbed by Greeks of their ' arnesia de lecto ' (Iudicum Venetorum in causis piraticis contra Graecos decisiones in Tafel und Thomas, III, pp. 243, 261, 275), and among the goods of a Marseille merchant which are taken from him by Venetian galleys in 1295 is a *lectus* (Tafel und Thomas, III, p. 374). Under the Venetian Statutes of Ziani, every merchant and mariner may carry free on board one mattress of a certain weight. If it exceeds the prescribed weight, or if he brings in a couch (*lectulus*), freight is payable for the mattress (St. maritt. Venez., p. 49). This provision is repeated in substance in the Venetian Statutes of Tiepolo (A, 31) and Zeno (56), and in the Statutes of Zara (IV, 26). See also Consulate of Sea, c. 73. Fynes Moryson uses his chest as a bed. Itinerary, p. 208.

The Statutes of Venice and of Zara restrict the merchant's free allowance of luggage to one trunk (cassella) (St. Ziani in St. maritt. Venez., p. 48; St. Tiepolo, A, 30; St. Zeno, 55; St. Zara, IV, 25); and they and the Statutes of Ragusa provide that no servant is to have a trunk (St. cited above, and St. Ragus. VII, 10).

10. A passenger is not to fry fish on board; the captain must not allow him.

The MSS. vary as to the latter clause, both in this and in the next chapter (see App. Crit.). Perhaps the original reading in both cases is ὁ ναύκληρος αὐτῷ μὴ συγχωρῶν, and we should translate 'unless the captain allows him'. The nominative absolute is common enough in Theophanes (see De Boor's Index, p. 761), but it may have offended scribes after the classical revival; and this would account for the variants. This chapter and the next are evidently intended to provide against the risk of fire. See Introduction, p. cxlix.

11. A passenger is not to split wood on board; the captain must not allow him.

12. A passenger on board is to take water by measure.

As to the importance of the water question in mediaeval voyages, see Introduction, p. cli.

Some of the MSS. specify the amount which the passenger is to take, as ὀγκίας or οὐγγίας [1] δύο (see App. Crit.).

13. Women on board are to have a space allowance of one cubit; and a boy . . . of half a cubit.

The use of the infinitive (γυναῖκας or possibly γυναῖκα . . . λαμβάνειν), of which there are many examples in the Sea-law, seems to have distressed the scribes (see App. Crit.).

It is possible that a line has dropped out and that we should read λαμβάνειν τόπον ⟨μῆκος πήχεων τριῶν, πλάτος⟩ πήχεως ἑνός. Whether the insertion is made or not, the sense of the passage must be the same.

τὸ τέλειον] My MSS. read either τὸ τέλειον or τέλειον. Venturi's MS. seems to have read τὸ μὴ τέλειον, which is adopted by the printed texts and translated 'puer nondum adultus' or 'puer necdum adultus'. παιδίον, according to Pollux (II, 4), on the authority of Hippocrates, is a boy up to seven. What τὸ παιδίον τὸ τέλειον means in this passage I do not know; it ought to mean 'a grown-up boy' (cp. Theophil. I, 4, 79 αὐτὸ δὲ τὸ παιδίον τέλειον γεγονός); this is impossible, but I do not see how the sense is bettered by inserting μή. Possibly we should read τὸ παιδίον τὸ ἔτειον, 'a boy from one year up' (Pollux, II, 8). A child under that age would come within the space allotted to the mother.

[1] The young men who miscollated for Pard. read this οὔτε, and the confiding Pard. adds a note, 'J'ai cru, sur la foi du manuscrit 1356, devoir admettre ces derniers mots, qui expliquent le véritable sens du mot μέτρῳ pour signifier *unam tantum mensuram*'.

14. If a passenger comes on board and has gold, let him deposit it with the captain. If he does not deposit it and says, 'I have lost gold or silver,' no effect is to be given to what he says, since he did not deposit it with the captain. 15. The captain and the passengers and the crew, who are on board together, are to take an oath upon the evangels.

These two chapters, though divided in the MSS., form in reality one chapter, and agree very closely with c. 13 of Part III. I have dealt in the Introduction (p. lxxvii) with the relation between these chapters and c. 13 of Part III, and (p. cc) with their subject-matter.

ἐν πλοίῳ] The Sea-law uses indifferently εἰσελθεῖν εἰς with the accusative and εἰσελθεῖν ἐν with the dative. Here D alone reads εἰς πλοῖον. In c. 13 all my MSS. (except CQ) read εἰσέλθῃ εἰς πλοῖον. In c. 39 we find first εἰσέλθῃ εἰς τόπον ἢ ἐν ἀκτῇ, where Y alone reads εἰς ἀκτήν; then εἰσελθεῖν εἰς τὸν τόπον ἐκεῖνον; and finally ἐν τῷ τόπῳ τούτῳ εἰσελθεῖν.

εἰ ... εἴπῃ] In conditional sentences introduced by εἰ the Sea-law uses most frequently the indicative, sometimes the subjunctive, but never the optative. The later MSS. often substitute the optative for the indicative or subjunctive of the better MSS. Clear cases of εἰ with the subjunctive are: c. 34, 8 εἰ ... προδιαμαρτύρηται; c. 36, 6 εἰ ... συμβῇ; c. 36, 10 εἰ ... ἀποκοιμηθῇ; c. 38, 3 εἰ ... βραχῇ; c. 39, 8 εἰ ... εἴπῃ; c. 44, 5 εἰ ... βλαβῇ. In cases of doubt as between indicative and subjunctive, I have generally put the indicative in the text; but the subjunctive is equally, if not more, in accordance with contemporary Byzantine usage. Soldier's law, 2 εἰ ... τύχῃ, 4 εἰ ... παρέλθῃ, 6 εἰ ... ἐπισχεθῇ, and in other places.

εἴτω] The tradition supports εἴτω or ἤτω here, c. ιζ΄, 3, c. 20, 2; εἴτωσαν c. 34, 12; but ἔστω c. ιθ΄, 4, c. 13, 4.

τὰ λεγόμενα ἐπεὶ τῷ ναυκλήρῳ οὐ παρέθετο] It will be seen from the App. Crit. that this reading is in part conjectural, and in part based upon BH.

c. 15. καὶ οἱ ναῦται] These words are omitted by good MSS., and those which give them put them some in one place and some in another. They may have been brought in from c. 13. In c. 13 there is no reference to οἱ ἐπιβάται, unless they come under the description of οἱ ἐμπλέοντες.

ὅρκον εὐαγγελίων] Some of the MSS. head this chapter περὶ ὅρκου ἀπαραιτήτου (see App. Crit.). The phrase ὅρκος ἀπαραίτητος does not seem to occur in legal texts, although ὅρκον παραιτεῖσθαι 'to refuse an oath' is common enough (Bas. XXII, 5, 34, 7; XXII, 5, 54). Ὅρκος ἀπαραίτητος is evidently the 'iusiurandum necessarium' of the Digest (XII, 2), which in the Basilica is

62

generally translated by ὅρκος νεκεσσάριος. Νεκεσσάριοι δέ εἰσιν οὓς ἐν δικαστηρίῳ τινὸς τῶν λιτιγατόρων ἐπὶ τὴν τούτου δόντος ἐπαγωγὴν ὁ δικαστὴς ἐπιφέρει (Schol. ad Bas. XXII, 5, 1; ed. Heimb. ii, p. 528). This Schol. uses ὅρκοι νεκεσσάριοι in an enlarged sense as including not merely those which ἐπὶ τομῇ παρέχονται πραγμάτων (the oath which our Sea-law contemplates), but also ὁ περὶ καλουμνίας ἤ ὁ περὶ τοῦ δικαίαν οἴεσθαι τὴν ἀντίρρησιν καὶ περὶ ὑπερθέσεως διδόμενος ὅρκος. The ὅρκος νεκεσσάριος is elsewhere used in a restricted sense, as equivalent to the oath of our Sea-law, no doubt because the other oaths mentioned had become obsolete (see Schol. ad Bas. XXII, 5, 31; ed. Heimb. ii, p. 557). This oath was not forced upon the defendant except where all other proofs were wanting (Schol. ad Bas. XXII, 5, 31; ed. Heimb. ii, p. 557; Πεῖρα, LXIX, 2. See also Schol. ad Bas. XXII, 5, 9; ed. Heimb. ii, p. 533), and it determined the result of the action (Schol. ad Bas. XXII, 5, 9, 1; ed. Heimb. ii, p. 532). The judgement, however, might be set aside, according to the better opinion, if evidence to contradict the oath was subsequently forthcoming (Schol. ad Bas. XXII, 5, 31; ed. Heimb. ii, p. 557).

Ὅρκος εὐαγγελίων is a strange phrase. It is possible that some words have dropped out, and that we should read ὅρκον ⟨κατὰ τῶν ἁγίων⟩ εὐαγγελίων. I find ὀμνύναι κατὰ τῶν ἁγίων εὐαγγελίων (Bas. VII, 6, 14), ἐν τῷ ἱερῷ καὶ θείῳ εὐαγγελίῳ (Prologo, p. 51. Compare E's reading in App. Crit.), εἰς τὰ ἅγια τοῦ θεοῦ εὐαγγέλια (Müller, Documenti, p. 42), πρὸς τῶν εὐαγγελίων (Procop. Hist. Arc. 5). The oaths to be taken in court begin κατὰ τὰ ἅγια εὐαγγέλια ταῦτα (Bas. XXII, 5, 1 Schol.).

As to the contents of the εὐαγγέλια see Ducange, col. 440, and as to the form of taking the oath see Bas. XXII, 5, 54; Ecloga, XVII, 2 ὁ . . . ἐξ ἐπαγωγῆς ἀντιδίκου ἐφαπτόμενος τῶν ἁγίων τοῦ θεοῦ εὐαγγελίων; Proch. XXXIX, 46 = Epanag. XL, 70; Ducange's note on Anna Comnena, ed. Bonn, ii, p. 670; Reiske's note on Const. Porph., ed. Bonn, ii, p. 436.

παρεχέτωσαν] ὅρκον παρασχεῖν is a regular formula (Bas. VII, 14, 20; Novellae Const. ed. Zach., p. 199).

16. A ship with all its tackle is to be valued at fifty pieces of gold for every thousand modii of capacity, and so is to come into contribution. Where the ship is old, it is to be valued at thirty pieces of gold for every thousand modii. And in the valuation a deduction is to be made of one third, and the ship is to come into contribution accordingly.

μοδισμός (cp. πηχισμός, σχοινισμός and their compounds) is found in the Tabula Heroniana apud Hultsch, Metrologicorum Scriptorum Reliquiae, I, p. 190, and Ducange, s. v., 942, App. 134, quotes passages from Theophylactus, archbishop of Bulgaria, and from Tzetzes on Hesiod.. It corresponds to Lat. *modiatio*, of which Godefroy gives examples (ad Cod. Theod. XIII, 5, 32, ed. Ritter, V, p. 95). Here it evidently means the capacity of the ship calculated in *modii*. The ship's capacity was reckoned either by the number of *modii* which it could contain or by its displacement in *modii* (see Introd., p. cliii). Ducange, s. v. μόδης, quotes from an arithmetic : ὁ θαλάσσιος μόδης ὀφείλει χωρεῖν σίτου καθαροῦ καὶ ἀρύπου λίτρας τεσσαράκοντα. This passage is also found in Palat. gr. 367, f. 88 r,[1] which adds ἡ φούκτας κϛ'· ἡ γὰρ φούκτα ἡ κού- μουλος ἡ λεγομένη ἀντλητὴ ἵστησι λίτρας αϛ'.

χρύσινοι are referred to here and in c. 7. The word is clearly masculine in c. 7, but in P. London, I, p. 204 (sixth century), we find χρύσινα (neut. pl.). χρύσινος, however, is much the commoner form (see Ducange, s. v. and Fabrot's Glossary to Nicetas Choniates, s. v.). It is equivalent to the ' solidus aureus ' or the νόμισμα, seventy-two of which made up a λίτρα χρυσίου (Ducange, de inferioris aevi numismatibus, lxxxvi, lxxxix, in Didot's ed. of the Latin glossary, vol. VII, pp. 188, 189).

ἐξαρτίας] All my MSS. (except A) give ἐξαρτίας. In the titles to c. 2 and c. 43 they give uniformly ἐξαρτίων, i. e. as if from ἐξάρτιον. ἡ ἐξαρτία here and in Bas. LIII, 2, ια', ὁ ἐξαρτισμός in Bas. LIII, 2, α', ἡ ἐξάρτησις in Synopsis minor, N, νθ', and τὰ ἐξάρτια all seem to come to the same thing, i. e. whatever the ship requires for the purpose of sailing. See also Ducange, s. v. ἐξάρτιον, col. 392, and Appendix, col. 70. An Etymologicum quoted by him gives a restricted meaning to ἐξάρτια as τὰ βαστά- ζοντα τὰ σχοινία καὶ τὴν ὀθόνην τοῦ πλοίου.

αὐτοῦ] This must refer to the ship, which has not been alluded to before. If the grammar is to be pressed, we must either say that αὐτοῦ refers to πλοίου in the title of the chapter (see App. Crit.), or we must insert after μοδισμοῦ some words like τοῦ καινοῦ πλοίου or τοῦ πλοίου τοῦ ἀπὸ σκαρίου.

τοῦ παλαιοῦ] It is singular that the age should not be more closely specified at which the ship's valuation is to be diminished. The Venetian Statutes, for instance, make a distinction for loading purposes between ships not five years old, ships between five and seven years old, and ships over seven years old (St. Zeno, 61); and one would expect similar precision here. In c. 11 πλοῖον παλαίον is referred to in the same indefinite way.

As to the length of life of mediaeval ships, see Canale (M. G.), Istoria di Genova, Firenze, 1860, vol. II, p. 584.

καὶ ἐν τῇ τιμήσει κτλ.] This passage evidently refers to new as well as to old ships.

τὸ τρίτον μέρος] Various mediaeval statutes lay down that

---

[1] This MS. (f. 88 r.-90) contains an interesting passage on the measurement of ships which the learned editor of the Νέος Ἑλληνο- μνήμων promises to publish (Νέος Ἑλλ. I, p. 125).

where a ship contributes to average, a deduction of one-third from its valuation is to be made for the tackle. St. Ragus. VII, 7; Ordin. Trani, 22; St. Ancon. 86, 87. Under the law as established by the Consulate of the Sea, there were two systems of valuing the ship for average purposes. Where the average loss is made by common accord, the ship contributes at one-half its value, reckoning in the tackle. Consulate, 50 (95), ed. Pard. II, p. 101, with a useful note of Pard.; 93, ed. Casaregi, p. 86; Targa, p. 325. Where the loss occurs from sudden necessity and is made without consultation, the ship contributes at two-thirds of its value, reckoning in the tackle. Consulate, 239 (284), ed. Pard. II, p. 323; 281, ed. Casaregi, p. 352; Targa, l. c. The latter system corresponds with that laid down in the Sea-law.

κουφιζέσθω] Cp. c. 40 κουφιζέσθωσαν τὴν ὑποτριβὴν καὶ τὴν ἀποβροχήν. 'κουφίζειν ist das technische Wort für entlasten (Schuldkonto),' Preisigke in P. Strassburg, I, p. 59, n. 4. Hence it is used here, and of forgiving debts (Polyb. VI, 17, 5; Plut. Caes. 37) or remitting taxes (Malal, p. 398, Bonn).

17. The law ordains: let them not write moneys lent at sea to be repaid out of property on land without risk. If they do write them, let them be invalid under the Rhodian law. But where loans are made on fields or on hills to be repaid out of property on land without risk, let them write them down in accordance with the Rhodian law.

The subject-matter of this and the two next chapters is dealt with in the Introduction, p. ccxxi.

ὁ νόμος κελεύει] It is a question whether ὁ νόμος is an extraneous law to which appeal is made or whether ὁ νόμος κελεύει is merely a rhetorical phrase to denote the sanction, equivalent to ' be it enacted' of English statutes. The same phrase in a different order (κελεύει ὁ νόμος) reappears c. 1; and ἐπὶ τὸν ῥόδιον νόμον (c. ιζ'), κατὰ τὸν ῥόδιον νόμον (cc. ιζ', ιη'), and κατὰ τὸν νόμον (c. 18) are also found. It is probable that in all these cases the phrase is merely added to enhance the authority of the proposition laid down.

τὰ ἐν τῇ θαλάσσῃ δεδανεισμένα] The opposition between this and τὰ ἐν ἀγροῖς ἢ ἐν ὄρεσι δανειζόμενα is taken by the learned editors to denote an opposition between loans made to travellers by sea and loans made to travellers by land. Pard. translates the latter phrase ' quae vero per agros et montes iter facientibus creduntur', and he is followed in substance by FM. The distinction in my opinion is rather between ' loans made on the security of ships and goods at sea' and ' loans made on the security of land whether cultivated or uncultivated '.

TRANSLATION AND COMMENTARY

ἔγγαια καὶ ἀκίνδυνα] The word ἔγγαια is sadly perplexing. In the two places in which it occurs in this chapter, the tradition is in favour of the spelling which I give in the text, but there is authority for ἔγγυα and ἔγγεα. In c. 16 and c. 18 there is the same diversity among the MSS. (see App. Crit.). In this chapter Pard. reads in both places ἔγγυα and translates ' cum (or sub) fideius-sione '. FM read ἔγγεα and translate 'fideiussoribus accedentibus'. In c. 16 Pard. also reads ἔγγυα and ἐγγύων, but his translation does not assist the reader to understand in what sense he took the word. FM who read ἔγγεα and ἐγγέων are also vague. In c. 18 Pard. reads ἐκ τῶν ἐγγυῶν which he translates ' a fideiussoribus ' and ἔγγυα which he translates ' sub fideiussione '. FM who read ἐγγέων and ἔγγεα adopt practically the same translation.

Now there is a well-known word ἔγγειος or ἔγγαιος. As to spelling, ἔγγαιος, which my best MSS. give, is strongly supported both by the inscriptions and the papyri; see also Lobeck, Phryn. 297. As to meaning, it means ' belonging to land ', ' on land.' Hence where it is used with χρήματα, it does not necessarily mean that the property consists of land; it equally well refers to mov-ables on land (see Dareste, Inscriptions, I, p. 331, n. 4; Billeter, Zinsfuss, p. 21). It is constantly used in opposition to ναυτικός or ὑπερπόντιος. Demosthenes contrasts ἔγγειοι τόκοι with ναυτικοὶ τόκοι (c. Phorm. 914), and συμβόλαιον ἔγγειον with συμβόλαιον ναυτικόν (c. Apat. 893); P. Elephantine, p. 20 καὶ ἐγγαίων καὶ ναυτικῶν (B. C. 310); Dareste, Inscr. II, p. 86 ἐπὶ ὑποθήκαις ἐγγαίοις (B. C. 200); Dareste, Inscr. I, pp. 313, 316 ἔγγαια καὶ ὑπερπόντια (second century B. C.; this and similar phrases are intended to sweep in all the party's property); Pollux, III, 84 and 115 ἔγγεια δανείσματα in contrast with ναυτικά; Iust. Nov. 106 εἰς τὸν τῶν ἐγγείων μεταχωρεῖν τρόπον; Synopsis Ambr. LIII, V, ις'; Ecloga pr. aucta, XI, 8; Epanag. aucta, XXII, 37. It is probable that ἔγγαιος is the right word in all these places of the Sea-law; ἔγγυα, though in one place (c. 16, 2) it has the authority of L, is mainly supported by the later MSS.

ἀκίνδυνος is found frequently in contracts of loan, deposit, hiring, and the like in reference to the property lent, deposited, or hired. It means that the property in question is to be free from risk, i. e. that the lender, depositor, or lettor is unconditionally entitled to have it replaced. It is applied both to the capital amount and to the interest, where interest is provided. It is sometimes found alone (Dareste, Inscriptions, I, p. 322, second century B. C.), sometimes in the form ἀκίνδυνος παντὸς κινδύνου (Dareste, op. cit., I, pp. 313, 316, second century B. C.; Berliner Gr. Urk. 1053, B. C. 13, 729, A. D. 144; P. Oxyrhynchus, III, p. 237, A. D. 169; P. Raineri, 35, p. 162, A. D. 216; Berliner Gr. Urk. 938, fourth century A. D.), or ἀπὸ παντὸς κινδύνου (Berliner Gr. Urk. 314, A. D. 630), sometimes in the fuller form ἀκίνδυνος παντὸς κινδύνου καὶ ἀνυπόλογος παντὸς ὑπολόγου or λόγου (Berliner Gr. Urk. 702,

A. D. 151; P. Raineri, 36, p. 163, A. D. 225; P. London, III, p. 175, A. D. 227).

What then is the meaning of ἔγγαια καὶ ἀκίνδυνα when applied to maritime loans? In my opinion the words are exactly equivalent to the phrase which occurs constantly in the Latin mediaeval documents, 'salva in terra.' Where money is made repayable, 'salvum in terra,' it is unconditionally repayable (salvum = ἀκίνδυνον), and it is repayable 'in terra'—out of the debtor's property on land as well as on sea. 'Inde in antea habetis salvum capitania et lucro hic in terra super omnia bona mea hereditatis et in rebus stabilia et mobilia' (Documents in Camera, 1, p. 433; II, p. xli). A receives money 'itinere maris in societate vel accomendatione vel mutuo ad statutum terminum vel ad statutum iter', A keeps it beyond the term or sends it on another route. Then the loan 'sit salva in terra scilicet in bonis' of A, and bears interest at twenty per cent. (St. Pera, IV, 4; cp. Sea-law, c. 18). On the same principle where money is lent ἔγγαιον καὶ ἀκίνδυνον, the money is unconditionally repayable, and the lender is entitled to recover it out of all the debtor's property, whether on land or at sea, and whether movable or immovable.

μὴ γραφέτωσαν] This direction may be simply addressed to parties about to enter into such contracts; but it sounds as if it was directed to a class charged with the execution of instruments. This class could only be the body of notaries. Although the preparation of legal documents was not confined to them, it is clear that they drew up the far greater number. As to the conditions required for the validity of instruments of loan, see Nov. LXXIII, 2 = Bas. XXII, 4, 1 = Epanagoge, XIII, 12; Novellae Const. ed. Zach, pr. 57; Ecloga XI, 2.

ἐπιγράφουσιν] This chapter affords a good illustration of the Byzantine passion for varying the expression, where there is no variation of the sense. There is δεδανεισμένα and δανειζόμενα; γραφέτωσαν and ἐπιγράφουσιν, ἐπιγραφέτωσαν; ἐπὶ τὸν ῥόδιον νόμον and κατὰ τὸν ῥόδιον νόμον.

18. A man borrows money at interest and for eight years pays the legal interest. After eight years it happens that there is a destruction or fire or inroad of barbarians. Let interest cease to be payable in accordance with the Rhodian law. If the man does not pay legal interest, the written contract prevails in accordance with the former agreement, as the writing bears on its face.

This chapter, like some others, has nothing to do with maritime law, and the reference to the Rhodian law is particularly out of place. Some of the MSS. entitule it 'concerning a loan on land' (see App. Crit.). As to its meaning, see Introduction, p. ccxxi.

ἐὰν δανείσηταί τις] The printed texts read ἐὰν δανείσῃ τις. Τις is in none of my MSS. The objection to δανείσῃ, which in one form or other is supported by all the MSS., is this. If it is the 3rd person sing. aor. subj. act., there is a difference of subject between it and τελέσῃ; 'if A lends and B pays.' If it is the 2nd person sing. aor. subj. middle, 'if thou borrowest,' then there is a change from the second to the third person. I have therefore written ἐὰν δανείσηταί τις, although the grammatical peculiarities of the Sea-law are such that to emend for the sake of removing one of them is perhaps superfluous.

ὀκτώ] This word is required to complete the sense, and, if expressed by η΄, would easily drop out after ἔτη.

συμβῇ] Grammar would require either συμβῇ ἀπώλεια or συμβῇ ἀπώλειαν γενέσθαι. In the Sea-law the accusative is always found after συμβῇ in the best MSS., whether γενέσθαι is added or not; but where it is not added there is a strong tendency among the later MSS. to put the nominative. This tendency exists even among the twelfth-century MSS., such as MQ. See the App. Crit. at cc. 2, 3; 10, 2, 4, 8; 15, 4; 17, 9; 28, 3; 29, 3; 36, 8; 39, 4, 11.

ἀπώλειαν . . . ἢ πυρκαϊὰν ἢ διαρπαγὴν βαρβάρων] This list of the casualties which may affect the borrower's property is strong evidence that we have to do with land and not with ships or goods at sea. The three misfortunes which may happen to things of the latter class are constantly described as fire, pirates, and shipwreck (cc. 17, 6; 28, 3; 29, 3). Now, although ἀπώλεια might be treated as equivalent to shipwreck, it is difficult to interpret διαρπαγὴ βαρβάρων of anything but a plundering on land.

τὰ ἔγγραφα κτλ.] This is a peculiarly clumsy phrase. It seems to mean nothing more than that the terms of the contract are to prevail. The contract is generally described as τὰ ἔγγραφα (title of c. 25; title of c. 29; cc. 20, 1; 21, 7, 9; 24, 4; 30, 8), sometimes as συνθῆκαι (c. 17, 8, 11), or συνθῆκαι τῶν ἐγγράφων (c. 22, 3).

19. Captains in actual command, where they contribute not less than three-fourths in value of the ship, wherever they are dispatched, may enter into agreements how they are to borrow money and send it on board ship either for the season or for a voyage, and what they have agreed upon is to prevail; and he who lent the money is to send a man to receive payment (?).

This chapter, as Pard. says, is 'fort obscur'. Francesco Venturi left it in the original Greek; and I should perhaps be wiser to imitate the discretion of the bishop. I have made as few altera-

68

tions in the tradition as were required to make the text intelligible; but it is probable that there is deep corruption somewhere.

οἱ ναύκληροι ναυκληροῦντες] See Introduction, p. cxxxiv.

συμβαλλομένου] I do not see what meaning can be given to this clause if we retain the MS. tradition. FM translate ' collata navi non minus tertia parte', which is as obscure as the original. By reading συμβαλλόμενοι we get this sense, that the owners in command in order to borrow must own three-quarters in value of the ship. As to the power of a majority in value of the owners to bind the minority, see Introduction, p. clxiv.

τοῦ τριμερίτου] I have translated this as if it was equivalent to τῶν τριῶν μερῶν, i. e. three parts out of four. This is rather doubtful. There is a word μερίτης which means a partner : οἱ μὲν διανεμόμενοι . . . μερῖται (Poll. VIII, 136), μερίτην· συμμερίστήν . . . μερίτης· ὁ τινὸς πράγματος μεταλαγχάνων (Suid. s. v., who cites from Polybius). ὁ τριμερίτης then would be a person who had three shares; but it is evident that, if the text is correct, the word cannot mean that.

καθὸ δεῖ] This clause is dependent on συνεγράψαντο, ' as they have agreed how they must, &c., so is it to prevail.'

χρηννύειν] Here the word seems to mean ' to borrow '. This form is not found elsewhere, but similar forms are found twice in the Characters of Theophrastus. Char. V καὶ τοῦτο περιὼν χρήννυναι (χρὴ νῦν ἀεὶ codices optimi) τοῖς φιλοσόφοις; Char. X ἀπαγορεῦσαι τῇ γυναικὶ μήτε ἅλας χρωννύειν μήτε ἐλλύχνιον κτλ. In both these places it appears to mean ' to lend '.

θερείαν] The MS. readings are meaningless. By reading θερείαν one gets a meaning which is in accordance with other authorities. Money might be lent for a single voyage (κατὰ πλοῦν). It might also be lent for the whole summer, i. e. the whole period during which the sea was open to navigation (see Introduction, p. cxlii). Another possible reading, which gives the same sense, would be κατὰ τὴν ὡραίαν. There is no authority in my MSS. for Pard.'s reading: καθ' ἑτερόπλουν καὶ κατ' ἀμφοτερόπλουν.

ἄνθρωπον] Where the loan was not to be repaid to the lender himself, he sent a man who could give a discharge. (Dig. XXII, 2, 4, 1; XLIV, 7, 23; XLV, 1, 122, 1.)

ἐπιχρήννυται] Leuncl. translates ' mutuum tradat '; FM ' mutuo tradat '; Pard. ' pecuniae invigilet '. H. Sieveking (Das Seedarlehen des Altertums, Leipzig, 1893) thinks that the ἄνθρωπος is a joint-lender (which is impossible) and tr. ' welcher seinerseits (Med.) mit (ἐπι) Gläubiger ist ' (p. 43). The word here ought to mean ' receive payment ' or ' give a discharge ' rather than ' hand over the money ' or ' look after it '. It is possible that ὃς ἂν ἐπιχ. refers, not to the ἄνθρωπος, but to ὁ χρήσας τὰ χ.

TRANSLATION AND COMMENTARY

CHAPTERS OF RHODIAN LAW BY WAY OF EXCERPT CONCERNING MARITIME AFFAIRS

The meaning of this and the other titles which are found in the MSS. is considered in the Introduction, p. lxvii. The table of chapters as given in the text is that contained in the oldest and best MSS. It attempts to give in a few words the pith of each chapter. In M we get a table of a different character, namely, one which gives the first three or four words of each chapter (Appendix C). There is still another table of chapters, which is given in the MSS. of the Ecloga ad Prochiron mutata, and is printed in Zach.'s ed., pp. 60, 61. I have not reproduced it, as it is clearly the work of an abridger. Some of the MSS. of Part II give a table of chapters which I have printed in Appendix B. This table is curious, because some of the headings aim at giving the substance of the chapter, while others merely give the first three or four words. MSS. which do not give this table of chapters of Part II occasionally give a heading either above or beside the respective chapter. For instance, c. ιθ´ has in some MSS. a heading which in others has got attached to the preceding chapter (see App. Crit.). As regards other law-books, the Farmer's Law has no table in any MS. which I have seen. The want of a table in this case would not be much felt, as the chapters themselves are for the most part very brief. The Soldier's Law has elaborate tables, both in L and in Vallicell. F, 47 (early eleventh century). These two tables, though they differ widely in detail, have this peculiarity in common, that they give the provenance of each chapter. They distinguish clearly the chapters which are derived from the Digest or the Code, and those which are derived ἐκ τῶν Ῥούφου [Ῥόφου Vall.] καὶ τῶν τακτικῶν (Vall. F, 47, f. 337 r., 339 r.; L, f. 339 v.). It is probable, therefore, that the table to the Soldier's Law in its original form was the work of the compiler of the law. A later scribe would not have been able to indicate the sources from which the book is made up. The other Byzantine law-books have headings to the τίτλοι, which are probably contemporaneous, and these headings are in some cases collected together in front of the book in the form of a πίναξ. The table prefixed to the Ecloga in Vall. F, 47 (f. 301 r.), is remarkable in this respect. In the body of the book each τίτλος has a title but not the individual chapters. In the table at the beginning each chapter has a title but the τίτλοι have not. For instance, in the table of chapters we get (f. 302 v.):—

Τίτλος ι´.

α´ περὶ δανειου καὶ ἐνεχύρων.
β´ περὶ δανείστοῦ ἐπιβάντος καὶ ἐνέχυρα λαβόντος.

70

TABLE OF PART III

γ´ περὶ τοῦ μὴ ἐνάγεσθαι τὴν γυναῖκα ὑπὸ τῶν ἀνδρικῶν χρεῶν
μὴ συνομολογησάσης.

δ´ περὶ κοινωνίας ἐγγράφου καὶ ἀγράφου.

On the other hand, in the text we get (f. 321 r.) :—

τίτλος ι´ περὶ δανείου ἐγγράφου καὶ ἀγράφου καὶ τῶν διδομένων ἐν
αὐτοῖς ἐνεχύρων.

As regards the indexes of the Basilica see Heimbach's Prolegomena, p. 118. On the whole, the tables which are prefixed to
Byzantine law-books in the best MSS. appear to be contemporaneous with the books themselves, if not the work of their
authors ; and the same is probably the case with this table to
Part III (see Introduction, p. lxix). We are therefore justified in
using the titles to interpret the substance of the chapters.

1. Concerning thefts of a ship's anchors.

κλαπέντων] It is common enough in Byzantine Greek to find
a masculine participle in agreement with a feminine substantive,
especially where the substantive is of the first declension and in
the genitive plural. See c. 29, 5 μὴ πληρωθέντων . . . τῶν ἡμερῶν ;
De Boor's index to Theoph. Simocatta, p. 369 ; Lobeck, Aglaoph.,
p. 216 ; Krumbacher, Geschichte, p. 251 ; Gradenwitz, Ein-
führung, p. 46 n. The Byzantines seem to have sometimes used
the form ἄγκυρον (see App. Crit. on c. 2, 2). In c. 11, 9, Mess.
reads ἄγκυρα.

2. Concerning thefts of anchors and other tackle.

3. Concerning a theft wrought by a sailor.

4. Concerning plundering of a ship by thieves or pirates.

κλεπτῶν ἢ πειρατῶν] The κλέπτης is a land-robber, e. g. a man
who cuts the ship's cables, or steals its anchors, or lays hands on
a merchant who has gone ashore. The πειρατής is a sea-robber.
In the Sea-law πειρατής and λῃστής are used indiscriminately.
The πειρατής appears to be distinguished from the λῃστής in
c. 15, 4, but the redundance is probably merely rhetorical. The
three misfortunes which may befal a ship are described in c. 17
as πῦρ, λῃσταί, or ναυάγιον ; in c. 28 and c. 29 they are described
as πυρκαιά, πειρατεία, or ναυάγιον. Originally λῃστής included the
sea-robber. Πειρατής, πειρατεία, πειρατήριον, are late words, not
to be found (according to Valck. ad Ammonium, p. 194) until
the Septuagint and Polybius. In Byzantine Greek there seems
to be no distinction between πειρατής and λῃστής. Dig. XIV, 2,
2, 3, apparently makes a distinction between *piratae* and *prae-*
dones. Both words are expressed by πειραταί in Synopsis Ambr.
LIII, 5, β´. Dig. XIII, 6, 18 pr. speaks of *latrones* and *piratae.*
Both words are expressed by λῃσταί in Bas. XIII, 1, 18. The

71

'latrones aut praedones' of Dig. IV, 6, 9 and the 'latrunculi ve. praedones' of Dig. XLIX, 15, 24 are rendered in Bas. (X, 35, 9; XXXIV, 1, 20), by λῃσταί.

5. Concerning injuries inflicted by sailors while fighting.

κύλλωμα is defined by LS as 'lameness', for which they cite Galen. The word seems to include in c. 5 any bodily injury. Cp. the Farmer's law, c. οβ΄ (M) ἐὰν ... συμβῇ κυλλωθῆναι κύνα τινά, where R substitutes τυφλωθῆναι.

6. Concerning homicide committed by sailors while fighting.

7. Concerning sailors who in a fight put out an eye or cause scrotal hernia.

ναυτῶν] The chapter includes captains and merchants. It is possible that the provision which formed the model of c. 7 did not extend to captains and merchants, and that they were included by the author of Part III. It is equally possible that the author of the table—whether he was the same as the author of Part III or not—was careless.

8. Concerning captain and sailors who take some one else's stock and run away with the ship.

ἐνθήκην] This word, which under the form of *hentica* plays so great a part in mediaeval commerce and law, is not classical. It occurs often in the Sea-law (Title 39, 40; cc. 11, 7; 21, 4; 32, 4). In some of these cases it seems to have merely the sense of γόμος or φορτία. In its proper sense, it is used of the merchant's trading capital when it is desired to lay stress upon the fact of his ownership. It corresponds to the classical ἀφορμή (Lob. Phryn. 223).

9. Concerning deliberations about jettison by captain and passengers.

ἀποβολῆς] The text of the chapter has (l. 1) ἐκβολῆς and (l. 6) ἐκβολή. In the Basilica, the words which regularly corresponded to *iactus, iacturam facere* are ἀποβολή, ἀποβάλλειν (see Synopsis Ambr. LIII, 3, *passim*). In the Sea-law, ἀποβολή is found here, Title 35 (of the mast), and c. 38, 8 (of goods); ἀποβάλλεσθαι is used of the mast breaking (c. 35, 2) and (in a doubtful passage) of the ship being lost (c. 39, 14). But the Sea-law uses ἐκβολή even more commonly in the sense of *iactus*. It is used of goods in Title 43; cc. 9, 1 and 6; 22, 7; 43, 1; and of the mast in Title 44; cc. 35, 1; 44, 1. ἐκβολή and ἐκ-

TABLE OF PART III

βάλλεσθαι are also used simply of unloading goods (Title 33 ; c. 33, 4); and this is the sense in which they are commonly used by Byzantine writers (Müller, Documenti, p. 44).

10. Concerning injury to ship or wreck.

11. Concerning the hiring of ships by merchants.

12. Concerning every deposit whether given in a ship or in a house.

13. Concerning disputes about a deposit of gold.

14. Concerning denial by a depositary of the deposit.

15. Concerning a merchant or passenger or slave who has been received in deposit remaining on shore, while the ship starts off to escape pillage or an attack of pirates.

παρατιθέντος] refers only to the δοῦλος. ἐν ἀκτῇ ἀπομείναντος refers to the merchant and passenger as well as to the slave. καί is superfluous. See note on c. 2 καὶ τούτων.

ἐπήρειαν] This word is used in Byzantine documents in a sense which the dictionaries do not notice. Primarily it denotes any 'despiteful treatment' (LS). Then it gets the special sense of obtaining money by threats, extortion, blackmail (C. I. G. 4957, l. 6; P. Fiorentini, 99, t. Domitian προορώμεθα μήποτε ἐπηρεάσῃ ἡμῖν of a dissolute son who was wasting his parents' substance; P. Grenfell, II, p. 132, A. D. 400 βούλεσθε οὖν τὸν κατασχεθέντα πάσης ἐπηρίας ἀπαλλάξαι). In one case it appears to equal πρόστιμον. P. Genève, II, p. 16 ὁ δὲ ἐπελευσόμενος τῷ ἑτέρῳ ἐπιστροφήσει ἐπηρίας λόγου (qy. λόγῳ) ἀργυρίου δραχμῶν μυριάδας τριακοσίας (A. D. 350). In the tenth century and thereafter it appears to denote an extraordinary tax levied by the public authority, something in the nature of the English 'benevolence'. In charters granting privileges to monasteries or religious persons there is always a provision freeing them from any ἐπήρεια or other impost. Examples are: Prologo, p. 36 (bis) (A. D. 999); Acta et Diplomata, VI, p. 3 (A. D. 1073); V, p. 138 (A. D. 1074); VI, p. 52 (A. D. 1088); Spata, p. 217 (A. D. 1109). In the privileges of the merchants of Ancona, confirmed by Andronicus Palaeologus senior, the merchants are to give so much ὑπέρ τε κομμερκίου καμπανιστικοῦ μεσιτικίου καὶ πάσης ἄλλης ἐπηρείας καὶ δόσεως (Acta et Diplomata, III, p. 17). The verb ἐπηρεάζεσθαι is similarly used in the sense of having tribute demanded (Acta et Diplomata, IV, p. 318 [A. D. 1175], p. 319 [A. D. 1189]). ἐπηρεαστής is also used of an official who levies exorbitant impositions: εἰ δὲ γενήσῃ ἐπηρεαστὴς δι' αἰσχρὸν κέρδος (Incerti de Officiis Regiis ad calcem Cecaumeni, p. 79). We may therefore justly apply it here to tribute demanded by corsairs or pirates.

73

TRANSLATION AND COMMENTARY

16. Concerning money lent out to be carried over sea.

ἐπιποντίων] The use of χρήματα ἐπιπόντια, in the sense of 'pecunia traiecticia,' and δάνειον ἐπιπόντιον in the sense of 'foenus nauticum', is not noticed in the dictionaries, but it is not uncommon in Byzantine text-books. Athanasius, XVII, 1 (Heimbach, 'Ανέκδοτα, p. 161) τὰ ἐπιπόντια χρήματα; Ecloga privata aucta, Tit. XI περὶ δανείου ἐπιποντίου; XI, 7 ἐπιπόντια δάνεια. The word διαπόντιος in this sense is much commoner. To the examples given by Ducange, 298, add Theod. Hermopolit. Brev. Nov. n. 106, ed. Zach., p. 102; Synopsis Ambrosiana, LIII, 1, θ΄; LIII, 5, ιε΄; Synopsis major LIII, 5, α΄ (Pard. I, p. 189); Index Basilicorum in MS. Coislin. 151 (Pard. I, p. 157); Epit. Seldeniana, f. 69 v.; Epitome, IX, 31; XVII, 87; see also Bruns on the Syrisch-Römisches Rechtbuch, p. 237, for another use of the word.

17. Concerning loans of gold and silver made on the footing of a share in profits.

κερδοκοινωνίᾳ] This word apparently only occurs here and in c. 9, 15, but its meaning fortunately is clear. The MSS. vary as to the spelling (see App. Crit.).

18. Concerning a man borrowing money for a fixed time and going abroad.

19. Concerning a man hiring a ship and giving an earnest.

20. Concerning a man hiring a ship and their agreeing in writing or coming to terms without writing.

συμφωνησάντων] The change from singular to plural is quite in accordance with Byzantine usage. The MSS. vary here, as they do in c. 17, 2, where I print ἐγγράψηται, though the plural, which is given by some of the best MSS., may be right.

21. Concerning disputes between two captains in partnership.

22. Concerning a merchant hiring the whole cargo-space of the ship.

γόμον] γόμος here seems to mean the whole carrying capacity of the ship. It generally means rather the cargo on board looked at as a whole,—the whole mass of goods which the ship is capable of receiving (Demosth. 883, 11; 1290, 19; Title 43; cc. 22, 3; 27, 1; 32, 1; 39, 5; 43, 2).

23. Concerning agreements between captain and merchant about cargo.

74

TABLE OF PART III

24. Concerning agreements between captain and merchant and the giving of half the freight and a subsequent change of intention.

τὰ ἡμίναυλα] is found here, cc. 24, 4 and 5; 27, 7; 30, 8; 32, 3; τὰ ἥμισυ τοῦ ναύλου in c. 20, 6; τὸ ἥμισυ ναῦλον in c. 20, 7, and τὰ ἥμισυ ναῦλα in c. 24, 1. τὰ ἡμίση ναῦλα is only found in inferior MSS. (see App. Crit.). The motive for these differences appears to be simply a love of variety; the meaning is always the same. As regards the grammar, cp. Title 37 and Title 41, in both of which cases there is a similar change to the accusative (or nominative) absolute.

25. Concerning a merchant not keeping to the time provided by the contract.

26. Concerning a ship wrecked while the sailors are sleeping on shore.

κλασματισθέντος] κλασματίζειν is not in LS. Ducange only cites it from Theophanes of cutting an army to pieces. Dind.-Steph. copies Ducange. The passage is p. 397 in De Boor's ed. The word is common in the table of chapters, but is nowhere found in the text of the Sea-law. It is found in Novellae Const., p. 451, where the sense is doubtful.

27. Concerning a ship which is wrecked on its way to be loaded by a merchant or partnership.

28. Concerning a ship which is wrecked from the fault of a merchant or partner.

29. Concerning a ship which is wrecked before the time fixed by the contract has arrived or after the time has arrived.

30. Concerning a ship with cargo which breaks to pieces, while the merchant is saved with gold on him.

31. Concerning disaster to ship and salvage of cargo in part.

φόρτου] The Sea-law appears to make no substantial difference in meaning between φόρτος, φορτίον, and φορτία. If a distinction can be drawn, it is this. ὁ φόρτος denotes the cargo on board, looked at as one mass without reference to its ownership (here, cc. 30, 3 (?) and 5; 38, 3 and 5; as to its meaning in c. 40, 10, see the Commentary). τὰ φορτία denotes the cargo looked at as an aggregate of goods belonging to different merchants (φορτία, Title 42; cc. 11, 1; 20, 8; 22, 4; 27, 4; 29, 2; 33, 1; 34, 3, 5, 7, 11; 35, 3; 39, 6, 11; 42, 1, 2; φορτίων, Title 34; cc. 10, 9; 34,

6; 43, 5; φορτίοις, cc. 16, 3; 27, 6). τὸ φορτίον only occurs once, and = ὁ φόρτος (c. 36, 5).

32. Concerning a ship hired or sailing in partnership and wrecked on its way through the strait.

ἐκπορίζειν] The spelling and sense of this word are equally doubtful. ἐκπορίζειν is used three times in Theophanes, ' de navibus per Hellespontum in mare Aegaeum devectis' (De Boor, Index graecitatis Theoph., p. 743). It is also found twice in the same sense in a sixth-century inscription; Dittenberger, Orientis Gr. Inscr. 521, vol. II, p. 179, where see note. The word therefore here would refer to a ship which had started on its voyage after having been loaded at Constantinople. There is nothing of this in the text of c. 32, unless it can be extracted from ἐπὶ γόμον ὑπάγῃ, as to which see Commentary.

33. Concerning a ship which is wrecked after unloading.

34. Concerning a ship which carries silk and injury wrought to the cargo from a storm or from bilge.

35. Concerning a ship which loses its mast.

36. Concerning a ship which in sailing runs down another ship.

37. Concerning a ship which is wrecked while the goods of the merchants or passengers are saved.

38. Concerning a ship loaded with corn and caught in a gale.

39. Concerning the loss of a ship which is loaded and salvage of the cargo.

βολήσαντος] if it = βολίσαντος ought to mean 'having cast the lead', which is impossible. The difficulty of explaining it as 'having made jettison' is that there is no allusion to jettison in the chapter. Possibly a line has dropped out and we should read βουλήσ⟨ει τοῦ ναυκλήρου καὶ τῶν ναυτῶν ναυαγήσ⟩αντος. See the text, l. 2.

40. Concerning a ship which is wrecked while ship and cargo are saved in part.

41. Concerning a ship which is destroyed while the goods of passengers are either saved or lost with it.

42. Concerning a ship which springs a leak while carrying cargo.

43. Concerning a ship which makes jettison of freight and tackle.

TABLE OF PART III

44. Concerning a ship which loses its mast or its tillers in a gale.

45. Concerning a man who brings something safe from the open sea to land from a ship which is wrecked.

46. Concerning a man who saves the long-boat from a ship which has broken off from it.

47. Concerning a man who saves something from the depths from a ship that is wrecked.

BEGINNING OF THE LAW

1. A ship is lying in harbour or on a beach and is robbed of its anchors. The thief is caught and confesses. The law lays down that he be flogged and that he make good twice over the damage he has done.

Chapters 1–3 are dealt with in the Introduction, p. lxxx.

πλοῖον] is the only word for ship used in the Sea-law, and ναῦται the only word for sailors.

ὁρμῇ] The MS. authority here is in favour of ὁρμᾷ, as it is in c. 2, 2 in favour of ὁρμῶντος where I read ὁρμοῦντος. In c. 36, 2, where I also read ὁρμοῦντος, the authority is more evenly balanced. In all these places the sense requires a form of ὁρμεῖν, ' to lie at anchor,' and not of ὁρμᾶν, ' to hasten.' It is possible that the Byzantines confused the two words. Theoph., p. 353, Bonn; p. 227, De Boor ἀπετέλεσε λιμένα, ὡς δύνασθαι ὁρμᾶν ἐν αὐτῇ πλοῖα πολλὰ παμμεγέθη. Here one would expect ὁρμεῖν, which De Boor suggests, but all his MSS. give ὁρμᾶν except h which gives ὁρᾶν. Theoph., p. 591, Bonn; p. 386, De Boor τοῦ δὲ τῆς πόλεως στόλου εἰς τὸν λιμένα τοῦ ἁγίου Μάμαντος ὁρμοῦντος, where there is no variant in De Boor's MSS. In this and similar cases it is impossible to be certain of the true reading, as the Byzantine writers of this age have lost all sense of linguistic precision.

ἐπὶ λιμένα ἢ ἐν ἀκτῇ] This phrase has no doubt the same sense as ἐν λιμένι ἢ ἐν ἀκτῇ (cc. 2, 2 ; 15, 3), and the difference is merely due to the unhealthy craving for varying the phrase. Cp. εἰς τόπον ἢ ἐν ἀκτῇ, c. 39, 3, and εἰς τὸ πλοῖον μείναντας, c. 26, 4. λιμήν is well defined in the Canonismata Homeri MSS. quoted by Ducange, s.v. σκάλα (App. 171) ἔστι δὲ λιμὴν μὲν κόλπος θαλάττης ταραχῆς ἀνέμων ἀπηλλαγμένος, ὅρμους ἐπιτηδείους ἔχων εἰς ὑποδοχὴν τῶν νεῶν. ὅρμος δέ, τὸ μέρος τοῦ λιμένος, εἰς ὃ ἑλκόμεναι αἱ νῆες δέδενται, ὃ οἱ κοινοὶ σκάλαν λέγουσι.

ἀγκυρῶν] In the mediaeval maritime statutes the number of

anchors which a ship was to carry was frequently determined by law, the number varying with the size of the ship; e. g. St. Zeno, 8 (St. maritt. Venez., p. 83); St. Ragus. VII, 3. Thefts of anchors or cables were a source of danger to travellers as late as the seventeenth century. ' They are naturally such thieves,' says Sir George Wheler, speaking of the Magnoti, ' that when any vessel cometh into their harbour, they will go by night and cut the cables of their ships [legendum, off their slips] when they can find nothing else to lay hold of, which sometimes endangers the vessels running ashore, when not discover'd in time ' (Journey into Greece, London, 1682, p. 47). Bernard Randolph tells a similar story (Present State of Archipelago, Oxford, 1687, p. 32).

κατασχεθείς] It seems superfluous to make the punishment of the thief conditional upon his being caught. In c. 3, 5 κατασχεθῇ is opposed to διὰ μαρτύρων ἐλεγχθῇ, and there it seems equivalent to ' is caught in the act '. It would have the same meaning here if the reading of E were adopted: κατασχεθῇ . . . ἢ ὁμολογήσῃ. Cp. Constitutiones Regni Siciliae, ed. 1786, p. 29 τοὺς . . . ταῖς τοιαύταις κλοπαῖς κατασχεθέντας ἢ ἐκουσίως ὁμολογοῦντας, where it translates ' in rapinis huiusmodi deprehensos '. In the earlier law-books, however, κατέχεσθαι or καταλαμβάνεσθαι is never used by itself in the sense of being caught in the act. E. g. Scholiast of Bas. LX, 12, 6 μανίφεστος μὲν κλοπή ἐστιν . . . ὅτε ὁ κλέπτης καταλαμβάνεται μετὰ τοῦ κλαπέντος πράγματος; Bas. LX, 53, 3 uses ὁ καταληφθεὶς ἐπὶ μυσαρᾷ τινι πράξει as a translation of ' in scelere deprehensus '. The regular phrase is ἐπ' αὐτοφώ(ο)ρῳ λαμβάνεσθαι. E. g. Scholiast, supra; Πεῖρα, LV, 2.

κελεύει ὁ νόμος] See p. 65.

βασανίζεσθαι] It is clear that the word here and in c. 3, 6 does not refer to the use of torture as a means of extracting truth. In this case the man has confessed, and in the other his guilt is proved by witnesses. βασανίζεσθαι here must be used of punishment, and, as this sense is not noticed in the dictionaries, it is worth while pointing out how it arose. βάσανος is strictly any means of proof. The word was then applied κατ' ἐξοχήν to a favourite method of proof, which consisted in inflicting physical pain with a view of extracting evidence; and so it came to denote the instruments themselves by which pain was inflicted for that purpose. κουεστίων δέ ἐστι τὸ ἐπαγαγεῖν βάσανον καὶ πόνον τῷ σώματι πρὸς κατάληψιν τῆς ἀληθείας (Bas. LX, 21, 14, 41, where βάσανον translates ' tormenta ', of Dig. XLVII, 10, 15, 41). It is obvious that some of the instruments by which pain is inflicted for the purpose of extracting evidence will inflict it equally well by way of punishment, especially where it is desired to make the punishment long drawn out.

According to Mommsen (Strafrecht, p. 985, n. 5) the rack is never used as a means of punishment. But the one use in some

PART III, CHAPTER I

cases slides gently into the other; e. g. if a man obstinately denies a crime while there is overwhelming evidence against him, you go on racking him as a punishment for his obstinacy. 'Si convictus ad proprium facinus detegentibus repugnaverit pernegando, sit eculeo deditus ungulisque sulcantibus latera perferat poenas proprio dignas facinore' (Cod. IX, 18, 7, 1). See paraphrase in Bas. LX, 39, 28, Sch. As a rule, however, the rack cannot have been convenient for the purpose of punishment; it was a heavy thing to move from the torture chamber to the open place of punishment; and where *torqueri*, αἰκίζεσθαι, are used of punishment (i. e. 'in eos qui inopia laborant corpus torquendum est', Dig. II, 1, 7, 3; ὁ ἐργασάμενος τεχνίτης . . . τὸ σῶμα αἰκισθεὶς τῆς πόλεως ἐξελαθήσεται, Cod. VIII, 10, 12, 5 e), what is meant is no doubt the infliction of the lash, which was equally serviceable for either purpose. Now just as βάσανος, βασανίζειν, are used of the lash where it is employed to get a confession (Nicet. Chron., p. 699, ed. Bonn βασάνοις ὑποβληθέντες ὅπως ἐκφήνωσι τοὺς συνίστορας, where B glosses βασ. ὑποβλ. by μαστιγωθέντες), so they are used of the lash where it is employed purely by way of punishment. A few instances may be given where the words are clearly used of punishment, and in some of these it is clear that the form of punishment was the lash. Iust. Nov. CXXIII, 20 βασάνοις ὑποβάλλεσθαι is represented in the Authenticum by ' verberibus subdi '. Ecloga XVII, μθ', distinguishes the case where a master λώροις ἢ ῥάβδοις τύψῃ his slave, and where he ἀμέτρως αὐτὸν ἐβασάνισεν. Soldier's Law, c. ιε' in L ὁ πρὸς τοὺς πολεμίους ἀποφυγὼν καὶ ὑποστρέψας βασανίζεται καὶ ἢ θηρίοις παραδίδοται ἢ εἰς φρουρὰν (lege φουρκὰν) καταδικάζεται. This passage, which is c. λγ' in Zach.'s text (Byz. Zeitschrift, III, p. 453) and c. 34 of Ecloga ad Proch. mutata, XXXIV, is a translation of Dig. XLIX, 16, 3, 10, where the word is *torquebitur*. In Bas. LVII, 1, 17, the word *torquentur* of the corresponding passage in the Digest (XLIX, 16, 7 pr.) is rendered by κολάζονται. Bas. VII, 6, 19 οἱ δὲ ἄρχοντες καὶ μεῖζον πρόστιμον καὶ τὰς περὶ σῶμα βασάνους ἐπιφέρειν δύνανται τοῖς ἐκβιβασταῖς, where the Latin original (Cod. III, 2, 3, 1) has 'corporales maculas'. Bas. LX, 21, 16, 5 τὸ μέτρον τῶν βασάνων translates the Latin 'modum verberum' (Dig. XLVII, 10, 17, 5). Macar. Omil. 32 λώροις αὐτὸν βασανίζει. Mich. Attal., p. 207, ed. Bonn παραδοὺς αὐτὸν τοῖς βασανισταῖς ξεσμοῖς ἀνηκέστοις διὰ βουνεύρων . . . αὐτὸν καθυπέβαλε. These authorities justify the translation of βασανίζεσθαι, which is given above.

ἀπολογεῖσθαι] in the sense of making damage good is not in the lexica.

2. The sailors of ship A by direction of their captain steal the anchors of ship B, which is lying in harbour or on a beach. Ship B is thereby lost. If this is con-

clusively proved, let the captain who directed the theft make good all the damage to ship B and its contents. If any one steals the tackle of a ship or any article in use on board, i. e. ropes, cables, sails, skins, boats, and the like, let the thief make them good twice over.

βουλήσει] There is probably no distinction in meaning between βουλήσει here and κελεύσει in the following chapter.

ἀγκύρας] This is the accusative after σύλα ποιήσωσιν. It has troubled the scribes. J's συμποιήσωσι is perhaps an attempt to get over the difficulty, but it is more likely to be a corruption. It is clear that ἀγκυρῶν, εἰς ἄγκυραν, and ἀφελόμενοι are conscious efforts to improve the grammar. There are traces of a reading ἄγκυρα, as if from ἄγκυρον. (See p. 71.)

καὶ τούτων] A superfluous καί or ἤ is not uncommon in the writings of this period, and is often got rid of by the later MSS. Farmer's Law, c. 9 ἐὰν γεωργὸς θερίσας . . . καὶ κουβαλίσῃ, where K and R omit καί; c. 47 ἐάν τις δοῦλος . . . κλέψας . . . ἤ ποιήσῃ, where R and Ferrini's MS. omit ἤ; Soldier's Law, c. 6, in L εἰ δέ τις βουλευσάμενος . . . καὶ ἐπισχεθῇ. See ante, Title 15, and post, c. 20 ὅς ἂν πλοῖον ναυλώσηται.

τὴν . . . ζημίαν ἐν τε τῷ πλοίῳ καὶ τὰ ἐν τῷ πλοίῳ σῶα] One would expect either τὴν ζημίαν ἔν τε τῷ πλοίῳ καὶ τοῖς ἐν τῷ πλοίῳ σῶαν or τὸ πλοῖον καὶ τὰ ἐν τῷ πλοίῳ σῶα. The difficulty seems to have been felt by the scribes (see App. Crit.). A somewhat similar phrase is ἐν τῇ ζημίᾳ τοῦ ναυαγίου καὶ τοῦ πλοίου (c. 10, 6).

τι τῶν ἐν τῷ πλοίῳ χρηματιζόντων] The editors agree with the translation given above : 'quid aliud navi necessarium et utile' (Leuncl., Pard.), 'quid eorum quae in navi adhibentur' (FM). Venturi translates 'aliquid eorum qui in navi mercaturam exercent', which is improbable.

σχοινίων] The MS. tradition varies greatly as between σχοινίον and σχοῖνος. See App. Crit. here; cc. 11, 10; 22, 2; 46, 1. It is impossible in these matters to do more than point out the diversity and leave the learned reader to take his choice. In P. London, III, p. 164 (A. D. 212) σχοινίον is found twice in a list of a boat's fittings. The word is always σχοινίον in Const. Porph. de Cerim., e. g. pp. 670, 18; 674, 20; 675, 12; 677, 7, ed. Bonn.

κανναβίων] Here καννάβιον appears to be different from σχοινίον. In c. 11, 10 σχοινία κανναβινα are referred to. In both cases there is great variety in the App. Crit. There appears to be no authority for the use of καννάβιον as a hempen-rope, except, perhaps, Const. Porph. de Cerim., p. 677, 9 κανάβιον λίτραιβ. Pollux, VII, 94, uses καννάβια of women's shoes of hemp. One thing is clear. The strongest ropes were made of hemp, but they might be made of other materials. Moschion apud Athen. 206 F εἰς δὲ σχοινία λευκέαν μὲν ἐξ Ἰβηρίας κάνναβιν δὲ καὶ πίτταν (κιττὸν A)

80

ἐκ τοῦ Ῥοδανοῦ ποταμοῦ [sc. ἡτοιμάσατο]; Dioscorid. III, 141 ; Plin.
N. H. XIX, 9, 56.

ἀρμένων] ἄρμενα is used in Byzantine Greek in the restricted
sense of 'sails'. Ducange, s. v.; Synopsis Ambr. LIII, B', ι';
Const. Porph. de Cerim. II, 45, pp. 671, 672, ed. Bonn.

διφθερῶν] The word occurs also cc. 11, 9; 34, 2; 38, 2. It
is clear from the last two references that it refers to coverings
which are put over the cargo to keep it dry.   See Böckh, Urkunden über das Seewesen, p. 106.

καράβων] The Basilica (LIII, II, α', ι', ια') refuse to allow that
the κάραβος or σκάφη is a part of the ship or entitled to be included under the term ἐξαρτισμός or ἐξαρτία.   This is merely
a paraphrase of various places in the Digest (VI, 1, 3, 1 ; XXI,
2, 44; XXXIII, 7, 29), and does not affect the inclusion in
common parlance of the ship's boat among its σκεύη or correda.
In Venice the ship's boat is not included among the correda (St.
maritt. Venez., p. 105), in Ragusa it is (St. Ragus. VII, 7).

ὁ τὰ σῦλα ποιήσας] τοῖς τὰ σῦλα παθοῦσιν of MN is perhaps
better, as it is easy to supply a subject for ἀποδιδότω from the
relative sentence.

3. A sailor by the captain's order robs a merchant or
passenger. The sailor is detected and caught. Let the
captain make good the damage twofold to those who
were robbed, and let the sailor receive a hundred blows.
If the sailor commits the theft of his own accord and is
caught or convicted by witnesses, let him be well beaten,
especially if the thing stolen is money, and let him make
good the loss to the person robbed.

ναύτης] The Greek mariner seems to have long had a tendency
to snap up unconsidered trifles.   An aged mariner admonishes
Fynes Moryson to lock up his goods 'lest the inferior marriners
should steale our shirts, or any other thing they found negligently
left, which they used to doe, especially at the end of any voyage '
(Itinerary, Part I, p. 270).

καταληφθεὶς κατασχεθῇ] This is merely an emphatic way of
saying 'if the thief is caught'.   There are many examples in the
Farmer's Law : α' εἰ δέ τις παρορίζων παρορίσει ; κα' εἰ δὲ ἀνανεύων
ἀνανεύει; μγ' ἐάν τις . . . διώκων συνδιώξῃ . . ., εἰ δὲ μηνύων ἐμήνυσε.
The same redundancy is found in mediaeval legal documents :
Sacerdoti, p. 26 'promittens promisisti'; p. 39 'committentes
committimus'; Baracchi, 17 ' promittens promitto.'

ὁ δὲ ναύτης λαμβανέτω] οἱ δὲ ναῦται λαμβανέτωσαν of DY is
illogical, as we have had ναύτης before, but that makes it none
the less likely to have been the original reading.

ξυλαγώγια] This word occurs only here, in c. I of Appendix D,

TRANSLATION AND COMMENTARY

and in M's reading in c. 38, 11. According to Schard it is 'genus supplicii nautici, cum quis sublevatus posteriori corporis parte ad lignum vehementi impulsu adigitur'. A similar punishment is thus described in an English treatise temp. Elizabeth. ' The ducking at the mayne yarde arme is, when a malefactor by having a rope fastened under his armes and abowte his myddle and under his breatche, is thus hoysed upp to the end of the yarde; from whence he is againe vyolentlie lett fall intoe the sea ' (cited in Diary of Henry Teonge, London, 1825, p. 19 n.). Among the Dutch this was a way used for training the young. ' Mos etiam apud nautas est, tyrones certo modo initiare ad ordinem nauticum, qui hic est, quod funi alligatos in aquas demittunt, et postea bene madidos malo nauis attundunt, in signum, quod multa in navigatione toleranda' (J. F. Stypmannus, Ius Maritimum, p. 358, ed. 1740). It is obvious that, if this or something not all unlike it was one ξυλαγώγιον, a hundred ξυλαγώγια must have been rather exhausting. As there is no authority to guide us, we may hope, for the sake of humanity, that the word merely means a beating. This is the view taken by the author of the Synopsis Minor (thirteenth century), who is probably referring to this passage. Lit. Ξ, 4, p. 187, ed. Zach., ξυλαγώγια παρὰ τῷ νόμῳ καλοῦνται αἱ διὰ ξύλων ἐπαγόμεναί τισι μάστιγες. The Byzantine vocabulary is exceptionally rich in words which denote a beating or the process of being beaten. The following list does not pretend to be complete : ἀβήννα (habena), αἰκίζεσθαι, ἀλλακτόν, βέργα (virga), βούνευρον, δαρμός (Livre du Préfet, pp. 18, 27; 24, 9; Schol. in Eclogam Leuncl., p. 127), ἐκστραορδινεύεσθαι, λῶρος, μαγλάβιον (Reiske ad Const. Porph., vol. 2, p. 53, ed. Bonn.), μάστιξ, παιδεία (Livre du Préfet, pp. 17, 3, 10; 21, 24), ῥάβδος (Bas. LX, 3, 17 Sch.; 59, 1), ῥόπαλον (Bas. LX, 34, 6 Sch.), σκυτάλη, σφραγίζεσθαι (Farmer's Law, νη´ (N), this may mean 'to be branded'), σωφρονίζεσθαι (Soldier's Law, μδ´ (L)), τύμπανον, φραγέλλιον. (See most of these words in Ducange, and also Zach., Geschichte, pp. 331, 332.)

ξύλον generally denotes an instrument of punishment, resembling the stocks (see Ducange, s. v. ξύλον and κοῦσπος. Mala mansio in Dig. XLVII, 10, 15, 41 is rendered in Bas. LX, 21, 14, 41 τὸ ἐμβαλεῖν τοὺς πόδας ξύλῳ). But ξύλα, in the Basilica, is also a translation of fustes (Bas. LX, 59, 1).

συλήσῃ μὲν κατασχεθῇ δέ] Here good MSS. read συλήσῃ κατασχεθῇ δέ, which may be right, and Σ συλήσας κατασχεθῇ. Cp. the variants in c. 1, 2 κατασχεθεὶς ... ὁμολογήσῃ, and in c. 30, 6 ἐκκομιζέτω ... δεκάτας δὲ ἀποδιδότω, where BGKS read in substance εἰ ἐκομίσατο ... δεκάτας ἀποδιδότω. It looks as if some scribes disliked δέ where there was no μέν to correspond, and altered the text accordingly.

κατασχεθῇ] If this word means, as the language suggests, ' be caught in the act,' the Sea-law disagrees with Roman law and

82

with the law of the Basilica, which oblige the thief to make the theft good fourfold when he is caught in the act, and twofold when he is not caught in the act (Πεῖρα, LV, β'). The doctrine of the Roman law is found in some of the maritime statutes. If a mariner is convicted of theft, 'si quidem repertus fuerit cum ipso furto antequam furtum perduxerit ad locum destinatum, solvat quadruplum . . . si vero iam pervenerat ad locum destinatum, duplum tantummodo solvat' (St. Zara, IV, 57). Under the law of Spalato, the thievish mariner had to make the loss good fourfold in every case (St. Spalat. VI, 57).

4. The captain brings the ship into a place which is infested by thieves or pirates, although the passengers testify to the captain what is at fault with the place. There is a robbery. Let the captain make the loss good to the sufferers. On the other hand, if the passengers bring the ship in in spite of the captain's protests and something untoward happens, let the passengers bear the loss.

κατάξῃ] may be intransitive, πλοῖον being the subject. It is more probable that πλοῖον is the object, and that ὁ ναύκληρος should be supplied as the subject from τῷ ναυκλήρῳ in next line. Cp. c. 11, 3 ἐὰν τοῦ πλοίου ἀρμενίζοντος πάθῃ, 'if the ship is injured while it is on the voyage'; c. 15, 7 τὰ τῶν ἐξελθόντων εἴδη καὶ σκεύη ἀπολαμβανέτωσαν, 'let those who have gone out recover their respective goods and chattels'; c. 30, 5 τὸ δὲ χρυσίον τοῦ ἐμπόρου ἐκκομιζέτω μεθ' ἑαυτοῦ, 'let the merchant take his gold with him.'

τὰ σύλα] I have inserted on the authority of C. The grammar seems defective without it, but it may be a gloss. Mess. adds, but after τοῖς συλ., τὸ ἄπερ ἀπόλεσαν.

καταγάγωσιν οἱ ἐπιβάται] The influence of the merchants and passengers in directing the navigation and determining the voyage is dealt with in the Introduction, p. cxli.

ὑποκείσθωσαν] This word occurs twice in c. 10 (lines 3 and 5), and there, as well as here, the MSS. vary as to the case which it is to govern.

5. If sailors set to fighting, let them fight with words and let no man strike another. If A strikes B on the head and opens it or injures him in some other way, let A pay B his doctor's fees and expenses and his wages for the whole time that he was away from work taking care of himself.

Discipline on board, which is the subject of chapters 5, 6, and 7, is dealt with in the Introduction, p. cxli; and the relation of these chapters to Roman law and the law of the Basilica is dealt with in the Introduction, p. lxxxiv.

λόγοις ποιείτωσαν] Pard. (I, p. 332, n. 2) contrasts this provision with a provision of the Rooles d'Oléron (Art. 12), which fines a sailor who gives the lie to another. The Rhodian compilation, he says, 'est beaucoup moins sévère, puisqu'il tolère les injures verbales entre les matelots. Notre article (i. e. Art. 12 of the Rooles) atteste le fait, reconnu par tous les auteurs, de la grande susceptibilité des peuples modernes, et surtout des Français, chez lesquels un démenti est une injure assez grave pour entraîner des voies de fait de la part de celui qui l'a reçu.' The distinction is in substance true, but this passage of the Sea-law does not really tolerate verbal injuries. To say that the sailors are to fight with words is merely an emphatic way of saying that they are not to come to blows. That it was easy enough even in Constantinople to pass from verbal to bodily injuries is shown by the story told in Πεῖρα, LXI, ϛ'.

μηδεὶς κρουέτω] As a rule, both in the Sea-law and the Farmer's Law, μή is found with the third person of the imperative: c. 11, 1 μὴ ἐμβαλλέτωσαν; c. 16, 2 μὴ χρηέσθωσαν; c. 22, 1 μὴ ἀγέτω; c. 37, 4 μὴ δότωσαν; Farmer's Law, c. 2 μὴ λαμβανέτω; c. 5 μὴ ἐπιδιδότωσαν; c. 12 μηδὲν λαμβανέτω; c. 13 μηδὲν λαμβανέτω. But the subjunctive is also found: Sea-law, c. 38, 11 μηδεὶς ποιήσῃ (ποιείτω some MSS.); Farmer's Law, c. 4 μὴ διαστρέψωσιν. The Sea-law has also (c. 32, 3) μὴ ἀπαιτεῖν.

τῆς ἀργίας] A reminiscence of Exod. xxi. 19 πλὴν τῆς ἀργείας αὐτοῦ ἀποτίσει καὶ τὰ ἰατρεῖα.

6. Sailors are fighting and A strikes B with a stone or log; B returns the blow; he did it from necessity. Even if A dies, if it is proved that he gave the first blow whether with a stone or log or axe, B, who struck and killed him, is to go harmless; for A suffered what he wished to inflict.

λίθῳ ἢ ξύλῳ] Three lines further down we have ἢ λίθῳ ἢ ξύλῳ ἢ σιδήρῳ. The difference throws some light on the composition of the Sea-law. It suggests that the chapter originally applied to fights on dry land; and that the compiler of the Sea-law, in adapting it to the conduct of sailors, added the σίδηρον, the carpenter's axe. Cp. Appendix A, line 49, ὁ πρωρεὺς καὶ ὁ ναυπηγὸς τὰ σίδηρα προσφερέτωσαν; Juvenal, xii, 61.

θάνῃ] is supported here by the tradition. In c. 7, 6 ἀποθάνῃ, and in c. 46, 3 ἀποθάνωσι are given by almost all the MSS.

7. One of the captains or merchants or sailors strikes a man with his fist and blinds him, or gives him a kick

and happens to cause a hernia. The assailant is to
pay the doctor's bill, and for the eye twelve gold pieces,
for the hernia ten. If the man who gets kicked dies,
his assailant will be liable to trial for murder.

τῶν ναυκλήρων] As a general rule the Sea-law speaks as if there
were only one ναύκληρος on board. Here and in c. 26 the plural
is used, as it is used in c. ιθ'. See on this point the Introduction,
p. cxxxiv.

γρόνθον] The tradition varies between γρόνθον and γρόνθῳ. It
is impossible to say which is right. We find in the Basilica
τυπτῆσαι λέγεται καὶ τὸ γρόνθον δοῦναι (LX, 21, 14, 40), where the
Synopsis has γρόνθῳ, and ῥάβδοις ἢ λώροις ἢ γρόνθοις τυπτήσει (LX,
3, 27, 17 Sch.).

πηρώσῃ] is here used absolutely in the sense of 'blind'.
LS. quote examples of πήρωσις in this sense, but none of the
verb.

δώσῃ] δοῦναι in the sense of to hit or wound is common in
Byzantine Greek. χειροκοπείσθω ὁ δεδωκώς, διὸ ὅλως μετὰ ξίφους
δοῦναι ἐτόλμησεν (Ecloga, XVII, μς') δώσει μετὰ ξίφους ἢ μετὰ ῥάβδου
ἢ μετὰ λίθου (Farmer's Law, ο᾽[M]). It is frequent in Theophanes
(see De Boor's Index Graecitatis, p. 738) and his continuators
(see Index Grammaticus to Bonn ed., p. 927).

τὰ ἰατρεῖα] although it has less manuscript support is probably
right, as it is the word used in Exod. xxi. 19, which the author
of c. 5 and this chapter evidently had in his mind.

ὑπὲρ μὲν τοῦ ὀφθαλμοῦ κτλ.] This passage is dealt with in the
Introduction, p. lxxxv. Under a Novel of the emperor Leo, he who
voluntarily puts out another's eye loses his own (Novellae Const.,
ed. Zach., p. 187). The Novel is reproduced in the Epanagoge
aucta (LII, 112, p. 364). The loss of an eye was evidently
a common consequence of a fight, and it is possible that the
lower classes of Constantinople indulged in gouging matches
such as were not infrequent a hundred years ago in some of the
southern states of the American Union. The object of each com-
batant in this form of sport was to enucleate his opponent's eye
(= πηρῶσαι) or tear off his testicles (perhaps the real meaning of
κήλην ποιῆσαι). See Isaac Weld, Travels through North America,
London, 1799, p. 110; J. B. McMaster, History of the U. S.,
II, p. 5.

8. The captain to whom the ship is entrusted sets sail
and runs away into another country with gold by will of
the sailors. All their possessions, movable, immovable,
and self-moving, as many as belong to them, are to be
seized. Unless the amounts which these fetch in a sale
make up the equivalent of the ship and the profits of the

time (during which they were absent), let the sailors
with the deputy captain be let out and make up the full
amount of the loss.

This chapter is considered in the Introduction, p. lxxxiii.

ὁ ναύκληρος πιστευθεὶς τὸ πλοῖον] As a rule in the Sea-law the
ναύκληρος or the ναύκληρος and ναῦται are treated as the owners
of ship. It is clear that in this chapter the ναύκληρος is not
owner. The recension given in Appendix F distinctly speaks of
ὁ κύριος τοῦ πλοίου. The only other reference to an owner of the
ship as apart from the ναύκληρος is in c. 26. In these cases the
ναύκληρος appears to correspond rather with the πιστικός of
the Basilica (Synopsis Ambr. LIII, 1, γ΄), and the words πιστευθεὶς
τὸ πλοῖον add to the resemblance. Moreover, he is called προναύκληρος at the end of the chapter, and this apparently means 'the
captain's agent'. Cp. προδανειστής, Dareste, Inscriptions I, p. 327.
See Introduction, p. cxxxii.

κινητὰ κτλ.] Cp. P. London, III, p. 264 (A. D. 558); P. London,
I, p. 233 (eighth century).

κατασχεθήσονται] As a rule, in Byzantine grammar and in the
Sea-law, a neuter substantive in the plural takes a plural verb.
To this rule the Sea-law makes the following exceptions. (a)
The verb εἶναι is generally found in the singular, especially in the
phrases ἄκυρα εἴτω (ἔστω) and κύρια ἔστω : cc. ιδ΄, 3 ; ιζ΄, 2 ; ιη΄, 10 ;
ιθ΄, 4 ; 9, 2 ; 13, 4 and 15, 10. (b) Where one substantive is followed
by two verbs, one verb is put in the plural and the other in the
singular, c. 9, 14. (c) The last rule is extended to cases where
two neuter plurals follow at short intervals, as here, ὑπάρχει . . .
κατασχεθήσονται; c. 9, 4. (d) The verb is put in the singular where
the substantive although plural in form expresses a singular idea,
e. g. τὰ φορτία, which = 'the cargo': cc. 34, 3 and 7 ; 42, 2. There
are one or two cases which cannot be brought under any of these
heads : cc. 9, 12 ; 21, 7 ; 36, 6 ; 37, 1.

αἱ τούτων ἐκτιμήσεις κτλ.] This phrase, as to which there is
great variety in the MSS., is clumsy, but it must mean 'if the
proceeds of sale of the properties seized do not amount to the
required sum'.

τῆς ἐργασίας τοῦ χρόνου] The captain and crew have run away
(as the title of the chapter says) with an ἐνθήκη, which would
have made profits. They are therefore liable, not only for the
value of the ship and for the money which they stole, but also for
the profits which would have been made by its employment during
the time that they had control of it. For the use of ἐργασία, to
denote profits, cp. Demosth. 1283, 28 ; Farmer's Law, c. 41
ἐάν τις κλέψῃ βοῦν . . . δώσει αὐτὸν καὶ τὴν ἐργασίαν αὐτοῦ πᾶσαν.
ἡ ἐργασία τοῦ χρόνου is a harsh phrase. Perhaps we should read
ἡ ἐργ. τοῦ χρυσίου.

προναυκλήρῳ] It is probable that the ναυκλήρῳ of some good

86

MSS. is merely a corruption and does not represent a different recension. MN, which give ναυκλήρῳ here, give προναυκλήρῳ in the other version of the chapter (Appendix F).

9. If the captain is deliberating about jettison, let him ask the passengers who have goods on board; and let them take a vote what is to be done. Let there be brought into contribution the goods ; the bedclothes and wearing apparel and utensils are all to be valued; and, if jettison takes place, with the captain and passengers the valuation is not to exceed a litra; with the steersman and mate, it is not to exceed half a litra; with a sailor, it is not to exceed three grammata. Slaves and any one else on board who is not being carried for sale are to be valued at three minas; if any one is being carried for sale, he is to be valued at two minas. In the same way if goods are carried away by enemies or by robbers or . . . together with the belongings of sailors, these too are to come into the calculation and contribute on the same principle. If there is an agreement for sharing in gain, after everything on board ship and the ship itself have been brought into contribution, let every man be liable for the loss which has occurred in proportion to his share of the gain.

The subject-matter of this important chapter is dealt with in the Introduction, p. cclviii.

χρήματα] here and in other places in this chapter must mean goods in general and not merely money or personal belongings. The ἐπιβάτης, as has been pointed out in the Introduction, p. cxl, was distinguished from the ἔμπορος simply by taking a smaller quantity of merchandise.

καὶ τὰ χρήματα] This does not mean that the goods are to be brought into contribution as well as something else ; but that the goods which have been referred to before are to be brought into contribution.

στρώματα] στρῶμα is the mattress. στρώματα is used in the Basilica as a rendering of culcitae (Bas. XLIV, 13, 3 = Dig. XXXIII, 10, 3 pr.). The passengers as a rule took their mattress and bedclothes with them. See ante, p. 60.

σκεύη] is used in the Sea-law for the ' instrumenta navis ' in general (cc. 2, 8 ; 30, 8 and 10), and εἴδη καὶ σκεύη is also used in a perfectly general sense of the passenger's goods and chattels (c. 15, 8). But here the context suggests that the word is used

TRANSLATION AND COMMENTARY

in a restricted sense of the cooking utensils which crew and passengers generally took with them for the purpose of the voyage. See *ante*, p. cl.

ἐκτιμάσθω] According to Pard. the valuation is to be made after jettison has taken place. He also thinks that the captain, passengers, officers and men contribute in respect of their persons. C. 35, which he cites in favour of this interpretation, does not support him. The language there is not to be pressed. It merely means that just as the ἔμποροι contribute in respect of τὰ φορτία, so the ναῦται contribute in respect of τὸ πλοῖον. The passage here means that the mattresses, &c. are to be valued—presumably when they are brought on board—but a limit is placed upon the valuation, and this limit varies with the presumed wealth of the owner. It was obviously highly convenient in such cases to fix a limit. Thus, the Table of Amalfi (c. 45) prescribes that if a mariner's clothes and coverings are lost and the colonna has to make them good, they are to be taken as worth six tareni unless the mariner can prove the value.

λίτρας ... ἡμιλίτρου ... γράμματα] As the bedding, &c., of the ship's officers is valued at one-half of the captain's, we may reasonably infer that the bedding, &c., of the seaman will be valued at not less than one-half of an officer's, and this inference is supported by the proportions in which they share the profits as determined by chapters α'–ζ'. If this is so, the λίτρα in this place = not more than twelve γράμματα and possibly less. Now neither the λίτρα nor the γράμμα is a coin, but they are occasionally found in accounts. A 3rd–4th century account is in λίτραι and γράμματα which are described as χρύσου γράμματα (P. London, III, No. 966, p. 58, where the learned editors observe that the γράμμα 'occurs very rarely in papyri'). A first century account is in λείτραι, ὀγκίαι, γράμματα (Berliner Gr. Urk. 781), and an account of A. D. 384–385 in χρυσοῦ λίτραι, οὐγκίαι, γράμματα (P. Leipzig, 62, Col. II). Now if we suppose that the λίτρα and γράμματα are of the same metal, whether it be gold or silver, this difficulty arises. The γράμμα as a weight was equivalent to the scruple or the twenty-fourth part of an ounce (Ducange, Dissertatio, p. 194 ; Glossaries, s. v. γράμμα, *scriptulus* and *scripulum*), and the ounce was equal to one-twelfth of the pound. The captain's valuation would then be ninety-six-fold the ordinary sailor's. This is impossible. The difficulty might be got over by supposing that the scribe of the archetype had misread the compendium for οὐγκία. Γο = οὐγκία and Γρ = γράμμα are easily confused. If the confusion was made, then instead of γράμματα τρία we should read οὐγκίαι τρεῖς. If this suggestion is right, it is clear that we cannot be dealing with weights of gold. No Byzantine skipper could have bedclothes and cooking utensils of an aggregate value of a pound of gold. The weights must both be silver. A way of getting over the difficulty, without altering the text, is

88

to suppose that the λίτρα is of silver and the γράμμα of gold. If this is so, what would be the ratio between the two? The γράμμα of gold is described as τέταρτον τοῦ χρυσίνου (Ducange, opp. cit.), and this is right, as the gold solidus or χρύσινος was made one-sixth of an ounce by the legislation of Valentinian (Godefroy on Cod. Theod. VII, 24, ed. Ritter, vol. II, p. 462). At this time five gold solidi went to the libra argenti, but gold afterwards appreciated, and four gold solidi went to the libra (Godefroy on Cod. Theod. XIII, 2, ed. Ritter, vol. V, p. 24. See also Cod. Theod. XV, 9, from which it appears that the libra argenti was coined as a rule into sixty pieces of silver. Each of these normal coins was the μιλιαρίσιον, which was equivalent to one-twelfth of a gold solidus, Ducange, Dissert., p. 192; Glossary, s. v.). If we take the later ratio, three γράμματα of gold would equal three-sixteenths of a λίτρα of silver, and this is a possible ratio between the captain's and the sailor's valuation. The difficulty of this interpretation is that it assumes the γράμμα to be not a weight but a coin, and there are hardly any references in the Byzantine authorities to the gold γράμμα as a coin.

It is possible that the gold γράμμα was not a Byzantine but a South Italian coin. There is a well-known South Italian coin, the tare or tari (later tarenus), which was also one-fourth of a solidus, and which first makes its appearance in the tenth century. The earliest instance which I find of it is in a document from Gaeta of the year 909 A.D. ('auri tari et livra una', Regii Neapolitani Archivi Monumenta, Neapoli, 1845, I, p. 11; 'auri tari et uncias duas,' op. cit., I, p. 13). In Naples it appears in 936 A.D. (op. cit., p. 87; Capasso (B.), Monumenta ad Neapolitani Ducatus Historiam pertinentia, T. 2, P. 1, Neapoli, 1885, p. 36). In Amalfi the earliest instance cited by Camera is in 957 A.D. (Camera (M.), Memorie... di Amalfi, Salerno, 1876, V.I, p. 174). The earliest instance of the ταρίον in Trinchera's documents is in 1005 A. D. (Trinchera, p. 13). That the tare was one-fourth of a gold solidus is proved by many authorities (Regii Neap. Arch. Mon. I, p. 172 = Capasso, op. cit., p. 54; Camera, op. cit., V. I, pp. 174, 176, 314). Perhaps the tare is simply the γράμμα under another name—probably of Arabic origin. The view that γράμμα = tare is supported by the passage already cited from the Italian version of the Table of Amalfi, c. 45. Having regard to the steady depreciation in the value of the tarenus, the six tareni of the Table of Amalfi are about equivalent to the γράμματα τρία of the Sea-law. In the beginning of the thirteenth century thirty tareni made an ounce of gold (Manduel, 1, in Blancard, I, p. 4).

The tare was divided into grana, and it seems to have origin-ally contained twelve (Camera, I, p. 179; II, p. xxxix), but the number varied, and in the fourteenth century it contained twenty (Muratori, Antiquit. Ital. II, 784). As the granum seems to have corresponded to the silver γράμμα, it is possible that the word is derived from γράμμα, although in the later Greek documents it is rendered κόκκος (Trinchera, pp. 218, 250, 403).

παῖδες κτλ.] The text draws a distinction between slaves who are not being carried for sale, e. g. the slaves who attend on a merchant (c. η΄) or the slave who is sent by a lender to see to the recovery of the loan (c. ιθ΄), and slaves who are carried for sale and who are merely merchandise. That a distinction was made for certain purposes between these two classes is shown by a ' lex censoria portus Siciliae ' cited in the Digest (L, 16, 203), which provides ' servos quos domum quis ducet *suo usu*, pro is portorium ne dato '. Cp. also Dig. XXXIX, 4, 16, 3 and 10. But what is the distinction here? It is tempting to read in the two places to which I have prefixed a dagger κατὰ τριῶν μνῶν (i. e. KATA Γ΄ MNΩN) and κατὰ δύο μνᾶς respectively, and to suppose that a slave not loaded on board for sale was valued for purposes of contribution at three minas, while a slave loaded on board for sale was valued at two minas. If these conjectures are right, ἐκτιμάσθωσαν should be supplied from ἐκτιμάσθω in the last sentence. What the μνᾶ is equivalent to in this place—assuming that my conjecture is right—is impossible to say. It is found for a sum of money in papyri of the Roman period, e. g. P. Leipzig, 10 (A. D. 240); P. London, III, p. 236 (fourth century). In late Byzantine authors it is used as equivalent to the λίτρα, whether of gold or silver. Thus one MS. of Nicetas Chon. always substitutes μνᾶ for λίτρα and vice versa in dealing with sums of money (ed. Bonn, pp. 67, 149, 713). The objection to my conjecture is this. The value of slaves varied greatly. See Cod. VII, 7, 1 = Bas. XLVIII, 14, 4 = Epanag. XXXVII, 8, where the lowest valuation is ten νομίσματα for a slave under ten years old, while a slave over that age is valued at twenty νομίσματα, and the valuation is much higher if the slave is a professional man (e. g. physician or mime) or an eunuch. It seems inequitable that one and the same valuation should be put upon all slaves who were being carried for sale, seeing that their real values might differ so greatly. This difficulty might be got over if we suppose that the cargoes contemplated in the chapter are exclusively of raw material on its way from the place of origin to a civilized slave-market, where it is to be instructed or castrated, as the case might be. If that was the general character of slaves carried for sale there is nothing unreasonable in fixing the same valuation for all, and the valuation would naturally be lower than that put upon slaves who were not being carried for sale and who were often no doubt well educated.

κατὰ τοῦτο δέ κτλ.] As to the right to contribution where the ship is ransomed by pirates or the property of individual passengers or mariners is taken, see Introduction, p. cclxxii.

στρατεία κοινή] These words cannot be right. The phrase is used in Polyb. XX, 6, 1 of a military expedition to be undertaken by confederates—in that case τὰ κοινὰ τῶν Βοιωτῶν, but it cannot have that meaning here. The passage evidently refers to three cases. The first case is where goods are taken by enemies; the second where they are taken by pirates; it is not an unreasonable inference that the third case is where they are taken by way of benevolence by the armed forces of one's own country. That in such a case contribution was due is proved by many authorities (St. Ragus. VII, 56, and Introduction, p. ccli).

We may therefore suspect that the meaningless στρατεί(ι)α κοινή conceals a genitive plural. One might have suggested στρατευτι-κῶν, which is found in Ducange, s. v. στρατευτικοί, were it not that in the passage from Zonaras which he quotes Büttner-Wobst reads στρατευταί with the better MSS. (ed. Bonn, III, p. 506).

τῶν διαφερόντων] τὰ διαφέροντα τοῖς ναύταις are the sailor's belongings. τὰ διαφέροντα αὐτοῖς = their property (Novellae Const., p. 281; Hase ad Leo Diac., p. 494, ed. Bonn). Possibly τὰ δια-φέροντα τοῖς ναύταις here are the *pacotilles* which mariners were often entitled to transport free in lieu of, or in addition to their pay. See Introduction, p. clxxiv.

εἰ δὲ σύμφωνον κτλ.] As to partnerships between ship and merchants, see Introduction p. ccxli. The passage is omitted by B and its followers. It is possible that the phrase was added when Part III was revised for insertion in the Basilica. Cp. c. 20, 9 ἡ δὲ πρᾶξις κτλ.

10. If the captain and crew are negligent and there is an injury or wreck, let the captain and crew be responsible to the merchant for making the damage good. If it is through the merchant's negligence that ship and cargo are lost, let the merchant be responsible for the loss caused by the shipwreck. If there is no default either of the captain or crew or merchant, and a loss or shipwreck occurs, what is saved of the ship and cargo is to come into contribution.

ἀμελήσῃ] ἀμέλεια and ἀμελεῖν are common in the Sea-law: cc. 26, 5, 7 (of mariners sleeping off the ship); 27, 3; 34, 11 (of merchants failing to bring up their cargo when there is bilge); 36, 8 (of a ship at rest failing to use signals); 10 (of negligence by the look out man of a ship in motion); 38, 3 (of sailors failing to use the pumps). The word is as indefinable as our 'negligence'. See the discussion by the Scholiast; Bas. LX, 10, 16 (vol. V, p. 442, ed. Heimb.).

11. The merchants and the passengers are not to load heavy and valuable cargoes on an old ship. If they load

91

them, if while the ship is on its voyage it is damaged or destroyed, he who loaded an old ship has himself to thank for what has happened. When merchants are hiring ships, let them make precise inquiry from the other merchants who sailed before them before putting in their cargoes, if the ship is completely prepared, with a strong sailyard, sails, skins, anchors, ropes of hemp of the first quality, boats in perfect order, suitable tillers, sailors fit for their work, good seamen, brisk and smart, the ship's sides staunch. In a word let the merchants make inquiry into everything and then proceed to load.

ἑαυτὸν ἀπὸ γῆς ἀπώλεσεν] Apparently a proverbial phrase. Cp. c. 36, 8 ἑαυτὸν ἀπώλεσεν.

ἐπιχειρίαν] ἡ ἐπιχειρία is not in the dictionaries, but it evidently means the whole equipment of the ship. Pap. 948 of the B. M. (P. London, III, p. 219) has : παρεχόμενος ὁ κυβερνήτης τοὺς αὐτάρκεις ναύτας καὶ τὴν τοῦ πλοίου πάσην ἐπιχρείαν, where the learned edd. needlessly suggest ἐπιχορίαν, i. e. ἐπιχορηγίαν. τὰ ἐπίχειρα are used by Byzantine authors not only in the senses given in LS., but also in the sense of 'preparations,' 'undertakings.' ἦν αὐτῷ μέγα τῶν ἐπιχείρων τὸ κατόρθωμα, εἰ μὴ τύχῃ τινὶ παρεσφάλη τοῦ ἐγχειρήματος (Theoph., p. 397, ed. Bonn ; p. 258, ed. De Boor) ; πυρὶ παρεδίδοσαν τὰ πρὸς ναυτιλίαν τούτων ἐπίχειρα (Theoph. Simocatta, VI, 4, 1 ; p. 246, ed. Bonn ; p. 226, ed. De Boor).

ἱστοκεραίαν] This word, as to which the MSS. vary, is supported by several authorities. Its meaning is determined by two passages of Artemidorus. I, 35, Hercher εἰ δέ τις πλέων ἴδοι τὸν ὄνειρον τοῦτον (i. e. that he has lost his head) ἀπολεῖσθαι τοῦ πλοίου τὴν ἱστοκεραίαν (εἰστοκεραίαν L, of eleventh century) σημαίνει, εἰ μὴ τῶν ναυτῶν τις εἴη ὁ ἑορακώς ; ἐπὶ γὰρ τούτων ἐτήρησα τοῖς ἄρχουσι θάνατον σημαῖνον . . . ἐπὶ δὲ τῶν ἐμπόρων καὶ ἐπιβατῶν κεφαλὴν ἄν τις λέγοι τὴν ἱστοκεραίαν (ἱστοκερδιάν L). II, 12. A bull, ναυτιλλομένοις . . . χειμῶνα σημαίνει καὶ πλήξας ναυάγιον τῆς ἱστοκεραίας (εἰστοκεραιάς L) παθούσης τι δεινόν . . . ἔοικε γὰρ τῷ ἱστίῳ καὶ τῇ καταρτίῳ διὰ τὴν βύρσαν καὶ τὰ κέρατα. It is singular that, while there is a reference to the sailyard, there should be none to the mast, and it is possible that we should read ⟨ἱστὸν καὶ⟩ ἱστοκεραίαν. See Böckh, Urkunden über das Seewesen, p. 129.

ἐξηρτισμένους] Here some of the MSS. read ἐξηρτημένους. just as in c. 42, 4, where I give ἐξηρτισμένον twice, there is a similar variety. But there can be little doubt that the verb is ἐξαρτίζειν. Cp. P. London, III, p. 164 (A. D. 212), σὺν κώπαις δυσὶ ἐξηρτισμένον.

In Bas. LIII, 5, 13, 14 ἐξαρτισθῆναι translates *armare*. There is the same variety in Theoph., p. 540, ed. Bonn, p. 353, ed. De Boor, ἐξαρτίσαντες στόλον μέγαν, where many MSS. read ἐξαρτήσαντες.

τοὺς ἀρκοῦντας] may mean 'sufficient in numbers', but it is more probable that it means 'sufficient for their work'. The mediaeval charter-parties constantly provide that the mariners are to be 'boni et sufficientes', and, as the number of mariners is specified, *sufficientes* must mean 'well-trained', or as another charter-party puts it 'in arte maris edocti sufficienter' (Authorities in Introduction, p. clxxxvi). In an Egyptian charter-party of A. D. 236 (P. London, III, p. 219) the skipper agrees to supply τοὺς αὐτάρκεις ναύτας.

γοργούς] γοργός in late Greek has the special meaning of 'swift, brisk, alert'. Thus in Nicet. Chon., p. 467, ed. Bonn, μετὰ νηῶν ταχυναυτουσῶν is given in B as μετὰ καὶ κατέργων γοργῶν, and the word is frequent in this sense in Anna Comnena (see Index Graecitatis of Bonn ed., vol. II, p. 766).

τὰ πλάγια μὴ παραλελυμένα] There is great variety here in the tradition. Some MSS. omit the phrase; M leaves out μὴ παραλελυμένα; many leave out μή. If it refers to the ship's sides, as I take it, it is out of place. It may be a gloss. It is observable that in this chapter words are more than once added by good MSS., e. g. line 8 τελείαν P; line 10 διαφόρους L; line 11 καλούς C. Each scribe apparently felt himself justified in adding to the description of a perfect ship and ship's company.

12. If a man makes a deposit in a ship or in a house, let him make it with a man known to him and worthy of confidence before three witnesses. If the amount is large, let him accompany the deposit with a writing. If the man who agreed to take charge of the deposit says that it is lost, he must show where the wall was broken through or how the theft took place and take an oath that there was no fraud on his part. If he does not show it, let him restore the goods safe as he received them.

The relation of this chapter and c. 13 to the older law is dealt with in the Introduction, p. lxxxvi, and their relation to the later law in the Introduction, p. cc. The chapter, as Pard. points out, has nothing to do with maritime law. The word διωρυγήν suggests that the chapter was originally confined to deposits made in a house, and it is probable that ἐν πλοίῳ ἢ ἐν οἴκῳ was added by the compiler of the Sea-law.

πιστικῷ] One cannot help suspecting that πιστικός here does not simply mean 'faithful', but has some connexion with ὁ πιστικός, the owner's agent on board ship (Synopsis Ambr. LIII, I, γ´;

TRANSLATION AND COMMENTARY

τὸν κριθέντα ἀξιόπιστον εἰς φυλακὴν πλοίου, πιστικὸν λέγουσι τῆς νηός Fragmenta de Verb. Signif. in calce Theophili, ed. Reitz, p. 975). If the chapter in its original form had merely γνωστῷ, the compiler of the Sea-law may have added καὶ πιστικῷ just as he probably added ἐν πλοίῳ ἢ ἐν οἴκῳ. B and its followers omit καὶ πιστικῷ. If this is so, we should translate ' let him make the deposit (if on land) with a man whom he knows, (if at sea) with the owner's agent.

ἐπὶ μαρτύρων τριῶν] See Introduction, p. lxxxix.

ἐὰν δὲ ᾖ τὸ θέμα βαρύ κτλ.] The Schol. on Bas. XXII, 5, 52 quotes Novel 88 as advising that deposits should always be made either in writing or before witnesses. If Novel 88 said this, it would supply an origin to this chapter; but Novel 88 does not say so either in its full form (ed. Schoell, p. 425) or in the epitomes of Theodore (Zach. Ἀνέκδοτα, p. 85) or Athanasius (Heimb. Ἀνέκδοτα, I, p. 81).

τὴν διωρυγήν] As to the spelling, see Lob. Phryn., p. 231. The word, however spelt, cannot refer to anything on board ship. It is never, so far as I know, used of a ship springing a leak or having a hole made in her by another ship; the words for this are τρυπᾶν, τρύπημα (see note on c. 42). Διω(ο)ρύττειν, διω(ο)ρυγή are used constantly of a hole made in a wall : Joseph. Antiq. Jud. 127 E; Clem. Alex. Strom. 764 B; Malalas, p. 466, ed. Bonn.

ὀμνύειν] According to the Code (IV, 1, 10) the plaintiff may offer (deferre) the oath to the defendant ' in actione depositi quae super rebus quasi sine scriptis datis movetur '. This passage is reproduced in the Basilica (XXII, 5, 52), and the Scholiast adds that the same rule applies where the deposit is made in writing (ed. Heimb., vol. II, p. 570).

13. If a passenger comes on board and has gold or something else, let him deposit it with the captain. If he does not deposit it and says 'I have lost gold or silver', no effect is to be given to what he says. But the captain and the sailors, all those on board together, are to take an oath.

See notes on cc. ιδ΄, ιε΄.

ὁμοῦ οἱ ἐμπλέοντες] Both here and in c. ιε΄ there is considerable variety among the MSS. as to who are to take the oath. In c. ιε΄ it is clear that the passengers are included. Here they are perhaps included under οἱ ἐμπλέοντες; but οἱ ἐμπλέοντες in c. 36, 4 and c. 46, 2 seems to mean only the sailors.

14. A man receives a deposit and then denies it. Evidence is taken in the matter. In due course the

94

deposit is found on him after he had taken an oath or denied his liability in writing. He is to make good the deposit twice over and suffer the penalty of his perjury.

ἐγγράφως ἀποταξαμένῳ] The depositee as an alternative to taking an oath ἐγγράφως ἀποτάσσεται. This must mean, as the editors agree, that he denies his liability in writing—denies in writing that he has the deposit; but I know no other instance of the word precisely in this sense. The word is common in Byzantine writers in the sense of parting from, renouncing, giving up, whether a person or a thing, and it takes genitive, dative or accusative, at the fancy of the author or his copyists. ἀποτάσσομαι τινι, 'I bid farewell to so-and-so' (Authorities in Lob. Phryn. 23); ἀποτάξασθαι αὐτῷ, 'to get rid of him' (P. Oxyrhynchus, II, pp. 299, first century); ἀνάβαινε πρός με ἵνα σοι ἀποτάξομαι, 'that I may take leave of you' (Berliner Gr. Urk, 884, 2nd–3rd century); ἀποταξάμενος τῇ αὐτοῦ γυναικί, 'having repudiated his wife' (Malal., p. 219, ed. Bonn); ἀποταξάμενοι τὸν τύραννον, 'having deserted the tyrant' (Theoph., p. 204, ed. De Boor); ἀποτάξασθαι τὴν βασιλείαν, 'to abdicate' (Theoph., p. 170, ed. De Boor); ἀπετάξατο τῆς βασιλείας, 'he abdicated' (Malal., p. 312, ed. Bonn). The word is also used absolutely of retiring from the world and entering into religion (Duc., s. v.). Hence in the Glossaries, rudiarii, ἀποταξάμενοι (Philox. I, p. 25; II, p. 161).

διπλῆν ταύτην ἀποδώσει κτλ.] A similar phrase occurs in P. Leipzig, 103 (Arabic period) ὁμολογῶ ... ὡς εἰ φανείην τι παραλείψας ἐν τῇ τοιαύτῃ καταγραφῇ ⟨παρασχεῖν⟩ ἐν διπλῇ ποσότητι μετὰ τοῦ ὑποκεῖσθαί μοι μετὰ τῆς ἐφιορκίας ἐγκλήματι.

15. A ship carries passengers or merchants or slaves whom the captain has taken in deposit. The captain comes to a city or harbour or shore, and some leave the ship. Robbers give chase or pirates make an attack and the captain gives the signal and gets away. The ship is saved with the property of the passengers and merchants that is on board. Let each receive back his own goods, and let those who went out receive back their respective goods and chattels. If any one is minded to pick a quarrel with the captain for leaving him on shore in a place infested by robbers, no effect is to be given to what he says because it was only when they were pursued that the captain and crew fled. If a merchant or passenger had somebody else's slave in deposit and

95

left him in any place, let him make the loss good to his master.

This chapter embraces two distinct points. (1) If merchants or passengers go on shore and the captain is obliged to put off suddenly for fear of pirates, he incurs no liability to merchants or passengers left behind. (2) If a merchant or passenger leaves behind a slave who has been deposited with him, he must make good the value to the owner. The first part of the chapter has evidently been altered by the compiler to bring in a reference to παραθήκη and thereby justify the position of this chapter among other chapters dealing with deposit. The first sentence would run perfectly smoothly if we left out παραθήκην . . . ἐν ἀκτῇ. As it is, it is not merely ungrammatical, which is a minor point, but inconsistent with a later passage. The person left behind attacks the captain for leaving him ἐν ἀκτῇ, whereas, in the passage which I would leave out, the captain comes ἐν᾽ πόλει τινὶ ἢ ἐν λιμένι ἢ ἐν ἀκτῇ.

ἐὰν ἐξελθόντων τινῶν] The risk of being left behind is a constant source of anxiety to the old travellers. See a thrilling account by Sir George Wheler, Travels, pp. 60 sqq. It is also provided for in statutes. Thus if a mariner is left behind without his fault, the shipowner must give him his agreed pay and his expenses of getting home (St. Massil. IV, 15).

κελεύσας] 'Nautica exhortatio denotari videtur,' says Schard ; cp. κέλευσμα, κελευστής.

ἐξειλήσῃ] ἐξειλῆσαι· τοῦτο λέγουσιν οἱ Ἀλεξανδρεῖς ἐπὶ τοῦ ἐκφυγεῖν (Etym. Mag. 348, 12). The word is used in this sense in Malalas, p. 121, 13 ; p. 438, 13, ed. Bonn ; in Chron. Pasch., p. 724, 13, ed. Bonn; in Theophanes, De Boor's Index Graecitatis, p. 745; and in the Basilica, e. g. L, 1, 43, ed. Heimb. vol. V, p. 44. The variants in the MSS. show that the word must have become obsolete by the thirteenth century, and illustrate the readiness of the later scribes to alter any word which they did not understand.

εἰ δὲ ἐμπόρων κτλ.] The merchant or passenger is made responsible for letting the slave go ashore.

16. Captains and merchants and whosoever borrow money on the security of ship and freight and cargo are not to borrow it as if it was a land loan . . . if the ship and the money are saved . . . lest a plot be laid against the money from the dangers of the sea or from pirates . . . let them pay back the loan from the property on land with maritime interest.

I have not found the key to this enigma. See Introduction, p. ccxxii.

ἐπὶ πλοίου κτλ.] I take this together with καὶ ναύλῳ καὶ τοῖς φορτίοις. There is nothing contrary to Byzantine usage in making ἐπί govern first a genitive and then a dative.

ἐπιβουλή] This is an extraordinary phrase. There is some authority for ἐπιβουλῆς, but if we read this ἐγγένηται is left without a subject.

ναυτικοῖς] if the text is right must mean 'with maritime interest' (Demosth. 893, 24 ναυτικοῖς ἐργάζεσθαι; Billeter, Gesch. des Zinsfusses, p. 36, n. 2.)

17. *A* gives gold or silver for the service of a partnership. The partnership is for a voyage, and he writes down as it pleases him till when the partnership is to last. *B*, who takes the gold or the silver, does not return it to *A* when the time is fulfilled, and it comes to grief through fire or robbers or shipwreck. *A* is to be kept harmless and receive his own again. But if, before the time fixed by the contract is completed, a loss arises from the dangers of the sea, it seemed good that they should bear the loss according to their shares and to the contract as they would have shared in the gain.

This chapter, which contains the first reference to the widely-spread doctrine of the commenda, is dealt with at length in the Introduction, p. ccxxxv.

χρείᾳ κοινωνίας] Here the tradition supports a division into two words; later on it gives χρεοκοινωνία in one word. In both cases there is some variety among the MSS. In the table of chapters the form is κερδοκοινωνία.

τοῦ χρυσίου] Observe that earlier in the chapter we have had χρυσίον ἢ ἀργύριον. Cp. c. ιδ΄, where we first get χρυσίον and then χρυσίον ἢ ἀργύριον. The difference is probably due merely to love of variety.

τοῦ κέρδους] τὸ κέρδος, which some MSS. give, is easier, but the genitive may be justified as depending loosely on τὰ μέρη.

ἔδοξε] suggests that we have here an actual legal decision.

18. A man borrows money and goes abroad. When the time agreed upon has expired, let them recover from his property on land according to law. If they cannot recover the debt, the capital of their loan shall be unconditionally repayable, but the interest shall be maritime interest for so long as he is abroad.

See Introduction, p. ccxxxv.

κομιζέσθωσαν] The subject is evidently the creditors.

κατὰ τὸν νόμον] See p. 65.

19. If a man hires a ship and gives earnest-money and afterwards says 'I have no need of it', he loses his earnest-money. But if the captain acts wrongfully, let him give back to the merchant double the earnest-money.

See Introduction, p. xcvii, ccvii.

μετέπειτα] seems to have become obsolete in later Greek. Just as many of the MSS. here give μετὰ ταῦτα, so in the Farmer's Law, νέ, where the best MSS. give μετέπειτα, Ferrini gives μετὰ ταῦτα from his worthless MS.

ἀπόλλειν] ἀπόλλω appears to be a Byzantine form of the verb at this epoch (c. 24, 3). There is, however, great variety among the MSS. In the Farmer's Law, α΄, ἀπόλλει occurs twice in the best MSS., while the later read ἀπόλλυσι.

ἄλλην] This word, which occurs again c. 24, 5, was evidently not understood by the later scribes (see App. Crit.). It is not in the lexica in this sense. Here and in c. 24, 5 ἄλλην ποιεῖν must mean 'to do something not contemplated by the contract'.

20. Where a man hires a ship, the contract to be binding must be in writing and subscribed by the parties, otherwise it is void. Let them also write penalties if they wish. If they do not write penalties, and there is a breach, either by the captain or by the hirer—if the hirer provides the goods . . . let him give the half of the freight to the captain. If the captain commits a breach, let him give the half-freight to the merchant. If the merchant wishes to take out the cargo, he will give the whole freight to the captain. These penalties shall be exacted as in cases where A brings a suit against B.

ὃς ἂν πλοῖον ναυλώσηται] The want of grammar is no reason for altering the text as some of the MSS. do. Cp. c. 30, 1 ἐὰν ὁ ἔμπορος φορτώσας τὸ πλοῖον . . . καὶ . . . συμβῇ; c. 33, 1 ἐὰν ὁ ναύκληρος θεὶς . . . καί τι πάθῃ τὸ πλοῖον; c. 36, 7 εἰ δὲ ἀμελήσας . . . καὶ συμβῇ ἀπώλειαν; c. 36, 9 εἰ δὲ καὶ ὁ ά. ἀμελήσας καὶ ὁ β. ἀποκοιμηθῇ; c. 39, 1 ἐὰν πλοῖον ἀρμενίζον . . . καὶ εἰσέλθῃ; Farmer's Law, ξέ (M) ὁ παραδοὺς πρὸς νομὴν κτήνη δούλῳ . . . καὶ ὁ δοῦλος πωλήσῃ αὐτὰ κτλ.

ἔγγραφα] As to the necessity for writing in the case of charter-parties see Introduction, p. xci.

συνεσφραγισμένα] means that the contract is to be subscribed—not necessarily sealed—by both parties. σφραγίς, σφραγίζειν have two meanings; σφραγίς is a seal, and σφραγίζειν means to seal. σφραγίς is also the sign of the cross, and σφραγίζειν means to apply the sign of the cross. ὁ δομέστικος κατασφραγίζει τοὺς δεσπότας (Const. Porph. de Cerim. I, 1, p. 12, ed. Bonn,

98

with Reiske's note 'facto manu signo crucis benedicit') : τὸ τοῦ σταυροῦ σημεῖον τῇ οἰκείᾳ ὄψει ἐπισφραγίσασθαι (Theoph. continuat., p. 237, ed. Bonn). See also Duc. s. v. 1499, and Appendix 179. In Byzantine documents both meanings are found, but the seal is only used in grants made by persons of quality, the grants themselves being called σφραγῖδες or σιγίλλια. σφραγισθὲν τῇ διαμολύβδῳ καὶ συνήθει σφραγίδι ἡμῶν (Trinchera, p. 6, A. D. 975). τῇ συνήθει ἡμῶν βούλλῃ τῇ ἰδιαμολύβδου σφραγίσαντες (Prologo, p. 33, A. D. 983). See also Trinchera, p. 17 (A. D. 1016), pp. 22–3 (A. D. 1026), p. 25 (A. D. 1032); Spata, p. 165 (A. D. 1091), p. 411 (A. D. 1123). On the other hand, where grants or contracts are made by ordinary people, the grantor or contracting party if he can write subscribes the grant or contract, and prefixes to his subscription the sign of the cross. The sign of the cross is not confined to illiterates. If the grantor or contracting party cannot write, he makes the sign of the cross and the subscription is made by another person, often a notary, by his direction. Marini, Pap. Dip., p. 281; P. Leipzig, 90 ἔγραψα ὑπὲρ αὐτοῦ γράμματα μὴ ἰδότος βαλόντος δὲ τῇ ἰδίᾳ αὐτοῦ χειρὶ τοὺς τρεῖς τιμίους σταυρούς; Bruns, Unterschriften, p. 127; Trinchera, pp. 7 (A. D. 981), 8, 13, 17, &c. ; Duc. 1434, s. v. σταυροὺς ποιεῖν. A document so subscribed is ἐσφραγισμένον just as much as if the seals of the parties were attached. Cp. Procop. Hist. Arc. 28 οἰκείοις ἐπισφραγίζων γράμμασιν.

The effect of συν in συνεσφραγισμένα is that the contract must be subscribed by both parties. To the example given by LS. add Berliner Gr. Urk. 86 (second century); Müller, Documenti, p. 58.

ἐπιτίμια] In the Byzantine authorities there is a clear distinction between ἐπιτίμιον (sometimes ἐπίτιμον or fem. sing. ἐπιτιμία) and πρόστιμον. ἐπιτίμιον is a penalty fixed by the law, whether for a breach of contract or for a delict. It may consist of a sum of money; it may consist of whipping, mutilation, or death. Where the law imposes a penalty for a breach of contract, that penalty may be, and often is, repeated in the contract, but it derives its efficacy not from the parties but from the law. πρόστιμον, on the other hand, is a penalty fixed by the parties to a contract for the breach of one or more of its stipulations. It always consists of a sum of money, which originally was payable to the party injured by the breach, but in later times often went either in part or whole to the fisc (Zach., Geschichte, pp. 298, 305). The difference between the ποινή and the πρόστιμον is well put in Schol. Bas. LX, 10, 7; ed. Heimb., vol. V, p. 431. This distinction is found in papyri of the sixth century and after. P. London, I, p. 202 (sixth century), a party who tries to break articles of compromise ἐνέχεσθαι ... τῷ τῆς ἐπιορκίας κινδύνῳ καὶ τοῖς ἄλλοις ἐπιτιμίοις τοῖς ὡρισμένοις κατὰ τῶν παραβαίνειν ἐπιχειρούντων ἐνομότους συνθήκας καὶ δοῦναι λόγῳ προστίμου καὶ παραβασίας τῷ ἐμμένοντι μέρει χρύσου οὐγκίας τέσσαρας. Other examples are Syro-Roman Law Book, London text, c. 85 ; P. London, III,

p. 254 (A. D. 507); Berliner Gr. Urk. 315 (Byz.); Berliner Gr. Urk. 404 (Arabic); P. London, I, p. 205 (sixth or seventh century), and I, p. 234 (testament of eighth century). In classical Greek the distinction does not exist. Demosthenes constantly uses ἐπιτίμιον of a penalty fixed by the contract : pp. 915, 1 ; 1286, 3 ; 1291, 11 ; 1296, 4. ἐπίτιμον is used in the same sense in P. Elephantine, III, p. 30 ; IV, p. 31 (B. C. 284–3). In the papyri of the Roman epoch ἐπίτιμον and πρόστιμον appear to be used indifferently. Thus ἐπίτιμον is used of a penalty fixed by the parties : Berliner Gr. Urk. 906, 987 (first century), 233, 350, 859, 998 (second century); and πρόστιμον of a penalty imposed by law : Berliner Gr. Urk. 1058 (t. Augustus), 282, 361, II, 542 (second century); P. Raineri, 5, p. 23 (A. D. 168). In the Code (IV, 21, 16) πρόστιμον and ἐπιτίμιον are used indifferently for a penalty payable to a plaintiff by a defendant who denies his own handwriting. In this chapter ἐπιτίμια is used, first, of penalties which the parties may or may not insert in the contract, and then of penalties which the law imposes where the parties have neglected to do so. We are justified therefore in dating the chapter before the distinction was made between ἐπιτίμιον and πρόστιμον, i. e. not later than the fifth century.

ἐὰν δὲ μὴ συγγράψωνται] Pard. translates ' quod si nullae scripturae factae fuerint ', i. e. ' if they do not put the contract in writing '; it means more probably ' if they do not lay down penalties for breach of the contract '. It has already been said that the contract is void (ἄκυρα) if not in writing and subscribed by the parties. It would be inconsistent after that to treat it as valid and subsisting. Moreover the passage at the end, ἡ δὲ πρᾶξις κτλ., suggests that the object of the chapter is not to supply the total want of a written contract, but to provide penalties where the parties have neglected to do so. The chapter, on this view of the case, gives three instances of breach of stipulation, and provides a penalty for each breach. As to the character of these stipulations see Introduction, p. cciii.

ἐπιφόρτου] ἐπίφορτος is not in the dictionaries. ἐπιφορτίζω is found in late authors (LS.), and is common in the Byzantines, e. g. Ignatius, Vita Nicephori, ed. De Boor, pp. 193–4 ; Theophylactus Simocatta (see De Boor's Index Graecitatis, p. 387); Anna Comnena, I, p. 270, ed. Bonn. ἐπιφορτισμός is in the glossaries (ἐπιφορτισμός honeratio, Corpus Gloss. Lat., II, p. 312); ἐπιφορτόω is given by some MSS. in Theophanes (De Boor's Index Graecitatis, p. 747); and Sophocles cites ἐπιφόρτωμα, ' an additional burden.' ἐπίφορτος here seems simply to mean ' the cargo ', but the passage is corrupt.

ἀποδιδότω . . . ἀποδότω . . . ἀποδώσει] Note the passion for varying the phrase.

ἡ δὲ πρᾶξις] The phrase is omitted by important MSS., and those which retain it vary as to the text. See next page.

ἐκδικήσει] ἐκδικεῖν, ἐκδίκησις are very general words meaning
to avenge, vengeance (see LS.). They are also used in a special
sense. Mitteis (Reichsrecht und Volksrecht, 1891, p. 501, n. 3)
gives examples of ἐκδικεῖν in the sense of 'vindicare, actione in
iudicium deducta vindicare'. Some examples may be added:
τὸν ἐπελευσόμενον . . . ἡμεῖς αὐτὸν ἀποστήσωμεν καὶ ἐκδικήσωμεν
(Berliner Gr. Urk. 13, A. D. 289); P. Leipzig, 33, col. 2, A. D. 368;
Theophilus, I, 5, 96; II, 1, 46; τὸν δὲ ἐπελευσόμενον ἢ ἀντιποιησό-
μενον . . . ἐκστήσω καὶ ἐκδικήσω καὶ καθαροποιήσω (P. Grenfell, I,
p. 99, A. D. 581); Journal of Philology, XXII, p. 274, t. Heraclius; Schol. Bas. XIII, 2, 1; ἵνα στίκω καὶ ἐκδικήσω σε ἀπὸ παντὸς
ἐναντίου προσώπου (Trinchera, p. 112, A. D. 1118); Müller, Documenti, p. 44, A. D. 1192; τὰ τιθέμενα πρόστιμα συμβολαίοις καὶ
συμφωνίαις ἐκδικείσθωσαν (Novellae Const., Coll. V, Nov. 6). The
word does not seem to refer to any special form of action and the
phrase simply means that the penalties may be recovered by legal
proceedings. This is not a very helpful statement and it is
possible that the text has been tampered with. A glance at the
App. Crit. (note especially the readings of D J L) suggests that
instead of καθάπερ εἰ ἐκδικήσει τίς τινα the original reading was
καθάπερ ἐκ δίκης, and this suggestion is strengthened by a consideration of the passages in which the phrase occurs. καθάπερ
ἐκ δίκης (of which many examples are given by Mitteis, Reichsrecht,
p. 404, and Dareste, Inscriptions, I, p. 333, n. 4) is equivalent to
καθάπερ ὠφληκὼς δίκην, and the passage would mean that one
party may enforce against the other the penalties mentioned in
the chapter as if that other had been sued and judgement given
against him, i. e. the party aggrieved can enforce his claims
against the property of the party in default by entry and sale,
or whatever the remedies of a judgement creditor may be, without the necessity of judicial process. A phrase constantly found
in the documents, with minor variations, is: γενομένης σοι τῆς
πράξεως ἔκ τε ἐμοῦ καὶ ἐκ τῶν ὑπαρχόντων μοι πάντων καθάπερ ἐκ
δίκης (Berliner Gr. Urk. 69, A. D. 120; P. London, III, p. 176,
A. D. 227; Fayum Towns, p. 225, A. D. 234; P. London, III,
p. 231, A. D. 315; P. Strassburg, I, p. 11, A. D. 510). Although
καθάπερ ἐκ δίκης is found in the Byzantine documents—other late
examples are P. Raineri, 30, p. 146, sixth century, καθωσὶ ἐκ
δίκης, Berliner Gr. Urk. 751, Byz.-Arab. period—nevertheless, as
far as one can judge from the scanty material published, it seems
to have been going out of use in the fourth century, and nothing
would be more natural than for the compiler of the Sea-law to
supplant it by the common Byzantine word ἐκδικεῖν. If καθάπερ
ἐκ δίκης is the true reading in this place, in would confirm the
date of the chapter which is suggested by the use of ἐπιτίμια.

21. Two persons make a partnership without writing.
Both the parties confess 'we made a partnership on

another occasion without writing and kept faith one to
the other and paid the tax on all occasions as if for a
single capital'. Something happens to one of the ships,
either while it is in ballast or when it is loaded. What
is saved is to contribute one-fourth part to the sufferer,
since they do not bring forward a contract in writing
but formed a partnership by word of mouth only. But let
contracts in writing subscribed by the parties be firm and
valid, and let the part saved contribute to the part lost.

This chapter has nothing to do with contracts of affreightment
between captain and merchant. It is only brought in here
because it deals with a case where the contract is not in writing,
and therefore has some connexion with the last chapter. In this
chapter the same person appears to be owner both of ship and
cargo. If it refers to partnerships between ναύκληροι, as the
title states—and this view is confirmed by Q's gloss on δύο—
then it deals with a commercial system quite different from
that which is at the back of cc. 20, 22–25. See Introduction.
p. cxlix.

τὰ μέρη] often in Byzantine Greek and earlier of the parties to
a contract or to a suit. P. Reinach, 44, p. 141 διὰ τὸ ἀμφοτέροις
τοῖς μέρεσι ὁμολογεῖσθαι.

ἑαυτοῖς] = ἡμῖν αὐτοῖς. See De Boor's Index Graecitatis Theoph.,
p. 741.

σαβουράτον] The MSS. vary in substance between this and
σάβουρον. In Latin saburra is the substantive and saburratus
the adjective. In Greek σαβούρα is the substantive and σάβουρος
or σαβουρός the adjective. Duc. s. v. 1315 and Appendix 166.
Duc. quotes no other passage for σαβουράτος but this, but he
quotes ἀσαβούρωτος from a glossary. The MSS. vary as to the
accent of σαβουράτος: L judiciously gives none. I make it
paroxytone, as that has rather more authority and may be
justified on the ground that the word, which is merely a transcription from the Latin, keeps its Latin accent.

22. Let the captain take nothing but water and provisions and the ropes which ships have need of, where
the merchant loads the whole ship according to their
written contract. If the captain is minded to put in
other cargo after this, if the ship has room, let him put it
in; if the ship has no room, let the merchant before
three witnesses resist the captain and sailors; and, if
there is jettison, it will rest with the captain; but if the

merchant does not prevent it, let him come to contribution.

ἐπὶ μαρτύρων τριῶν] See Introduction, p. lxxxix.

23. If there is a contract in writing between captain and merchant, let it be binding; but if the merchant does not provide the cargo in full, let him provide freight for what is deficient, as they agreed in writing.

πλῆρες] πλήρης is sometimes used indeclinably. F. Blass, Grammar of New Testament Greek, London, 1905, p. 81; P. London, III, p. 261 (A. D. 556). In cc. 33, 3; 46, 4 the tradition is in favour of εἰς πλῆρες. εἰς πλήρης is found in Berliner Gr. Urk. 319 (seventh century) and 371 (Arabic).

24. The captain takes the half-freight and sails and the merchant wishes to return. They made and subscribed a contract in writing. The merchant loses his half-freight by reason of his hindrance. Where there is a contract in writing and the captain commits a breach, let him return the half-freight and as much again.

συνεσφράγισαν] See ante, p. 98.
διὰ δέ] δέ is here used to introduce the apodosis.
τὴν ἐμπόδιον] I can give no other instance of this phrase than c. 28, 4.
ἀπόλλειν] See ante, p. 98.
ἄλλην ποιήσῃ] See ante, p. 98.

25. If the limit of time fixed by the contract passes, let the merchant provide the sailors' rations for ten days. If the second limit also passes, above all things let the merchant make up the full freight and go away. But if the merchant is willing to add so much to the freight, let him give it and sail as he pleases.

ἡ προθεσμία] is the time fixed either by law or by contract within which certain things have to be done—in this case the time fixed by the charter-party within which the merchant has to provide the agreed cargo at the place of loading (see Introduction, p. clxxxvii). The chapter seems to mean this. After the time fixed by the charter-party for loading has passed, the merchant has a second period of grace, ἡ δευτέρα προθεσμία, lasting ten days, during which he must provide the sailors their rations. If this second period passes, the merchant becomes

liable for the whole freight, while the captain is relieved from
any further obligation.
The chapter is far from clear. The rhythm of the passage
suggests that the break comes after δέκα, and in that case we
should have to translate 'if the limit of time fixed by the contract passes up to ten days'. The objection is that the limit
fixed by the contract for loading was necessarily variable, and
might be either less or more than ten days. Moreover, the second
limit is a statutory one, and unless ἕως ἡμερῶν δέκα refers to it,
its duration is not fixed. 'Das zehntägige Zeitintervall,' says
Mitteis (P. Raineri, I, p. 83), 'ist im römischen Rechtsleben über-
haupt eine beliebte Grösse.' He gives many instances.

σιταρχίας] Most of my MSS. spell the word with χ, and I see
no reason for changing χ to κ. According to Dind.-Steph. there
are two words 'annona militaris' which is spelt with a κ, and
'munus praefecti annonae' which is spelt with a χ. LS. make
the same distinction; σιταρκία is 'sufficiency of provisions', and
σιταρχία is the 'office of supplying a town or army, the com-
missariat'. It is, however, the fact that in most of the passages
which the lexicographers cite for σιταρκία meaning 'rations,'
which is the meaning that the word has here, the best MSS. give
σιταρχία. Thus, in Arist. 1350, 36, although Bekker gives in the
text σιταρκίαν, his best MSS. give χ; in 1351, 12 and 16 the
MSS. agree in giving χ. In the passages quoted by Dind.-Steph.
from Polybius (V, 75, 1; I, 70, 3; I, 52, 5; XI, 25, 10; V, 50,
2; I, 66, 6) Hultsch always spells the word with χ. In only
one instance (I, 70, 3) does he mention a variant; there the later
MSS. give κ. Herwerden, s. v., p. 741, quotes two passages
from the Amherst Papyri (II, pp. 29, 32, B.C. 250) in which the
word is spelt with χ, and adds 'quam autem antiquum sit hoc
vitium, si vitium est, luculenter hic locus docet'. The gram-
marians spell the word in both senses with χ. σιταρχία· τὸ σῖτον
διδόναι τοῖς ἐπιβάταις, Bekker, Anecd. 301, 26; σιταρχία· τὸ εἰς
ὀψώνιον διατεταγμένον δαπάνημα, Hesych. Sitarchia is also the
spelling of F in Apuleius, Metamorph., ed. Eyssenhardt, II, c. 11
('haec enim sitarchia navigium Veneris indiget sola'), of the
Scholiast to Juvenal, XII, 61, p. 349, ed. Jahn ('inter sitarchiam
et securem necessariam putato ad navem vehendam'), and of the
glossaries ('sitos triticum unde sitarchia,' Corpus Gloss. Lat. II,
p. 202; 'sitarchos tutartus,' Corpus Gloss. Lat. III, p. 205).
I do not lay stress upon σιταρχίαν in Berliner Gr. Urk. 948 (4th–
5th century) because it is in an illiterate letter. The only
authority for σιταρκία is Synopsis Ambros. LIII, 3, β', p. 162, ed.
FM. This cloud of witnesses raises a suspicion that there is
only one word, viz. σιταρχία, and that the distinction is a late
Byzantine invention, working upon a false etymology. Thus
Photius, who evidently had before him the definition of σιταρχία
given above from Bekker, Anecd., alters it into ἡ σῖτον διδοῦσα

τοῖς ἐπιβάταις. There is some authority for σιταρκεῖν. Diod.
Excerpt. Vat., p. 59, vol. II, p. 183, ed. Dind.; Eustathius, 626,
55 ὁ τὸ σιταρκεῖν φάμενος σῖτον ἐπαρκεῖν. In Strabo, 833, however,
Meineke gives σιταρχούμενον. σιτάρκησις κάστρων is used in Acta
et Diplomata, V, p. 137 (A. D. 1074) in the sense of 'the duty of
supplying troops with corn'. In mediaeval Latin sitarchia or
sitarcia—perhaps from a supposed connexion with arca—came
to mean the receptacle in which the rations are placed, and this
is the only meaning given by Duc. 1375, s. v. σιτάρκιον.

προσθεῖναι ποσότητα τῷ ναύλῳ] is not necessarily, as Pard.
translates ' summam aequam naulo adiicere '. ποσότης is simply
an amount, and the vagueness of such a direction is not out of
keeping with the general tone of the Sea-law.

ἐμπλεέτω] I agree with Pard. in translating naviget. FM.
translate adiciat—probably from want of thought.

26. If one of the crew or captains sleeps off the ship
and the ship is lost whether by day or night, all the
damage regards the members of the crew or captains
who slept off the ship, while those who remained on
board go harmless. Those who were negligent must
make good to the owner of the ship the damage which
was done by reason of their negligence.

ναυκλήρων] As to the possibility of more than one ναύκληρος
being on board see Introduction, p. cxxxvii, and note on c. ιθ΄.

ἐκκοιτοῦντος] LS. translate the word 'sleep out, keep night-
watch'. Here it evidently means 'to sleep off the ship'. The
mediaeval statutes often contain provisions intended to secure
the constant presence on board of a certain proportion of the
crew. See Introduction, p. clxxvii.

νυκτὸς ἢ ἡμέρας] This phrase is no doubt added to prevent it
from being suggested that the chapter only refers to injuries
arising at night.

ἐφορᾶν] 'regards.' It governs τοὺς ἐξωκ. cc. 29, 4 ; 36, 3.

τοὺς ἐξωκοιτοῦντας] Note the love of variety. Before we had
the singular and ἐκκοιτεῖν; here we have the plural and ἐξωκοιτεῖν.

τοὺς δὲ ἀμελήσαντας . . . ζημίαν] This phrase seems to be a mere
repetition of the previous passage πᾶσαν τὴν ζημίαν . . . ναυκλήρους.

τῷ δεσπότῃ τοῦ πλοίου] Here the owner of the ship is distinguished from the captain. See Introduction, p. cxxxii.

27. A ship is on its way to be freighted by a merchant
or a partnership. The ship is damaged or lost by the
negligence of sailors or of the captain. The cargo which
lies in the warehouse is free from claims. If evidence is
given that the ship was lost in a storm, what is saved of

105

TRANSLATION AND COMMENTARY

the ship is to come into contribution together with cargo and the captain is to retain the half-freight. If one of the partners denies the partnership and is convicted by three witnesses, let him pay his share of the contribution and suffer the penalty of his denial.

ἀπέρχηται εἰς γόμον] This phrase probably means 'is on its way to receive a cargo'. If this is so, τὰ φορτία τὰ ἐν ὅρια κείμενα are the goods which are in the warehouses waiting to be loaded. The captain would have received τὰ ἡμίναυλα on the signing of the contract and before the ship started for its port of loading. This explanation of ἀπέρχηται εἰς γόμον is supported by the position of this chapter in the Sea-law. Chapters 28 and 29 deal with the loading of the ship in the place fixed by the contract. Chapters 30 and 31 deal with the ship on its voyage. Chapter 33 deals with the ship after it has unloaded in the place fixed by the contract. The only doubt is occasioned by c. 32, which uses the phrase ἐπὶ γόμον ὑπάγῃ. It is not improbable that this chapter is simply another form of c. 27, although in that case we should rather expect it to follow immediately after c. 27.

κοινωνίας] See Introduction, p. cclxii.

τὰ ἐν ὅρια κείμενα] This is a case where an early corruption has preserved the true reading. Many of the MSS. read ἐνόρια as if it was one word. The scribes who saw that it was really ἐν ὅρια were so disgusted with the grammar and the spelling that they corrected it into ἐν ὁρίω (ὠρείω) or ἐν ὡραίοις (see App. Crit.). The same thing happened in c. 33, 4 τὰ ἐν ὅρια ἐκβεβλημένα (see App. Crit.). The spelling of the word varies greatly in the MSS. Duc. 1793 gives ὠρεῖον ὁρεῖον ὅριον ὁρρεον (see also Bast, Epist. Crit., p. 62); but where it is possible to get at the reading of the oldest MSS. the spelling seems to be ὅριον. In the Farmer's Law, ξγ′ (M) ὁρίω is read by M, while G reads ὡρίω and R ὠρείω. In Theophanes, De Boor reads ὅρια twice (pp. 150, 384), both times with his best MSS. In Const. Porph. de Cerim. II, 51, p. 699, ed. Bonn, the text gives ὁρρία. In Malalas, the printed text gives always ὡρεῖα, but Barocc. 182, which I have examined, has once (f. 23 r = p. 60, Dind.) ὁρία corrected into ὡρία; once (f. 193 r = p. 307, Dind.) ὡρεῖα ; and once (f. 254 r = p. 399, Dind.) ὡρεῖα. The papyri give as dat. pl. ὁρίοις (B. G. U., 1011, 2nd cent.) ὁρίοις (P. Fiorent, 75, p. 157, A. D. 380) and ὁρρίοις (B. G. U. 838, A.D. 578).

μαρτύρων τριῶν] See Introduction, p. lxxxix.

τὴν τιμωρίαν] See Introduction, p. lxxxvii.

28. If a ship is hindered in the loading by a merchant or partner, and the time fixed for loading passes, and it happens that the ship is lost by reason of piracy or fire

or wreck, let him who caused the hindrance make good the damage.

ἐμβολῇ] The word here means merely 'loading'—a use to which LS. do not advert. As regards this meaning, and its more technical meaning to denote the annual contribution of corn made to Rome and afterwards to Constantinople, see the authorities in Herwerden, s. v. ; Rostowzew, Kornerhebung und-transport in griech.-römisch. Aegypten in Archiv für Papyrusforschung, III, p. 221.

29. If the merchant does not provide the cargo at the place fixed by the contract, and the time fixed for loading passes, and a loss happens by reason of piracy or fire or wreck, all the injury to the ship regards the merchant. But if the days of the allowed time have not passed when something of this sort happens, let them come to contribution.

The first part of this chapter repeats in a slightly different form what was laid down in the last one.

πληρωθέντων] See ante, p. 71.

30. If the merchant loads the ship and there is gold with him and the ship happens to suffer one of the maritime risks and the cargo is lost and the ship goes to pieces, let what is saved from the ship and the cargo come to contribution, but let the merchant take his gold with him on paying a tenth. If he was saved without clinging to any of the ship's spars, let him pay the half-fare in accordance with the contract; if he had to cling for safety to one of the spars, let him pay one-fifth.

ἐὰν ὁ ἔμπορος κτλ.] The grammar is peculiar and attempts have been made in some MSS. to regularize it, but see note on c. 20 ὃς ἂν πλοῖον ναυλώσηται.

καὶ ὁ φόρτος . . . διαλυθῇ] This phrase may be a gloss. It rather impedes the sense, as it is clear from the next phrase that part at least of the cargo is saved. The reading is very doubtful.

ἐὰν δὲ μή κτλ.] This passage is obscurely worded, but the sense is fairly clear. Whether the merchant was saved by clinging to a spar or not, he must pay the half-freight; but if he was saved without clinging to one, he must pay 10 per cent. of the value of his gold. If he had to cling to one to be saved, he must pay 20 per cent. See Introduction, p. cclxiii.

TRANSLATION AND COMMENTARY

31. If the merchant loads the ship and something happens to the ship, all that is saved is to come into contribution on either side; but the silver, if it is saved, is to pay a fifth; and the captain and the sailors are to give help in salving.

32. If a ship is on its way to be loaded, whether it is hired by a merchant or goes in partnership, and a sea-disaster takes place, the merchant is not to ask back the half-freight, but let what remains of the ship and the cargo come to contribution. If the merchant or the partner has also given an advance, let their agreement made in writing prevail.

ἐπὶ γόμον ὑπάγῃ] See note on c. 27 ἀπέρχηται εἰς γόμον.
κοινωνίᾳ] See Introduction, p. ccxlii.
τὰ δὲ τοῦ πλοίου] One would expect σωζόμενα after τοῦ πλοίου.
προχρείαν] The MSS. vary between this, προσχρείαν and προχειρίαν (see App. Crit.). προχρεία is clearly the true reading. Dig. XIX, 2, 15, 6 runs: 'item cum quidam naue amissa uecturam, quam pro mutua acceperat, repeteretur, rescriptum est ab Antonino Augusto non immerito procuratorem Caesaris ab eo uecturam repetere, cum munere uehendi functus non sit.' Cyril paraphrases this passage as follows: ὁ προχρήσας τὸν ναῦλον, εἰ ἀπόληται ἡ ναῦς, ἀναλαμβάνει αὐτόν (Schol. ad Bas. XX, 1, 15; ed. Heimb. II, p. 345). It is paraphrased in the Synopsis Ambr. (LIII, I, νθ'): τοῦ πλοίου ναυαγήσαντος, ἀποδίδωσιν ὁ ναύκληρος τὰ ναῦλα, ἅπερ ἔλαβεν ἐν προχρείᾳ ὡς μὴ μετακομίσας. The latter paraphrase is frequently found; τὰ τῶν ἐπιβατῶν φορτία is sometimes added (Prochiros, XVII, 8; Epanagoge, XXIV, 9; Epit. Selden., f. 78 v.; Appendix F, ι'; Appendix G (g); Harmenop. II, xi, 21; ed. Heimb., p. 332). The glossaries have πρόχρεια antecessum or in antecessum (Cyrilli Glossaria, ed. 1682, Part I, p. 163; Part III, p. 13). The word occurs constantly in the papyri, especially in the form ἐν προχρείᾳ or λόγῳ προχρείας. These authorities show that προχρεία is primarily an advance. It is used in a more general sense in Anecdota Bekk., p. 472: ἀφορμή· ἰδίως παρὰ Ἀττικοῖς ἡ πάροδος λέγεται, ἣν νῦν πολλοὶ πρόχρειαν καὶ ἐνθήκην λέγουσι. The word here is probably used in its strict sense, of an advance in respect of freight beyond the half-freight, which would normally be paid at the execution of the contract. It is also possible that the word is used loosely, of an advance analogous to the mediaeval commenda, made either to the ναύκληρος or to a merchant (see p. ccxxxv).

108

33. If the captain puts the cargo in the place fixed by the contract and the ship comes to grief, let the captain recover the freight in full from the merchant, but the goods which have been unloaded into warehouses are safe from those which are on board the ship with the ship, but let what are found on the ship together with the ship come into contribution.

εἰσκομιζέσθω] A curious phrase, ' let the captain get his freight brought in in full by the merchant.'

ἀκίνδυνα εἶναι κτλ.] i. e. where goods have been unloaded no claim is to be made upon them for contribution, either by those which remain on board or by the ship.

ὑπὸ τῶν συμπλεόντων] I have translated as if the nominative was τὰ συμπλέοντα τοῦ πλοίου, which would be equivalent to τὰ εὑρισκόμενα ἐν τῷ πλοίῳ. The meaning is not altered if the nominative is οἱσυμπλέοντες.

34. If a ship is carrying linen or silk, let the captain supply good skins, in order that in a storm no harm may be done to the freight by the dashing of the waves. If the water rises in the hold, let the captain say so at once to those who have the cargo on board, in order that it may be brought up. If the passengers make it manifest to the captain and for all that the cargo is injured, the captain is responsible together with the sailors. If the captain declares beforehand together with the sailors that the water is rising in the ship and the goods must come up, but those who loaded the goods neglect to bring them up, let the captain and sailors go harmless.

ὀθόνην] Linen here is probably an independent cargo; it may also be an adjunct to the cargo of silk, as linen was used to wrap up silken garments (λόγῳ ἐνδυμάτων τῶν βαμβακίνων χιτώνων, Livre du Préfet, p. 39). Ὀθόνη also denoted the ship's sail (carbasus ὀθόνη πλοίου, Corpus Gloss. Lat. II, p. 379) and the ship's flag (Duc., Appx. 144).

βέστην] Pard. translates this word vestes; FM. vestem. Duc. 192 translates it vestis, and βεστιοπράτηρ qui vestes vendit, sutor. But it was also used in a special sense of silk. Livre du Préfet, p. 26 οἱ βεστιοπράται ὀφείλουσιν ἐξωνεῖσθαι σηρικὰς ἐσθῆτας, οὐ μὴν ἄλλην τινὰ ἐμπορείαν.

ἐπικλύσει] though it has less MSS. authority, is probably right. The Schol. ad Thuc. III, 89, defines ἐπίκλυσις as κύματος ἐξόρμησίς τις ἐπὶ τὴν γῆν, but it must be equally appropriate of waves swamping a ship. The Byzantines used it of immersion in the baptismal font (Duc. 422). Ἐπίκλασις, which has the weight of MSS. authority, apparently does not occur elsewhere. It might be used of the waves breaking over the ship.

ἔκθεσις] here apparently means the bringing up of the cargo from below.

οἱ ἐπιβάται] This is A's reading; my other MSS. give οἱ ναῦται. It is obvious that οἱ ναῦται cannot stand if the rest of the sentence is right. If the mariners warn the captain, and in spite of that the goods are injured, it would be iniquitous to make them responsible. One would expect, however, οἱ ἔμποροι rather than οἱ ἐπιβάται. The editors get over the difficulty, while they retain οἱ ναῦται, by putting μή before φανερόν; none of my MSS. support this. A better plan, if one kept οἱ ναῦται, would be to leave out ἅμα τοῖς ναύταις in line 8. It might easily have crept in from the line below.

35. If a ship makes jettison of its mast, whether it breaks of its own accord or is cut, let all the sailors and the merchants and the goods and the ship so far as saved come into contribution.

As to contribution where part of the ship's tackle is jettisoned, see Introduction, p. cclxxiii.

πάντες οἱ ναῦται καὶ οἱ ἔμποροι] This does not necessarily imply, as Pard. thinks, that 'les personnes mêmes sont assujetties à la contribution'. The passage may equally well be understood as a rhetorical way of saying that the sailors are to contribute in respect of ship and the merchants in respect of goods. See Introduction, pp. cclx, cclxxvii.

36. If a ship in sail runs against another ship which is lying at anchor or has slackened sail, and it is day, all the collision and the damage regards the captain and those who are on board. Moreover let the cargo too come into contribution. If this happens at night, let the man who slackened sail light a fire. If he has no fire, let him shout. If he neglects to do this and a disaster takes place, he has himself to thank for it, if the evidence goes to this. If the sailsman was negligent and the watchman dozed off, the man who was sailing perished as if he ran on shallows and let him keep harmless him whom he strikes.

As to the doctrine of collision in Roman law, see Introduction, p. cclxxxv.

τοὺς ἐμπλέοντας] The other passages in which οἱ ἐμπλέοντες are found in the Sea-law leave it doubtful whether it is confined to the mariners or extends to merchants and passengers. It is clear from the next passage that the cargo was to some extent liable.

πῦρ ἀπτέτω] The fire no doubt was to be lighted on the mast. Cp. Procop. de Bello Vandal. I, 13, ed. Bonn, p. 366 κοντούς τε ὀρθοὺς ἀναστήσας ἐν πρύμνῃ ἑκάστῃ ἀπεκρέμασεν ἀπ' αὐτῶν λύχνα, ὅπως ἔν τε ἡμέρᾳ καὶ νυκτὶ αἱ τοῦ στρατηγοῦ νῆες ἔκδηλοι εἶεν.

κραυγὰς παρεχέτω] The sailors probably took it in turns to sing through the night.

ἀμελήσας] See note on c. 20 ὃς ἂν πλοῖον ναυλώσηται. The MSS. vary greatly; see App. Crit.

ἑαυτὸν ἀπώλεσεν] Cp. c. 11 ἑαυτὸν ἀπὸ γῆς ἀπώλεσεν.

εἰ δὲ καὶ κτλ.] The chapter contemplates three possibilities: (a) Ship A (πλοῖον ἀρμενίζον) in the daytime runs down ship B, which is at rest. (b) The same thing happens at night, ship B having neither lighted a fire nor made a noise (εἰ δὲ ταῦτα . . . μαρτυρηθῶσιν. (c) The third hypothesis deals with the case where the commander of ship A (ὁ ἀρμενίζων) is also negligent. In that case ὡς εἰς βράχη ἀπώλετο, 'he is lost as if he had run against shoals,' i. e. ship B incurs no liability to ship A; on the contrary, ship A must make the damage good to ship B (ὃν κρούσει ἀζήμιον φυλαττέτω).

ἀρμενιστής] Not in the lexica.

ἀμελήσας] See note on c. 20 ὃς ἂν πλοῖον ναυλώσηται.

βιγλεοφόρος] The MSS. vary between this or some form of it and βι(η)γλάτωρ (see App. Crit.). Duc. 199, s. v. βιγλάτωρ, cites several authorities, to which add Niceph. Phoc. de Velitatione Bellica apud Leo. Diac., p. 225, 13, ed. Bonn. He cites no authority for βιγλεοφόρος but this passage.

The watch on board ship was not a special office, but was taken in turn by merchants, passengers, mariners, and servants. St. Zeno, 94 = St. Zara, IV, 37 = St. Spalat. VI, 66; St. Ancon. 8; Consulate of Sea, c. 206.

37. If the ship comes to grief and the property of the merchants or passengers is saved while the ship is lost, let the debentures which are saved provide one-fifteenth, but let not the merchant and the passengers give the ship to the captain.

τῶν ἐμπόρων] Yet two lines lower down we have ὁ ἔμπορος.

γραμμάτια] Some of the scribes found difficulties in this word, and the editors agree that it is corrupt. This is wrong. There are few commoner words in the Byzantine law-books. The γραμμάτιον or γραμματεῖον is an instrument by which A acknowledged indebtedness to B. It contained a statement of the securities given for the debt, the time fixed for repayment, and the rate of interest, if any. It might either be written by the debtor himself (ἰδιόχειρον), in which case it required the subscriptions of three witnesses, or take the form of a notarial act (ἀγοραῖον). (Ecloga Privata Aucta, XI, 2; Epanagoge, XIII,'8). The transfer of the γραμμάτιον transferred the right to sue for and recover the debt. Its intentional destruction by the creditor extinguished the debt; and if it was destroyed by chance, while the debt was still subsisting, the creditor was naturally placed at a great disadvantage in recovering the debt, as his failure to produce the γραμμάτιον raised a presumption that the debt was gone. Moreover, the debtor was entitled to have the γραμμάτιον back when he paid off the debt, and, if the creditor could not restore it to him, he was obliged to guarantee him against the risk of its improper use by a third person (Epanagoge, XIII, 5; Bas. XXII, 1, 24, 64; XXIII, 1, 35; LX, 6, 11, 1 Sch.; Πεῖρα, XXVI, ιη', p. 126). It was therefore only natural that, as the owners of silver paid 20 per cent. when it was recovered from a wreck, and the owners of gold 10 per cent., the owners of γραμμάτια should pay 7½ per cent.

The spelling is doubtful (see App. Crit.). The papyri vary greatly, the same document often giving both spellings. γραμμάτιον occurs in P. Amherst, 147, p. 179 (early fifth); P. London, III, p. 271 (A.D. 539); P. Oxyrhynchus, I, p. 207 (A.D. 550); P. Grenfell, II, p. 140 (sixth cent.); P. Amherst, 150, p. 183 (A.D. 592); γραμματεῖον in P. Leipzig, 41 (fourth cent.); P. London, III, p. 271; P. Grenfell, II, p. 138; P. Reinach, 58, p. 169 (sixth cent.); P. Amherst, 151 (A.D. 610–640); B. G.U. 808 (Byz.); P. Fiorentini, 70 (seventh cent.), P. London, I, p. 233 (8th cent.).

δότωσαν] δωσάτωσαν, which is found in many MSS. (see App. Crit.), may be right. See De Boor's Index Graecitatis Theoph., s. v. δίδωμι (p. 738); Malal., pp. 26, 4, and 328, 14, ed. Bonn.

38. If a ship loaded with corn is caught in a gale, let the captain provide skins and the sailors work the pumps. If they are negligent and the cargo is wetted by the bilge, let the sailors pay the penalty. But if it is from the gale that the cargo is injured, let the captain and the sailors together with the merchant bear the loss; and let the captain together with the ship and the sailors receive the six-hundredths of each thing saved. If goods are to be thrown into the sea, let the merchant be the first to throw and then let the sailors take a hand. Moreover none of the sailors is to steal. If any one steals, let the robber make it good twofold and lose his whole gain.

τὰς δὲ ἐξ ἐκατοστάς] The scribes evidently found great difficulty in the text (see App. Crit.). The conjecture which I propose is supported more or less by passages in other maritime codes. See Introduction, p. cclxxxix.

ἅμα τοῦ πλοίου καὶ τοῖς ναύταις] The rule in the Sea-law appears to be that where the substantive governed by ἅμα is an inanimate object it is put in the genitive (cc. 33, 6 ἅμα τοῦ πλοίου : 41, 6 ἅμα τῆς συμβολῆς : 43, 4 ἅμα τῆς τιμῆς), where it is a living being, in the dative (cc. 10, 1; 34, 8, 9 ἅμα τοῖς ναύταις : c. 38, 6 ἅμα τῷ ἐμπόρῳ : c. 46, 2 ἅμα καὶ τοῖς ἐμπλέουσιν). In this instance the rule is carried out, but, even apart from the rule, there appears to have been a strong tendency in the Byzantine grammar of this period, where ἅμα, or any other preposition, is followed by two substantives, to put those substantives into different cases. Malal., p. 219, 22, ed. Bonn, ἅμα τῷ αὐτῷ Ἀγρίππᾳ στρατηγῷ καὶ στρατιωτικῶν δυνάμεων αὐτοῦ. De Boor, in his Index Graecitat. Theoph. s. v. ἅμα, σύν, gives many examples, some of which he unnecessarily corrects.

πρῶτος ῥιπτέτω] As to the custom for the owner of cargo to throw first, see Introduction, p. cclxviii ; and cp. Juvenal, xii, 37.

τοῦ κέρδους] the profit which he would have made by receiving a percentage of the valuables saved.

39. A ship with a cargo of corn or wine or oil is in full sail. By wish of the captain and crew who slacken sail, the ship goes into a place or on a beach against the wish of the merchant. It happens that the ship is lost, but the cargo or goods are saved. The merchant is to suffer no harm from the loss of the ship, since he did not wish to go into that place. If while the ship is in full sail, the merchant says to the captain 'I want to go into this place ', and the place is not comprised in the charter-party, and it happens that the ship is lost while the goods are saved, let the captain have his ship made good by the merchant. If it is by wish of both parties that the ship is cast away, let everything come to contribution.

This chapter may be compared with c. 4; and with Ordin. Trani, 8.

ἐὰν πλοῖον . . . ἀρμενίζον . . . καὶ εἰσέλθῃ] See note on c. 20 ὃς ἂν πλοῖον ναυλώσηται.

μεστὸν σίτου ἢ οἴνου ἢ ἐλαίου] There seems no reason why the provisions of this chapter should be confined to ships carrying certain cargoes. It is possible that the chapter comes from some collection of rules relating to the *navicularii* who supplied Rome and afterwards Constantinople. σῖτος and ἔλαιον were two of their principal imports (Dig. L, 6, 6 (5), 6).

TRANSLATION AND COMMENTARY

40. A ship is wrecked, and part of the cargo and the ship is saved. The passengers have on them gold or silver or whole silks or pearls. Let the gold that is saved provide a tenth, and the silver contribute a fifth. Let the whole silks, if they are saved dry, contribute a tenth, as being equal to gold. If they are wetted, let an allowance be made for the abrasion and the wetting, and let them come into contribution on that footing. Let the pearls according to their valuation contribute to the loss like a cargo of gold.

ὁλοσηρικά] ὁλοσηρικός is an adjective (ὁλοσήρικα ἱμάτια, Theoph., p. 322, 7, ed. De Boor; στολὴν ἄσπρον ὁλοσηρικόν, Malal., p. 287, 15 and 310, 11; χλαμύδα ἄσπρον ὁλοσήρικον, Malal., p. 413, 12; χλαμύδιν ἄσπρον ὁλοσηρικόν, Chron. Pasch., p. 613, 20), but τὸ ὁλοσηρικόν, τὰ ὁλοσηρικά are not infrequently found substantively (τὴν τιμὴν παντὸς τοῦ ὁλοσηρήκου, Edictum apud Zach. 'Ανέκδοτα, p. 263, n. 46; φοροῦντας ὁλοσήρικα, Chron. Pasch., p. 721, 11, ed. Bonn; ὥσπερ γὰρ ἐνδεδυμένος ὁλοσήρικον, Dorotheus de Doctrina, l. 2; ὥσπερ γυνὴ ἔχουσα ὁλοσήρικα, Macar. Omil. 17, 19; Σῆρες .. ὄνομα ἔθνους ὅθεν ἔρχεται καὶ τὸ ὁλοσήρικον, Hesych. The corresponding word in Latin is holosericus (Lamprid. Vita Heliog. c. 26; Vita Alex. Severi, c. 40; Vopisc. Vita Aureliani, c. 45; Vita Taciti, c. 10; Cod. Theodos. XV, 9, 1; Symmachus, Epist. IV, 8), but the substantival form is holoserica (fem. sing.) : 'cum subsutura holosericae' (Edict. Diocl. de pretiis rerum venalium, 7, 49). The authorities vary greatly as to the accentuation. I print ὁλοσηρικά, in agreement with LS., Pard., and many of my MSS., but there is good authority for ὁλοσήρικα. In Malalas, Barocci, 182, which I have examined, always gives ὁλοσήρικον; f. 179 r = p. 287 Dind.; f. 195 v = p. 310 Dind.; f. 264 r = p. 413 Dind. De Boor's MSS., in Theoph., l. c., all give ὁλοσήρικα or ὁλοσήρικα. In the Edict published by Zach. from Selden, 10, f. 58 v, the MS. (which I have examined) has τοῦ ὁλοσηρήκου, as Zach. prints it.

ὡς ὅμοια ὄντα τοῦ χρυσίου] In the time of Aurelian, a pound of silk cost a pound of gold ('libra enim auri tunc libra serici fuit', Vopisc. Vita Aureliani, c. 45). Justinian, according to Procop., Hist. Arcana, 25, forbade merchants to sell clothes made from silk (ἱμάτια τὰ ἐκ μετάξης) at more than eight gold-pieces per pound. The merchants could not carry on business on these terms and a royal monopoly was established, under which silk of ordinary quality (βαφῆς μὲν τῆς προστυχούσης) was sold at six gold-pieces the ounce, while silk of extra quality (βάμματος δὲ τοῦ βασιλικοῦ, ὅπερ καλεῖν ὁλόβηρον νενομίκασι) was sold at twenty-four gold-pieces and more. A price of six gold-pieces per ounce means that the pound of silk cost a pound of gold; and Zach.

quotes this passage from the Sea-law to show that the same price
lasted till the eighth century (see his paper, 'Eine Verordnung
Justinians über den Seidenhandel aus den Jahren 540-547' in
Mémoires de l'Académie Impériale des Sciences de St.-Pétersbourg,
VIIᵉ Série, Tome IX, Nᵒ 6, St.-Pétersbourg, 1865). But the
language here cannot be pressed to that extent. It does not
necessarily mean that whole silks were worth their weight in
gold (ἰσοστάσια τῷ χρυσίῳ), but merely that they were to pay ten
per cent. on account of their great value.

εἰ δὲ βραχῶσι κτλ.] does not mean that the whole silks are to
pay less than ten per cent. if they are wetted, but that they are
to pay ten per cent. on a reduced valuation.

χρυσίου φόρτον κτλ.] This is an obscure phrase, which the
editors do not make less obscure. Leuncl. translates 'onus auri
exaequantes, navis exitium compensent'; Pard. 'ut onus auri
exaequantes, damnum resarciant'; FM. 'ad onus auri redacta
ad reparationem interitus contribuant'. It certainly cannot mean
that a pound of pearls are to pay the same amount as a pound of
gold; it must mean that they are to pay the same proportion, i. e.
ten per cent. of their value. It is difficult to get this out of the
words, and I am tempted to read καθὼς ἐκτιμηθῶσι ⟨ὡς⟩ χρυσίου
φόρτος τελείτωσαν κτλ.

41. If there are passengers on board and the ship is
injured or destroyed, but the goods of the passengers
are saved, let the passengers make a payment towards
the loss of the ship. If passengers two or three lose
their gold or their goods, let them receive from all
according to their capacity towards the loss together
with the contribution of the ship.

This chapter is remarkably vague for a legal code. The first
provision, namely, that passengers whose goods are saved are to
contribute to ship, merely repeats in general and not quite
accurate language (see Introduction, p. cclxii) what has been laid
down before with particularity in respect to some special classes
of passengers' belongings. The second provision is of a hortatory
nature. ⸱ How is one to determine the relative capacities of those
whose goods are saved to contribute to those whose goods are
lost?

ἢ διαφθαρῇ ἢ ἀπόληται] The compiler of the Sea-law uses a
surprising variety of expressions to denote injury to, or destruction of a ship, and it is impossible to draw any clear distinction
between them. We have (always of ship) cc. 11, 3 πάθῃ ἢ διαφθαρῇ; 27, 2 παθεῖν ἢ διαφθαρῆναι; 45, 1 στραφῇ ἢ διαφθαρῇ. It
is probable that here he did not make any distinction in his mind
between διαφθαρῇ and ἀπόληται, but was led on by the second-
rate conveyancer's passion for accumulating synonyms.

δύο ἢ τρεῖς] This phrase, as Brunner justly says (Syrisch-Römisches Rechtsbuch, p. 276), is 'unjuristisch'. It is perhaps due to an unseasonable reminiscence of scripture. κατὰ τὴν δύναμιν is also vague.

ἅμα τῆς συμβολῆς] This probably means that the passengers are to contribute to their fellow passengers as well as to the ship. It may possibly mean that ship is to contribute to the passengers who have lost. Leuncl. and Pard., who translate ' navi in collationem veniente ' seem to take the latter view.

42. If a ship springs a leak while it is carrying goods and the goods are taken out, let it lie with the captain, whether he wishes to carry the goods in the ship to the trading-place agreed upon, if the ship is repaired. If the ship is not repaired but the captain takes another ship to the trading-place agreed upon, let him give the whole freight.

Although the grammar of this chapter is more faulty than usual the sense is fairly clear. If a ship springs a leak with goods on board, the captain has two alternatives. He may have the ship repaired and carry the goods in it to the place prescribed in the contract. He may put the goods into another ship. This chapter is considered on p. ccviii, and cp. C. Tortosa, IX, 27, cc. 33, 34.

τρυπήσῃ] The intransitive use of τρυπᾶν is apparently not classical. The word is used transitively in Bas. LX, 3, 27, 24 (ὁ πλοῖον τρυπήσας).

ἐὰν δὲ θελήσῃ] δέ is apparently used here to introduce the first of two alternatives. For another superfluous δέ see c. 24, 3.

ἐν τῷ συγκ. ἐμπορίῳ] here = εἰς τὸ συγκ. ἐμπόριον. εἰς τὸ συγκείμενον ἐμπόριον occurs in Demosth. 1293, 2 ; 1294, 2.

διδότω] As to the subject of this verb, see p. ccviii.

43. If a ship is caught in a storm and makes jettison of its cargo, and breaks its sailyards and mast and tillers and anchors and rudders, let all these come into contribution together with the value of the ship and of the goods which are saved.

κεράτων] Dind.-Steph. cite, for κέρας in this sense, Synesius, Ep. 4; Lucian, Amor. c. 6; Anth. Pal. V, 204. To these examples add Inscription of A. D. 90 in Dittenberger, Orientis Gr. Inscr. 674, vol. II, p. 418; P. London, III, p. 164 (A. D. 212); Apollodorus, Poliorcetica in Wescher's Poliorcétique des Grecs, p. 179 μακρὰ σανὶς ὥσπερ τὰ ἐν τοῖς πλοίοις κέρατα; Hesych., s. v. καρχήσια; Corpus Gloss. Lat. III, p. 29 κέρας, *antemna*. The Byzantine form was κερατάριον. To the examples given by Duc. 637 and Appx. 99 add Const. Porph. de Cerim, II, 44, ed. Bonn, p. 659.

καταρτίου] Here the authority is overwhelming for καταρτίου. In Title 35, Title 44, and c. 35, 1 the MSS. agree in τῆς καταρτίας. In c. 44, 2 most give τῆς καρτίας, but there is some authority for τῶν καταρτίων. The common Byzantine form is τὸ κατάρτιον, of which Duc. 612 gives many instances, to which add Const. Porph. de Cerim. II, 44, p. 659. ἡ κατάρτιος is also found (examples in LS., to which add Appendix A, p. 41 and ' catorcios arbor ' in Corpus Gloss. Lat. III, p. 205), but apparently ἡ καταρτία occurs only in the Sea-law and in Chron. Pasch., p. 720, 6, ed. Bonn.

ἐφολκίων] LS. give ἐφόλκαιον, a rudder, for which their only authority is Homer, and ἐφόλκιον, a small boat towed after a ship. Leuncl., Pard., and FM. take the word here and in c. 44, 3 in the latter sense. In c. 46, 6 Leuncl. is vague. Pard. and FM. translate ' cum instrumentis '. It is difficult to believe that in that place the word means a small boat, a trailer, and it is probable that in all three places it means the same thing, rudders. There is no doubt that the word often means a ship's boat; but there is enough authority to show that it may also mean a rudder. Hesych. ἐφόλκιον· διὰ τοῦ ί τὸ πηδάλιον ἀπὸ τοῦ ἐφέλκεσθαι; Apollonius ἐφόλκεον . . . σημαίνει δὲ καράβια μικρά. οἱ δέ, τὸ πηδάλιον; Eustath. 1533, 45 τὸ δὲ πηδάλιον ὅτι καὶ ἐφόλκιον λέγεται δηλοῦσιν οἱ παλαιοί; Eustath. 1761, 12 and 46 distinguishes between ἐφόλκαιον, the rudder, and ἐφόλκιον, a kind of boat. It is improbable that the κάραβος had small boats attached to it, but it is clear that the ship's boat had a rudder or rudders (St. Ancon. del Mare, 34).

44. A ship has a cargo, and in a gale the mast is jettisoned or the tillers broken or one of the rudders lost. If it happens that the cargo gets wet from the gale, there is every necessity that these should come to contribution. But if the cargo is hurt more from the bilge and not from the gale, let the captain take the freight and hand the goods over dry and in quantity as he took them.

As to the captain's liability in cases of bilge see Introduction, p. cxcix.

45. If in the open sea a ship is overset or destroyed, let him who brings anything from it safe on to land

117

receive instead of reward the fifth part of that which
he saves.

Salvage, with which this and the two next chapters deal, is
dealt with in the Introduction, p. cclxxxviii.

46. A boat breaks the ropes and gets off from its ship
and is lost with all hands. If those on board are lost or
die, let the captain pay their annual wages for the full
year to their heirs. He who saves the boat with its
rudders will give them all back as he in truth finds
them and receive the fifth part of what he saves.

This chapter, like some others, deals with matters which are
quite disparate—the wages of the seamen who are lost and the
salvor's reward. It gives the impression in consequence of representing a judicial decision.

τὰ σχοινία] Acts, xxvii, 32 ; Cic. de Invent. II, 51 ' Tempestas
iactare coepit usque adeo ut dominus navis, cum idem gubernator
esset, in scapham confugeret et inde funiculo, qui a puppi religatus
scapham annexam trahebat, navi, quoad posset, moderaretur '.

τοῖς ἐμπλέουσιν] Cp. Petron. 102 ' unum nautam stationis per-
petuae interdiu noctuque iacere in scapha '.

ἀπόλωνται ἤ ἀποθάνωσι] The phrase is redundant, unless we
take ἀπόλωνται to mean ' are lost ', ' disappear ', while ἀποθάνωσι
implies that the captain has knowledge of their fate. Some of
the scribes at any rate felt the redundancy, and omitted one or
other word (see App. Crit.).

τὸν μισθὸν κτλ.] The word μισθός does not necessarily imply
that the mariners received a fixed wage. It is equally consistent
with their receiving a share of profits (see α'–η). The word
ἐνιαυσιαῖος does imply that, whether they received fixed wages or
a share of profits, their engagement was for a year. The word
year, however, in this context is not necessarily a calendar
year. It no doubt starts from the time when the sea became
open to navigation. If the mariner was back at his home port
by the time that navigation was over, the ' year ' would no doubt
terminate then. If the mariner found himself at a foreign port
when the sea was closed, the year would no doubt include the
winter months during which the ship was laid up, and the
mariner, where he was paid fixed wages, received an allowance.
This chapter determines that, where the mariner dies, under the
circumstances mentioned, in the course of a ' year's ' service, his
relatives are to receive the amount which he would have received
if he had lived through the year. See Introduction, p. clxviii.

καθὼς κτλ.] There is great diversity of reading among the
MSS. here, but the sense is clear. The passage means that, if

118

the salvor restores everything that he has found, he receives one-fifth. See a similar passage from M in Appendix F, ς΄.

47. If gold or silver or anything else is raised from the sea from a depth of eight fathoms, let the salvor receive one-third. If it is raised from a depth of fifteen fathoms, let the salvor receive one-half by reason of the danger of the sea. Where things are cast from sea to land and found there or carried to within one cubit of the land, let the salvor receive one-tenth part of what is salved.

ὀργυιῶν] The classical ὀργυιά was equal to four πήχεις and measured 1·85 metres (Hermann-Blümner, p. 441). Just as in Byzantine times there was a longer and a shorter πῆχυς (see note, p. 59), so there was a longer and a shorter ὀργυιά. The longer was used ἐν ταῖς βασιλικαῖς ἀπογραφαῖς, and the shorter was used in sales. Pediasimus in Hultsch, Metrologicorum Scriptorum Reliquiae, vol. II, pp. 148, 166. See also Hultsch, Beiträge zur ägyptischen Metrologie, in Archiv für Papyrusforschung, III, p. 440. The MSS. indulge (lines 2 and 3) in every variety of spelling and accentuation. The South Italian form seems to have been ὀργία (pl. ὀργίες, Trinchera, p. 190, A. D. 1147; ὀργίας, Trinchera, p. 436, A. D. 1267). Duc. 1066 gives examples of οὐργυιά, to which add Pasini, Codices MSS. Bibl. Taurinensis, Taurini, 1749, I, p. 224 (A. D. 1319) οὐργυιῶν βασιλεικῶν δέκα, χειροσπηθάμων ἐγδοήκοντα πέντε. According to this the royal ὀργυιά equalled eight and a half σπιθαμαί, which is inconsistent with either the longer or the shorter πῆχυς as given by Hero (see note on p. 59).

ἢ ἐπιφερομένων] should perhaps be left out with some of the best MSS. (see App. Crit.); εὑρισκομένων ἐπὶ πῆχυν ἕνα would then mean ' found within a cubit's length of land '.

APPENDIX A

PROLOGUE

FIRST FORM.

Sea-law of the Rhodians, which was promulgated by the divine emperors, Adrianus Tiberius Lucius Septimius Severus Pertinax semper augusti.

Tiberius Caesar Augustus pontifex maximus, in the thirty-second [year] of his tribunician power, says as follows. The sailors, captains, and the merchants having approached me in order that events at sea in a storm may come to contribution, Nero answered and said: 'Greatest, wisest, and most steadfast Caesar, what is established by your greatness I think it necessary to display, without passing over a single statement, having carefully sought out in Rhodes and imparted all matters relating to those who sail on ships, captains and merchants and passengers, and to deposits of capital and partnerships, and to purchases and sales of ships, and works of shipbuilding, and to deposits of gold and silver and of various goods.' All these things Tiberius Caesar determined by his vote, and sealed and handed over to Antoninus the illustrious consul. They bring it before consuls in the most fortunate city, head of all others, Rome, in the consulship of the illustrious Laurus and Agrippina. These brought it before the emperor Vespasian, and having sealed it in the presence of the senate Ulpius Trajanus determined that it was the Rhodian law together with the illustrious senate. But let the law of the sea be determined by the nautical law. The same was determined by the divine Augustus.

SECOND FORM.

[The second form, after going on much as above, has this addition.]

The emperor Adrian in the consulship of Clarus and Alexander having sealed it laid down that the Rhodian law was just and had authority. Tiberius Caesar said: I say there is no greater danger than to come into contribution when the mast breaks off of its own accord. If it is necessary, let the mate and the ship's carpenter bring their axes and cut the mast in order that the ship may not sink, and let this come to contribution.

I have dealt with this rigmarole in the Introduction (p. lxxi) at as much length as it deserves.

APPENDIX D

I. If a sailor sent on business be a shareholder, one who receives a share under contract, he must execute every commission of the ship and may go away when his time is expired. If he wishes to go away before the time is expired, let him receive seventy blows and so he is to sail. If he is found stealing, he is to receive one hundred blows and let him lose his share.

II. If a sailor who is sent by the captain for wood or elsewhere goes with comrades and is left behind, let the captain pay him. If he does not go with comrades, if any accident happens to him who is sent, let the captain pay him.

III. If a sailor hires himself out, let him know that he is a slave and has sold himself, and that he is to execute every commission. And if he is sent out let him perform his duty faithfully, committing no theft or wrongdoing, but acting with zeal and goodwill worthily, receiving in full his additional salary. If he steals gold or silver, let him lose his freedom and salary and become a slave, having handed himself over to punishment.

IV. If a slave is let out by his master to a workshop or a business, let his master tell the truth about his trustworthiness. If the master does not tell and the slave commits a theft and runs away, the theft and the flight and the death are to be made up by the master out of his wages.

These chapters are not found in any MS. earlier than the fourteenth century, but the third and fourth are given in a different form in M (see Appendix F). According to Zach., who published them in his edition of the Ecloga ad Prochiron mutata, ' ita barbare conceptae sunt, ut critica arte sanari non possint ' (p. 169). The meaning, however, of all except II is tolerably clear.

I. ἀποτακτάρις] Zach., who reads ἀποτακτάρις ἢ μερίτης, regards ἀποτακτάρις as distinguished from μερίτης. ' Ein ναύτης, der statt bestimmten Lohnes einen solchen Antheil (i. e. am Gewinn) erhält, heisst μερίτης, im Gegensaze zu einem ἀποτακτάρις, d. h. einem solchen, der auf einen Gewinnantheil verzichtet hat und festen Lohn erhält (Das Wort ἀποτακτάρις in Ecl. ad Proch. mut. XL, 40 hat Pardessus p. 258 ganz irrthümlich mit mandatarius übersezt ') (Geschichte, p. 317, n. 1076). This is all very well, but Zach.'s translation of ἀποτακτάρις is derived from the passage itself—the word does not seem to occur elsewhere, and the etymology does not support him. Ναύτης ἀποτακτάρις, if we consult the etymology, is more likely to mean ' a sailor who is sent on an errand '. ἀποτάσσειν is used of detailing a person on some business. Examples in LS., Dittenberger, Orientis Gr. Inscr. 229, vol. I, p. 375 (B.C. 244), 738 ; vol. II, p. 481 (c. B.C. 115); and P. Oxyrhynchus, III, 475, p. 159 ἀξιῶ ἐὰν δόξῃ σοι ἀποτάξαι ἕνα τῶν περὶ σὲ ὑπηρετῶν εἰς τὴν Σ. (A. D. 182). I have ventured to read ᾖ instead of ἤ, and translate ' If a sailor who is sent on the ship's business is a μερίτης', i. e. one who receives a part by virtue of a contract, &c. The mediaeval statutes deal with such cases not infrequently (see St. Ragus. VII, 31, 52 ; Table Amalfi, 13, 46). Observe that the last words of the chapter τὸ μέρος ἀπολλέτω, which refer to the subject of the chapter, can only refer to a μερίτης.

εἰ δὲ εὑρεθῇ κτλ.] This is evidently a reminiscence of c. 3.

II. One thing is clear about this chapter. It refers to a sailor who is sent by his captain to fetch wood or for some other purpose. Then, if we adopt the addition given in H, we find three cases provided for successively. (a) ἐὰν ναύτης συνέλθῃ καὶ παραλειφθῇ κτλ. : (b) ἐὰν μὴ συνέρχηται κτλ. : (c) ἐὰν δέ τις τῶν πεμφθέντων ἀποθάνῃ κτλ. The third hypothesis is clear enough. If one of the sailors who are sent off dies, the captain is to bury him at his, the captain's, expense. This passage, whatever its authority may be, throws light upon the others. It suggests that the other passages also refer to untoward events which may happen to a sailor who is sent off. The text is so doubtful, and the words used, even if we were certain about the text, are so vague, that it is impossible to do more than make a guess.

The first passage possibly means, if the sailor goes with comrades (συνέλθῃ) and is left behind (παραλειφθῇ) the captain is to pay him his share. The Table of Amalfi refers to such a case (c. 46), 'Se alcuno compagno restasse in terra mandato ad utilità della colonna, lo quale non fosse per suo difetto, che non potesse sequire lo viaggio, deve havere la sua parte del guadagno di tutto lo viaggio.' It was common enough to send sailors on shore for wood. Diplomi Pisani, ed. Bonaini, in Arch. Stor. It. S. 1, T. 6, P. 2, Suppl. 1, p. 23 n. 'galeotti eiusdem hostis inciderunt ligna in ipsa silva ubi volebant ad utilitatem galearum' (A. D. 1156). The second passage possibly refers to a case where something untoward happens to the sailor— reading νεώτερον for νεώτερος of the MSS. Even if he does not go with comrades (ἐὰν μὴ συνέρχηται) yet if anything untoward happens to the man who is sent (ἐὰν νεώτερον γένηται κατὰ τοῦ πεμφθέντος) the captain is to pay him his share. This may be brought into connexion with Table of Amalfi, c. 14 'Si aliquis nautarum vel sociorum esset apprehensus a piratis . . . durante navigio, non obstante quod non serviat societati, habeat partem suam '; St. Ragus. VII, 31 'Si vero marinarius aliquis iret in terram de voluntate patroni vel nauclerii, et sibi dampnum aliquod acciderit, ipsum dampnum restitui debeat de comunitate navis vel ligni'; St. Ancon. 17. One has only to look at Pard.'s translation of this chapter (which is based, however, on a different and inferior text) to see how doubtful the matter is.

III, IV. We get into smoother water in the following chapters— smoother because here we have the assistance of a much better MS. (M). Just as chapters I and II refer, in my opinion, to the sailor who is a μερίτης, so III refers clearly to a free man who hires himself out as a sailor, and IV to a slave who is hired out by his master. III, in the elaborate form in which it is given in F H and Par. gr. 1720, states in the first place that the free man who hires himself out as a sailor is to execute all commissions, &c. It is probable that τὰς ἐπιμισθίας, which the sailor is to get if he behaves himself, do not simply mean 'integram mercedem', as Pard. takes it, but refer to the allowance, in addition to wages, which a sailor received who was sent on shore. Table of Amalfi, c.13 'Si aliquis nautarum vel sociorum remanserit in terra ad utilitatem societatis, habeat pro suis expensis ut infra declarabitur'.

The second part of the chapter provides that if the sailor commits a theft he is to lose his freedom and wages and become a slave. This passage is consonant with the latter part of c. 8 as it appears in M.

There is no reference on the face of c. IV to ships or sailors. The chapter is a perfectly general one, and refers to every slave who is hired out by his master εἰς ἐργαστήριον ἢ εἰς ἐργασίαν. The master in hiring him is to give his character. If he gives a wrong character and the slave steals and runs away, the master is liable to pay damages out of the wages received or receivable by him. Pard. (I, p. 259 n.) does not understand θάνατος: 'La mort de cet esclave voleur n'est une perte que pour son maitre; il ne doit d'indemnité à celui à qui il l'avait loué que pour la privation des services.' The meaning seems to me this. θάνατος does not necessarily refer to a slave who runs away. There are two alternatives. The slave may run away, or he may die. If he dies in the course of the period for which he was hired, an allowance is to be made to the hirer out of the total wages paid or payable for that period.

APPENDIX E

48. Let him who robs from captains make it good fourfold.

49. Let him who puts his private load on the public load and compels the captain to this course not only be fined and have no remedy in case of shipwreck but also be severely punished.

50. Let those who seize anything from the pitiable condition of the shipwrecked or who gain anything from them by fraud make it good fourfold to those whom they have wronged. He who with force and violence carries things off from a shipwreck is to make them good, and, in addition, if he is free, he is relegated for three years; if they are persons of low rank, they are put into a public work for the same period; if they are slaves, they are sent off to harder labour under the fisc.

Many of the MSS. which give these chapters state accurately where they come from. Thus c. 48 is stated in the MSS. to be derived from Cod. XI, 2; c. 49 from Cod. XI, 5; and c. 50 from Dig. XLVII, 9. (Pard.'s references in his ed. are all wrong.)

Cod. XI, 2 (1), 3 (5) runs as follows: 'Ab his, qui in naucleros praedas egerunt, uolumus eorum commodis satisfieri. et

ideo, ne crescat in posterum eorum audacia, sancimus ut, qui-
cumque in rapinis fuerit deprehensus, poena quadrupli teneatur.'
This passage is evidently, as the MSS. say it is, the origin of
c. 48. Pard. says that c. 48 is derived from Cod. VI, 2, 18.
This passage runs as follows: 'In eum, qui ex naufragio uel
incendio cepisse uel in his rebus damni quid dedisse dicitur,
infra annum utilem ei cui res abest quadrupli, post in simplum
actionem proditam praeter poenam olim statutam edicti forma
perpetui declarat.' Obviously this is not the origin of c. 48.
Pard.'s error was due partly to his reading ναυαγίων (which none
of my MSS. give) instead of ναυκλήρων. C. 49 is an almost
literal translation of Cod. XI, 5 (4). It is worth noticing that
τὸν ναύκληρον translates ' portitores frumenti'.

C. 50 is a singular mixture. οἱ ἐκ τῆς ἐλεεινοτάτης down to
πονηρόν is a translation of Dig. XLVII, 9, 3, 8 'eos autem, qui
quid ex miserrima naufragorum fortuna rapuissent lucratiue
fuissent dolo malo'. But the passage in the Digest goes on ' in
quantum edicto praetoris actio daretur, tantum et fisco dare
debere', while c. 50 has simply τὸ τετραπλοῦν τοῖς ἀδικηθεῖσι
παρεχέτωσαν. This passage is given in the same words (with the
substitution of ἀποφάσεως for ὑποστάσεως) in Appendix H (l),
where I cite other authorities. Another form of the passage of
the Digest is given by Heimb. as Bas. LIII, 3, 31 (ed. Heimb. V,
p. 116) from Balsamon, and by me in Appendix H (n) from K.
The second part of c. 50 (ὁ δὲ βαρυτέρᾳ πρέδᾳ κτλ.) is a free translation of Dig. XLVII, 9, 4, 1. The following points of difference
deserve notice : (a) μετὰ τὴν τούτων ἀποκατάστασιν is not in the
original. (b) The original provides that the freemen are to be
beaten *fustibus* and the slaves *flagellis*. (c) 'in metallum' is
rendered by εἰς βαρύτερον ἔργον τοῦ φίσκου. The same passage of
the Digest is given in another form in Appendix H (o), and was
evidently given in the Synopsis from which Venturi translated
(see FM., p. 184).

INDEXES

I. CHAPTERS OF THE SEA-LAW REFERRED TO IN THE INTRODUCTION

Part II

CHAP.	PAGE
α′–ζ′	clxvii
η′	cxl
ι′	cxlix
ια′	cxlix
ιβ′	cl
ιδ′, ιε′	lxxvii, cc
ις′	clii, cclxxvi
ιζ′	ccxxi
ιη′	ccxxi
ιθ′	ccxxii

Part III

1	lxxx
2	lxxxi
3	lxxxi
4	cxlii
5	lxxxv, clxvii
6	lxxxvi
7	lxxxv
8	lxxvii, lxxxiii
9	ccxliii, cclviii, cclxxv
11	lxxvi, clxxxii
12	lxxvi, lxxxvii, xc
13	lxxvii, cc
14	lxxxix
15	cxlvii
16	ccxxii
17	xci, ccxxxv
18	ccxxxv
19	xcii, xcvii
20	xci, ccii, cciv, ccvi

CHAP.	PAGE
21	xci, ccxxxvi
22	cl, clxxxvii, cclix, cclxxiii
23	cciv
24	xcvii, cxciv, cciv, ccvi
25	cl, clxxxvii, cciv
26	cxxxii
27	lxxxvii, cxciv, cxcvi, ccxlii, cclx
28	clxxxvii, ccxlii
29	clxxxvii, cclxi
30	cxciv, cxcvi, cclxi, cclxiii
31	cclxi, cclxiii
32	cxciv, cxcvi, ccxlii
33	cxciv, cclxi
34	cxcix
36	cclxxxv
37	cclxi
38	cxcix, cclix, cclxii, cclxxxix
39	cxlii
40	cclxii
41	cclxii
42	cxciv, ccviii
43	cclix
44	cxciv, cxcix
45	cclxiv, cclxxxix
46	clxvii, cclxxxix
47	cclxxxix

Appendix A		lxxi–lxxiv
" B		lxxi
" D		clxviii
" F		lxxvii, lxxxiii

126

II. GREEK WORDS AND PHRASES

ἄγκυρα, 71, 77, 80.
ἀκίνδυνος, ccxxi, 66.
ἄλλην, 98.
ἅμα, 112.
ἀμέλεια, 91.
ἀπαραίτητος, 62.
ἀποβολή, 72.
ἀπόλλειν, 98.
ἀπολογεῖσθαι, 79.
ἀποτακτάρις, 122.
ἀποτάσσεσθαι, 95.
ἀπώλεια, 68.
ἀρκοῦντες, 93.
ἄρμενα, clxxxiv, 81.
ἀρμενιστής, 111.
ἀρραβών, xcii–xcviii.
βασανίζεσθαι, 78.
βέστις, 109.
βιγλεοφόρος, 111.
βολήσαντος, 76.
γόμος, 74.
γοργός, clxxxvi, 93.
γράμμα, 88.
γραμμάτιον, 111.
γρόνθος, 85.
δεσπότης τοῦ πλοίου, cxxxii.
διαπόντιος, 74.
διαρπαγή, 68.
διαφέροντα (τά), 91.
διπλοῦν (εἰς τό), 79.
διφθέρα, clxxxiv, 81.
διωρυγή, 94.
δοῦναι, 85.
δύο ἢ τρεῖς, xc, 116.
ἔγγαια, ccxxi, 66.
ἔγγραφα, 68.
εἰ with subj., 62.
εἴτω, 62.
ἐκβολή, 72.
ἐκδικεῖν, 101.
ἐκκοιτεῖν, 105.
ἐκπορίζειν, 76.
ἐμβολή, 107.
ἐμπλέοντες, 94.

ἔμπορος, cxxxix.
ἐνθήκη, 72.
ἐξαρτία, 64.
ἐξαρτίζειν, 92.
ἐξειλῆσαι, 96.
ἐπήρεια, 73.
ἐπιβάτης, cxxxix.
ἐπίκλυσις, 109.
ἐπιμισθία, 123.
ἐπιπόντιος, 74.
ἐπιτίμιον, 99.
ἐπίφορος, 100.
ἐπιχειρία, 92.
ἐπιχρήννυναι, 69.
ἐργασία, 86.
εὐαγγελίων (ὅρκος), 63.
ἐφόλκιον, 117.
ἡμίναυλα, cxciv, 75.
θερεία, 69.
ἰατρεῖα, 85.
ἱστοκεραία, clxxxiv, 92.
καθάπερ ἐκ δίκης, 101.
καννάβιον, 80.
καραβίτης, 58.
κάραβος, clxxxv, 81.
κατάρτιος, 117.
κατέχεσθαι, 78, 82.
κελεύει ὁ νόμος, 65, 78.
κέρας, 116.
κερδοκοινωνία, 74.
κερμακόλουθος, ccxix.
κεφάλαια, 57.
κλασματίζειν, 75.
κλέπτης, 71.
κοινωνία, ccxxxiv.
κουφίζεσθαι, 65.
κυβερνήτης, cxxxi.
κύλλωμα, 72.
ληστής, 71.
λιμήν, 77.
λίτρα, 88.
μέρη, 102.
μετέπειτα, 98.
μισθός, clxvii, 57, 118.

μνᾶ, 90.
μοδισμός, cliii, 63.
ναύκληρος, cxxxi–cxxxv, 58.
ναυπηγός, 58.
ναυτικόν, 97.
ξυλαγώγιον, 81.
ὀγκία, οὐγκία, 61, 88.
ὀδύνη, 109.
ὀλοσηρικός, 114.
ὀργυιά, 119.
ὁρμᾶν and ὁρμεῖν, 77.
ὅριον=ὡρεῖον, 106.
παῖδες, 59, 90.
παρα(ε)σχαρίτης, 58.
πειρατής, 71.
πηρῶσαι, 85.
πῆχυς, 59.
πιστικός, cxxxii, 86, 93.
πλήρης, 103.
ποσότης, 105.
προθεσμία, 103.
προναύκληρος, 86.
πρόστιμον, 99.
προχρεία, 108.
πρωρεύς, 58.
σαβουράτος, 102.
σίδηρον, 84.
σιταρχία, 104.
σκεύη, 87.
στρώματα, 87.
συσφραγίζειν, 98.
σχοινίον, clxxxiv, 80, 118.
τέλειος, 61.
τόπος, 60, 61.
τριμερίτης, 69.
τρυπᾶν, 116.
ὑποθήκη, ccxiii.
φόρτος, 75.
χρεοκοινωνία, 97.
χρηματίζειν, 80.
χρηννύειν, 69.
χρύσινοι, 64.

INDEXES

III. WORDS AND PHRASES IN LATIN AND OTHER LANGUAGES

PAGE

accomandum ccxlv
accomendacio ccxxxvii
agumine clxxxv
apertum scriptum . . clxxxviii
avaria ccli
barcha clxxxv
calcare clxxxiii
camerarius cxxxvii
cantaro=kantare . . . cliv
carati clxiv
caricum clxxv
collegantia ccxxxvii
columna, colonna . . . ccxlvi
conciare clxxxiii
conductus clxx
conserva cxlviii
entega ccxlix
extrahi per pilum . . . cc
famuli=fanti . . clxvi, clxxxvi
galiotus clxvi
gomene clxxxv
granum 89
imbolium clvii
incama(e)rata cxciii
indagarii clxxxv
loca clxiv
marinariciam (ad) . clxix, clxx

PAGE

miliare . . . . clxxiii, clxxv
milliarium=migliaio . . cliv
modiatio 64
modii cliii
mudua . . . . cxlviii, clxxi
nauclerus cxxxvi
parabulusum cclxxvii
paraspodia clxxv
partem (marinarius ad) clxviii,
clxix
patronus cxxxvi
portionarii cxxxv
praepositus cxxxvi
quaternus . . cxxxvii, cxxxviii
recomandigio ccxxxvii
scriba, scribanus . . . cxxxvii
soldum (marinarius ad) clxxi,
clxxii
suprapositus cxxxvi
tabula=tavola . . . ccxlvi
tara (lordo, netto di) . . cxciii
tare, tari, tarenus . . . 89
terzariam (ad) . clxxi, clxxiii
timoni clxxxv
traiecticia pecunia . . ccxvii
varea (see also avaria) . cclxxiv
viciati cclxxvii

IV. THE SUBJECT-MATTER

Abstracts, collections of notarial, cxxv.
Advance, in respect of freight, cxcvi, 108.
Aequitas, as foundation for doctrine of contribution, cclvi.
Agermanament, cclxvi.
Amalfi (Table of), system of column in, ccxliv–ccxlviii.
law of jettison in, cclxix.
Ambrosian Synopsis, ci–ciii.
Anchors, how many required on board, clxxxiv.

Anchors, frequent thefts of, 77.
Ancona, system of, with regard to contribution, cclxxviii.
rules of, as regards collision, cclxxxvi.
as regards salvage, ccxci.
Arra, Arrha, 'Αρραβών, in Greek and Roman law, xcii–xcviii.
in mediaeval law, ccvii.
given to mariners on taking service, clxvi.
Assault, how dealt with, in Sealaw, lxxxiv–lxxxvi.
Average, ccli–cclxxxv.

Ballasting, of ship, clvi.
Basilica, LIII, relation of Sea-law to, xcviii–cxii.
contents of, civ–cviii.
Bilge, shipowner's liability for, cxcix.
Boats, how many required with ship, clxxxv.
reward for bringing in, cclxxxix, ccxc.

Cabin, size of, in middle ages, 60.
Cables, how many required on board, clxxxiv.
when cutting of, gives claim to contribution, cclxx.
Cambium, in mediaeval law, ccxxv, ccxxix.
Capacity, of ship, clii–clv.
Caravans (mudue), of ships, cxlvii, ccxxvii.
Cargo (transportation of), clxxix–ccix.
Charter-parties, must be in writing, xci.
abstracts of two, clxxix–clxxxii.
Collision, cclxxxv–cclxxxviii.
Column, system of, at Amalfi, ccxliv–ccxlviii.
Commenda, in mediaeval law, ccxxxvii–ccxl.
liability to *avarie*, in cases of, cclii.
Commercial Documents. *See* Documents.
Comune, Comunitas, on board, ccxliii.
Consulate of Sea, its character, cxx.
payment of mariners in, clxxiii.
remedies for breach of contract in, ccv, ccvi.
contribution in, cclxxix–cclxxxiv.
salvage in, ccxcii.
Consultation, as preliminary to jettison, cclxiv, cclxviii, cclxxiv.
Contingency, loans upon, ccx, ccxvii.
Contracts, conditions of their validity in Sea-law, xc.
Contribution, law of, cx–cxii, ccli–cclxxx.
Corsairs, whether distinguishable from pirates, clxiv.

Critical apparatus, method of, xxxii–xxxiv.
Custom, references to, in statutes and documents, cxxii.
Customs, list of, used in Part III, cxv.
date of, cxix, cxx.

Dareste, M., his text of Sea-law, xlv.
Demosthenes, maritime loans in, ccxii.
Deposit, law of, in Sea-law, lxxxvii–lxxxix, 94.
on board ship, cc.
Discipline on board, cxli, cxlii, clxxviii, clxxix.
Documents, list of, used for Part III, cxv–cxix.
how they illustrate maritime law, cxxv–cxxviii.
Drink, supply of, during voyage, cl, clii.

Earnest-money. *See* Arra.
Ecloga, relation of, to Sea-law, lxxviii.
table of chapters in, 70.
Editions of Sea-law, xli–xlvi.
Emperors, list of, who established Sea-law, lxviii.
Emptio, in mediaeval law, ccxxv, ccxxix.
Entega, system of, at Ragusa, ccxlviii–ccli.
Exercitor, in Roman law, cxxx, cxxxi, clix–clxiii.
Eye, punishment for putting out, lxxxv, 85.

Farmer's Law, lxxxii, xc, cxiv.
Ferrini-Mercati, their two texts of Sea-law, xliv.
Fire, danger of, on board ship, cxlix.
Food, supply of, on board ship, cl–clii.
Freight, principles on which determined, clxxxix–cxcvii.
how far liable to make contribution, cclxxvi.

Godefroy, Jacques, his view as to Prologue, lxxi–lxxiii.

INDEXES

Goldschmidt, his view as to contribution, cclxiv–cclxvii.
Gubernator, in Roman law, cxxxi.

Homicide, how punished in Sea-law, lxxxiv, lxxxvi.
Hypothecation (maritime), ccxii, ccxviii, ccxxix, ccxxxii.

Indexes of Basilica, xcix.
Interest, in Roman law, ccxvi.
in Byzantine law, ccxx.
on agricultural loans, ccxxi.
ecclesiastical prohibition of, ccxxiii.
in Constitutum Usus of Pisa, ccxxxiv.

Jettison, ccli–cclxxxv.
Joint-ownership of ship, clxiii–clxvi.
Justum impedimentum, ccviii.

Land-robbers, dangers from, cxliii, cxliv, 78.
Lash, a favourite Byzantine punishment, 79, 82.
Leunclavius, his edition of Sea-law, xlii.
Loading and Unloading of Cargo, by whom done, clxxvi.
provisions as to loading, clvii.
time within which loading must take place, clxxxvii.
system under which goods were loaded, clxxxviii.
provisions as to unloading, cxcvii, cxcviii.
injuries done to cargo during unloading, cc.
Loan (maritime), ccix–ccxxxiv.
Lombard (law), influence of, on Sea-law, lxxxv.
Luggage, free allowance of, cxl, 60.
responsibility of captain for, cc.

Magister nauis, cxxx, cxxxi.
how far his contracts bind exercitor, clxi, clxii.
Manuscripts, description of those used, xvii–xxxii.

Manuscripts, list of those not used, xxxiv–xli.
estimate of their merits, liv–lx.
Mariners, clxvi–clxxix.
want of discipline among, cxlii.
supply of food to, cli.
how many required on ship, clxxxvi.
liability of, to make contribution, cclxxvi.
various shares of, in profits, 57.
pay of, 118.
various classes of, 122–124.
Mark, on ship, to prevent overloading, clviii.
of merchants, on goods, clxxxviii.
Masts, how many required on board, clxxxiv.
contribution when cut down, ccliv, cclxx.
Measures of length, in Sea-law, 59, 119.
Men-at-arms, accompanying merchantmen, cxlvi.
Merchant, distinguished from passenger, cxxxviii–cxl.
Moneys, in Sea-law, 64, 88-90.
Monkey, as minister of divine vengeance, cci.
Mutuum, in mediaeval law, ccxxiv.

Name of ship, clv.
Navigation, damages and difficulties of, cxli–clii.
Notarial abstracts, as illustrating maritime law, cxxv.

Oath, of scriba, cxxxvii.
of mariners, clxxvi.
necessary, 62, 63.
in actions of deposit, 94.
Offences, for which mariners may be dismissed, clxxviii.
Overloading, provisions against, clviii.

Pacotille of mariners, clxxiv–clxxvi.
whether liable to contribute, cclxxvii.
Pardessus, his edition of Sea-law, xliv.

430

Partnership between merchants, ccxxxiv–ccxli.
between ship and cargo, ccxli–ccli.
Passenger, distinguished from merchant, cxxxviii–cxl.
liability of shipowner for effects of, cc.
bed and bedclothes of, 60.
space-allowance on board, 60.
Pay of mariners, clxvi–clxxiv.
Penal clauses, in charter-parties, ccii.
in maritime loans, ccxviii.
in the commenda, ccxxxix.
in Byzantine law, 99.
Pepper, as form of currency, ccxxiv.
Perjury, punishment of, in Sea-law, lxxxvi, lxxxvii.
Permutatio, in mediaeval law, ccxxv, ccxxix.
Person (offences against), in Sea-law, lxxxiv.
Pilgrim traffic, cli.
Pirates, in Roman empire and middle ages, cxliii.
contribution when ship is redeemed by, ccliv, cclxxii.
Pisa (Constitutum Usus of), formation of, cxxi.
doctrine of, on maritime loans, ccxxxiv.
on contribution, cclxix.
on collision, cclxxxvi.
on salvage, ccxcii.
Pledge. *See* Hypothecation.
Prologue of Sea-law, date of, lxii, lxxi–lxxiv.
Proof, in Sea-law, lxxxix.
Punishments, in Sea-law for theft, lxxx–lxxxiv, 78, 82.
for assault or homicide, lxxxv, lxxxvi.
for perjury, lxxxvii.
of mariners, for disobedience, clxxviii.

Ragusa, payment of mariners at, clxviii–clxx.
system of entega at, ccxlviii–ccli.
Reprisals, cxlv, cxlvi.
Risk (maritime), ccx, ccxvii.
Rogancia or **Rogadia,** in mediaeval law, ccxl.

Ropes, 80, 102, 118. *See* Cables.

Safety of ship, provisions to insure, clvi–clviii.
Sailors. *See* Mariners.
Sails, how many required on board, clxxxiv.
Salvage, cclxii, cclxxxviii–ccxciii.
Schard (Simon), his edition of Sea-law, xli.
Scribe of ship, duties and authorities of, cxxxvii, cxxxviii.
duties in reference to cargo, clxxxviii.
Sea, closing of, in winter, cxlii, cxliii.
Servants (famuli), number of, on board, clxxxvi, 59.
Ship, capacity and valuation of, clii–clv, cclxxvi, 63, 65.
name of, clv.
provisions to insure safety of, clvi–clviii.
divisions of, for purposes of ownership, cxxxv, clxiii.
as subject of commenda, ccxxxvii.
injuries to, as giving right to contribution, ccliii.
Shipowner, clix–clxvi.
Silk, value of, at different epochs, 114.
Slaves, valuation of, 90.
Societas, in mediaeval law, ccxl, ccxli.
Soldier's law, cxiv, 70.
Statutes, list of, used in Introduction, cxv–cxix.
date of, cxix, cxx.
character of, cxxi.
maritime distinguished from city, cxxii.
borrowings of, one from another, cxxiii.
Sugar, how packed in middle ages, cxcii.
Synopsis Major, ciii, civ.
chapters of Sea-law in, xxxi.
manuscripts of, xxxi.

Table of Chapters of Sea-law, lxix.
in legal manuscripts, 70.
Tackle, how far loss of, is subject of contribution, cclxxiii.

INDEXES

Tackle, when not liable to make contribution, cclxxvi.

Theft, how dealt with, in Sea-law, lxxviii–lxxxiv.

responsibility of exercitor for sailors', clx, clxi.

Tillers, how many required on board, clxxxv.

Titles given to Sea-law in manuscripts, lxvii.

Torture, as form of punishment, 78.

Tow and Pitch, expenses of, how borne, clxxiv.

Trani, Ordinamenta of, date of, cxx.

breaches of contract in, cciv.

rules of, with regard to contribution, cclxxix.

rules of, as to salvage, ccxci.

Transhipping, when captain is justified in, ccviii.

Valuation, of ship for contribution, cclxxviii, 64.

Valuation, of goods for contribution, cclxxviii, 88.

of slaves, 90.

of mariners' goods, 91.

Venturi (Francesco), manuscript of, xxvii–xxix.

synopsis of, xcix, ci.

Watch, on board, how kept, 111.

Water, supply of, on board, cli, 61.

Weapons, ship when required to carry, cxlvi.

Winter, closing of sea in, cxlii.

Witnesses, three required in Sea-law, lxxxix.

Wreck, duty of mariners to help in, clxxxvii, clxxxix.

Wreckers, dangers from, cxliii.

Writing, when contracts required to be in, xc, xcii.

Zara, payment of mariners at, clxx–clxxiii.

www.ingramcontent.com/pod-product-compliance
Lightning Source LLC
Chambersburg PA
CBHW021428180326
41458CB00001B/177